NEW GOSPEL STUDIES 5/2

THE INFLUENCE
OF THE GOSPEL OF SAINT MATTHEW

NEW GOSPEL STUDIES 5/2

THE INFLUENCE
OF THE GOSPEL OF SAINT MATTHEW
ON CHRISTIAN LITERATURE
BEFORE SAINT IRENAEUS

Book 2
The Later Christian Writings

by
Édouard Massaux

translated by
Norman J. Belval
and
Suzanne Hecht

edited and with an introduction and addenda by
Arthur J. Bellinzoni

PEETERS   **MERCER**

ISBN 0-86554-382-8

*The Influence of the Gospel of Saint Matthew
on Christian Literature before Saint Irenaeus.*
Book 1. *The First Ecclesiastical Writers.*
English translation copyright ©1990 ©1992
Mercer University Press, Macon, Georgia 31207
Translation—by arrangement with Peeters Press—of book 2 of
*Influence de l'Évangile de saint Matthieu
sur la littérature chrétienne avant saint Irénée*
Réimpression anastatique présentée par Frans Neirynck
Supplément bibliographie 1950–1985 par Boudewijn Dehandschutter
Bibliotheca Ephemeridum Theologicarum Lovaniensium 75
(ISBN 90-6186-214-0) ©1986 (¹1950) by Leuven University Press/
Presses Universitaires de Louvain/Universitaire Pers Leuven
Published by Uitgeverij Peeters/Peeters Press, Leuven (Belgium)
All rights reserved
Printed in the United States of America

Library of Congress Cataloging-in-Publication Data

Massaux, Édouard.
   The influence of the Gospel of Saint Matthew on Christian literature before Saint Irenaeus.

   (New gospel studies ; 5)
   Translation of: Influence de l'Évangile de saint Matthieu sur la littérature chrétienne avant saint Irénée.
   Includes bibliographical references and indexes.
   Contents: bk. 1. The first ecclesiastical writers — bk. 2. The later Christian writings.
   1. Bible. N.T. Matthew—Criticism, interpretation, etc.—History—Early church, ca. 30–600. 2. Christian literature, Early—History and criticism. 3. Fathers of the church. I. Bellinzoni, Arthur J. II. Title. III. Series.
BS2575.2.M29513   1990   226.2'009'015   90-38747
ISBN 0-86554-377-1 (bk. 1 : alk. paper)
ISBN 0-86554-382-8 (bk. 2 : alk. paper)   CIP

Table of Contents

Book 1
The First Ecclesiastical Writers
First Clement, Barnabas, and the Letters of Ignatius of Antioch

(New Gospel Studies 5/1, 1990)

Book 2
The Later Christian Writings
Second Clement, Polycarp, Apocalypses, Noncanonical Gospels,
the Agrapha, and Some Gnostic Writings

Book 3
The Apologists and the Didache
Aristides, Justin Martyr, Tatian, Apollinaris of Hierapolis,
Athenagoras of Athens, and Theophilus of Antioch; and the Didache

(New Gospel Studies 5/3, forthcoming)

Preface to the English Translation

The question of the influence of the Gospel of Matthew on second century Christian literature is central to an understanding of the development of the church's fourfold Gospel canon. Such a study is also closely related to a study of early church history and the history of early Christian theology.

These subjects have had renewed attention, especially in the last two or three decades. Just as the discovery of the Dead Sea Scrolls in 1947 reopened the question of the canon of the Jewish Bible, so too has the discovery of the Coptic Gnostic library near Nag Hammadi stimulated interest in the study of the New Testament canon, especially the question of the status of Christian books in the second and third centuries. Although the Nag Hammadi library was discovered in 1945, only about half of it had been published by 1966, and an English translation of the entire collection did not appear until 1978.[1]

The diversity of early Christianity was perceived even earlier, when in 1934 Walter Bauer published his classic study *Orthodoxy and Heresy in Earliest Christianity*.[2] There has also been an enhanced appreciation of this diversity with the publication in German and then in an English translation of Edgar Hennecke's *New Testament Apocrypha*.[3] Until the publication in English of Hennecke's collection in 1963 and 1965, English-speaking scholars were largely limited to the collection of apocrypha of M. R. James.[4] It is not surprising that there was so little scholarly interest in the Christian apocryphal literature. The material was often regarded as an extracanonical, heretical curiosity, and it was generally of little interest to New Testament scholars and only of peripheral interest to patristic scholars and to historians of early Christian doctrine. James M. Robinson and Helmut Köster have

---

[1]James M. Robinson, *The Nag Hammadi Library in English* (New York: Harper and Row, 1978).

[2]Walter Bauer, *Rechtglaübigkeit und Ketzerei im ältesten Christentum* (Tübingen: Mohr/Siebeck, 1934; corr. repr. 1964); ET by the Philadephia Seminar on Christian Origins, ed. Robert A. Kraft and Gebhard Krodel (Philadelphia: Fortress Press, 1971).

[3]Edgar Hennecke, *New Testament Apocrypha*, ed. Wilhelm Schneemelcher, ET ed. R. McL. Wilson (Philadelphia: The Westminster Press, vol. 1, 1963; vol. 2, 1965).

[4]Montague Rhodes James, *The Apocryphal New Testament* (Oxford: Clarendon, 1924; corr. repr. 1953).

built substantially upon the work of Bauer, in part at least by focusing attention on extracanonical Christian literature.[5] Also the diversity within early Christianity has been made more evident, even within the books of the canonical New Testament itself, and the discussion of this diversity within the earliest church has begun to find its way into basic introductions to the New Testament.[6]

The use of first-century Christian writings in second-century Christian literature is, of course, not identical to the question of the history of the canon or of the canonical status of individual books. A book can be used by a church father of the patristic period without in any way implying that that book is authoritative, much less canonical. The development of the New Testament canon was a long and protracted process that extended into the fifth century. However, the period leading up to Irenaeus was clearly the most critical in establishing the core of the New Testament canon, in particular the emergence of the quadriform gospel, thirteen letters of Paul, the Acts of the Apostles, and 1 Peter and 1 John. By the beginning of the third century twenty of the twenty-seven books of the New Testament canon were widely cited by many of the church fathers alongside the already canonical Old Testament.

The history of the New Testament canon involves much more than an examination of the citation of individual books. Yet a study of the citation of individual documents is a useful place to begin any study of the history of the canon. Édouard Massaux's *The Influence of the Gospel of Saint Matthew on Christian Literature before Saint Irenaeus* first appeared in French in 1950 and was reprinted with additional bibliographical entries in 1986. In this monumental volume Massaux identified the Gospel of Matthew as the New Testament book that most influenced primitive Christian literature. In spite of the title of this important book, Massaux's study included a discussion not only of the influence of the Gospel of Matthew, but also the influence of Mark, Luke, John, the Pauline letters, and some of the catholic letters on most of the Christian literature written up to the time of Irenaeus and known at the time that Massaux wrote in 1950. The Nag Hammadi material was, of course, not known to Massaux at the time of his research.

It is Massaux's contention that the Gospel of Matthew was both known and used by the end of the first or the early part of the second century and with increasing frequency as time passed. Not all scholars have agreed with Massaux's conclusions. As Frans Neirynck has indicated in his introduction to the 1986 edition (see below, pp. xi-xix), Massaux's thesis found a strong opponent in the study

---

[5]See esp. James M. Robinson and Helmut Köster, *Trajectories through Early Christianity* (Philadelphia: Fortress Press, 1971).

[6]Joseph B. Tyson, *The New Testament and Early Christianity* (New York: Macmillan Publishing Company, 1984) esp. 353-87.

of Helmut Köster,[7] who argued that the Apostolic Fathers were primarily dependent not on the written gospels but on the church's oral tradition. The differences between the positions of Massaux and Köster are limited principally to the writings of the Apostolic Fathers. The issue has recently been reexamined by Wolf-Dieter Köhler,[8] whose conclusions are basically compatible with those of Massaux. Köhler tries to develop criteria for determining what constitutes evidence for the status of the Gospel of Matthew in a particular writing and has the advantage of treating some of the Gnostic literature unknown when Massaux wrote in 1950. But Massaux's treatment is much more thorough.

Modern studies of the development of the New Testament canon tend to divide the second century into two parts: the period before Marcion, and the period between Marcion and Irenaeus (or the Muratorian Canon). Whether one agrees with Massaux that the earliest fathers of the church knew our Gospel of Matthew or with Köster that they were dependent primarily on the same presynoptic oral and/or written tradition upon which Matthew depends, a study of the influence of the Gospel of Matthew on Christian literature up to the time of Irenaeus is critical to an understanding of both the development of the canon and the rich diversity of second-century Christianity, in what would later be viewed as both its orthodox and its heterodox manifestations.

Massaux's volume is still seminal to the question, and no other study has attempted to cover so much material so fully. Obviously the question of the use of the Gospel of Matthew in the second century has not been resolved to everyone's satisfaction. At this time, when there is a renewed interest in second-century Christianity, the work of Massaux, out-of-print for many years, still serves as an invaluable resource. Massaux has provided a clearly stated argument of his position backed up by detailed and exhaustive analyses of the relevant texts. He argues for a relatively simple solution to the problem by rejecting an appeal to the use by the Apostolic Fathers of presynoptic oral or written sources and by arguing for the use of the text of the Gospel of Matthew by the turn of the first Christian century.

Massaux's study is divided into three books, which will be published in English in three volumes: (1) The Earliest Christian Writings (1 Clement, Barnabas, and the Letters of Ignatius of Antioch); (2) The Later Christian Writings (2 Clement, Polycarp, Apocalypses, Noncanonical Gospels, the Agrapha, and Some Gnostic Writings); and (3) The Apologists (Aristides, Justin Martyr, Tatian, Apollinaris of Hierapolis, Athenagoras of Athens, and Theophilus of Antioch) and the Didache. In each chapter Massaux examines first the question of the use of the Gospel of Matthew generally by looking initially at parallels to the text of the Ser-

---

[7]Helmut Köster, *Synoptische Überlieferung bei den apostolischen Vätern*, TU 65 (Berlin: Akademie Verlag, 1957).

[8]Wolf-Dieter Köhler, *Die Rezeption des Mattäusevangeliums in der Zeit vor Irenäus*, WUNT 2/24 (Tübingen: Mohr-Siebeck, 1987).

mon on the Mount and then at parallels to other Matthean passages and then proceeds to an examination of the influence of other New Testament writings (Mark, Luke, John, the letters of Paul, etc.) on the second-century Christian literature. He often divides his discussion into texts in which the use of Matthew is certain, probable, possible, doubtful, and excluded.

The work of Massaux heretofore has been available only in French. With the publication of this classic in English it is hoped that we can renew additional interest in the question of the influence of gospel or gospel-like tradition on Christian literature of the second century. A fuller understanding of second-century Christianity will ultimately afford us a clearer picture of first-century Christianity as well and will enable us better to understand the diversity within the early church and the development toward catholic Christianity.

The first draft of the translation of this volume into English was done by Norman J. Belval (S.T.D.), Archdiocesan Director of the Archdiocese of Hartford, Connecticut. A substantial reworking of this translation was then undertaken by my colleague, Suzanne Hecht (Ph.D.), Sara Niles Flowers Georges '18 Professor of Foreign Languages and Literatures at Wells College. I worked closely with Professor Hecht on this revised translation, which was then returned to Norman Belval for his comments and further suggestions. I did the final editing of their translation. Out of this synthesis we believe we have produced a superior translation of this invaluable classic.

Massaux does not provide French translations of those Greek passages in the Later Christian Writings in which literary dependence on the Gospel of Mattew is either doubtful or to be dismissed. To make this English edition of Massaux's work more useful, I have included English translations for all of these passages and noted that they were added by the editor.

In addition, at the end of each chapter I have provided an addendum listing those passages in the Later Christian Writings that are judged to contain citations or allusions to the Gospel of Matthew according to Köster, Köhler, and *Biblia Patristica*. These addenda hopefully make this English edition more useful to the contemporary critic.

The bibliography to the English edition has synthesized into one listing Massaux's original bibliography and the supplementary bibliography of Boudewijn Dehandschutter of works published between 1950 and 1985.

Aurora, New York   *Arthur J. Bellinzoni*
1 September 1991   Professor of Religion, Wells College

Preface to the Reprint

The work presented here is a reprint of a magisterial thesis in theology defended at Louvain in 1950. The same author earlier presented a study on "The Influence of Saint Matthew's Gospel on the Didache," published in *ETL* 25 (1949): 5-41. To my knowledge, Édouard Massaux returned only once to one of the problems studied in this book, namely in an article on "The Text of the Sermon on the Mount Used by Saint Justin," published in *ETL* 28 (1952): 411-48. The dissertation, inspired and directed by Professor Lucien Cerfaux, was by no means unnoticed. To describe its welcome in Louvain and elsewhere, I propose to quote the synthesis of reviews written in 1954 by Jules Cambier.

> It is traditionally said that Mt. is the New Testament document that has most influenced primitive Christian literature. Massaux wanted to determine in as precise a way as possible the place occupied by the first gospel in Christian writings prior to Irenaeus. He also wanted to assess the influence of the other New Testament writings on this same literature. He was thus able to conclude in favor of the prevalent influence of the Gospel of Matthew in the primitive Church. It is generally admitted (cf. Fascher, Héring, Botte, etc.) that Massaux has attained his goal. The nine pages that Audet devoted to this work in *RB* emit a unique sound; independent of some valid observations, it seems that these remarks can be acknowledged only with much reservation, not to speak of the "tone" which seemed to many to be other than "respectfully candid."
>
> Has the author examined all Christian literary texts of the second century, as some critics concede to him? There are some who still quote this or that document whose analysis could have added to the enormous mass of material already cited here. It is clear that Massaux had reasons not to dwell on this or that Christian document which happens to be at the periphery of the vast field that he had the courage to clear. Maybe he could have let us know the reasons for his choice, at least in some cases that were discussed by his critics, for example, in the *Epistle to Diognetus*. But let us not allow a detail to prevent us from seeing the overall purpose: the mass of materials investigated here demands, writes Héring, an astonishing knowledge of primitive Christian literature. E. Fascher acknowledges the careful examination of details pursued with meticulous precision; Massaux's work also presents the

practical synthesis of analyzed facts. For Héring, "all the writings on the N.T. have been studied by the author with accuracy beyond reproach." However, other critics pointed out that one or another analysis concluded too firmly in favor of a dependence on Matthew; but this remark, even if it were founded, does not change the general tenor of the conclusions which the author reached.

I had occasion to mention above the extent of Massaux's investigations. When it is known that many points were and will no doubt still remain obscure for a long time, it is not astonishing to see Massaux propose on some matters of detail other solutions than those advanced by his predecessors. On that score, one could ask whether some relatively free citations of logia that are found in the first gospel are not to be linked rather to a primitive document like the Aramaic logia translated into Greek, which Papias mentions and to which one readily turns today in order to clarify somewhat the synoptic problem. This is the opinion of several critics. Héring also wished to see the influence of apocryphal writings more widely stressed, be they Jewish or Christian. But, as Kilpatrick remarks, if the author is sometimes found too categorical in his presentation of this or that solution, it must be recognized that he has provided us with a very useful work which will be profitably consulted.

Let us refer to some other particular points discussed by the reviewers. Massaux has provided a work copious in textual criticism, sometimes completing the work of his predecessors and sometimes adopting another solution: thus, instead of referring to an extracanonical gospel, as Bousset often does, to explain an influence on a given text, Massaux prefers to explain this coloration as coming from a Matthean logion. (Let us recall that Massaux presented several more confirmations of his views against Bousset's position in *ETL* 1952.) Again, from the point of view of textual criticism, Héring is happy to observe that this book confirms "that the so-called Western text was actually the only text known to Christianity in the second century." Several reviewers have pointed out Massaux's merit in having shown the different way, ever more precise and more literal, in which our first Christian authors cite the documents of the New Testament, particularly the Gospel of Matthew.

Discussions on the subject of the dating of the Didache are well known. Massaux opts for a much later era than the one traditionally accepted. The argument that Audet puts forth and which receives approval, notably from Kilpatrick and Fascher, is the disappearance of the anti-Jewish barb which is found in the earlier Christian writings: Christianity lives henceforth its own life; we are no doubt at the time of Justin or a bit later.

Anyone who has used Massaux's book will not wonder that all scholars declared themselves pleased with the very rich instrument which this work offers in its abundant bibliography, its very valuable tables, and the vast material assembled and analyzed. As Professor Descamps says, "The exegete and the historian who will ponder over these conclusions [= of Massaux's book] will gradually deduce, it seems, its various implications"; and he proposes an example, that of the history of synoptic tradition.

Let us end with a general consideration of Fascher: it is possible to have different views on certain points; but we shall readily agree that the author has assembled many details that are dispersed in commentaries and monographs, and has studied them from a clearly defined point of view. Massaux's book improves our knowledge of early Christian literature as well as of the development of some exegetical practices of the primitive Church. In the same vein, Father Botte concluded: "Whatever disagreements there may be [= on the solution of some problems], the work of Massaux is bound to afford a great service to those who study early Christian literature as well as to those interested in textual criticism of the New Testament."[1]

The section that examines Matthew's influence on the Didache is a literal rendering of Massaux's article of 1949 (pp. 604-41; 644, 1st line of 3rd paragraph). The relationship between the article of 1952 and the section on Justin (orig. pp. 464-570) is a bit more complex. In the article on "The Text of the Sermon on the Mount,"[2] Justin's passages are grouped under three headings: (1) Justin's text is practically identical to Matthew's; (2) Simple changes of style appear; and (3) The dependence on Matthew could be more distant. In order to facilitate the comparison of passages Massaux has examined, I list below a synoptic table.

		1950	1952		App.	Sec.		
1 Apol	15.1-3	466-60	416-21	=	730-35	(2)		
	15.9-10	471-74	428-33	=	742-47	(3)		
	15.11	474-75	421-23	=	735-37	(2)		
	15.13	477-79	433-34	=	747-48	(3)		
	15.14-16	479-81	434-38	=	748-52	(3)		
	15.17	481-82	438-39	=	752-53	(3)		
	16.1-2	482-84	439-42	=	753-56	(3)		
	16.5	484-85	423-25	=	737-39	(2)		
	16.9	487	415	=	729	(1)		
	16.11	489-90	425-27	=	739-41	(2)		
	16.13	491-92	415-16	=	729-30	(1) 13c		
			427-28	=	741-42	(2) 13ab		
Dial	35.3	514-17	427-28	=	741-42	(2)	1 Apol	16.13
	76.5	522-23	425-27	=	739-41	(2)		16.11
	96.3	531-32	433-34	=	747-48	(3)		15.13
	105.6	538	414-15	=	728-29	(1)		
	133.6	545	429-31	=	743-45	(3)		15.9b

[1]*ETL* 30 (1954): 478-80. J. Cambier refers to the following reviews: J. P. Audet, *RB* 58 (1951): 600-608; B. Botte, *Bulletin de théologie ancienne et médiévale* 6 (1951): 197-98; J. Cambier, *RHE* 26 (1951): 210-13; A. Descamps, *Revue diocésaine de Tournai* 6 (1951): 369-70; E. Fascher, *TLZ* 78 (1953): 281-83: J. Héring, *RHPR* 33 (1953): 74-75; G. D. Kilpatrick, *JTS* 2 (1951): 199-200; J. Levie, *NRTh* 73 (1951): 874-76.

[2]Reproduced in an appendix, original pp. 725-62; in vol. 3 of this English edition.

The version of 1952 is distinguished from that of 1950 primarily by its critical apparatus of the text of Matthew, established thanks to the editions of Legg, Nestle, Merk, von Soden, and Tischendorf, and by a more complete inventory of patristic citations. Several references can be noted to the study of 1950 (see notes 15, 21, 47, 67, 68, 70, 82, 95, 97, 107, 125). He sometimes adds a supplementary argument (n.21: *1 Apol.* 15.3; n.70: *1 Apol.* 15.9b), or he is simply satisfied to repeat what has been said, and well said, in 1950 (n.47, regarding *1 Apol.* 15.12). It is undoubtedly more important to remark that a new nuance occasionally appears in the article of 1952. Thus, for example, in *1 Apol.* 16.5, it is no longer a matter of a simple change of style:

> I believe that the hypothesis to hold is that the meaning in Mt. (5:37) has been modified, and that the Matthean logion thus changed continued to exist in the tradition side by side with the text of Mt. from which it derives. Instinctively, Justin and his parallels picked it up as it existed within the tradition. (425 = 739)

He proposes a similar hypothesis regarding *1 Apol.* 15.13; *Dial.* 96.3:

> I would be rather easily inclined to admit here a traditional logion, namely one existing within the tradition rather than a precise source. This logion may have derived from the Matthean text which tradition has rendered more precise. (434 = 748)

Since its appearance, Massaux's book was destined to become one of the classical works on the acceptance of New Testament writings in primitive Christianity. Of course, it cannot be said that his position on the date of the Didache has been accepted. The fate of Jean-Paul Audet's opposing thesis has not fared much better: it is now regarded as "romantic oversimplification" (Draper). Criticism seems to have rediscovered its equilibrium around a consensus that tends to place the Didache at the beginning of the second century. But the problem of the contacts with Matthew remains posed.[3]

The basic thesis of the influence of canonical gospels and of the preponderance of Matthew found a formidable opponent in the book of Helmut Köster, *Synoptische Überlieferung bei den Apostolischen Vätern* (1957). Köster presented his thesis in Marburg in 1954 without knowing Massaux's book.[4] He studies the Apostolic Fathers and, in his conclusion, notes a very marked difference with regard to Justin's writings:

---

[3]See F.-M. Braun's reaction in *Jean le Théologien et son évangile dans l'Église ancienne*, EBib (Paris, 1959) 259.

[4]He mentions it in an additional note, and proposes to answer it "in einer bereits in Angriff genommenen Arbeit über die Evangelienzitate Justins" (2n.1); cf. below, n.6.

Ein ganz anderes Bild bietet sich schon wenige Jahrzente später bei Justin, bei dem bereits im grossen Masse die Evangelien "verwendet" werden. Die Quellen der synoptischen Tradition sind bei Justin fast ausschliesslich unsere Evangelien, die Geschichte der Tradition ist bei Justin mithin erstmalig eine Geschichte der Auslegung unserer Evangelien. (267)[5]

The confrontation of the two theses, therefore, directly concerns only the Apostolic Fathers. Massaux establishes thereby Matthew's influence and explains the freedom in the use of the gospel texts (particularly in the writings he deems the oldest: Clement of Rome, Barnabas, and Ignatius of Antioch) thanks to a certain familiarity with the Gospel of Matthew. According to Köster, the use of the synoptic gospels cannot be demonstrated, and one must turn to a *formgeschichtlich* solution: the similarities with the gospel texts are explained by the survival of oral tradition, independent of the written gospels. Henceforth, two hypotheses and two names are juxtaposed in the introductions to the New Testament to note that "to the present day there is no unity on the question whether 1 Clem and Ignatius did [Massaux] or did not [Köster] know a written gospel."[6]

Köster's name is omnipresent in recent studies. The most-qualified authors refer to Massaux's book as well. I think for instance of Arthur J. Bellinzoni's work on Justin and Donald A. Hagner's on Clement of Rome.[7] The name of Massaux

---

[5]He sees in it the subject of a further study: "wäre Aufgabe einer Untersuchung der Evangelienzitate Justins." Cf. "Septuaginta und synoptischer Erzählungsstoff im Schriftbeweis Justins des Märtyrers," inaugural dissertation (Heidelberg, 1956). The study has never been published. The sayings of Jesus in the writings of Justin have been studied under his direction in Arthur J. Bellinzoni's doctoral dissertation (Harvard, 1963); cf. below, n.7.

[6]W. G. Kümmel, *Einleitung in das Neue Testament*, 12th ed. (Heidelberg, 1963) 353 (= [21]1983, 424; = 1975 ET, 480). The sentence is repeated in A. Wikenhauser, *Einleitung in das Neue Testament*, 6th ed. wholly rev. by Josef Schmid (Freiburg, 1973) 28 ("bis jetzt keine Übereinstimmung . . . "); see also p. 247, a long note on Massaux's book (already in Wikenhauser's 1st ed. [1953] 145.)

I found no reference to Massaux's work in H. Köster's introduction (*Einführung in das Neue Testament* [Berlin/New York, 1980]; *Introduction to the New Testament*, 2 vols. [Philadephia: Fortress Press, 1982]). Köster does refer to Massaux in "Überlieferung und Geschichte der frühchristlichen Evangelienliteratur," in *Aufstieg und Niedergang der Römischen Welt*, II. *Principal*, pt. 25/2 (Berlin/New York, 1984) 1463-542: "Nachweise . . . sind vollständig gesammelt und ausführlich besprochen . . . Jedoch ist Massaux oft nicht kritisch genug und schliesst aus blossen Anklängen oder Zitaten aus der freien Überlieferung bereits auf Benutzung des 'Matthäusevangeliums' " (1480n.89). Contact with Matthew seems only apparent ("scheinbare Bekanntschaft") in 1 Clement, Barnabas, Ignatius, and the Didache (cf. *Synoptische Überlieferung*). Köster admits to "Kenntnis und Benutzung des Matthäus" in Polycarp, 2 Clement (cf. *Synoptische Überlieferung*), Justin, and Ptolemy's *Letter to Flora* (n.91: he refers to Massaux "für sonstige Nachweise").

[7]A. J. Bellinzoni, *The Sayings of Jesus in the Writings of Justin Martyr*, NovTSup 17 (Leiden, 1967) (cf. above, n.5); D. A. Hagner, *The Use of the Old and the New Testaments in Clement of Rome*, NovTSup 34 (Leiden, 1973; diss. written under the direction of F. F. Bruce, Manchester).

is absent in K. P. Donfried's book on 2 Clement. To illustrate the complexity of the problem of citations, Donfried notes that "the two most thoroughgoing studies on the matter at hand . . . come to completely different conclusions on most issues"[8]: he refers to Köster's book (1957) on the one hand, and to the *The New Testament in the Apostolic Fathers* (1905) of the Oxford Committee on the other hand.

Several authors show skepticism towards the use of the Gospel of Matthew, and, in order to explain the same points of similarity, they prefer to refer to an influence of Matthew's sources. Even L. Cerfaux used the study of Massaux to bring out the idea that the Sermon on the Mount existed separately before being incorporated into a gospel.[9] The existence of collections of the sayings of Jesus is very widely recognized. The hypothesis of a source peculiar to Matthew has its supporters: Joost Smit Sibinga has Ignatius dependent on a pre-Matthean writing, the source M,[10] and according to John S. Kloppenborg, Did. 16 represents an apocalyptic tradition which Matthew knew and used.[11] Reading the collection of articles just published by D. Wenham, the hypothesis of a direct influence of the Gospel of Matthew is no longer acceptable. Even pertaining to Did. 1.3b–2.1— which Köster still believes is an "insertion" whereby Matthew's and Luke's influence can be seen[12]—Jonathan Draper is categorical: "In none of these sayings from the Jesus tradition and the wisdom tradition can a dependence on either Matthew or Luke be demonstrated."[13] D. A. Hagner examines the Apostolic Fathers and comes to the same conclusion regarding Clement of Rome, Ignatius, Polycarp, Didache, and Barnabas.[14] His judgment is more delicately nuanced when it

---

[8]K. P. Donfried, *The Setting of the Second Clement in Early Christianity*, NovTSup 38 (Leiden, 1974) 57. According to Donfried, "the large majority, if not all, of 2 Clement's citations of early Christian tradition are taken from pre-or noncanonical materials" (79).

[9]"En marge de la question synoptique" (1957), in *Recueil Lucien Cerfaux* 3 (Gembloux, 1962; new and rev. ed. BETL 71, 1985) 102.

[10]J. Smit Sibinga, "Ignatius and Matthew," *NovT* 8 (1965–1966): 263-83. Cf. below, n.16.

[11]J. S. Kloppenborg, "Didache 16.1-8 and Special Matthaean Tradition," *ZNW* 70 (1979): 54-67.

[12]Cf. F. Neirynck, "Paul and the Sayings of Jesus," in A. Vanhoye, ed., *L'Apôtre Paul*, BETL 73 (Leuven, 1986) 265-321, 298n.175.

[13]J. Draper, "The Jesus Tradition in the Didache," in D. Wenham, ed., *The Jesus Tradition Outside the Gospels*, Gospel Perspectives 5 (Sheffield, 1985) 269-87, esp. 273-79. J. Draper is the author of a dissertation on the Didache: "A Commentary on the Didache in the Light of the Dead Sea Scrolls and Related Documents" (Cambridge, 1983).

[14]D. A. Hagner, "The Sayings of Jesus in the Apostolic Fathers and Justin Martyr," in *The Jesus Tradition*, 233-68. One may note a quite considerable transition compared to the conclusions of his dissertation (cf. above, n.7). See *The Use of the Old and New Tes-*

pertains to 2 Clement, Hermas, and Justin. The last article in this collection is written by Richard Bauckham.[15] Meant as a synthesis and an article on methodology, it becomes an argument for the hypothesis of a gospel source used by Ignatius (and by the authors of the Ascension of Isaiah, the Didache, and the Gospel of Peter)[16] and slightly different from the source M, which Matthew used; and finally: "The differences would be readily explicable if in both cases M were the oral tradition of the church of Antioch, on which Matthew drew some twenty or thirty years before Ignatius wrote."[17]

Massaux's thesis has by no means been abandoned. To be sure, most critics have reservations on the large number of literary contacts Massaux is ready to accept, and many have the feeling he uses too readily the word "sure" when it would be more suitable to say "probable" or "possible." In his recent commentary, Ulrich Luz briefly summarizes the question of the use of the Gospel of Matthew. I quote him.

Vieles ist hier umstritten. Ich beschränke mich darauf, thetisch meine Sicht darzulegen, die im ganzen näher bei Massaux als bei Köster liegt. In der Didache wird die Mt-Redaktion zweifellos vorausgesetzt. Stellen wie Kap. 8 oder—weniger sicher—10,5 oder Kap. 16 lassen eine fast sichere Hypothese zu: Die Didache ist in einer durch Mt geprägten Gemeinde entstanden. Leider ist aber Didache nicht genau datierbar.

Ignatius ist nicht primär durch das Mt-Ev geprägt. Er hat es aber gekannt, denn es gibt Stellen, die Mt Redaktion voraussetzen (Sm 1,1 = Mt 3,15,vgl. Phld 3,1 = Mt 15,13). Polykarp kennt Mt in seinem (2.) Brief sicher (Pol 2,3 = Mt 7,1f; 5,3.6.10; Pol 7,2 = Mt 6,13; 26,41). Da die Datierung aber nicht sicher ist, können wir nur sagen: Vielleicht war Mt um 115 im Smyrna bekannt. Denkbar scheint mir, daß es Berührungen zwischen dem Barnabasbrief und Mt gibt (vgl. bes. 5,8-12 mit 5-7.8f.23f!), aber es gibt keine Beweismöglichkeit. Ähnliches gilt für den 1 Clemensbrief (vgl. bes. 24,5 mit

---

taments in Clement of Rome, 178, on the "probability" that Clement knew one or more synoptic gospels (cf. 15.2; 24.5); 279: "The most satisfactory explanation of the Synoptic material in these epistles is that Ignatius is dependent upon his memory of the written Synoptics"; 280: "Polycarp appears to know sayings of Jesus from oral tradition, but also one or more of the Synoptic Gospels, which he quotes loosely and from memory"; 280: "It seems clear enough that the Gospel of Matthew is used in the Didache" (Did 1; 9.5; 11.7; 13.1; 16); 281: "it appears that, of the Synoptics, Barnabas knew at least Matthew."

[15]R. Bauckham, "The Study of Gospel Traditions Outside the Canonical Gospels. Problems and Prospects," in *The Jesus Tradition,* 369-403.

[16]Ibid. 380: "Matthew's special source: of all the putative sources of the Synoptic Gospels, the one for which there is the best evidence outside the Synoptic Gospels." See esp. §5 on "Ignatius and Matthew as a Paradigm Case" (386-98): a clarification regarding Smit Sibinga's article (cf. above, n.10).

[17]Ibid, 398.

Mt 13,3-9 und 46,6-8 mit Mt 18,6f). Es ist also möglich, daß Mt vor 100 in Rom und etwas später in Ägypten bekannt war. Justin schließlich setzt m.E. die Evangelien voraus; das Mt-Ev benutzt er am meisten.[18]

Under the direction of Ulrich Luz, Wolf-Dietrich Köhler prepared a doctoral dissertation that reexamines the matter in its entirety: "Die Rezeption des Matthäusevangeliums in der Zeit vor Irenäus."[19] Here is his conclusion.

Berücksichtigt man nur die einegermaßen sicher zu datierenden Schriften, so ergibt sich immerhim doch, daß ab der Zeit Justins generell mit der Kenntnis des Mt gerechnet werden kann; vor Justin ist für alle Schriften/Verfasser Mt-Kenntnis und -Benutzung zumindest möglich; nie war die Aufnahme vorsynoptischer mündlicher Tradition wahrscheinlich zu machen.
Eingezeichnet in ein Koordinatensystem, dessen Achsen durch die Positionen von Köster (Überlieferung) und Massaux (Influence) gekennzeichnet sind, ergibt sich für die frühe Zeit der Rezeption des Mt eine Einordnung der erhobenen Befunde zumeist deutlich näher an Massaux als an Köster, nie näher an Köster als an Massaux und immerhin in einigen Fällen direkt an oder sogar auf der Linie der Massauxschen Position.[20]

The last critical edition of the Didache takes the same position. Without referring to Massaux's work, Klaus Wengst enters into a dialog with Köster regarding Did. 7.1; 8.1,2; 9.5; 11.3,7; 13.1-2; 15.3,4, to conclude:

In der Gemeinde des Didachisten war wahrscheinlich das Matthäusevangelium als "das Evangelium" bzw. "das Evangelium unseres Herrn" bekannt, und es wurde von ihm für seine Schrift benutzt.[21]

---

[18]U. Luz, *Das Evangelium nach Matthäus*, 1. Teilband: *Mt 1-7*, EKKNT I/1 (Zürich-Neukirchen, 1985) 75-76. On Ignatius, see *ZNW* 62 (1971): 170n.121; cf. W. G. Kümmel, *Einleitung* (1963) 70 (= 90): Eph. 17:1; Sm. 1:1; 6:1; Pol. 1:3; 2:2. See also M. Hengel, *Die Evangelienüberschriften*, SAH (Heidelberg, 1984) 20 (n.45: reference to Massaux).

[19]Diss. presented at Bern, November 1985 (Tübingen: Mohr, 1987; xviii + 609 pp.). Following an introduction (statement of the question and methodology), Köhler examines one by one all the writings with numerous references to Massaux's work. The inventory of texts has been brought up to date: see the section on the Nag Hammadi texts, 379-428.

[20]Cf. 525. See in appendix "Tabellarische Überblick über die Rezeption des Mt vor Irenäus" (539-71), to be compared with the "Table of New Testament Quotations: Matthew" in Massaux's work (orig. 664-77). Massaux's list points out all the passages admitting comparison; an asterisk indicates cases of sure literary contact. Köhler distinguishes between *wahrscheinlich* (w); *möglich bis wahrscheilich* (m +); *möglich, aber nicht zwingend* (m); *möglich aber nicht naheliegend* (m −); *unwahrscheinlich* (uw); *auszuschliessen* (a).

[21]K. Wengst, *Didache (Apostellehre), Barnabasbrief, Zweiter Klemensbrief, Schrift an Diognet*, Schriften des Urchristentums 2 (Darmstadt, 1984) 30; cf. 25-30; and cf. 19 on "the interpolation" in 1:3b–2:1.

At a time when a new discussion of the influence of the Gospel of Matthew seems to be surfacing, Massaux's book, out of print for several years, can still be of use. It affords a point of view that is clearly stated and substantiated with a thorough analysis of the texts. The essential thesis of the book—a certain preponderance of the influence of Matthew—is still valid. Massaux allows a principle of simplicity to guide him in his interpretation: a source which is "unknown" does not attract him. It is, it seems to me, a lesson to consider when faced with the multiplicity of pre-, para-, and postsynoptic sources that are afloat today.

It is unusual to publish the reprint of a dissertation that dates from 1950.[22] I am happy to be able to present it to its author, my former professor of New Testament textual criticism and the honorary rector of the Catholic University of Louvain in Louvain-la-Neuve.

Louvain, 1 July 1986 *Frans Neirynck*

---

[22]I would like to thank my colleague Boudewijn Dehandschutter who was willing to prepare a bibliographical supplement covering the years 1950–1985.

Introduction

It is more and more prevalent today, especially among Catholic exegetes, to claim that the Gospel of Matthew is more important than the others, and that it could easily be called "the Gospel par excellence." It is said that this assertion would agree with the thinking of the first Christian generations who used principally the first gospel. Yet, quite often, this view is based on conclusions of a general nature such as verbal coincidence or the similarity of ideas between the Gospel of Mt. and that of the ecclesiastical writers of the first two centuries. There are, of course, overall studies which look at the links between early Christian literature and the New Testament;[1] yet a detailed and exhaustive study considering the place and influence of Matthew in the first centuries would still have its usefulness. Moreover, these general works propose the most diverse and contradictory opinions. These reasons have led me to examine in detail and in a systematic fashion how and in what measure the influence of Mt. has exerted itself from early Christian times until St. Irenaeus. I have stopped at the threshold of Irenaeus's *Adversus Haereses* where the fourfold gospel is clearly mentioned.

My focus of interest does not point directly to the manner in which the exegesis of Mt. was done, nor is it my goal to reestablish the primitive text of the gospel. My attention focuses on the presence of and the more or less important place occupied by Mt. in the early literature. This is why I have chosen to limit the examination to texts in which literary influence of the first gospel is manifested.

In the course of my study, I shall often speak of literary contact. I mean to use the term in a rather strict sense of the word, requiring, when speaking of contact, sufficiently striking verbal concurrence that puts the discussion in a context

---

[1]Cf., e.g., A Committee of the Oxford Society of Historical Theology, *The New Testament in the Apostolic Fathers* (Oxford, 1905), which takes into consideration all the writings of the New Testament; W. von Löwenich, *Das Johannesverständnis im zweiten Jahrhundert*, Beihefte zur ZNW 13 (Giessen, 1933), who attends to the fourth gospel; E. Aleith, *Paulusverständnis in der alten Kirche*, BZNW 18 (Berlin, 1937), who pays particular attention to the Pauline writings. Some monographs are devoted to certain authors, esp. Saint Justin, such as that of W. Bousset, *Die Evangeliencitate Justins des Märtyrers in ihrem Wert für die Evangelienkritik* (Göttingen, 1891).

that already points towards the gospel of Mt. These literary contacts do not exhaust the literary influence of the gospel; one can expect, without a properly so-called literary contact, the use of typically Matthean vocabulary, themes, and ideas.

In order to determine exactly and define the extent of the influence of Mt., the attitude of authors towards other New Testament writings ought to be examined as a basis for comparison.

My work is divided into three books, each corresponding to a stage of this influence. The first considers the early ecclesiastical writers, who have used, generally in a free way, the sayings of Christ drawn from the Gospel of Mt. The second looks to the later writings, which manifest a wider usage and contain citations more and more faithful not only to the legislative sayings of Jesus but also to the parables and narratives of Mt. The third finally examines the Apologists, whose writings constitute a well-defined literary genre and who give witness progressively to a more bookish use of the first gospel. In each of these books, I have by and large followed a chronological order, yet grouping at times those works that belong to the same literary genre.

In concluding this dissertation, I am happy to express my gratitude to those who facilitated bringing it to fruition. First of all, I thank the professors of the Faculty of Theology to whom I owe my scholarly formation.

It is a special pleasure to express publicly my gratitude to Canon Lucien Cerfaux. Having initiated me to New Testament exegesis, he pointed out to me the significance of this study, and has continually assisted me with wise counsel and encouraged me with inalterable good will; I owe a great deal to his lessons in exegesis, his directives and his suggestions. May he accept the dedication of this work as a testimony of my heartfelt and respectful gratitude.

I must also thank in a special way Canons L. Jansens and R. de Langhe designated by the Faculty of Theology as readers of my dissertation.

My thanks are also expressed to Canon É. van Cauwenbergh, librarian of the University of Louvain, whose dedication and accessibility are known to all researchers. I also wish to underscore the kind assistance of the reverend librarians of the Abbey of Mont-César and the theological College of the Society of Jesus in Louvain. Finally I wish to thank the abbé Marien who helped me in the particularly dry task of compiling the indexes.

Louvain   *Édouard Massaux*
On the feast of the Annunciation of Our Lady 1950

Abbreviations

Journals, Series, Reference Works

ABR *Australian Biblical Review* (Melbourne)
ACW *Ancient Christian Writers*
AJT *The American Journal of Theology* (Chicago)
AKG *Arbeiten zur Kirchengeschichte*
AnBoll Analecta Bollandiana
ATAbh Alttestamentliche Abhandlungen
ATANT Abhandlungen zur Theologie des Alten und Neuen Testaments
ATR *Anglican Theological Review* (Evanston IL)
Aug *Augustinianum* (Rome)
BBB *Bonner biblische Beiträge*
BETL Bibliotheca ephemeridum theologicarum lovaniensium (Louvain)
BFChTh *Beiträge zur Förderung christlichen Theologie*
BGBE *Beiträge zur Geschichte der biblischen Exegese*
BHT *Beiträge zur historischen Theologie*
BJRL *Bulletin of the John Rylands University Library of Manchester*
BLE *Bulletin de littérature ecclésiastique* (Toulouse)
BWANT Beiträge zur Wissenschaft vom Alten und Neuen Testament
BZ *Biblische Zeitschrift* (Paderborn)
BZNW *Beihefte zur Zeitschrift für die neutestamentliche Wissenschaft* (Berlin)
CH *Church History* (Wallingford PA)
CivCatt *La Civiltà Cattolica* (Rome)
CorpAp *Corpus apologetarum christianorum saeculi secundi*
CQR *The Church Quarterly Review* (London)
CSCO Corpus scriptorum christianorum orientalium
CThM *Concordia Theological Monthly* (St. Louis MO)
DR *Downside Review* (Bath)
DTC *Dictionnaire de théologie catholique*
DT(F) Divus Thomas (Fribourg, Switzerland)
DT(P) Divus Thomas (Piacenza, Italy). Commentarium de philosophia et theologia

EBib Études bibliques
EKKNT *Evangelisch-katholischer Kommentar zum Neuen Testament*
EQ *Evangelical Quarterly* (London)
ETL *Ephemerides Theologicae Lovanienses* (Louvain)
EvTh *Evangelische Theologie* (Munich)
ExpTim *The Expository Times* (Birmingham, England)
FKD *Forschungen zur Kirchen- und Dogmengeschichte*
FRLANT Forschungen zur Religion und Literatur des Alten und Neuen Testaments
FZPhTh *Freiburger Zeitschrift für Philosophie und Theologie* (Fribourg, Switzerland)
GNT *Grundrisse zum Neuen Testament*
GOTR *Greek Orthodox Theological Review*
Greg *Gregorianum. Commentarii de re theologica et philosophica* (Rome)
HeyJ *Heythrop Journal*
HNT Handbuch zum Neuen Testament
HNT/E Handbuch zum Neuen Testament. Ergänzungsband (Supplements)
HTR *The Harvard Theological Review* (Cambridge MA)
IKC *Internationale Kirchliche Zeitschrift* (Berne)
JAC *Jahrbuch für Antike und Christentum*
JBL *Journal of Biblical Literature* (Atlanta)
JEH *Journal of Ecclesiastical History* (Cambridge and New York)
JPh *The Journal of Philosophy* (New York)
JQR *The Jewish Quarterly Review* (Philadelphia)
JR *The Journal of Religion* (Chicago)
JSJ *Journal for the Study of Judaism in the Persian, Hellenistic, and Roman Period* (Leiden)
JSNT *Journal for the Study of the New Testament* (Sheffield)
JTC *Journal for Theology and the Church* (New York)
JTS *The Journal of Theological Studies* (Oxford)
KlT Kleine Texte für (theologische und philologische) Vorlesungen und Übungen
MScRel *Mélanges de science religieuse*
NAK *Nederlands Archief voor Kerkgeschiedenis* (Leiden)
NedTTs *Nederlands theologisch tijdschrift* (The Hague)
NKZ *Neue kirchliche Zeitschrift*
NorTT *Norsk teologisk tidsskrift/Norwegian Theological Journal* (Oslo)
NovT *Novum Testamentum* (Leiden)
NovTSup Novum Testamentum Supplements
NRTh *Nouvelle revue théologique* (Louvain)
NTAbh Neutestamentliche Abhandlungen
NTS *New Testament Studies* (Cambridge)
NTTijd *Nieuw Theologisch Tijdschrift*
OCP *Orientalis christians periodica*
OrChr *Oriens christianus*

OrChrAn *Orientalia christiana Analecta*
   PG Patrologia graeca, ed. J. P. Migne, 162 vols. (1857–1866)
   PL Patrologia Latina, ed. J. P. Migne, 221 vols. (1844–1864)
   PTR *The Princeton Theological Review*
   PTS Patristische Texte und Studien
   RAp *Revue apologétique* (Paris)
 RAsMy *Revue d'ascétique et de mystique*
   RB *Revue Biblique* (Jerusalem)
  RBen *Revue Bénédictine. De critique, d'histoire et de littérature religieuses* (Maredsous, Belgium)
   REA *Revue des études anciennes*
RelStRev *Religious Studies Review* (Macon GA)
 RevistB *Revista biblica* (Buenos Aires)
RevScRel *Revue des sciences religieuses* (Strasbourg)
RevThom *Revue thomiste*
   RHE *Revue d'histoire ecclésiastique* (Louvain)
  RHLR *Revue d'histoire et de littérature religieuses*
  RHPR *Revue d'histoire et de philosophie religieuses* (Strasbourg)
   RHR *Revue de l'histoire des religions* (Paris)
   ROC *Revue de l'orient chrétien*
   RQH *Revue des questions historiques*
 RSPhTh *Revue des sciences philosophiques et théologiques* (Paris)
   RSR *Recherches de science religieuse* (Paris)
 RThAM *Recherches de théologie ancienne et médiévale* (Louvain)
   RTL *Revue théologique de Louvain* (Louvain)
   RTP *Revue de théologie et de philosophie* (Lausanne)
   RUO *Revue de l'université d'Ottawa*
   SAH Sitzungsberichte der Heidelberger Akademie der Wissenschaften, philosophische-historische Klasse
   SAQ Sammlung ausgewählter kirchen- und dogmengeschichtlicher Quellenschriften
   SC Sources chrétiennes
  SCatt *Scuola Cattolica* (Varese, Italy)
   Scr *Scripture*
   SJT *Scottish Journal of Theology* (Edinburgh)
   SP *Studia patristica*
  SPAW Sitzungsberichte der preussischen Akademie der Wissenschaften
   StEv *Studia Evangelica* (Berlin)
   StTh *Studia Theologica* (Lund)
  TDNT *Theological Dictionary of the New Testament*, 10 vols., ed. G. Kittel and G. Friedrich, trans. G. Bromiley (1964–1976). ET of *TWNT: Theologisches Wörterbuch zum Neuen Testament*, 10 vols. (1933–1976)
   TGl *Theologie und Glaube* (Paderborn, Germany)
   Th *Theology. A Journal of Historic Christianity* (London)

ThJ   *Theologische Jahrbücher* (Tübingen)
ThLB   *Theologisches Literaturblatt*
ThPh   *Theologie und Philosophie* (Frankfurt)
ThQ   *Theologische Quartalschrift* (Tübingen)
ThR   *Theologische Rundschau* (Tübingen)
ThRv   *Theologische Revue* (Münster)
ThT   *Theologisch Tijdschrift* (Leiden)
ThZ   *Theologische Zeitschrift* (Basel)
TLZ   *Theologische Literaturzeitung* (Leipzig)
TS   *Theological Studies* (Washington)
TSK   *Theologische Studien und Kritiken* (Hamburg)
TTh   *Tijdschrift voor Theologie* (Nijmegen)
TU   Texte und Untersuchungen
TVers *Theologische Versuche* (Berlin)
VC   *Vigiliae christianae*
VD   *Verbum domini* (Rome)
VetChr *Vetera Christianorum* (Bari, Italy)
VigChr *Vigiliae Christianae. A review of early Christian life and language* (Amsterdam)
VS   *Verbum salutis*
WUNT   Wissenschaftliche Untersuchungen zum Neuen Testament
ZKG   *Zeitschrift für Kirchengeschichte* (Stuttgart)
ZKTh   *Zeitschrift für katholische Theologie* (Vienna)
ZKWL   *Zeitschrift für kirchliche Wissenschaft und kirchliches Leben* (Leipzig)
ZNW   *Zeitschrift für die neutestamentliche Wissenschaft und die Kunde der älteren Kirche* (Berlin)
ZThK   *Zeitschrift für Theologie und Kirche* (Tübingen)
ZWT   *Zeitschrift für wissenschaftliche Theologie* (Jena)

Miscellaneous

corr.   correction, corrected (e.g., corr. repr.)
diss.   dissertation
ed(s). edition, edited by, editor(s)
ET   English translation
n.   note (29n.3 = page 29, note 3)
n.s.   new series
orig.   original
repr.   reprint(ed)
trans. translation, translated by, translator(s)

Book 2

THE LATER CHRISTIAN WRITINGS

I have examined in volume 1 the works of the earliest church writers. I now proceed to later Christian writings, in which there emerges progressively not only the use of the sayings of Christ drawn from the Gospel of Mt., but an influence of this gospel as a whole. In this second volume, I also consider a few Gnostic writings which I have investigated from a point of view that interests me. Six chapters divide this second volume, the last ones grouping, as far as possible, writings which belong to the same literary genre:

1. 2 Clement.
2. Polycarp and the *Martyrdom of Polycarp*.
3. The Apocalypses.
4. The noncanonical gospels.
5. The *Agrapha*.
6. Some Gnostic writings.

Chapter 1

SECOND CLEMENT

The first work which I consider is the so-called *Second Epistle of Clement of Rome to the Corinthians,* which is generally dated in the first half of the second century, and more precisely between the years 120 and 140. As I examine it according to my focus of interest, I consider in the first section its relationship to the Gospel of Mt., and I save the second section for other New Testament writings in order to give solid grounds to a comparative judgment on the place and influence of the Gospel of Mt. in this writing.

Section 1
SAINT MATTHEW

The first paragraph concentrates on the texts of 2 Clement where a Matthean influence is certain. A second paragraph is reserved for those texts where this influence is less certain or to be excluded.[1]

§1. Texts in Which the Literary Influence of Matthew Is Certain

1. 2 Clem. 2:4

Καὶ ἑτέρα δὲ γραφὴ λέγει, ὅτι οὐκ ἦλθον καλέσαι δικαίους, ἀλλὰ ἁμαρτωλούς.

And another Scripture says: "I came not to call the just, but sinners."

This phrase, attributed to Scripture, can be found in Mt. 9:13, Mk. 2:17, and Lk. 5:32. These New Testament parallels immediately raise the question: does the

---

[1] I quote the texts of 2 Clement according to the edition of K. Bihlmeyer, *Die Apostolischen Väter,* Sammlung ausgewählter Kirchen- und Dogmengeschichter Quellenschriften, zweite Rehe, erstes Heft, erster Teil (Tübingen, 1924) 71-81. [The English text of 2 Clement, trans. Francis X. Glimm, is taken from *The Apostolic Fathers,* trans. Francis X. Glimm, Joseph M. F. Marique, and Gerald G. Walsh, *The Fathers of the Church, A New Translation,* vol. 1 (Washington DC: The Catholic University of America Press, 1962). Editor's note.]

author of 2 Clement actually grant the value of Scripture to a saying from the New Testament, whereas elsewhere he seems to grant it only to the Old Testament, and no other logion of Christ is quoted as γραφή?[2]

Authors generally agree that this particular point testifies in favor of a "Scripture" of the New Testament. D. Van Den Eynde challenges this way of thinking, and asserts that it is doubtful, at the very least, that the anonymous author of 2 Clement wished to quote as Scripture a gospel text. In Pseudo-Clement's mind, the so-called quotation of the New Testament would be drawn from prophetic writings. In order to establish that Christ saved us through his sufferings, he would first provide a text from Isaiah, then this particular text which to him was also prophetic. "The reason for this error seems quite clear," writes D. Van Den Eynde, "provided that the quote is reset in its context in Matthew. Here it is: 'Jesus says: "Those who are well have no need of a physician, but those who are sick. Go and learn what this means: *I desire mercy, and not sacrifice.* For I came not to call the righteous, but sinners." ' The italicized words, which are lacking in the parallel passages from Mark and Luke, are borrowed from Hosea.[3] The words which follow in fact restore the actual words of Christ, but it could also be thought—to err is easy—that they still belonged to the prophecy of Hosea. This is why I believe that the author of 2 Clement was mistaken. I have proof that he drew his quote from the Gospel of Matthew or, at least, from a writing which offers that same context, because, as he explains the words 'I came not to call the righteous, but sinners,' he also draws from the words of Hosea: 'I *desire mercy* and not *sacrifice,*' although he did not quote them. Indeed, he writes: 'So, also, Christ willed to save the things that were perishing, and He saved many men, when He had come and called us who were, even now, perishing. Since, then, He has bestowed such *mercy* on us, first that we the living do not sacrifice to gods who are dead. . . . ' The paraphrase includes more than the quote led us to anticipate; the author remembered simultaneously both parts of the 'prophecy': the words of Hosea and those of Christ. It is, therefore, doubtful, at the very least, that the anonymous author of 2 Clement wished in this case to quote as Scripture a gospel text."[4]

This hypothesis is quite plausible. But there is another and maybe simpler one, which would explain the presence of the word γραφή, even if in the author's mind the quote came from Mt. It must be acknowledged that the meaning of γραφή at-

---

[2]Cf. 2 Clem. 4:5; 5:2; 5:4; 6:1; 8:5; 9:11; 12:2; 13:4 (this last reference is introduced by λέγει ὁ θεός).

[3]Mt. translates the Hebrew text of Hosea 6:6; the text of the LXX says διότι ἔλεος θέλω ἢ θυσίαν.

[4]Cf. D. Van Den Eynde, *Les Normes de l'Enseignement Chrétien dans la littérature patristique des trois premiers siècles* (Gembloux, Paris, 1933) 47-49.

tributed to the Old Testament does not extend to the gospels.[5] Their significance comes from the fact that they bear witness to the sayings of Christ. But a significance equivalent to Scripture could be attributed to a saying of Christ, not simply because it comes from the gospel in which it is written, but because it is a saying of Christ who is the Word of God.[6] However, this problem is not within my focus of interest. My concern is to know with which of the parallels the author is in literary contact.

In any hypothesis, it must be acknowledged that 2 Clement depends on Mt.

The similarity of the synoptic parallels among themselves and with the text of 2 Clem. 2:4 is very great: a synoptic table shows it clearly:

2 Clem. 2:4	Matt. 9:13	Mark 2:17	Luke 5:32
καὶ ἑτέρα δὲ γραφὴ λέγει ὅτι οὐκ ἦλθον καλέσαι δικαίους, ἀλλὰ ἁμαρτωλούς.	πορευθέντες δὲ μάθετε τί ἐστιν· ἔλεος θέλω καὶ οὐ θυσίαν· οὐ γὰρ ἦλθον καλέσαι δικαίους, ἀλλὰ ἁμαρτωλούς.	οὐκ ἦλθον καλέσαι δικαίους ἀλλὰ ἁμαρτωλούς.	οὐκ ἐλήλυθα καλέσαι δικαίους ἀλλὰ ἁμαρτωλούς.

The texts of Mt. and Mk. are practically identical to that of 2 Clem. 2:4, which seems, indeed, to have kept the phraseology of Mt. or Mk., rather than Lk.; the latter, in fact, uses ἐλήλυθα. Now, if the author of 2 Clem. was inspired by Lk., he actually reproduces the remainder of the text so faithfully that it would be hard to explain why he has ἦλθον instead of ἐλήλυθα.

But between Mt. and Mk., which one should be given preference? The absence of the particle γάρ is not sufficient to tip the scale towards Mk., so it is clear that only the context can resolve the question. Now, in the context of 2 Clem. 2:4, reference to the mercy of God is made more than once, in 1:7 and 3:1, the first passage appearing a few verses before, and the second a few verses after the text in question. But it is precisely in Mt. 9:13 that a reference is made to the mercy of God following the text of Hosea. This is why it can be asserted that the author is here in literary contact with the text of Mt., which he quotes literally.

D. Van Den Eynde suggested that the author may have drawn from a writing presenting the same context as Mt. The sheer simplicity of it prevents me from subscribing to this view, for this other source from which the author is supposed to have drawn is unknown to us, and it is a mere presupposition. Moreover, we

---

[5]Cf. F. C. Overbeck, "Über das Verhältnis Justinus des Märtyrers zur Apostelgeschichte," *ZWT* 15 (1872): 406; Overbeck, a review of *Patrum apostolicorum opera*, fasc. 1, by de Gebhart, Harnack, Zahn, in *TLZ* 1 (1876) col. 338.

[6]However, I must stress that , for my purpose, the saying of Christ is considered as written, because of the lemma ἑτέρα δὲ γραφὴ λέγει. When Pseudo-Clement invokes elsewhere a saying of Christ, he uses the lemma εἶπεν ὁ κύριος (2 Clem. 9:11) or λέγει δὲ καὶ αὐτός (2 Clem. 3:1-2).

have in hand the Gospel of Mt., whose text and context in this passage furnish an excellent parallel to 2 Clem. 2:4.

2. 2 Clem. 3:1-2

. . . τίς ἡ γνῶσις ἡ πρὸς αὐτόν, ἢ τὸ μὴ ἀρνεῖσθαι δι᾽ οὗ ἔγνωμεν αὐτόν; λέγει δὲ καὶ αὐτός· Τὸν ὁμολογήσαντά με ἐνώπιον τῶν ἀνθρώπων, ὁμολογήσω αὐτὸν ἐνώπιον τοῦ πατρός μου.

. . . what is true knowledge concerning Him except not to deny Him through whom we knew the Father? He Himself says: He who confessed me before men, I will confess him before my Father.

These words recall several gospel texts: Mt. 10:32-33: Πᾶς οὖν ὅστις ὁμολογήσει ἐν ἐμοὶ ἔμπροσθεν τῶν ἀνθρώπων, ὁμολογήσω κἀγὼ ἐν αὐτῷ ἔμπροσθεν τοῦ πατρός μου τοῦ ἐν τοῖς οὐρανοῖς· ὅστις δ᾽ ἂν ἀρνήσηταί με ἔμπροσθεν τῶν ἀνθρώπων, ἀρνήσομαι κἀγὼ αὐτὸν ἔμπροσθεν τοῦ πατρός μου τοῦ ἐν τοῖς οὐρανοῖς; Lk. 12:8-9: Λέγω δὲ ὑμῖν, πᾶς ὃς ἂν ὁμολογήσῃ ἐν ἐμοὶ ἔμπροσθεν τῶν ἀνθρώπων, καὶ ὁ υἱὸς τοῦ ἀνθρώπου ὁμολογήσει ἐν αὐτῷ ἔμπροσθεν τῶν ἀγγέλων τοῦ θεοῦ· ὁ δὲ ἀρνησάμενός με ἐνώπιον τῶν ἀνθρώπων ἀπαρνηθήσεται ἐνώπιον τῶν ἀγγέλων τοῦ θεοῦ; and also 2 Tim. 2:12: . . . εἰ ἀρνησόμεθα, κἀκεῖνος ἀρνήσεται ἡμᾶς.

The absence of the verbs ὁμολογέω and ἀρνέομαι in Mk. 8:38 and Lk. 9:26, texts sometimes proposed as parallels, excludes thereby a literary influence on the author of 2 Clem.

Pseudo-Clement depends here on Mt. 10:32-33. In fact, in 2 Clement, just as in the Matthean text, the second part of the sentence is in the first person (ὁμολογήσω) whereas in Lk. it is in the third person (ὁμολογήσει) with the Son of Man as subject, an expression absent from the text of 2 Clement. Moreover, in the second part of the sentence, as in Mt., Christ confesses before his Father and not, as in Lk., before the angels of God, those who confessed him before men. It can, therefore, be thought that ἀρνεῖσθαι of verse 1 is also inspired by Mt. rather than by Lk. or by 2 Tim., since it is in the same context that Mt. speaks of denying Christ.[7]

---

[7]The presence in 2 Clem. of ἐνώπιον, which is also found in Lk., could possibly bring to mind a reminiscence of the text of Lk. Let me note, however, that in Lk. 12:9 ἐνώπιον is placed after ἀρνεῖσθαι whereas in 2 Clem. it is read after ὁμολογέω; Lk. 12:8, after ὁμολογέω, reads ἔμπροσθεν just as in Mt. 10:32, and I base my opinion of asserting a literary dependence on the text which contains ὁμολογέω.

3. 2 Clem. 3:5

Λέγει δὲ καὶ ἐν τῷ Ἡσαΐᾳ· Ὁ λαὸς οὗτος τοῖς χείλεσίν με τιμᾷ, ἡ δὲ καρδία αὐτῶν πόρρω ἄπεστιν ἀπ' ἐμοῦ.

And He (Christ) says also in Isaias: "This people honors me with their lips, but their heart is far from me."

We have already seen this quotation of Isaiah in 1 Clem. 15:2, and I pointed out in that instance that Clement of Rome was inspired by Mt. 15:8 rather than by Isaiah 29:13 or Mk. 7:6.

The reasons I gave to support this opinion are equally valid in this present case. First of all, 2 Clem. is very close to Mt. 15:8, which as a matter of fact reads: ὁ λαὸς οὗτος τοῖς χείλεσίν με τιμᾷ, ἡ δὲ καρδία αὐτῶν πόρρω ἀπέχει ἀπ' ἐμοῦ. In addition, Pseudo-Clement also has a motive to think of Mt. rather than the text of the LXX of Isaiah: indeed, he invites the reader to confess Christ sincerely so as to honor him not only with lip service but from the heart and spirit (2 Clem. 3:4). Now, Mt. militates precisely against the hypocrisy of the Pharisees whom he depicts through the quote in question. Finally, Mk. cannot have exercized its influence here, since no other text of 2 Clement seems to have been inspired by the second gospel.

But does the author refer to a text which the oral tradition might have preserved? It is not probable: the context which recommends an unequivocal attitude in the service of the Lord suggests the text of Mt., and it can be supposed, because of the way he quotes, that 2 Clem. uses a written text.[8]

Let it not be said that Pseudo-Clement referred explicitly to Isaiah and that, as a result, he borrowed the text in question from the prophet. Indeed, it was in Mt. that he found the mention of Isaiah.

4. 2 Clem. 4:2

Λέγει γάρ· Οὐ πᾶς ὁ λέγων μοι· Κύριε κύριε, σωθήσεται, ἀλλ' ὁ ποιῶν τὴν δικαιοσύνην.

For He (Christ) says: "Not everyone who says to me Lord, Lord, shall be saved, but he who works justice."

This saying of Christ recalls Mt. 7:21: Οὐ πᾶς ὁ λέγων μοι κύριε κύριε, εἰσελεύσεται εἰς τὴν βασιλείαν τῶν οὐρανῶν, ἀλλ' ὁ ποιῶν τὸ θέλημα τοῦ πατρός μου τοῦ ἐν τοῖς οὐρανοῖς, and Lk. 6:46: Τί δέ με καλεῖτε· κύριε κύριε, καὶ οὐ ποιεῖτε ἃ λέγω;

At first reading, it seems that the text of 2 Clement is much closer to Mt. than to Lk. A definite literary contact with Mt. 7:21 can be asserted. In fact, in the first

---

[8]Cf. book 1, 20-21.

gospel and in the letter of Pseudo-Clement, the same words are found: οὐ πᾶς ὁ λέγων μοι· κύριε κύριε and ἀλλ' ὁ ποιῶν; moreover, the identical meaning between σωθήσεται of 2 Clement and εἰσελεύσεται εἰς τὴν βασιλείαν τῶν οὐρανῶν of Mt. cannot be doubted. Finally, ποιεῖν δικαιοσύνην is equivalent to ποιεῖν τὸ θέλημα τοῦ πατρός μου τοῦ ἐν τοῖς οὐρανοῖς of Mt. In addition, not only is there equivalence, but Pseudo-Clement comments excellently on the Matthean thought, since for Mt., justice consists precisely in accomplishing the commandments, the expression of the will of God.

Let me note that it is the Lord who speaks when it says λέγει γάρ or λέγει δέ (2 Clem. 3:5). But he speaks sometimes in the gospel, other times in Isaiah (ἐν τῷ Ἠσαΐᾳ, 2 Clem. 3:5). He is the one who expresses himself in the prophetic word. However, if this is so, then there is a parallel between the saying of Jesus written in Isaiah and that which is written in the gospel. This would, as such, allude to a written word.

This would explain that a saying of Jesus in the gospel could already be Scripture; since it is Scripture in Isaiah, it is also scripture in the gospel.

5. 2 Clem. 6:2

Τί γὰρ τὸ ὄφελος, ἐάν τις τὸν κόσμον ὅλον κερδήσῃ, τὴν δὲ ψυχὴν ζημιωθῇ;

For what is the advantage if a man gain the whole world and lose his soul?

This saying refers us to the synoptic gospels: Mt. 16:26; Mk. 8:36; and Lk. 9:25.

2 Clem. 6:2	Matt. 16:26	Mark 8:36	Luke 9:25
Τί γὰρ τὸ ὄφελος ἐάν τις τὸν κόσμον ὅλον κερδήσῃ, τὴν δὲ ψυχὴν ζημιωθῇ;	Τί γὰρ ὠφελυθήσεται ἄνθρωπος, ἐὰν τὸν κόσμον ὅλον κερδήσῃ τὴν δὲ ψυχὴν αὐτοῦ ζημιωθῇ;	τί γὰρ ὠφελεῖ ἄνθρωπον κερδῆσαι τόν κόσμον ὅλον καὶ ζημιωθῆναι τὴν ψυχὴν αὐτοῦ;	τί γάρ ὠφελεῖται ἄνθρωπος κερδήσας τὸν κόσμον ὅλον ἑαυτὸν δὲ ἀπολέσας ἢ ζημιωθείς;

The sentence in 2 Clement is identical in meaning to that of the synoptics, but a literary contact is certain only with the Gospel of Mt. The author of 2 Clement quotes the latter almost literally. He has preserved from Mt. the turn of phrase, the disposition of the words, and the tense of the verbs. Some slight differences are, however, evident: Pseudo-Clement uses τὸ ὄφελος instead of ὠφεληθήσεται. (Mk. and Lk. do not have either.) He has replaced ἄνθρωπος of Mt. with τις and has dropped αὐτοῦ after ψυχήν.

The difference between Mk. and Lk., on the one hand, and 2 Clem. 6:2, on the other, is much stronger: first of all, the expression τὸν κόσμον ὅλον in 2 Clem., which as in Mt. precedes the verb κερδήσῃ, follows it in the two other synoptics; then a similar remark is in order for τὴν ψυχήν and the verb ζημιωθῇ; finally, 2

Clement does not have the infinitive forms κερδῆσαι, ζημιωθῆναι of Mk. nor the participial forms κερδήσας, ζημιωθείς of Lk., but rather the personal forms κερδήσῃ and ζημιωθῇ of Mt.

6. 2 Clem. 9:11

Καὶ γὰρ εἶπεν ὁ κύριος· ᾿Αδελφοί μου οὗτοί εἰσιν οἱ ποιοῦντες τὸ θέλημα τοῦ πατρός μου.

For the Lord said: "Those who do the will of my Father are my brethren."

This saying of Christ recalls the synoptics: Mt. 12:49b-50; Mk. 3:34-35; and Lk. 8:21.

2 Clem. 9:11	Matt. 12:49b-50	Mark 3:34-35	Luke 8:21
᾿Αδελφοί μου οὗτοί εἰσιν οἱ ποιοῦν-τες τὸ θέλημα τοῦ πατρός μου.	ἰδοὺ ἡ μήτηρ μου καὶ οἱ ἀδελφοί μου· ὅστις γὰρ ἂν ποιήσῃ τὸ θέλημα τοῦ πατρός μου τοῦ ἐν οὐρανοῖς, αὐ-τός μου ἀδελφὸς καὶ ἀδελφὴ καὶ μήτηρ ἐστίν.	ἴδε ἡ μήτηρ μου καὶ οἱ ἀδελφοί μου· ὃς ἂν ποιήσῃ τὸ θέλημα τοῦ θεοῦ, οὗτος ἀδελφός μου καὶ ἀδελφὴ καὶ μήτηρ ἐστίν.	μήτηρ μου καὶ ἀδελφοί μου οὗτοί εἰσιν οἱ τὸν λόγον τοῦ θεοῦ ἀκούον-τες καὶ ποιοῦντες.

Contrary to certain commentators who assert that the words of 2 Clement do not come from the texts of one of our gospels, but rather from a noncanonical source,[9] I believe it can be said that Pseudo-Clement is literarily dependent on the Gospels of Mt. and Lk.

First of all, let me note that the idea in 2 Clem. 9:11 is similar to that in the synoptic tradition. Let me mention also that the text itself is closer to Mt. than to Mk. or Lk.: indeed, all the words of the author are found in Mt. 11:49b-50. In Mk. or Lk., instead of τοῦ πατρός μου we find simply τοῦ θεοῦ, and Lk. does not even have the substantive θέλημα.

Moreover, it can easily be understood that Pseudo-Clement did not use the words ἡ μήτηρ μου. In the context, indeed, he writes in verse 10: "Let us, then, give Him everlasting praise, not only from our mouth, but also from our heart, that He may receive us as sons (υἱούς)." He proves, therefore, in verse 11 that we can be received as sons when he records a saying of Christ who, being the Son of God, has called us his brothers. He thus implies that we can be the sons of God, since we are the brothers of his Son. We see, therefore, that the mention of ἡ μήτηρ μου would have been out of place in the thinking of the author.

---

[9]Cf. de Gebhardt and Harnack, *Clementis Romani ad Corinthios quae dicuntur epistulae,* 125; Knopf, *Die Lehre der zwölf Apostel, Die zwei Clemensbriefe,* 167.

Based on the analogous quote of Epiphanius, who claimed it to be borrowed from the *Gospel of the Ebionites*,[10] some commentators have thought that this quote came from that gospel. But as Lightfoot observes, it simply proves that the *Gospel of the Ebionites* had appropriated pieces from the canonical gospels.[11]

Let me add that 2 Clem. 9:11 is very close to Lk.: ἀδελφοί μου οὗτοί εἰσιν οἱ . . . ποιοῦντες; the author may have combined the texts of Lk. and Mt.

§2. Texts in Which the Literary Influence of Matthew Is Less Certain or to Be Excluded

1. 2 Clem. 2:7

Οὕτως καὶ ὁ Χριστὸς ἠθέλησεν σῶσαι τὰ ἀπολλύμενα, καὶ ἔσωσεν πολλούς, ἐλθὼν καὶ καλέσας ἡμᾶς ἤδη ἀπολλυμένους.

So, also, Christ willed to save the things that were perishing, and He saved many men, when He had come and called us who were, even now, perishing. [The English translation of this passage has been added by the editor.]

Several texts are generally linked to this passage: Mt. 18:11 which is omitted in excellent manuscripts: ἦλθεν γὰρ ὁ υἱὸς τοῦ ἀνθρώπου σῶσαι τὸ ἀπολωλός; Lk. 19:10: ἦλθεν γὰρ ὁ υἱὸς τοῦ ἀνθρώπου ζητῆσαι καὶ σῶσαι τὸ ἀπολωλός; and 1 Tim. 1:15: πιστὸς ὁ λόγος καὶ πάσης ἀποδοχῆς ἄξιος, ὅτι Χριστὸς Ἰησοῦς ἦλθεν εἰς τὸν κόσμον ἁμαρτωλοὺς σῶσαι.

The texts of Mt. (Western) and of Lk. are almost identical. The best manuscripts of Mt. in this group read ζητῆσαι,[12] a word present in Lk. The absence of this word ζητῆσαι in 2 Clem. 2:7 justifies the opinion that Pseudo-Clement is literarily dependent on the Matthean text, presuming it already had the Western form of Mt.

Yet this opinion is not certain, since many witnesses of Mt., the Syriac Sinaitic and the Jerusalem versions, the Coptic Sahidic and Bohairic versions, the Ethiopic version and the Georgian version do not include this verse; and among those which include it— generally the representatives of the Western text—a few, nevertheless a small number, read the verb ζητῆσαι as does Lk.

---

[10] Cf. Epiphanius, *Panarion Haer.* 30.14.

[11] Cf. Lightfoot, *The Apostolic Fathers*, part 1, *S. Clement of Rome*, 2:231.

[12] Against G and many minor miniscules, the Hierosolymite Syriac version, the Bohairic Coptic version (a few witnesses), and the Ethiopic version.

2. 2 Clem. 11:2- 3

Λέγει γὰρ καὶ ὁ προφητικὸς λόγος˙ Ταλαίπωροί εἰσιν οἱ δίψυχοι, οἱ διστάζοντες τῇ καρδίᾳ, οἱ λέγοντες˙ Ταῦτα πάλαι ἠκούσαμεν καὶ ἐπὶ τῶν πατέρων ἡμῶν, ἡμεῖς δὲ ἡμέραν ἐξ ἡμέρας προσδεχόμενοι οὐδὲν τούτων ἑωράκαμεν. Ἀνόητοι, συμβάλετε ἑαυτοὺς ξύλῳ˙ λάβετε ἄμπελον˙ πρῶτον μὲν φυλλοροεῖ, εἶτα βλαστὸς γίνεται, μετὰ ταῦτα ὄμφαξ, εἶτα σταφυλὴ παρεστηκυῖα.

For the prophetic word says: ''Miserable are the double-minded, who hesitate in their heart and say: All these things we have heard even in our fathers' time, but we have waited from day to day and have seen none of them. O foolish men, compare yourselves to a tree. Take a vine; first it sheds its leaves, then there comes a bud, after this a sour berry, then the bunch of ripe grapes.'' [The English translation of this passage has been added by the editor.]

This text has already been examined in the study of 1 Clem. 23:3-4 in view of the fact that some authors linked it at times with Mt. 24:32-33.[13] It suffices to revert to the conclusion reached in that context: no text from the Old or New Testament can be taken into consideration here. This passage can be considered only as a reference to an apocryphon.

3. 2 Clem. 6:7

Ποιοῦντες γὰρ τὸ θέλημα τοῦ Χριστοῦ εὑρήσομεν ἀνάπαυσιν˙ εἰ δὲ μήγε, οὐδὲν ἡμᾶς ῥύσεται ἐκ τῆς αἰωνίου κολάσεως, ἐὰν παρακούσωμεν τῶν ἐντολῶν αὐτοῦ.

For if we do the will of Christ, we shall find repose; but if not, nothing shall save us from eternal punishment, if we neglect His commandments. [The translation of this passage has been added by the editor.]

The expression αἰώνιος κόλασις brings to mind Mt. 25:46: καὶ ἀπελεύσονται οὗτοι εἰς κόλασιν αἰώνιον, οἱ δὲ δίκαιοι εἰς ζωὴν αἰώνιον.

These words of Mt. are drawn from the Discourse on the Parousia and envision, therefore, the future world. However, these simple words are not sufficient a base to assert a literary contact with the first gospel. Indeed, the remainder of the sentence of 2 Clement does not resemble Mt. in any way. I shall merely point out that this expression αἰώνιος κόλασις is unique in Mt. for all the New Testament. 1 Jn. 4:18 does use the term κόλασις but without the qualifier αἰώνιος.

The author of 2 Clement knows the Gospel of Mt. He is literarily dependent on it in many parts of his writing. I have pointed out that in certain passages in which he is under a Matthean literary influence, Pseudo-Clement follows the Matthean text fairly closely, sometimes keeping even the verbal forms of the Mat-

---

[13]Cf. book 1, 27-28.

thean sentence.[14] He even quotes literally a text of Mt.,[15] most probably as Scripture.

Section 2
THE OTHER NEW TESTAMENT WRITINGS

The author of 2 Clement knows and uses still other New Testament writings besides the Gospel of Mt., or shows at times common thoughts with some of them. According to their more or less frequent use of these writings, I propose to consider first the other synoptics, then the letters of Paul, next the catholic epistles of James and Peter, and finally the Johannine writings.

§1. The Other Synoptics

Since no passage of 2 Clement is in literary contact with the Gospel of Mk., this paragraph considers only the various texts which reveal a definite or probable use of the Gospel of Lk.; I also add those sections in 2 Clement which are in agreement with the synoptic tradition, but which do not demonstrate a particular affinity with one of the synoptics. I shall consider first the texts which show a relationship with the Gospel of Lk.

Speaking of the necessity to confess Christ, not only in words, but in deeds, Pseudo-Clement writes in 2 Clem. 4:5: "For this reason, provided you do these things, the Lord said: 'If ye be gathered together with Me in My bosom and do not carry out My commandments, I will cast you off (ἀποβαλῶ ὑμᾶς) and will say to you: Depart from me; I know not whence you come, you workers of iniquity (καὶ ἐρῶ ὑμῖν. Ὑπάγετε ἀπ' ἐμοῦ, οὐκ οἶδα ὑμᾶς πόθεν ἐστέ, ἐργάται ἀνομίας).' '' For this saying of Christ, the commentators usually refer to an unknown source; for some, this source is the *Gospel according to the Egyptians*.[16] It is usually noted that the tone is indeed that of the commandments of Christ, to which the entire context speaks, and that the author must have had before him an apocryphal gospel.[17]

To be sure, the words "if ye be gathered with Me in My bosom and do not carry out My commandments, I will cast you off . . . " find no parallel in our gospels. As a result, some have thought of the *Gospel according to the Egyptians*; but the proposition "Depart from me; I know not whence you come, you workers of iniquity" can be compared to Mt. 7:23; Lk. 13:27; and Ps. 6:9.

---

[14]Cf. 8-9, above: 2 Clem. 6:2 and Mt. 16:26.

[15]Cf. 3-6, above: 2 Clem. 2:4 and Mt. 9:13.

[16]Lightfoot, *S. Clement of Rome*, 2:218.

[17]Cf. Knopf, *Die Lehre der zwölf Apostel, Die zwei Clemensbriefe*, 159.

2 Clem. 4:5b does not coincide literally with any of the parallels. Yet it is closer to Lk. than to Mt. Indeed, we find in Lk. 13:27 the words οὐκ οἶδα πόθεν ἐστέ and ἐργάται, absent in Mt. 7:23, which has nothing in common with 2 Clem. 4:5b other than ἀπ' ἐμοῦ and ἀνομία. This last word is absent in Lk.

It is, therefore, easier to believe that the author of 2 Clement is literarily dependent on Lk., which he has probably colored with a slight Matthean tint recognizable by the use of the substantive ἀνομία, which can also come from Ps.

In this part of 2 Clement, there would, therefore, be two sayings of Christ: the first from an unknown source, the *Gospel according to the Egyptians* in the opinion of several scholars; the second inspired by the Gospel of Lk.

Naturally, there is still the possible hypothesis that both quotes come from an apocryphon which might itself have drawn from Lk. However, it can as easily be understood that the first saying of Christ, which ends in the apocryphon with ἀποβαλῶ ὑμᾶς, reminded Pseudo-Clement of the text of Lk., which he simply joined to the quote drawn from the apocryphon.

In 2 Clem. 5:2-4, the author relates a dialogue between Jesus and Peter: "For the Lord said: 'You shall be as lambs in the midst of wolves.' And Peter answered and said to Him: 'What if the wolves should tear the lambs?' Jesus said to Peter: 'The lambs should not fear the wolves after they are dead. And so with you—fear not those who kill you and can do nothing more to you; but fear Him who after your death has power over soul and body, to cast them into hell fire.' "

All the commentators see here a quote of an apocryphal gospel, but they note that this conversation between Jesus and Peter has a flavor which recalls Mt. 10:16, 28 and Lk. 10:3; 12:4-5.

The principal argument in favor of an apocryphal gospel rests on the form of the dialogue in this passage and on the presence of the words "what if wolves should tear the lambs" and "the lambs should not fear the wolves after they are dead," two phrases absent in the canonical gospels.

A synoptic comparison illustrates the similarity of this text to the gospels.

2 Clem. 5:2-4	Matt. 10:16, 28	Luke 10:3; 12:4-5
² . . . Ἔσεσθε ὡς ἀρνία ἐν μέσῳ λύκων. ⁴ . . . ὑμεῖς μὴ φοβεῖσθε τοὺς ἀποκτέννοντας ὑμᾶς καὶ μηδὲν ὑμῖν δυναμένους ποιεῖν, ἀλλὰ φοβεῖσθε τὸν μετὰ τὸ ἀποθανεῖν ὑμᾶς ἔχοντα ἐξουσίαν ψυχῆς καὶ σώματος τοῦ βαλεῖν εἰς γέενναν πυρός.	¹⁶ . . . ὑμᾶς ὡς πρόβατα ἐν μέσῳ λύκων. ²⁸καὶ μὴ φοβεῖσθε ἀπὸ τῶν ἀποκτεννόντων τὸ σῶμα, τὴν δὲ ψυχὴν μὴ δυναμένων ἀποκτεῖναι. φοβεῖσθε δὲ μάλλον τὸν δυνάμενον καὶ ψυχὴν καὶ σῶμα ἀπολέσαι ἐν γεέννῃ.	³ . . . ὑμᾶς ὡς ἄρνας ἐν μέσῳ λύκων. ¹²:⁴⁻⁵μὴ φοβηθῆτε ἀπὸ τῶν ἀποκτεννόντων τὸ σῶμα καὶ μετὰ ταῦτα μὴ ἐχόντων περισσότερόν τι ποιῆσαι. ὑποδείξω δὲ ὑμῖν τίνα φοβηθῆτε· φοβήθητε τὸν μετὰ τὸ ἀποκτεῖναι ἔχοντα ἐξουσίαν ἐμβαλεῖ εἰς τὴν γέενναν.

This synoptic table, especially with reference to 2 Clem. 5:4, would possibly indicate that 2 Clement or the apocryphon combined here Lk. and Mt. In Lk. 10:3, in fact, we find the word ἄρναι, which corresponds to ἀρνία as opposed to πρόβατα in Mt. The beginning of verse 4 corresponds more to Mt. 10:28a, where we find the formula of 2 Clem. μὴ φοβεῖσθε against μὴ φοβηθῆτε of Lk., and the participle δυναμένων parallel to δυναμένους, absent in Lk. The end of verse 4 is closer to Lk. 12:5 because of the words ἔχοντα ἐξουσίαν, which are found in 2 Clem. but lacking in Mt.; because of the verb βαλεῖν, which is closer to ἐμβαλεῖν of Lk. than to ἀπολέσαι of Mt.; and because of the expression εἰς γέενναν, which is a more faithful parallel to εἰς τὴν γέενναν of Lk. than to ἐν γεέννῃ of Mt. Let me add finally the verb ποιῆσαι in Lk., which is present in the form ποιεῖν in 2 Clem. but which Mt. does not use here.

But this hypothesis of a combination of texts of Mt. and of Lk. has against it a serious argument which detracts significantly from its validity: 2 Clem. 5:4 is an integral part of the preceding verses and, as has been said, none of our gospels relates a similar conversation between Jesus and Peter. The use of an apocryphal source is, therefore, more likely.[18] Yet, the author of this apocryphal source may have used Mt. and Lk. This concerns the question of the apocryphal gospels which we examine later.

We read in 2 Clem. 6:1: "The Lord says: 'No servant can serve two masters. If we desire to serve both God and Mammon, it is no good to us (οὐδεὶς οἰκέτης δύναται δυσὶ κυρίοις δουλεύειν. Ἐὰν ἡμεῖς θέλωμεν καὶ θεῷ δουλεύειν καὶ μαμωνᾷ, ἀσύμφορον ὑμῖν ἐστίν).'" As we read these words, they seem to echo Mt. 6:24 and Lk. 16:13. There is an unquestionable literary contact with one of the two gospels, whose texts are almost identical. The only difference between the text of Mt. and that of Lk. consists in the fact that the text generally preserved in Mt. does not contain the reading οἰκέτης, which is corroborated only by L, Δ, Φ, and some minuscules. It is clear that the author's idea is absolutely similar to that of the gospels. The first sentence in Pseudo-Clement coincides literally with the first sentence in the gospels; and in the words which follow immediately in 2 Clement, the words of Mt. 6:24 and Lk. 16:13 can still be read. The absence of the word οἰκέτης in the generally received text of Mt. 6:24 and its presence in Lk. 16:13 make the balance lean in favor of the latter as having had a literary influence on 2 Clem. 6:1.[19]

Having said that it is in keeping the commandments of the Lord that we shall obtain eternal life, the author writes in 2 Clem. 8:5: "For the Lord says in the Gos-

---

[18]Justin, *I Apol.* 19.7 has a quote which also recalls the same gospel texts and reveals an affinity with 2 Clem.: μὴ φοβεῖσθε τοὺς ἀναιροῦντας ὑμᾶς καὶ μετὰ ταῦτα μὴ δυναμένους τι ποιῆσαι, εἶπε, φοβήθητε δὲ τὸν μετὰ τὸ ἀποθανεῖν δυνάμενον καὶ ψυχὴν καὶ σῶμα εἰς γέενναν ἐμβαλεῖν. Cf. also Clement of Alexandria, *Excerpta ex Theod.* 14.3; Irenaeus, *Adv. Haer.* 3.18.5.

[19]Cf. E. Nestle, *Novum Testamentum graece et latine,* 19th ed. (Stuttgart, 1949) notes "p" with regard to Mt. 6:24, thereby signifying that the reading οἰκέτης has been introduced under the influence of a parallel text, namely Lk. 16:13.

pel: 'If you do not keep what is small, who will give you what is great? For I say to you, that he who is faithful in that which is least is faithful also in that which is great (ὅτι ὁ πιστὸς ἐν ἐλαχίστῳ καὶ ἐν πολλῷ πιστός ἐστιν).' '' Lk. 16:10-12 is usually pointed out as a parallel: "He who is faithful in a very little is faithful also in much (ὁ πιστὸς ἐν ἐλαχίστῳ καὶ ἐν πολλῷ πιστός ἐστιν); and he who is dishonest in a very little is dishonest also in much. If then you have not been faithful in the unrighteous mammon, who will entrust to you the true riches? And if you have not been faithful in that which is another's, who will give you that which is your own (τὸ ἡμέτερον τίς δώσει ὑμῖν)?'' The first part of the quote from 2 Clement strays a good deal from the gospel text; the second part coincides literally with the beginning of the Lucan parallel. This saying is supposed to have been uttered by our Lord in the gospel; the author gives no other determination, and he means the gospel in general. Let me note that the first part of the quote may come from an apocryphal tradition, and the second part from Lk. There obviously remains the plausible hypothesis that Pseudo-Clement found the entire quotation in an apocryphal source.[20] But, in any case, a literary contact with Lk. is still possible. Hemmer remarks, moreover, that the text of Lk., in and of itself, is not without difficulty and confusion as is borne out by various opinions regarding the text.[21]

When he deals with the scandal of the pagans, 2 Clem. 13:4 writes: "For, when they (the pagans) hear from us that God says: 'It is no credit to you, if you love them that love you, but it is a credit to you if you love your enemies and those who hate you (οὐ χάρις ὑμῖν, εἰ ἀγαπᾶτε τοὺς ἀγαπῶντας ὑμᾶς, ἀλλὰ χάρις ὑμῖν, εἰ ἀγαπᾶτε τοὺς ἐχθροὺς καὶ τοὺς μισοῦντας ὑμας). . . . ' '' These words echo the words of the gospels as found in Mt. 5:44, 46-47 and Lk. 6:27, 32-35. It is quite apparent that the text of 2 Clem. is closer to Lk. than to Mt. Indeed, 2 Clement has the participle τοὺς μισοῦντας, which is absent from Mt. but present in Lk. 6:27, as well as the expression χάρις ὑμῖν, which is lacking in Mt. but which is found in Lk. 6:34. As for the rest of the words, they are found equally in Mt. and Lk. It is quite clear, therefore, that Pseudo-Clement seems to have been inspired by the Lucan text.

Let me add that 2 Clem. 2:2 uses the verb ἐγκακέω in a context where the issue is perseverance in prayer. Lk. 18:1 also uses this verb in a similar context, yet the Lucan sentence is too far removed from 2 Clem. to allow us to believe in the

---

[20]Irenaeus still seems to know quite well the context of this Logion: *Adv. Haer.* 2.34.3: "Et ideo dominus dicebat ingratis existentibus in eum: si in modico fideles non fuistis, quod magnum est quis dabit vobis? significans quoniam qui in modica temporali vita ingrati exstiterunt ei qui eam praestitit, iuste non percipient ab eo in saeculum saeculi longitudinem dierum"; cf. also Hippolytus, *Refutation* 10.33.7: ὑπάκουε τῷ πεποιηκότι καὶ μὴ ἀντίβαινε νῦν, ἵνα ἐπὶ τῷ μικρῷ πιστὸς εὑρεθεὶς καὶ τὸ μέγα πιστευθῆναι δυνηθῇς.

[21]Cf. Hemmer, *Clément de Rome*, 148.

slightest literary relationship.[22]

Since we are considering the Gospel of Lk., let me add a few words concerning Luke's other writing, the Acts of the Apostles. No text of Acts had a literary influence on 2 Clement. If we read in 2 Clem. 1:1 the expression applied to Christ "judge of the living and the dead (κριτὴς ζώντων καὶ νεκρῶν)," which is found literally in Acts 10:42, it must be recognized that an analogous formula, κρίνειν ζῶντας καὶ νεκρούς, can also be read in 2 Tim. 4:1 and 1 Pet. 4:5, and this cripples somewhat the hypothesis of a literary dependence on the Acts of the Apostles.

As for the words ἡ ὁδὸς ἡ εὐθεῖα of 2 Clem. 7:3, they constitute too obvious an expression to allow us to believe in a literary contact with Acts 13:10 where the phrase is found in a text inspired by Hosea 14:10. Moreover, 2 Pet. 2:15 has a very similar expression: ὁδὸς εὐθεῖα.

Just as in 2 Clem. 13:1, the verbs μετανοέω and ἐξαλείφω are found joined in the same text in Acts 3:19, but in Acts the verb νήφω of 2 Clem. is missing.

We read in 2 Clem. 20:5: ". . . the Savior and Prince of Immortality (τὸν σωτῆρα καὶ ἀρχηγὸν τῆς ἀφθαρσίας)." These words are drawn from the final doxology of 2 Clement. They probably belong to liturgical formulas. Let me simply mention the following: in Acts 5:31, ἀρχηγὸν καὶ σωτῆρα; in Acts 3:15, ἀρχηγὸν τῆς ζωῆς; in Heb. 2:10, τὸν ἀρχηγὸν τῆς σωτηρίας; and in Heb. 12:2, τὸν τῆς πίστεως ἀρχηγόν.

Beyond instances in which the dependence on the Gospel of Lk. is certain or probable, several texts remain which are consistent with the synoptic tradition but which cannot be placed in literary relationship with any one of the synoptics in particular.

So it is that in 2 Clem. 3:4, pointing out how we shall confess Christ, the author writes: "By doing what He says, and not disobeying His commandments, and honoring Him not only with our lips but with all our heart and all our mind (ἀλλὰ ἐξ ὅλης καρδίας καὶ ἐξ ὅλης τῆς διανοίας)." The last formula recalls Mt. 22:37; Mk. 12:30; and Lk. 10:27 which refer to Deut. 6:5. But the author of 2 Clement reveals no particular affinity with one or the other of these parallels.

When 2 Clem. 14:1 says: " . . . ; but if we do not do the will of the Lord, we shall verify the Scripture which says: My house has become a den of thieves," the author draws from the same text of Jer. 7:11 as does Mt. 21:13; Mk. 11:17; and Lk. 19:46.

Let me note, moreover, in 2 Clem. 17:7 the expression πῦρ ἄσβεστον, which is present in Mt. 3:12; Mk. 9:43; and Lk. 3:17.

Finally, when the author writes in 2 Clem. 11:6: "For He is faithful who promised to pay to each the wages of his works (τὰς ἀντιμισθίας ἀποδιδόναι

---

[22]The verb ἐγκακέω appears again in the N.T. in 2 Cor. 4:1, 16; Gal. 6:9; Eph. 3:13; and 2 Thess. 3:13.

ἑκάστῳ τῶν ἔργων αὐτοῦ),'' he articulates a very Jewish norm of retribution,[23] taken up frequently in the New Testament,[24] without disclosing a dependence on a specific text.

The author of 2 Clement certainly knew the Gospel of Lk. He does not refer to it explicitly, he does not quote it word for word, but he is at times very close to it, demonstrating clearly that he is inspired by it. Yet, the texts are few where the literary dependence on the third gospel is certain; in most instances, the dependence is very probable and does not exclude the hypothesis of the use of an apocryphal source.

§2. The Pauline Writings[25]

The letters of Saint Paul do not seem to have strongly influenced 2 Clement: very few texts are found which indicate a reference to a Pauline parallel. On the other hand, many images and expressions recalling those of the apostle are found in 2 Clement.

As he invites his readers to keep their flesh chaste, Pseudo-Clement writes in 2 Clem. 9:3: "We must, therefore, guard the flesh as a temple of God (ὡς ναὸν θεοῦ).'' The expression ναὸς θεοῦ applied to the body is quite Pauline: it is read in 1 Cor. 3:16; 6:19; and 2 Cor. 6:16. From the point of view of meaning, the parallel closest to this passage is 1 Cor. 6:19, where the Apostle aims at individual Christians and recommends purity of their body, just as Pseudo-Clement does in the immediate context (2 Clem. 8:6).[26] Yet, in the Pauline passage, we do not read the expression ναὸς θεοῦ, but ναὸς τοῦ ἁγίου πνεύματος. A literary contact with this precise Pauline text is, therefore, not absolutely certain. But it can at least be asserted that the author uses, as does Paul, the theme of the spiritual temple which is also present in the Christian tradition.[27] Given the similarity of the context dealing with purity, it is plausible to believe that the author was thinking of the Pauline theme.

Another theme, quite Pauline as well, appears in 2 Clem. 14:2: "I do not think that you are ignorant that the living Church is 'the body of Christ (ὅτι ἐκκλησία ζῶσα σῶμά ἐστιν Χριστοῦ).' For the Scripture says: 'God made man male and female'; the male is Christ and the female is the Church.'' Although the expression ἐκκλησία ζῶσα is found nowhere in Paul, the concept of the Church as the body of Christ is certainly Pauline. It is found in Rom. 12:5; 1 Cor. 10:17; 12:27;

---

[23]Cf., e.g., Ps. 28(27):4; 62(61):13; Prov. 24:12; Jer. 17:10.

[24]Cf. Mt. 16:27; Rom. 2:6; 2 Tim. 4:14; Rev. 22:12.

[25]In this chapter, I do not consider the texts of Paul mentioned when I examined texts which are related to Mt. and the synoptics.

[26]Cf. Cerfaux, *La Théologie de l'Église suivant saint Paul*, 113-14, and 114n1.

[27]Cf. *Barn.* 5:15; 16:8; Ignatius, *Ephes.* 15:3; *Philad.* 7:2.

Col. 1:18, 24; 2:19; 3:15; but the Epistle of the Ephesians, 1:23; 2:16; 4:4; 5:23; and 5:28-32, is the one to compare with this text. 2 Clement develops and explains this image of the Church as the body of Christ, when he speaks of a heavenly syzygy between the preexisting Christ and the preexisting Church, and when he explains the order of procreation in Gen. 1:27 as given to this syzygy. Now, this theme where σῶμα and syzygy are united is also found in Eph. 5:30-32, where woman is the body of man and they become one flesh in their union of love. Later we find Valentinus' syzygy in Irenaeus: Ἄνθρωπος (heavenly man) καὶ Ἐκκλησία. However, if there is a similarity of theme, we must admit that it is not expressed in the same terms as Eph. 5:28-32 which does not stress the terms ἄρσεν καὶ θῆλυ. We can, therefore, admit only the presence of a similar theme.[28]

Beyond these Pauline themes, I must point out in 2 Clement ideas similar to those of the apostle. However, the words which express these ideas do not give a clue that allows us to conclude that there is a literary dependence on Saint Paul.

Thus, as he develops in 2 Clem. 1:4 the thought that God has given us the gift of light, Pseudo-Clement declares: "He has spoken to us as a father to his sons." This teaching that we are the sons of God, that God is the Father who called us his sons, is present in Rom. 8:15; 9:26; 2 Cor. 6:18; Gal. 4:4-5; and 1 Jn. 3:1, but its expression in the parallels mentioned is different from 2 Clement, and it does not recommend a literary influence from any of them.

Elsewhere, in 2 Clem. 5:6, as he proposes a way to secure the peace of the future kingdom and eternal life, the author prescribes no other means than "to conduct ourselves in holiness and justice and regard these things of the world as foreign to us and not desire them." Paul, in 1 Cor. 7:29-31 asserts also, but in totally different words, that the Christian must not cling to anything in this world which passes away.

When, in 2 Clem. 9:1, Pseudo-Clement writes: "And let not any one of you say that this flesh is not judged and does not rise again," he simply gives evidence of a difficulty which existed at the time concerning faith in the resurrection, which 1 Cor. 15:12-19 and 2 Tim. 2:18 had already revealed. But in any case, he does not depend on these texts. It can merely be said that the author had to answer to difficulties concerning the resurrection, difficulties which were already known at the time of the apostle.

2 Clem. 19:4 teaches more or less like Rom. 8:18; 2 Cor. 4:17; and 1 Pet. 4:12-13 when it says: "Let not the godly man grieve, then, if he be distressed in these present times. A time of blessedness awaits him; he shall live again above with the fathers and rejoice in an eternity without sorrow." However, again, the expression of this teaching is so different from the Pauline texts that it excludes a

---

[28]Cf. Lightfoot, *S. Clement of Rome*, 2:243, notes that 2 Clem. could be placed between the doctrine of Paul and that of the Valentinians, who consider the Church as an eternal Aeon.

literary reference to any one of them.

Several images used by 2 Clement recall Pauline images, but the texts which depict them do not furnish necessary and sufficient elements to establish a literary influence.

In 2 Clem. 7, the author uses the image of the contest to paint a canvas of Christian life. This metaphor was prevalent in that time in popular literature and moral philosophy.[29] Paul uses it as well in 1 Cor. 9:24-26. If the epithet φθαρτός (2 Clem. 7:1) is found in this passage of 2 Clement with reference to the contest, in Paul it qualifies the crown. Moreover, let me add that the homilist does not establish, as did Paul, a contradiction between the perishable *crown* and the imperishable *crown*, but between perishable *contests* and imperishable *contests*. Hence, this text of 2 Clem. probably shows nothing more than the use of a current metaphor.

When he urges penance, the author writes in 2 Clem. 8:2: "For we are as clay for the hand of the workman. Just as the potter, if he makes a vessel and it bends or breaks in his hands, shapes it over again, but if he has gone so far as to put it into the fiery oven, can do nothing to help any more; so let us also, while we are still in this world, repent with our whole heart of the evil things we have done in the flesh, that we may be saved by the Lord while we have time for repentance." The image of the potter is found in Rom. 9:21, but developed in an entirely different manner: the apostle speaks of the potter who can make from the same mass one vase for luxury and another for vile uses. Again, this is a common image. It is found in Jer. 18:4-6; Test. of the XII Patriarchs, Naphtali 2; and especially Theophilus, *Ad Autol.* 2.26.

It happens that Pseudo-Clement uses quotations from the Old Testament, also used by Saint Paul, without, however, having been influenced by the way the apostle uses them.

Thus, in 2 Clem. 2:1: "Rejoice, O thou barren, thou bearest not; sing forth and shout, thou that dost not travail; for many are the children of the desolate, more than heirs that hath a husband," the author refers to Is. 54:1 as does Gal. 4:27.

When he speaks of the assurance of promises, Pseudo-Clement writes in 2 Clem. 11:7: "If, then, we perform justice before God, we shall enter into His kingdom and receive the promises which 'ear has not heard, nor eye seen, nor has it entered into the heart of men (ἃς οὓς οὐκ ἤκουσεν οὐδὲ ὀφθαλμὸς εἶδεν, οὐδὲ ἐπὶ καρδίαν ἀνθρώπου ἀνέβη).' " This quotation of Isaiah 64:3 has already been examined with reference to 1 Clem. 34:8.[30] Given the similarity to the Pauline text of 1 Cor. 2:9, and the divergence from that of Isaiah, it is not impossible that the

---

[29]Cf. Knopf, *Die Lehre der zwölf Apostel, Die zwei Clemensbriefe,* 163.
[30]Cf. book 1, 49.

author depends on the text given by Paul. Yet, nothing in the context suggests such a reference to 1 Cor. 2:9. Pseudo-Clement perhaps draws the quote from a rabbinical tradition which transmitted in this form the text of Isaiah.[31] The same remark applies equally to 2 Clem. 14:5, where we read a part of the quote of Is. 64:3, taken up in 1 Cor. 2:9.

Finally, a series of words and expressions familiar or peculiar to Paul are used by the author of 2 Clement without literary dependence. These expressions are ὁσίως καὶ δικαίως,[32] ὡς ἔχομεν καιρόν,[33] πιστὸς γὰρ ὁ ἐπαγγειλάμενος,[34] τοῖς ἔξω referring to the pagans,[35] ἀφορμὴν λαμβάνω,[36] τὸ αὐτὸ φρονέω,[37] καλὴ συνείδησις,[38] δικαιοσύνην διώκω,[39] σκοτίζω τὴν διάνοιαν,[40] τῷ μονῷ θεῷ at the closing of the letter,[41] the words ἀποτίθημι meaning to put off,[42] ἀντιμισθία,[43] ἐπιφανεία to signify the coming at the last days,[44] ἀνθρωπάρεσκος,[45]

---

[31]Cf. J. Huby, *Saint Paul, Première Épître aux Corinthiens*, Verbum Salutis 13 (Paris, 1946) 90-91 and notes, where he writes: "As to the origin of the quote, the ancients were already in disagreement. . . . Origen said that it was borrowed from the *Apocalypse of Elijah*, an apocryphal work which we no longer possess in its original and integral text. St. Jerome contested neither the presence of the Pauline formula in this apocryphon nor in the *Ascension of Isaiah*, but he explained it rather as a paraphrase of Is. 64:3. To this first text, the borrowing of the formula: 'what has not entered into the heart of man' from Is. 64:16 must be added. Rather than attributing to St. Paul this 'paraphrase' and this fusion of the two texts, I prefer the explanation that makes it depend not on the apocryphal *Apocalypse of Elijah*, but on a rabbinical tradition which transmitted in this form the text of Isaiah." References which support this hypothesis will be found in Huby's book in the pages and notes indicated above.

[32]Cf. 2 Clem. 5:6 and 1 Thess. 2:10 where there also is καὶ ἀμέμπτως.

[33]Cf. 2 Clem. 9:7 and Gal. 6:10.

[34]Cf. 2 Clem. 11:6 and Heb. 10:23.

[35]Cf. 2 Clem. 13:1 and Col. 4:5; 1 Thess. 4:12; 1 Tim. 3:7; and perhaps 1 Cor. 5:12-13.

[36]Cf. 2 Clem. 16:1 and Rom. 7:8, 11.

[37]Cf. 2 Clem. 17:3 and Rom. 12:16; 2 Cor. 13:11; Phil. 2:2; 4:2: it is one of the parenetic formulas of unity in Paul (cf. L. Cerfaux, *La Théologie de l'Église suivant saint Paul*, 188).

[38]Cf. 2 Clem. 16:4 and Heb. 13:18.

[39]Cf. 2 Clem. 18:2 and 1 Tim. 6:11; 2 Tim. 2:22.

[40]Cf. 2 Clem. 19:2 and Eph. 4:18; Rom. 1:21 has ἐσκοτίσθη ἡ ἀσύνετος αὐτῶν καρδία.

[41]Cf. 2 Clem. 20:5 which recalls the expression of 1 Tim. 1:17.

[42]Cf. 2 Clem. 1:6 and Eph. 4:22, 25; Col. 3:8; Heb. 12:1; and also 1 Pet. 2:1.

[43]Cf. 2 Clem. 11:6 and Rom. 1:27; 2 Cor. 6:13.

[44]Cf. 2 Clem. 12:1; and only in this sense in the pastoral epistles: 1 Tim. 6:14; 2 Tim. 1:10; 4:1, 8; Tit. 2:13.

[45]Cf. 2 Clem. 13:1 and Eph. 6:6; Col. 3:22.

and οἱ ἄσοφοι.[46]

Let me also add that 2 Clem. 1:8: "He called us when we were naught, his will has made us pass from nothingness to being" is sometimes compared to Rom. 4:17. This comparison is not justified since the idea is totally different. In 2 Clem. 1:8, the author recalls the creation: we were not; God has called us to being. In Rom. 4:17, God raises the dead and calls the things that were not as if they already were. I believe that this similarity is due solely to a verbal assonance between ἐκ μὴ ὄντος εἶναι in 2 Clement and τὰ μὴ ὄντα ὡς ὄντα in Romans.

In conclusion, it cannot be said that the literary influence of the texts of the Pauline epistles on 2 Clement was very great. I can merely point out the presence of images and ideas which are read in Paul, but which do not necessarily come into 2 Clement from the texts of the apostle. Finally, I emphasize the use by Pseudo-Clement of words and expressions familiar to the Pauline vocabulary.

§3. The Catholic Epistles of James and Peter[47]

Any one of the Catholic epistles could have been consided by the author of 2 Clement.

First of all, I propose to look at the Epistle of James.

When Pseudo-Clement writes in 2 Clem. 15:1, "For the reward (μισθός) is not small for having converted (ἀποστρέψαι εἰς τὸ σωθῆναι) a straying and per-ishing soul (πλανωμένην ψυχὴν καὶ ἀπολλυμένην) to salvation," indeed he seems to remember the text of Jas. 5:19-20: "My brethren, if any one of you wan-ders (πλανηθῇ) from the truth and some one brings him back (ἐπιστρέψῃ), let him know that whoever brings back (ὁ ἐπιστρέψας) a sinner from the error (ἐκ πλάνης) of his way will save (σώσει) his soul from death and will cover a mul-titude of sins."[48] The meeting of thought is striking: to "the reward is not small," James has the corresponding "will save his soul from death and will cover a mul-titude of sins;" "for having converted a straying and perishing soul to salvation" of 2 Clem. corresponds to "if any one of you wanders from the truth and some one brings him back, let him know that whoever brings back a sinner from the error of his way. . . ." The similarity of expressions is no less remarkable: πλανωμένην (2 Clem) and πλανηθῇ, πλάνης (Jas.); ἀποστρέψαι (2 Clem.) and ἐπιστρέψῃ, ἐπιστρέψας (Jas.); σωθῆναι (2 Clem.) and σώσει (Jas.). Let me add, however, that the term μισθός, which 2 Clement stresses, is absent in James, which expresses a similar idea. Moreover, the words of James, "[he] will cover

---

[46]Cf. 2 Clem. 19:2 and Eph. 5:15: unique in the N.T.

[47]I consider here only those texts which have not been mentioned in the preceding parts of my study.

[48]Cf. A. Charue, *Les Épîtres Catholiques, Épître de saint Jacques, La Sainte Bible* of L. Pirot 12 (Paris, 1938) 433.

a multitude of sins,'' are missing in 2 Clement. A literary reminiscence of the text of James could, therefore, easily be expected.

In the midst of an enumeration of vices to avoid and virtues to practice, 2 Clem. 4:3 reads: ''μηδὲ καταλαλεῖν ἀλλήλων, nor speaking against one another.'' In the New Testament, only Jas. 4:11 has this expression and develops at length the idea which it implies. Yet, I hesitate to see here a literary reminiscence of this text of James, for this failing must have been widespread enough for Pseudo-Clement not to need to refer to a specific text.[49]

In noting in 2 Clem. 6:3 that ''This world and the future world are two enemies,'' the author expresses, but in different terms, an idea more or less similar to that of Jas. 4:4, which asserts that a friendship with the world cannot be maintained without accepting, by the same token, to be an enemy of God.[50]

Let me add as well that 2 Clem. 20:3, with the sentence ''No one of the just has reaped fruit quickly, but he waits for it,'' calls for patience in waiting for the earned reward. Jas. 5:7-11, in a different manner, invites us also to wait with patience for the coming of the Lord.

I propose now to go on to the Epistles of Peter.

''Charity covers a multitude of sins (ἀγάπη δὲ καλύπτει πλῆθος ἁμαρτιῶν),'' says 2 Clem. 16:4, in a context in which he exhorts conversion because of the nearness of the judgment. A literally identical assertion is found in 1 Pet. 4:8, on which Pseudo-Clement most probably depends. In Peter, this text is also found in a passage about the end of all things and the need to prepare for it through a Christian life, especially a life of charity.[51] Jas. 5:20 has a similar text, but the word ἀγάπη is missing.

2 Clem. 16:3 reads: ''But you know that 'the day' of judgment 'is now coming,' kindled as a furnace, and the power of heaven shall dissolve and the whole earth shall be as lead melting in the fire.'' The burning and destruction of the universe by fire are mentioned by 2 Pet. 3:7-10. Morevoer, it was a common theme already present in many noncanonical Jewish texts,[52] in later Christian writings,[53] and also in Graeco-Roman, Iranian and other literatures.[54]

Let me note finally, in 2 Clem. 11:2, the expression ὁ προφητικὸς λόγος, which is also present in 2 Pet. 1:19.

---

[49]Cf. Knopf, *Die Lehre der zwölf Apostel, Die zwei Clemensbriefe*, 158.

[50]Cf. Charue, *Les Épîtres Catholiques, Épître de saint Jacques*, 420.

[51]Cf. Charue, *Les Épîtres Catholiques, Première Épître de saint Pierre*, 467; *Épître de saint Jacques*, 433.

[52]Cf. Strack-Billerbeck, *Kommentar zum Neuen Testament aus Talmud und Midrasch* (Munich, 1922-1928) 3:775.

[53]Cf. Hermas, *Vis.* 4.3.3; *Ethiopic Apoc. Pet.* 5.

[54]Cf. Charue, *Les Épîtres Catholiques, Seconde Épître de saint Pierre*, 498.

The literary influence of the Catholic Epistles of James and Peter on 2 Clement is, therefore, minimal. One text of James and one text of Peter may possibly have literarily inspired Pseudo- Clement.

§4. The Johannine Writings[55]

Few texts of 2 Clement find parallels in the Johannine writings.

It is sometimes mentioned that 2 Clem. 3:1: "what is true knowledge (τίς ἡ γνῶσις) concerning Him [the Father of truth] except not to deny Him through whom we knew the Father (δι' οὗ ἔγνωμεν αὐτόν)?" could be linked with Jn. 17:3. Yet, this link is rather weak since, in fact, the notion of knowledge in the Johannine sense does not exist in the text of 2 Clement. The author has in mind simply the fact that we have come to the knowledge of a single God as opposed to the dead and multiple gods of paganism. Moreover, the terms of Pseudo-Clement are too removed from those of Jn. to allow us to believe in a literary dependence.[56]

In 2 Clem. 9:5, as we read: "If Christ the Lord, who saved us, being spirit at first, became flesh (ὢν μὲν τὸ πρῶτον πνεῦμα, ἐγένετο σάρξ) and so called us," the temptation is to think of Jn. 1:14: καὶ ὁ λόγος σὰρξ ἐγένετο. But πνεῦμα means here spiritual nature, as its opposition to σάρξ indicates, and as the author explicitly says in 2 Clem. 14:2-3.

The expression σὺ ἧς of 2 Clem. 17:5 uttered by the unbelievers, could be an echo of Jn. 8:25, 28 and 13:19. I also note in 2 Clem. 5:5; 8:4 and 6 the Johannine expression ζωὴ αἰώνιος.

We find in 2 Clem. 1:6: "Blinded in our understanding, we bowed down to sticks (ξύλα) and stones (λίθους) and gold (χρυσόν) and silver (ἄργυρον) and brass (χαλκόν), the works of men." Rev. 9:20 has a somewhat similar enumeration to brand idolatry. Yet, Pseudo-Clement does not seem to depend upon it: this enumeration is, in fact, traditional when speaking of idolatry.[57]

It can be concluded that actually none of the Johannine writings exercized an influence of a literary sort on 2 Clement.

At the conclusion of this first chapter, it can be asserted that, of all the New Testament writings, only the Gospel of Matthew has exercised a definite literary

---

[55] I consider only those Johannine texts which were not mentioned previously.

[56] Knopf, *Die Lehre der zwölf Apostel, Die zwei Clemensbriefe*, 157, notes: "Aber den johanneischen Begriff der 'Erkenntnis' können wir hier nicht entragen. Die Gnosis Gottes, die II Clem. meint, ist der Monotheismus. Die Logik von τίς ἡ γνῶσις κτλ. ist etwas gewaltsam. Aber der Satz, dass die wahre Gotteserkenntnis im Bekenntnis zu Christus bestehe, hat seinen Sinn darin, dass Christus allein diese Erkenntnis vermittelt."

[57] Cf. Pss. 115:4(113:12); 135(134):15; Wis. 13:10-19; Dan. 5:23.

influence on certain passages of 2 Clement. The absence of all reference to the Gospel of Mk. must be noted. Among the other New Testament writings, the Gospel of Lk. seems to have been known by Pseudo- Clement, who probably referred to it, and yet quite rarely. Let me add as well that in the numerous cases in which I asserted a possible literary reminiscence from Lucan texts, I left the door open to the hypothesis which considers an inspiration drawn from an apocryphal gospel. For Saint Paul, I mentioned simply the resemblance of themes, of images and expressions. Yet his literary influence, if it existed, must have been very slight. Traces of the Catholic epistles of James and Peter, as well as traces of Johannine writings, are almost nonexistent in 2 Clement.

Let me also mention that when 2 Clement is under the literary dependence of Mt., it follows fairly closely the texts of the first gospel, to the point of citing a passage literally[58] and thereby giving it most likely the value of Scripture, and even sometimes preserving the verbal forms.[59] This phenomenon was not as noticeable in the Christian writings previously studied.

In 2 Clement, from the point of view of literary influence, the place of the Gospel of Mt. is preponderant not only over the other gospels but also over the other writings of the New Testament.

---

[58]Cf. 3-6, above: 2 Clem. 2:4 and Mt. 9:13.
[59]Cf. 8-9, above: 2 Clem. 6:2 and Mt. 16:26.

Editor's Addendum to Chapter 1

According to Helmut Köster (*Synoptische Überlieferung bei den apostolischen Vätern*, 62-111), 2 Clement contains several citations that reflect a revisional reworking of Matthew (2 Clem. 2:4; 3:2; and 6:2), and in many of the citations the parallels in Matthew and Luke have quite obviously been harmonized or bear similarities to harmonizations found in the texts of Justin Martyr (2 Clem. 9:11; 4:2, 5; 5:2-4). Köster argues that 2 Clement did not use Matthew (and Luke) directly. Rather 2 Clement probably drew from a harmonizing collection of sayings which was itself composed on the basis of Matthew and Luke.

Wolf-Dietrich Köhler (*Die Rezeption des Matthäusevangeliums in der Zeit vor Irenäus*, 129-49) concludes the following with respect to 2 Clement's use of the Gospel of Matthew.

1. Passages for which dependence on Matthew is probable

2 CLEMENT	MATTHEW
3:2	10:32
4:2	7:21
6:2	16:26

2. Passages for which dependence on Matthew is quite possible

2 CLEMENT	MATTHEW
2:4	9:13
6:7a	11:29
9:11	12:50

3. Passages for which dependence on Matthew is at most theoretically possible

2 CLEMENT	MATTHEW
3:4	7:24
3:5	15:8
5:5	11:29
6:7b	25:46
11:6	16:27
14:1	21:13
17:7	31:12

4. Passages for which dependence on Matthew is very improbable

2 CLEMENT	MATTHEW
6:1	6:24
13:4a	5:44
4:5	7:23
5:2, 4	10:28
8:5	25:21-23

   Biblia Patristica (*Index des Citations et Allusions Bibliques dans la Littéra-ture Patristique, Des origines à Clément d'Alexandrie et Tertullien*, vol. 1 [Paris, 1975] 223-93) lists the following citations or allusions to the Gospel of Matthew in the text of 2 Clement.

2 CLEMENT	MATTHEW
17:7	3:12
6:1	6:24
4:2	7:21
4:5	7:23
2:4	9:13
5:2	10:16
5:4	10:28
3:2	10:32
6:7	11:29
9:11	12:49-50
3:5	15:8
6:2	16:26
11:6	16:27
2:7	18:11
14:1	21:13
3:4	22:37
11:2	24:32-36
8:5	25:21-23
6:7	25:46

Chapter 2

POLYCARP

I will now turn my attention to two works which revolve around the person of Polycarp, bishop of Smyrna. The first is a letter he addresses to the Phillipians; the second is the narrative of his martyrdom. Each of these works will be the subject of a special section.

Section 1
THE LETTER OF POLYCARP TO THE PHILIPPIANS

The entire *Letter of Polycarp* has come down to us only in a Latin version, which contains fourteen chapters. We also have the Greek text through chapter 9.[1] Chapters 9 and 13, less the last sentence, have been preserved in Greek by Eusebius;[2] Zahn did a Greek version of the missing chapters;[3] Lightfoot's contribution, done independently of Zahn,[4] was to translate them as well.[5]

Following my customary method dictated by my primary interest, I shall examine in the first paragraph the literary relationships which exist between the *Letter of Polycarp* and the Gospel of Mt. A second paragraph considers the other New Testament writings.

---

[1]For the *Letter of Polycarp to the Philippians*, I rely on the edition of K. Bihlmeyer, *Die Apostolischen Väter*, SAQ 2nd ser. 1 (Tübingen, 1924) 114-20. [The English text of Polycarp's *Letter to the Philippians*, trans. Francis X. Glimm, is taken from *The Apostolic Fathers*, trans. Francis X. Glimm, Joseph M. F. Marique, and Gerald G. Walsh, *The Fathers of the Church, a New Translation*, vol. 1 (Washington: The Catholic University of America Press, 1962). Editor's note.]

[2]Cf. Eusebius, *Hist. Eccl.* 3.36.13-14.

[3]Cf. Th. Zahn, *Ignatii et Polycarpi Epistulae, Martyria, Fragmenta, Patrum Apostolicorum opera*, fasc. 2, (Leipzig, 1876) 124-32.

[4]Cf. J. B. Lightfoot, *The Apostolic Fathers*, part 2, *S. Ignatius, S. Polycarp*, vol. 3 (London, New York, 1889) 320.

[5]Cf. ibid., 338-47; 349-50.

§1. Saint Matthew

A few gospel citations in the letter obviously do not depend on the Gospel of Mt. As a result, I thought it better to consider them separately. This is why the first part will consist of a study of the texts where the Matthean influence is certain, and the second will consider instances in which this influence is possible or doubtful.

A. Texts in Which the Influence of Matthew Is Certain

1. Pol. Phil. 2:3a

Μνημονεύοτες δὲ ὧν εἶπεν ὁ κύριος διδάσκων· Μὴ κρίνετε, ἵνα μὴ κριθῆτε· ἀφίετε, καὶ ἀφεθήσεται ὑμῖν· ἐλεᾶτε, ἵνα ἐλεηθῆτε· ᾧ μέτρῳ μετρεῖτε, ἀντιμετρηθήσεται ὑμῖν.

No! Remember what the Lord said when he taught: "Judge not, that you may not be judged. Forgive, and you shall be forgiven. Be merciful, that you may obtain mercy. With what measure you measure, it shall be measured to you in return."

These words call to mind several texts of Mt. and Lk., as well as 1 Clem. 13:2. The following synoptic chart better discloses the similarity of these texts.

Polyc. 2:3a	Matt. 5:1; 7:1; 5:7; 6:14-15	Luke 6:37-38	1 Clem. 13:1-2
μνημονεύοντες δὲ ὧν εἶπεν ὁ κύριος	καὶ ἀνοίξας τὸ στόμα αὐτοῦ ἐδί-δασκεν αὐτοὺς λέγων·		μάλιστα μεμνημέ-νοι τῶν λόγων τοῦ κυρίου Ἰησοῦ, οὓς ἐλάλησεν διδάσκων
διδάσκων· Μὴ κρίνετε, ἵνα μὴ	Μὴ κρίνετε, ἵνα μὴ κριθῆτε· ἐν ᾧ γὰρ κρίματι κρίνετε, κριθήσεσθε, καὶ ἐν ᾧ μέτρῳ με-τρεῖτε, μετρηθήσ-εται ὑμῖν. Μακάριοι οἱ ἐλεή-μονες, ὅτι αὐτοὶ ἐλεηθήσονται	καὶ μὴ κρίνετε, καὶ οὐ μὴ κριθῆτε . . . ᾧ γὰρ μέτρῳ με-τρεῖτε. ἀντιμε-τρηθήσεται ὑμῖν.	ἐπιείκειαν καὶ μακ-ροθυμίαν. Οὕτως γὰρ εἶπεν· Ἐλεᾶτε, ἵνα ἐλε-ηθῆτε· ἀφίετε, ἵνα ἀφεθῆ ὑμῖν· . . . ὡς κρίνετε, οὕτως κριθήσεσθε . . . ᾧ μέτρῳ με-τρεῖτε, ἐν αὐτῷ μετρηθήσεται ὑμῖν.
κριθῆτε· ἀφίετε καὶ ἀφεθήσ-εται ὑμῖν· ἐλεᾶτε, ἵνα ἐλεη-θῆτε, ᾧ μέτρῳ με-τρεῖτε, ἀντιμε-τρηθήσεται ὑμῖν.	Ἐὰν γὰρ ἀφῆτε τοῖς ἀνθρώποις τὰ παρ-απτώματα αὐτῶν, ἀφήσει καὶ ὑμῖν ὁ πατὴρ ὑμῶν ὁ οὐρ-άνιος. Ἐὰν δὲ μὴ ἀφῆτε τοῖς ἀν-θρώποις, οὐδὲ ὁ πατὴρ ὑμῶν ἀφήσει τὰ παραπτώματα ὑμῶν.		

The rhythm in the words of Christ reported by Polycarp is striking. We find ourselves in the presence of a kind of quatrain:

Μὴ κρίνετε, ἵνα μὴ κριθῆτε·
ἀφίετε, καὶ ἀφεθήσεται ὑμῖν·
ἐλεᾶτε, ἵνα ἐλεηθῆτε·
ᾧ μέτρῳ μετρεῖτε, ἀντιμετρηθήσεται ὑμῖν.

The first and third sentences contain an intentional subordinate introduced by ἵνα and end with an identical rhyme in –θῆτε. The second and the fourth sentences end also with a rhyme in –θήσεται ὑμῖν. Now, Polycarp does not usually write in this particular style. It can, therefore, be assumed that this text was already present in a mnemotechnic form and that he borrowed it. Is it not apparent that one of the parallels mentioned in the above synoptic chart is the source from which he drew?

All of Polycarp's formulas are found in Mt., although some are structured differently. This is not so for Lk. from which the clause ἐλεᾶτε ἵνα ἐλεηθῆτε is missing. Nevertheless, let me point out that Polycarp, like Lk., uses the compound verb ἀντιμετρηθήσεται.

The text of Polycarp is too removed from Mt. and Lk., especially from a stylistic viewpoint, to allow the conjecture of a direct reference to one or the other. Moreover, Polycarp does not strictly follow the order of the Matthean sentences. Let me also add that, as far as the sentences which could be derived from Mt. are concerned, not only do they not reproduce his text word for word, but they are also simpler and shorter. Finally, Lk. can be excluded, since he does not have the sentence ἐλεᾶτε, ἵνα ἐλεηθῆτε.

As for 1 Clem. 13:2, the similarity is somewhat striking: the same way of introducing the sayings of the Lord: μεμνημένοι (Clem.), μνημονεύοντες (Pol. Phil.), διδάσκων (Clem. and Pol. Phil.); and all the formulas of Polycarp are produced by Clement of Rome, which also contains others. A few slight differences of style are to be noted: instead of μὴ κρίνετε, ἵνα μὴ κριθῆτε, Clement says ὡς κρίνετε οὕτως κριθήσεσθε; instead of ἀντιμετρηθήσεται, Clement reads ἐν αὐτῷ μετρηθήσεται ὑμῖν.

The resemblance with 1 Clement is unquestionably more noteworthy. Now, I have already asserted that this passage of 1 Clement was drawn from a sort of primitive catechism inspired by the Sermon on the Mount, which must have played an important role in early Christian times.[6]

Is a direct dependence on Clement of Rome possible? Since Polycarp omitted a few sentences that are characteristic of Clement, I believe that in this instance he draws rather from this primitive catechism, which had reached the last stage of

---

[6]Cf. book 1, 10.

its evolution and whose point of departure was the Matthean Sermon on the Mount. Indeed, Polycarp's formulas have the characteristics of a finished work, of a completed structure, which the catechism, the source of Clement of Rome, had not yet attained, even though it shows an attempt at simplification and improvement. Clement of Rome would, therefore, appear to be a stage in the evolution of this catechism.

Yet, Polycarp introduces his citation in the manner of the Bishop of Rome with the words μνημονεύοντες δὲ ὧν εἶπεν ὁ κύριος διδάσκων, which recall μάλιστα μεμνημένοι τῶν λόγων τοῦ κυρίου Ἰησοῦ οὓς ἐλάλησεν διδάσκων. Moreover, we know that the Bishop of Smyrna knew Clement's *Epistle to the Corinthians*; the table of citations and references to 1 Clement drawn up by Lightfoot[7] shows eloquently that Polycarp had in hand and used the letter of Clement of Rome. It is, therefore, likely that in this case he draws from it as well.

Still, the fact that Polycarp drops certain of Clement's sentences which were already clad with a particular rhythm,[8] and which were thus easy to remember and likely to be easily reproduced, and the fact that he changes others and simplifies the whole, allow me to believe that he broke away from the text of Clement.

Naturally, it can still be inferred that it is Polycarp himself who simplified the text of 1 Clement and gave it this remarkable form of a quatrain; but this is contrary to the practice of the Bishop of Smyrna.

2. Pol. Phil. 2:3b

(μνημονεύοντες δὲ ὧν εἶπεν ὁ κύριος διδάσκων) . . .
καὶ ὅτι μακάριοι οἱ πρωχοὶ καὶ οἱ διωκόμενοι ἕνεκεν δικαιοσύνης, ὅτι αὐτῶν ἐστὶν ἡ βασιλεία τοῦ θεοῦ.

(Still keeping in mind what the Lord said when he taught us) . . . And again: "Blessed are the poor, and they who are persecuted for justice's sake, for theirs is the Kingdom of God."

Again, we find parallels with the Sermon on the Mount in Mt. 5:3, 10: Μακάριοι οἱ πτωχοὶ τῷ πνεύματι, ὅτι αὐτῶν ἐστιν ἡ βασιλεία τῶν οὐρανῶν. . . . Μακάριοι οἱ δεδιωγμένοι ἕνεκεν δικαιοσύνης, ὅτι αὐτῶν ἐστιν ἡ βασιλεία τῶν οὐρανῶν, and Lk. 6:20: Μακάριοι οἱ πτωχοί, ὅτι ὑμετέρα ἐστιν ἡ βασιλεία τοῦ θεοῦ.

Compared with the text of Mt., Polycarp does not have τῷ πνεύματι, and he uses the expression βασιλεία τοῦ θεοῦ instead of βασιλεία τῶν οὐρανῶν.

---

[7]Cf. J. B. Lightfoot, *The Apostolic Fathers*, part 1, *S. Clement of Rome*, vol. 1 (London, New York, 1890) 149- 52.

[8]The sentences of Clement that are absent in Pol. Phil. are ὡς ποιεῖτε, οὕτω ποιηθήσεται ὑμῖν· ὡς δίδοτε, οὕτως δοθήσεται ὑμῖν· ὡς χρηστεύεσθε, οὕτως χρηστευθήσεται ὑμῖν.

On the other hand, he mentions the beatitude οἱ διωκόμενοι ἕνεκεν δικαιο-σύνης. This last beatitude is missing in Luke; if it were there, the text of Polycarp would be an exact replication of the text of the third gospel.

In this case, Polycarp is literarily dependent on the Matthean text. First of all, he reports a beatitude present only in the first gospel. Then, this beatitude contains precisely the word δικαιοσύνη, an important term in the first gospel. Moreover, if Polycarp borrows the second beatitude from Mt., why would he have turned to Luke for the first since Mt. has it as well? It is simpler to believe that he dropped the words τῷ πνεύματι. Finally, let me note that the words of Polycarp are a summary of the beatitudes and that he noticed that the first and the last use the same formula: αὐτῶν ἐστιν ἡ βασιλεία τῶν οὐρανῶν.

With the words καὶ ὅτι, this sentence of Polycarp still depends on the intro-ductory formula μνημονεύοντες δὲ ὧν εἶπεν ὁ κύριος διδάσκων. Now, from a stylistic point of view, it is totally different from the sentences which immediately precede it in the same verse, and which pick up the introductory lemma as well, and for which I postulated dependence on a primitive catechism which was itself drafted from Matthew's Sermon on the Mount.

Thus, in the whole of verse 3, Polycarp refers to Matthew's Sermon on the Mount, being at the same time under the influence of a catechism which he knows represents the substance of the Sermon.

3. Pol. Phil. 7:2

. . . δεήσεσιν αἰτούμενοι τὸν παντεπόπτην θεὸν μὴ εἰσενεγκεῖν ἡμᾶς εἰς πειρασμόν, καθὼς εἶπεν ὁ κύριος· Τὸ μὲν πνεῦμα πρόθυμον, ἡ δὲ σὰρξ ἀσθενής.

. . . beseeching the all-seeing God in petitions "not to lead us into tempta-tion," as the Lord said, "The spirit indeed is willing, but the flesh is weak."

The last sentence is an explicit reference to a saying of the Lord (καθὼς εἶπεν ὁ κύριος). It is found in the narrative of the agony of Christ in Mt. 26:41: γρηγο-ρεῖτε καὶ προσεύχεσθε ἵνα μὴ εἰσέλθητε εἰς πειρασμόν· τὸ μὲν πνεῦμα πρόθυμον, ἡ δὲ σὰρξ ἀσθενής and in Mk. 14:38, whose text is identical to that of Mt.; Lk. 22:46 does not have τὸ μὲν πνεῦμα πρόθυμον, ἡ δὲ σὰρξ ἀσυενής.

The texts of Mt. and Mk. mention precisely the prayer not to enter into temp-tation: we find here, therefore, all the elements of Polycarp's sentence whose ma-terial identity with these gospel texts is remarkable. Polycarp cites Mt. 26:41, but modifies it slightly under the influence of the Our Father where these words are read: μὴ εἰσενεγκεῖν ἡμᾶς εἰς πειρασμόν (Mt. 6:13). The influence of the Our Father, close to the Matthean tradition, tends to attribute the reference to Mt.

The Oxford Committee, having noted that the citation introduced by καθὼς εἶπεν ὁ κύριος coincides literally with Mt. and Mk. and appears in a context quite similar to that which is read in the gospel, asserts that it may be due to an

oral tradition or may come from a parent document of the gospels, and not necessarily from the gospels themselves.[9]

I do not see the need to multiply hypotheses unnecessarily, since the text of
Mt. was within reach and since Polycarp, just as the first gospel, establishes a relationship between "to enter into temptation" and "the spirit indeed is willing,
but the flesh is weak." Why then turn to an oral tradition or to a parent document
of the gospels, whose existence is hypothetical?

B. Texts in Which the Influence of Matthew Is Possible or Doubtful

1. Pol. Phil. 6:2

Εἰ οὖν δεόμεθα τοῦ κυρίου, ἵνα ἡμῖν ἀφῇ, ὀφείλομεν καὶ ἡμεῖς ἀφι-
έναι.

If, then, we beseech the Lord to forgive us, we should also forgive.
[The English translation has been added by the editor.]

The verb δέομαι indicates that it is here a question of a prayer; this prayer is
the Our Father where the request in question is also found in the Matthean as well
as in the Lucan form: Mt. 6:12: καὶ ἄφες ἡμῖν τὰ ὀφειλήματα ἡμῶν, ὡς καὶ ἡμεῖς
ἀφήκαμεν τοῖς ὀφειλέταις ἡμῶν, and Lk. 11:4: καὶ ἄφες ἡμῖν τὰς ἁμαρτίας
ἡμῶν, καὶ γὰρ αὐτοὶ ἀφίομεν παντὶ ὀφείλοντι ἡμῖν.

A similar idea is read several times in Mt., principally in the Sermon on the
Mount, in Mt. 6:14-15, and also in 18:35; yet the verb δέομαι leads naturally to
the Lord's Prayer.

Polycarp may very well have referred directly to the Our Father, a common
prayer in early Christianity, without necessarily thinking of one of the two gospels
which report it. Let me note, however, that the context contains ideas from Matthew's Sermon on the Mount, namely: no anger among the presbyters, an idea
which can be likened to Mt. 5:22; no covetousness, to be likened to Mt. 6:19; and
no unjust judgments, as in Mt. 7:1-2. These clues are too weak to assert with certainty a literary dependence on Mt. rather than on the Our Father, the prayer of
the community.

2. Pol. Phil. 5:2

. . . πορευόμενοι κατὰ τὴν ἀλήθειαν τοῦ κυρίου ὃς ἐγένετο διάκονος
πάντων.

. . . walking according to the truth of the Lord, who became the servant of
all. [The English translation has been added by the editor.]

---

[9]Cf. *The New Testament in the Apostolic Fathers*, 103.

In several places in the gospel, Christ introduces himself as having come to serve: Mt. 20:28 and Mk. 10:45, both of which read: ὁ υἱὸς τοῦ ἀνθρώπου οὐκ ἦλθεν διακονηθῆναι, ἀλλὰ διακονῆσαι καὶ δοῦναι τὴν ψυχὴν αὐτοῦ λύτρον ἀντὶ πολλῶν. Lk. 22:27 is similar: ἐγὼ δὲ ἐν μέσῳ ὑμῶν εἰμι ὡς ὁ διακονῶν.

Other gospel texts even put the term διάκονος into the mouth of Christ, such as Mt. 23:2 and Mk. 9:35. This latter text contains literally the expression of Polycarp πάντων διάκονος but does not apply it to Christ. Moreover, as we shall see, in the absence of any other reference to the second gospel, it can be inferred that the bishop of Smyrna was not inspired by it.

3. Pol. Phil. 6:1

Καὶ οἱ πρεσβύτεροι . . . ἐπισκεπτόμενοι πάντας ἀσθενεῖς.

And the presbyters (also must be) . . . visiting all the sick.

[The English translation has been added by the editor.]

In the discourse of the Judge at the Parousia who, in the condemnation of the damned, identifies himself with the weak, with the one in prison, etc., Mt. 25:36, 43 reads, . . . ἠσθένησα καὶ ἐπεσκέψασθέ με . . . ἀσθενὴς καὶ ἐν φυλακῇ καὶ οὐκ ἐπεσκέψασθέ με.

Could the text of Polycarp demonstrate a concrete application for the presbyters to follow in the general duty of all Christians, such as the Matthean texts imply? The presence of the verb ἐπισκέπτομαι and the word ἀσθενής speak in favor of this interpretation.

4. Pol. Phil. 12:3

Orate . . . pro persequentibus et odientibus vos.

Pray . . . for those who persecute and hate you.

[The English translation has been added by the editor.]

This recalls Mt. 5:44: καὶ προσεύχεσθε ὑπὲρ τῶν διωκόντων ὑμᾶς, and Lk. 6:28: προσεύχεσθε περὶ τῶν ἐπηρεαζόντων ὑμᾶς. But the absence of the original Greek text prevents me from drawing a conclusion; let me simply note a similar idea in both gospels.

The bishop of Smyrna knows the Gospel of Mt.; not only is he literarily dependent on it, but he also cites certain texts literally; his use of this gospel is not limited to the Sermon on the Mount. With 2 Clement, the letter of Polycarp is one of the first works in which we notice a greater fidelity towards the texts which inspire it.

The letter of Polycarp testifies to the existence of a primitive catechism, a sort of abridged version of Matthew's Sermon on the Mount.

§2. The Other New Testament Writings

The letters of Saint Paul and 1 Peter have influenced rather strongly the composition of several passages of Polycarp's *Letter to the Philippians*. As for the remainder of the New Testament literature, its influence was practically nil. I shall first say a few words regarding the Gospels of Mk. and Lk., the Johannine writings and the Acts of the Apostles. I shall then consider the literary relationships with reference to the Pauline letters. I shall finally consider 1 Peter.

A. Mark, Luke, the Johannine Writings, the Acts of the Apostles

No passage of the letter of Polycarp bears a trace of a definite literary dependence on the Gospel of Mk. or Lk. In the paragraph devoted to Saint Matthew, I demonstrated that several texts were more or less parallel to either Mk. or Lk.; but in each case, preference was given to Mt., or a decision in favor of one of the synoptics in particular was impossible to reach.

This observation pertains also to the Fourth Gospel and to the Book of Revelation, a startling phenomenon when it is known that, according to tradition, Polycarp was a disciple of the apostle John.[10] One single passage of the letter of the bishop of Smyrna reveals a clearly Johannine tint. He recalls texts, not from the Gospel of Jn., but from his letters. It is in Pol. Phil. 7:1: "For everyone who does not confess that Jesus Christ has come in the flesh (πᾶς γάρ, ὃς ἂν μὴ ὁμολογῇ 'Ιησοῦν Χριστὸν ἐν σαρκὶ ἐληλυθέναι) is an antichrist (ἀν- τίχριστός ἐστιν)." These words echo 1 Jn. 4:2-3: πᾶν πνεῦμα ὃ ὁμολογεῖ 'Ιησοῦν Χριστὸν ἐν σαρκὶ ἐληλυθότα (ἐληλυθέναι: Β, lat.) ἐκ τοῦ θεοῦ ἐστιν, καὶ πᾶν πνεῦμα ὃ μὴ ὁμολογεῖ τὸν 'Ιησοῦν ἐκ τοῦ θεοῦ οὐκ ἔστιν· καὶ τοῦτό ἐστιν τὸ τοῦ ἀντιχρίστου, and 2 Jn. 7: οἱ μὴ ὁμολογοῦντες 'Ιησοῦν Χριστὸν ἐρχόμενον ἐν σαρκί· οὗτός ἐστιν ὁ πλάνος καὶ ὁ ἀν- τίχριστος.

A literary contact with these texts is beyond doubt: Polycarp cites them almost literally, and he expresses the same idea.

As for the Acts of the Apostles, it is so dubious that the author was inspired by it that its use can be called into question.[11] However, one text of Acts might have influenced Pol. Phil. 1:2, which reads: "unto our Lord Jesus Christ, who for our sins endured to face even death. 'Whom God has raised up, having broken the pangs of Hell' (ὃν ἤγειρεν ὁ θεός, λύσας τὰς ὠδῖνας τοῦ ᾅδου)." Acts 2:24 states an idea similar to the second part of this text: ὃν ὁ θεὸς ἀνέστησεν λύσας τὰς ὠδῖνας τοῦ θανάτου (ᾅδου: D, lat., pesh.).

---

[10]Cf. A. Schwegler, *Das Nachapostolische Zeitalter in den Hauptmomenten seiner Entwicklung*, vol. 2 (Tübingen, 1846) 156n3.

[11]E. Zeller, "Die älteste Überlieferung über die Schriften des Lukas," *ThJ* 7 (1848): 532-33.

The presence of the participle λύσας and of ὠδῖνας τοῦ θανάτου (ᾅδου) in a text which carries the very same meaning suggests a literary contact. To be sure, the expression ὠδῖναι θανάτου is read in 2 Sam. 22:6; Ps. 18 (17):5; 116 (114):3, but it is not in conjunction with the participle λύσας; the words λύσας τὰς ὠδῖνας τοῦ ᾅδου surely point to a reference to Acts, and the text of Polycarp, bearing ᾅδου, would support the Western reading.

The formula μνημονεύοντες δὲ ὧν εἶπεν ὁ κύριος διδάσκων in Pol. Phil. 2:3 to introduce sayings of Christ can also be noted. It may recall the very similar one in Acts 20:35; but I stated above that Polycarp had in mind to cite 1 Clem. 13:1-2, where this lemma is found, even though he gets farther away from the text of the bishop of Rome when he cites the actual words of Christ. [12]

In Pol. Phil. 2:1, Christ is introduced as "the judge of the living and of the dead (κριτὴς ζώντων καὶ νεκρῶν)"; but this is merely a common idea to which Acts 10:42; 2 Tim. 4:1; and 1 Pet. 4:5 testify.

Finally, let me mention in Pol. Phil. 1:2 the use of the expression ἐξ ἀρχαίων χρόνων, which is rather similar to ἀφ' ἡμερῶν ἀρχαίων of Acts 15:7; the presence in Pol. Phil. 6:3 of the term ἔλευσις peculiar to Lk. 21:7 (D), 23:42 (D), and Acts 7:52; and the two Latin terms *sors* and *pars* in Pol. Phil. 12:2, which correspond perhaps to κλῆρος and μερίς from Acts 8:21.

B. The Letters of Saint Paul

Having praised the faith of the Philippians, Polycarp notes that their joy is beyond words, and he gives the following reason in 1:3: "knowing that 'by grace you are saved, not through works' (εἰδότες ὅτι χάριτί ἐστε σεσωσμένοι, οὐκ ἐξ ἔργων), but by the will of God through Jesus Christ." The words εἰδότες ὅτι introduce a reference to a written document. [13] It seems quite apparent that the author was alluding to Eph. 2:5, 8-9; indeed, striking parallels are found: "even when we were dead through our trespasses, [God] made us alive together with Christ (by grace you have been saved [χάριτί ἐστε σεσωσμένοι])" (Eph. 2:5). "For by grace you have been saved (τῇ γὰρ χάριτί ἐστε σεσωσμένοι) through faith (διὰ πίστεως); and this is not your own doing, it is the gift of God—not because of works (οὐκ ἐξ ἔργων), lest any man should boast" (Eph. 2:8-9). Other than a similar idea, we find in Polycarp expressions from this epistle of Paul: χάριτί ἐστε σεσωσμένοι, οὐκ ἐξ ἔργων. This observation is sufficient to allow the assertion that Polycarp depends here on the text of Eph.

In the course of a pericope devoted to fidelity to the precepts of the Lord, Polycarp writes in 2:2: "Now 'He who raised him' from the dead 'will also raise us' (ὁ δὲ ἐγείρας αὐτὸν ἐκ νεκρῶν καὶ ἡμᾶς ἐγερεῖ)." This calls to mind 2

---

[12] Cf. above, 29-30.
[13] Cf. A Committee of the Oxford Society, *The N. T. in the Apostolic Fathers*, 84.

Cor. 4:14: εἰδότες ὅτι ὁ ἐγείρας τὸν κύριον Ἰησοῦν καὶ ἡμᾶς σὺν Ἰησοῦ ἐγερεῖ. The parallelism is not absolutely strict, Paul having in addition σὺν Ἰησοῦ; but except for this difference, all of Polycarp's terms are read in the Pauline sentence. In addition to the words ὁ ἐγείρας applied to God as in Paul, the καὶ ἡμᾶς is remarkable: it recalls clearly 2 Cor. and compels recognition of a literary contact. 1 Cor. 6:14 offers a parallel as well, but it is less compelling.

It is interesting to note that Polycarp knows that Paul wrote to the Philippians. He says it himself in 3:2: "For neither I, nor anyone like me, is able to rival the wisdom of the blessed and glorious Paul, who, when living among you, carefully and steadfastly taught the word of truth face to face with his contemporaries and, when he was absent, wrote you letters. By the careful perusal of his letters you will be able to strengthen yourselves in the faith given to you." It is infinitely probable from this text that Polycarp knew the existing letter.

"Now the beginning of all difficulties is love of money (ἀρχὴ δὲ πάντων χαλεπῶν φιλαργυρία)," writes Polycarp in 4:1 at the beginning of a passage concerning this vice. 1 Tim. 6:10 states a similar maxim: ῥίζα γὰρ πάντων τῶν κακῶν ἐστιν ἡ φιλαργυρία; two words of Polycarp are there: πάντων and φιλαργυρία. It may be surprising not to find in Polycarp the substantive ῥίζα characteristic of this Pauline text; yet it must be recognized that the bishop of Smyrna indeed depends on 1 Tim., for in the sentence which immediately follows, he is in definite literary contact with 1 Tim. 6:7. Indeed, he writes: "Since we know then (εἰδότες οὖν ὅτι) that 'we have brought nothing into this world, and can take nothing out of it either' (οὐδὲν εἰσηνέγκαμεν εἰς τὸν κόσμον, ἀλλ' οὐδὲ ἐξενεγκεῖν τι ἔχομεν), let us arm ourselves with the armor of righteousness (τοῖς ὅπλοις τῆς δικαιοσύνης) and learn first to advance in the commandment of the Lord." The first part of this sentence corresponds exactly to 1 Tim. 6:7: οὐδὲν γὰρ εἰσηνέγκαμεν εἰς τὸν κόσμον, ὅτι οὐδὲ ἐξενεγκεῖν τι δυνάμεθα, which Polycarp cites almost literally.

Let me add another definite reminiscence of the Pauline metaphor of the armor in Rom. 6:13; 2 Cor. 6:7 (where the expression ὅπλα δικαιοσύνης is read explicitly), and Rom. 13:12. I would also like to emphasize that Polycarp, by introducing his sentence with εἰδότες οὖν ὅτι, was himself giving notice that he was about to make a citation.

Moving onward to the examination of the duties of deacons, Polycarp, in 5:1, again introduces a citation: "Knowing, then (εἰδότες οὖν ὅτι) that 'God is not mocked' (θεὸς οὐ μυκτηρίζεται), we ought to walk in a manner worthy of His commandment and glory." This citation is found literally in Gal. 6:7 (μὴ πλανᾶσθε, θεὸς οὐ μυκτηρίζεται) in a similar context which invites us to act according to the law (Gal. 5:14) and which enumerates a series of prescriptions. Let me add that in the New Testament only Gal. 6:7 uses the verb μυκτηρίζω.

In his advice to deacons, Polycarp says in 5:3: "For it is good to be cut off from the lusts in the world, because 'all lust wars against the Spirit,' and 'neither fornicators nor the effeminate nor sodomites (καὶ οὔτε πόρνοι οὔτε μαλακοὶ οὔτε ἀρσενοκοῖται) shall inherit the Kingdom of God' (βασιλείαν θεοῦ κληρονομήσουσιν), nor those who do unnatural things (οὔτε οἱ ποιοῦντες τὰ ἄτοπα).'' This enumeration of a series of vices echoes 1 Cor. 6:9-10. The bishop of Smyrna is literarily dependent on it. Paul's list of sinners is partially found in Polycarp: πόρνοι, μαλακοί, ἀρσενοκοῖται, as well as the expression βασιλείαν θεοῦ κληρονομήσουσιν. The addition made by Polycarp at the end of his sentence, οὔτε οἱ ποιοῦντες τὰ ἄτοπα, indicates that he is conscious of the omission of certain categories of sinners in the list which precedes. His sentence already finished, he, therefore, retraces his steps and slips in these few words which are general enough to include all those he omitted.

In his advice to the presbyters, Polycarp gives the reason which justifies our obligation to exercise forgiveness. He writes in 6:2: ''for we stand before the eyes of the Lord God, and we 'must all stand before the judgment-seat of Christ,' and 'each must give an account of himself' (πάντας δεῖ παραστῆναι τῷ βήματι τοῦ Χριστοῦ καὶ ἕκαστον ὑπὲρ αὐτοῦ λόγον δοῦναι).'' Parallels which are generally recognized are Rom. 14:10, 12 and 2 Cor. 5:10. Polycarp is literarily dependent on the first which says, πάντες γὰρ παραστησόμεθα τῷ βήματι τοῦ θεοῦ . . . ἄρα [οὖν] ἕκαστος ἡμῶν περὶ ἑαυτοῦ λόγον δώσει [τῷ θεῷ]. The bishop of Smyrna follows almost literally the text of Rom. from which he takes up the propositions πάντες παραστησόμεθα τῷ βήματι τοῦ θεοῦ and ἕκαστος ἡμῶν περὶ ἑαυτοῦ λόγον δώσει. He may have added δεῖ and changed θεοῦ to Χριστοῦ under the influence of 2 Cor., however, he alone is responsible for this change.[14]

Polycarp refers explicitly to a Pauline text in 11:2: ''Or do we forget 'that the saints shall judge the world,' as Paul teaches (aut nescimus quia sancti mundum judicabunt, sicut Paulus docet)?'' This sentence is found in 1 Cor. 6:2: ἢ οὐκ οἴδατε ὅτι οἱ ἅγιοι τὸν κόσμον κρινοῦσιν. Given that we have only the Latin version of this text, we can wonder whether the Latin translator was the one who added the words ''sicut Paulus docet''; this hypothesis would at least inform us as to how the Latin translator understood the Greek text deemed as coming from Paul.

In Polycarp's Phil. 11:4, I must also point out the presence of two Pauline metaphors, that of the body[15] and that of construction.[16] Unfortunately, we possess only the text of the Latin version of this passage: ''do not consider such persons (Valens and his wife) enemies, but invite them back as sinful and erring members (sicut passibilia membra), that you may heal the whole body of you (ut omnium vestrum corpus salvetis). By doing this you edify one another (vos ipsos

---

[14] A Committee of the Oxford Society, *The New Testament in the Apostolic Fathers,* 90.
[15] Cf. 1 Cor. 12:12-27; Rom. 12:4- 5.
[16] Cf. Rom. 15:2, 20; 1 Cor. 3:9; 6:19; 14:12, 26; 2 Cor. 6:16; 12:19; Eph. 2:20- 21.

aedificatis).'' Polycarp may have thought of 1 Cor. 12:26 (καὶ εἴτε πάσχει ἓν μέλος, συμπάσχει πάντα τὰ μέλη), particularly for the metaphors of the body and the sinful members.

Prompting moderation towards Valens, Polycarp writes in 12:1: ''Now, as it is said in these Scriptures: 'Be angry and sin not (irascimini et nolite peccare),' and 'Let not the sun go down upon your wrath (et sol non occidat super iracundiam vestram).' '' A parallel is found in Eph. 4:26: ὀργίζεσθε καὶ μὴ ἁμαρτάνετε· ὁ ἥλιος μὴ ἐπιδυέτω ἐπὶ παροργισμῷ ὑμῶν. Only one difference appears in the Pauline text: Polycarp links the citation of Ps. 4:5 and the passage ''sol non occidat super iracundiam vestram'' with the conjunction ''and.'' In Paul, both sentences are juxtaposed, the second seeming indeed to be a commentary on the first. The fact that the bishop of Smyrna joins these two passages is proof enough of his dependence on the Pauline text.

Other passages of Polycarp's *Letter to the Philippians*, while not revealing an absolute literary dependence on Pauline writings, can nevertheless be considered as having very probable reminiscences.

Thus when Pol. Phil. 1:1 reads ''I greatly rejoice with you in our Lord Jesus Christ (συνεχάρην ὑμῖν μεγάλως ἐν τῷ κυρίῳ ἡμῶν ᾽Ιησοῦ Χριστῷ),'' I cannot help but note that it is precisely in St. Paul's Letter to the Philippians that a very similar sentence is read in 4:10: ἐχάρην δὲ ἐν κυρίῳ μαγάλως. The similarity in sentences leads me to believe that the text of Polycarp is probably a literary reminiscence.

'' . . . [the faith] which is the mother of us all (ἥτις ἐστὶν μήτηρ πάντων ἡμῶν),'' Polycarp writes in Pol. Phil. 3:3, ''with hope (τῆς ἐλπίδος) following and charity (τῆς ἀγάπης) leading, charity toward God and Christ and our neighbor. For, if a person remain with these, he has fulfilled the commandment of righteousness (πεπλήρωκεν ἐντολὴν δικαιοσύνης); for he who has charity is far from all sin.'' This text likely contains various reminiscences from Paul. First of all, the words ἥτις ἐστὶν μήτηρ πάντων ἡμῶν are found literally in Gal. 4:26,[17] but applied to the heavenly Jerusalem, a symbol of the Church. Then Rom. 13:8-10, rather than Gal. 5:14 whose development is shorter, may have been the source of Polycarp's terms: indeed, the verb πληρόω, and the words ἐντολή and ἀγάπη are found. Although the mention of faith and hope is lacking, the similarity of thought favors a contact.

In his advice to the deacons, Polycarp writes in 5:2: ''If we be pleasing to Him in this world, we shall receive the future world in accordance with His promises to raise us up from the dead, and, if we act in a manner worthy of Him (ἐὰν πολιτευσώμεθα ἀξίως αὐτοῦ), 'we shall also reign with Him' (συμβασιλεύ-

---

[17]The generally recognized text of Gal. 4:26 reads ἐστὶν μήτηρ ἡμῶν; but some witnesses (A, H, L, several minuscules, the Syriac Harclean version) add πάντων as does Polycarp in his text.

σομεν), provided we believe (εἴγε πιστεύομεν)." The words "if we act in a manner worthy of Him" recall those of Phil. 1:27. But it is also possible, given his knowledge of 1 Clement, that Polycarp is referring to 1 Clem. 21:1 which reads: ἐὰν μὴ ἀξίως αὐτοῦ πολιτευόμενοι, all the more so since the words "if we be pleasing to Him" (ᾧ ἐὰν εὐαρεστήσωμεν) of Polycarp find a parallel (τὰ καλὰ καὶ εὐάρεστα ἐνώπιον αὐτοῦ ποιῶμεν) in this same passage of 1 Clem. As for the verb συμβασιλεύω, unique in the Apostolic Fathers, it can be believed that the author borrowed it from 2 Tim. 2:12: εἰ ὑπομένομεν, καὶ συμβασιλεύσομεν. This same verb is also read in 1 Cor. 4:8; yet, if the words of Polycarp εἴγε πιστεύομεν are to be read as referring to "faith," this interpretation of faithfulness gives preference to the text of 2 Tim. 2:12.

In addressing the presbyters, the Bishop of Smyrna in 6:1 urges them to be "always providing what is good before God and men (προνοοῦντες ἀεὶ τοῦ καλοῦ ἐνώπιον θεοῦ καὶ ἀνθρώπων)." Three parallel texts are often pointed out: Prov. 3:4; Rom. 12:17; and 2 Cor. 8:21. The text of Rom. 12:17 has not inspired Polycarp: the absence of the words θεοῦ καί is enough to exclude it. 2 Cor. 8:21 depends on Prov. 3:4; it would, therefore, be awkward to insist on a parallel between 2 Cor. 8:21 and Pol. Phil. 6:1, particularly if we know as well that the number of passages which may prove that Polycarp makes use of the Old Testament is minimal.[18] It can, therefore, be inferred that he refers directly to 2 Cor., since the contexts are again similar: Paul, as does Polycarp, gives a series of moral precepts. Yet, it must be noticed that, since the words οὐ μόνον ἀλλὰ ἐνώπιον of 2 Cor. 8:21 are missing, and because the construction of Prov. 3:4 is simpler, the latter passage is closer to Pol. Phil. 6:1.

When he proposes the patience of martyrs as an example, Polycarp declares in 9:2, "(. . . practice all endurance. . . .) Be convinced that all these 'ran not in vain' (οὐκ εἰς κενὸν ἔδραμον), but in faith and in righteousness." Two texts of the apostle, Gal. 2:2 and Phil. 2:16, contain the expression εἰς κενὸν τρέχω. In Gal. 2:2, the subject is the disagreement which arose between Peter and Paul; the context is, therefore, far from resembling that of Polycarp. In Phil. 2:16, on the other hand, the context may favor a literary contact: indeed, in this passage Paul invites the Philippians to obtain their salvation in his absence, so that he may act as a witness in the midst of the Gentiles and so that he may be certain that he has not run in vain. Inasmuch as Polycarp is addressing the Philippians, he assumes that they are convinced that Paul and the other apostles did not run in vain.

Still in the same exhortation to patience, Polycarp adds in 10:1: "Stand fast, therefore, in this conduct and follow the example of the Lord, 'firm and unchangeable in faith (firmi in fide et immutabiles) . . . ' " The last words suggest 1 Cor. 15:58 and Col. 1:23. The expression "in fide" is missing in 1 Cor., but

---

[18]Cf. A Committee of the Oxford Society, *The N. T. in the Apostolic Fathers*, 91.

the order of the principal words and the words themselves may be similar in Polycarp and in 1 Cor. Let me add that, in the opinion of some, the bishop of Smyrna's
use of the Letter to the Colossians is very doubtful.[19] This is why it is deemed that
1 Cor. 15:58 is the passage which may have been the source for Polycarp. Yet it
so happens that, here again, the original Greek text is missing, an inconvenience
which weighs heavily on the conclusions.

Still in Phil. 10:1, the words "lovers of the brotherhood, loving each other
(fraternitatis amatores, diligentes invicem)" may come from Rom. 12:10. But here
again we have only the Latin version from which to try to draw a conclusion. Let
me point out that the Vulgate in 1 Pet. 3:8 has "fraternitatis amatores," and that
similar thoughts are read in Jn. 13:34 and 15:12, 17.

When he considers Valens' abuse of trust, Polycarp notes in 11:2: "If any
man cannot control himself in these things, how can he recommend it to another
(Qui autem non potest se in his gubernare, quomodo alii pronuntiat hoc)?" There
is here a possible reminiscence of 1 Tim. 3:5, but, given the absence of the Greek
text, it cannot be inferred with certainty.

Polycarp recalls in 11:3 that "(Paul) boasts about you in all the Churches (de
vobis etenim gloriatur in omnibus ecclesiis). . . . " The similarity with 2 Thess.
1:4 is quite striking. It has been said that, due to a memory lapse, the Bishop of
Smyrna attributed to the Philippians what Paul had said about the Thessalonians.[20]

In advocating moderation towards Valens, Polycarp says in 11:4: "Therefore, be temperate yourselves in this regard, and do not consider such persons enemies (et non sicut inimicos tales existimetis). . . . " 2 Thess. 3:15 gives an
excellent parallel, which reads: καὶ μὴ ὡς ἐχθρὸν ἡγεῖσθε.

The stylistic formula of Pol. Phil. 12:1: " . . .I believe that this is so with you
(quod ego credo esse in vobis)" could be a reminiscence of the language of 2 Tim.
1:5.

The meeting in the same sentence of "sempiternus pontifex" and "Dei filius" in Pol. Phil. 12:2 suggests a dependence on Heb. 6:20 and 7:3. Yet, Clement
of Rome characterizes Christ several times as ἀρχιερεύς;[21] the use that Polycarp makes of 1 Clement is known in other respects.

As he ends his letter, Polycarp invites his readers to prayer in 12:3: "'Pray
for all the saints (pro omnibus sanctis orate).' 'Pray also for the emperors (orate
etiam pro regibus),' and authorities, and rulers, and 'for those who persecute and
hate you' and for 'the enemies of the Cross (et pro inimicis crucis),' that the result
of your effort may be manifest to all men (ut fructus vester manifestus sit in omnibus). . . . " In this passage we can find many probable reminiscences of Pau-

---

[19]Cf. ibid., 86.
[20]Cf. ibid., 95.
[21]Cf. 1 Clem. 36:1; 61:3; 64.

line texts: the invitation to prayer for all the saints recalls Eph. 6:18, for emperors 1 Tim. 2:1-2; the expression "inimici crucis" recalls Phil. 3:18 where it is found literally; finally the clause "ut fructus vester manifestus sit in omnibus" finds an eloquent parallel in 1 Tim. 4:15.

In addition to the passages in which a definite or probable literary dependence can be pointed out, several other passages can be found which state ideas similar to those of the apostle, even though their literary dependence is not clear. Thus, when he insists on fidelity to the precepts of the Lord in 2:1, Polycarp notes that: "To Him (Jesus) are subject all things in Heaven and on earth (ᾧ ὑπετάγη τὰ πάντα ἐπουράνια καὶ ἐπίγεια), Him every breath serves and He will come as 'the judge of the living and the dead.' . . . " The bishop of Smyrna states here an idea similar to 1 Cor. 15:28. So it is when he invites women to practice purity in Pol. Phil. 4:2, which corresponds to 1 Tim. 3:11; when he invites widows in Pol. Phil.4:3 "to be prudent in the faith of the Lord, and to pray without ceasing for all," a parallel thought is found in 1 Tim. 5:5. When Polycarp in 9:2 recalls that the martyrs "are with the Lord, with whom they also suffered (ᾧ καὶ συνέπαθον), in the place which they have deserved," it echoes the idea of Rom. 8:17: εἴπερ συμπάσχομεν, ἵνα καὶ συνδοξασθῶμεν.

In this *Letter to the Philippians* by Polycarp, let me add several terms and expressions of the Pauline vocabulary: καρποφορέω,[22] οἰκοδομέω,[23] κατὰ πρόσωπον,[24] τὰ κρύπτα τῆς καρδίας,[25] δίλογοι applied to deacons,[26] εὐλάβεια,[27] λόγος δικαιοσύνης,[28] ὁ νῦν αἰών,[29] poenitentiam dare.[30]

Finally, there remain several texts in which some scholars wished sometimes to see a reminiscence of the apostle. Neither the uncertainty of the meaning, nor its obscurity, nor the expressions allow us to believe in a Pauline influence. Thus in Pol. Phil. 11:2: "If a man does not abstain from avarice, he will be defiled by idolatry, and will be judged as one of the pagans, who 'know not the judgment of

---

[22]Cf. Pol. Phil. 1:2 and Rom. 7:4, 5; Col. 1:6, 10 and also Mt. 13:23; Mk. 4:20, 28; Lk. 8:15.

[23]Cf. Pol. Phil. 3:2 and Rom. 15:20; 1 Cor. 8:1, 10; 10:23; 14:4, 17; Gal. 2:18; 1 Thess. 5:11 and also Mt. 7:24, 26; 16:18; 21:33, 42; 23:29; 26:61; 27:40; Mk. 12:1, 10; 14:58; 15:29; Lk. 4:29; 6:48, 49; 7:5; 11:47, 48; 12:18; 14:28, 30; 17:28; 20:17; Acts 7:47, 49; 9:31; 20:32; 1 Pet. 2:5, 7.

[24]Cf. Pol. Phil. 3:2 and 2 Cor. 10:1, 7; Gal. 2:11; and also Lk. 2:31; Acts 3:13; 25:16.

[25]Cf. Pol. Phil. 4:3 and 1 Cor. 14:25.

[26]Cf. Pol. Phil. 5:2 and 1 Tim. 3:8.

[27]Cf. Pol. Phil. 6:3 and Heb. 5:7; 12:28.

[28]Cf. Pol. Phil. 9:1 and Heb. 5:13.

[29]Cf. Pol. Phil. 9:2 and 1 Tim. 6:17; 2 Tim. 4:10; Tit. 2:12.

[30]Cf. Pol. Phil. 11:4 and 2 Tim. 2:25.

the Lord.' '' Some scholars have sometimes thought of Eph. 5:5 and Col. 3:5,[31] but the idea does not seem similar and the agreement is due solely to the mention of idolatry. So it is with Pol. Phil. 11:3: "However, I have not found nor heard anything of the kind among you, among whom blessed Paul toiled, who were yourselves his epistles in the beginning," where scholars thought of 2 Cor. 3:2. Strictly speaking, these words of Polycarp are somewhat obscure; does he wish to say simply that they are the ones whom Paul addresses at the beginning of his letter?

It is, therefore, a fact that Polycarp knows the Pauline literature: he uses it, he cites it in many passages and almost literally; he seems to have come under very strong influence from the writings of the apostle. But I wish to point out that all the Pauline passages on which he depends have a clearly marked moral character, or else they are introduced in moral contexts. Polycarp does not follow Paul on the path of high theological concepts. This is why, if there is a conjecture that he uses the Pauline metaphors of the body and construction, he does not give them the weight they bear in the hand of the apostle; moreover, he merely refers discreetly to them.[32]

C. 1 Peter

Eusebius already mentioned that Polycarp used in his *Letter to the Philippians* testimonies drawn from 1 Peter.[33] In fact, the letter of Polycarp is full of citations and reminiscences of this epistle.

In the introduction of his letter, Polycarp, in 1:3, praises the faith of the Philippians in Jesus Christ: "In Him, though you see him not, you believe with unspeakable glorious joy (εἰς ὃν οὐκ ἰδόντες πιστεύετε χαρᾷ ἀνεκλαλήτῳ καὶ δεδοξασμένῃ), to which joy many desire to come (εἰς ἣν πολλοὶ ἐπιθυμοῦσιν εἰσελθεῖν). . . . '' 1 Pet. 1:8 offers a remarkable parallel: ὃν οὐκ ἰδόντες ἀγαπᾶτε, εἰς ὃν ἄρτι μὴ ὁρῶντες πιστεύοντες δὲ ἀγαλλιᾶσθε χαρᾷ ἀνεκλαλήτῳ καὶ δεδοξασμένῃ. The literary contact is definite: the idea is absolutely similar, the terms are practically identical; Polycarp simply omitted a few.[34] Indeed, ὃν οὐκ ἰδόντες, πιστεύοντες, χαρᾷ ἀνεκλαλήτῳ καὶ δεδοξασμένῃ is found in the text of the bishop of Smyrna. Furthermore, 1 Pet. 1:12: εἰς ἃ ἐπιθυμοῦσιν ἄγγελοι παρακύψαι, which follows fairly closely 1 Pet. 1:8, has most probably influenced the rest of the sentence cited by Polycarp.

When he preaches fidelity to the precepts of the Lord, Polycarp orders in 2:1: "Wherefore, girding up your loins (διὸ ἀναζωσάμενοι τὰς ὀσφύας ὑμῶν), serve

---

[31]Cf. A Committee of the Oxford Society, *The N. T. in the Apostolic Fathers*, 93.

[32]Cf. Pol. Phil. 11:4.

[33]Cf. Eusebius, *Hist. Eccl.* 4.14.3-8; cf. Lelong, *Ignace d'Antioche et Polycarpe de Smyrne*, lii.

[34]Mt. 13:17 has sometimes been mentioned as a parallel, but this text is much less close to Pol. Phil. 1:3 than is the text of 1 Pet. 1:8.

God in fear. . . . " 1 Pet. 1:13 contains literally the words of Polycarp: διὸ ἀναζωσάμενοι τὰς ὀσφύας τῆς διανοίας ὑμῶν. The literary contact is undeniable: identity of idea, identity of words, and furthermore, Pol. Phil. 2:1 follows Pol. Phil. 1:3 where it was determined that the author came under the literary influence of 1 Pet. 1:8 and 12, verses which precede the text of Peter to which I now appeal.

Still in Pol. Phil. 2:1, Christians are invited to believe "in Him who raised our Lord Jesus Christ from the dead and gave Him glory (πιστεύσαντες εἰς τὸν ἐγείραντα τὸν κύριον ἡμῶν ᾽Ιησοῦν Χριστὸν ἐκ νεκρῶν καὶ δόντα αὐτῷ δόξαν), and a throne at His right hand." The author cites almost literally 1 Pet. 1:21. Indeed, in addition to the identical idea, the terms are almost perfectly identical; furthermore, Polycarp still follows the verses of chapter 1 of 1 Peter, inspired here by 1 Pet. 1:21, having been inspired shortly before by 1 Pet. 1:13. He adds, however, to the text of Peter the words "and a throne at His right hand," stating thereby an idea similar to Pol. Phil. 2:10.

Still recommending fidelity to the precepts of the Lord, Polycarp writes in 2:2: "not rendering evil for evil, nor abuse for abuse (μὴ ἀποδιδόντες κακὸν ἀντὶ κακοῦ ἢ λοιδορίαν ἀντὶ λοιδορίας) or blow for blow, or curse for curse." Here again, we find the literary influence of 1 Pet. 3:9, which is cited literally. Polycarp adds, probably of his own invention: "blow for blow, curse for curse."

When he exhorts young people to curb their least evil desires, the bishop of Smyrna gives the reason for this counsel in 5:3: "For it is good to be cut off from the lusts in the world, because 'all lust wars against the spirit' (πᾶσα ἐπιθυμία κατὰ τοῦ πνεύματος στρατεύεται). . . . " The author has perhaps fused here the text of Gal. 5:17 (ἡ γὰρ σὰρξ ἐπιθυμεῖ κατὰ τοῦ πνεύματος) with 1 Pet. 2:11 (ἀγαπητοί, παρακαλῶ ὡς παροίκους καὶ παρεπιδήμους ἀπέχεσθαι τῶν σαρκικῶν ἐπιθυμιῶν, αἵτινες στρατεύονται κατὰ τῆς ψυχῆς). But the presence in 1 Peter of the verb στρατεύομαι indicates that this text served as a basis for the editing of the passage of the *Letter to the Philippians.*

"Let us be watchful in prayers (νήφοντες πρὸς τὰς εὐχάς)," says Polycarp in 7:2. The expression he uses here coincides so strictly with 1 Pet. 4:7 (νήψατε εἰς προσευχάς) that there is just cause to conclude that he borrowed it from 1 Pet.

In inviting us to imitate Christ, Polycarp writes in 8:1: "Without interruption, therefore, let us persevere by our hope and by the guarantee of our righteousness, which is Jesus Christ, who bore our sins in His own body on the tree (ὃς ἀνήνεγκεν ἡμῶν τὰς ἁμαρτίας τῷ ἰδίῳ σώματι ἐπὶ τὸ ξύλον), who did no sin, nor was deceit found in His mouth (ὃς ἁμαρτίαν οὐκ ἐποίησεν, οὐδὲ εὑρέθη δόλος ἐν τῷ στόματι αὐτοῦ); but for our sake, that we might live in Him, He endured all things." In some parts, this text follows almost literally 1 Pet. 2:22 and 24: ὃς ἁμαρτίαν οὐκ ἐποίησεν οὐδὲ εὑρέθη δόλος ἐν τῷ στόματι αὐτοῦ . . . ὃς τὰς ἁμαρτίας ἡμῶν αὐτὸς ἀνήνεγκεν ἐν τῷ σώματι αὐτοῦ ἐπὶ τὸ ξύλον.

Peter refers to Is. 53:4, 9, 12;[35] but Polycarp does not follow the text of the prophet. It is definitely closer to 1 Pet. from which he takes up words absent in the text of Is., such as ἁμαρτίαν before οὐκ ἐποίησεν and ἐν τῷ σώματι αὐτοῦ ἐπὶ τὸ ξύλον after ἀνήνεγκεν.

In drawing the conclusion from the conduct of the martyrs, Polycarp says in 10:2: '' . . . keep your conduct free from reproach among pagans, so that from your good works you may receive praise . . . (conversationem vestram irreprehensibilem habentes in gentibus, ut ex bonis operibus vestris et vos laudem accipiatis).'' Although the original Greek text of this passage is missing, a very probable literary dependence on 1 Pet. 2:12 can be asserted. In fact, in addition to a similar thought, the Latin text follows very closely the Greek text of Peter. In Pol. Phil. 8:2, ''if we suffer for His name (ἐὰν πάσχομεν διὰ τὸ ὄνομα αὐτοῦ), let us praise Him (δοξάζωμεν αὐτόν),'' there is quite probably a literary reminiscence of 1 Pet. 4:15-16, which reads in particular εἰ δὲ ὡς χριστιανός (τις πασχέτω) . . . δοξαζέτω δὲ τὸν θεὸν ἐν τῷ ὀνόματι τούτῳ, and which is found in almost identical form in the text of Polycarp.

When in 12:2, Polycarp speaks of ''His Father, who raised Him up from the dead (patrem qui resuscitavit eum a mortuis),'' he may have been inspired by 1 Pet. 1:21, but this statement constitutes one of the commonplace themes of primitive Christian preaching.[36]

Let me also point out the use of the word εὔσπλαγχνοι in Pol. Phil. 5:2 and 6:1, which is found in 1 Pet. 3:8;[37] and the expression ζηλωταὶ περὶ τὸ καλόν in Pol. Phil. 6:3, which is similar to τοῦ ἀγαθοῦ ζηλωταί in 1 Pet. 3:13.[38]

Finally, let me add that Pol. Phil. 10:2: ''You must all be subject to one another . . . (omnes vobis invicem subjecti estote),'' sometimes linked to 1 Pet. 5:5, depends rather on 1 Clem. 38:1, which reads ὑποτασσέσθω ἕκαστος τῷ πλησίον αὐτοῦ.

This examination of the letter of Polycarp in relation to 1 Peter reveals that Polycarp uses 1 Peter and is literarily dependent on it in numerous passages. Polycarp follows very closely the texts of Peter, which it reproduces sometimes literally.

No trace of a definite influence can be mentioned from the letter of James or from 2 Peter.

A basic conclusion emerges from this section: the bishop of Smyrna uses only one of our gospels, namely the Gospel of Matthew. He gives witness to a fairly

---

[35]Cf. Is. 53:4, 9, 12: οὗτος τὰς ἁμαρτίας ἡμῶν φέρει καὶ περὶ ἡμῶν ὀδυνᾶται καὶ ἡμεῖς ἐλογισάμεθα αὐτὸν εἶναι ἐν πόνῳ καὶ ἐν πληγῇ καὶ ἐν κακώσει . . . ὅτι ἀνομίαν οὐκ ἐποίησεν, οὐδὲ εὑρέθη δόλος ἐν τῷ στόματι αὐτοῦ . . . καὶ αὐτὸς ἁμαρτίας πολλῶν ἀνήνεγκεν καὶ διὰ τὰς ἁμαρτίας αὐτῶν παρεδόθη.

[36]Cf. Acts 2:24; 3:15; Rom. 4:24; 10:9; Gal. 1:1; Col. 2:12.

[37]Cf. also Eph. 4:32.

[38]Let me also mention ζηλωτὴς καλῶν ἔργων in Tit. 2:14.

remarkable fidelity to the texts he uses, and he even goes as far as to cite some literally. When he reports a saying of Christ, he borrows it from the first gospel. There is no reference to other gospels, a fairly strange phenomenon, particularly in reference to the fourth gospel, since tradition holds that Polycarp was a disciple of the apostle John. Therefore, it must be inferred that, for Polycarp, the Gospel of Mt. is the source which is usually referred to and from which the words of the Lord are drawn.

An equally important place must be made for the epistles of Saint Paul in Polycarp's *Letter to the Philippians*: the Pauline texts from which he draws are quite numerous. He cites some almost literally. Let me emphasize that the passages which he draws from Saint Paul have a moral character, or he inserts them in contexts which consider human activity. He does not refer to the more theological texts of Paul.

1 Peter was also one of Polycarp's principal sources. He drew copiously from it, citing entire phrases. He seems to use it in the same way he uses the texts of Saint Paul: sometimes he inserts passages of Paul and Peter in the thread of his account; sometimes he draws more freely from them.

Section 2
THE MARTYRDOM OF POLYCARP

Few passages in this narrative find parallels in the Gospel of Mt. and in the New Testament in general. Possible comparisons with several specific texts are subject to caution. They are, in fact, made with texts drawn from Christ's Passion narrative. The author of the *Martyrdom of Polycarp* asserts in 1:1 his intention to present the narrative of a martyrdom which resembles the Passion of Christ as told in the gospel, and he ends his narrative by pointing out, in 19:1, the analogy between the martyrdom of the bishop of Smyrna and the Passion of the Lord. Now, in primitive Christianity, the events of the Passion would no doubt have been told often: its main characteristics were engraved in the memory of Christians. It is not necessary, therefore, to presume that the author will follow a specific text, particularly since he seems to be inspired solely by the essential characteristics of the Passion which he finds in the martyrdom of Polycarp. Various points of contact between this narrative and the Passion may be mentioned briefly: Polycarp was betrayed by someone from his household (6:1): Judas, the traitor, was one of the Twelve (Mt., Mk., Lk., Jn.); the name of the irenarch who was charged to lead Polycarp to the stadium is Herod (6:2): this name is explicitly linked to that of Herod in the gospel (Lk.); he who betrays the bishop of Smyrna comes to get him, accompanied by a band of armed men (7:1): Judas was accompanied by soldiers and armed men (Mt., Mk., Lk., Jn.); Polycarp could have escaped, but he preferred the will of God (7:1): in agony, Christ asks his Father to take the chalice away from him, but resolves to do the will of his Father (Mt., Mk., Lk.); the appearance of Polycarp provokes astonishment and stupor in those who came to arrest him (7:2): the soldiers who come to seize Christ fall backwards when Christ asks them: "Whom do you seek?" (Jn.); Polycarp is made to mount a donkey and so to enter into the city on a day of great sabbath (8:1): Christ enters triumphantly into Jerusalem, mounted on a donkey (Mt., Mk., Lk., Jn.); Polycarp does not answer the questions which Herod and his father Nicetus ask him (8:2): Christ keeps silent before his interrrogators (Mt., Mk., Jn.); Polycarp is showered with abuse and is made to suffer (8:3): Christ is flagellated (Mt., Mk., Jn.); the bishop of Smyrna is threatened with beasts (11:1): confronting the silence of Christ, Pilate reminds him that he has the power to have him crucified (Jn.); the proconsul is disconcerted (12:1): a disconcerted Pilate washes his hands (Mt.); the crowd demands loudly the death of Polycarp (12:2-3): the crowd demands the death of Christ (Mt., Mk., Lk., Jn.); Polycarp takes off his garments (13:2): Christ is stripped of his garments (Mt., Mk., Lk., Jn.); Polycarp is placed on the stake (13:3): Christ is placed on the cross (Mt., Mk., Lk., Jn.); Polycarp prays on the stake (14): Jesus prays on the cross (Mt., Mk., Lk.); wonders happen near the stake (15): wonders accompany the death of Christ (Mt., Mk., Lk.); Polycarp is pierced with a dagger (16): the side of Christ is opened with a lance (Jn.); Nicetus intervenes to ask the governors to deny the body of Polycarp to the Christians (17): the chief priests and the Pharisees ask Pilate to guard the sepulchre against an eventual snatching of the body by the disciples of Christ (Mt.)

There is no doubt that the author of the *Martyrdom of Polycarp* refers to traits of the Passion of Jesus which are in one or another of the evangelists; it can, therefore, be assumed that he does not follow a specific gospel; he is inspired rather by the substance of the Passion as tradition preserved it.

Such a statement will necessarily influence any assertions that the author of the *Martyrdom of Polycarp* is referring to a specific gospel text. These assertions cannot be absolutely certain, since the very likely hypothesis of resorting to tradition will always remain open. Nevertherless, while still holding on to this last hypothesis, I propose to point out first several passages which are closer to a specific Matthean parallel. I shall then go on to the other New Testament writings.

§1. Saint Matthew

1. Polyc. Martyr. 7:1

Ἔχοντες οὖν τὸ παιδάριον τῇ παρασκευῇ περὶ δείπνου ὥραν ἐξῆλθον διωγμῖται καὶ ἱππεῖς μετὰ τῶν συνήθων αὐτοῖς ὅπλων ὡς ἐπὶ λῃστὴν τρέχοντες. Καὶ ὀψὲ τῆς ὥρας συνεπελθόντες ἐκεῖνον μὲν εὗρον ἔν τινι δωματίῳ κατακείμενον ἐν ὑπερῴῳ· κἀκεῖθεν δὲ ἠδύνατο εἰς ἕτερον χωρίον ἀπελθεῖν, ἀλλ' οὐκ ἠβουλήθη εἰπών· Τὸ θέλημα τοῦ θεοῦ γενέσθω.

So they brought the little boy along and on Friday, about supper time, the police and horsemen with their usual arms came out as if against a bandit. And late in the evening they converged on Polycarp and found him resting in an upper room. Though it was still in his power to get away to another locality, he did not wish to, saying, "The will of God be done."[39]

The words ὡς ἐπὶ λῃστὴν τρέχοντες recall the words of Jesus to those who came to arrest him. Mt. 26:55; Mk. 14:48; Lk. 22:52 all three read ὡς ἐπὶ λῃστὴν ἐξήλθατε μετὰ μαχαιρῶν καὶ ξύλων. Given the concern of the author to establish a parallel between the martyrdom of Polycarp and the Passion of the Savior, these words certainly allude to the arrest of Christ at Gethsemane. The author, therefore, consciously refers to it. The identity of the texts of the three synoptics does not allow us to decide which one he had in mind.

The final words τὸ θέλημα τοῦ θεοῦ γενέσθω recall Mt. 6:10: γεηθήτω τὸ θέλημά σου; 26:42: εἰ οὐ δύναται τοῦτο παρελθεῖν ἐὰν μὴ αὐτὸ πίω, γενηθήτω τὸ θέλημά σου; Lk. 22:42: πλὴν μὴ τὸ θέλημά μου ἀλλὰ τὸ σὸν γινέσθω; and Acts 21:14: τοῦ κυρίου τὸ θέλημα γινέσθω. Only Mt. 26:42 and Lk. 22:42 can be considered. The text of the *Martyrdom of Polycarp* is much closer to that of Mt. than to that of Lk. In Lk., in fact, the sentence is more entangled, and he makes a parallel between the will of Christ and the will of the Father. Mt. is simpler; the Matthean text and of the *Martyrdom* are almost identical.

Now, I pointed out above that the words ὡς ἐπὶ λῃστὴν τρέχοντες of this same verse 1 found an identical parallel in the three synoptics in the context of the arrest of Christ. It is reasonable, therefore, to infer that for this sentence, preference ought to be given to Mt. 26:55 as a possible source for the author of the *Martyrdom*.

As for the description of the armed men who came to arrest Christ, it could also have been inspired by Mt. 26:47. Yet, only Jn. 18:3 uses the word ὅπλα which is also present in the *Martyrdom*.

2. Polyc. Martyr. 8:1

. . . τῆς ὥρας ἐλθούσης τοῦ ἐξιέναι, ὄνῳ καθίσαντες αὐτὸν ἤγαγον εἰς τὴν πόλιν, ὄντος σαββάτου μαγάλου.

So they placed him on an ass, and brought him into the city on a great Sabbath.

------

[39]For the *Martyrdom of Polycarp*, I follow the edition of K. Bihlmeyer, *Die Apostolischen Väter*, SAQ 2nd ser. 1 (Tübingen, 1924) 120-32. [The English text of the *Martyrdom of St. Polycarp*, trans. Francis X. Glimm, is taken from *The Apostolic Fathers*, trans. Francis X. Glimm, Joseph M. F. Marique, and Gerald G. Walsh, *The Fathers of the Church, A New Translation*, vol. 1 (Washington: The Catholic University of America Press, 1962). Editor's note.]

The fact that Polycarp is made to mount upon an ass and is brought into the city is a new trait of martyrdom (κατὰ τὸ εὐαγγέλιον).[40] All the gospels report the entry of Christ into Jerusalem on an ass: Mt. 21:1-9; Mk. 11:1-10; Lk. 19:29-38; Jn. 12:12-16; but only Mt. 21:2, 7 uses the substantive ὄνος as does this text, too thin a clue, however, to conclude in favor of a literary dependence. For σάββατον μέγα, Jn. 19:31 comes to mind.

Both of these texts suggest that a dependence on Mt. is quite probable. The following passages suggest that a literary reminiscence of the Matthean texts is possible.

1. Polyc. Martyr. 4

Διὰ τοῦτο οὖν, ἀδελφοί, οὐκ ἐπαινοῦμεν τοὺς προσιόντας ἑαυτοῖς, ἐπειδὴ οὐχ οὕτως διδάσκει τὸ εὐαγγέλιον.

For this reason, therefore, brethren, we do not approve those who give themselves up, because the Gospel does not teach us this. [The English translation of this passage has been added by the editor.]

All the commentators have wondered where such a teaching of the gospel is read. They generally go back to Mt. 10:23; Jn. 7:1; 8:59; 10:39, where the teaching of Christ and his example show that persecutors can be fled from and that it is not necessary to wait for them. Polycarp, moreover, will leave his city to escape from those who seek him, as is told in chapter 6. Nothing in the text indicates that the author refers to one or the other of the texts mentioned above. The verb διδάσκει, however, fits better with a saying of Christ like the one in Mt. 10:23 than with a series of examples from the life of Christ from which the intent of the teaching would proceed.

2. Polyc. Martyr. 6:1

Καὶ μὴ εὑρόντες συνελάβοντο παιδάρια δύο, ὧν τὸ ἕτερον βασανιζόμενον ὡμολόγησεν. Ἦν γὰρ καὶ ἀδύνατον λαθεῖν αὐτόν, ἐπεὶ καὶ οἱ προδιδόντες αὐτὸν οἰκεῖοι ὑπῆρχον.

But, not finding him, they seized two slave boys, of whom one turned informer after being tortured. For, it was not really possible for him to remain hidden, since those who betrayed him were of his own household. [The English translation of this passage has been added by the editor.]

The word οἰκεῖοι echoes the saying of Christ in Mt. 10:36: καὶ ἐχθροὶ τοῦ ἀνθρώπου οἱ οἰκιακοὶ αὐτοῦ, which is a free citation of Mic. 7:6. Is the author perhaps making a casual reference to this saying? The presence of the term οἰκεῖ-

---

[40]Cf. Lelong, *Ignace d'Antioche et Polycarpe de Smyrne*, 138.

οι is fairly close to οἰκιακοί, and the fact that only Mt. reports this saying of the Lord could be a clue. The text of Mic. 7:6 cannot here be taken into consideration; there is neither οἰκεῖοι nor οἰκιακοί.

Let me mention also the participle σταθείς in 7:3, which describes the posture of Polycarp in prayer. Mt. 6:5 and Lk. 18:11, 13 use the same verb to describe as well the posture of persons in prayer. Let us notice also the term ποτήριον in 14:2, which is present in the gospels in Mt. 10:42; 20:22, 23; 23:25, 26; 26:27, 39; Mk. 9:41; 10:38, 39; 14:23, 36; Lk. 11:39; 22:17, 42; and Jn. 18:11.[41]

In conclusion, it can be noted that not one passage of the *Martyrdom of Polycarp* is under the definite literary influence of a text of the first gospel; some specific passages might be admitting of a dependence.

§2. The Other New Testament Writings

The other New Testament writings do not seem to have played a special role in the drafting of the *Martyrdom of Polycarp*. However, certain texts must be mentioned because commentators sometimes refer to them.

Not one passage can be clearly linked with the Gospel of Mk.; the same applies to the Gospel of Lk. Yet, I would like to point out the use of the verb αἱρέω in 3:2 with the same meaning as Lk. 23:18; Acts 21:36; 22:22, and the expression κατὰ πόλιν in 5:1, which is present in Lk. 8:1, 4; Acts 15:21; 20:23,[42] without proving in the least that there is the slightest literary influence from these texts.

With reference to the Johannine texts, only 14:2 deserves some attention: "I bless Thee, for having made me worthy of this day (τῆς ἡμέρας) and hour (καὶ ὥρας ταύτης); I bless Thee, because I may have a part, along with the martyrs, in the chalice of Thy Christ, 'unto resurrection in eternal life' (εἰς ἀνάστασιν ζωῆς αἰωνίου), resurrection both of soul and body in the incorruptibility of the Holy Spirit." The term ὥρα has sometimes been linked with Jn. 12:27 where the meaning is similar; there is no mention of a specific day or hour. In fact, the words which follow, "worthy because I may have a part in the chalice of Christ," indicate clearly that ἡμέρα refers to the period of sufferings, and ὥρα is the climax within that period.[43] The point at hand is the day of the martyrdom and hour of the death of Polycarp. This minimal clue does not lead to the conclusion of a literary influence. I am simply emphasizing that Jn. also has the term ὥρα, which refers to the Passion of Christ.

The words εἰς ἀνάστασιν ζωῆς αἰωνίου recall Jn. 5:29, which does not have the adjective αἰωνίου; the context is different. Jn., indeed, notes that judg-

---

[41]This term is read also in 1 Cor. 10:16, 21; 11:25, 26, 27, 28; Rev. 14:10; 16:19; 17:4; 18:6.

[42]This expression is also found in Tit. 1:5.

[43]Cf. Lightfoot, *S. Ignatius, S. Polycarp*, 3:387.

ment belongs to the Son. To be sure, the author of the *Martyrdom of Polycarp* may have taken the expression ready made from Jn., but there is no element in the text to suggest it. On the contrary, the words which follow, "of soul and body in the incorruptibility of the Holy Spirit," do not lead to Jn. 5:29.

The expression κύριε ὁ θεὸς ὁ παντοκράτωρ of 14:1 at the beginning of the prayer of Polycarp is found in Rev. 4:8; 11:17; 15:3; 16:7; but the author may have taken it from the liturgy.

The Acts of the Apostles in 2:29; 4:29, 31; 28:31 and Heb. 4:16 have the expression μετὰ παρρησίας, which is present in 10:1.

Some texts state ideas similar to those of Saint Paul, thus in 1:2: "For, like the Lord, he (Polycarp) waited to be betrayed, that we might become his imitators, not regarding ourselves alone, but also our neighbors (μὴ μόνον σκοποῦντες τὸ καθ' ἑαυτούς, ἀλλὰ καὶ τὸ κατὰ τοὺς πέλας)," an idea similar to Phil. 2:4 is stated in the last clause. The presence of the verb σκοπέω and the opposition expressed by μὴ μόνον and ἀλλὰ καί could be a hint of a literary reminiscence of the Pauline text.

2:3 reads, " . . . for they kept before their eyes the escape from eternal and unquenchable fire, and with the eyes of their heart they looked up to the good things which are stored up for those who have persevered, 'which neither ear hath heard nor eye hath seen, nor hath it entered into the heart of man' (ἃ οὔτε οὖς ἤκουσεν οὔτε ὀφθαλμὸς εἶδεν οὔτε ἐπὶ καρδίαν ἀνθρώπου ἀνέβη)." The author uses here a citation which is closer to 1 Cor. 2:9 than to Is. 64:4; I have already pointed out that this citation may have come from a rabbinical tradition which transmitted in this form the text of Isaiah.[44] In this case, the author may also have drawn from this tradition, since no element of the text and context leads to 1 Cor. 2:9.

The words βασανιζόμενοι τῆς σαρκὸς ἀπεδήμουν of 2:2, " . . . at the time of their torture the noble martyrs of Christ were absent from the flesh . . . , " may have been suggested by 2 Cor. 5:6.[45]

10:2: " . . . for we have been taught to give honor, as is proper, to rulers and authorities appointed by God, provided it does not harm us . . . "; submission due to the authorities is affirmed in Rom. 13:1-7; 1 Pet. 2:13-14.

I would like to mention as well some expressions and terms in the *Martyrdom of Polycarp* which are present in Paul: such as ἄνωθεν meaning "anew,"[46] τῷ δὲ δυναμένῳ,[47] ὁ γράψας,[48] and κατὰ πάντα τόπον.[49]

---

[44]Cf. book 1, 49.

[45]Cf. Lightfoot, *S. Ignatius, S. Polycarp*, 3:366.

[46]Cf. 1:1 and Gal. 4:9.

[47]Cf. 20:2 and Rom. 16:25; Eph. 3:20; also Jude 24.

[48]Cf. 20:2 and Rom. 16:22.

[49]Cf. the inscription and 1 Cor. 1:2 where a similar expression reads ἐν παντὶ τόπῳ.

The *Martyrdom of Polycarp* bears no definite trace of a literary influence from the catholic epistles. At best, the similarity of the formula of the inscription ἔλεος, εἰρήνη καὶ ἀγάπη θεοῦ πατρὸς καὶ τοῦ κυρίου ἡμῶν 'Ιησοῦ Χριστοῦ πληθυνθείη can be compared to the text of Jude 2: ἔλεος ὑμῖν καὶ εἰρήνη καὶ ἀγάπη πληθυνθείη.

As a whole, this second section does not furnish any definite element in favor of the use of and literary influence from the first gospel. The other New Testament writings do not furnish better information. The author most likely followed the usual practice by turning to the tradition found in the Passion Narrative of Christ and combining features present sometimes in one gospel, sometimes in another. I would like to stress, however, that it is again the Gospel of Mt. which furnishes the best parallel to some texts of the *Martyrdom of Polycarp*. The dependence is attributed either to the *Martyrdom* or to the tradition.

An overview of this second chapter as a whole shows that only Polycarp's *Letter to the Philippians* is interesting for the focus of my interest. He uses the Gospel of Mt. and reproduces its texts almost literally. Polycarp shows no attraction to the other gospels, not even to the gospel of the apostle John whose disciple he was. Whenever the letters of Paul and 1 Peter are also rather frequently cited, these texts have a particular, clearly marked moral tone, most often framed in the unfolding of the life of the Christian community. In short, Mt. seems indeed to be the gospel: this is the gospel to depend on for the sayings of Christ.

Editor's Addendum to Chapter 2

According to Helmut Köster (*Synoptische Überlieferung bei den apostolischen Vätern* and *Introduction to the New Testament*, vol. 2, *History and Literature of Early Christianity* [Philadelphia: Fortress Press, 1982] 112-23), Polycarp not only knows and uses 1 Clement, but also corrects the quotations of sayings of Jesus in 1 Clement 13:2 according to the text that had been established by the Gospels of Matthew and Luke (Pol. Phil. 2:3); a knowledge of the text of those gospels is also shown elsewhere (Pol. Phil. 7:2). Following the thesis of Paul N. Harrison (*Polycarp's Two Letters to the Philippians* [Cambridge: Cambridge University Press, 1936]), Köster regards chapters 1–12 of Polycarp's letter as a later document than the original text of the epistle consisting of chapter 13 and possibly chapter 14.

Wolf-Dietrich Köhler (*Die Rezeption des Matthäusevangeliums in der Zeit vor Irenäus*, 97-110) concludes the following with respect to Polycarp's *Letter to the Philippians*.

1. Passages for which dependence on Matthew is probable

PHILIPPIANS	MATTHEW
2:3b	5:3 and 5:10
12:3	5:44 and 5:16, 48

2. Passages for which dependence on Matthew is quite possible

PHILIPPIANS	MATTHEW
6:2	6:12 (cf. 18:23-35)
7:2	6:13 and 26:41

3. Passages for which dependence on Matthew is at most theoretically possible

PHILIPPIANS	MATTHEW
5:2	20:28
6:1	25:36, 43

4. Passages for which dependence on Matthew is very improbable

PHILIPPIANS	MATTHEW
2:3a	5:7 and 18:33
1:3	25:21 and 13:17
10:1	18:10
11:2	18:17
6:1	13:14-15

Biblia Patristica (*Index des Citations et Allusions Bibliques dans la Littérature Patristique, Des origines à Clément d'Alexandrie et Tertullien,* vol. 1 [Paris, 1975] 223-93) lists the following citations or allusions to the Gospel of Matthew in the text of Polycarp's *Letter to the Philippians.*

PHILIPPIANS	MATTHEW
2:3	5:3
2:3	5:10
12:3	5:44
6:2	6:12
7:2	6:13
6:2	6:14-15
2:3	7:1-2
7:2	26:41

With respect to the Martyrdom of Polycarp, Wolf-Dietrich Köhler (*Die Rezeption des Matthäusevangeliums in der Zeit vor Irenäus,* 487-89) concludes the following.

1. Passages for which dependence on Matthew is quite possible

MARTYRDOM OF POLYCARP	MATTHEW
4	10:23
6:2	10:36; 27:5
7:1	26:55; 6:10
8:1	21:7
11:2	25:46
14:2	20:22-23

2. Passages for which dependence on Matthew is only theoretically possible but in no way compelling

MARTYRDOM OF POLYCARP	MATTHEW
2:3	25:46

Chapter 3

THE APOCALYPSES

Assembled in this present chapter are writings which can be categorized in the literary genre of apocalypses. Studied in succession are: the Christian parts of the *Ascension of Isaiah*, the *Odes of Solomon*, the *Sibylline Oracles*, the *Apocalypse of Peter*, and the *Shepherd of Hermas*.

Section 1
THE CHRISTIAN PARTS OF THE ASCENSION OF ISAIAH

Scholars in this century who have studied the work known as the *Ascension of Isaiah* generally distinguish three parts. The first, of Jewish origin, written before the year 100 on the basis of a pre-Christian Jewish tradition and called the *Martyrdom of Isaiah*, includes the following passages: 1:1-2a, 6b-13a; 2:1-3:12; 5:1-14. The second, a kind of Christian apocalypse sometimes called the *Testament of Hezekiah*, which dates from the end of the first century or the first years of the second, extends from 3:13 to 4:18. The third, of Christian origin, which dates from about the middle of the second century, is called the *Vision of Isaiah*, and includes 6:1 to 11:40. These three parts were compiled soon after the year 150.[1]

I shall be concerned only with the Christian parts of the *Ascension of Isaiah*. As in the first chapter, my focus of interest leads me to examine in a first paragraph the literary influence of Mt.; a second paragraph is devoted to the other New Testament writings.

---

[1]For the history of this book, cf. E. Tisserant, *Ascension d'Isaïe, translation from the Ethiopic version with the principal variants from the Greek, Latin, and Slavonic versions, introduction, and notes*, Documents pour l'Étude de la Bible, published under the direction of F. Martin (Paris, 1909) 32-61; R. H. Charles, *The Ascension of Isaiah translated from the Ethiopic version, which together with the new Greek fragment, the Latin versions and the Latin translation of the Slavonic version, is here published in full* (London, 1900) xxxvi-xliii; from the same author, *The Martyrdom of Isaiah*, in R. H. Charles, *The Apocrypha and Pseudepigrapha of the Old Testament in English*, vol. 2, *Pseudepigrapha* (Oxford, 1913) 155; F. Flemming-H. Duensing, *Die Himmelfahrt des Jesaja*, in E. Hennecke, *Neutestamentliche Apocryphen* 24, 2nd ed. (Tübingen, 1924) 303 [ET 2:642-43].

The original of the *Ascension of Isaiah* is lost; there remains only one complete Ethiopic version, a few fragments of a Greek text,[2] of two Latin versions,[3] and of a translation into old Slavonic. This fact constitutes a serious handicap for the task I have proposed to perform. Yet, in the translations I use, I may find enough elements to link a particular passage to the first gospel or to a particular New Testament writing.

§1. Saint Matthew

Two texts of the *Ascension of Isaiah* have special affinity with the Gospel of Mt.

1. Asc. Is. 3:17-18a

. . . and that Beloved, sitting on their shoulders (of the angels), will come forth and send his twelve disciples, and they will teach all nations and every tongue the resurrection of the Beloved. . . .[4]

These words seem to constitute a reminiscence of Mt. 28:19. They occur, in fact, in a context which summarizes the life and the activities of Christ, and undoubtedly refer to the mission of the apostles after the resurrection; only the first gospel reports this mission. Moreover, the Matthean text contains the principal elements of the passage from the *Ascension of Isaiah*; it is also to the apostles that Christ addresses himself;[5] Christ sends them (πορευθέντες) and orders them to teach all nations (μαθητεύσατε πάντα τὰ ἔθνη). It can, therefore, be assumed that the author is inspired by the Matthean text, noting, however, an addition which is absent from the text of the gospel, namely the expression "every tongue the resurrection of the Beloved."

The fragments preserved in the Greek text of the *Ascension of Isaiah* have this passage;[6] it reads: μαθητεύσουσιν πάντα τὰ ἔθνη, which corresponds very well to the Matthean parallel. This Greek text, which dates probably from the 5th or 6th century, somehow confirms my position, since the words of Matthew are there.

---

[2]Cf. B. P. Grenfell and A. S. Hunt, *The Amherst Papyri, Being an Account of the Greek Papyri*, vol. 1 (London, 1900) 1-22.

[3]Cardinal Mai, *Scriptorum veterum nova collatio*, vol. 3, pt. 2 (Rome, 1828) 238.

[4][Editor's note.] The English text of *The Ascension of Isaiah*, trans. M. A. Knib, is taken from *The Old Testament Pseudepigrapha*, vol.2, ed. James H. Charlesworth (Garden City NY: Doubleday and Company, 1985).

[5]Cf. Mt. 28:16.

[6]The fragments of the Greek text of the *Ascension of Isaiah* are found in Grenfell and Hunt, *The Amherst Papyri, Being an Account of the Greek Papyri*, 1:1-22; the text of Asc. Is. 3:17-18a is found on p. 11.

Indeed, the author of the Greek text either understood the text he wrote to depend on Mt. 28:19 or he found such a text and transmitted it as is.

2. Asc. Is. 11:2-4

[2] And I saw a woman of the family of David the prophet whose name (was) Mary, and she (was) a virgin and she was betrothed to a man whose name (was) Joseph, a carpenter, and he also (was) of the seed and family of the righteous David of Bethlehem in Judah. [3] And he came into his lot. And when she was betrothed, she was found to be pregnant, and Joseph the carpenter wished to divorce her. [4] But the angel of the Spirit appeared in this world, and after this Joseph did not divorce Mary, but did not reveal this matter to anyone.

Numerous details of Matthew's infancy narrative coincide with the whole of this passage; some, however, are found also in Lk., others are absent from the texts of the gospels.

While the *Protevangelium of James* and Ignatius of Antioch clearly testify that Mary was of the lineage of David,[7] the texts of the New Testament do not explicitly state this tradition, but they assume it.[8] Moreover, the virginity of Mary, her engagement to Joseph, the Davidic origin of the latter, and the name of the virgin are read in Mt. 1:16, 18, 20 and Lk. 1:27; 2:4. I agree with E. Tisserant that, according to this text, Mary and Joseph had their usual residence in Bethlehem.[9] Mt. 2:1 also allows this assumption; Lk. 1:26 thinks rather of Nazareth, considering Bethlehem (Lk. 2:4) only as the place to which Mary and Joseph had to go for the census, implying thereby that they did not ordinarily live there.

As for Joseph's intention to divorce Mary (v. 3), only Mt. 1:18-19 reports it: μνηστευθείσης τῆς μητρὸς αὐτοῦ Μαρίας τῷ Ἰωσήφ, πρὶν ἢ συνελθεῖν αὐτοὺς εὑρέθη ἐν γαστρὶ ἔχουσα ἐκ πνεύματος ἁγίου. Ἰωσὴφ δὲ ὁ ἀνὴρ αὐτῆς, δίκαιος ὢν καὶ μὴ θέλων αὐτὴν δειγματίσαι, ἐβουλήθη λάθρα ἀπολῦσαι αὐτήν.

A similar intention is read also in Prot. Jas. 14:1. An influence of the first gospel cannot be stated with absolute certainty, since birth narratives about Christ, embellished with wonderful details, one more than the other, may have circulated at that time. The numerous apocryphal gospels prove it. Yet, the striking parallel with Mt. leads to the assumption that there is here a reminiscence of the Matthean text. Indeed, the words "when Mary was betrothed" correspond to Mt.'s genitive absolute μνηστευθείσης τῆς μητρὸς αὐτοῦ Μαρίας; "she was found to be

---

[7]Cf. Prot. Jas. 10:1; Ign. Eph. 18:2.

[8]Cf. Lk. 1:32, 69; Acts 2:30; Rom. 1:3-4; 2 Tim. 2:8.

[9]Cf. Tisserant, *Ascension d'Isaïe*, 203.

pregnant'' corresponds to εὑρέθη ἐν γαστρὶ ἔχουσα; and ''Joseph the carpenter wished to divorce her'' is equivalent to ἐβουλήθη λάθρα ἀπολῦσαι αὐτὴν. For as much as can be judged through a translation, in both texts the construction of the sentence is quite similar and many words correspond to the point that a dependence can easily be believed.

All the details of verse 4 are not read in Mt., which, alone among the gospels, mentions at least two, and these can be completed with the help of the *Protevangelium of James,* which contains them all. First of all, the appearance of the angel of the Spirit corresponds to Mt. 1:20 and to Prot. Jas. 14:2; then Joseph decides not to send Mary away, but to keep her close to him: a similar trait is reported in Mt. 1:24 and in Prot. Jas. 14:2. Finally, Joseph's silence is mentioned only by Prot. Jas. 15:4.

Since verse 3 is almost certainly a reminiscence of Mt., it can be concluded that in this entire passage, the author has very probably narrated these events by drawing them from the Matthean narrative, but he amplified them according to the apocryphal infancy narratives or simply according to the embellishments of the oral tradition.

§2. The Other New Testament Writings

The *Ascension of Isaiah* shows no particular relationship either with the other synoptics, with the Acts of the Apostles, with the Johannine literature, or with the catholic epistles. It betrays, principally in the part considered as an apocalypse (3:13-4:18), the use of traditional themes and ideas; moreover, in comparison with the Pauline letters, certain texts deserve special consideration. This is why I consider first the other New Testament writings with the exception of the letters of Paul, which I shall treat separately. Finally, I shall pay particular attention to traditional ideas and themes.

A. The Other New Testament Writings
with the Exception of the Letters of Saint Paul

Regarding Asc. Is. 3:20, ''and there will be many signs and miracles in those days,'' it has been pointed out that only Mk. 16:17-18 mentions the miracles accomplished by the disciples of Christ; Mk. goes so far as to report them in detail. The author of the *Ascension of Isaiah* merely states the fact. But in so doing, he does not necessarily depend on the second gospel, for he may well have in mind the miracles and wonders which occurred in the early days of the Church, such as are told for example in different passages of the Acts of the Apostles.[10]

---

[10]Cf. Acts 8:7; 28:3-6, 8.

The sentence in Asc. Is. 9:14, "and they will lay their hands upon him and hang him upon a tree, not knowing who he is," recalls the saying of Christ in Lk. 23:34. However, a dependence on this passage seems excluded. The *Ascension of Isaiah* indeed, beyond the fact that it does not report a saying of Christ, draws attention to the very person of Christ (who he is); in Lk., the words of Christ have in mind the very action of the executioners (τί ποιοῦσιν).

Asc. Is. 7:37 contains the expression "One . . . unique,"* whereas ordinarily the formula is "the Beloved." That this is the language of Jn.[11] can simply be observed, but there is no clue in the immediate context to lead us towards a specific Johannine text.

In a context which relates the marvelous birth of Jesus, Asc. Is. 11:14b reads: "And they were all blinded concerning him (the child); they all knew about him, but they did not know from where he was." These last words have sometimes been linked with Jn. 7:27.[12] The parallel does not seem valid; in Jn., in fact, the words "they did not know from where he was" refer to a characteristic which, according to a Jewish concept, distinguished the Christ; this passage on the other hand, as the context suggests,[13] refers to the birth of Jesus which had occurred unknown to all.

In the vision of Isaiah related in Asc. Is. 6:1-11:40, the passage 7:21 recalls strangely two texts of Revelation which are also very similar: Rev. 19:10 and 22:8-9. The apocryphon says it thus: "And I fell on my face to worship him, and the angel who led me would not let me, but said to me, 'Worship neither throne, nor angel from the six heavens, from where I was sent to lead you, before I tell you in the seventh heaven.' " Both passages of Revelation describe a similar scene. First of all, the contexts are very similar; the subject matter throughout these texts is that of a vision: in the *Ascension of Isaiah,* an angel shows Isaiah the second heaven; in Rev. an angel shows Babylon (19:10) or Jerusalem (22:8-9) to the seer. Then the sentence "and I *fell* on my face to *worship* him" agrees with Rev. 19:10: "Then I *fell* down (ἔπεσα) at his feet to *worship* him (προσκυνῆσαι)," and Rev. 22:8: "And when I heard and saw them, I *fell* down (ἔπεσα) to *worship* (προσκυνῆσαι) at the feet of the angel who showed them to me." Furthermore, the angel's interdiction to adore him finds its equivalent in Rev. 19:10 and 22:8-9 in the formula pronounced by the angel: ὅρα μή. Finally, the order to adore only him who is in the seventh heaven, meaning God, as it appears in Asc. Is. 9, is identical to the order given by the angel in Rev. 19:10 and 22:8-9: τῷ θεῷ προσκύνησον. All these parallels lead to the belief that the author was inspired by one of these

---

*Massaux's text reads "Fils unique" (only Son). [Editor's note]

[11]Cf. Jn. 1:14, 18; 3:16, 18; 1 Jn. 4:9.

[12]Cf. Tisserant, *Ascension d'Isaïe,* 205.

[13]Cf. Asc. Is. 11:12-14a, notably v. 14a: "But many said, 'She did not give birth; the midwife did not go up (to her), and we did not hear (any) cries of pain.' "

scenes from the Book of Revelation.[14]

B. The Letters of Saint Paul

Several texts, not many, may be compared with some passages in the Pauline letters.

Asc. Is. 10:6 reads: "And I heard the angel who led me, and he said to me, 'This is the Most High of high ones, who dwells in the holy world, who rests among the holy ones, who will be called by the Holy Spirit in the mouth of the righteous the Father of the LORD.' " The last words find a remarkable parallel in Gal. 4:6; indeed, the idea is absolutely identical: it is through the Holy Spirit that the righteous can name the Father. A dependence is possible because throughout, the subject matter is the Holy Spirit who dwells in the righteous, the Holy Spirit who, through the righteous, calls God the Father.

Three passages in Asc. Is., 9:15; 10:11; 11:6, speak of the ignorance of angels with respect to the Incarnation. This statement, common up to Saint Augustine, may be based on 1 Cor. 2:7-8; Eph. 3:10.

When the author writes in Asc. Is. 10:15: " . . . and then the princes and the powers of that world will worship you," he expresses an idea similar to Phil. 2:10. Note that the Latin version printed in Venice in 1522 reads, regarding this passage: "Then the princes and the powers and all the angels and all the rulers of heaven and earth and hell will adore you"; and the Slavonic version, according to Bonwetsch's Latin translation, reads: "And then the princes and the powers and the angels and each of their rulers in heaven and on earth and in hell will adore you."[15] The additions of these versions to the Ethiopic version remind us all the more of Phil. 2:10.

According to Asc. Is. 4:2b, "Beliar will descend . . . in the form of a man, a king of iniquity. . . . " This man, Nero as they believed, represents the Antichrist. Paul in 2 Thess 2:3 uses the formula "man of lawlessness" to designate the Antichrist.

C. Traditional Themes

Many passages in the *Ascension of Isaiah* reveal a great fidelity to traditional themes whose traces are found in the texts of the New Testament.

Thus, a splendid apocalyptic tableau is set up in Asc. Is. 3:21-4:18. I must point out the presence of traditional themes of apocalyptic literature even though, as E. Tisserant remarked, the description of the troubles which afflicted the nascent Church can be found as well. "The subject matter deals simultaneously with

---

[14]Cf. E. B. Allo, *Saint Jean, L'Apocalypse*, EBib (Paris, 1921) 277.

[15]Cf. Tisserant, *Ascension d'Isaïe*, 197.

what took place at the end of the first century and the ills which were expected at the end of the world; both tableaus are blended into one."[16] This is why the apocalyptic themes are mixed with the depiction of the ills of the primitive church already mentioned in the New Testament.

This tableau is divided into three distinct parts as is usual to the apocalyptic genre: first, the disturbances which precede the coming of Christ (Asc. Is. 3:21-31), then the appearance of the Antichrist (Asc. Is. 4:1-13), finally the coming of the Lord (Asc. Is. 4:14-18). Each of these parts contains traditional traits. In the first, the disturbances preceding the coming of Christ include the renunciation of the teaching of the apostles,[17] of the faith,[18] of love[19] and of purity,[20] the struggle in the last days,[21] the shepherds as oppressors of their flock,[22] respect for people,[23] the absence of true prophets which assumes the presence of false prophets,[24] the presence of the spirit of error and of fornication and the love of gold among the servants of Christ,[25] mutual hatred,[26] the search for what pleases one's self and his own desires coupled with the forgetting of prophecies.[27] The second part describes the coming of the Antichrist with characteristics which are just as traditional: he is the king of iniquity[28] who tries to pass himself off as Christ[29] and to seduce.[30] The third part presents, still with very traditional colors, the coming of the Lord: awaited by all,[31] the Lord will appear with the angels,[32] with the saints,[33]

---

[16]Cf. Tisserant, *Ascension d'Isaïe*, 112.

[17]Cf. Asc. Is. 3:21 and 1 Tim. 1:3-4; 4:1; 2 Tim. 4:3-4.

[18]Cf. Asc. Is. 3:21 and 1 Tim. 4:1.

[19]Cf. Asc. Is. 3:21 and Mt. 24:12.

[20]Cf. Asc. Is. 3:21 and Jude 4.

[21]Cf. Asc. Is. 3:22 and Mt. 24:6; Mk. 13:7; Lk. 21:9.

[22]Cf. Asc. Is. 3:24 and Acts 20:29-30.

[23]Cf. Asc. Is. 3:25 and Jas. 2:1-13.

[24]Cf. Asc. Is. 3:27 and Mt. 24:6, 11, 24; Mk. 13:22a.

[25]Cf. Asc. Is. 3:28 and 2 Tim. 3:2-4; 2 Pet. 2:2-3; 1 Jn. 4:6; Jude 4.

[26]Cf. Asc. Is. 3:29 and Mt. 10:21; 24:10; Mk. 13:12a; Lk. 21:16a.

[27]Cf. Asc. Is. 3:30-31 and 2 Tim. 4:3; 2 Pet. 3:3.

[28]Cf. Asc. Is. 4:2b and 2 Thess. 2:3.

[29]Cf. Asc. Is. 4:6 and Mt. 24:5, 23-24; Mk. 13:6, 21-22; Lk. 21:8; 2 Thess. 2:4.

[30]Cf. Asc. Is. 4:9 and Mt. 24:5, 24; Mk. 13:6, 22; Lk. 21:8; 2 Thess. 2:8-10; 2 Jn. 7.

[31]Cf. Asc. Is. 4:13 and 1 Cor. 1:7; 1 Thess. 1:10; Heb. 9:28.

[32]Cf. Asc. Is. 4:14 and Mt. 16:27; 24:31; 25:31; Mk. 8:38; 13:27; Lk. 9:26; 2 Thess. 1:7.

[33]Cf. Asc. Is. 4:14 and Mt. 24:31; 25:31; Mk. 13:27; 1 Thess. 3:13; Jude 14.

with splendor.[34] Beliar, meaning Satan, and his followers will go to eternal fire;[35] a special lot will be reserved for those who will be still living at the Parousia,[36] the saints will be clothed in a robe,[37] and fire will consume the impious.[38]

Besides this vast apocalyptic picture with traditional tints, many other texts express ideas which are common to New Testament literature. So it is that many facts in the life of Christ are highlighted which are the common weal of the tradition, such as the Incarnation,[39] the persecution which Christ must suffer and the torments which the children of Israel must inflict upon him,[40] the coming of the twelve apostles to Jesus and the teaching they have received from him,[41] the crucifixion before the Sabbath[42] with criminals,[43] the burial in a sepulchre,[44] the scandal of the apostles before the events of the Passion,[45] the guard at the tomb,[46] its opening by two angels.[47] There can also be added the mission of the Judge attributed to the Son,[48] the seating of Christ at the right hand of the Father.[49]

Among other traditional ideas or themes which are still present in the *Ascension of Isaiah,* I would like to add the preaching of the resurrection of the Savior,[50] the charisma of the word to the faithful,[51] the crowns given to the righteous as a

---

[34]Cf. Asc. Is. 4:14 and Mt. 24:30; 25:31; Mk. 13:27; 1 Thess. 4:16.

[35]Cf. Asc. Is. 4:14 and Mt. 25:41; Rev. 19:20; 20:10.

[36]Cf. Asc. Is. 4:15 and 1 Thess. 4:17; 2 Thess. 1:7.

[37]Cf. Asc. Is. 4:16 and 2 Cor. 5:4; Rev. 3:4, 5, 8; 4:4; 6:11; 7:9, 13, 14.

[38]Cf. Asc. Is. 4:18 and Mt. 3:12; 13:41, 50; 25:41; Lk. 3:17; 2 Thess. 1:8.

[39]Cf. Asc. Is. 3:13.

[40]Cf. Asc. Is. 3:13.

[41]Cf. Asc. Is. 3:13.

[42]Cf. Asc. Is. 3:13 and Mk. 15:42; Jn. 19:31.

[43]Cf. Asc. Is. 3:13 and Mt. 27:38; Mk. 15:27; Lk. 23:33; Jn. 19:18.

[44]Cf. Asc. Is. 3:13 and Mt. 27:60; Mk. 15:46b; Lk. 23:53b; Jn. 19:41.

[45]Cf. Asc. Is. 3:14 and Mt. 26:31; Mk. 14:27.

[46]Cf. Asc. Is. 3:14 and Mt. 27:65-66; 28:11.

[47]Cf. Asc. Is. 3:16 and Mt. 28:2; Lk. 24:4; Jn. 20:12; Gospel of Peter 36-37.

[48]Cf. Asc. Is. 10:12 and Mt. 24 and 25; Mk. 13; Lk. 21:27.

[49]Cf. Asc. Is. 11:32 and Mt. 22:44; 26:64; Mk. 14:62; Lk. 22:69; Acts 7:55; Rom. 8:34; Eph. 1:20; Col. 3:1; Heb. 1:3; 8:1; 10:12; 12:2; 1 Pet. 3:22; Ps. 110(109):1.

[50]Cf. Asc. Is. 3:18 and Acts 3:15; 4:10; 5:30; 10:40; 13:30, 37; Rom. 4:24; 6:4, 9; 8:11, 34; 10:9; 1 Cor. 6:14; 15:4, 12, 17, 20; 2 Cor. 4:14; Gal. 1:1; Eph. 1:20; Col. 2:12; 1 Thess. 1:10; 2 Tim. 2:8.

[51]Cf. Asc. Is. 3:19; 6:10 and 1 Cor. 12:3.

reward,[52] the idea of the Church in the heavens, the assembly of the elect.[53]

Among similar expressions, I note the formula "some of the twelve" designating an apostle,[54] the expression "they were like angels" to describe the state of the righteous in heaven,[55] the name "his Chosen One" definitely used to indicate the chosen of God,[56] the expression "in the last days" to mark the Messianic times,[57] and the expression "doers of righteousness."[58]

By way of conclusion, it is important to note the very great fidelity in the Christian parts of the *Ascension of Isaiah* to ideas and themes already present in the New Testament writings. I focused on two passages which show a very probable dependence on texts of the first gospel. Yet, the absence of the original text does not allow us to affirm a definite literary dependence. The absence of any reference to the other gospels places Mt. in a privileged position.

I would like to repeat that the description of the "Vision of Isaiah" is probably inspired by one of two scenes in Rev. 19:10 or 22:8-9. Finally, a few texts of Paul, but with a very slight degree of probability, are likely to bear a definite relationship to passages in the *Ascension of Isaiah*.

Section 2
THE ODES OF SOLOMON

Only a Syriac version of this work, based on the Greek original, is available.[59] It is generally considered Christian[60] since the theory of Harnack[61] and Spitta[62] has been almost unanimously abandoned: they assumed that a primitive draft of the *Odes* was written by a Jewish author, and that it was subsequently interpolated by a Christian author.

---

[52]Cf. Asc. Is. 8:26 and 1 Cor. 9:25; 1 Thess. 2:19; 2 Tim. 4:8; Jas. 1:12; 1 Pet. 5:4; Rev. 2:10; 3:11; 4:4, 10.

[53]Cf. Asc. Is. 3:15 and Gal. 4:26; Heb. 12:22; Rev. 3:12; 21:2; Enoch 38.

[54]Cf. Asc. Is. 4:3 and Mt. 26:14; Mk. 14:10, 20; Lk. 22:3, 47; Jn. 6:71; 20:24; in the N.T., except in Jn. 20:24, this formula "one of the Twelve" designates Judas; here, in Asc. Is., it designates Peter. [Massaux's text reads "un des Douze," or "one of the Twelve." Editor's note.]

[55]Cf. Asc. Is. 9:9 and Mt. 22:30; Mk. 12:25; Lk. 20:36.

[56]Cf. Asc. Is. 8:7; this name is given by Isaiah to the servant of Yahweh (Is. 42:1), to the Messiah by Lk. 23:35; Enoch 40:5 has "the Elect One" without any complement; again Enoch 49:2, 4; 51:3; 52:6; in Enoch 39:6, it is "the Elect One of righteousness and of faith."

[57]Cf. Asc. Is. 9:13 and Is. 2:2; Dan. 2:28; 10:14; Acts 2:17; Hermas, Sim. 9.12.3.

[58]Cf. Asc. Is. 6:17 and Ecclus. 20:30; Ezek. 18:19; Acts 10:35.

[59]The text of the Syriac version was published for the first time in 1909 by R. Harris, *The Odes and Psalms of Solomon, now first published from the Syriac version* (Cambridge,

Still driven by the same focus of interest, I examine in the first paragraph the possible literary relationships with the Gospel of Mt.; the second paragraph considers the other New Testament writings.

§1. Saint Matthew

The absence of the original Greek text of the *Odes of Solomon* renders our task difficult in the search for the literary influence which the first gospel may have had on this writing. I am, therefore, restricted to point out certain passages in which relationships are more or less close to the Matthean texts. Yet, these relationships can be such as to lead to the belief in a dependence on the first gospel. As a whole, passages admitting of being linked to texts of Mt. are rare.

1. Ode 14:5

Let me be pleasing before you, because of your glory,
and because of your name let me be saved from the Evil One.[63]

The last words recall the end of the Lord's Prayer of Mt. 6:13: καὶ μὴ εἰσενέγκῃς ἡμᾶς εἰς πειρασμόν, ἀλλὰ ῥῦσαι ἡμᾶς ἀπὸ τοῦ πονηροῦ.

1909); a new edition appeared in 1916, by R. Harris and A. Mingana, *The Odes and the Psalms of Solomon, Re-edited for the Governors of the John Rylands Library*, 2 vols. (Manchester, London, New York, Bombay, Calcutta, Madras, 1916); I follow this 2nd ed. [The English text of *The Odes of Solomon*, trans. J. H. Charlesworth, is taken from *The Old Testament Pseudepigrapha*, vol. 2, ed. James H. Charlesworth (Garden City NY: Doubleday and Company, 1985). Editor's note.]

[60]Cf. on this subject Labourt and Batiffol, *Les Odes de Salomon*, 45-52, where the critics' opinions are set forth. Those who believe that it is a Christian work are: Labourt and Batiffol, *Les Odes de Salomon*, 116; M.-J. Lagrange, in a review of A. Harnack's book, in RB 19 (1910): 593-99; P. Lejay, in reviewing the same work of Harnack, in *Bulletin d'ancienne littérature et d'archéologie chrétiennes* (1911): 57; A. Loisy, reviewing the same work of Harnack, in *Revue critique* (Feb. 1911): 101-105; A. Headlam, "The Odes of Solomon," *Church Quarterly Review* (1911): 277-87; Th. Zahn, "Die Oden Salomos," NKZ 21 (1910): 760.

[61]Cf. A. Harnack, *Ein jüdisch-christliches Psalmbuch aus dem ersten Jahrhundert* (Leipzig, 1910) 74-77; 104-106; 110-12.

[62]Cf. F. Spitta, "Zum Verständnis der Oden Salomos," ZNW 11 (1910): 193-203; 250-90.

[63]H. Gressmann's translation, *Die Oden Salomos*, 450, respects the parallelism less than the translation given; Gressmann in effect reads, "Lass mich dir wohlgefallen um deiner Ehre und deines Namens willen! Lass mich erlöst werden von dem Bösen!" The Syriac text contains this parallel (cf. Harris and Mingana, *The Odes and Psalms of Solomon*, vol. 1, ad loc.).

Odes Sol. 14 consists of a prayer of the Son to his Father.[64] Now in Mt. the Lord's Prayer begins precisely with the words: Πάτερ ἡμῶν. Moreover, only the Matthean text has this request, which is absent in Lk. An influence from the first gospel seems possible.

Yet, it would be difficult to speak in terms of a literary contact, since the Greek text of the *Odes of Solomon* is lacking. Moreover, R. Harris's remark cannot be ignored when he states that, in all the Syriac versions of Mt., the phrase "Deliver us from evil" is rendered by the verb ـܦܨ, while in this ode it is expressed with the verb ܢܙܒ. This difference in phraseology is remarkable.[65]

2. Ode 22:12

And the foundation of everything is your rock.
And upon it you have built your kingdom,
and it became the dwelling place of the holy ones.[66]

Several scholars see a parallel with Mt. 16:18-19a: "And I tell you, you are Peter, and on this rock I will build my church, and the powers of death shall not prevail against it. I will give you the keys of the kingdom of heaven. . . . "[67]

R. Harris even suggests that it is coincident with the Matthean text: the words expressing build,[68] kingdom,[69] and rock[70] in the Peshitta are found in this ode.[71] The texts which served as a basis for the Peshitta and for the Syriac version of the ode had, therefore, the same Greek terms, unless the author of the Syriac version of the *Odes* was here inspired by the Peshitta. Hence, a literary influence of the Matthean text on the Greek text of the passage of this ode is very probable, all the more since Mt. has no parallel in the other gospels. Yet, in the *Pistis Sophia* (ch. 72) where this ode is read, I would like to point out that, instead of the word "rock,"

---

[64]Cf. Gressmann, *Die Oden Salomos*, 450; cf. also v. 1 of the Ode: "As the eyes of a son upon his father, / so are my eyes, O Lord, at all times toward you."

[65]Cf. Harris and Mingana, *The Odes and Psalms of Solomon*, 2:123.

[66]P. Batiffol in Labourt and Batiffol, *Les Odes de Solomon*, 81, translates, "Que ton rocher devienne le fondement de tout." There follows also this translation by Gressmann, *Die Oden Salomos*, 457: "Auf dass dein Fels das Fundament des Alls werde"; and Harris and Mingana, *The Odes and Psalms of Solomon*, 2:326: "And that the foundation for everything might be thy rock."

[67]Cf. Harris and Mingana, *The Odes and Psalms of Solomon*, 2:121; Gressmann, *Die Oden Salomos*, 547.

[68] ܒܢܐ.

[69] ܡܠܟܘܬܐ.

[70] ܐܒܐ.

[71]Cf. Harris and Mingana, *The Odes and Psalms of Solomon*, 2:121.

the Coptic has the word "light."[72]

In the texts which follow, a relationship with Mt. is less clear.

Ode 8:18c-19a

And upon my right hand I have set my elect ones.
And my righteousness goes before them.

In the second part of the ode from which these words are taken, the Lord himself speaks through the mouth of Solomon. In the entire New Testament, only Mt. 25:34 offers a practically similar expression: "Then the King will say to those at his right hand: 'Come, O Blessed of my Father.' . . . "

Ode 23:17

The letter was one of command,
and hence all regions were gathered together.[73]

This ode 23 is a sort of apocalypse. The letter in question seems indeed to be Christ, the thought of God sent like an arrow. Men ran after this letter to "know where it would land" (v. 10). Now, the text says that the letter expressed an order prescribing the gathering of all the regions on earth. Does it not echo the saying of Christ in Mt. 28:19: "Go therefore and make disciples of all nations. . . . "?[74]

Ode 42:6

Then I arose and am with them,
and will speak by their mouths (of those who believe in me).

This sentence recalls the last words of Christ to his apostles after his resurrection in Mt. 28:19-20: "Go therefore and make disciples of all nations, baptizing them in the name of the Father and of the Son and of the Holy Spirit, teaching them to observe all that I have commanded you; and lo, I am with you always, to the close of the age."

Is it possible to see here a reference to the text of the first gospel? But it may also be the simple application of a traditional theme in the description of martyr-

---

[72]Cf. Labourt and Batiffol, *Les Odes de Salomon*, 24.

[73]I stray slightly from J. Labourt's translation, in Labourt and Batiffol, *Les Odes de Salomon*, 25, which reads, "La lettre était une lettre de commandement, aussi furent réunies en un seul endroit. . . . " This translation does not preserve the intentional value of ܪ ܐܬܠܡ.

[74]Cf. Labourt and Batiffol, *Les Odes de Salomon*, 82-83.

dom, Christ speaking through the mouth of those who are persecuted; the following verse of this ode speaks indeed of persecution.[75]

Ode 42:7b-8

> and I threw over them the yoke of my love.
> Like the arm of the bridegroom over the bride,
> so is my yoke over those who know me.

The term ''yoke'' suggests a reminiscence of Mt. 11:29-30. ''Take my yoke upon you, and learn from me; for I am gentle and lowly in heart, and you will find rest for your souls. For my yoke is easy, and my burden is light.'' But no clue in the context allows us to determine with certainty that the author of the ode had the Matthean text in mind.

§2. The Other New Testament Writings

In different passages, the *Odes of Solomon* can be compared with Johannine and Pauline texts. Otherwise, they do not seem to show a special relationship with the rest of the other New Testament writings.

A. The Johannine Writings

It is rarely possible to demonstrate that texts of the *Odes* depend on the Johannine literature. I pause a bit to examine passages which seem to show a special relationship with Jn. As to the others, I simply mention the ideas which seem to echo those of Jn.

Odes Sol. 10:4-5a reads, ''I took courage and became strong and captured the world, / and it became mine for the glory of the Most High, and of God my Father. / And the gentiles who had been scattered were gathered together. . . . '' This ode certainly stresses the conversion of the Gentiles, who have been saved by entering the Church. In the first three verses, the author introduced himself as the evangelist of the new faith;[76] he then begins to speak in the name of Christ. When Christ states that he made the world captive, it recalls ''I have overcome the world'' of Jn. 16:33 and ''I will draw all men to myself'' of Jn. 12:32. But the sentence ''the gentiles who had been scattered were gathered together'' recalls the thought of the evangelist in Jn. 11:51-52, which relates the prophecy of Caiaphas. ''He (Caiaphas) did not say this of his own accord, but being high priest that year he prophesied that Jesus should die for the nation, and not for the nation only, but to gather into one the children of God who are scattered abroad.'' In this prophecy which

---

[75]Cf. Odes Sol. 42:7: ''For they have rejected those who persecute them; . . . ''

[76]Cf. Harris and Mingana, *The Odes and Psalms of Solomon*, 2:264-65.

has the Gentiles in mind, the text addresses the dispersion and return to unity[77] as does the ode: the parallel is remarkable.

In Odes Sol. 17:10, Christ says, "And I shattered the bars of iron, / for my own iron(s) had grown hot and melted before me." The agreement with Jn. 10:7 and 9 is quite striking.

Odes Sol. 18:6: "Let not light be conquered by darkness, / nor let truth flee from falsehood." The contrast between light and darkness has a Johannine flavor (Jn 1:5). Yet, whereas Jn. speaks of the "comprehension" of the light by darkness, the ode wishes for the victory of light over darkness.

Odes Sol. 30:1, 2, 5: "[1] Fill for yourselves the water from the living spring of the Lord. . . . [2] And come all you thirsty and take a drink, / and rest beside the spring of the Lord. . . . [5] because it flowed from the lips of the Lord, / and it named from the heart of the Lord." The image of the water which gushes from the living spring of the Lord recalls Jn. 4:10, 14; 7:37-38; Rev. 22:17.

It would be difficult to deny a literary parallel between Ode 41:14: "And light dawned from the Word / that was before time in him" and Jn. 1:1: ἐν ἀρχῇ ἦν ὁ λόγος, καὶ ὁ λόγος ἦν πρὸς τὸν θεόν. The parallel is all the more significant because in Jn. 1:5, the Word is called τὸ φῶς.

Finally, Odes Sol. 3:3 reads "For I should not have known how to love the Lord, / if he had not continuously loved me." As. R. Harris and A. Mingana rightfully remark, this ode seems to be a hymn written on the theme: "We love, because he first loved us" of 1 Jn. 4:10 and 19.[78] The similarity of thought between the two texts is undeniable: the love of God for mankind calls for the love of mankind for God. To this must be added—for as much as a translation can reveal it—the nearly perfect identity of the sentences and formulas of the ode and of 1 Jn.

In addition to the passages mentioned up to now, fairly numerous texts seem to echo Johannine ideas.

Odes Sol. 6:8, 10-12: "[8] For there went forth a stream. . . . [10] For it spread over the face of all the earth, / . . . [11] Then all the thirsty upon the earth drank, / and thirst was relieved and quenched; [12] For from the Most High the drink was given." This Odes Sol. 6 deals with the knowledge of God, and it recalls the symbolism of the Johannine images of Jn. 4:13-14; 7:37-38 and Rev. 22:17.[79] Water in the fourth gospel (Jn. 7:37) is a symbol of the Spirit; with this author, it is a symbol of knowledge, and it echoes a frequent theme which compares the blessings of life, either present or future, with living water. This is how wisdom, the

---

[77]Cf. Jn. 10:16 which expresses a similar idea.

[78]Cf. Harris and Mingana, *The Odes and Psalms of Solomon*, 2:218.

[79]Cf. Labourt and Batiffol, *Les Odes de Salomon*, 62.

word of God, and salvation are symbolized by water in the Old Testament.[80]

In verse 18 of this same ode, the expression "living water of eternity" sounds like Jn. 4:10-11, 14; 7:37 and Rev. 22:17.[81]

In the passage of Odes Sol. 7:3b-6, which speaks of the Incarnation, verse 4 reads "He became like me, that I might put him on." Two ideas are linked here: one is Johannine, the incarnation and the welcome of the Word (Jn. 1:12); the other is Pauline, putting on Christ (Rom. 13:14; Gal. 3:27).

When we find in Odes Sol. 7:16a, "And because of his salvation he will possess everything," it recalls Mt. 11:27a; Lk. 10:22a; Jn. 3:35 and 17:2. Jn. 17:2 is particularly significant: the Father has given the Son power (ἐξουσία) over all flesh.[82]

In verse 12 of the same ode, "He has allowed them to appear to them that are his own; / in order that they may recognize him that made them, / and not think that they came of themselves," the words "to appear to them who are his own" recall Jn. 1:11.

An idea similar to that of Jn. 3:16 is in Odes Sol. 9:7: "And also that those who have known him (the purpose of the Most High) may not perish, / and so that those who receive (him) may not be ashamed." In the ode, the fact of receiving the purpose of the Most High, meaning the truth,[83] is enough to be saved; for Jn., faith saves from perdition and gives eternal life.[84]

In Odes Sol. 12:7, the Word is called "light and dawning of thought." Jn. 1:9 comes immediately to mind, but, according to general opinion, this entire ode deals with the word of God just as the Book of Wisdom (9:1) and Ecclesiasticus (42:15; 43:26) speak of it.[85] In verse 12, "For the dwelling place of the Word is man," the sentence is indeed very close to Jn. 1:14 and 18 ("And the Word became flesh and dwelt among us . . . "), but the entire ode does not go beyond the concept of the word in the wisdom literature (cf. 12:1).

Odes Sol. 16:18 reads, "And there is nothing outside the Lord, / because he was before anything came to be." Two texts express a similar idea: Jn. 1:3 and

---

[80]Cf. Ecclus. 15:3; Is. 8:6; 12:3; 55:1.

[81]Cf. Labourt and Batiffol, *Les Odes de Salomon*, 62-63.

[82]The Syriac verb (cf. Harris and Mingana, *The Odes and Psalms of Solomon*, vol. 1, Odes Sol. 7:16a) ܐܚܘܕ corresponds normally to the Greek κρατεῖν (cf. ܐܚܘܕ ܠܐ : παντοκράτωρ); it also means at times ἐξουσία; anyway, there is not much difference between ἐξουσία and κρατεῖν.

[83]Cf. Labourt and Batiffol, *Les Odes de Salomon*, 102.

[84]Is. 28:16 has a more or less similar idea.

[85]Cf. Labourt and Batiffol, *Les Odes de Salomon*, 108-109; Harris and Mingana, *The Odes and Psalms of Solomon*, 2:275. On the concept of the Word in the wisdom literature, cf. W. Bousset, *Die Religion des Judentums* (Berlin, 1903) 341; J. Lebreton, *Les origines du dogme de la Trinité*, vol. 1 (Paris, 1910) 119-20.

Col. 1:17; the latter, which insists more explicitly than Jn. 1:3 on the preexistence of the Lord before all things, is even closer to this ode than is Jn.[86]

Christ says in Odes Sol. 28:18-19, "And they sought my death but were unsuccessful, / because I was older than their memory; / and in vain did they cast lots against me. / And those who were after me / sought in vain to destroy the memorial of him / who was before them." The sentence "I was older than their memory" recalls the saying of Christ in Jn. 8:58. The words "of him who was before them" may suggest the testimony of John the Baptist in Jn. 1:15, 27, 30.

Odes Sol. 31:4 reads: "Then he raised his voice towards the Most High, / and offered to him those that had become sons through him." Critics take pleasure in sighting verses 3-6 of this ode as understood to come from Christ.[87] Verse 4 seems to echo Jn. 17:9 in the priestly prayer of Christ.

Addressing the saints, the author of Odes Sol. 9 writes in verse 11, "Put on the crown in the true covenant of the Lord, / and all those who have conquered will be inscribed in his book." A parallel idea is found in Rev. 3:5, where there is mention of a book of life in which those who are victorious are inscribed.[88]

When the author says in Odes Sol. 20:7, "But put on the grace of the Lord generously, / and come into his Paradise, / and make for yourself a crown from his tree," he alludes to the tree of paradise in Genesis which Rev. 2:7 also has in mind. But this allusion may very well depend on an idea according to which the righteous receive a share in the eschatological blessings, which is developed with the theme that invites mankind to return to the sources.[89]

Odes Sol. 22:5 reads: "He (Christ) who overthrew by my hands the dragon with seven heads, / and placed me at his roots that I might destroy his seed." The Book of Revelation also speaks of the dragon.[90]

Odes Sol. 23:8b-9a speaks of a letter, which represents the thought of God, or maybe Christ,[91] and which is sealed. Many enemy hands rushed to catch it, but "they were afraid of it and of the seal which was upon it. / Because they were not allowed to loosen its seal." It may be noted that in Rev. 5:1-5, only the lion of Judah can open the book and the seven seals; but there is no positive clue to lead us towards this precise passage.

---

[86]Cf. Harris and Mingana, *The Odes and Psalms of Solomon*, 2:286, who also note this coincidence with Col. 1:17.

[87]Cf. Labourt and Batiffol, *Les Odes de Salomon*, 88-89.

[88]Cf. E. B. Allo, *Saint Jean, L'Apocalypse*, EB (Paris, 1921) 38 and 67-68; mention is also made of a book in Rev. 5:8, 9; 13:8.

[89]Cf. Rev. 22:1-2; Is. 41:4; 43:18 ff; Ezek. 34:25.

[90]Cf. Rev. 12:3, 4, 7, 9, 13, 16, 17; 13:2, 4, 11; 16:13; 20:2.

[91]Cf. Labourt and Batiffol, *Les Odes de Salomon*, 82.

Starting with verse 14 of Odes Sol. 42, the author describes the preaching of Christ to the righteous who are imprisoned in Sheol. Verse 20 reads, "And I placed my name upon their head, / because they are free and they are mine." In Rev. 7:3; 9:4; 14:1; and 20:4, the sign pertaining to Christ is also indicated with a seal placed on the forehead of the chosen, but the preaching of Christ in hell is not mentioned.

The name of "Life" for Christ (Odes Sol. 3:9) is Johannine (Jn. 1:4; 11:25; 14:6).[92]

In conclusion, it must be stated that, if Johannine expressions or ideas are found in the *Odes of Solomon,* it cannot be said that the author necessarily took them from the Johannine writings; the impression is rather that they originated in a similar atmosphere.

If the fourth gospel is not an influence per se, could this more or less profound similarity of feelings and thoughts with Jn. not be explained by a source upon which the *Odes of Solomon* depended? Such a source may have existed. According to R. Bultmann, one of the sources of the Gospel of Jn. was related to the *Odes of Solomon* and was made up, as he says himself, of *Offenbarungsreden.*[93] It is not my purpose to determine whether this source existed or not. Anyway, the elements I used in my study are insufficient to solve the point. Yet, the relationship between the *Odes of Solomon* and the Johannine literature can be satisfactorily understood through an environment of identical ideas, without having to resort to a source.

B. The Pauline Letters

In this segment, I deal first with passages which show a special relationship with texts of Paul; I then merely mention those which simply recall a Pauline idea.

In Odes Sol. 6, where the author states that the universe will come to the knowlege of the Lord and will be quenched with its living water,[94] verse 6 reads, "The Lord has multiplied his knowledge, / and he was zealous that those things should be known which through his grace have been given to us." This passage echoes 1 Cor. 2:12: "Now we have received not the spirit of the world, but the Spirit which is from God, that we might understand the gifts bestowed on us by God." A literary reminiscence of the text of Paul seems here to be almost certain: first of all, the last words of Paul coincide almost literally with the end of verse 6 of the ode; then, throughout the ode, a special act of the Lord makes known the gifts of God. Finally, I propose to add an important comment from R. Harris and

---

[92]Cf. also Rev. 1:17-18, where Christ is called "the living one."

[93]Cf. R. Bultmann, *Das Evangelium des Johannes,* Kritisch-exegetischer Kommentar über das Neue Testament (Göttingen, 1941) 4n.5. [ET: *The Gospel of John* (Philadelphia, Westminster Press, 1971) 17n.5. Editor's addition.]

[94]Cf. Labourt and Batiffol, *Les Odes de Salomon,* 63.

A. Mingana: according to them, this passage of the ode is closer to the Greek text of 1 Cor. than to the Peshitta.[95]

Odes Sol. 17:15-17: "Then they received my blessing and lived, / and they were gathered to me and were saved; / Because they became my members, and I was their head. / Glory to you, our Head, O Lord Messiah." The last words recall the Pauline image of the body of Christ such as it is found in Rom. 12:5; 1 Cor. 11:3; 12:27; Eph. 4:15-16; 5:23. The term "body" does not appear in the ode, but it is certainly subjacent and present in the mind of the author: the words "members" and "head" suggest it. In addition, the ideas are also quite Pauline: the unity of the faithful in Christ and the salvation of the members of the body of Christ. The author seems altogether under the influence of the ideas and the metaphor of Paul.

Since he feels justified, the author says in his own behalf in Odes Sol. 28:3, "I trusted, consequently I was at rest; / because trustful is he in whom I trusted." The ode's expression "I trusted, consequently I was at rest" coincides closely with Heb. 4:3: "For we who have believed enter that rest. . . "[96] 1 Cor. 1:9, sometimes mentioned as a parallel, expresses faithfulness to God.

In Odes Sol. 28:4-5, Solomon, who represents the justified soul, says, "He has greatly blessed me, / and my head is with him. / And the dagger shall not divide me from him, / nor the sword." This entire ode is Christological and, as R. Harris stated, it bears "the melody of the *Quis me separabit* of Saint Paul (Rom. 8:35-39)"; the righteous man believed and found rest; nothing can separate him from the Lord.[97]

Odes Sol. 33:13 says, "My elect ones have walked with me, / and my ways I shall make known to them who seek me; / and I shall promise them my name." In this section of the ode, these words are spoken by Wisdom which certainly represents Christ;[98] they are linked with Col. 2:6: "As therefore you received Christ Jesus the Lord, so live in him. . . . " For the words "walk with me" (Ode) and "live in him" (Col.), there is a perfectly tangible coincidence between the Odes Sol. and the Greek or Syriac version of Col.[99] A parallel can be drawn not only with the texts but with the contexts as well. In the ode, Christ brings a message,

---

[95]Cf. Harris and Mingana, *The Odes and Psalms of Solomon*, 2:123-24.

[96]Cf. Harris and Mingana, *The Odes and Psalms of Solomon*, 2:124-25.

[97]I would like to note, however, that this idea is expressed in Rom. 8:35 in different terms from those used in the ode; where the ode uses ܦܠܐ to express separation, the Syriac version of Rom. uses ܦܪܫ ; and when the ode designates the sword with the word ܣܝܦܐ , the Syriac of Rom. has ܚܪܒܐ .

[98]On Wisdom as a figure of Christ in this ode, cf. Harris and Mingana, *The Odes and Psalms of Solomon*, 2:124; Labourt and Batiffol, *Les Odes de Salomon*, 112.

[99]Cf. Harris and Mingana, *The Odes and Psalms of Solomon*, 2:124.

which is to be accepted on faith in order to be saved. The elect of Christ walk with him, he lets them know his ways.[100] In cautioning the Colossians against false teachers, Paul proclaims that their first duty is to be faithful to the teaching they received from Christ and to live in Christ, following his precepts.[101] Faithfulness to the teaching received from Christ and the accomplishment of his precepts (Col.) correspond rather well to "know the way of Christ" (Ode). All these remarks, both about the text and the context, point toward a literary dependence.

Odes Sol. 38:17-22 is very closely parallel to the idea of 1 Cor. 3:6 and 10. The author of the ode says: "For I was established and lived and was saved, / and my foundations were laid on account of the Lord's hand; / because he has planted me. / For he set the root, / and watered it and adapted it and blessed it, / and its fruits will be forever. / It penetrated deeply and sprang up and spread out, / and it was full (with sap) and was enlarged. / And the Lord alone was praised,/ in his planting, and in his cultivation; / In his care and in the blessing of his lips, / in the beautiful planting of his right hand; / And in the attainment of his planting, / and in the understanding of his mind." In the passages indicated above, Paul explains that even though he has planted and Apollos has watered, both are really only collaborators of the divine work, to such an extent that the planting is ultimately from God. As for the author of the ode, he attributes everything to the work of the Lord, the planting, the watering, and the tilling of the whole, as well as the growth of the field of the Lord. It is quite possible that the author has the Pauline texts in mind.[102]

Odes Sol. 41 is a hymn to the saints; the saints speak (vv. 1-8), then Christ appears and is a source of wonder to those who see him because he is of another race (vv. 8-11), and the song of the saints resumes (vv. 11-16).[103] In this last section, verses 11-13 read, "And his Word is with us in all our way, / the Savior who gives life and does not reject ourselves. / The Man who humbled himself, / but was raised because of his own righteousness. / The Son of the Most High appeared / in the perfection of his Father." The words "the Man who humbled himself, but was raised because of his own righteousness" recall Phil. 2:8-9, whose Syriac version uses the same words as the ode.[104]

---

[100]Cf. Labourt and Batiffol, *Les Odes de Salomon*, 112.

[101]Cf. J. Huby, *Saint Paul, Les Épîtres de la captivité*, VS 8 (Paris, 1935) 57.

[102]Cf. Harris and Mingana, *The Odes and Psalms of Solomon*, 2:124.

[103]Cf. Labourt and Batiffol, *Les Odes de Salomon*, 109-10.

[104]Cf. Harris and Mingana, *The Odes and Psalms of Solomon*, 2:122. In Phil., humiliation is designated by the verb ܡܟܟ and exaltation with ܪܡܪܡ (palpel of ܪܘܡ); the ode expresses humiliation with the same verb ܡܟܟ and exaltation with ܐܬܬܪܝܡ (aphel of ܪܘܡ). It can, therefore, be assumed that the Greek texts which were the basis of both translations had identical verbs; this would demonstrate a dependence on the Pauline text.

The presence in the *Odes of Solomon* of ideas similar to those of Paul and expressions of Pauline vocabulary must also be mentioned.

Odes Sol. 3:6: "And I shall be no foreigner, / because there is no jealousy with the Lord Most High and Merciful." Cf. Eph. 2:19: "So then you are no longer strangers and sojourners, but you are fellow citizens with the saints and members of the household of God."

3:7b: "because I love him that is the Son, I shall become a son" recalls Gal. 4:4-5.

3:8: "Indeed he who is joined to him who is immortal, / truly will be immortal" expresses an idea similar to 1 Cor. 6:17: "But he who is united to the Lord becomes one spirit with him."[105]

3:10a: "This is the Spirit of the Lord, which is not false" corresponds to "it is impossible that God should prove false" in Heb. 6:18.

4:11: "For there is no regret with you; that you should regret anything which you have promised" echoes Rom. 11:29: "The gifts and the call of God are irrevocable." It could also remind us of Num. 23:19 and Ps. 110 (109):4.

5:13-15: "Even if everything should be shaken, / I shall stand firm. / And though all things visible should perish, / I shall not die; / Because the Lord is with me, / and I with him." It instinctively recalls the statement of Rom. 8:38-39 which proclaims that nothing "will be able to separate us from the love of God in Christ Jesus our Lord" (cf. Odes Sol. 28:4).

6:3: "For he destroys whatever is foreign, / and everything is of the Lord." This entertains a new situation where all that is foreign will be subdued or annihilated by God, where nothing will be an obstacle to God. Eph. 2:19 celebrates also the new state of converted pagans: " . . . you are fellow citizens with the saints and members of the household of God. . . . "

7:24: the choir of saints marching is heard: "And let there not be any person / that is without knowledge or voice." These words perhaps recall 1 Cor. 14:10: " . . . none is without meaning. . . . "

8:1: "Open, open your hearts to the exultation of the Lord, / and let your love abound from the heart to the lips." This sounds like numerous calls to joy by the apostle in Phil. 2:18; 3:1; 4:4; and 1 Thess. 5:16.

8:10b: the counsel "keep my faith, you who are kept by it" recalls the words of Paul: "Fidem servavi" of 2 Tim. 4:7.

8:11a: if H. Gressmann's translation is to be considered: "Erkennt meine Erkenntnis, die ihr wahrhaft von mir erkannt seid,"[106] it could lead to a reminiscence of 1 Cor. 13:12; but this translation does not respect the text which was transmitted, and which is translated as: "And understand my knowledge, you who

---

[105]Cf. Harris and Mingana, *The Odes and Psalms of Solomon*, 2:218.

[106]Cf. Gressmann, *Die Oden Salomos*, 444.

know me in truth." Such a translation no longer leads to a comparison with the Pauline text.[107]

Just as in Eph. 2:8,[108] in Odes Sol. 9:5 salvation is the work of "grace."

If Heb. 4:12 has sometimes been linked with Odes Sol. 12:5 ("For the subtlety of the Word is inexpressible, / and like his expression so also is his swiftness and his acuteness, / for limitless is his path"), the best parallel is still Wis. 7:24, all the more so since, according to critics, the writer seems to use in this ode many wisdom terms which are found in chapter 7 of Wisdom.[109]

Odes Sol. 14:10 says of God, "For you are sufficient for all our needs." This is like an echo of Phil. 4:19: "God will supply every need of yours."[110]

15:8-9: "I have put on incorruption through his name, / and stripped off corruption by his grace. / Death has been destroyed before my face, / and Sheol has been vanquished by my words." This passage implies the Pauline opposition of 1 Cor. 15:53-55 between corruptibility and incorruptibility, between mortality and immortality.

Just as Heb. does in 4:4, it is to Gen. 2:2 that Odes Sol. 16:12 refers: "And he set the creation and aroused it, / then he rested from his works."

31:4: "Then he raised his voice towards the Most High, / and offered to him those that had become sons through him" may recall Heb. 2:13 which, for its part, refers to Is. 8:17-18.

32:1: "To the blessed one the joy is from their heart, / and light from him who dwells in them"; Eph. 3:14-19 states a parallel idea concerning the dwelling of God; the Apostle formulates the wish that Christ dwells in the hearts of the Ephesians as a source of light to understand the vastness of the divine gift of the love of Christ.[111]

33:12: "And they who have put me on will not be rejected, / but they will possess incorruption in the new world"[112] recalls Eph. 4:24.

41:15a: "The Messiah in truth is one" may recall 1 Cor. 8:6, which states that Jesus Christ is unique.

---

[107]Cf. J. Dupont, *Gnosis. La connaissance religieuse dans les Épîtres de saint Paul* (Louvain, Paris, 1949) 64. The Syriac text is found in Harris and Mingana, *The Odes and Psalms of Solomon*, vol. 1, Odes Sol. 8.

[108]Cf. Huby, *Saint Paul, Les Épîtres de la captivité*, 186-87.

[109]Cf. Harris and Mingana, *The Odes and Psalms of Solomon*, 2:274.

[110]Cf. ibid., 124 and 280.

[111]Cf. Huby, *Saint Paul, Les Épîtres de la captivité*, 186-87.

[112]H. Gressmann, *Die Oden Salomos*, 466, translates as does J. Labourt: "sondern die neue, unvergängliche Welt gewinnen"; Harris and Mingana, *The Odes and Psalms of Solomon*, 2:375, translate: "but they shall possess incorruption in the new world."

As for Odes Sol. 23:10-14, P. Batiffol's hypothesis must be considered.[113] The text of the Ode reads, "But those who saw the letter ran after it; / that they might know where it would land, / and who should read it, / and who should hear it. / But a wheel received it, / and it (the letter) came over it. / And with it was a sign, / of the Kingdom and of providence. / And everything which was disturbing to the wheel, / it mowed it and cut it down. / And it restrained a multitude of adversaries; / and bridged rivers." P. Batiffol notes that the letter certainly represents a living person, in this context it is Christ. The word τρόχος may also mean a torture rack, and as such, it could then mean the cross. The letter has been attached to the cross: Saint Paul wrote that the decree of our condemnation has been nailed to the cross by Jesus Christ (Col. 2:14). There might, therefore, be a reminiscence of Col. 2:14.

In the translations of the *Odes of Solomon*, especially in H. Gressmann's, numerous references to Pauline texts are found. In most cases, a simple similarity of terms led to the comparison, and the main examples are: the way of Faith,[114] drunkenness,[115] the cloud overhead,[116] to strip and to put on,[117] pleroma,[118] for the glory of the Most High and of God, his Father,[119] holiness,[120] raise one's arms to pray,[121] captivity.[122]

In conclusion, I merely wish to state briefly that, if the *Odes of Solomon* contain ideas similar to those of Paul, the grandiose dogmatic constructions of the apostle are not to be found. The Odes are inspired rather by the moral and mystical traits of the Pauline epistles. However, the great number of similarities, even of literary dependencies, must be emphasized.

C. The Remainder of the New Testament Writings

The *Odes of Solomon* show no special affinity with the Gospel of Mk.; the same is true for the Gospel of Lk. Yet, regarding the latter, a few texts which are at times linked with the third gospel ought to be mentioned, even if I may not be able to assert a dependence upon it. For example, the expression "the Way in his peace" in Odes Sol. 11:3 is similar to that of Lk. 1:79, "the way of peace" in the

---

[113]Cf. Labourt and Batiffol, *Les Odes de Salomon*, 83-84.

[114]Cf. Odes Sol. 39:13 and Rom. 4:12.

[115]Cf. Odes Sol. 11:8 where the term "intoxication" has been linked with "come to your right mind" of 1 Cor. 15:34.

[116]Cf. Odes Sol. 35:1 and 1 Cor. 10:1-2 where the cloud in the desert is recalled.

[117]Cf. Odes Sol. 21:3 and 2 Cor. 5:2-3.

[118]Cf. Odes Sol. 7:11 and Eph. 1:10, 23; 3:19; 4:13; Col. 1:19; 2:9.

[119]Cf. Odes Sol. 10:4 and Phil. 2:11: "to the glory of God the Father."

[120]Cf. Odes Sol. 7:16 and 1 Thess 3:13.

[121]Cf. Odes Sol. 21:1 and 1 Tim. 2:8.

[122]Cf. Odes Sol. 10:2-3 and Eph. 4:8, which cites Ps. 68 (67):19.

hymn of Zachariah.

A reference to Lk. 1:35 has sometimes been seen in Odes Sol. 19:6-8a;[123] but the uncertainty of the original text does not allow a safe conclusion.[124]

Odes Sol. 28:2 reads, "My heart continually refreshes itself and leaps for joy, / like the babe who leaps for joy in his mother's womb." The expression "leaped for joy in her womb" is found in Lk 1:41, 44. The ode and Lewis's Syriac versions and the Peshitta of Lk. 1:44 use the same words.[125] It is simply a technical expression.

In Odes Sol. 29, which is a song of thanksgiving for liberation from the enemy, verse 8 reads, "And he gave me the scepter of his power, / that I might subdue the thoughts of the gentiles, / and humble the strength of the mighty." This expresses an idea very similar to that of Lk. 1:51-52 in the Magnificat of the Virgin.[126]

Odes Sol. 31:12-13 reads, "And I bore their bitterness because of humility; / that I might save my nation and instruct it. / And that I might not nullify the promises made to the patriarchs, / to whom I was promised for the salvation of their offspring." We find here the theme of faithfulness to the promises, a very common theme in the Old Testament. It is also present in Lk. 1:54-55, 70-73, in the hymn to the Virgin and in the hymn of Zachariah, both of which are also filled with reminiscences of the Old Testament.

With reference to Odes Sol. 37:2, "And I spoke with the lips of my heart, / and he heard me when my voice reached him," R. Harris notes that the idea of a voice reaching its destination is expressed in Lk. 1:44 in the same way as in this ode, the only difference being the use of the particle of indirect complement.[127] There is nothing more here than a simple similarity of phraseology.

---

[123]Cf. Labourt and Batiffol, *Les Odes de Salomon*, 75-76.

[124]A translation of this text by Lactantius is available, *Instit.*, 4.12.3: "Salomon in ode undevicesima ita dicit: Infirmatus est uterus virginis et accepit fetum et gravata est, et facta est in multa miseratione mater virgo." Diverse hypotheses regarding this text can also be seen in Labourt and Batiffol, *Les Odes de Salomon*.

[125]Cf. Harris and Mingana, *The Odes and Psalms of Solomon*, 2:121. These words are ܟܪܣܐ ܕܐܡܗ ܕܝ.

[126]Cf. ibid., 2:364. Yet, it does not seem that Lk. 1:51-52 served as a basis for the author of the ode; R. Harris's remark on this subject is, in fact, very suggestive: "Verse 8 is composite," he says; "the first sentence is based on Ps 110(109):2: for 'scepter of power' the Odes Sol. has ܚܝܠܬܢܘܬܝ ܕܫܘܠܛܢܐ and the Peshitta has ܫܘܠܛܢܐ ܕܥܘܫܢܟ. The second sentence is drawn from Ps. 33(32):10, and the Odes Sol. may be compared with the Peshitta: Ode, ܡܚܫܒܬܐ ܕܥܡܡܐ ; Peshitta, ܡܣܪܚ ܠܬܪܥܝܬܐ ܕܥܡܡܐ These different coincidences," he adds, "can still be very natural; I cannot, therefore, conclude with certainty a dependence on the Ode."

[127]Cf. ibid., 2:122. The particle is ܠܘܬ in the Odes Sol. and ܒ in the Peshitta and in Lewis's text.

Except for Odes Sol. 4:9, "You have given to us your fellowship, / not that you were in need of us, / but that we are always in need of you," which contains an idea similar to Acts 17:25: "as though he (God) needed anything," there is no passage in the *Odes of Solomon* that reveals a particular relationship with either the Acts of the Apostles or with the catholic epistles.

Moreover, several texts of the *Odes of Solomon* contain traditional Christian features or express ideas common to several New Testament writings, without leading to a conclusion that asserts a literary dependence on a specific text.

Odes Sol. 6:13-18 describes allegorically the diffusion in the universe of the knowledge of God and of faith:[128] "Blessed, therefore, are the ministers of that drink, / who have been entrusted with his water. / They have pleased the parched lips, / and have restored the paralyzed will. / Even lives who were about to expire, / they have seized from Death. / And members which had fallen, / they have restored and set up. / They gave power for their coming, / and light for their eyes. / Because everyone recognized them as the Lord's, / and lived by the water of eternity." The ministers who preach this faith have, therefore, by dint of its dissemination, gained something like physical power. The description of its results recalls Mt. 11:4-5; and Lk. 7:22. Certain elements of the ode and of the quoted gospel passages may be linked, such as: "the ministers of this water have given light to the eyes of men" (Ode) and the "blind see" (Mt. and Lk.); "they have given power for their coming, they have restored the paralyzed will" (Ode) and "the dead rise" (Mt. and Lk.). These agreements are even more telling if we add that in this ode, "the author grows excited at the thought that the whole universe will come to know the Lord."[129] This echoes "the Good News is announced to the poor" in Mt. and Lk.

It is easy to recognize in the last words of Odes Sol. 7:15: " . . . he was well pleased by the Son," a reminiscence of the words of the Father at the baptism of Christ reported through the synoptic tradition in Mt. 3:17b; Mk. 1:11b and Lk. 3:22b.

Odes Sol. 7:16-17 opens a small apocalypse[130] which includes verses 16b-25: "And the Most High will be known by his holy ones: / To announce to those who have songs of the coming of the Lord, / that they may go forth to meet him and may sing to him, / with joy and with the harp of many tones." These words have a gospel tone and bring to mind different passages from the New Testament: Mt. 21:9; 23:39; Mk. 11:9-10; Lk. 19:37-38; Jn. 12:13 and Rev. 22:20. Among these texts, those which refer to the triumphal entry of Christ into Jerusalem must be particularly mentioned. Two things simply need to be noted: among the texts which

---

[128]Cf. Labourt and Batiffol, *Les Odes de Salomon*, 63.

[129]Cf. ibid., 63.

[130]Cf. ibid., 65.

tell of the triumphal entry of Christ, only Jn. 12:13 mentions that the crowd went to meet the Lord, a formula present in the ode; secondly, in the Syriac version, for the expression "to announce," a single word translates the Greek εὐαγγε-λίζεσθαι.[131]

In Odes Sol. 8:15, "I am pleased by them, / and am not ashamed by them," one word in the last sentence might recall Mk. 8:38 and Lk. 9:26, where the Savior declares that whoever is ashamed of him, of him will the Son of man be ashamed on the last day.

Odes Sol. 11 describes the joy and happiness of paradise, and verse 20 says: "Behold, all your laborers are fair, / they who work good works, / and turn from wickedness to your kindness." In this ode, the author states positively an idea similar to that of Mt. 7:23 and Lk. 13:27. The ode asserts that, in the kingdom, the workers turn away from iniquity; the gospels, on the other hand, note that in the kingdom there is no place for workers of iniquity.

In Odes Sol. 17, where the author is engaged in describing the work of God as revealed in Christ, the sentence in verse 14a reads, "And I sowed my fruits in hearts. . . . " Critics have said that this may have been suggested by the gospels' image of the sower who sows the word of God (Mt. 13:3-23; Mk. 4:3-20; Lk. 8:5-15).[132]

The words of Odes Sol. 20:7b-8, "and come into his Paradise, / and make for yourself a crown from his tree. / Then put it on your head and be refreshed, / and recline upon his serenity" are a remote reminiscence of Mt. 8:11; 26:29; Lk. 13:29; 22:29-30; and Rev. 19:9.

Odes Sol. 22:1, "He who caused me to descend from on high, / and to ascend from the regions below," refers perhaps to Christ ascending from Hades. This allusion usually leads to Eph. 4:9-10 and 1 Pet. 3:19, which recall the descent of Christ into hell.

Odes Sol. 24:1-3 reads, "The dove fluttered over the head of our Lord Messiah, / because he was her Head. / And she sang over him, / and her voice was heard. / Then the inhabitants were afraid, / and the foreigners were disturbed." In the general opinion of scholars, these words refer to the narrative of the Holy Spirit who came down to Christ in the form of a dove at his baptism. This episode of the baptism of Christ is told by the synoptics in Mt. 3:16; Mk. 1:10 and Lk. 3:21b-22a. The first verse of this ode allows us to establish only one thing: the agreement with the synoptic tradition concerning the apparition of a dove at the baptism of Christ. But the fear of the inhabitants mentioned in the third verse is noted by certain codices of the Itala, a and g[1], immediately before verse 16 of Mt. 3: "Et cum

---

[131]Cf. Harris and Mingana, *The Odes and Psalms of Solomon*, vol. 1, ad locum: ܡܣܒܪ.

[132]Cf. Labourt and Batiffol, *Les Odes de Salomon*, 73.

baptizaretur lumen ingens circumfulsit de aqua ita ut timerent omnes qui advenerant.'' However, fear this time comes from the apparition of fire rising from water. The theme of fear before a manifestation of the divine nature is too commonplace to allow a conclusion in favor of a relationship between the ode and the variant.

The idea of Odes Sol. 24:8, ''For they labored from the beginning; / and the end of their labor was life,'' recalls ''Nisi granum frumenti . . . '' in Jn. 12:24 as well as in 1 Cor. 15:36.

Odes Sol. 31:9 reads, ''Then they divided my spoil, / though nothing was owed them.'' In this ode which deals with the offering of the Son of God, Christ recalls his passion and his crucifixion. This verse refers undoubtedly to the allotment of his garments as narrated in Mt. 27:35; Mk. 15:24; Lk. 23:34b and Jn. 19:23-24.

Verse 10 of this same ode reads, ''But I endured and held my peace and was silent, / that I might not be disturbed by them.'' If, as is occasionally thought, the words of verse 8a, ''when I stood up,'' as well as those of verse 11, ''But I stood undisturbed like a solid rock'' point to the crucifixion,[133] there is a striking agreement with the Gospel of Peter 10; indeed, this gospel draws attention to the silence of Christ on the cross. If, on the other hand, ''I have stood up'' means ''to stand before a tribunal,'' there is a link in this verse with the gospels' mention of silence during the Passion (Mt. 26:63; 27:14; Mk. 15:5; Lk. 23:9 and Jn. 19:9).

Odes Sol. 39:9 reads, ''The Lord has bridged them by his word, / and he walked and crossed them on foot.'' This may recall the miracle of walking on the water in Mt. 14:25-33; Mk. 6:45-52 and Jn. 6:15-21.

Finally, in Odes Sol. 42:15b, the supplication ''Son of God, have pity on us'' brings to mind several passages of the gospels: Mt. 9:27; 15:22; 20:30-31; Mk. 10:47-48; Lk. 16:24; 17:13 and 18:38-39.

Some expressions which are also read in the New Testament writings still need to be pointed out. In Odes Sol. 3:11, the words ''Be wise and understanding and vigilant'' are linked to 1 Pet. 5:8: ''Be sober, be watchful''; Odes Sol. 5:3a: ''Freely did I receive your grace'' recalls Mt. 10:8: ''You received without paying''; the expression ''announce peace'' is read in Odes Sol. 9:6a and Acts 10:36.

Some scholars such as H. Gressmann multiply the references to the New Testament writings. These are usually only expressions whose similarity is coincidental and whose influence is to be taken only in the broadest sense.[134]

---

[133]Cf. ibid., 90.

[134]These expressions are: the term ''crown'' in Odes Sol. 1:3 and 1 Pet. 5:4; the adverb ''generously'' in Odes Sol. 7:3 and Jas. 1:5; the expression ''abundant grace (of God)'' in Odes Sol. 7:10 and 1 Pet. 1:3; the verb ''keep'' in Odes Sol. 8:10 and Jude 21; the substantive ''fruit'' in Odes Sol. 11:23 and 2 Pet. 1:8; the expression ''the door of his light''

In concluding this section, I would like to remind the reader that, first of all, with the original text of the *Odes of Solomon* missing, only the Syriac version was used as a basis of this study. This fact quite often prevented me from drawing with absolute certainty conclusions concerning possible literary contacts with the New Testament writings. Nevertheless, I believe I was able to detect a definite influence of the first gospel in the composition of a few odes, not that the author goes back explicitly to the Gospel of Matthew or cites it literally, but that he is inspired by certain Matthean texts.

Moreover, the author of the *Odes* gives no indication of any affinity with the Gospel of Mk., and the same is equally true for the Gospel of Lk., the Acts of the Apostles, and the pastoral epistles.

It is evident, therefore, that Mt. held a privileged place compared with the other synoptics, and I could even go as far as to say, very simply, compared with the other gospels. Indeed, numerous similarities between the Odes and the Johannine literature can probably be explained otherwise than through a direct literary influence. As mentioned above,[135] the impression is rather that there is a similar atmosphere of feelings and thoughts of a mystical character.

As for the Pauline letters, they have influenced the author of the *Odes of Solomon* with their moral and mystical touches: Paul's deeper dogmatic statements have not influenced the author of the Odes.

Finally, I pointed out many ideas common to the Odes and to the New Testament writings, especially the synoptics. This is probably how the author paid his tribute to the tradition.

Section 3
THE SIBYLLINE ORACLES

As a whole, the *Sibylline Oracles* seem to have been organized in their present form in the second century by Oriental Christians who used Jewish writings as their sources. They consisted of fourteen books, the ninth and tenth of which have not yet been found. Critics generally agree that books 6, 7, and 8 are Christian, while books 3.97-828, 4, and 5 are Jewish. However, they hesitate as to the Jewish or Christian character of books 13 and 14, while they identify Christian inter-

---

in Odes Sol. 12:3, considered a parallel to "door of faith" in Acts 14:27; the substantive "mirror" in Odes Sol. 13:1 and Jas. 1:23; the words "(he) exalted me" in Odes Sol. 17:7 linked with "you may grow up to salvation" in 1 Pet. 2:2; the words "world to corruption, that everything might be broken" in Odes Sol. 22:11 and "all these things . . . to be dissolved" in 2 Pet. 3:11; "I rested on the spirit of the Lord" in Odes Sol. 36:1 and "the spirit of glory and of God rests upon you" in 1 Pet. 4:14.

[135]Cf. above, 70.

polations in the other books, even though these may have been included much later.[136]

I propose to limit my inquiry to books 6, 7, and 8 whose Christian character is beyond doubt.

The first paragraph is devoted to the Gospel of Mt., and I set aside a second paragraph for other New Testament writings.[137]

§1. Saint Matthew

The Gospel of Mt. did not particularly influence the Christian books of the *Sibylline Oracles*. References to the Matthean texts will sometimes be found in the writings of certain authors, but on the whole, these Matthean passages have parallels in the other gospels. This observation indicates that the *Sibylline Oracles* are rather faithful to Christian traditions as reflected in the gospels.

I examine below various passages which give leave to possible references to the gospels, and where some of the references include a text of Mt.

1. Sib. Or. 8.190

Ἄστρα πεσεῖται ἄπαντα θαλάσσης ἀντίπρῳρα.
All the stars will fall directly into the sea. . . .*

Sib. Or. 8.107-216 describes the last times.[138] This description mentions here the fall of the stars. Eschatological scenes usually proclaim this fall of the stars: many texts bear witness to it:

Is. 34:4: All the host of heaven shall rot away,
and the skies roll up like a scroll.
All their host shall fall (πάντα τὰ ἄστρα πεσεῖται),
as leaves fall from the vine,

---

[136]Cf. on this subject: H. C. O. Lanchester, *The Sibylline Oracles,* in R. H. Charles, *The Apocrypha and Pseudepigrapha of the Old Testament, in English,* vol. 2, *Pseudepigrapha* (Oxford, 1913) 368-74; J. Geffcken, *Christliche Sibyllinen,* in E. Hennecke, *Neutestamentliche Apocryphen* 30, 2nd ed. (Tübingen, 1924) 401; R. Cornely-A. Merk, *Manuel d'Introduction historique et critique à toutes les Saintes Écritures,* 1, *Ancien Testament* (Paris, 1928) 92; B. Altaner, *Patrology,* trans. H. Graef (New York: Herder and Herder, 1960) 91-93; E. Schürer, *Geschichte des jüdischen Volkes im Zeitalter Jesu Christi* 3, 4th ed. (Leipzig, 1909) 555ff.

[137]I rely on the Greek text of the *Sibylline Oracles* given by J. Geffcken, *Die Oracula Sibyllina, Griechische Christliche Schriftsteller 8* (Leipzig, 1902).

*The English text of the *Sibillyne Oracles,* trans. J. J. Collins, is taken from *The Old Testament Pseudepigrapha,* vol. 1, ed. James H. Charlesworth (Garden City NY: Doubleday and Company, 1983). [Editor's note.]

[138]Cf. Geffcken, *Christliche Sibyllinen,* 405.

like leaves falling from the fig tree.

Mt. 24:29: Immediately after the tribulation of those days the sun will be darkened, and the moon will not give its light, and the stars will fall from heaven (ἀστέρες πεσοῦνται ἀπὸ τοῦ οὐρανοῦ), and the powers of the heavens will be shaken.''

Mk. 13:24-25: But in those days, after that tribulation, the sun will be darkened, and the moon will not give its light, and the stars will be falling from heaven (καὶ οἱ ἀστέρες ἔσονται ἐκ τοῦ οὐρανοῦ πίπτοντες), and the powers in the heavens will be shaken.''

Rev. 6:13: . . . and the stars of the sky fell (καὶ οἱ ἀστέρες τοῦ οὐρανοῦ ἔπεσαν) to the earth as the fig tree sheds its winter fruit when shaken by a gale.

It is with the text of Isaiah that the actual agreement with this text is strongest. Like the prophet, in fact, it uses the word ἄστρα and not ἀστέρες found in the other parallels, and it has the adjective πάντα , which is ignored by the other texts. Yet, there is perhaps here nothing more than one of the features of the usual picture of the last times. Besides, the *Oracles*[139] themselves repeat several times this theme of the fall of the stars.[140]

2. Sib. Or. 8.205b-208

. . . νεκρῶν δ' ἐπανάστασις ἔσται˙
καὶ χωλῶν δρόμος ὠκύτατος καὶ κωφὸς ἀκούσει
καὶ τυφλοὶ βλέψουσι, λαλήσουσ' οὐ λαλέοντες,
καὶ κοινὸς πάντεσσι βίος καὶ πλοῦτος ἐσεῖται.

There will be a resurrection of the dead
and most swift racing of the lame, and the deaf will hear
and the blind will see, those who cannot speak will speak,
and life and wealth will be common to all.

Many scriptural texts come to mind:

Is. 35:5-6: Then the eyes of the blind (τυφλῶν) shall be opened,
and the ears of the deaf unstopped (ὦτα κωφῶν ἀκούσονται);
then shall the lame man (ὁ χωλός) leap like a hart,
and the tongue of the dumb shall sing for joy.

---

[139]When I speak of *Oracles* or *Sibylline Oracles*, I mean only the Christian books 6, 7, 8 of the *Sibylline Oracles*.

[140]Cf. Sib. Or. 2.202: ἄστρα γὰρ οὐρανόθεν τε θαλάσσῃ πάντα πεσεῖται [''For all the stars will fall together from heaven on the sea.'' (Editor's addition.)]; 8.341: ἄστρα γὰρ οὐρανόθεν φωστήρων πάντα πεσεῖται [''For all the stars of luminaries will fall from heaven.'' (Editor's addition.)]

Mt. 11:5: . . . the blind receive their sight (τυφλοὶ ἀναβλέπουσιν) and the lame walk (χωλοὶ περιπατοῦσιν), lepers are cleansed and the deaf hear (κωφοὶ ἀκούουσιν), and the dead are raised up (νεκροὶ ἐγείρονται), and the poor have good news preached to them.

Lk. 7:22 is identical to Mt. 11:5.

The comparison should be made with the texts of Mt. and Lk. rather than with that of Isaiah. Indeed, the verb βλέπω is found in both gospels in the form of the composite verb ἀναβλέπω, whereas it is absent in Isaiah. The terms τυφλός, χωλός, and κωφός are read in the *Oracles* and in the three parallels mentioned. The mention of the resurrection of the dead is missing in Isaiah. Moreover, the actual construction of the sentences of the *Sibylline Oracles* looks much more like that of the gospels: sentences whose parts are very brief and which seem to enumerate.

Furthermore, only Isaiah mentions the dumb, but the term he uses, μογιλάλων, is missing in the text of the *Oracles*. All things considered, more elements of the *Oracles* are found in the gospel texts. It appears that the author was inspired by one of them without being able to determine which one, given the identity of the texts of Mt. and of Lk., and he added the comment about the dumb as well as the words: ''life and wealth will be common to all.''

In Sib. Or. 1.353-55, there is an excellent parallel to this text which is generally recognized as a Christian interpolation.[141]

3. Sib. Or. 8.231

Θρῆνος δ' ἐκ πάντων ἔσται καὶ βρυγμὸς ὀδόντων.

A lament will rise up from all and gnashing of teeth.

This passage takes up the description of the end of times, written in acrostic verses. It recalls many texts of the gospels: Mt. 8:12b; 13:42b, 50b; 22:13b; 24:51b; 25:30b; Lk. 13:28.

All these texts are identical and read ἐκεῖ ἔσται ὁ κλαυθμὸς καὶ ὁ βρυγμὸς τῶν ὀδόντων.

The second part of the verse of the *Sibylline Oracles* coincides completely with all the parallels mentioned. Only the first part differs, particularly the word θρῆνος instead of κλαυθμός. Yet, the substitution of θρῆνος for κλαυθμός is likely

---

[141]Sib. Or. 1.353-55:

Βλέψουσιν δέ τυφλοί, ἀτὰρ βαδίσουσί τε χωλοί,

κωφοί τ' εἰσαΐσουσι, λαλήσουσ' οὐ λαλέοντες.

δαίμονας ἐξελάσει, νεκρῶν δ' ἐπανάστασις ἔσται.

[''The blind will see, and the lame will walk. / The deaf will hear; those who cannot speak will speak. / He will drive out demons, there will be a resurrection of the dead.'' (Editor's addition.)]

to be intentional; it can, indeed, be explained by the very composition of the passage: the word κλαυθμός could not be suitable for the author whose composition in acrostic verses required in this place a word beginning with the letter θ to form the first letter of Θεός.

This surmise allows for a literary contact with one or another text of the gospels, without being able to determine which specific one, given the identity of the texts. Let me simply point out that the expression ὁ βρυγμὸς τῶν ὀδόντων is more familiar to Mt., where it is read six times, than to Lk., who uses it only once.

4. Sib. Or. 8.239-40

Σάλπιγξ δ' οὐρανόθεν φωνὴν πολύθρηνον ἀφήσει
'Ωρύουσα μύσος μελέων καὶ πήματα κόσμου.

A trumpet from heaven will issue a most mournful sound,
wailing for the defilement of limbs and the woes of the world.

The trumpet (σάλπιγξ) is a classic element in the scenario of the last days in the eschatological literature. Thus, it is found in the great discourse in Mt. 24:31: "and he will send out his angels with a loud trumpet call (σάλπιγγος), and they will gather his elect from the four winds. . . ." It appears again in 1 Cor. 15:52: "in a moment, in the twinkle of an eye, at the last trumpet (σάλπιγγι). For the trumpet will sound (σαλπίσει), and the dead will be raised imperishable, and we shall be changed." We meet it also in 1 Thess. 4:16: "For the Lord himself will descend from heaven with a cry of command, with the archangel's call, and with the sound of the trumpet (ἐν σάλπιγγι) of God. And the dead in Christ will rise first. . . ."

In the texts mentioned, the trumpet serves to resurrect the dead. In the *Oracles,* on the other hand, it is an instrument of lamentation. It follows that the author seems to have simply taken up the mention of the trumpet, which was almost foisted upon him by his description of the last times, but he assigned a new quality to it, that of an instrument of lamentation. The same comparison can also be made with "the seven trumpets" in the Revelation of Jn. (8:6, 8, 10, 12; 9:1, 13; 10:7).

5. Sib. Or. 8.272

Πάντα λόγῳ πράσσων, πᾶσαν δὲ νόσον θεραπεύων.
. . . doing all with a word, healing every disease.

This passage is drawn from the description of the being of Christ and of his activity. The last words have a gospel tone and recall above all Mt. 4:23: "And he (Jesus) went about all Galilee, teaching . . . preaching . . . and healing every disease (θεραπεύων πᾶσαν νόσον) and every infirmity among the people." Mt. 9:35: "And Jesus went about all the cities and villages, teaching . . . preaching

. . . and healing every disease (θεραπεύων πᾶσαν νόσον) and every infirmity.'' Cf. Mt. 10:1.

As for Mk. 1:39; 6:7 and Lk. 9:1, given sometimes as parallels, the former does not speak of healing disease and the latter does not have the expression πᾶσαν νόσον, but only νόσους.

In the context, the *Sibylline Oracles* seem to sketch a rough outline of the various activities of Christ; the author could very well have summarized in three words the healings of Christ without referring necessarily to a text of Mt. Yet, the concrete identity of expression leads to the belief that it depends on the Matthean text.

6. Sib. Or. 8.273-78

> Τοὺς ἀνέμους παύσειε λόγῳ, στορέσει δὲ θάλασσαν
> μαινομένην ποσὶν εἰρήνης πίστει τε πατήσας.
> ἐκ δ' ἄρτων ἅμα πέντε καὶ ἰχθύος εἰναλίοιο
> ἀνδρῶν χιλιάδας ἐν ἐρήμῳ πέντε κορέσσει,
> καὶ τὰ περισσεύοντα λαβὼν τότε κλάσματα πάντα
> δώδεκα πληρώσει κοφίνους εἰς ἐλπίδα λαῶν.

> He will stop the winds with a word. He will calm
> the raging sea by walking on it with feet of peace and with faith.
> From five loaves and a fish of the sea
> he will satisfy five thousand men in the desert,
> and taking all the leftover fragments,
> he will fill twelve baskets for the hope of the peoples.

This passage recalls Christ's walking on water and the multiplication of the loaves, two narratives tightly bound together in the gospel tradition.

The miracle of the multiplication of the loaves finds parallel texts in Mt. 14:15-26; Mk. 6:35-49; Lk. 9:12-17 and Jn. 6:5-19. A comparison between the *Oracles* and these gospel texts reveals first of all a series of words and expressions which the *Oracles* have in common with the four gospels: these are ἐκ ἄρτων πέντε,[142] ἀνδρῶν,[143] κλάσματα,[144] δώδεκα κοφίνους.[145] Two terms, ἰχθύς[146] and ἐν ἐρήμῳ, in the form of ἐρήμος τόπος,[147] are peculiar to the synoptics. Whereas the *Sibylline Oracles* do not determine the number of fish, the gospels, on the other hand,

---

[142]Cf. Mt. 14:17, 19; Mk. 6:38, 41; Lk. 9:13, 16; Jn. 6:9.

[143]Cf. Mt. 14:21; Mk. 6:44; Lk. 9:14; Jn. 6:10.

[144]Cf. Mt. 14:20; Mk. 6:43; Lk. 9:17; Jn. 6:13.

[145]Cf. Mt. 14:20; Mk. 6:43; Lk. 9:17; Jn. 6:13.

[146]Cf. Mt. 14:17, 19; Mk. 6:38, 41; Lk. 9:13, 16. Jn. 6:9 uses ὀψάριον.

[147]Cf. Mt. 14:15; Mk. 6:35; Lk. 9:12; this expression is missing in the Johannine narrative.

recall that there were two fish.¹⁴⁸ In addition, instead of χιλιάδας πέντε, all the gospels have πεντακισχίλιοι;¹⁴⁹ τὰ περισσεύοντα finds corresponding terms in the gospels¹⁵⁰ except in Mk.; and πλυρώσει has a parallel only in Mt. and Mk.¹⁵¹ Finally, the *Sibylline Oracles* have εἰναλίοιο, χορέσσει, λαβών, εἰς ἐλπίδα λαῶν, words absent in the narrative of the gospels.

Did the author follow the text of one of the gospels in this passage? As far as the walking on water is concerned, it could be assumed that he summarized this miracle in his own way; none of the words he uses find their equivalent in the narrative of the gospels. As for the story of the multiplication of the loaves, Mk. can be rejected as a source of this narrative since the words τὰ περισσεύοντα are missing. The Lucan text can also be excluded since it does not have anything corresponding to πληρώσει. Jn. can also be eliminated since he does not mention that the scene takes place in a desert area, and because he calls the fish ὀψάριον and not ἰχθύς.

Consequently, there remains only the Matthean narrative which includes all the elements derived by the story in the *Sibylline Oracles*.

It can be assumed that the author is familiar with the text of the first gospel. Note, for example, the allegorical interpretation of the twelve baskets. By the way, Sib. Or. 1.356-59¹⁵² is a parallel to this text.

7. Sib. Or. 8.287-89

Εἰς ἀνόμων χεῖρας καὶ ἀπίστων ὕστερον ἥξει,
δώσουσιν δὲ θεῷ ῥαπίσματα χερσὶν ἀνάγνοις
καὶ στόμασιν μιαροῖς ἐμπτύσματα φαρμακόεντα.

Later he will come into the hands of lawless and faithless men,
and they will give blows to God with unholy hands
and poisonous spittings with polluted mouths.

---

¹⁴⁸Cf. Mt. 14:17, 19; Mk. 6:38, 41; Lk. 9:13, 16; Jn. 6:9.

¹⁴⁹Cf. Mt. 14:21; Mk. 6:44; Lk. 9:14; Jn. 6:10.

¹⁵⁰Cf. Mt. 14:20; Lk. 9:17; Jn. 6:13.

¹⁵¹Cf. Mt. 14:20; Mk. 6:44.

¹⁵²Sib. Or. 1.356-59:

Κύματα πεζεύσει καὶ ἐρημαίῳ ἐνὶ χώρῳ
ἐξ ἄρτων πέντε καὶ ἰχθύος εἰναλίοιο
χιλιάδας κορέσει πέντε, τὰ δὲ λείψαντα τούτων
δώδεκα πληρώσει κοφίνους εἰς ἐλπίδα λαῶν.

[" . . . he will walk the waves, and in desert places / he will satisfy five thousand from five loaves / and a fish of the sea, and the leftovers of these / will fill twelve baskets for the hope of the people." (Editor's addition.)]

There is no doubt that these words refer to the episode of the flagellation during which Christ was struck and spat upon. The narrative is found in Mt. 26:67; Mk. 14:65 and Lk. 23:63-65.

Mt. 26:67: Then they spat in his face (ἐνέπτυσαν), and struck him; and some slapped him (ἐρράπισαν). . . .

Mk. 14:65: And some began to spit (ἐμπτύειν) on him, and to cover his face, and to strike him, saying to him, "Prophesy!" And the guards received him with blows (ῥαπίσμασιν).

Lk. 22:63-65: Now the men who were holding Jesus mocked him and beat him (ἐνέπαιζον); they also blindfolded him and asked him, 'Prophesy! Who is it that struck you?' And they spoke many other words against him, reviling him.

Since Luke's narrative does not mention spitting into the face of Christ, it could not have been a source for the author. The words ῥαπίσματα and ἐμπτύσματα lead to a probable literary contact. With Mt. or Lk.? Since there is proof that the *Sibylline Oracles* know Mt., it is the obvious choice. Another parallel may be mentioned, probably a Christian interpolation in Sib. Or. 1.365-66.[153]

8. Sib. Or. 8.292-295

Καὶ κολαφιζόμενος σιγήσει μή τις ἐπιγνῷ,
τίς τίνος ὢν πόθεν ἦλθεν, ἵνα φθιμένοισι λαλήσει.
καὶ στέφανον φορέσει τὸν ἀκάνθινον· ἐκ γὰρ ἀκανθῶν
τὸ στέφος ἐκλεκτῶν αἰώνιόν ἐστιν ἄγαλμα.

Beaten, he will be silent, lest anyone recognize
who he is, whose son, and whence he came, so that he may speak to the dead;
and he will wear the crown of thorns. For, made of thorns,
the crown of chosen men is an eternal delight.

This language recalls various events of the Passion: Christ beaten, his silence before his interrogators, his crowning with thorns.

The blows given to Christ are expressed with the same verb κολαφίζω in Mt. 26:67 and Mk. 14:65; the silence of Christ is mentioned in Mt. 26:63; 27:13; Mk. 14:61; 15:4; Lk. 23:9; and Jn. 19:9, but never with the verb σιγάω. The questionings to which Christ was subjected are manifold: Christ is interrogated by the

---

[153]Sib. Or. 1.365-66:

Καὶ τότε δὴ κιλάφους καὶ πτύσματα φαρμακόεντα
'Ισραὴλ δώσει μυσαροῖς ἐνὶ χείλεσι τούτῳ.

[Then indeed Israel, with abominable lips / and poisonous spittings, will give this man blows. (Editor's addition.)]

High Priest about his messianism and his divine sonship (Mt. 26:63; Mk. 14:61; Lk. 22:67): the words τίς τίνος ὤν in the *Oracles* may reflect this; Pilate (Mt. 27:11; Mk. 15:2; Lk. 23:3; Jn. 18:33) interrogates him about his kingship over the Jews: the query πόθεν ἦλθεν of the *Oracles* may recall the question of the Roman procurator in Jn. 19:9: πόθεν εἶ σύ;

As for the crowning with thorns, it is described in Mt. 27:29; Mk. 15:16b and Jn. 19:2.

The difference between the texts of the *Oracles* and the parallels mentioned is too great to favor a literary influence. However, the author may have read a gospel and commented upon it in his own way; there would then be a dependence. I lean toward Mt. who, as mentioned above, was well-known to the author. But the hypothesis of a rather full dependence on the traditional narrative of the Passion cannot be excluded.

9. Sib. Or. 8.297-98

> Ἐκ καλάμων γὰρ σειομένων ὑπὸ πνεύματος ἄλλου
> πρὸς κρίματα ψυχῆς ἐτράφη ὀργῆς καὶ ἀμοιβῆς.

This text is rather dubitable and its meaning is fairly obscure.[154] It is translated as: "For by winds shaken by another wind / the inclinations of the soul are turned from wrath and change."

The first words recall the words of Christ concerning John the Baptist in Mt. 11:7 and Lk. 7:24: "What did you go out into the wilderness to behold? A reed (κάλαμον) shaken (σαλευόμενον) by the wind?" Did the author compare the precursor to a reed shaken by the wind?

The uncertainty of the Greek text, the identity of these parallels, the mention of wrath in Mt. 3:7 as in Lk. 3:7 do not lead me to determine whether this passage is dependent on the New Testament texts mentioned above.

10. Sib. Or. 8.302

> Ἐκπετάσει χεῖρας καὶ κόσμον ἅπαντα μετρήσει.

He will stretch out his hands and measure the entire world.

The author is very likely alluding to the crucifixion of Christ; the gospels report it in Mt. 27:35; Mk. 15:24; Lk. 23:33 and Jn. 19:18a; but not a single expression of the *Sibylline Oracles* is found in the gospel texts. A similar formula in Sib. Or. 1.372,[155] generally considered as a Christian interpolation, may be men-

---

[154]Cf. Geffcken, *Die Oracula Sibyllina,* 161.

[155]Cf. Sib. Or. 1.372: 'Αλλ' ὅταν ἐκπετάσῃ χεῖρας καὶ πάντα μετρήσῃ. [But when he will stretch out his hands and measure all. (Editor's addition.)]

tioned.

11. Sib. Or. 8.303

Εἰς δὲ τὸ βρῶμα χολὴν καὶ πιεῖν ὄξος ἔδωκαν.
They gave him gall for food and vinegar to drink.

The gospels narrate in Mt. 27:34, 48; Mk. 15:36a; Lk. 23:36 and Jn. 19:29 that Christ was given to drink on Calvary; all the gospels mention the vinegar. Only Mt. 27:34 speaks of gall (χολή) as well, but he does not say that this gall was given for food (εἰς τὸ βρῶμα), and he does not combine in the same phrase the mention of gall and vinegar. The best parallel is in the text of Ps. 69(68):22 by which the gospels were inspired and which reads: καὶ ἔδωκαν εἰς τὸ βρῶμά μου χολὴν καὶ εἰς τὴν δίψαν μου ἐπότισάν με ὄξος. The text of Ps. 69 is almost exactly the same as the text of the *Oracles*; the words ἔδωκαν, εἰς τὸ βρῶμα, χολήν, ὄξος are present, only the verb πίνω is missing, but it is very close to ποτίζω. Here again a parallel is conspicuous in Sib. Or. 1.367,[156] probably a Christian interpolation.

12. Sib. Or. 8.305-306

Ναοῦ δὲ σχισθῇ τὸ πέτασμα καὶ ἤματι μέσσῳ
νὺξ ἔσται σκοτόεσσα πελώριος ἐν τρισὶν ὥραις.
The veil of the Temple will be rent, and in midday
there will be dark monstrous night for three hours.

Two events are to be distinguished in this passage: the tearing of the veil of the temple and the heavy darkness.
The first is narrated by the synoptics:

Mt. 27:51: And behold, the curtain of the temple (τὸ καταπέτασμα τοῦ ναοῦ) was torn (ἐσχίσθη) in two, from top to bottom. . . .

Mk. 15:38: And the curtain of the temple (τὸ καταπέτασμα τοῦ ναοῦ) was torn (ἐσχίσθη) in two, from top to bottom.

Lk. 23:45: . . . the curtain of the temple (τὸ καταπέτασμα τοῦ ναοῦ) was torn (ἐσχίσθη) in two.

The *Sibylline Oracles* have the word ναός and the verb οχίζω in common with the synoptics, but they have πέτασμα instead of the composite καταπέτασμα in the synoptics.

---

[156]Cf. Sib. Or. 1.367: Εἰς δὲ τὸ βρῶμα χολὴν καὶ εἰς ποτὸν ὄξος ἄκρατον. [For food they will give him gall and for drink unmixed vinegar. (Editor's addition.)]

Faced with the similarity of the texts of the synoptics, it is impossible to decide upon which one of the texts the *Oracles* may depend. I shall simply state that the author follows tradition such as is found in the synoptics.

The second event concerns the coming of thick darkness. It is described in Mt. 27:45; Mk. 15:33; Lk. 23:44; all three mention that darkness covered the land from the sixth to the ninth hour, but they do not stress particularly that it was night at noon. The Gospel of Peter 15:18[157] notes that the intensity of darkness at noon was such that many stumbled despite their lighted lamps. Moreover, it would be difficult to find a literary link between this text of the *Oracles* and that of the synoptics; only the word σκοτόεσσα may, at best, correspond to σκότος of the gospels. The author seems rather to follow here an unusual tradition or he draws inspiration from his own invention.

I would like to point out again a Christian interpolation to this passage in Sib. Or. 1.375-78.[158]

13. Sib. Or. 8.324-28

Χαῖρ' ἁγνὴ θύγατερ Σιών, πολλὰ παθοῦσα·
αὐτός σου βασιλεὺς ἐπιβὰς ἐπὶ πῶλον ἐσάγει
πρᾶος πᾶσι φανείς, ἵνα τὸ(ν) ζυγὸν ἡμῶν
δοῦλον δυσβάστακτον ἐπ' αὐχένι κείμενον ἄρῃ
καὶ θεσμοὺς ἀθέους λύσῃ δεσμούς τε βιαίους.

Rejoice, holy daughter Sion, who have suffered much.
Your king himself comes in, mounted on a foal,
appearing gentle to all so that he may lift our yoke
of slavery, hard to bear, which lies on our neck
and undo the godless ordinances and constraining bonds.

---

[157]Cf. Gos. Pet. 5.15, 18: Ἦν δὲ μεσημβρία καὶ σκότος κατέσχε πᾶσαν τὴν Ἰουδαίαν καὶ ἐθορυβοῦντο καὶ ἠγωνίων μήποτε ὁ ἥλιος ἔδυ, ἐπειδὴ ἔτι ἔξη . . . περιήρχοντο δὲ πολλοὶ μετὰ λύχνων νομίζοντες ὅτι νύξ ἐστιν, (καὶ) ἐπέσαντο. ["Now it was midday and a darkness covered all Judea. And they became anxious and uneasy lest the sun had already set, since he was still alive . . . And many went about with lamps, (and) as they supposed that it was night, (they went to bed *or* they stumbled)." (Editor's addition.)]

[158]Cf. Sib. Or. 1.375-78: Νὺξ ἔσται σκοτόεσσα πελώριος ἤματι μέσῳ·
καὶ τότε δὴ ναὸς Σολομώνιος ἀνθρώποισιν
σῆμα μεγ' ἐκελέσει, ὁπόταν Ἀιδωνέος οἶκον
βήσεται ἀγγέλων ἐπαναστασίην τεθνεῶσιν.
[. . . there will be monstrous dark night in midday. / And then indeed the temple of Solomon will effect / a great sign for men, when he goes to the house of Adonis / announcing the resurrection to the dead. (Editor's addition.)]

Two parts can be distinguished in this passage: the first recalls the entry of Christ into Jerusalem, the second deals with an unbearable yoke.

The first reports an acclamation which welcomed Christ upon his triumphal entry into Jerusalem. It is found in Mt. 21:5 and Jn. 12:15. These texts of the New Testament are inspired by Zech. 9:9.

Mt. 21:5: Tell the daughter of Zion (θυγατρὶ Σιών),
Behold, your king (ὁ βασιλεύς σου) is coming to you,
humble (πραΰς), and mounted on an ass (ἐπιβεβηκὼς ἐπὶ ὄνον),
and on a colt (ἐπὶ πῶλον), the foal of an ass.

Jn. 12:15: Fear not, daughter of Zion (θυγάτηρ Σιῶν);
behold your king (ὁ βασιλεύς σου) is coming,
sitting on an ass's colt (καθήμενος ἐπὶ πῶλον ὄνου)!

Zech. 9:9: Rejoice greatly, O daughter of Zion (χαῖρε . . . θύγατερ Σιῶν)!
Shout aloud, O daughter of Jerusalem!
Lo, your king (ὁ βασιλεύς σου) comes to you;
triumphant and victorious is he,
he is humble (πραΰς) and riding on an ass, on a colt the foal of an ass (ἐπιβεβηκὼς ἐπὶ ὑποζύγιον καὶ πῶλον νέον).

The absence of the term πραΰς and the substitution of ἐπιβαίνω by καθίζω in Jn. are reasons enough to exclude a literary influence from the latter.

The general tone of this piece is rather important. The author follows a gospel, in this case Mt. This does not prevent him from referring as well to underlying oracles which are well known in the literature of the second century: this would explain the presence of χαῖρε, which is absent in Mt. but present in Zechariah.

The second part of this text states that Christ has come "so that he may lift our yoke of slavery, hard to bear, which lies on our neck and to undo the godless ordinances and constraining bonds." The presence of the term ζυγός has sometimes suggested a reference to Mt. 11:29.[159] The anti-Jewish literature played on the term ζυγός: yoke of the law—yoke of Christ. There would, therefore, be here an implicit reference to the Matthean text.

14. Sib. Or. 8.476

Καινοφαὴς δὲ μάγοισι σεβάσθη θέσφατος ἀστήρ.
A wonderous, new-shining star was venerated by Magi.

These words recall Mt. 2:2: "For we (the Magi) have seen his star (αὐτοῦ τὸν ἀστέρα) in the East, and have come to worship him." The *Sibylline Oracles* have embellished this event reported in Mt., by making clear the very sense that

---

[159]Cf. Geffcken, *Christliche Sibyllinen*, 408.

Mt. gave to the star: a wonderous, new-shining star. By the way, βηθλεέμ in Sib. Or. 8:479, is called the homeland of the Logos, of Christ; in so doing, the *Oracles* are consistent with Mt. and Lk.

15. Sib. Or. 8.481-82

Καὶ πάντων ἀγαπᾶν τὸν πλησίον ὥσπερ ἑαυτόν·
καὶ θεὸν ἐκ ψυχῆς φιλέειν, αὐτῷ δὲ λατρεύειν.

and, above all, love your neighbor as yourself,
and love God from the soul and serve him.

There are numerous parallels to this passage; they are found in Mt. 22:37, 39; Mk. 12:30, 31 and Lk. 10:27; to these must be added Deut. 6:5 and Lev. 19:18.

Only the New Testament combines the love of God with the love of neighbor. This simply establishes the faithfulness of the *Sibylline Oracles* to this great Christian precept. In view of the similarity of the texts of the three synoptics, it is impossible to state that this text of the *Oracles* is in literary contact with one rather than with another: the text is consistent with the synoptic tradition. Some differences are still to be noted: the single mention of ἐκ ψυχῆς instead of the enumeration ἐκ καρδίας, etc., in the synoptics; the verbs φιλεῖν and λατρεύειν, which are absent from the texts of the gospels.

I would like to mention also the verb ἀστράπτω in Sib. Or. 6.18, sometimes linked with Mt. 24:27 and Lk. 17:24[160] only because the corresponding substantive ἀστραπή is found in these gospel texts.

Sib. Or. 7.134-35 seems to use a metaphor similar to Mt. 7:15 where the shrewdness of those who deceive is described in the image of people who put on sheep's clothing (δυσάμενοι προβάτων λασιότριχα ῥινά). In Mt., the false prophets are clothed in sheepskins even though they are ravenous wolves.

When the *Sibylline Oracles*, in 8.334, state that "Since he is imperishable he pays no attention to perishable sacrifices," it echoes more or less Mt. 9:13 and 12:7 which moreover cite Hosea 6:6: "For I desire steadfast love and not sacrifice."

Finally, Sib. Or. 8.417-18, Mt. 25:32-33 and Ezek. 34:17 have in common the idea of a division which the Judge will make among all those who are subject to his judgment: "I will set ram by ram and shepherd by shepherd / and calf by calf, near each other for trial."

In general, scholars acknowledge the Christian character of the first 96 verses of book 3 of the *Sibylline Oracles*. Some of these verses deserve consideration.

---

[160]Cf. Geffcken, *Die Oracula Sibyllina*, 131; also *Christliche Sibyllinen*, 412.

Sib. Or. 3.63-70

'Εκ δὲ Σεβαστηνῶν ἥξει Βελίαρ μετόπισθεν
καὶ στήσει ὀρέων ὕψος, στήσει δὲ θάλασσαν,
ἠέλιον πυρόεντα μέγαν λαμπράν τε σελήνην
καὶ νέκυας στήσει καὶ σήματα πολλὰ ποιήσει
ἀνθρώποις· ἀλλ' οὐχὶ τελεσφόρα ἔσσετ' ἐν αὐτῷ,
ἀλλὰ πλανᾷ καὶ δὴ μέροπας, πολλούς τε πλανήσει
πιστούς τ' ἐκλεκτούς θ' Ἑβραίους ἀνόμους τε καὶ ἄλλους
ἀνέρας, οἵτινες οὔπω θεοῦ λόγον εἰσήκουσαν.

Then Beliar will come from the *Sebastenoi*
and he will raise up[161] the height of mountains, he will raise up the sea,
the great fiery sun and shining moon,
and he will raise up the dead, and perform many signs
for men. But they will not be effective in him.
But he will, indeed, also lead men astray, and he will lead astray
many faithful, chosen Hebrews, and also other lawless men
who have not yet listened to the word of God.

This apocalypse deals with the personification of the Antichrist and the description of his activity. The gospels speak of it as well in Mt. 24:24 and Mk. 13:22; other parallels include 2 Thess. 2:8-12 and Rev. 13:13-14a.

Mt. 24:24: For false Christs and false prophets will arise and show great signs and wonders (σημεῖα μεγάλα καὶ τέρατα), so as to lead astray (πλανῆσαι), if possible, even the elect (καὶ τοὺς ἐκλεκτούς).

Mk. 13:22: False Christs and false prophets will arise and show signs and wonders (σημεῖα καὶ τέρατα), to lead astray (ἀποπλανᾶν), if possible, the elect (τοὺς ἐκλεκτούς).

2 Thess. 2:8-12: And then the lawless one (ὁ ἄνομος) will be revealed, and the Lord Jesus will slay him with the breath of his mouth and destroy him by his appearing and his coming. The coming of the lawless one by the activity of Satan will be with all power and with pretended signs and wonders (ἐν πάσῃ δυνάμει καὶ σημείοις καὶ τέρασιν ψεύδους), and with all wicked deception for those who are to perish, because they refused to love the truth and so be saved. Therefore God sends upon them a strong delusion (πλάνης), to make them believe what is false (τῷ ψεύδει), so that all may be condemned who did not believe the truth but had pleasure in unrighteousness.

Rev. 13:13-14a: It (the other beast) works great signs (σημεῖα μεγάλα), even making fire come down from heaven to earth in the sight of men; and by the signs which it is allowed to work in the presence of the beast, it deceives (πλανᾷ) those who dwell on earth. . . .

---

[161]For the difficult meaning of στήσει, cf. Lanchester, *The Sibylline Oracles*, 380.

Of all these Christian parallels, the closest seems to be that of Saint Paul: Beliar and the lawless one both perform pretended signs and wonders, both seduce a multitude of followers. But since this piece of the *Oracles*, according to B. Rigaux, dates probably from the year 30,[162] Paul was influenced by it rather than the opposite.

It follows from the analysis of all these texts that the literary influence of the Gospel of Mt. must be acknowledged. In addition to the passage which deals with the miracle of the loaves (Sib. Or. 8.273b-78), several expressions are more familiar to the first gospel.[163] In addition, there are several definite contacts with Mt., which is not true for the other synoptics. I pointed out also that, if the gospel narrative is based on Mt., it also refers to the Old Testament and to the apocrypha in accordance with the literature of this period.[164] Particularly in the traditional Passion Narrative, the *Sibylline Oracles* demonstrate that Mt. was the source, and that it exerted influence together with a common tradition of which the Gospel of Peter has left traces.[165]

§2. The Other New Testament Writings

Few passages of the *Sibylline Oracles* have a literary dependence on a New Testament text other than the first gospel. For the sake of clarity, and because of the relative number of references which can be mentioned with any of these writings, I consider first the Johannine literature, then the epistles of Saint Paul, and finally the remainder of the New Testament writings.

A. The Johannine Literature

Sib. Or. 8.254b-255 reads: "(so that the people might know that he is elect) and the stone (τὸν λίθον) he promised. / The one who has believed in him will have eternal life (ὃν ὁ πιστεύσας ζωὴν αἰώνιον ἕξει)." The metaphor of the stone which supports the edifice, applied to Christ, is found in 1 Pet. 2:6, which is inspired by the text of Is. 28:16. The last sentence of the *Oracles* has a clearly marked Johannine flavor and recalls Jn. 3:36: ὁ πιστεύων εἰς τὸν υἱὸν ἔχει ζωὴν αἰώνιον. The texts of the *Oracles* and Jn. coincide almost literally: the same verb πιστεύω, the same expression ζωὴν αἰώνιον ἐχεῖν, the same object of faith:

---

[162]Cf. Rigaux, *L'Antéchrist*, 200.

[163]Cf. above, 83-84: ὁ βρυγμὸς τῶν ὀδόντων in Sib. Or. 8.231; above, 84-85: πᾶσαν νόσον θεραπεύων in Sib. Or. 8.272.

[164]Cf. above, 90-91: Sib. Or. 8.324-28; 91-92: Sib. Or. 8.476.

[165]Cf. above, 90, as well as Sib. Or. 8.296 which I consider later, below, 95.

Christ. It is clear, therefore, that the author seems to be literarily dependent on this Johannine text.

As Sib. Or. 8.296 reads: "They will stab his sides with a reed on account of their law (πλευρὰς νύξουσιν καλάμῳ διὰ τὸν νόμον αὐτῶν)," it could be construed at first glance that it refers to the blows which the soldiers gave Christ during the flagellation; the crucifixion is in fact mentioned in the *Oracles* a few verses further, in 8.302. However, the verb νύσσω, hapax in the New Testament in Jn. 19:34, and the substantive πλευρά recall the piercing of Christ narrated in Jn. 19:34 where all these terms are found. The same goes for the reference to the Jewish Law (Jn. 19:31). The Gospel of Peter has a text quite similar to that of the *Oracles*.[166] The author follows perhaps a special tradition to which the Acts of John could be another wintess;[167] he may have transposed before the crucifixion the episode of the piercing narrated by Jn., which he touches up slightly in substituting καλάμῳ for λόγχῃ, influenced perhaps by ὑσσώπῳ (Jn. 19:29). I would like to point out a parallel also found in Sib. Or. 1.372-375, which is generally considered a Christian interpolation.[168]

I wish also to note in Sib. Or. 8.316b an expression typical of Jn. 3:3, 7: γεννηθέντες ἄνωθεν.

Sib. Or. 8.248, "An iron shepherd's rod will prevail (ῥάβδος ποιμαίνουσα σιδηρείη γε κρατήσει)," recalls many parallels: Rev. 2:27; 12:5; 19:15 and Ps. 2:9. They all agree almost perfectly with this text: we find the verb ποιμαίνω, the words ῥάβδος σιδήρα. A literary dependence seems to be quite in line; but given the similarity of Ps. and of the texts of Revelation, it is difficult to determine the author's source. As in Sib. Or. 8.217-44, there is a description of the last days which would lead towards a preference for the texts of Revelation where indeed the Messiah appears to destroy the Antichrist. However, the author may have taken this image from Ps. 2 which speaks of the triumph of Christ over the nations.

In a description of the last days, Sib. Or. 8.353 reads: "and they will call death fair (καὶ καλέσουσι καλὸν τὸ θανεῖν) and it will evade them (φεύξετ' ἀπ' αὐτῶν)." This is an apocalyptic feature (Rev. 9:6) on which the *Sibylline Oracles* seem indeed to depend. The fairly pronounced coincidence of the texts, in fact,

---

[166]Gos. Pet. 2.9: . . . ἕτεροι καλάμῳ ἔνυσσον αὐτόν. [" . . . others nudged him with a reed. . . ." (Editor's addition.)]

[167]Cf. Acts Jn. 97: καὶ λόγχαις νύσσομαι καὶ καλάμοις. [" . . . and pierced with lances and reeds. . . . " (Editor's addition.)].

[168]Sib. Or. 1.372-75: 'Αλλ' ὅταν ἐκπετάσῃ χεῖρας καὶ πάντα μετρήσῃ
καὶ στέφανον φορέσῃ τὸν ἀκάνθινον ἠδέ τε πλευράν
νύξωσιν καλάμοισιν, ὅτου χάριν ἐν τρισὶν ὥραις
νὺξ ἔσται σκοτόεσσα πελώριος ἤματι μέσσῳ.

[But when he will stretch out his hands and measure all, / and bear the crown of thorns— and they will stab / his side with reeds—on account of this, for three hours / there will be monstrous dark in midday. (Editor's addition.)]

speaks favorably of this literary dependence: ἐπιθυμήσουσιν ἀποθανεῖν of Rev. corresponds to the words καλέσουσι καλὸν τὸ θανεῖν in Sib. Or.; φεύγει ὁ θάνατος ἀπ' αὐτῶν of Rev. agrees with the phrase φεύξετ' ἀπ' αὐτῶν in Sib. Or.

Sib. Or. 3.15-16[169] says: "but he himself, eternal, revealed himself / as existing now (ὄντα), and formerly (πρὶν ἐόντα) and again in the future (ἀτὰρ πάλι καὶ μετέπειτα)." Rev. 1:8 and 4:8 state a similar idea but in different terms.

Sib. Or. 3.81b-82 reads: "when God who dwells in the sky / rolls up the heaven (οὐρανὸν εἰλίξῃ) as a scroll is rolled (καθ' ἅπερ βιβλίον εἰλεῖται)." Is. 34:4 and Rev. 6:14 use an absolutely identical image. I would, however, give preference here to the text of Isaiah since the term οὐρανός is in direct relation with the verb ἐλίσσω as it is in the *Oracles*, whereas in Rev. 6:14 the verb ἐλίσσω is related to the scroll, and the verb ἀποχωρίζω is related to οὐρανός.

Finally, I would like to point out the presence of the word δράκων in Sib. Or. 8.88, which is also present in Rev. 12:3, and the word σφραγίς in Siob. Or. 8.244, which is common in the New Testament.[170]

B. The Epistles of Saint Paul

In Sib. Or. 8.408, "and provide for me, the living one (τῷ ζῶντι), a living sacrifice (ζῶσαν θυσίαν)," we find the expression ζῶσα θυσία, which is peculiar to Rom. 12:1 in the New Testament. In this text, Paul invites the Romans to offer their body to God as a living host, holy, pleasing to God. There could be a literary dependence with respect to this text, especially since the point is an offering to God as it is in Saint Paul; however, it may be asked whether the participle ζῶσα was placed as a kind of parallel to ζῶντι which is applied to God in the same passage.

Sib. Or. 8.414-415 reads: "and then I will raise the dead, having undone fate / and the sting of death (θανάτου κέντρον), and later I will come to judgment." The expression θανάτου κέντρον is read in 1 Cor. 15:55 which draws from Hosea 13:14. Yet, the prophet does not speak of "the sting of death" but of Hades. This Sibylline text is inserted in a passage quite similar to 1 Cor. 15:55; the last days are there and the dead are raised. A reminiscence of the Pauline text is, therefore, probable.

Sib. Or. 8.444-45 states, "Though he is mortal all the things of the world will serve him; when he is fashioned of clay (χοϊκῷ πλασθέντι) we will subject all things to him." The qualifier χοϊκός applied to Adam is read in 1 Cor. 15:47. It reappears in verses 48 and 49 of the same chapter and only in these passages of

---

[169]I pointed out above, on 80, that the first 96 verses of bk. 3 were acknowledged as Christian. [This claim is actually made not on p. 80 but on p. 92. (Editor's note.)]

[170]Cf. Rom. 4:11; 1 Cor. 9:2; 2 Tim. 2:19; Rev. 5:1, 2, 5, 9; 6:1, 3, 5, 7, 9, 12; 8:1; 9:4.

the New Testament. Yet, Gen. 2:7 offers an interesting parallel; indeed, the words ἔπλασεν χοῦν in Gen. are easily linked to the expression χοϊκῷ πλασθέντι in Sib. Or. The presence of the verb πλάσσω combined with the qualifier χοῦς— two words which are also present in Sib. Or.—leads me to believe that it is the narrative of Genesis rather than the Pauline text which has literarily influenced the author of the *Oracles*. This hypothesis seems all the more sound when we know that Sib. Or. 8.429-55 deals with the creation.[171]

In the description of Christ in acrostic verses, Sib. Or. 8.246 reads: "(Christ will be) the life of pious men, but the scandal of the world (πρόσκομμα δὲ κόσμου)." Is. 8:14 had prophesied that the Lord would be a stumbling-block to some; Rom. 9:32-33 and 1 Pet. 2:8 were inspired by this prophecy; all three texts use the word πρόσκομμα. We have here a Christian theme which goes back to Is. 8:14 to explain how some people did not believe in Christ.

When Sib. Or. 8.300-301 states: 'then for him (Christ) every law will be dissolved which from the beginning / was given in teachings to men, on account of a disobedient people," it sets forth an idea similar to Rom. 7:4-6, but it does not lead us to suspect the slightest literary contact. There is here, perhaps, a reminiscence of Col. 2:14.

Finally, I would like to point out the expression παρθένος ἁγνή which is common to Sib. Or. 8.291 and 2 Cor. 11:2.

It can be stated, therefore, that there was a definite knowledge of the Pauline epistles which has exerted an influence on the composition of several passages of the *Sibylline Oracles*. Nevertheless, there are not many parallels with the texts of the apostle.

C. The Remainder of the New Testament Writings

In The *Sibylline Oracles*, there is not the slightest trace of a definite literary influence from a text of Mk. I pointed out in the first paragraph on Saint Matthew some parallels drawn from Mk., but I was not able to conclude in any instance that there was a definite literary influence from the second gospel. The same is true with respect to the Gospel of Luke.[172]

Speaking of Christ, The *Sibylline Oracles* 8.331 state: "and love him from your soul and bear his name (τοὔνομα βάστασον αὐτοῦ)." The expression τοὔνομα βάστασον recalls Acts 9:15; it is the same formula, unique in Acts for the whole New Testament; the Lord speaks here of Paul to Ananias. Does the author

---

[171]Cf. Geffcken, *Christliche Sibyllinen*, 410.

[172]Sib. Or. 8.245: τὸ ξύλον ἐν πιστοῖς, τὸ κέρας τὸ ποθούμενον ἔσται ["the wood among the faithful, the desired horn" (Editor's addition.)] has sometimes been compared with Lk. 1:69 (cf. Geffcken, *Die Oracula Sibyllina*, 157), but only because of the presence of the term κέρας.

depend on Acts? Nothing in the context leads towards this text of Acts. The *Sibylline Oracles* recall no other text of the Acts of the Apostles.

The catholic epistles do not seem to have played a role in the composition of the *Sibylline Oracles*. Let me simply point out that, when Sib. Or. 8.310-11 states: "He (Christ) will come to Hades announcing (ἀγγέλλων) hope for all / the holy ones, the end of ages and last day," it states a fact known by Eph. 4:9 and 1 Pet. 3:19; 4:6. In addition, the verb εὐαγγελίζω found in 1 Pet. 4:6 is more or less alluded to with ἀγγέλλων in the text of the *Oracles*.

By way of conclusion of this section, I have demonstrated that the *Sibylline Oracles* show a certain affinity for the Gospel of Mt.;[173] on the other hand, they go back to many ideas found in the gospel tradition. But the *Sibylline Oracles* disclosed that this tradition was based on the Gospel of Mt., and that it blended features taken from the apocrypha and added references from prophetic passages in the Old Testament. The Passion and Infancy Narratives in the *Oracles* bear witness to this.

The *Sibylline Oracles* know the Gospel of Jn., which exerted a definite literary influence: in several passages, although not many, I pointed out formulas which are quite Johannine. The same is true of Revelation.

As for the epistles of Paul, they are not foreign to the composition of several verses of the *Sibylline Oracles*, although they are few in number.

Section 4
THE APOCALYPSE OF PETER

Of the *Apocalypse of Peter*, there survive only one Greek passage known as the Akhmîm fragment, discovered by Bouriant in 1886-1887, and several other Greek fragments dispersed in the works of ecclesiastical writers.[174] The complete text of this work was published only in 1910 in an Ethiopic version by S. Grebaut.[175] A German translation based on this Ethiopic version was done by H. Wei-

---

[173]Cf. above, 94.

[174]For these fragments, I follow the edition of E. Klostermann, *Apocrypha 1, Reste des Petrusevangeliums, der Petrusapokalypse und des Kerygma Petri*, KlT 3 (Berlin, 1933) 8-13. See also E. Preuschen, *Antilegomena, Die Reste der ausserkanonischen Evangelien und christlichen Überlieferungen* (Giessen, 1905) 84-88.

[175]S. Grébaut gives the Ethiopic text and the French translation in *Revue de l'Orient Chrétien*, 2nd ser. 5 (15) (1910): 197-214; 307-17; on 318-23, 425-39 of the same review, the author continues his text and translation, but these passages stem from pseudo-Clementine literature and no longer belong to the *Apocalypse of Peter*. (Cf. Altaner, *Patrology*, 83-84.)

nel in the Neutestamentliche Apokryphen in E. Hennecke.[176]

I follow H. Weinel's translation for the passages missing from the Greek text. Obviously, when I identify a literary contact with a text of the New Testament in the Ethiopic version, this contact may be due to the author responsible for the Ethiopic version; indeed, he may have been inspired by a text of the New Testament. The decisive merit of these literary contacts in the Ethiopic version can be ascertained only by comparing them with literary contacts found in the Greek fragments parallel to the Ethiopic version.

Following my usual way of proceeding, I consider in a first paragraph the texts which relate to the Gospel of Mt. A second paragraph is devoted to other New Testament writings.

§1. Saint Matthew

1. Apoc. Pet. 1

And when he was seated on the Mount of Olives, his own came unto him, and we entreated and implored him severally and besought him, saying unto him, "Make known unto us what are the signs of thy Parousia and of the end of the world, that we may perceive and mark the time of thy Parousia and instruct those who come after us, . . ."

This recalls Mt. 24:3 and its parallels Mk. 13:3-4 and Lk. 21:7:

Mt. 24:3: As he sat on the Mount of Olives (καθημένου δὲ αὐτοῦ ἐπὶ τοῦ ὄρους τῶν ἐλαιῶν), the disciples came to him (προσῆλθον αὐτῷ οἱ μαθηταί) privately (κατ' ἰδίαν), saying (λέγοντες), "Tell us (εἰπὲ ἡμῖν), when will this be, and what will be the sign of your coming and of the close of the age (καὶ τί τὸ σημεῖον τῆς σῆς παρουσίας καὶ συντελείας τοῦ αἰῶνος)?"

Mk. 13:3-4: And as he sat on the Mount of Olives (καὶ καθημένου αὐτοῦ εἰς τὸ ὄρος τῶν ἐλαιῶν) opposite the temple, Peter and James and John and Andrew asked him privately (κατ' ἰδίαν), "Tell us (εἰπὸν ἡμῖν) when will this be, and what will be the sign (τί τὸ συμεῖον) when these things are all to be accomplished?"

Lk. 21:7: And they asked him, "Teacher, when will this be, and what will be the sign (καὶ τί τὸ σημεῖον) when this is about to take place?"

---

[176]Cf. H. Weinel, *Offenbarung des Petrus*, in E. Hennecke, *Neutestamentlich Apokryphen* 25, 2nd ed. (Tübingen, 1926) 314-27. [ET: *New Testament Apocrypha*, vol. 2, trans. H. Duensing (Philadephia: Westminster Press, 1965) (Editor's note.)]

An examination of these texts shows, so long as the Ethiopic version is faithful to the original text, that the question of the apostles in the *Apocalypse of Peter* is the same as what is found in Mt., and not what is found in Mk. or Lk.

Elements of this writing are found only in the first gospel. First of all, the expression "the signs of thy Parousia" finds a parallel only in Mt. (τῆς σῆς παρουσίας); Mk. and Lk. merely say: "what will be the sign (τί τὸ σημεῖον)?" Yet, codex D of Lk. reads τῆς σῆς ἐλεύσεως. Next, the mention of the end of the world is found only in Mt. Finally, only Mt. notes, as does the *Apocalypse of Peter*, that Christ, when seated on the Mount of Olives, has disciples who approach him.

2. Apoc. Pet. 1

And our Lord answered and said unto us, "Take heed that men deceive you not and that ye do not become doubters and serve other gods."

The synoptics furnish excellent parallels to this passage.

Mt. 24:4: And Jesus answered them (ἀποκριθείς), "Take heed that no one leads you astray (βλέπετε μή τις ὑμᾶς πλανήσῃ)."

Mk. 13:5: And Jesus began to say to them, "Take heed that no one leads you astray (βλέπετε μή τις ὑμᾶς πλανήσῃ)."

Lk. 21:8: And he said, 'Take heed that you are not led astray (βλέπετε μὴ πλανηθῆτε)."

It is the Matthean text which, here again, is literarily at the basis of the *Apocalypse of Peter*, at least in the Ethiopic version. In fact, Lk. may be excluded since it does not use the construction μή τις which corresponds to "no one"; in addition, Mt. alone, contrary to Mk. and Lk., has the verb ἀποκρίνω which corresponds to "answered" in Apoc. Pet.; finally, the context is still about the discourse of Christ on the Mount of Olives, in which, in the passage previously analysed, I demonstrated why the Matthean text had my preference.

3. Apoc. Pet. 1

Many will come in my name saying "I am the Christ." Believe them not and draw not near unto them.

Still within the context of Christ's great apocalyptic discourse on the Mount of Olives:

Mt. 24:5: For many will come in my name (πολλοὶ γὰρ ἐλεύσονται ἐπὶ τῷ ὀνόματί μου), saying, "I am the Christ" (λέγοντες· ἐγώ εἰμι ὁ Χριστός), and they will lead many astray. 24:26: . . . do not believe it (μὴ πιστεύσητε).

Mk. 13:6: Many will come in my name, saying, "I am he!" (πολλοὶ ἐλεύσονται ἐπὶ τῷ ὀνόματί μου λέγοντες ὅτι ἐγώ εἰμι) and they will lead many astray.

Lk. 21:8: . . . for many will come in my name, saying, "I am he!" (πολλοὶ γὰρ ἐλεύσονται ἐπὶ τῷ ὀνόματί μου λέγοντες· ἐγώ εἰμι) and, "The time is at hand!" Do not go after them (μὴ πορευθῆτε ὀπίσω αὐτῶν).

Here again, the Matthean text was the literary source of the *Apocalypse of Peter*. In fact, the phrase "I am the Christ" is read only in Mt. where the word Χριστός is explicitly mentioned. Moreover, Mt. alone has the words μὴ πιστεύσητε which correspond to "Believe them not" of the *Apocalypse of Peter*. Finally, the context is still the eschatological discourse on the Mount of Olives for which Mt. holds a privileged place. However, there might also be an influence of the text of Lk., which has μὴ πορευθῆτε ὀπίσω αὐτῶν, an expression which might correspond to "draw not near unto them."

4. Apoc. Pet. 1

. . . like the lightning which shineth from the east to the west, so shall I come on the clouds of heaven with a great host in my glory; . . .

Still in the context of the same apocalyptic discourse of Christ in the synoptics, there are close parallels to this passage:

Mt. 24:27: For as the lightning comes from the east and shines as far as the west (ὥσπερ γὰρ ἡ ἀστραπὴ ἐξέρχεται ἀπὸ ἀνατολῶν καὶ φαίνεται ἕως δυσμῶν), so will be the coming of the Son of man. 24:30: . . . then will appear the sign of the Son of man in heaven, and then all the tribes of the earth will mourn, and they will see the Son of man coming on the clouds of heaven with power and great glory (ὄψονται τὸν υἱὸν τοῦ ἀνθρώπου ἐρχόμενον ἐπὶ τῶν νεφελῶν τοῦ οὐρανοῦ μετὰ δυνάμεως καὶ δόξης πολλῆς)."

Mk. 13:26: And then they will see the Son of man coming in clouds with great power and glory (ὄψονται τὸν υἱὸν τοῦ ἀνθρώπου ἐρχόμενον ἐν νεφέλαις μετὰ δυνάμεως πολλῆς καὶ δόξης).

Lk. 17:24: For as the lightning flashes and lights up the sky from one side to the other, so will the Son of man be in his day. 21:27: And they will see the Son of man coming in a cloud with power and great glory (ὄψονται τὸν υἱὸν τοῦ ἀνθρώπου ἐρχόμενον ἐν νεφέλῃ μετὰ δυνάμεως καὶ δόξης πολλῆς).

Lk. 17:24 is not the source of the author, for the expression "from the east to the west" is missing. Only the text of Mt. uses the image of lightning and remains as the literary source of the *Apocalypse of Peter*.

As for the passage on the coming of Christ, Mt. again is the source since it is the only one which has the complete expression of the *Apocalypse of Peter*: "on the clouds of heaven"; Mt. 24:30 actually writes: ἐπὶ τῶν νεφελῶν <u>τοῦ οὐρα-</u>

νοῦ, whereas Mk. 13:26 and Lk. 21:27 have ἐν νεφέλαις and ἐν νεφέλῃ.

H. Weinel notes that the expression "my glory" corresponds to a reading of the text D in Lk. 9:26 as opposed to Mt. 16:27 and Mk. 8:38.[177] Such a comment does not speak in favor of a Lucan influence, since the point deals simply with the glory of Christ. The author has Christ speaking in the first person, and this is how I understand the presence of the expression "my glory."

5. Apoc. Pet. 1

. . . when my Father will place a crown upon my head, that I may judge the living and the dead and recompense every man according to his work.

The role of judge of the living and the dead granted to the Son of God is mentioned also in 2 Tim. 4:1; 1 Pet. 4:5, and in Peter's speech in Acts 10:42. It is difficult to determine upon which of these texts the author may actually depend, since these parallels are very similar. In any case, there is certainly here a theme common in early Christianity on the role of the judge attributed to the Son. It might refer also to Mt. 25:31-34 (cf. βασιλεύς: v. 34).

The *Apocalypse of Peter* continues: ". . . and recompense every man according to his work." Mt. 16:27 expresses this idea of recompense similarly: ". . . he (the Son of man) will repay every man (ἀποδώσει ἑκάστῳ) for what he has done (κατὰ τὴν πρᾶξιν αὐτοῦ)." 1 Pet. 1:17: ". . . him who judges each one impartially according to his deeds (κρίνοντα κατὰ τὸ ἑκάστου ἔργον)" is also a parallel worth noting, but the idea of recompense is not as clearly expressed as in the *Apocalypse of Peter*. Ps. 62 (61):13 and Prov. 24:12 express the idea of recompense, but the expression κατὰ τὰ ἔργα does not correspond as well to the words of the *Apocalypse of Peter* as does Mt.'s κατὰ τὴν πρᾶξιν, "for what he has done," literally "according to his deed." Hence, preference must be given to the Matthean text as the literary basis of this passage. I would like to add that Apoc. Pet. 6 again makes the same statement on reward and in the same terms. There is, therefore, reason to assert that there is, here again, a literary dependence on the text of Mt. 16:27.

6. Apoc. Pet. 2:1

And ye, receive ye the parable of the fig-tree thereon: as soon as its shoots have gone forth and its boughs have sprouted, the end of the world will come.

Several texts of the synoptics are likely parallels to this passage:

---

[177]Cf. Weinel, *Offenbarung des Petrus*, 318.

Mt. 24:32-33: From the fig tree learn its lesson (ἀπὸ δὲ τῆς συκῆς μάθετε τὴν παραβολήν): as soon as its branch becomes tender and puts forth its leaves (ὅταν ἤδη ὁ κλάδος αὐτῆς γένηται ἀπαλὸς καὶ τὰ φύλλα ἐκφύῃ), you know that summer is near. So also, when you see all these things, you know that he is near, at the very gates.

Mk. 13:28-29: From the fig tree learn its lesson (ἀπὸ δὲ τῆς συκῆς μάθετε τὴν παραβολήν): as soon as its branch becomes tender and puts forth its leaves (ὅταν ἤδη ὁ κλάδος αὐτῆς ἀπαλὸς γένηται καὶ ἐκφύῃ τὰ φύλλα), you know that summer is near. So also, when you see these things taking place, you know that he is near, at the very gates.

Lk. 21:29-30: And he told them a parable (παραβολήν): "Look at the fig tree (τὴν συκῆν), and all the trees; as soon as they come out in leaf, you see for yourselves and know that the summer is already near. So also, when you see these things taking place, you know that the kingdom of God is near."

Lk. was not here the source of the *Apocalypse of Peter*; indeed, the introductory statement, "receive ye the parable of the fig tree," is missing; moreover, the Lucan text extends to all trees the parable of the fig tree, and it does not have any clause corresponding to "as soon as its shoots have gone forth," which we do read in Mt. and Mk.

But faced with the similarity between the texts of Mt. and Mk., it is impossible to decide which of the two is the basis for this particular passage of the *Apocalypse of Peter*. Yet, until now, I have consistently found that the author showed considerable fidelity to Mt., but I have never found a text where the influence of Mk. was felt. I am led to believe that the same is true in this case, and that the author follows, here again, the Matthean text.

7. Apoc. Pet. 2

Verily, I say to you: when its boughs have sprouted at the end, then shall deceiving Christs come, and awaken hope (with the words): "I am the Christ, who am (now) come into the world."

When he writes "Verily, I say to you: when its boughs have sprouted at the end," the author takes up the words of the preceding passage. As for the remainder of the text, the assertion "I am the Christ" is sufficient, as stated above,[178] to allow us to believe that the author is literarily dependent on Mt. 24:5, and not on the parallels in Mk. 13:6 and Lk. 21:8.

The last clause, "who am (now) come into the world," may echo Jn. 1:9: "The true light . . . was coming in the world (ἦν τὸ φῶς τὸ ἀληθινόν . . . ἐρχόμενον εἰς τὸν κόσμον)."

---

[178]Cf. above, 100.

8. Apoc. Pet. 2

> Enoch and Elias will be sent to instruct them that this is the deceiver who must
> come into the world and do signs and wonders in order to deceive.

Whereas, generally speaking, a certain parallelism with Mt. 24:24 and Mk. 13:22
may be drawn (ἐγερθήσονται ψευδόχριστοι καὶ ψευδοπροφῆται), there is still
a link to be made with 2 Thess. 2:3-12 and Rev. 19:19-20. In these passages, the
man of lawlessness (2 Thess.) and the beast (Rev.) bring to mind a human being.
Now this text speaks as well of a human being, the deceiver. The author uses,
therefore, a theme known in the early days of Christianity. The gospels do not
seem to be aware of the idea of an individual Antichrist.[179]

9. Apoc. Pet. 3

> And he (Christ) showed me . . . how the righteous and the sinners shall be
> separated. . . .

The same idea of separation between the righteous and the sinners is found in
Mt. 25:32-46, and only in this gospel. The *Apocalypse of Peter* offers a summary.

10. Apoc. Pet. 3

> And I asked him (Christ) and said: "Lord, allow me to speak thy word con-
> cerning these sinners: 'it were better for them that they had not been cre-
> ated'." And the Saviour answered and said: "O Peter, why speakest thou thus,
> 'that not to have been created were better for them'?"

The sentence "it were better for them that they had not been created" recalls
Mt. 26:24: "It would have been better for that man if he had not been born (καλὸν
ἦν αὐτῷ εἰ οὐκ ἐγεννήθη ὁ ἄνθρωπος ἐκεῖνος)" and Mk. 14:21: "It would
have been better for that man if he had not been born (καλὸν [ἦν: D, Θ] αὐτῷ εἰ
οὐκ ἐγεννήθη ὁ ἄνθρωπος ἐκεῖνος)."
It is quite probable that the author of the *Apocalypse of Peter*, inspired by this
text of the gospel, applies it to all sinners and no longer to Judas alone. The identity of the parallel texts is somewhat perplexing, but the fact that the influence of
Mk. in the passages analyzed above is nil causes the scale to tilt in favor of the
Matthean text.

---

[179]Cf. on this subject, F. Amiot, *Saint Paul, Épître aux Galates, Épîtres aux Thes-
saloniciens*, VS 14 (Paris, 1946) 364-73.

11. Apoc. Pet. 6:1

And all will see how I come upon an eternal shining cloud, and the angels of God who will sit with me on the throne of my glory at the right hand of my heavenly Father.

Several texts of the synoptics are parallel to this passage: Mt. 24:30; 25:31; Mk. 13:26; Lk. 21:27 on the one hand, and then again Mt. 16:27; Mk. 8:38 and Lk. 9:26.

Mt. 24:30: . . . and they will see the Son of man coming on the clouds of heaven with power and great glory (ὄψονται τὸν υἱὸν τοῦ ἀνθρώπου ἐρχόμενον ἐπὶ τῶν νεφελῶν τοῦ οὐρανοῦ μετὰ δυνάμεως καὶ δόξης πολλῆς). 25:31: When the Son of man comes in his glory, and all the angels with him, then he will sit on his glorious throne (ὅταν δὲ ἔλθῃ ὁ υἱὸς τοῦ ἀνθρώπου ἐν τῇ δόξῃ αὐτοῦ καὶ πάντες οἱ ἄγγελοι μετ' αὐτοῦ, τότε καθίσει ἐπὶ θρόνου δόξης αὐτοῦ).

Mk. 13:26: And then they will see the Son of man coming in clouds (καὶ τότε ὄψονται τὸν υἱὸν τοῦ ἀνθρώπου ἐρχόμενον ἐν νεφέλαις) with great power and glory.

Lk. 21:27: And then they will see the Son of man coming in a cloud (καὶ τότε ὄψονται τὸν υἱὸν τοῦ ἀνθρώπου ἐρχόμενον ἐν νεφέλῃ) with power and great glory.

Mt. 16:27 and its parallels, Mk. 8:38 and Lk. 9:26 may be excluded from this comparison, since they do not mention the sitting on the throne of glory. In describing the precursory signs of the Parousia, the author of the *Apocalypse of Peter* has set us in the mood of the Matthean texts of Christ's great apocalyptic discourse. Only Mt. 25:31-46 describes the Parousia itself. Mt. 25:31 speaks also of the angels who will accompany the Lord and of the sitting on the throne of glory. The author has, therefore, used Mt. 25:31 as his literary basis.

I also wish to add that the final expression "at the right hand of my heavenly Father" can also be linked with Mt. 26:64; Mk. 14:62 and Lk. 22:69.

12. The Transfiguration

The narrative of this event is present for the most part in the Akhmîm fragment (4-20),[180] and in its entirety in the Ethiopic version (15-17).

Chapter 4 of the Akhmîm fragment introduces the narrative: Καὶ προσθεὶς ὁ κύριος ἔφη· ἄγωμεν εἰς τὸ ὄρος, εὐξώμεθα: "And the Lord continued and said, 'Let us go to the mountain and pray.'" The Ethiopic version gives as a parallel: "And my Lord Jesus Christ, our King, said to me, 'Let us go into the holy moun-

---

[180]Cf. Hennecke-Schneemelcher, 2:680-83.

tain'" (15:1). The *Apocalypse of Peter* may be compared to Mt. 17:1; Mk. 9:2 and Lk. 9:28. Yet, I am inclined to believe that it depends rather on the Lucan text, the only one to mention prayer: ἀνέβη εἰς τὸ ὄρος προσεύξασθαι.

Further on, chapter 6 reads, Καὶ εὐχομένων ἡμῶν ἄφνω φαίνονται δύο ἄνδρες ἑστῶτες ἔμπροσθε τοῦ κυρίου πρὸς οὓς οὐκ ἐδυνήθημεν ἀντιβλέψαι: "And as we prayed, suddenly there appeared two men, standing before the Lord, on whom we were not able to look." The Ethiopic version says: "And behold, there were two men, and we could not look on their faces . . ." The parallels are Mt. 17:2-3; Mk. 9:2, 4; and Lk. 9:29-30, 32. Rather than Mt. or Mk., the literary source of the author might have been the Gospel of Lk., which is the only one to point out, in 9:29, that the Transfiguration takes place while Christ is praying (ἐν τῷ προσεύχεσθαι αὐτόν); the *Apocalypse of Peter* also mentions prayer, but it is a prayer of all the apostles. Moreover, Lk., and again he alone, has the words δυὸ ἄνδρες (9:30, 32). Let me point out, however, that ἔμπροσθεν is absent in the Lucan text, yet present in the *Apocalypse of Peter,* and this presence may proceed from Mt. 17:2 or Mk. 9:2.

The remainder of the Greek text of the narrative of the Transfiguration (7-20) is quite independent of the narrative in the synoptics (Mt. 17:1-9; Mk. 9:2-9; and Lk. 9:28-36). The same applies to the parallel texts of the Ethiopic version (15-16). Only a few elements are likely to be linked more or less to one of the synoptics. Thus chapter 7: ἐξήρχετο γὰρ ἀπὸ τῆς ὄψεως αὐτῶν ἀκτὶν ὡς ἡλίου; the Ethiopic parallel (15) has: "for a light came from them which shone more than the sun. . . . " In Mt. 17:2, it is the face of Christ which shone like the sun.

Chapter 8 of the Akhmîm fragment: οὓς ἰδόντες ἐθαμβώθημεν; the Ethiopic (15) writes: "And when we suddenly saw them, we marvelled." The fear of the apostles is mentioned in Mt. 17:8 and Lk. 9:34 with the verb φοβέω, and in Mk. 9:6 with the adjective ἔκφοβοι.

Chapter 8 of the Akhmîm fragment: τὰ μὲν γὰρ σώματα αὐτῶν ἦν λευκότερα πάσης χιόνος ["For their bodies were whiter than any snow." Editor's addition]; the Ethiopic (15) reads, "and their raiment also was glistening. . . . " The texts we usually read in Mt. 17:2 and Mk. 9:3 mention the whiteness of the garments of Christ. Codex D of these same texts adds that this whiteness was of snow; Lk. 9:29 simply mentions the whiteness of the garment of Christ.

Finally, I would like to point out in Akhmîm 9-20 and in its Ethiopic parallel 15-16 the presence of elements which are absent from the gospels, such as the remarks on the radiance of the garments of those transfigured, on the beauty of their faces, on the pink complexion mingled with the whiteness of their body, on their styled and perfumed hair.

On the whole, it can be said that up to now, in the narrative of the Transfiguration, the author felt quite free and did not seem to have been inspired by any text in particular, although a slight preference might be granted to Lk.

The end of the narrative of the Transfiguration is known to us only through the Ethiopic version (16-17) which I now propose to examine.

Chapter 16 reads, "And I said to him (Christ), 'My Lord, wilt thou that I make here three tabernacles, one for thee, one for Moses, and one for Elias?'"

This passage agrees very well with Mt. 17:4; Mk. 9:5 and Lk. 9:33:

Mt. 17:4: And Peter said to Jesus, "Lord, it is well that we are here; if you wish (εἰ θέλεις), I will make three booths here, one for you and one for Moses and one for Elijah."

Mk. 9:5: And Peter said to Jesus, "Master, it is well that we are here; let us make three booths, one for you and one for Moses and one for Elijah."

Lk. 9:33: And as the men were parting from him, Peter said to Jesus, "Master, it is well that we are here; let us make three booths: one for you and one for Moses and one for Elijah."

Lk. 9:33 (codex D): And, as they were parting from him, Peter said to Jesus, "Master, it is well that we are here; do you wish that I make (θέλεις ποιήσω) three booths here: one for you and one for Moses and one for Elijah."

Mk. 9:5 was not used as a source by the author of the *Apocalypse of Peter*, because we do not find in his text the words "do you wish"; the same goes for the usual reading of Lk. 9:33. On the other hand, Mt. 17:4 as well as the reading of D of Lk. 9:33 have the words "if you wish" or "do you wish," which are found in this passage. The similarity between Mt. and Lk. (D) prevents me from deciding which one of the two influenced the *Apocalypse of Peter*. It is, however, likely that it is Mt. The harmonizing variant of Lk. simply shows that the text of Mt. was well known.

Chapter 17 reads, "And behold there came suddenly a voice from heaven saying: 'This is my Son, whom I love and in whom I have pleasure. . . .'"

In the context of the Transfiguration, these words recall the texts of the synoptics:

Mt. 17:5: . . . and a voice from the cloud said, "This is my beloved Son, with whom I am well pleased (καὶ ἰδοὺ φωνὴ ἐκ τῆς νεφέλης λέγουσα· οὗτός ἐστιν ὁ υἱός μου ὁ ἀγαπητός, ἐν ᾧ εὐδόκησα); listen to him."

Mk. 9:7: . . . and a voice came out of the cloud, "This is my beloved Son (καὶ ἐγένετο φωνὴ ἐκ τῆς νεφέλης· οὗτός ἐστιν ὁ υἱός μου ὁ ἀγαπητός); listen to him."

Lk. 9:35: And a voice came out of the cloud, saying, "This is my Son, my Chosen (καὶ φωνὴ ἐγένετο ἐκ τῆς νεφέλης λέγουσα· οὗτός ἐστιν ὁ υἱός μου ὁ ἐκλελεγμένος); listen to him!"

Codex D has here again a special reading for Lk. 9:35:

Lk 9:35 (codex D): And a voice came out of the cloud saying, "This is my beloved Son in whom I am well pleased (καὶ φωνὴ ἦλθεν ἐκ τῆς νεφέλης λέγουσα˙ οὗτός ἐστιν ὁ υἱός μου ὁ ἀγαπητός ἐν ᾧ ηὐδόκησα); listen to him."

The text of Mk. and the standard text of Lk. cannot have been a source of the *Apocalypse of Peter,* because they do not mention the words ἐν ᾧ εὐδόκησα, which are present in this Apocalypse. Only Mt. 17:5 has these words and is the literary source. Codex D of Lk., a harmonizing reading, indicates here again that Mt. was well known.

Chapter 17 reads, "And there came a great and exceeding white cloud over our heads and bore away (from sight) our Lord and Moses and Elias."

The synoptics point out this detail:

Mt. 17:5: He was still speaking, when lo, a bright cloud (νεφέλη φωτεινή) overshadowed them (ἐπεσκίασεν). . . .

Mk. 9:7: And a cloud (νεφέλη) overshadowed them (ἐπισκιάζουσα). . . .

Lk. 9:34: As he said this, a cloud (νεφέλη) came and overshadowed them (ἐπεσκίαζεν). . .

Once again, only Mt. has in his text φωτεινή, which corresponds to "exceedinly white" in the *Apocalypse of Peter.* Again, it is probable that the author was inspired by the Matthean text.

Let me again point out in chapter 16: "And he said to me in wrath, 'Satan maketh war against thee . . .'" This saying of Christ recalls Mt. 16:23 and Mk. 8:33. The parallelism is not very close, but it can be assumed that there is here an echo of this saying of Christ to Peter. Furthermore, in the absence of another reference to Mk. in the *Apocalypse of Peter,* preference may be given to the Matthean text.

As a whole, in the Greek text as well as in the Ethiopic version of the narrative of the Transfiguration, the author takes considerable liberty with respect to the gospel narrative. The Greek text and its Ethiopic parallel perhaps reveal a slight preference for Lk., whereas, in those passages that are peculiar to it, the Ethiopic version is clearly under the influence of Mt. It is quite possible that the original combined the texts of Mt. and Lk.

Except for the narrative of the Transfiguration, all the passages of the *Apocalypse of Peter* that I just examined are drawn from the Ethiopic version of this work, and none of them has a parallel in the Greek fragments known to date. In this Ethiopic version, I have pointed out a considerable number of texts which are literarily dependent on the Gospel of Mt. and which testify to the powerful influence which this gospel has exercised. Quite often, the author of the *Apocalypse of Peter* is content to take up almost literally the Matthean texts.

My conclusions touch only indirectly on the original Greek text, since it is still possible that the Ethiopic translator was under the influence of the text of Mt. I would like, at least, to point out that the *Apocalypse of Peter* led the Ethiopic translator to the first gospel.

§2. The Other New Testament Writings

Among the other New Testament writings which had some influence on the composition of the *Apocalypse of Peter*, special attention must be devoted to the Gospel of Lk. For this reason I consider it separately.

A. The Gospel of Luke

In the Ethiopic version of the *Apocalypse of Peter*, the parable of the barren fig tree (chapter 2) is linked with the third gospel:

Even as a man (from the house of Israel) hath planted a fig tree in his garden and it brought forth no fruit, and he sought its fruit for many years. When he found it not, he said to the keeper of his garden, "Uproot the fig tree that our land may not be unfruitful for us." And the gardener said to God, "We thy servants (?) wish to clear it (of weeds) and to dig the ground around it and to water it. If it does not then bear fruit, we will immediately remove its roots from the garden and plant another one in its place."

This parable of the fig tree is read only in the Gospel of Lk. in 13:6-9. The *Apocalypse of Peter* is literarily dependent on it. The text of Lk. served as a basis for the author. I propose merely to point out the evidence of this literary dependence. "A man hath planted a fig tree in his garden" corresponds to Lk. 13:6: συκῆν εἶχέν τις πεφυτευμένην ἐν τῷ ἀμπελῶνι αὐτοῦ. "And he sought its fruit for many years" agrees with Lk. 13:6: ἦλθεν ζητῶν καρπὸν ἐν αὐτῇ, and Lk. 13:7: ἰδοὺ τρία ἔτη ἀφ' οὗ ἔρχομαι ζητῶν καρπόν. "When he found it not" recalls οὐχ εὗρεν of Lk. 13:6 and οὐκ εὑρίσκω of Lk. 13:7. "He said to the keeper of his garden, 'Uproot the fig-tree that our land may not be unfruitful for us'" imitates the style of Lk. 13:7: ἔκκοψον αὐτήν ἰνατί καὶ τὴν γῆν καταργεῖ. Finally, "And the gardener said to God, 'We thy servants wish to clear it of weeds and to dig the ground around it and to water it. If it does not then bear fruit, we will immediately remove its roots from the garden and plant another one in its place'" is a development taken from the text of Lk. 13:8-9: "And he answered him, 'Let it alone, sir, this year also, till I dig about it and put on manure. And if it bears fruit next year, well and good; but if not, you can cut it down.'"

I would also like to point out that the statement in Apoc. Pet. 1:5, "For the coming of the Son of God will not be manifest," echoes Lk. 17:20: "The kingdom of God is not coming with signs to be observed."

The Ethiopic version leads us to assume that the *Apocalypse of Peter* was under the literary influence of the Gospel of Lk. It takes up the parable of the fig tree, which it follows almost literally. This conclusion is just as valid for the Greek text of the *Apocalypse of Peter* insofar as this Greek text has been faithfully translated by the author of the Ethiopic version.

B. The Remainder of the New Testament Writings

Not a single passage of the *Apocalypse of Peter* shows the least literary dependence on Mk. The same is true with respect to the Gospel of Jn.

As for the Revelation of John, it must be pointed out that, in all probablity, it influenced the composition of Apoc. Pet. 4, which reads: ". . . and he will command hell to open its bars of steel and to give up all that is in it." Also in the context of the last judgment, Rev. 20:13 reads, "Death and Hades gave up their dead (τοὺς ἐν αὐτοῖς). . . ."

Let me again point out Apoc. Pet. 17: "And we prayed and went down from the mountain, and we praised God who hath written the names of the righteous in heaven in the book of life." "The book of life" is an expression well known from the Book of the Revelation of John.[181]

As for the Pauline literature, I have already mentioned above[182] in connection with the deceiver the use of a primitive Christian theme, evidence for which is found in 2 Thess. 2:3-12.

I may also stress that, when Apoc. Pet. states in chapter 4: "Behold and consider the corns of wheat which are sown in the earth," in a context that speaks of the resurrection of the dead, it uses the same image as Paul does in 1 Cor. 15:36.

Finally, when Apoc. Pet. 14 mentions "the portion of the righteous," it uses an expression fairly similar to Col. 1:12: ἡ μερὶς τοῦ κλήρου τῶν ἁγίων.

As a result, as much as the Ethiopic version allows a definite conclusion, two writings of the New Testament have especially had a literary influence on the *Apocalypse of Peter*: the Gospel of Mt. and the Gospel of Lk.

The Gospel of Mt. played a very important role. In almost every case in the Ethiopic version, this gospel has been the basis of the passages which can be compared to the gospels, except for the parable of the barren fig tree, which is absent from Mt. and for which the author has turned to the Lucan text. The Greek narrative of the Transfiguration and its Ethiopic parallel reveal a slight preference for Lk.; yet, in the same narrative, the passages peculiar to the Ethiopic version are under the literary influence of the first gospel. It is, therefore, most probable that the author combined the texts of Mt. and Lk.

---

[181]Cf. Rev. 3:5; 13:8; 17:8; 20:12, 15; 21:27.

[182]Cf. above, 104.

It is obvious that, when the author of the *Apocalypse of Peter* used the first gospel, he leaned quite heavily on the text of Mt. and cited it almost literally, but he, nevertheless, did not refer to it explicitly.

Section 5
THE SHEPHERD OF HERMAS

This section is devoted to a very long work, the *Shepherd of Hermas*, which may be classified among the apocalypses. It contains, in fact, many revelations. My focus of interest leads me to consider separately, first the literary relationships between the *Shepherd of Hermas* and the Gospel of Mt.; a second paragraph will deal with the other New Testament writings.

§1. Saint Matthew

Despite its scope, the *Shepherd of Hermas*[183] contains very few passages which show a definite literary influence from Mt. On the other hand, ideas parallel to the synoptics are found in many places, but it is practically impossible to determine whether these parallels have influenced Hermas in his composition and, accordingly, to which one of the gospels the leading role belongs. In many cases, the question remains whether Hermas simply takes up a traditional idea that is merely witnessed by the synoptics.

This is why, in this paragraph devoted to the Gospel of Mt., I consider first the texts of the *Shepherd*, in which the Matthean influence is definite or very probable; I then proceed to the passages where texts of Mt. are among possible parallels, and I finally go on to those places in which the influence of the first gospel is to be excluded.

A. Texts for Which the Influence of Matthew Is Definite or Very Probable

1. Vis. 1.1.8[184]

'Επὶ τὴν καρδίαν σου ἀνέβη ἡ ἐπιθυμία τῆς πονηρίας. ἢ οὐ δοκεῖ σοι ἀνδρὶ δικαίῳ πονηρὸν πρᾶγμα εἶναι, ἐὰν ἀναβῇ αὐτοῦ ἐπὶ τὴν καρδίαν ἡ πονηρὰ ἐπιθυμία; ἁμαρτία γέ ἐστιν, καὶ μεγάλη, φησίν.

"In your heart there has arisen the desire for evil. Surely, you think that it is

---

[183]For the text of the *Shepherd of Hermas*, I follow the edition of A. Lelong, *Le Pasteur d'Hermas*, Greek text, French translation, introduction and index, *Textes et Documents, Les Frères Apostoliques* 4 (Paris, 1912); I also draw from the translation of this author. See also P. Bonner, *A Papyrus Codex of the Shepherd of Hermas (Simil. 2-9) with a Fragment of the Mandates* (Ann Arbor MI, 1934). [The English text of the *Sheperd of Hermas*, trans. Joseph M.-F. Marique, is taken from *The Apostolic Fathers*, trans. Francis X. Glimm, Joseph M.-F. Marique, and Gerald Walsh, *The Fathers of the Church, A New Translation*, vol. 1 (Washington: The Catholic University of America Press, 1962). Editor's note.]

[184]I set this text in the first part of this paragraph, because only Mt. states a similar teaching, even though its influence is not absolutely certain in this instance.

evil that an evil desire arises in the heart of a good man. It is a sin,'' she said, ''yes, a great sin.''

In this first vision, Hermas sees once more the woman to whom his master had sold him, whom he had loved and wished to marry. This Rhode—so was she called—appears to him and accuses him of having sinned against her. Hermas denies it, and Rhode replies with the above-mentioned text.

The idea of sin through desire recalls a passage characteristic of Mt. in the Sermon on the Mount. Indeed, Mt. 5:28 reads, ἐγὼ δὲ λέγω ὑμῖν ὅτι πᾶς ὁ βλέπων γυναῖκα πρὸς τὸ ἐπιθυμῆσαι αὐτὴν ἤδη ἐμοίχευσεν αὐτὴν ἐν τῇ καρδίᾳ αὐτοῦ. Evil desire alone is already adultery, and thus a sin.

Except for ἐπιθυμία in Hermas, which may be compared with ἐπιθυμῆσαι in Mt., and the presence here and there of καρδία, there is not the slightest resemblance between Hermas and Mt. from the standpoint of words and expressions.

Given the dissimilarity of these texts, it is not necessary to look for an influence of Mt. in Hermas' teaching of sin through simple desire; indeed, this teaching might have gained acceptance by that time. Yet, it is important to point out that it is characteristic of Mt. in the New Testament. Hence, the first gospel may very well have been its source.

2. Mand. 4.1.1

Ἐντέλλομαί σοι, φησίν, φυλάσσειν τὴν ἁγνείαν, καὶ μὴ ἀναβαινέτω σου ἐπὶ τὴν καρδίαν περὶ γυναικὸς ἀλλοτρίας ἢ περὶ πορνείας τινὸς ἢ περὶ τοιούτων τινῶν ὁμοιομάτων πονηρῶν. τοῦτο γὰρ ποιῶν μεγάλην ἁμαρτίαν ἐργάζῃ.

"I command you," he said, "to guard purity. Let it not enter your heart to think of another man's wife, nor about fornication, nor any such thing. If you do, you will commit a serious sin."

Hermas takes up here, in a different form, the same teaching given in Vis. 1.1.8; the parallel to point out is again Mt. 5:28, which may be the source of this teaching which the *Shepherd* propounds.

Dibelius sees in the words of Hermas a legacy from non-Christian parenesis; for example, Pseudo-Phocylides states, στέργε τεὴν ἄλοχον· τί γὰρ ἡδύτερον καὶ ἄρειον, ἢ ὅταν ἀνδρὶ γυνὴ φρονέῃ φίλα γήραος ἄχρις καὶ πόσις ἢ ἀλόχῳ.[185] Yet, the pagans' interest is not so much in chastity per se as in the pleasure of life. Hermas is actually a Christian. The Oxford Committee also points out the similarity with Mt. 5:28.[186]

---

[185]M. Dibelius, *Der Hirt des Hermas*, HNT/E 4 (Tübingen, 1923) 505.

[186]Cf. A Committee of the Oxford Society, *The New Testament in the Apostolic Fathers*, 121.

3. Mand. 6.2.4

Ὅρα νῦν καὶ τοῦ ἀγγέλου τῆς πονηρίας τὰ ἔργα. πρῶτον πάντων ὀξύχολός ἐστι καὶ πικρὸς καὶ ἄφρων, καὶ τὰ ἔργα αὐτοῦ πονηρά, καταστρέφοντα τοὺς δούλους τοῦ θεοῦ· ὅταν οὖν οὗτος ἐπὶ τὴν καρδίαν σου ἀναβῇ, γνῶθι αὐτὸν ἀπὸ τῶν ἔργων αὐτοῦ.

Now observe the deeds of the angel of wickedness. First of all, he is of a violent temper, bitter, and silly. His deeds are evil, the undoing of the servants of God. So, when he enters your heart, know him from his deeds.

The last statement recalls surprisingly the words of Mt. 7:16 and Lk. 6:44. This is where Mt. speaks of the distinction between true and false prophets who will be distinguished by their deeds: ἀπὸ τῶν καρπῶν αὐτῶν ἐπιγνώσεσθε αὐτούς. Lk. 6:44 states ἕκαστον γὰρ δένδρον ἐκ τοῦ ἰδίου καρποῦ γινώσκεται in a parable inserted in a context which describes the behavior required of disciples of Christ.

A similarity of thought between Hermas and these two gospel passages is undeniable, and a literary influence of the Matthean text is very probable. First of all, in fact, ἀπὸ τῶν καρπῶν αὐτῶν of Mt. may correspond to ἀπὸ τῶν ἔργων αὐτοῦ in Hermas, and ἐπιγνώσεσθε of Mt. may have inspired γνῶθι in Hermas. Moreover, the Matthean text is concerned with the distinction between true and false prophets; the context of the Shepherd is also concerned with telling the difference between the angel of justice and the angel of wickedness. Besides, Lk. states that the tree is known by its fruit. I must finally add, however, that when Lk. uses the preposition ἐκ instead of ἀπό, and when he adds ἰδίου, it does not favor the possibility of a literary influence on Hermas.

4. Mand. 11.16

Ἔχεις ἀμφοτέρων τῶν προφητῶν τὴν ζωήν· δοκίμαζε οὖν ἀπὸ τῶν ἔργων καὶ τῆς ζωῆς τὸν ἄνθρωπον τὸν λέγοντα ἑαυτὸν πνευματοφόρον εἶναι.

The life of the two kinds of prophets has just been given you. Test, then, by life and actions the man who says he is inspired.

This recalls again Mt. 7:16 and Lk. 6:44.

Notwithstanding the absence of the verb γιγνώσκω and the addition of the substantive ἡ ζωή in the text of Hermas, the similarity of thought with the texts of the gospels is indubitable. If we consider the presence of the term προφητῶν and the fact that Hermas discusses the distinction between true and false prophets, it becomes obvious that he is much closer to Mt. than to Lk.

5. Mand. 12.1.2

. . . (ἡ ἐπιθυμία ἡ πονηρὰ) δαπανᾷ δὲ τοὺς τοιούτους τοὺς μὴ ἔχοντας ἔνδυμα τῆς ἐπιθυμίας τῆς ἀγαθῆς, ἀλλὰ ἐμπεφυρμένους τῷ αἰῶνι τούτῳ· τούτους οὖν παραδίδωσιν εἰς θάνατον.

For, evil desire is fierce and is tamed with difficulty; it is fearsome in its ferocity and wastes men. In particular, if a servant of God becomes entangled in it and has no prudence, it works dreadful havoc with him. But it costs a heavy price to those who have not the cloak of good desire and are engrossed with this world. Such men it hands over to death. [Editor's addition]

The Oxford Committee refers to Mt. 22:11-13, pointing out that this passage of Hermas may have been suggested by the parable of the marriage feast, but that the similarity is rather loose.[187]

The presence of the word ἔνδυμα in Hermas was probably the reason for the agreement with Mt. 22:11-13. Although the text of Hermas is in contact with Stoicism,[188] I agree with Dibelius that the image which is traditionally depicted in Stoicism with the verb δαπανᾶν is missing. The Stoa usually says, διαφεύγει γὰρ οὐδὲν . . . τὴν ἐπιθυμίαν, ἀλλ' οἷα φλὸξ ἐν ὕλῃ νέμεται δαπανῶσα πάντα καὶ φθείρουσα.[189] It is, therefore, possible that Hermas was inspired more or less by the gospel parable. However, comparison with a garment is not that unusual.

6. Sim. 3.3 is a prelude to the following *Similitude,* and together they form a literary unit.[190]

In the preamble of the pericope, Hermas puts forward the thought that the righteous and sinners are not differentiated in this world. In Sim. 4, he states that this distinction will be possible in the future world.

Many authors, after recalling that Sim. 3 and Sim. 4.3 are quoted by Origen in his commentary on Mt. 24:32,[191] refer as a rule to the parable of the good wheat and the weeds in Mt. 13:24-30 and to its explanation in Mt. 13:38-40, adding that the passage in Hermas may surely have been suggested by the parable of the weeds, since the general idea is similar. They further note that it is Hermas's custom to transform the ideas he uses and to adapt them to his own composition.[192] The par-

---

[187]Cf. ibid., 119.

[188]Cf. M. Dibelius, *Der Hirt des Hermas,* 544.

[189]Cf. ibid., 544.

[190]Cf. Lelong, *Le Pasteur d'Hermas,* 148; Dibelius, *Der Hirt des Hermas,* 557-58.

[191]Cf. Origen, *Comment. in Mt.,* PG 13:1683.

[192]Cf. F. X. Funk, *Patres apostolici,* vol. 1 (Tübingen, 1901) 527; O. De Gebhardt and A. Harnack, *Hermae Pastor graece addita versione latina recentiore e codice Palatino, Patrum Apostolicorum Opera* 3 (Leipzig, 1887) 139; A Committee of the Oxford Society, *The New Testament in the Apostolic Fathers,* 119.

able of the weeds and the good wheat is peculiar to Mt.

Sim. 3.3

῞Ωσπερ γὰρ ἐν τῷ χειμῶνι τὰ δένδρα, ἀποβεβληκότα τὰ φύλλα, ὅμοιά εἰσι καὶ οὐ φαίνονται τὰ ξηρὰ ποῖά εἰσιν ἢ τὰ ζῶντα, οὕτως ἐν τῷ αἰῶνι τούτῳ οὐ φαίνονται οὔτε οἱ δίκαιοι οὔτε οἱ ἁμαρτωλοί, ἀλλὰ πάντες ὅμοιοί εἰσιν.

For, just as in winter trees that have shed their leaves are alike and do not look dry, as they really are, or living, so in this world neither the just nor sinners look as they are, but all are alike.

Mt. 13:24-30 is usually given as a parallel to this kind of prelude: weeds are shown as growing in the midst of good wheat; the master of the field forbids the removal of the weeds for fear of uprooting the good seeds as well, urging to wait for harvest time. A general idea similar to that of Hermas may be acknowledged: in this age—Mt. explains and stresses that the harvest is the consummation of the age—weeds (evil), and good wheat (the righteous) grow together and cannot be removed separately. In winter, says Hermas, trees shed their leaves; the shriveled and the living cannot be recognized; it is the same in the present age: sinners and righteous are mixed together and cannot be distinguished.

But in the other world it is summer, continues Hermas in Sim. 4.2-4, and in summer the living trees are in bloom and the shriveled ones are without leaves:

"Those that are in bloom," he said, "are the just (οἱ δίκαιοί εἰσιν), destined to live in the world to come (εἰς τὸν αἰῶνα τὸν ἐρχόμενον). For, the world to come is summer (θερεία) for the just (τοῖς δικαίοις), but it is winter (χειμών) for sinners (τοῖς δὲ ἁμαρτωλοῖς). When the Lord's mercy shines forth, then will God's servants be made manifest. So will all be made manifest. Just as in summer the fruits of every single tree come to light and we know what they are, so will the fruits of the just (τῶν δικαίων) be manifest, and it will be known that all are flourishing in that (future) world. Pagans and sinners (οἱ ἁμαρτωλοί), the dry trees you see, will be found to be dry and fruitless in that world. They will be burned (κατακαυθήσονται) as firewood and will be manifest, because their activity in life was wicked. Sinners (οἱ ἁμαρτωλοί) will be burned (καυθήσονται) because they sinned without repenting; pagans, because they did not know their Creator."

Although some details find more or less exact similarities in other New Testament texts, Hermas's general idea is an easy parallel to Mt. 13:30, 38, 40.

The distinction will be made between the righteous and sinners, between blossoming trees and withered trees fit to be burned. In Mt., at harvest time which is the fullness of time, the weeds will be separated from the wheat and thrown into the fire; the weeds represent the ungodly who will be thrown into the fire (Mt.

13:40). The comparison between the last day and the blossoming trees is found in Mt. 24:32 and in its parallels, Mk. 13:28 and Lk. 21:30. Finally, the mention that the tree is known by its fruit is found in Mt. 7:16-19 and Lk. 6:43-44.

7. Sim. 5.2

[1] Let me tell you the parable I have in mind relative to fasting. [2] A man had a field and numerous servants. One part of the field he planted as a vineyard (ἐφύτευσεν ἀμπελῶνα). Then he chose a dependable, respected, and honest servant, summoned him and said, ''Take this vineyard I planted and fence it in till I come. Do not do anything else to the vineyard. Do this and you will receive from me your freedom.'' Then the master of that slave went off to a foreign country (ἐξῆλθε δὲ ὁ δεσπότης τοῦ δούλου εἰς τὴν ἀποδη-μίαν). [3] When he had left, the slave took the vineyard and fenced it in (ἐχ-αράκωσε τὸν ἀμπελῶνα). After finishing it, he noticed that the vineyard was full of weeds. [4] He thought the matter over to himself and said (ἐν ἑαυτῷ οὖν ἐλογίσατο λέγων), ''I have done what my master ordered. I shall next dig this vineyard; it will be neater after having been dug. Without weeds it will yield more fruit, since the fruit will not be choked by weeds (μὴ πνιγό-μενος ὑπὸ τῶν βοτανῶν).'' So he went and dug the vineyard and plucked up all the weeds that were in it. Then the vineyard became very neat and flour-ishing, without any weeds to choke it. [5] After a while the master of the slave and of the field returned (μετὰ χρόνον ἦλθεν ὁ δεσπότης τοῦ δούλου καὶ τοῦ ἀγροῦ) to his vineyard. When he saw that the vineyard had been fenced in properly and, over and above this, had been dug and cleared of weeds and that the vines were flourishing, he was exceedingly glad at the work of his slave. [6] So, he summoned his beloved son who was his heir (τὸν υἱὸν αὐ-τοῦ τὸν ἀγαπητόν, ὃν εἶχε κληρονόμον) and his friends who were his ad-visers and told them what he had ordered his slave to do and what he found. They, also, were happy at the master's testimony in favor of his slave. [7] The latter said to them, ''I promised freedom to this slave, if he observed the order I gave him. He has kept my order and, besides, to my great pleasure, has done a good work in the vineyards. [8] So, as a reward for this, I wish to make him joint heir with my son (θέλω αὐτὸν συγκληρονόμον τῷ υἱῷ μου ποιῆσαι) because, when the good thought came, he did not neglect it, but put it into execution.'' With this intention of his the son of the master agreed: the slave should be joint heir. [9] A few days later, his master had a banquet (δεῖπνον ἐποίησεν ὁ οἰκοδεσπότης αὐτοῦ), and sent him many dainties from the feast. The slave, however, took from the dainties sent him by his master only what was sufficient for himself and distributed the remainder to his fellow slaves. [10] Then the fellow slaves, in their joy at receiving the dainties, began pray-ing in his behalf, that he might find even greater favor with his master, for he treated them so well. [11] All this his master heard, and once more was ex-ceedingly pleased with his conduct. So, he called together his friends once more and his son, and let them know what he had done with the dainties he

had received. Those called together were all the more agreed that he should be joint heir with the son (συνευδόκησαν γενέσθαι τὸν δοῦλον συγκληρονόμον τῷ υἱῷ αὐτοῦ).

This *Similitude* has parallels in the synoptics and in the Old Testament: the parable of the vineyard in Mt. 21:33-42; Mk. 12:1-12; Lk. 20:9-19; Is. 5:1-2; Jer. 2:21; the parable of the talents in Mt. 25:14-31; Lk. 19:12-27; and the parable of the sower in Mt. 13:7; Mk. 4:7; Lk. 8:7. Other parallels are also sometimes indicated: Mt. 13:24; Mk. 13:34; Lk. 12:17.

The following table, which points out these parallels, demonstrates that Hermas was inspired by the three parables mentioned.

Sim. 5.2.2:	ἐφύτευσεν ἀμπελῶνα	—Jer. 2:21: ἐγὼ δὲ ἐφύτευσά σε ἄμπελον —Is. 5:1: ἐφύτησα ἄμπελον	
		—Mt. 21:33: ἐφύτευσεν ἀμπελῶνα —Mk. 12:1: ἀμπελῶνα . . . ἐφύτευσεν —Lk. 20:9: ἐφύτευσεν ἀμπελῶνα	in the parable of the vineyard
	εἰς τὴν ἀποδημίαν	—Mt. 21:33: ἀπεδήμησεν —Mk. 12:1: ἀπεδήμησεν —Lk. 20:9: ἀπεδήμησεν	in the parable of the vineyard
		—Mt. 25:14: ἀποδημῶν —Mt. 25:15: ἀπεδήμησεν —Mk. 13:34: ἀπόδημος	in the parable of the talents
Sim. 5.2.3:	ἐχαράκωσε τὸν ἀμπελῶνα	—Is. 5:2: ἐχαράκωσα	
Sim. 5.2.4:	ἐν ἑαυτῷ οὖν ἐλογίσατο λέγων	—Lk. 12:17: διελογίζετο ἐν ἑαυτῷ λέγων	
	μὴ πνιγόμενος ὑπὸ τῶν βοτανῶν	—Mt. 13:7: καὶ ἀνέβησαν αἱ ἄκανθαι καὶ ἀπέπνιξαν αὐτά —Mk. 4:7: καὶ ἀνέβησαν αἱ ἄκανθαι καὶ συνέπνιξαν αὐτό —Lk. 8:7: καὶ συμφυεῖσαι αἱ ἄκανθαι ἀπέπνιξαν αὐτό	in the parable of the sower
Sim. 5.2.5:	μετὰ χρόνον ἦλθεν ὁ δεσπότης τοῦ δούλου . . .	—Mt. 25:19: μετὰ δὲ πολὺν χρόνον ἔρχεται ὁ κύριος τῶν δούλων ἐκείνων	in the parable of the talents
Sim. 5.2.6:	τὸν υἱὸν αὐτοῦ τὸν ἀγαπητόν	—Mt. 21:37: τὸν υἱὸν αὐτοῦ —Mk. 12:6: υἱὸν ἀγαπητόν —Lk. 20:13: τὸν υἱόν μου τὸν ἀγαπητόν	in the parable of the vineyard
	ὃν εἶχε κληρονόμον	—Mt. 21:38: οὗτός ἐστιν ὁ κληρονόμος· δεῦτε ἀποκτείνωμεν αὐτὸν καὶ σχῶμεν τὴν κληρονομίαν αὐτοῦ	
		—Mk. 12:7: . . . ὅτι οὗτός ἐστιν ὁ κληρονόμος . . . καὶ ἡμῶν ἔσται ἡ κληρονομία —Lk. 20:14: . . . οὗτός ἐστιν ὁ κληρονόμος . . . ἵνα ἡμῶν γένηται ἡ κληρονομία	in the parable of the vineyard

Sim. 5.2.7: συγκληρονόμον τῷ υἱῷ μου ποιῆσαι: cf. Sim. 5.2.6

Sim. 5.2.9:	ἐποίσεν	—Mt. 13:27: οἱ δοῦλοι τοῦ οἰκοδεσπό-	in the parable
	ὁ οἰκοδεσπότης αὐτοῦ	του	of the sower
		—Mt. 21:33: ἄνθρωπος ἦν οἰκοδεσπότης	in the parable
		ὅστις	of the vineyard

Sim. 5.2.11.: τὸν δοῦλον συγκληρονόμον τῷ υἱῷ αὐτοῦ: cf. Sim. 5.2.6

Such are the possible parallels, based on the presence in Hermas of words and expressions of the synoptics. I must add the indubitable similarity of thought: the planting of the vineyard, the attitude of the slave comparable to that of the good servant in the parable of talents, the choking of the vineyard by weeds identical to the choking of the good seed by thorns.

An examination of the preceding table reveals that only Mt. has the parable of the talents and the term οἰκοδεσπότης in the parables of the sower and of the vineyard. On the other hand, he uses neither the phrase ἐχαράκωσε τὸν ἀμπελῶνα of Sim. 5.2.3, which is also absent in all the synoptics, nor the words ἐν ἑαυτῷ ἐλογίσατο λέγων in Sim. 5.2.4, which have a parallel only in Lk. 12:17 and whose context is other than the parables, nor the term τὸν ἀγαπητόν in Sim. 5.2.6, which is present in the two other synoptics.

Mk. lacks the parable of the talents, the term οἰκοδεσπότης in the parables of the sower and of the vineyard, the phrase ἐχαράκωσε τὸν ἀμπελῶνα of Sim. 5.2.3, and the words ἐν ἑαυτῷ ἐλογίσατο λέγων of Sim. 5.2.4. On the other hand, Mk. has the word ἀγαπητόν of Sim. 5.2.6.

As for Lk., he uses neither the parable of the talents, nor the word οἰκοδεσπότης of the parables of the sower and of the vineyard, nor the expression ἐχαράκωσε τὸν ἀμπελῶνα of Sim. 5.2.3. But he uses in 12:17 the words διελογίζετο ἐν ἑαυτῷ λέγων, which are parallel to ἐν ἑαυτῷ ἐλογίσατο λέγων of Sim. 5.2.4, and he has the term τὸν ἀγαπητόν of Sim. 5.2.6.

When Mt. is compared with the other synoptics, the odds are, as a whole, very much in his favor. It follows then that Hermas drew his inspiration from the Matthean parables which he freely developed, influenced as well by expressions taken from Isaiah, Lk. or Mk. The author does not slavishly follow the text of Mt.; it is rather the foundation upon which he builds his own parable, while probably taking the phrase ἐχαράκωσε τὸν ἀμπελῶνα from Isaiah, the words ἐν ἑαυτῷ οὖν ἐλογίσατο λέγων possibly from Lk., and the term τὸν ἀγαπητόν from Lk. or Mk.

This way of thinking is corroborated by Hermas himself in Sim. 5.5.2, a text which gives specifically a second explanation of the parable proposed in Sim. 5.2, the first having been given in Sim. 5.3. It reads, ὁ ἀγρὸς ὁ κόσμος οὗτός ἐστιν· ὁ δὲ κύριος τοῦ ἀγροῦ ὁ κτίσας τὰ πάντα: "The field is this world. The lord of the field is the One who has created everything. . . . " Now, here again, when Mt. explains the parable of the sower, he also writes in 13:38, ὁ δὲ ἀγρός ἐστιν ὁ κόσμος. This explanation is peculiar to Mt. I have shown that, in Sim. 5.2, Hermas seems to have drawn his inspiration from the three parables of the Matthean text, one of which is the parable of the sower. As Hermas explains here his own parable, he draws from the explanation of the parable of the sower which Mt. provides. It follows then that he was already influenced by Mt. when he proposed the *Similitude*.

8. Sim. 6.3.6

. . . λαμβάνοντες παρὰ τοῦ κυρίου πάντα ὅσα ἂν αἰτῶνται.

. . . receiving from the Lord everything they (those who have made penance) ask for.

A similar idea, in almost identical terms, is expressed in Mt. 21:22: καὶ πάντα ὅσα ἂν αἰτήσητε ἐν τῇ προσευχῇ πιστεύοντες λήμψεσθε; in Mk. 11:24: διὰ τοῦτο λέγω ὑμῖν, πάντα ὅσα προσεύχεσθε καὶ αἰτεῖσθε, πιστεύετε ὅτι ἐλάβετε καὶ ἔσται ὑμῖν; and in 1 Jn. 3:22: καὶ ὃ ἐὰν αἰτῶμεν λαμβάνομεν ἀπ' αὐτοῦ. A literary influence from 1 John is excluded, because the formula πάντα ὅσα is missing. On the other hand, both Mt. and Mk. have the words of Hermas: αἰτέω, λαμβάνω, πάντα ὅσα. One clue may tilt the scale in favor of a Matthean influence: πάντα ὅσα ἂν αἰτῶνται is a replica of πάντα ὅσα αἰτήσητε in Mt.

9. Sim. 9.20.2

Οἱ δὲ πλούσιοι . . . οἱ τοιοῦτοι οὖν δυσκόλως εἰσελεύσονται εἰς τὴν βασιλείαν τοῦ θεοῦ.

Such persons (the rich), then, will enter the Kingdom of God only with difficulty.

At the reading of this sentence, well known passages from the synoptics come spontaneously to mind: Mt. 19:23: ἀμὴν λέγω ὑμῖν ὅτι πλούσιος δυσκόλως εἰσελεύσεται εἰς τὴν βασιλείαν τῶν οὐρανῶν; Mk. 10:23: πῶς δυσκόλως οἱ τὰ χρήματα ἔχοντες εἰς τὴν βασιλείαν τοῦ θεοῦ εἰσελεύσονται; Lk. 18:24: πῶς δυσκόλως οἱ τὰ χρήματα ἔχοντες εἰς τὴν βασιλείαν τοῦ θεοῦ εἰσπορεύονται.

Hermas never uses Mt.'s formula: εἰς τὴν βασιλείαν τῶν οὐρανῶν, but rather that of Mk. and Lk.: εἰς τὴν βασιλείαν τοῦ θεοῦ, which became very early a technical phrase in Christianity.[193]

Moreover, Hermas, just as Mt., has the substantive πλούσιος whereas Mk. and Lk. designate the rich with a periphrasis. This difference with Mk. and Lk.

---

[193]Cf. Acts 1:3; 14:22; 19:8; 28:23; Rom. 14:17; 1 Cor. 4:20; 6:9, 10; 15:50; Gal. 5:21; Eph. 5:5; Col. 4:11; 1 Thess. 2:12; 2 Thess. 1:5.

is even more significant. It follows then that Hermas depends most probably on the Matthean text. Furthermore, Hermas does not use an exclamatory sentence as do Mk. and Lk. who write πῶς δυσκόλως, but he states as simply, as does Mt., the affirmation that the rich will enter the Kingdom with difficulty (δυσκόλως).

In the following verse, in Sim. 9.20.3, there is a statement similar to the one we have just seen: Ὥσπερ γὰρ ἐν τριβόλοις γυμνοῖς ποσὶ περιπατεῖν δύσκολόν ἐστιν, οὕτω καὶ τοῖς τοιούτοις δύσκολόν ἐστιν εἰς τὴν βασιλείαν τοῦ θεοῦ εἰσελθεῖν: "So, for these persons it is just as hard to enter into the Kingdom of God as it is to walk among thorns without shoes."

Hermas abandons the comparison in the synoptics of the camel which goes through the eye of a needle. This may reveal a sign of considerable independence with regard to the texts from which he draws his inspiration.

Finally, I would like to add Vis. 2.2.7, where the expression θλίψις μεγάλη is used to designate the tribulation of the last times as in Mt. 24:21;[194] Vis. 3.8.9 where the term συντέλεια, which is typically Matthean, signifies the end of time;[195] and the formula ὁ βασιλεύς ὁ μέγας in Vis. 3.9.8, which is also present in Mt. 5:35.[196]

B. Texts Where One of the Possible Parallels Is Matthean

This section deals with passages of Hermas with which various New Testament parallels may be identified, including texts of Mt., but where the source cannot be more precisely determined.

1. Vis. 2.2.8

For the Lord has sworn by His Son that those who have denied their Christ (τοὺς ἀρνησαμένους τὸν κύριον αὐτῶν) have been rejected from their Life; I mean those who are on the point of denying (τοὺς νῦν μέλλοντας ἀρνεῖσθαι) in the days to come. However, to those who have denied Him formerly (τοῖς δὲ πρότερον ἀρνησαμένοις), mercy has been granted because of His great mercy.

The thought of the denial of the Lord recalls the words of Mt. 10:32-33; Mk. 8:38; Lk. 9:26; and 2 Tim. 2:12. Hermas seems to know this theme of early Christianity which the synoptic tradition and Paul relate. He uses the same verb ἀρνέομαι as Mt. and Paul. However, he does not render this theme in its pristine

---

[194]Rev. 2:22 also has this expression.

[195]This word συντέλεια is found six times in the New Testament, namely, five times in Mt. (13:39, 40, 49; 24:3; 28:20) and once in Heb. 9:26.

[196]This expression is fairly common in the book of Psalms: 47(46):3; 48(47):3; 95(94):3; Tobit 13:16 also uses it.

state. The gospels and Paul are more absolute: he who denied Christ or was ashamed of him will be denied in the last days, or the Lord will be ashamed of him. As for Hermas, he distinguishes different periods, and according to these periods he distinguishes those who will be saved: the Lord has had pity on those who denied him until this day; but those who will deny him in the days to come are condemned. This leads to the belief that Hermas knows the theme in its pristine state, and he develops it here and accommodates it according to the needs of the thesis which he proposes: his children have sinned; God instructs him to exhort them to penance, his children as well as all guilty Christians; at this juncture, but for this one time only, God is willing to promise all sinners forgiveness for their past sins whatever they may be; but those who will subsequently deny him are lost.[197]

2. Vis. 3.6.5

"Lady, who are the white, round stones that do not fit into the building?" She answered and said: "How long are you going to be foolish and senseless? All these questions! Do you not understand anything? They are those who have the faith (οὗτοί εἰσιν ἔχοντες μὲν πίστιν), but also the riches of this world (ἔχοντες δὲ καὶ πλοῦτον τοῦ αἰῶνος τούτου). When persecution comes (ὅταν γένηται θλῖψις), they deny their Lord (ἀπαρνοῦνται τὸν κύριον αὐτῶν), because of their riches and their business."

The Oxford Committee thinks that this passage could very well indicate a knowledge of the parable of the sower, although it is impossible to show a connection with a particular gospel.[198] The specific texts to be linked with this text of Hermas are: Mt. 13:20-22; Mk. 4:16-20 and Lk. 8:13-15.

Several of the *Shepherd's* words or similar expressions are found in the passages of the synoptics mentioned above: ἔχοντες πίστιν may correspond to ἀκούων τὸν λόγον καὶ λαμβάνων αὐτόν in Mt. 13:20—Mk. 4:16 uses the same expressions as Mt.—and above all to πιστεύουσιν in Lk. 13:13; ἔχοντες πλοῦτον may be set as a parallel with ἡ ἀπάτη τοῦ πλούτου in Mt. 13:22 and Mk. 4:19, and with ὑπὸ πλούτου πορευόμενοι in Lk. 8:14; τοῦ αἰῶνος τούτου finds an echo in the words μέριμνα τοῦ αἰῶνος of Mt. 13:22, μέριμναι τοῦ αἰῶνος of Mk. 4:19, and in μέριμναι τοῦ βίου of Lk. 8:14; the phrase ἀπαρνοῦνται τὸν κύριον αὐτῶν may be equivalent to διὰ τὸν λόγον εὐθὺς σκανδαλίζεται (σκανδαλίζονται) in Mt. 13:21 and Mk. 4:17, and to ἀφίστανται in Lk. 8:13.

A similarity of thought with the synoptic tradition seems to be thrust upon us, a similarity all the more striking that the same words or very close expressions are

---

[197]Cf. Lelong, *Le Pasteur d'Hermas*, xi.

[198]Cf. A Committee of the Oxford Society, *The New Testament in the Apostolic Fathers*, 119.

found here and there. But it is practically impossible to determine definitively which of the synoptics may have influenced the composition of this passage.

3. Vis. 3.6.6

> Just as the round stone cannot be made square, unless it be cut and lose something, so also the rich (οἱ πλουτοῦντες) in this world cannot be made useful for the Lord (τῷ κυρίῳ εὔχρηστοι γενέσθαι), unless their riches have been cut out of them.

The synoptics, Mt. 19:21-24; Mk. 10:21-25; and Lk. 18:22-25, also mention the necessity to get rid of wealth in order to enter the Kingdom.

If this text of the *Shepherd* is to be considered alone, its difference with the synoptics does not allow the thought of a literary contact with any one of them. I shall simply point out that, just as they do, it states the difficulty for the wealthy to please the Lord, thus testifying on behalf of a concept which was common in early Christian times. Hermas abandons again the synoptic comparison of the camel and the eye of the needle. In Sim. 9.20.2 and 3, a parallel passage, I have concluded that there is an influence of the Matthean text.[199]

4. Vis. 3.7.3

> Do you wish to know who are the other stones that have fallen near the waters and cannot roll there? They are the ones who hear the word (οὗτοί εἰσιν οἱ τὸν λόγον ἀκούσαντες) and wish to be baptized in the Name of the Lord, but then change their mind when they recall the purity of the truth and return to their evil desires.

The words οἱ τὸν λόγον ἀκούσαντες are also read in Mt. 13:20 and 22; Mk. 4:18 and Lk. 8:15 in the parable of the sower.

I have already called upon these texts of the synoptics to link them with Vis. 3.6.5.[200] Their context is the same as in Hermas; they explain a parable containing many points, each of which requires a clarification. The synoptics speak of different soils where the seed has been sown; Hermas speaks of different kinds of stone needed for the construction of the tower.

The attitude of "the ones who hear the word" in the gospels agrees fairly well with the attitude of those who, having heard the word and desired to be baptized in the name of the Lord, change their mind and return to their previous mistakes.

However, the details of the narrative of the synoptics and of the *Shepherd* are too different to maintain a definite literary contact. Yet, it cannot be denied that

---

[199]Cf. above, 119-20.
[200]Cf. above, 121-22.

there is a very great similarity of thought, reinforced by the use of the parabolic genre as in the gospels.

A definite literary influence due to the expression οἱ τὸν λόγον ἀκούσαντες could perhaps be argued, but in that case, it is impossible to determine which one of the gospels ought to be given preference, since all three synoptics use this expression.

5. Vis. 3.8.3

The first of them (the women), with the strong hands, is called Faith (Πίστις). God's elect are saved by her (διὰ ταύτης σώζονται οἱ ἐκλεκτοὶ τοῦ θεοῦ).

Hermas states simply a traditional idea (Mt. 9:22; Mk. 5:34; 10:52; Lk. 7:50; 8:48, 50; 17:19; 18:42; Acts 14:9; 26:18; Rom. 3:22, 28; 5:1; 1 Cor. 1:21; Eph. 2:8, etc.).

6. Vis. 4.2.6

Alas for those who hear these remarks and disobey them! It were better for them that they had not been born (αἰρετώτερον ἦν αὐτοῖς τὸ μὴ γεννηθῆναι).

The last words sound like an echo of Mt. 26:24 and Mk. 14:21. Indeed, Hermas uses the verb γεννηθῆναι; yet the *Shepherd* puts the sentence in the plural; futhermore, instead of καλόν in the gospels, he uses αἰρετώτερον; and instead of a conditional phrase (εἰ οὐκ . . .), he has the simple infinitive γεννηθῆναι.

Surely, as the Oxford Committee points out, this sentence may be derived from a saying of the synoptics; the variations are no more substantial than may be expected from a quote which is not meant to be explicit.[201] But it is impossible to determine if Hermas quotes from Mt. or Mk.

7. Mand. 9.4

Then ask (αἰτοῦ) of the Lord and you will receive (ἀπολήψῃ) all. You cannot fail to obtain all your requests (αἰτημάτων) provided you ask (αἰτήσῃς) the Lord without wavering.

The gospels have similar statements about the efficacy of prayer in Mt. 7:7, 11; 21:22; Mk. 11:24 and Lk. 11:9. Hermas does not show any more literary affinity with one than with the other. All the texts mentioned have the verb αἰτέω

---

[201]Cf. A Committee of the Oxford Society, *The New Testament in the Apostolic Fathers*, 121.

as does Hermas, and the simple verb λαμβάνω instead of the composite verb ἀπο-
λαμβάνω in the *Shepherd*.

8. Mand. 10.1.5

> Just as good vineyards, when not cared for, grow barren with thorns (χερ-
> σοῦνται ἀπὸ τῶν ἀκανθῶν) and various weeds (βοτανῶν), so believers (οἱ
> ἄνθρωποι οἱ πιστεύσαντες), who become involved in the aforementioned
> numerous occupations (εἰς ταύτας τὰς πράξεις), lose their understand-
> ing and are altogether without perception of justice.

The numerous encumbrances to which Hermas referred earlier, in verse 4 of
the same chapter, are business, wealth, friendship with pagans, and other com-
mitments of this world (πραγματεῖαι καὶ πλοῦτος καὶ φιλίαι ἐθνικαί καὶ ἄλλαι πολλαὶ πραγματεῖαι τοῦ αἰῶνος τούτου). The need to be free from every
occupation of that period in order to understand the word of God and receive its
fruits is explicitly stated in the synoptics as well, in the context of the explanation
of the parable of the sower, in Mt. 13:22; Mk. 4:18-19; and Lk. 8:14.

Here again, a fairly clear similarity of thought can be asserted: χερσοῦνται
ἀπὸ τῶν ἀκανθῶν may correspond to ὁ εἰς τὰς ἀκάνθας σπαρείς in Mt. 13:22,
to οἱ εἰς τὰς ἀκάνθας σπειρόμενοι in Mk. 4:18, and to τὸ εἰς τὰς ἀκάνθας
πεσόν in Lk. 8:14. οἱ ἄνθρωποι οἱ πιστεύσαντες of Hermas may be set as a
parallel to ὁ τὸν λόγον ἀκούων of Mt. 13:22, to οἱ τὸν λόγον ἀκούσαντες of
Mk. 4:18, and to οἱ ἀκούσαντες of Lk. 8:14. As for εἰς ταύτας τὰς πράξεις
of Hermas, I have shown that it referred to πραγματεῖαι καὶ πλοῦτος καὶ φιλίαι ἐθνικαί καὶ ἄλλαι πολλαὶ πραγματεῖαι τοῦ αἰῶνος τούτου, and its
parallels may be found in ἡ μέριμνα τοῦ αἰῶνος καὶ ἡ ἀπάτη τοῦ πλούτου of
Mt. 13:22, in αἱ μέριμναι τοῦ αἰῶνος καὶ ἡ ἀπάτη τοῦ πλούτου καὶ αἱ περὶ
τὰ λοιπὰ ἐπιθυμίαι of Mk. 4:19, and in μέριμναι καὶ πλοῦτος καὶ ἡδοναὶ
τοῦ βίου of Lk. 8:14.

It is obvious that the kinds of encumbrances the *Shepherd* points out were already specified in the gospels. Their gathering in Hermas may come from a source
other than the gospels, since the words are indeed too different to maintain a literary contact. It could also be inferred that Hermas expresses his own experience
or that of his associates.

9. Sim. 5.3.3

> But, if you do some good over and above God's commandment, you will ac-
> quire all the greater glory and will be held in that much greater honor in the
> sight of God, with whom you are destined to be. Therefore, if you also per-
> form these additional services, while keeping God's commandments, joy will
> be yours, provided you observe them in accordance with my commands.

This passage of Hermas could easily be considered a development of the words on perfection in Mt. 19:21; Mk. 10:21 and Lk. 18:22. In the *Shepherd*, there is not one word which allows the conclusion that Hermas, speaking of works of supererogation, has in mind the sayings of Christ in the synoptics. This is a case of simple similarity of thought.[202]

10. Sim. 5.6.1 and 4

[1] . . . The Son of God is not represented in the form of a slave, but is represented with great power (εἰς ἐξουσίαν μεγάλην κεῖται) and majesty. . . . [4] So you see . . . that He Himself is Lord of His people, because He has all power from His Father (ἐξουσίαν πᾶσαν λαβὼν παρὰ τοῦ πατρὸς αὐτοῦ). . . .

The fact that the Son received all power from his Father is read also in Mt. 28:18; other passages of the New Testament state it just as well: Jn. 3:27-35; 13:3; 17:2; 1 Cor. 15:27-28; Eph. 1:20-21; Phil. 2:9-10; Rev. 12:10.

These many texts to which I refer testify in favor of a hypothesis that this was a common theme in primitive Christianity. Particularly with reference to the Matthean text, I would perhaps tend to agree with the Oxford Committee that Hermas's words are sufficiently close to suggest a dependence, but there are too few of them to allow me to reach this conclusion with any certainty.[203] This is why I prefer to say that Hermas expresses here a common theme.

I must point out here, as literarily closer to Mt. 28:18, the text of Sim. 5.7.3: "He (God) has all power (αὐτοῦ γάρ ἐστι πᾶσα ἐξουσία)."

11. Sim. 6.3.6

. . . They declare that God is a just judge (δίκαιος κριτής) and that they suffered each in the measure of his actions (ἕκαστος κατὰ τὰς πράξεις αὐτοῦ).

The idea of God as an impartial judge, paying each according to his actions is common in the Scripture; it is found in Mt. 16:27; 2 Cor. 11:15; 1 Pet. 1:17; Rev. 2:23; Ps. 62(61):13; Prov. 24:12; and Ecclus. 35:22. The context of this passage in Hermas does not lead us particularly to one as opposed to another of these texts. Could the term πράξεις in Hermas tilt the balance in favor of a literary parallel with Ecclus. 35:22, which also has πράξεις, instead of πρᾶξις in Mt. and ἔργα in the other parallels?

---

[202]Cf. Dibelius, *Der Hirt des Hermas,* 566, agrees with this view up to a point.

[203]Cf. A Committee of the Oxford Society, *The New Testament in the Apostolic Fathers,* 119.

12. Sim. 9.13.2

It will be found that no man will enter the Kingdom of God in any other way, unless they (the virgins) clothe him with their raiment (τὸ ἔνδυμα αὐτῶν).

The Oxford Committee turns to Mt. 22:11-13, a passage drawn from the parable of the wedding guests where one of the guests is expelled because he is not dressed in wedding garments, and it points out that this passage of Hermas may have been suggested by this parable but that the similarity is not really precise.[204]

The presence of the word ἔνδυμα would be a sign of dependence.

13. Sim. 9.20.1

. . . The thorns are the rich (οἱ πλούσιοι) and the thistles (αἱ ἄκανθαι) are those involved in various business affairs.

This recalls Mt. 13:22; Mk. 4:18-19 and Lk. 8:14. The presence in Hermas of the words πλούσιοι and ἄκανθαι, and its idea similar to that of the synoptics may very well reveal here a knowledge of the parable of the sower, although it is impossible to link this passage of the *Shepherd* with a specific gospel.

14. Sim. 9.28.6

Therefore, count yourselves blessed (οὐκοῦν μακαρίζετε ἑαυτούς). Consider that you have performed a mighty deed, if one of you suffers for God (διὰ τὸν θεὸν πάθῃ).

The thought which is expressed here is clearly similar to that of Mt. 5:11 and Lk. 6:22. Hermas was most probably inspired by these words of the Sermon on the Mount. Did he draw his inspiration from Mt. or Lk.? There is no clue in the text or in the context that allows an answer to this question.

15. Sim. 9.29.3

You who will remain constant . . . and will be like babes (ὡς τὰ βρέφη), without evil guile, will be more glorious than all the aforementioned. Every child is glorious in God's sight and comes to Him before all others.

The mention of small children and the admonition to imitate them suggest many texts of the synoptics: Mt. 18:3; 19:14; Mk. 10:14 and Lk. 18:16. The statement that the Kingdom of God is open to those who have the innocence of children (Sim. 9.29.2) confirms this reference. Here again, there is a resemblance between the text of Hermas and the idea expressed by the synoptics, but there is no clue

---

[204]Cf. ibid., 119.

which allows us to determine a literary reference with one or another of the texts mentioned above.

The same applies for Sim. 9.31.3 which also mentions the innocence of small children: "I, the angel of penance, consider you all happy, you who are innocent as babes (quicumque estis innocentes sicut infantes), because your part is good and in honor in God's sight."

I would like to close this section with the reminder that, when Hermas says in Mand. 12.4.4, "But, the persons who have the Lord on their lips, while their heart is hardened, who are in fact far from the Lord (οἱ δὲ ἐπὶ τοῖς χείλεσιν ἔχοντες τὸν κύριον, τὴν δὲ καρδίαν αὐτῶν πεπωρωμένην καὶ μακρὰν ὄντες ἀπὸ τοῦ κυρίου) for them these mandates are difficult and hard to fulfill," he refers to Is. 29:13 as do Mt. 15:8 and Mk. 7:6. Again after the example of Mt. 4:4 and Lk. 4:4, Hermas is probably inspired by Deut. 8:3, when he says in Sim. 9.11.8, " 'Sir,' I said, 'our supper all night was the words of the Lord.' "

I would also like to add the use by Hermas of certain words and expressions present in several New Testament texts, such as Mt.: σκληροκαρδία,[205] πρωτο-καθεδρία, πρωτοκαθεδρίται,[206] and λογὸν ἀποδίδωμι to express how men will render account in the last days,[207] κατασκήνωσις,[208] ψυχὴν ἀπόλλυμι.[209]

C. Texts for Which Matthean Influence Is to Be Excluded

I call attention to these texts because the reading of some commentaries often leads to the belief that they are related literarily to Mt., since they are sometimes attributed to Matthean passages. Now there are cases in which this reference does not signify in the least a literary influence from the first gospel; it merely indicates either the use of an identical word or a rather vague similarity of thought; in many

---

[205]Cf. Vis. 3.7.6 and Mt. 19:8 and Mk. 10:5; 16:14; W. Bauer, *Griechisch-deutsches Wörterbuch zu den Schriften des Neuen Testaments und der übrigen urchristlichen Literatur*, 3rd ed. (Berlin, 1937) col. 1259, points out that this word follows the prevailing biblical and ecclesiastical use, and he adds to the given references Deut. 10:16; Jer. 4:4; Ecclus. 16:10; T. 12 Patr., Sim. 6.2.

[206]Cf. Vis. 3.9.7 and πρωτοκαθεδρία in Mt. 23:6; Mk. 12:39; Lk. 11:43; 20:46. It may be asked whether this term in Vis. 3.9.7 is a simple title or a reproof; some ancient interpreters, under the influence of the texts of the gospels, have opted for reproof: i.e., the versio vulgata which translates "qui amatis primos consessus," and the versio palatina which says "qui amatis primas sessiones." Later on, the parallel with προηγούμενοι makes it now generally accepted that it is a simple title (cf. Funk, *Patres apostolici*, 1:452; Dibelius, *Der Hirt des Hermas*, 476); it is not solely because they occupy the place of honor that leaders are censured, but for various reasons, hence the rift.

[207]Cf. Vis. 3.9.10 and Mt. 12:36; Lk. 16:2; Acts 19:40; Rom. 14:12; Heb. 13:17; 1 Pet. 4:5.

[208]Cf. Sim. 5.6.7 and Mt. 8:20; Lk. 9:58.

[209]Cf. Sim. 9.26.3 and Mt. 10:28, 39; 16:25; Mk. 8:35; Lk. 6:9; 9:24; 17:33; Jn. 12:25.

cases, a Matthean influence is even to be excluded.

1. Mand. 5.2.7

> Then, when He (the spirit) has left, the man in whom He dwelled becomes emptied of the righteous spirit; he is filled with evil spirits afterwards and disorderly in all his actions, dragged here and there by evil spirits.

For some, this recalled Mt. 12:43 and Lk 11:24. But there is an essential difference between Hermas and the texts of the gospel: whereas in Hermas the case in point is the flight of the Holy Spirit, in the gospels it is the evil spirits who flee. I believe that it is solely the idea of the departure of the Spirit which is the basis of the agreement.

2. Mand. 7.4

> There are two kinds of fear, then. If you wish to do evil, fear the Lord and you will not do it. So, too, if you wish to do good, fear the Lord and you will do it.

In pointing out this formula of the two fears, Dibelius refers to Mt. 10:28 and Lk. 12:4-5.[210] But in both texts as well as in Hermas, the two fears do not have the same object. The first concerns those who may lose the body, but not the soul; the second aims at him who may lose body and soul in gehenna.

3. Mand. 12.5.4

> In the same way the devil comes and tempts all the servants of God. Those who are strong in the faith resist him and he goes away from them, because he cannot find entrance. So, he goes then to the empty and, finding an entrance, he goes into them. Thus he accomplishes in them whatever he pleases and makes them his slaves.

This text is sometimes linked with Mt. 12:43-45 and Lk. 11:24-27. But such a reference seems highly improbable. Indeed, if in Hermas the devil tries first to enter into those who have faith and is met with stiff resistance, nothing similar appears in the gospels. Moreover, in the narrative of the *Shepherd*, the cast out devil does not go to seek help as he does in the gospel.

---

[210]Cf. Dibelius, *Der Hirt des Hermas*, 525.

4. Sim. 5.3.2-3

[2] Keep the commandments of the Lord (τὰς ἐντολὰς τοῦ κυρίου φύλασσε), and you will be well pleasing to God; you will be inscribed in the number of those who keep His commandments. [3] . . . while keeping God's commandments (φυλάσσων τὰς ἐντολὰς τοῦ θεοῦ). . . .

The expression τὰς ἐντολὰς φυλάσσω has suggested a number of parallels: Eccl. 12:13; Mt. 19:17; Mk. 10:19; and Lk. 18:20. But it is obvious that, if there is a literary contact, it is not with the text of Mt. or with any other gospel, but with Ecclesiastes which has literally the expression in question.

5. Sim. 5.3.8

If you perform your fast, then, in the way I have just commanded, your sacrifice will be acceptable in the sight of God (ἔσται ἡ θυσία σου δεκτὴ παρὰ τῷ θεῷ). . . .

Various references are generally given for this passage: Prov. 15:8; Ecclus. 35:6; Is. 56:7; Mt. 5:24; Phil. 4:18; and 1 Pet. 2:5.

Technically, the texts of Ecclesiasticus and the Letter to the Philippians are closest to the words of Hermas. But if there is a literary contact, I would give preference to the text of Ecclesiasticus which, in the preceding context in 34:26, treats of fasting just as Hermas does in this passage of the *Shepherd*.

6. Sim. 8.7.6

Life belongs to all who keep the Lord's commandments. Now, in the commandments there is nothing about first places and any point of honor but about man's long-suffering and humility. The life of the Lord, then, is to be found in men of this kind, but death is among those of doubtful heart and among transgressors.

Commentators point out as parallels Mt. 18:4 and 23:12, and then even add sometimes that when Hermas wrote these reported words, he had in mind the sayings of the Lord in Mt. 23:6-12.[211] These commentators might also have mentioned Lk. 14:11 and 18:14. But in reading these texts of the gospels, I cannot help but note that it is only the mention of humility in the *Shepherd* that led to these texts of Mt. or Lk.

---

[211]Cf. de Gebhardt and Harnack, *Hermae Pastor*, 191; Funk, *Patres apostolici*, 1:571.

7. Sim. 9.31.6

And, if the shepherds are scattered, how will they answer for their flocks?

Mt. 26:31 and Mk. 14:27 have sometimes been considered as parallels. But it would be better to emphasize the differences between Hermas and these gospel texts than to speak of their parallelism. Indeed, the *Shepherd* deals with the scattering of the shepherds, whereas Mt. and Mk. envisage the scattering of the flocks. Here again, a simple word, "scattering," brought about this comparison.

In conclusion, if I may state that Hermas knew the Gospel of Mt. and seemed indeed to refer to it, I must also point out that the literary influence of Mt. is of a somewhat particular nature. To be sure, certain Matthean texts have inspired several passages of the *Shepherd,* but Hermas merely let himself be governed by Matthean ideas. He follows the texts of Mt. at a distance, as though they were but a canvas which he adorns. He transforms the ideas of the first gospel and adapts them to his own composition, and in this way he creates an original work. He never cites Mt. literally, nor does he refer to it explicitly. Considering the *Shepherd*'s wide scope, few passages are literarily dependent on Mt. Moreover, Hermas has many more passages which agree with the synoptic tradition upon which he seems to rely.

§2. The Other New Testament Writings

The *Shepherd of Hermas* reveals literary relationships with almost all the other New Testament writings. Hermas seems, as a matter of fact, to show a knowledge of the Gospel of Mk., whereas the Gospel of Lk. does not seem to have inspired him very much. Some sentences in the *Shepherd* have a striking resemblance to passages in Jn. He also looked through certain epistles of Paul. He shows as well a remarkable affinity with the Epistle of James.

This is why I consider first the two other synoptics and the Acts of the Apostles; I then go on to the Johannine literature, next to the Pauline epistles, and finally to the catholic epistles and, in particular, to the Epistle of James.

A. Mark and the Writings of Luke[212]

Mand. 4 makes recommendations on chastity and deals with the matter of adultery. Concerning the latter, Mand. 4.1.6 reads, "'Sir,' I said, 'what then is he to do, if the wife continues in this passion?' 'Let him divorce her,' he (the Shepherd) said, 'and remain single. But, if he divorces her and marries another woman, he himself commits adultery (ἐὰν δὲ ἀπολύσας τὴν γυναῖκα ἑτέραν

---

[212]In this paragraph, I do not plan to return to the texts of Hermas which have parallels in several New Testament texts including Mk. or Lk.; I already pointed these out in connection with Mt., where I dealt with those texts which had a possible Matthean parallel; cf. above, 120-27.

γαμήση καὶ αὐτὸς μοιχᾶται)."' The Shepherd's answer to Hermas recalls Mt. 5:32; 19:9; Mk. 10:11 and Lk. 16:18. It repeats almost literally the text of the synoptics. Yet, a literary influence from Mt. on Hermas's composition is to be excluded. Indeed, what distinguishes Mt. from the other parallels is a restriction he brings to the statements of Mk. and Lk., and this restriction is simply absent from the text of Hermas: in the *Shepherd*, there is no hint of either παρεκτὸς λόγου πορνείας (Mt. 5:32) or μὴ ἐπὶ πορνείᾳ (Mt. 19:9). As for the texts of Mk. and Lk., even though their phraseology is almost identical, it is more probable that Hermas depends here on Mk.; in fact, he has kept the verbal forms γαμήση and μοιχᾶται, whereas Lk. has the participle γαμῶν and the present μοιχεύει.[213]

In the interpretation of the parable of the willow tree, Sim. 8.6.4 reads: "The persons whose rods were discovered to be dry and worm-eaten are apostates and traitors to the Church, who baspheme the Lord by their sins. Furthermore, they were ashamed of the Name of the Lord (ἐπαισχυνθέντες), the Name invoked upon them." The expression "ashamed of the Name of the Lord" refers undoubtedly to Mk. 8:38 and Lk. 9:26, where the verb ἐπαισχύνομαι is found in the context of persecution: those who have been ashamed of Christ and his sayings in this world, the Son of man will be ashamed of them at the end of times. Mt. 10:33, also a parallel, uses the verb ἀρνέομαι. We are, therefore, left with the impression that when Hermas refers to this gospel saying, he does not have in mind the words of Christ as reported by Mt., but rather those sayings in the other two synoptics. There is no contextual factor to tilt the balance in favor of one or the other.

The same remark applies to Sim. 9.14.6 and Sim. 9.21.3 where we find the same expression "ashamed of His name." The first of these texts says in fact: "Do you see the kind of persons He (the Son of God) supports? Those who bear His name with their whole heart. Therefore, He has been made their foundation and gladly gives them support, because they are not ashamed (ἐπαισχύνονται) to bear His name." The second reads: "Just as their weeds wither at the sight of the sun, so also do persons who are doubters worship idols in their cowardice and are ashamed (ἐπαισχύνονται) of the Name of their Lord when they hear of persecution."

Also to be mentioned is the use of the parabolic theme in Hermas. For Hermas, the parable is to be understood as in Mk. 4:10-12 and Jn. 16:25, namely as an enigma which hides more than it enlightens and which, therefore, requires a solution, meaning an explanation.[214] Hermas states the theme with the words ἡ

---

[213]Cf. Dibelius, *Der Hirt des Hermas*, 506.

[214]Cf. on this subject Dibelius, *Der Hirt des Hermas*, 479, 567-68; L. Cerfaux, "'L'aveuglement d'esprit' dans l'Évangile de saint Marc," in *Muséon* 59/1-4, *Mélanges L. Th. Lefort* (Louvain, 1946) 267-79; M. Hermaniuk, *La Parabole Évangélique. Enquête exégétique et critique* (Paris, Louvain, 1947) 357-65.

καρδία μου πεπώρωται (Mand. 4.2.1), which approximate Mk. 3:5; 6:52; 8:17.²¹⁵

As for Vis. 3.6.3: "'Who are the stones with cracks in them?' 'They are those opposed in their hearts and not at peace with one another (εἰρηνεύοντες ἐν ἑαυτοῖς),'" some critics and commentators refer to 1 Thess. 5:13; Mk. 9:50; Rom. 13:11 for the expression εἰρηνεύοντες ἐν ἑαυτοῖς.²¹⁶ Strictly speaking, only 1 Thess. 5:13 actually uses this expression.

As for the Gospel of Lk., Hermas seems to have drawn very little from it. There may be in Mand. 9.8 a reminiscence of the third gospel. Hermas writes in this section: "Do not let up, then, in the request of your soul. But, if in your request you grow faint (ἐὰν δὲ ἐκκακήσῃς) and doubt, blame yourself and not the Giver." The Oxford Committee refers to Lk. 18:1, and points out that the idea of Hermas is related to it and that the expression is exact enough to suggest a dependence.²¹⁷ The verb ἐγκακέω is used also by Paul in 2 Cor. 4:1, 16; Gal. 6:9; Eph. 3:13 and 2 Thess. 3:13, but it does not refer to prayer.²¹⁸ The idea of Hermas is close to that of Lk. Now, the latter is the only one of the synoptics to insist on the necessity of persevering prayer and to use the verb ἐγκακέω. These remarks suggest that Hermas perhaps referred to the Lucan text.

Some texts of the *Shepherd* recall various passages of the Acts of the Apostles.

In the commentary on the symbolism of the stones of the tower under construction, Vis. 3.7.3 reads, "Do you wish to know who are the other stones that have fallen near the waters and cannot roll there? They are the ones who hear the word and wish to be baptized in the Name of the Lord (βαπτισθῆναι εἰς τὸ ὄνομα τοῦ κυρίου). . . . " The expression βαπτισθῆναι εἰς τὸ ὄνομα seems to be a common formula, and Hermas may have simply bowed to common usage. I would still like to point out that, followed by τοῦ κυρίου, this expression appears literally in Acts 8:16 and 19:5.²¹⁹

Speaking of the forthcoming great troubles and having learned from Hermas himself that he had escaped from the monstrous beast, the woman says to him in

---

²¹⁵We also find in the New Testament the expression πώρωσις τῆς καρδίας in Eph. 4:18, and the verb πωρόω in Jn. 12:40; Rom. 11:7; 2 Cor. 3:4.

²¹⁶Cf. Lelong, *Le Pasteur d'Hermas*, 40.

²¹⁷Cf. A Committee of the Oxford Society, *The New Testament in the Apostolic Fathers*, 120.

²¹⁸2 Clem. 2:2 also uses the verb ἐγκακέω in a passage which mentions prayer: τὰς προσευχὰς ἡμῶν ἁπλῶς ἀναφέρειν πρὸς τὸν θεόν, μὴ ὡς αἱ ὠδίνουσαι ἐγκακῶμεν.

²¹⁹This expression, which became traditional in the community (cf. Mt. 28:19; Acts 2:38; 8:16; 10:48; 19:5; 1 Cor. 1:13, 15), probably alludes to the baptismal liturgy (cf. W. Heitmüller, "Im namen Jesu," FRLANT, W. Bousset and H. Gunkel (Göttingen, 1903): 88-93, 115-16, 266-336; for Hermas, 92 and 297-98). It is consequently difficult to claim that Hermas has been directly influenced by a specific N.T. writing; the only possible observation is that the formula he uses is closer to that which is found in Acts 8:16; 19:5.

Vis. 4.2.4, "'Yes, indeed,' she said, 'you escaped, because you cast your care on God and you opened up your heart to the Lord, in the assurance that you can be saved by nothing except His great and glorious Name' (ὅτι δι' οὐδενὸς δύνῃ σωθῆναι εἰ μὴ διὰ τοῦ μεγάλου καὶ ἐνδόξου ὀνόματος)." A very striking parallel appears in Acts 4:12: οὐδὲ γὰρ ὄνομά ἐστιν ἕτερον ὑπὸ τὸν οὐρανὸν τὸ δεδομένον ἐν ἀνθρώποις ἐν ᾧ δεῖ σωθῆναι ἡμᾶς. According to the context of this passage in the Acts of the Apostles, it is clear that the name in question is the name of Jesus. In fact, it is in the name of Jesus Christ that Peter performs a healing (Acts 3:20); he is arrested with John for the preaching of this name; they are interrogated so as to know by what name and by what power they performed this miracle (Acts 4:7), and Peter answers that it is in the name of Jesus Christ and adds that it is only by this "name" that we are saved (Acts 4:12). However, there is much more to this ὄνομα of Acts than a simple name; the assumption is that the "name" is related to the very person of the Son of God. A comparison with Acts 4:12 seems at least possible. That Hermas added the epithets μέγα καὶ ἐνδόξον to ὄνομα is not surprising: I noted more than once that Hermas does not refrain from adjusting the texts which inspire him in order to suit his own composition. Anyway, such a formula may be one more sign of the pronounced Judaic character of the *Shepherd of Hermas.*[220] However, I would like to point out that the absolute rendering of ὄνομα is rather frequent with Hermas,[221] and seems to presuppose an archaic theology of the "name," traces of which can be found particularly in the first chapters of the Acts of the Apostles and perhaps in Ignatius of Antioch.[222]

In explaining in Sim. 9.28.2 who are the believers who came from the eleventh mountain, the *Shepherd* says, "(they are) those who have suffered for the sake of the Name of the Son of God (οἱ παθόντες ὑπὲρ τοῦ ὀνόματος τοῦ υἱοῦ τοῦ θεοῦ) who bore sufferings readily with their whole heart, and who have given up their lives (παρέδωκαν τὰς ψυχὰς αὐτῶν)." The reading of this text recalls Acts 5:41 and 15:26. The text of Acts 5:41 recalls Mt. 5:10-12. The traditional theme of the witness is probably present in all these passages where the best testimony is given by the martyrs who give their lives for Christ. In Acts 15:26, the

---

[220]Cf. 2 Macc. 8:15: ἕνεκα τῆς ἐπ' αὐτοὺς ἐπικλήσεως τοῦ σεμνοῦ καὶ μεγαλοπρεποῦς ὀνόματος; 3 Macc. 2:9: πρὸς δόξαν τοῦ μεγάλου καὶ ἐντίμου ὀνόματός σου; and the letter of Clement of Rome, in passages clearly influenced by the Old Testament: 1 Clem. 58:1; 59:2; 60:4; 64.

[221]Cf. Vis. 3.1.9; 3.2.1; 3.3.5; 4.2.4; Sim. 8.10.3; 9.13.2; 9.13.3; 9.17.4; 9.19.2; 9.28.3; 9.28.5.

[222]Cf. L. Cerfaux, "La première communauté chrétienne à Jérusalem," *ETL* 16 (1939): 24-26, where on p. 25 the author advances, "It may be asked whether, in these texts (particularly those from the first chapters of Acts), the 'name' is not a remote echo of the hypostasis of the Word, somewhat like δύναμις θεοῦ and σοφία θεοῦ in Saint Paul."

expressions ὑπὲρ τοῦ ὀνόματος τοῦ κυρίου and παραδεδωκόσι τὰς ψυχὰς αὐτῶν are similar to those of the *Shepherd*. Hermas follows perfectly the traditional path of the theme of the witness; but the formulation of this theme in Hermas may have been drawn from from Acts 15:26.

I would also like to mention the expression ἐργάζομαι τὴν δικαιοσύνην, which is present in Vis. 2.2.7; Mand. 12.3.1; 12.6.2; and Sim. 9.13.7, which Acts 10:35 also has, which is found as well in Heb. 11:33, and which Ps. 14:2 already had.

In Vis. 3.9.2, Hermas uses the verb ἀντιλαμβάνομαι, which is present in Acts 20:35; Hermas follows it with ἀλλήλων, and this is what sets him closer to παραλαμβάνομαι ἀλλήλων in Rom. 15:7.

As for καρδιογνώστης which Hermas used in Mand. 4.3.4, I would like to point out that it is peculiar to Acts 1:24 and 15:8 in the entire New Testament.

Finally, Vis. 1.3.4: "Behold the God of Hosts, who has created the world (κτίσας τὸν κόσμον) with His invisible power, strength, and surpassing wisdom," has sometimes suggested Acts 17:24 where God is called ὁ ποιήσας τὸν κόσμον. Let me note at once that the Acts of the Apostles does not have here the participle κτίσας, but rather ποιήσας. Moreover, this entire fourth verse in Hermas has the character of a liturgical hymn,[223] and this hymn is woven around reminiscences of the Old Testament. Therefore, this text ought rather to be linked with the Old Testament; and, actually, the expression in 2 Macc. 7:23, ὁ τοῦ κόσμου κτίστης, is much closer to the formula of Hermas. Besides, the mention of creation finds its place in liturgy (cf. Rev. 4:11; 1 Clem. 60:1).

B. The Johannine Writings

When Sim. 5.6.3 reads, "By cleansing their sins in person, He (the Son of God) showed them the ways of life and gave them the law which He received from his Father (δοὺς αὐτοῖς τὸν νόμον, ὃν ἔλαβε παρὰ τοῦ πατρὸς αὐτοῦ)," the last clause sounds like an echo of Jn. 10:18; 12:49-50; 14:31 and 15:10. Jn. 10:18 and 12:49-50 deserve special attention: the first, because it includes almost literally Hermas's clause ταύτην τὴν ἐντολὴν ἔλαβον παρὰ τοῦ πατρός μου; the second, inasmuch as it includes the word ἐντολή, which also pertains to life. To be sure, instead of ἐντολή, Hermas uses the word νόμος, but as we know, he is not given to following word for word the texts from which he draws his inspiration. At the very least, it may be acknowledged that this passage has a clearly Johannine flavor.

---

[223]Cf. Dibelius, *Der Hirt des Hermas*, 440; Lelong, *Le Pasteur d'Hermas*, 13. E. Norden, in *Agnostos Theos, Untersuchungen zur Formengeschichte religiöser Rede* (Leipzig, 1913) 202ff., analyzes this passage of Hermas.

We find in Sim. 9.12.1 and 3: "'In the very first place,' I said, 'tell me this: What is the rock and the gate?' 'This rock and this tower,' he said, 'is the Son of God (ἡ πέτρα, φησίν, αὕτη καὶ ἡ πύλη ὁ υἱὸς τοῦ θεοῦ ἐστί).' . . . Because,' he said, 'He has manifested Himself in the last days of the consummation of things, and for this reason the gate (ἡ πύλη) is new. In this way those who are destined to be saved enter the Kingdom of God through the gate' (ἵνα οἱ μέλλοντες σῴζεσθαι δι' αὐτῆς εἰς τὴν βασιλείαν εἰσέλθωσι τοῦ θεοῦ)." In 1 Cor. 10:4, in recalling the miracle of the water flowing from the rock in the desert, Paul identifies the rock with Christ. In Jn. 10:7, 9, just as in Hermas, Christ is also called the door in a passage which deals with salvation; but Jn. uses the word θύρα whereas Hermas uses πύλη, and the latter recalls Mt. 7:14 in a section which also deals with salvation. The use of the word πύλη is all the more remarkable since Hermas, in Vis. 3.9.6, in his commentary on the construction of the tower, used θύρα to designate the door.

It is quite possible that we have, gathered in this text, several vague recollections of the New Testament. If a Johannine tone tends to flavor this passage as a whole, thanks to the identification of Christ with the door which must be crossed so as to be saved, Hermas may still have remembered that Paul identifies the rock with Christ, and that Mt. designates the door which leads to life as πύλη. Yet, it is equally possible that such ideas were prevalent enough among Christians and beyond any direct literary influence of one of the texts mentioned above.[224]

But finally, I still give preference to a strong Johannine influence with a reminiscence of Mt. and Paul, and that is because of the following verse of Hermas in Sim. 9.12.4, which reads: "For that reason also, nobody enters the Kingdom of God without receiving the Name of His Son (οὕτω, φησίν, εἰς τὴν βασιλείαν τοῦ θεοῦ οὐδεὶς εἰσελεύσεται, εἰ μὴ λάβοι τὸ ὄνομα τοῦ υἱοῦ αὐτοῦ)." There is an important parallel to this statement in Jn. 3:5: ἐὰν μή τις γεννηθῇ ἐξ ὕδατος καὶ πνεύματος οὐ δύναται εἰσελθεῖν εἰς τὴν βασιλείαν τοῦ θεοῦ. In Hermas, the expression λαβεῖν τὸ ὄνομα τοῦ υἱοῦ τοῦ θεοῦ is certainly linked to Christian baptism;[225] now Jn. 3:5 also refers to Christian baptism. Furthermore, this Johannine text includes Hermas's expression εἰσελθεῖν εἰς τὴν βασιλείαν τοῦ θεοῦ. It is, therefore, easy to assume that Hermas refers to this declaration of Christ to Nicodemus; he simply replaced the formula ἐὰν μή τις γεννηθῇ ἐξ ὕδατος καὶ πνεύματος with one of his usual expressions to designate baptism.[226]

---

[224]Cf. A Committee of the Oxford Society, *The New Testament in the Apostolic Fathers*, 123.

[225]Cf. Sim. 9.16.3, where the correlative expression "he receives the Name of the Son of God" is in a context which asserts the necessity of baptism.

[226]The other expression to designate baptism is "he receives the seal" in Sim. 9.16.3-4.

Sim. 9.12.1 and 3 belong to the same context as Sim. 9.12.4; it follows then that they are also literarily dependent on Jn. 3:5 with reminiscences of Paul and Mt.

Insofar as it elucidates verse 4, I may add that Sim. 9.12.5 is logically influenced by Jn. as well when it says: "In the same way that you cannot enter a city, except through this gate, so no human being can enter the Kingdom of God, except by means of the Name of His Beloved Son."

Besides, there is no doubt that Hermas is literarily dependent on John in the entire chapter 12 of Sim. 9. Sim. 9.12.6 confirms it again: "But the gate is the Son of God (ἡ δὲ πύλη ὁ υἱὸς τοῦ θεοῦ ἐστίν), the only entrance to the Lord. Therefore, no one goes in to Him except through his Son (αὕτη μία εἴσοδός ἐστι πρὸς τὸν κύριον. ἄλλως οὖν οὐδεὶς εἰσελεύσεται πρὸς αὐτὸν εἰ μὴ διὰ τοῦ υἱοῦ αὐτοῦ)." This passage repeats almost literally Jn 14:6: Λέγει αὐτῷ Ἰησοῦς· ἐγώ εἰμι ἡ ὁδὸς καὶ ἡ ἀλήθεια καὶ ἡ ζωή· οὐδεὶς ἔρχεται πρὸς τὸν πατέρα εἰ μὴ δι’ ἐμοῦ. The text of Hermas is literarily dependent on it. In addition to similarity of thought, the same words and the same sentence construction are there. The following simple synoptic table is in itself sufficient proof.

Sim. 9.12.6	John 14:6
εἴσοδος . . .	ὁδός . . .
οὐδείς	οὐδείς
εἰσελεύσεται	ἔρχεται
πρὸς αὐτὸν (κύριον)	πρὸς τὸν πατέρα
εἰ μὴ διὰ	εἰ μὴ δι’
τοῦ υἱοῦ αὐτοῦ.	ἐμοῦ.

A difficulty may arise, and that is that Hermas dropped ἀλήθεια and ζωή from the Johannine text. The answer lies in the fact that in verse 6, Hermas is still busy commenting on verse 1 where he called the Son of God πύλη. Now, the word ὁδός agrees better with πύλη. Besides, let me recall once more that when he follows a text, Hermas does not follow it word for word. As for his use in this context of the expression ὁ υἱὸς τοῦ θεοῦ, one of his typical characteristics is never to use the words Ἰησοῦς and Χριστός.

At the conclusion of the entire passage, which comments on the rock and the door, Sim. 9.12.8 says: "Anyone who fails to receive His Name will not enter into the Kingdom of God (ὃς ἂν τὸ ὄνομα αὐτοῦ μὴ λάβῃ, οὐκ εἰσελεύσεται εἰς τὴν βασιλείαν τοῦ θεοῦ)." The author takes up Sim. 9.12.4 whose literary dependence on Jn. 3:5 has been mentioned earlier.

In Sim. 9.15.2, it may be deemed that Hermas is still influenced by Jn. 3:5 when he has the Shepherd say: "The person who bears these names and that of the Son of God can enter into the Kingdom of God (ταῦτα τὰ ὀνόματα ὁ φορῶν καὶ τὸ ὄνομα τοῦ υἱοῦ τοῦ θεοῦ δυνήσεται εἰς τὴν βασιλείαν τοῦ θεοῦ εἰσελθεῖν)." Indeed, these words seem to take up positively what had been said negatively in Sim. 9.12.4, which betrays the literary influence of Jn. 3:5.

Jn. 3:5 still comes to mind when Hermas, speaking of baptism, writes in Sim. 9.16.2: "'They had to ascend,' he (the Shepherd) said, 'by means of water in order to be made living. Otherwise, if they had not shed the death of their former life, they could not enter into the Kingdom of God' (οὐκ ἠδύναντο γὰρ ἄλλως εἰσελθεῖν εἰς τὴν βασιλείαν τοῦ θεοῦ).'' There remains to be pointed out in this text one more reminiscence of the Pauline image drawn from Rom. 6:4 and Col. 2:12.

Still in Sim. 9, the text of 16.3-4 leads to Jn. 3:5; it says, "Those, also, who were deceased so received the seal of the Son of God (τὴν σφαγῖδα τοῦ υἱοῦ τοῦ θεοῦ) and entered the Kingdom of God (εἰσῆλθον εἰς τὴν βασιλείαν τοῦ θεοῦ). For, a man is dead before he receives the Name of God, but, when he receives the seal, he puts off death and receives life. The seal, therefore, is water (ἡ σφραγὶς οὖν τὸ ὕδωρ ἐστίν). The dead go down into the water and come out of it living. Therefore, this seal was proclaimed to them and they put it to use to enter the Kingdom of God (ἵνα εἰσέλθωσιν εἰς τὴν βασιλείαν τοῦ θεοῦ).'' The identification of the seal with water recalls baptism; the expression εἰσελθεῖν εἰς τὴν βασιλείαν τοῦ θεοῦ may, therefore, depend on Jn. 3:5. To be sure, this is a traditional formula if considered in isolation, but it belongs to a sentence whose first part, "received the seal," is explained by Hermas himself to mean Christian baptism, and the context is the same as in Jn. 3:5. I would like to repeat here a reference to the Pauline teaching in Rom. 6:4 and Col. 2:12 on the effective symbolism of baptism.

The Exegesis of Hermas on Jn. 3:5. All the preceding remarks, together with a careful reading of Sim. 9.12-16, lead me to question whether Hermas, in this passage, simply divulges his own, perhaps a bit personal, understanding of Jn. 3:5. I have just demonstrated that a literary reference to Jn. 3:5 seems to be rather compelling: the Johannine text functions as a leitmotiv for this passage, and he refers to it many times.

It is well known that, in Hermas, the formulas "to receive or bear the Name," and "to receive or bear the seal" are related to baptism. Besides, Hermas maintains more than once the Spirit's affinity with virtues and his opposition to vices. The presence of virtues is favorable to the indwelling of the Spirit; the presence of vices drives it away; virtues and vices are sometimes personified and even called πνεύματα or δυνάμεις. So it is that a bad conscience cannot dwell with the spirit of truth which requires us to walk in truth (Mand. 3.4); patience is favorable to the Holy Spirit while anger drives it away (Mand. 5.1.2-3). The Holy Spirit leaves the man who is riddled with anger, folly, fickleness, madness, bitterness, animosity, hatred, and takes refuge in a gentle and calm abode (Mand. 5.2.6); sadness distresses the Spirit and drives it away (Mand. 10.1.2; 2.1; 2.2; 2.4; 2.5-6; 3.2; 3.3). A spirit given by God has the force of divinity; it comes from the power of the Divine Spirit (Mand. 11.5). The spirit from below is weak, without any power (Mand. 11.6). A man who has the spirit of God is meek, calm, humble; he abstains from evil and vain desires of this world (Mand. 11.8); the spirit from below is inane, powerless, foolish (Mand. 11.11). The man from below is proud, insolent, impudent, gossiping; he lives in pleasures and deceits (Mand. 11.12).

From this relationship between the Spirit and the presence of virtues, and from its incompatibility with vice, Hermas may have seen in the Spirit a particular aspect which I would call "moral," in the sense that the Holy Spirit is only there where virtues are found, and is absent where vices dominate. Πνεύματα presides over these virtues and these vices; it inspires or symbolizes them and, consequently, there is a narrow connection between these πνεύματα and the Holy Spirit. Even if he does not necessarily identify them, Hermas goes as far as passing easily from the πνεύματα to the Holy Spirit, assigning to one of them what he says of the Spirit and vice versa. This is how he was able to glide quite easily towards a more ethical aspect of the concept of the Holy Spirit.

A text of Sim. 9 is remarkable on this subject. In Sim. 9.13.2 the virgins around the door are called ἅγια πνεύματα; we know from Sim. 9.15.2 that these holy spirits preside over or symbolize virtues. Now, in Sim. 9.24.2, speaking of believers who came from the seventh mountain and entered the tower, the Shepherd notes that they are clothed with the Holy Spirit of the virgins (ἐνδεδυμένοι τὸ πνεῦμα τὸ ἅγιον τούτων τῶν παρθένων). The presence of the participle ἐνδεδυμένοι recalls clearly Sim. 9.13.2 where the virgins are called πνεύματα and where the Shepherd affirms the necessity of receiving the garment of the virgins (ἐνδύσωσι τὸ ἔνδυμα αὐτῶν); thus far, Hermas has not spoken of the Holy Spirit of the virgins but of the holy spirits of the virgins. In Sim. 9.24.2, this transformation takes place explicitly: we go from πνεύματα of the virgins to πνεῦμα τὸ ἅγιον of the virgins. To be clad with the spirits of the virgins is equivalent in Hermas's mind to putting on the Holy Spirit of the virgins, to such a point that all the good πνεύματα may be seen as powers of the Holy Spirit, which emanate from it and which may be easily blended with it. On the other hand, evil πνεύματα are the powers of the devil which are, therefore, easily identified with him; this last remark is inferred, on the one hand, from Mand. 5.1.3, where Hermas says that the devil dwells in anger, and, on the other hand, from Mand. 2.4-5, where Hermas ranks anger among the evil πνεύματα.

Influenced by the moral side of the Spirit, Hermas is not consistent in his way of speaking. He passes with ease from the Holy Spirit to the spirits which preside over or symbolize the virtues, and reverses himself just as easily. This is how, in Hermas, the Holy Spirit seems to correspond sometimes to an action according to the Spirit.

Having commented on the Spirit in Hermas, and referring to the consideration of Sim. 9.12-16 in the literary climate of Jn. 3:5, I wonder whether Hermas finds in the Johannine text two elements necessary to enter the Kingdom: the first is baptism, and it corresponds to ἐξ ὕδατος in Jn.; the second, equivalent to ἐκ πνεύματος, is what may be designated by a single expression: "acting according to the Spirit." Hermas describes this second element in various forms, namely to put on the virgins' garments, to bear their names, to carry their virtues, and to follow the commandments. But let us examine those texts.

First of all, the first element required to enter the Kingdom is baptism. Hermas expresses it with two formulas; in the first, it is necessary to bear or to have received the Name; in the second, it is necessary to carry or to have received the seal.

The first formula (it is necessary to carry or to have received the Name) reappears several times in the following chapters of the Shepherd: in Sim. 9.12.4: "For that reason also, nobody enters the Kingdom of God without receiving the Name of His Son"; in Sim. 9.12.5: "no human being can enter the Kingdom of God, except by means of the Name of His Beloved Son"; in Sim. 9.12.8: "Anyone who fails to receive His Name will not enter into the Kingdom of God."

The second formula (it is necessary to carry or to have received the seal) appears in Sim. 9.16.3: "Those, also, who were deceased so received the seal of the Son of God and entered the Kingdom of God"; in Sim. 9.16.4: "Therefore, this seal was proclaimed to them and they put it to use to enter the Kingdom of God."

Yet this first element, baptism, does not suffice to enter the Kingdom. It is not enough to have the Name or the seal; something more is required to enter into the Kingdom. Considering the concept of the Spirit as it is formulated by Hermas, this is at least what emerges from certain texts of the *Shepherd* which mention a second necessary element that corresponds to an "action according to the Spirit," and may correspond to ἐκ πνεύματος in Jn. 3:5. Listen to the Shepherd on this subject: Sim. 9.13.2: "no man will enter the Kingdom of God in any other way, unless they clothe him with their raiment." "These virgins," he says in the same verse, "are holy spirits, . . . (they) are the powers of the Son of God. If you bear the Name without His power, you are bearing the Name to no purpose." Sim. 9.13.3: "Even the Son of God Himself bears the names of these virgins." In Sim. 9.15.1-2, we find the list of the names of the virgins: "Faith, Continence, Fortitude, Long-suffering, Simplicity, Innocence, Purity, Cheerfulness, Truth, Understanding, Concord, and Love." A second element necessary to enter into the Kingdom must include, therefore, the garments of the virgins which must be worn, the virtue of the Son of God which we must possess, the names of the virgins which we must carry.

Both aforementioned elements, baptism and "action according to the Spirit," must be present together in order to enter the Kingdom of God. Hermas says it best, namely in Sim. 9.13.2: "If you bear the Name (first element), without His power (second element), you are bearing the Name (first element) to no purpose." The Shepherd established this last statement with the help of features he drew from the parable he set forth, namely in exposing the significance of the stones which were rejected: "Now, the stones which you saw rejected," says Sim. 9.13.2-3, "are those who bore the Name (first element), but did not put on the virgins' raiment (second element)." The Shepherd then resumes his statement: "Anybody who bears the Name of the Son of God (first element) is also bound to bear their names. Even the Son of God Himself bears the names of these virgins (second element).'' This is how he then explains a part of his parable in Sim. 9.13.4: ''All the stones . . . that you saw going into the building of the tower and distributed by the hand of the virgins to remain in the building are clothed with the power of the virgins (second element).'' Hermas refers many times to this important statement, sometimes combining it with the Pauline image of the unity of the body: Sim. 9.13.5: ''And so, those who believed in the Lord through His Son, and have clothed themselves with these spirits, will be one spirit, one body, with a single color to their garment.'' Sim. 9.15.2: ''The person who bears these names (the virgins') (second element) and that of the Son of God (first element) can enter into the Kingdom of God.''

The presence of only one of these two elements mentioned—for there may be one without the other— does not entitle anybody to enter into the Kingdom. This is what happened to those who bore the Name and the spirits of the virgins, but abandoned the latter, as Hermas states it in Sim. 9.13.6-9: '''Now, sir,' I said, 'these rejected stones—why are they rejected? They have come through the gate (first element)[227] and have been set in the building by the hands of the virgins (second element).'[228]—'Since you show interest,' he said, 'and enquire accurately, I shall tell you about the rejected stones. They all received the Name of the Son of God (first element), as well as the power of the virgins (second element). So, on receiving these spirits, they obtained power and were associated with the servants of God; theirs was one spirit, one body and one raiment, for they had the same mind and practiced justice.[229] However, after some time they were led astray by the beautiful women you saw dressed in black garments, with bare shoulders and hair hanging down loosely and beautiful in form. At their sight they were filled with desire for them, clothed themselves with their power, and shed the power of the virgins (second element). Therefore, they were ejected from the house of God and handed over to the women.''

Yet, the loss of this second element is not beyond remedy; it may be recovered through penance, and this is how Hermas touches on the great problem which interests him and which is the central focus of his work: penance. This is, indeed, what he says in Sim. 9.14.1-2: '''Now, sir, suppose,' I said, 'that these men, in spite of their condition, should repent and put off their desire for these women and return to the virgins? And suppose, also, that they walk in their power

---

[227]Indeed, ''to come through the gate'' and ''to receive the Name'' are almost identical, since only those who bear his Name may pass through the gate, who is the Son of God; cf. Sim. 9.12.5.

[228]It is, indeed, from the hands of the virgins that man is clothed with their raiment; cf. Sim. 9.13.2.

[229]This passage is interwoven with Pauline images: Rom. 12:16; 2 Cor. 13:11; Eph. 4:4; Phil. 2:2; 3:16; 4:2.

and in their deeds (second element): Will they not enter the Kingdom of God?' 'They will enter,' he said, 'if they cast off the works of these women and assume the power of the virgins, so as to walk in their deeds (second element). That is the reason there was a pause in the building, so they could repent and return to the building of the tower. However, if they do not repent, then others will enter and they themselves will be finally rejected.'''

He who possesses only the first element is excluded from the Kingdom, for Sim. 9.15.3 says, "The servant of God who bears these names (the names of the women dressed in black)[230] can, indeed, see the Kingdom of God, but cannot enter it."

Nor will those who have the spirits of the virgins (second element), but do not carry the Name (first element) enter into the Kingdom. This is what happened to the righteous of the Old Testament. Since baptism is absolutely necessary, the apostles and the Christian doctors went to hell after their death in order to baptize them.[231] This is the teaching which Hermas develops in Sim. 9.16.1-4: '''Why,' I said, 'did the stones that had borne these spirits go up from the abyss (first element), and why were they put into the building (second element)?' 'They had to ascend,' he said, 'by means of water (first element) in order to be made living. Otherwise, if they had not shed the death of their former life, they could not enter the Kingdom of God. Those, also, who were deceased so received the seal of the Son of God (first element) and entered the Kingdom of God. For, a man is dead before he receives the Name of the Son of God (first element), but, when he receives the seal (first element), he puts off death and receives life. The seal, therefore, is water. The dead go down into the water and come out of it living.[232] Therefore, this seal was proclaimed to them (first element) and they put it to use to enter the Kingdom of God.'''

Hermas considers then the case of the apostles and the doctors who, according to his vision, rose also from the bottom of the water although they had already received the seal. Now, according to the teaching of the Shepherd himself, they could normally enter into the Kingdom. Why must they still rise from the water? The Shepherd gives the answer to this problem in Sim. 9.16.5-6: "Because, . . . the Apostles and teachers who preach the Name of the Son of God, after having been laid to rest in power and faith in the Son of God, preach also to those who have been laid to rest before them. To the latter they themselves passed on the seal

---

[230]The names of these women dressed in black are Unbelief, Incontinence, Disobedience, Deceit, Grief, Wickedness, Licentiousness, Irascibility, Lying, Foolishness, Slander, and Hatred.

[231]This tradition appears also in Clement of Alexandria, Strom. 2.9, PG 8:980; 6.6, PG 9:269.

[232]Here again is the Pauline image of Rom. 6:4; Col. 2:12.

(first element) they proclaimed. So, they went down with them into the water and came up again. But, the Apostles and teachers, though they were alive, went down and returned alive."[233]

In light of this teaching of Hermas and with the help of Sim. 9.14.5, another decree can be added as a second element needed to enter the Kingdom: "Now, if the whole of creation is supported by the Son of God, what do you think of those who are called by Him, who bear His Name[234] and walk in His commandments?" This sentence includes the first element, namely "they bear His Name"; the second, according to the teaching of Hermas, is expressed with the words: "and walk in His commandments." Consequently, the fulfilling of the commandments must be included in the notion of the second element required in order to enter the Kingdom.

In short, Hermas, who is under the literary influence of Jn. 3:5 in Sim. 9.12-16, quite probably understands this Johannine teaching in his own personal way. He saw in the first part of the Johannine verse two conditions needed to enter into the Kingdom: water and the Spirit. The first of these conditions is baptism, which Hermas expresses with his own formulas: to bear or to receive the Name, to bear or to receive the seal. The second condition requires that man put on the garments of the virgins, that he put on their virtues, that he put on their spirits, that he bear their names, that he follow the commandments. The expression ἐκ πνεύματος means all that to Hermas, because, as far as he is concerned, there is a close relationship between the Spirit and the virtues whose images are symbolic; they represent, in fact, the condition of the indwelling of the Spirit, and this is how Hermas can easily establish in his mind an identity between the presence of these virtues and that of the Spirit: where there are virtues, there is the Spirit. For Hermas, admission to the Kingdom is conditioned not only by receiving baptism but also by "acting according to the Spirit."

Sim. 9.24.4 reads, "All your descendants will dwell with the Son of God, for you have received from His spirit." The first words may be based on Jn. 17:24 where Christ prays for his Church and asks that his own be with him. Yet, this link does not go beyond the point of sheer possibility, because there is no clue in the text to lead us to Jn. 17:24 other than a vague similarity of idea.

When Sim. 9.31.2 states, "They (those who have not received the seal) must enter God's Kingdom," because of what I said above, it usually recalls Jn. 3:5.

I would still like to add that the expression τηρέω τὰς ἐντολάς in Sim. 5.1.5 is especially Johannine (Jn. 14:15, 21; 15:10; 1 Jn. 2:3; 3:22; Rev. 12:17; 14:12), even if it is read as well in the New Testament in Mt. 19:17 and 1 Tim. 6:14.

Let me now move on to 1 John and Revelation.

---

[233]Again the Pauline image of Rom. 6:4; Col. 2:12.

[234]The καί which precedes τὸ ὄνομα φοροῦντες may be the explicative καί.

In Mand. 3.1: "since the Lord is truthful (ἀληθινός) in every word and there is no lie in Him (καὶ οὐδὲν παρ' αὐτῷ ψεῦδος)," only a similarity of idea may be assumed with 1 Jn. 2:27, where Saint John writes καὶ οὐκ ἔστιν ψεῦδος regarding the anointing of the Spirit.

Vis. 4.2.1 reads, "After I had gone approximately thirty feet past the beast, behold, there met me a virgin, decked out like a lady coming from a bridal chamber (κεκοσμημένη ὡς ἐκ νυμφῶνος ἐκπορευομένη), all in white and with white sandals. She was veiled to the forehead and her headdress was a turban. But her hair was white." The verse identifies this virgin with the Church. A similarity of rhetorical image may be assumed here, even perhaps to the point of a literary contact with the description of the heavenly Jerusalem which Rev. 21:2 describes in the same vein, and where the phrase ὡς νύμφην κεκοσμημένην is found.

In Sim. 8.3.3, where Hermas calls the angel Michael "The great and glorious angel . . . who has power over this people and is their captain," it follows the traditional path[235] and cannot refer to Rev. 12:7, which merely mentions this archangel.

Again in Sim. 8.2.1, where Hermas mentions the crowns bestowed on those whose rods were covered with buds and fruit and who enter the tower, this theme of the crown bestowed on the elect is often mentioned in Revelation.[236]

As for the term σφραγίς which Hermas uses frequently,[237] it often appears in Revelation;[238] so it is with the expression λευκὸς ὡς χιών in Sim. 8.2.3, which is also found in Rev.[239]

In Vis. 1.3.2 and Sim. 2.9, there is mention of the "book of life." This image suggested by the idea of the judgment is common in all Jewish and Christian literature. Beyond its presence in passages of the Old and New Testaments,[240] it is also found in other Jewish and Christian writings.[241]

Vis. 4.1.6 relates Hermas's encounter with a sea monster. The description of this monster is sometimes linked to Rev. 11:7 and 12:3-4, but this agreement rests only on the simple fact that there is a description of a monster in Rev. as well. This monster, according to Vis. 4.1.10 had four colors on its head: black, red as the color of fire and blood, gold, and white. In Rev. 6:2, 4, 5, 8, four horsemen

---

[235]Cf. Dan. 10:13, 21; 12:1; Enoch 20:5; 24:6.

[236]Cf. Rev. 2:10; 3:11; 4:4, 10; 6:2; 9:17; 12:1; 14:14.

[237]Cf. Sim. 8.2.2 and 4; 8.6.3; 9.16.3, 4, 5, 7; 9.17.4.

[238]Cf. Rev. 5:1, 2, 5, 9; 6:1, 3, 5, 7, 9, 12; 7:2; 8:1; 9:4; σφραγίζω: Rev. 7:3, 4, 5, 8; 10:4; 20:3; 22:10.

[239]Cf. Rev. 1:14.

[240]Cf. Ex. 32:32-33; Ps. 69(68):29; Dan. 12:1; Rev. 3:5; 13:8; 17:8; 20:12, 15; 21:27.

[241]Cf. Enoch 47:3; 89:2 ff.; Jub. 30:20ff.; Apoc. Syr. Bar. 24.1; Hermas, Mand. 8.6; Sim. 2.9; 5.3.2.

appear, each on a horse of a different color: white, fiery red, black, and yellowish-green. Here again, the parallel is due only to the mention of four colors.

In conclusion, it can be asserted that few texts of Jn. have inspired Hermas literarily. A Johannine influence is certain and is clearly delineated in Sim. 9.12-16 in particular; in this section, two texts of the fourth gospel exerted a definite literary influence; Jn. 3:5, in particular, was probably the basis for Hermas to write a great part of the ninth Similitude. Yet, Hermas does not follow word for word the Johannine texts which inspire him; he drops some of its elements or substitutes others to suit his own composition.[242]

Some expressions of Hermas correspond to Revelation—namely, the description of the heavenly Jerusalem may have inspired the description of the Church in Vis. 4.2.1.

C. The Epistles of Saint Paul

Hermas certainly knew some of the Pauline epistles. He shows it in different parts of his work which reveal the apostle's influence in text as well as in context.

Hermas deals with second marriages in Mand. 4.4.1-2: "'Sir,' I said, 'if a wife or husband is deceased (ἐὰν γυνή . . . ἢ πάλιν ἀνήρ τις κοιμηθῇ) and either one of the survivors marries again (καὶ γαμήσῃ τις ἐξ αὐτῶν), does he or she sin by marrying (μήτι ἁμαρτάνει ὁ γαμῶν)?' 'There is no sin (οὐχ ἁμαρτάνει),' he said. 'But, anyone who remains single achieves greater honor for himself and great glory before the Lord (περισσοτέραν ἑαυτῷ τιμὴν καὶ μεγάλην δόξαν περιποιεῖται πρὸς τὸν κύριον). But, even in remarriage there is no sin (ἐὰν δὲ καὶ γαμήσῃ, οὐχ ἁμαρτάνει).'" Hermas is very probably inspired by the advice which Paul gives to the Corinthians in 1 Cor. 7:8-9, 28, 38-40. Almost all his expressions are found there: thus, ἐὰν ἀνήρ τις κοιμηθῇ corresponds to 1 Cor. 7:39; ἐὰν γαμήσῃ, to 1 Cor. 7:28; and οὐχ ἁμαρτάνει, to 1 Cor. 7:28; as for the sentence: "But, anyone who remains single achieves greater honor for himself and great glory before the Lord," it may be considered as a development of the words of Paul: "To the unmarried and the widows I say that it is well for them to remain single as I do" (1 Cor. 7:8); or: "and he who refrains from marriage will do better" (1 Cor. 7:38); or also: "But in my judgment she (a widow) is happier if she remains as she is" (1 Cor. 7:40). We know also that when Hermas is inspired by a text, he is not chained to it word for word; he develops it in his own way to suit the needs of his composition, often revealing his source with a similar idea and several words or expressions. We can, therefore, easily agree that in this particular case, he drew his inspiration in chapter 7 from 1 Corinthians.

Mand. 10 deals with reflections and advice on melancholy. It seems obvious that Hermas's account has been literarily influenced by two passages from Paul:

---

[242]Cf. above, 134-42.

Eph. 4:30 and 2 Cor. 7:10. The Shepherd says in Mand. 10.1.2: "You are a senseless man . . . not to know that sorrow (ἡ λύπη) is more wicked than all spirits and most dangerous to servants of God. More than all spirits it destroys a human being and wears out the Holy Spirit (καταφθείρει τὸν ἄνθρωπον καὶ ἐκτρίβει τὸ πνεῦμα τὸ ἅγιον)—but again saves it (καὶ πάλιν σῴζει)." The Shepherd then develops this statement in Mand. 10.2.1-6: "Let me tell you now, slow-witted man, how melancholy wears out the Holy Spirit (πῶς ἡ λύπη ἐκτρίβει τὸ πνεῦμα τὸ ἅγιον) and again lightens it (καὶ πάλιν σῴζει). When the man of divided purpose applies himself to any practice and fails in it because of his divided purpose, this melancholy (ἡ λύπη) enters into him and the Holy Spirit is in gloom and is worn out (λυπεῖ τὸ πνεῦμα τὸ ἅγιον). So, also, when violent anger clings to the man about some matter and he is very much embittered, melancholy (ἡ λύπη) enters the heart of the angry man. He is then distressed at the action he performed and repents (μετανοεῖ) because he did evil. Now, this melancholy seems to bring salvation, because he repents of having done evil (αὕτη οὖν ἡ λύπη δοκεῖ σωτηρίαν ἔχειν, ὅτι τὸ πονηρὸν πράξας μετενόησεν). So, both deeds distress the Spirit (λυποῦσι τὸ πνεῦμα): the divided purpose, because he has not succeeded in the action itself; the anger distresses the Spirit (λυπεῖ τὸ πνεῦμα), because he committed evil. The two, then, divided purpose and anger, are saddening to the Holy Spirit (λυπηρά ἐστι τῷ πνεύματι τῷ ἁγίῳ). Remove melancholy (τὴν λύπην), then, and do not oppress the Holy Spirit (καὶ μὴ θλῖβε τὸ πνεῦμα τὸ ἅγιον) dwelling within you, lest He pray to God to depart from you. For, the Spirit of God that was given to this flesh does not endure melancholy and confinement (ταύτην λύπην οὐχ ὑποφέρει οὐδὲ στενοχωρίαν)." In Mand. 10.3.2, the Shepherd repeats his statement: "The melancholy man . . . by bringing melancholy to the Holy Spirit (λυπεῖ τὸ πνεῦμα τὸ ἅγιον) he commits grave sin.

Throughout this passage, a leitmotiv recurs and echoes the words of Eph. 4:30: καὶ μὴ λυπεῖτε τὸ πνεῦμα τὸ ἅγιον τοῦ θεοῦ; this echo resounds more than once and expresses forcefully the baneful consequences of melancholy which concerns this Mandate of the Shepherd.

Yet, for Hermas, whose fervent desire is to see men saved, melancholy contains a salutary aspect which he finds expressed in another of Paul's texts, 2 Cor. 7:10, which states that melancholy brings out repentance, thanks to which he who sinned is saved: ἡ γὰρ κατὰ θεὸν λύπη μετάνοιαν εἰς σωτηρίαν ἀμεταμέλητον ἐργάζεται. There seems to be no doubt that Hermas depends on it in Mand. 10.2.4 where he has the Shepherd say, αὕτη οὖν ἡ λύπη δοκεῖ σωτηρίαν ἔχειν, ὅτι τὸ πονηρὸν πράξας μετενόησεν. In this sentence, he establishes the same teaching as Paul; furthermore, the term σωτηρία and the verb μετενόησεν correspond to μετάνοια in Paul.

In short, Eph. 4:30 and 2 Cor. 7:10 were the sources from which Hermas drew. Wishing to caution against the disastrous effects of melancholy, Hermas finds in

Eph. 4:30 the main reason for this caution: the sad man does evil in saddening the Holy Spirit. Yet, melancholy is not entirely baneful, because finally—and this is where Hermas thinks of 2 Cor. 7:10—it brings out a salutary repentance.

Eph. 4:30 may also be compared to Mand. 3.4, in which the Shepherd blames Hermas for his past behavior. "It was really your duty, as the servant of God, to walk in truth and not allow an evil conscience to dwell in the company of the Spirit of truth. Neither ought you to cause grief to the Spirit of truth and holiness (μηδὲ λύπην ἐπάγειν τῷ πνεύματι τῷ σεμνῷ καὶ ἀληθεῖ)." The last words recall Eph. 4:30, which was used by the author as noted previously. It is, therefore, quite possible that here again Hermas refers to it, notwithstanding the difference which did not exist in the passage mentioned above and which I must point out, namely: instead of τὸ πνεῦμα τὸ ἅγιον, Hermas has here the expression τὸ πνεῦμα τὸ σεμνὸν καὶ ἀληθές, but—and we know this—he does not refrain from changing the source which inspires him.

In the parable of the construction of the tower, the Shepherd identifies the rock with the Son of God in Sim. 9.12.1: "This rock (ἡ πέτρα) and this tower . . . is the Son of God (ὁ υἱὸς τοῦ θεοῦ ἐστί)." This reminds us naturally of Paul who, recalling the events in the desert, writes in 1 Cor. 10:4, ἡ πέτρα δὲ ἦν ὁ Χριστός. There may be here an allusion to this Pauline text; the absence of Χριστός, replaced by ὁ υἱὸς τοῦ θεοῦ is normal in Hermas.

In his commentary on Sim. 9, Hermas has the Shepherd say in 13.5-7: "And so, those who believe in the Lord through His Son, and have clothed themselves with these spirits, will be one spirit, one body (ἓν πνεῦμα, ἓν σῶμα), with a single color to their raiment (καὶ μία χρόα τῶν ἱματίων αὐτῶν) . . . theirs was one spirit, one body and one raiment (ἓν πνεῦμα καὶ ἓν σῶμα καὶ ἓν ἔνδυμα), for they had the same mind and practiced justice (τὰ γὰρ αὐτὰ ἐφρόνουν)." There is no doubt that Hermas took up the Pauline formulas, but he interpreted them somewhat closer to the Hellenistic way of thinking.[243] I would also like to note in this context the expression τὸ αὐτὸ φρονεῖν, which is one of the parenetic formulas of unity in Paul.[244] Moreover, this ninth Similitude is devoted to the allegory of the tower, which represents the building of the Church here on earth, and the allegory of the construction is either present or hinted at in Paul in Rom. 9:32-33; 15:2; 15:20; 1 Cor. 3:9; 14:12, 26; 2 Cor. 6:16; 12:19; and Eph. 2:21-22; 4:12. Incidentally, Eph. 2:10-22 may be linked with Sim. 9.4.3, in which different stones are identified as having been used for the construction of the tower, εἰς τὴν οἰ-

---

[243]Cf. L. Cerfaux, *La Théologie de l'Église suivant saint Paul*, Unam Sanctam 10, 2nd ed. (Paris, 1948) 180n.2. For the idea of unity in Greek and Hellenistic philosophy, cf. S. Hanson, *The Unity of the Church in the New Testament* (Upsala, 1946) 46-47.

[244]Cf. Cerfaux, *La Théologie de l'Église suivant saint Paul*, 187-88.

κοδομὴν τοῦ πύργου.[245]

Still in this ninth Similitude, other Pauline formulas of unity are found. Namely in Sim. 9.17.4: "all the nations that dwell under the heavens, after hearing and believing, are called by one Name, that of the Son of God. So, when they receive the seal, they have one understanding (μίαν φρόνησιν ἔσχον) and one mind (καὶ ἕνα νοῦν). Their faith (καὶ μία πίστις) and love (μία ἀγάπη) make them one. . . . " This passage recalls the formulas of Eph. 4:3-6.[246] The same is true for Sim. 9.18.4: "the Church of God will become one body (ἓν σῶμα), one understanding (μία φρόνησις), one mind (εἷς νοῦς), one faith (μία πίστις), and one love (μία ἀγάπη)."

A Pauline literary influence stands out throughout the texts of Sim. 9, even though not one of the apostle's texts can be found literally. But the similarity of thought and the presence of identical words leave no doubt with respect to Hermas's source of inspiration in his concept of the unity of the Church.

Sim. 9.16.2-4, 6 also needs to be mentioned because of the evidence of Pauline teaching; I have already examined this passage in connection with Jn.[247] Hermas borrowed from Rom. 6:3-5 and Col. 2:12 Paul's ideas on the meaning of the baptismal ritual; namely, through baptism we are buried into death in order to obtain a new life.[248] He expresses this idea in his own way to suit the needs of his own composition: rising through the water, we receive life; receiving the seal divests us of death and invests us with life; and above all, we descend into the water dead and rise up alive. According to Saint Paul, this is what the efficacious symbolism of baptism represents. It is, therefore, likely that Hermas had in mind these Pauline texts.

Other passages from Hermas, while not necessarily revealing a literary dependence on Pauline texts, still express ideas similar to those of Paul.

In Mand. 3.1, the Shepherd instructs Hermas, "Love truth and let nothing but truth issue from your mouth, in order that the spirit which God has settled in this flesh of yours may be found to be truthful in the sight of all men." A somewhat similar idea appears in Eph. 4:25, in the sense that Paul invites his readers to speak the truth and forsake lying. But it hardly seems probable that Hermas referred to this text, for, except for the presence of ψεῦδος and ἀλήθεια in Hermas and in Paul, the motive for having to speak the truth is different for each author:

---

[245]Cf. A Committee of the Oxford Society, *The New Testament in the Apostolic Fathers*, 107.

[246]Cf. Cerfaux, *La Théologie de l'Église suivant saint Paul*, 180.

[247]Cf. above, 137 and 141.

[248]Cf. Cerfaux, *Une lecture de l'Épître aux Romains*, Bibliothèque de l'Institut Supérieur des Sciences Religieuses de l'Université Catholique de Louvain 2 (Tournai, Paris, 1947) 60.

in the *Shepherd*, truth must be told so that the authenticity of the spirit, which God has lodged in the flesh of man, stands out in the eyes of mankind; in Eph., truth must be told because Christians are unified into one membership.[249]

Speaking of the one-time repentance, Mand. 4.3.1-2 says, "'Sir,' I said, 'I have been told by some teachers that there is no other repentance (ἑτέρα μετάνοια οὐκ ἔστιν) except the one [that was vouchsafed us], when we went into the water (εἰς ὕδωρ κατέβημεν) and received remission of our former sins.' He said to me, 'You have been correctly told; such is the case. For, the person who has received remission of sins must no longer sin, but live in purity.'" Heb. 6:4-6 expresses a similar teaching; just as in Hermas, the subject matter in Heb. is sins committed after baptism, because the author of the Epistle to the Hebrews denotes the baptized with the expression ἅπαξ φωτισθέντας, as does Hermas with the words εἰς ὕδωρ κατέβημεν. Nevertheless, the parallel with Heb. is limited to this simple similarity of idea, since Hermas's language does not retrace in any way that of the Epistle to the Hebrews, except for the term μετάνοια. Hermas probably merely reported a teaching common at that time. This is, in fact, what he seems to imply when he writes: "I have been told by some teachers."

In Sim. 4.4, the Shepherd says to Hermas, "Sinners will be burned, because they sinned without repenting; pagans, because they did not know their Creator (ὅτι οὐκ ἔγνωσαν τὸν κτίσαντα αὐτούς)." This recalls Rom. 1:20-21 in which we read a similar idea regarding persons whose bad dispositions have posed an obstacle to the knowledge of God and who, therefore, yielded to the vanity of their thoughts.

Sim. 8.2.9 reads, "For, He who created this tree (with the rods) wishes all who have taken branches from it to live." The affirmation of the universal salvific will of God is present also in 1 Tim. 2:4, but in a language so different that the Pauline text could not have been the source of the sentence in Hermas.

In Sim. 9.12.2, wishing to explain that the rock which is the Son of God is very ancient, the Shepherd says, "The Son of God is born before all His creation (πάσης τῆς κτίσεως αὐτοῦ προγενέστερός ἐστιν) and, so, is counselor to His Father in His creation." This statement could be compared to the picture of the origins of Wisdom in Prov. 8:22-30; moreover, Col. 1:15 reports a similar teaching and contains the expression πρωτότοκος πάσης κτίσεως, which can easily be linked to πάσης τῆς κτίσεως αὐτοῦ προγενέστερος in Hermas. Yet, a literary contact with the text of Paul is out of the question, because the characteristic word of the Pauline passage πρωτότοκος is missing in Hermas.

---

[249]It is difficult to see how the Oxford Committee (*The New Testament in the Apostolic Fathers*, 107) could write on this passage, "Both language and idea are common enough to indicate a borrowing." There is a similarity of idea, but where is the similarity of language?

The exhortation of the Shepherd at the end of Sim. 9.31.6 states: "I, also, am a shepherd, and I have the gravest obligation to give an account for you." Heb. 13:17 also acknowledges that the shepherd must account for his flock, thus presenting a similar teaching.

In recommending leniency to Hermas, the aged woman says to him in Vis. 2.3.2, "However, your refusal to fall away from the Living God, your simplicity, and your great continence are saving you (τὸ μὴ ἀποστῆναί σε ἀπὸ θεοῦ ζῶντος)." The last words of this passage recall particularly the last words of Heb. 3:12: Βλέπετε, ἀδελφοί, μήποτε ἔσται ἔν τινι ὑμῶν καρδία πονηρὰ ἀπιστίας ἐν τῷ ἀποστῆναι ἀπὸ θεοῦ ζῶντος. The identity is perfect; both texts have τὸ ἀποστῆναι ἀπὸ θεοῦ ζῶντος. Given the identity of expression, it is tempting to assert a literary contact; but the difference in contexts is, however, not favorable to this notion. Wis. 3:10, sometimes given as a parallel, has a somewhat different expression: τοῦ κυρίου ἀποστάντες. The same goes for Vis. 3.7.2, in which the symbol of the stones is explained thus: "Those (stones) who fall into fire and are burned are the ones who have finally rebelled from the living God (οὗτοί εἰσιν οἱ εἰς τέλος ἀποστάντες τοῦ θεοῦ τοῦ ζῶντος). . . . "

The convergence in Hermas of expressions similar or very close to Paul must also be mentioned, such as δοξάζω τὸ ὄνομα τοῦ κυρίου,[250] εἰρηνεύοντες or εἰρηνεύετε ἐν ἑαυτοῖς,[251] ἡ ἀνακαίνωσις τῶν πνευμάτων,[252] ἀντιλαμβάνεσθαι ἀλλήλων,[253] the word ἱλαρότης,[254] the expressions ὁ κτίσας τὰ πάντα[255] and δίκαιος κριτής.[256]

I propose now to examine some of Hermas's texts which have sometimes been linked to Pauline writings, but which are certainly not inspired by them.

In Mand. 12.2.4, Hermas uses the image of armor: "As for you, put on the desire of justice and, armed with the fear of the Lord, resist them." This passage has sometimes been compared with Eph. 6:13.[257] The context of Eph. describes the Christian's armor, and the breastplate of righteousness is among the elements which compose it; but Hermas does not speak of the Christian's armor in such de-

---

[250]Cf. Vis. 2.1.2 and 2 Thess. 1:12 and also Ps. 86(85):9, 12; Is. 24:15; 46:5.

[251]Cf. Vis. 3.6.3; 9.2; 9.10; 12.3, and 1 Thess. 5:13 and also Mk. 9:50.

[252]Cf. Vis. 3.8.9 which can be linked with ἀνακαινώσις τοῦ νοός in Rom. 12:2 and with ἀνανεοῦσθαι δὲ τῷ πνεύματι τοῦ νοὸς ὑμῶν in Eph. 4:23.

[253]Cf. Vis. 3.9.2 to be compared with προσλαμβάνεσθαι ἀλλήλους in Rom. 15:7 and with ἀντιλαμβάνομαι in Acts 20:35.

[254]Cf. Mand. 10.3.1 and only in Rom. 12:8 in the N.T..

[255]Cf. Sim. 5.5.2; 7.4 and Eph. 3:9, and also Rev. 4:11 and Ecclus. 18:1.

[256]Cf. Sim. 6.3.6 and 2 Tim. 4:8 and also Ps. 7:12; 2 Macc. 12:6.

[257]Cf. Lelong, *Le Pasteur d'Hermas*, 128.

tail as Paul does. Moreover, the fear of the Lord is not mentioned in Eph. 6:13. This parallel is most likely due only to the metaphor of the armor common to both Hermas and Paul.

As for the name Hermas in Vis. 1.1.4, I would like to note that this name is found in Rom. 16:14 among those whom Paul greets in that Church. This name was too common[258] to allow us to believe that Hermas was necessarily the one whom Paul addressed.

Vis. 1.3.4: "Behold the God of Hosts . . . He is moving away the heavens, the mountains (μεθίστανει τοὺς οὐρανοὺς καὶ τὰ ὄρη), the hills, and seas . . . ," has sometimes been linked with 1 Cor. 13:2 in which the expression ὄρη μεθιστάναι is found. Hermas does not refer to this text of Paul because, first of all, the subject matter in the *Shepherd* is not faith but God, whose power moves heaven and earth. Next, this entire passage in Hermas is full of reminiscences of the Old Testament, particularly the Book of Psalms; now then, Ps. 46 (45):3 and Is. 54:10 have this specific expression.

Finally, when Vis. 3.13.4 reads, "Here you have the complete revelation. Do not ask for anything more about a revelation, but if anything is necessary it will be revealed to you," some critics thought it to be an idea similar to Phil. 3:15b. The idea may seem similar when this passage is read out of context, but this similarity decreases when it is seen in its context. In this case, the parallel between Hermas and Paul rests probably on the presence of the word ἀποκάλυψις in both authors.

Some of the apostle's texts and ideas have, therefore, exerted their influence on the composition of several passages in the *Shepherd*. Hermas, however, does not refer explicitly to Saint Paul, and even when he is literarily dependent on him, he does not follow his texts to the letter. Except for the effective symbolism of baptism and the Pauline formulas on unity, which he interprets anyway in a more Hellenistic manner, most of Paul's texts which have influenced Hermas or include a similar idea have, in Hermas, a clearly distinct moral character or they are inserted in a context of moral nature. None of the high theological constructions of the apostle are found in the *Shepherd*.

D. The Pastoral Epistles and the Epistle of James in Particular

Whoever has read a commentary or a study on the *Shepherd of Hermas* notices immediately a very large number of references to the Epistle of James. In fact, authors generally agree in stressing the strong affinity between the *Shepherd* and the Letter of James: Hermas knew it and was inspired by it in many passages.

In Mand. 1.1, the Shepherd says, "First of all, believe that there is one God (πρῶτον πάντων πίστευσον ὅτι εἷς ἐστιν ὁ θεός . . .)" Zahn thinks that when

---

[258]Cf. de Gephardt and Harnack, *Hermae Pastor,* 5.

Hermas wrote these words, he had in mind Mk. 12:28-29[259] in which there is as well a reference to Deut. 6:4-5. Gaâb proposes Jas. 2:19: σὺ πιστεύεις ὅτι εἷς ἐστιν ὁ θεός as a parallel.[260] The presence in Hermas of the words πρῶτον πάντων, in a context which speaks of commandments (ἐντολή)[261] draws attention initially to Mk. 12:28, which speaks of ἐντολὴ πρώτη πάντων, and not to Deut. 6:4-5 or Jas. 2:19 whose contexts do not speak of commandment (ἐντολή). Nevertheless, and for various reasons, I am inclined to believe that Hermas refers here to Jas. First of all, Jas. 2:19 is tangibly very close to the text of Hermas; he shares ὅτι εἷς ἐστιν ὁ θεός with him, and he has πιστεύεις, which corresponds to πίστευσον. In the second place, Hermas does not interpret πρῶτον πάντων to refer to the first commandment as coming first in a series of others; in fact, had he intended it this way, the expectation would be for him to speak subsequently of a second commandment. Well, nowhere is there subsequent mention of a second commandment; πρῶτον πάντων, therefore, does not imply the presence of a second commandment, but signifies simply "above all." In the third place, a reference by Hermas to the text of Mk. is impossible: if Hermas was referring to this πρῶτον and was insisting on this πρῶτον, it would be impossible psychologically for him to have changed the substance of Mk.'s first commandment by substituting for the love of God faith in the oneness of God. Finally, the absence of the verb πιστεύω in Deut. 4:5-6 leads me to believe that Hermas did not take this text into consideration. Therefore, the only solution which remains is that Hermas referred to Jas. 2:19.

In Mand. 9.1-7, the Shepherd gives several pieces of advice on doubt and on confidence in prayer. Many scholars think that Hermas is inspired by Jas. 1:5-9. Dibelius, however, is not convinced of this affinity; since the similarity is insufficient, he explains it by recourse to a common tradition.[262] Here is what Hermas wrote:

> Cast off indecision and doubt not in the least, when asking anything from God (ἆρον ἀπὸ σεαυτοῦ τὴν διψυχίαν καὶ μηδ' ὅλως διψυχήσῃς αἰτήσασθαί τι παρὰ τοῦ θεοῦ). Do not say "How can I ask and receive anything (αἰτήσασθαι) from the Lord after having committed so many sins?" Do not entertain such thoughts, but with your whole heart turn to the Lord and ask Him without wavering (καὶ αἰτοῦ παρ' αὐτοῦ ἀδιστάκτως). You will learn His superabundant mercy. He will not leave you in the lurch. No! He will fulfill the request of your soul. God is not like human beings who bear a grudge.

---

[259]Cf. Th. Zahn, *Der Hirte des Hermas* (Gotha, 1868) 449ff.

[260]Cf. E. Gaâb, *Der Hirte des Hermas* (Basel, 1866) 98.

[261]Cf. Vis. 5.6 and 7; the division into Visions, Mandates, and Similitudes goes back to Hermas himself; cf. on this subject Lelong, *Le Pasteur d'Hermas*, viii.

[262]Cf. Dibelius, *Der Hirt des Hermas*, 529.

He is without malice and has mercy on what He has made. Cleanse your heart, then, of all the vanities of this world and of the vices mentioned above. Then ask of the Lord (καὶ αἰτοῦ παρὰ τοῦ κυρίου) and you will receive all (ἀπολήψῃ πάντα). You cannot fail to obtain all your requests, provided you ask the Lord without wavering (ἐὰν ἀδιστάκτως αἰτήσῃς παρὰ τοῦ κυρίου). However, if you waver in your heart, you will not receive a single one of your requests (ἐὰν δὲ διστάσῃς ἐν τῇ καρδίᾳ σου, οὐδὲν οὐ μὴ λήψῃ τῶν αἰτημάτων σου). Those who are divided in purpose are they who waver before the Lord (οἱ γὰρ διστάζοντες εἰς τὸν θεόν, οὗτοί εἰσιν οἱ δί-ψυχοι) and altogether fail to obtain any of their requests (καὶ οὐδὲν ὅλως ἐπιτυγχάνουσι τῶν αἰτημάτων αὐτῶν). But those who are wholly perfect in the faith ask everything with reliance on the Lord and they receive, because they ask without wavering, without divided purpose (οἱ δὲ ὁλοτελεῖς ὄν-τες ἐν τῇ πίστει πάντα αἰτοῦνται πεποιθότες ἐπὶ τὸν κύριον καὶ λαμβάνουσιν ὅτι ἀδιστάκτως αἰτοῦνται, μηδὲν διψυχοῦντες). Every man of divided purpose will be saved with difficulty, unless he repents (πᾶς γὰρ δίψυχος ἀνήρ, ἐὰν μὴ μετανοήσῃ, δυσκόλως σωθήσεται). Cleanse your heart, then, of divided purpose (διψυχίας), clothe yourself with faith (πίστιν), because it is strong, and put your trust in God, confident that you will receive every request you make of Him (πίστευε τῷ θεῷ, ὅτι πάντα τὰ αἰτήματά σου ἃ αἰτεῖς λήψῃ). Now, if some time or other, after hav-ing made it, you receive your request from the Lord rather slowly, do not doubt (μὴ διψυχήσῃς) because you did not receive your soul's request quickly. In general, you receive your request slowly because of some temptation or some shortcoming of which you are not aware.

As a whole, there certainly seems to be a similarity of idea between Jas. 1:5-9 and this passage in Hermas. Throughout both texts, there is an exhortation to pray with confidence and without any doubt. But is there something more, namely, is there a literary connection between Hermas and the Letter of James? Hermas uses James's words: δίψυχος, αἰτέω, παρὰ θεοῦ αἰτέω ἐν πίστει, λαμβάν-ομαι; however, James does not once use Hermas's characteristic word διστάζω; he uses rather the verb διακρίνω, which is also repeated many times in the pas-sage examined. Yet, as a whole, we must acknowledge that Hermas's texts them-selves are fairly removed from those of James. Is Hermas simply commenting, in his own way, on the words of James? If, on the other hand, we can demonstrate that Hermas use the Epistle of James freely, the hypothesis of a reference will be confirmed.

Still in the context of the need to trust in prayer, Mand. 9.11 reads, "'You see then,' he (the Shepherd) says, 'that faith is from above from the Lord (ἡ πίσ-τις ἄνωθέν ἐστι παρὰ τοῦ κυρίου), and its power is great, whereas divided purpose is an earthly spirit, from the Devil (ἐπίγειον πνεῦμά ἐστι παρὰ τοῦ διαβόλου), lacking in power.'" This passage recalls Jas. 1:17 and 3:15. Hermas expresses the antithesis between faith and doubt in a way which is very similar to

Jas. 3:15; Hermas says ἄνωθέν ἐστι . . . ἐπίγειον . . . παρὰ τοῦ διαβόλου;
James writes ἄνωθεν . . . ἐπίγειος, δαιμονιώδης. Moreover, what Hermas says
about faith resembles what James writes of the gift of God in 1:17; faith ἄνωθέν
ἐστι παρὰ τοῦ κυρίου, notes the Shepherd; the gift ἄνωθέν ἐστιν ἀπὸ τοῦ πατρός, declares James. While the antithesis ἄνωθεν–ἐπίγειος is obvious, the hypothesis of a dependence is plausible given the great similarity of expressions.

Bearing in mind the distinction between true and false prophets, Hermas writes
in Mand. 11.5, "For, no spirit granted by God (πᾶν γὰρ πνεῦμα ἀπὸ θεοῦ δοθέν)
has to be consulted. It speaks everything with the Godhead's power, because it is
from above (ὅτι ἄνωθέν ἐστιν), from the power of the Divine Spirit." I have
just noted in the preceding paragraph that Hermas was probably inspired by Jas.
1:17, applying to faith what James said of the gift of God in general. This particular text supplies us with another serious clue which demonstrates that Hermas
knew this text of Jas. 1:17 and was inspired by it. James writes, πᾶσα δόσις ἀγαθὴ
καὶ πᾶν δώρημα τέλειον ἄνωθέν ἐστιν καταβαῖνον ἀπὸ τοῦ πατρὸς τῶν φώτων.
The presence in Hermas of πᾶν and δοθέν is an important element in favor of a
reference to the text of James, because these words echo rather faithfully πᾶσα
δόσις. Both also use the common expression ἄνωθέν ἐστιν. Hermas merely applies to the Spirit James's general statement about the divine gift.

I would add that a parallel with Jas. 3:15 is suggested by the following verse
in Mand. 11.6: "But, the spirit that is consulted and speaks according to the desires of men is earthy (ἐπίγειον) and weak, without any power." As a result, the
perception is that Hermas connects Jas. 1:17 and 3:15, linking ἄνωθεν in Jas. 1:17
with ἐπίγειον in Jas. 3:15. Moreover, Hermas continues to develop freely in
Mand. 11 the idea expressed in verse 5, pointing out the characteristics of the spirit
from above and contrasting them with those of the spirit here below, somewhat
like Jas. 3:15-17, which speaks of the wisdom from above and the wisdom here
below, yet without borrowing a single word from the text of James.

Speaking of good and evil desires, the Shepherd makes in Mand. 12 many
similar statements which I have compiled below.

Mand. 12.2.4: "If evil desire sees you armed with the fear of God (καθωπλισ-
μένον τῷ φόβῳ τοῦ θεοῦ) and resisting (ἀνθεστηκότα), it will flee far away
and you will not set eyes on it, because it fears your arms."

Mand. 12.4.6-7: "Be converted, you who walk in the commandments of the
Devil (τοῦ διαβόλου), commandments that are hard, bitter, cruel, and foul.
And do not fear the Devil either, because he has no power against you (μὴ
φοβήθητε τὸν διάβολον, ὅτι ἐν αὐτῷ δύναμις οὐκ ἔστιν καθ᾽ ὑμῶν). I,
the Angel of Repentance, who have overcome the Devil, am on your side.
The Devil only causes fear, but his fear is of no consequence. Do not fear
him, then, and he will flee from you (μὴ φοβήθητε οὖν αὐτόν, καὶ φεύξεται ἀφ᾽ ὑμῶν)."

Mand. 12.5.2: "'The Devil cannot lord it over those who are servants of God (οὐ δύναται καταδυναστεύειν τῶν δούλων τοῦ θεοῦ) with their whole heart and who place their hope in Him. The Devil can wrestle with, but not overcome them. So, if you resist him (ἐὰν οὖν ἀντισταθῆτε αὐτῷ), he will flee from you in defeat and confusion (νικηθεὶς φεύξεται ἀφ' ὑμῶν). But empty men,' he said, 'fear him, as if he had power.'"

All these statements sound like an echo of Jas. 4:7: ὑποτάγητε οὖν τῷ θεῷ· ἀντίστητε δὲ τῷ διαβόλῳ καὶ φεύξεται ἀφ' ὑμῶν. The words and the idea are sufficiently close to James to justify the conclusion that they are probably based on the epistle.[263] The text of James is particularly close to Mand. 12.5.2. But, if we acknowledge that Hermas is literarily dependent on James in this passage, this conclusion may be extended to all the other cited passages as expressing an idea similar to that of Mand. 12.5.2.

Still other texts are sometimes given as parallels. Thus, resistance to the Devil is read in 1 Pet. 5:9,[264] the flight of the demon is mentioned in the Testament of the XII Patriarchs, Simeon 3, Issachar 7, Napht. 8.[265] The ideas expressed in these last parallels are found in Hermas, but none of them has assembled in one text the resistance to the demon and his flight, as they are in the *Shepherd* and in Jas. 4:7. This is why I think that Hermas depends on the text of James. The contexts are moreover similar: they both have in mind to establish the powerlessness of the demon. But here again, I emphasize that Hermas develops in his own way, and according to the needs of his own composition, the text from which he draws inspiration.

In a context inviting the reader not to fear the Devil, the Angel of Repentance says to Hermas in Mand. 12.6.3: "Listen to me: Fear Him who has power to save and to destroy. Keep all the mandates (τὸν πάντα δυνάμενον σῶσαι καὶ ἀπολέσαι καὶ τηρεῖτε τὰς ἐντολὰς ταύτας). . . . " The words "who has power to save and to destroy" echo a series of New Testament texts: Mt. 10:28; Lk. 6:9; 9:24, 56; 12:5; 17:33; Jas. 4:12. It is obvious that the text of Hermas states an idea which has a strong parallel with some of these New Testament texts, namely with Mt. 10:28; Lk. 6:9; and Jas. 4:12. Yet, literarily, contact is made with the words of Jas.; he is the only one, in fact, who actually uses both verbs σῶσαι and ἀπολέσαι as does Hermas; and as in the *Shepherd,* they are preceded by the participle δυνάμενος; finally, the context in Hermas deals with keeping the command-

---

[263]Cf. A Committee of the Oxford Society, *The New Testament in the Apostolic Fathers,* 112; A. Charue, *Les Épîtres Catholiques, Épître de saint Jacques, La Sainte Bible* de L. Pirot, 12 (Paris, 1938) 422.

[264]1 Pet. 5:9: ᾧ (διαβόλῳ) ἀντίστητε στερεοὶ τῇ πίστει.

[265]*Test. 12 Patr.*, Simeon 3: ἀποτρέχει τὸ πονηρὸν πνεῦμα ἀπ' αὐτοῦ; Issachar 7: πᾶν πνεῦμα τοῦ βελιὰρ φεύξεται ἀφ' ὑμῶν; Napht. 8: ὁ διάβολος φεύξεται ἀφ' ὑμῶν.

ments, and the same text of James has the word νομοθέτης which is able to lead the spirit to the idea of laws and commandments. It is also interesting to point out that, with regard to this passage, the Oxford Committee, which is usually reluctant to admit a literary contact, resigns itself to it this time: "Here, the identity of expressions and the similarity of context strongly suggest a literary dependence; it is possible that both authors use a common document, but in this case, there is no proof of this document."[266]

Thinking of the excellence of the Shepherd's precepts, Hermas writes in Sim. 6.1.1: "While seated in my house and praising the Lord for all I had seen, I also reflected on the mandates. I thought that they were noble, possible of fulfillment, joyous, glorious, and capable of saving man's soul (δυνάμεναι σῶσαι ψυχὴν ἀνθρώπου)." The last words, δυνάμεναι σῶσαι ψυχὴν ἀνθρώπου, recall Jas. 1:21 where, speaking of the practice of the gospel, it says, διὸ ἀποθέμενοι πᾶσαν ῥυπαρίαν καὶ περισσείαν κακίας ἐν πραΰτητι δέξασθε τὸν ἔμφυτον λόγον τὸν δυνάμενον σῶσαι τὰς ψυχὰς ὑμῶν. A literary reminiscence of this text seems quite probable; first of all, there is an almost tangible identity between the end of the text of Hermas and the end of the text of James; moreover, the Logos in question in the epistle is the gospel, which James considers as the main source of what is prescribed; finally, James 1:22 speaks of the "doers of the word," namely those who keep Hebraism in mind and "carry out what has been imposed."[267] As a result, when Hermas speaks of the mandates which have been received, he may very well have thought of the text of James and remembered the words which this apostle applies to the gospel which can save souls.

In the eighth Similitude in which he uses the parable of the willow and the rods, Hermas considers in a given moment the great number of penitents; in 8.6.4, he has the Shepherd say: "The persons whose rods were discovered to be dry and worm-eaten are apostates and traitors to the Church, who blaspheme (βλασφημή-σαντες) the Lord by their sins. Furthermore, they were ashamed of the Name of the Lord, the Name invoked upon them (ἐπαισχυνθέντες τὸ ὄνομα κυρίου τὸ ἐπικληθὲν ἐπ' αὐτούς)." I have already pointed out that, because of the presence of the verb ἐπαισχύνομαι, Hermas certainly alluded to the text of Mk. 8:38 or Lk. 9:26, where this verb is found in a context alluding to the persecutions which the disciples of Christ will have to bear.[268] The expression τὸ ἐπικληθὲν ἐπ' αὐ-

---

[266]Cf. A Committee of the Oxford Society, *The New Testament in the Apostolic Fathers*, 109.

[267]Cf. Charue, *Les Épîtres Catholiques, Épître de saint Jacques*, 403.

[268]Cf. above, 131.

τούς recalls several texts of the Old and New Testament,[269] and it probably means belonging to the Lord. It is literally found in Jas. 2:7: οὐκ αὐτοὶ βλασφημοῦσιν τὸ καλὸν ὄνομα τὸ ἐπικληθὲν ἐφ' ὑμᾶς. This formula, "the Name invoked upon them," may have come to Hermas from the Old Testament. But I just reminded the reader that Hermas had already been inspired in this verse by the New Testament. It is, therefore, reasonable to believe that he is still referring to it for this particular formula, and that he assembled and arranged two New Testament texts in his own way. This hypothesis is all the more plausible inasmuch as this formula in James is actually unique in the scripture, and inasmuch as the text of James includes the verb βλασφημέω, which is also present in Sim. 8.6.4.

In his commentary on the symbolism of the sixth mountain, the Shepherd says in Sim. 9.23.4: "Now, our God and Lord, who is Lord of all things and has power over all His creation, holds no grudge against those who have confessed their sins, but is indulgent. How is it, then, that a corruptible man, full of sins, holds a grudge as if he were able to destroy and to save (ὡς δυνάμενος ἀπολέσαι ἢ σῶσαι αὐτόν)?" The last words of this passage recall Jas. 4:12: εἷς ἐστιν νομοθέτης καὶ κριτής, ὁ δυνάμενος σῶσαι καὶ ἀπολέσαι. With the formula δυνάμενος ἀπολέσαι ἢ σῶσαι, Hermas seems to suggest that this power to destroy or to save belongs to God; in fact, in this verse he sets the behavior of God against that of the vindictive: God forgets and forgives, but man dares to remember as though he could destroy or save! Applied to God, this formula recalls Jas. 4:12 with which it agrees. A literary contact is compelling, all the more since the context of Jas. 4:11 condemns also the one who judges his brother badly, since God is the Judge who can destroy or save.[270]

Vis. 2.2.7 may also be added to the list of the texts of Hermas that are literarily dependent on Jas., to wit: "Blessed are those of you who will endure the great persecution that is to come (μακάριοι ὑμεῖς ὅσοι ὑπομένετε τὴν θλῖψιν τὴν ἐρχομένην τὴν μεγάλην). . . . " This echoes Jas. 1:12: μακάριος ἀνὴρ ὅς ὑπομένει πειρασμόν. Both texts are very similar: the word μακάριος and the verb ὑπομένω are found in both. It is very possible that Hermas considers the persecution to come as a trial; besides, this is an idea which is found in the synoptic tradition in Christ's discourse on the last times.[271] In this particular case, the literary dependence on Jas. 1:12 becomes even more probable, even though Dan.

---

[269]Regarding references to the O.T., see in E. Hatch and H. A. Redpath, *A Concordance to the Septuagint and the other Greek Versions of the Old Testament, including the Apocryphal Books* (Oxford, 1897), under the term ἐπικαλέω; commentators generally refer this text to Gen. 2:19-20; 48:16; Deut. 14:23; 28:10; the N.T. references are Acts 15:17 and Jas. 2:7.

[270]I have already pointed out Hermas's use of Jas. 4:12: cf. above, 154; the remark of the Oxford Committee on p. 155 might also be noted.

[271]Cf. Mt. 24; Mk. 13; Lk. 21.

12:12 also has the expression μακάριος ὁ ὑπομένων, but neither in the context of trial nor of the great persecution.

Beyond these several passages in which Hermas seems to be literarily dependent on the Letter of James, other texts of the Shepherd deserve to be mentioned as expressing an idea similar to the statements of James, although they do not have any literary contact.

Exhorting the faithful, the aged woman says in Vis. 3.9.6: "Now, then, you who pride yourselves on your wealth, take care lest the indigent (οἱ ὑστερούμενοι) groan at any time, and their groan mount up to the Lord (ἀναβήσεται πρὸς τὸν κύριον). . . . '' The teaching that the groans of the poor mount up to God is particularly present in Deut. 24:14-15 and Jas. 5:1 and 4; as for the exploitation of the poor by the rich, parallels have sometimes been found also in Lev. 19:13; Deut. 24:14-15; Jer. 22:13; Mal. 3:5; Tob. 4:15; Job 24:9; Ecclus. 4:1-6; Ps. 12(11):6; Jas. 5:1; and Enoch 94:7-10. The similarity of idea is especially noteworthy in Deut. 24:14-15 and Jas. 5:1 and 4; but Hermas's expressions are not close enough to any of these texts to lead to the conclusion of a literary influence from either one; at best, it can be said that the word ὑστερούμενοι may be found, if need be, in ὁ ἀφυστερημένος of Jas. 5:4.

In Mand. 3.1 and Sim. 5.6.5, Hermas uses the verb κατοικίζω to describe the indwelling of the Holy Spirit. This verb is peculiar to Jas. 4:5 in the entire New Testament. It seems to be the set term to describe the indwelling of the Holy Spirit in us.[272]

In Mand. 8.10 and Sim. 1.1.8, Hermas attaches special attention to the consideration to be shown to widows and orphans. His formula is χήρας καὶ ὀρφάνους ἐπισκέπτεσθαι. This same expression is read in Jas. 1:27. The mention of widows and orphans as particularly deserving of charity is absolutely traditional and even goes back to the Old Testament.[273] Yet Hermas's formula does not appear, as such, in the Old Testament and is unique to James in the New Testament.

Applying to the rich and the poor the parable of the vine hooked on the oak, the Shepherd says in Sim. 2.5: "So, when a rich man goes up to a poor man and helps him in his needs, he has the assurance that what he does for the poor man can procure a reward from God (for the poor man is rich in his [power of] intercession with God and in his confession)." The idea of the poor man who, because he is poor, is rich in spiritual life is common to Hermas and to Jas. 2:5, but it is not peculiar to James; it is common in the New Testament, namely in Mt. 5:3; Lk. 6:20; 12:21; 16:19-31; and 2 Cor. 6:10. As for the teaching of the great power of prayer with God, it is also present in Jas. 1:5-6, but spelled out in different words.

---

[272]Cf. O. Michel, κατοικίζω in *TDNT* 5:156, where he also refers to Mand. 5.2.5; 10.2.6; Sim. 3.2.

[273]Cf. Charue, *Les Épîtres Catholiques, Épître de saint Jacques,* 404.

In Sim. 8.2.1; 3.6; and 4.6, the Shepherd points out that the elect, those who can enter the tower, are crowned. The theme of the crown which adorns the elect is particularly developed in Revelation;[274] the crown is the sign of victory and symbolizes participation in the Kingdom of Christ. It is to that effect that Paul speaks of the "crown of righteousness,"[275] Saint Peter of the "crown of glory,"[276] Saint John[277] and Saint James[278] of the "crown of life."[279] It is clear, therefore, that there is no need for a special parallel with Jas. 1:12; they all simply use the same theme.

Coming to the case of the renegades symbolized by those who presented rods, two-thirds withered and one-third green, the Shepherd says in Sim. 8.9.1, "However, they did not fall away from God, but clung to the faith, without doing its works." Jas. 2:14 also expresses this antithesis between the fact of having faith and not having it blossom through deeds: Τί τὸ ὄφελος, ἀδελφοί μου, ἐὰν πίστιν λέγῃ τις ἔχειν ἔργα δὲ μὴ ἔχῃ. But he expresses this antithesis in such different terms that only a simple similarity of idea can be acknowledged.

Explaining that the believers who come from the second mountain are hypocrites and teachers of perversity, the Shepherd declares in Sim. 9.19.2: "These, also, are like the first, without fruits of justice (μὴ ἔχοντες καρπὸν δικαιοσύνης)." The expression καρπὸς δικαιοσύνης is common to several texts of the New Testament and is also read in the Old Testament: Phil. 1:11; Jas. 3:18; Heb. 12:11 and Prov. 3:9; 11:30. Now, there is no clue in these texts that leads us to determine that any one in particular was the source for Hermas. The expression was perhaps traditional, and Hermas may simply have conformed to this tradition. However, I could readily give a slight preference to Jas. 3:18 as being closer to this text. The Shepherd states in fact that hypocrites and teachers of perversity do not produce any fruit of justice; now James, in the context of 3:17, states that "the wisdom from above is first pure, then peaceable, gentle, open to reason, full of mercy and good fruits, without uncertainty or insincerity."[280] James's linkage of the absence of hypocrisy and justice may provide a context similar to that of Hermas where hypocrisy is related to the absence of the fruit of justice.

In the message which the elderly lady has given to Hermas, she tells him concerning his wife in Vis. 2.2.3, "she also fails to put a check on her tongue and

---

[274]Cf. Rev. 2:10; 3:11; 4:4, 10; 6:2; 9:17; 12:1; 14:14.

[275]Cf. 2 Tim. 4:8.

[276]Cf. 1 Pet. 5:4.

[277]Cf. Rev. 2:10.

[278]Cf. Jas. 1:12.

[279]Cf. Charue, *Les Épîtres Catholiques, Épître de saint Jacques,* 398.

[280]Cf. Charue, *Les Épîtres Catholiques, Épître de saint Jacques,* 419.

thus she commits sin." Jas. 3:1-12 develops at length a series of remarks on the bad use of the tongue, a source of many evils. It is interesting to point out that James is the only book in the New Testament to speak of the sins of the tongue. Yet, there is no statement in Hermas's text which recalls the sins of James; the only possible parallel between the two texts rests on the fact that both acknowledged that the tongue may be a source of sins.

Other words and expressions in Hermas may also be read in Jas. without necessarily assuming a reference to this letter; yet several words or expressions are peculiar to James in the New Testament or even in the Bible: πολυσπλαγχνία,[281] ἀκατάστατος,[282] καθαρὸς καὶ ἀμίαντος,[283] χαλιναγωγέω,[284] σπαταλάω.[285]

Finally, several texts from the *Shepherd* deserve to be compared with certain passages of 1 Peter and suggest that Hermas knew this letter.

Explaining to Hermas in Vis. 3.11 why the elderly lady appeared to him old and seated in a chair, the angel told him that it showed that his spirit had grown old, wasted away and powerless as a natural consequence of listlessness and doubt, and he adds in 3.11.3, "For, just as old men, without hope of renewing their youth, have no other thing to look forward to except their final rest, so you also, weakened by temporal affairs, surrendered to indifference, instead of throwing your cares on the Lord (ἐπερρίψατε ἑαυτῶν τὰς μερίμνας ἐπὶ τὸν κύριον)." The reading of the last words, "instead of throwing your cares on the Lord," recalls Ps. 55(54):23 and 1 Pet. 5:7. Hermas's words suggest a literary influence from either one. Let me add, however, that Hermas does not cite word for word the text of Ps. from the LXX (ἐπίρριψον ἐπὶ κύριον τὴν μέριμνάν σου), and that the word κύριος, which Hermas has set down, is missing in 1 Pet. The presence in Ps. and in the *Shepherd* of the formula ἐπὶ κύριον, as opposed to ἐπὶ θεόν in 1 Pet., may constitute enough of a clue to lead us to give preference to the text of Ps. as having influenced Hermas.

Speaking of the martyrs, in the explanation of the eleventh mountain, the Shepherd states in Sim. 9.28.5, "You who have suffered for His Name (οἱ πάσχοντες ἕνεκεν τοῦ ὀνόματος) ought to praise God (δοξάζειν ὀφείλετε τὸν θεόν), because He has deemed you worthy of bearing His name and of healing all sins." This statement of the Shepherd recalls the beatitude of Mt. 5:11 and Lk. 6:22, but its formulation does not allow us to believe that there is a literary

---

[281]Cf. Vis. 1.3.2 and Jas. 5:11 which has the adjective that corresponds to πολύσπλαγχνος, and which is unique in the LXX and in the N.T.

[282]Cf. Mand. 2.3; 5.2.7; Jas. 1:8; 3:8; and also Is. 54:11.

[283]Cf. Mand. 2.7; Sim. 5.7.1 and Jas. 1:27 (unique in the N.T.).

[284]Cf. Mand. 12.1.1 and Jas. 1:26; 3:2; this word is not found in the LXX and is not read in Jas. in the N.T.

[285]Cf. Sim. 6.1.6 and Jas. 5:5 as well as 1 Tim. 5:6.

contact. Moreover, 1 Pet. 4:13-16 is an excellent parallel, because it mentions the advice to glorify God (δοξαζέτω τὸν θεόν) after having suffered in the Name of Christ. This mention of the glorification of God, expressed with δοξάζω, may allow us to see in the text of Hermas, beyond a similarity of idea, a reference to the text of Peter.[286]

In the conversation of the Woman with Hermas, in the course of which she reveals to him that the tower is the Church, Vis. 3.3.5 reads, "'Why, lady, is the tower built on waters?' . . . '(Because) your life has been saved by water (διὰ ὕδατος ἐσώθη) and will be so saved.'" This teaching on salvation through water, by baptism, is found in 1 Pet. 3:20-21 where Noah and his family are saved by the waters which, while supporting the ark, drowned the sinners. Moreover, 1 Pet. 3:20 has the verb διεσώθησαν and the expression δι' ὕδατος. Hermas, on the other hand, has the verb ἐσώθη and the expression δι' ὕδατος; yet, Hermas refers neither to the ark nor to Noah. The idea of salvation through water is simply similar. It may have come directly from the practice and necessity of baptism, and may easily suggest the figurative foundation of the tower ἐπὶ ὑδάτων.[287]

In his explanation of the rock and the door, the Shepherd says in Sim. 9.12.2-3: " 'The Son of God is born before all His creation (πάσης τῆς κτίσεως προγενέστερός ἐστιν) and, so, is counselor to His Father in His creation. For this reason He is ancient.' 'But, sir, why is the gate new?' I said. 'Because,' he said, 'He has manifested Himself in the last days of the consummation of things (ἐπ' ἐσχάτων τῶν ἡμερῶν τῆς συντελείας φανερὸς ἐγένετο), and for this reason the gate is new.'" Commentators put forward numerous texts from the New Testament: Jn. 1:1; Col. 1:15; Heb. 1:2; 1 Pet. 1:20; 1 Jn. 1:2; 3:5, 8. I have already pointed out the similarity of thought with Col. 1:15.[288] Let me add that in 1 Pet. 1:20, the use of the participle φανερωθέντος is to be linked with Hermas's φανερός, and the expression ἐπ' ἐσχάτου τῶν χρόνων is very similar to the *Shepherd*'s ἐπ' ἐσχάτων τῶν ἡμερῶν. Moreover, none of these parallels mentioned above expresses as clearly as 1 Pet. the antithesis which Hermas emphasizes between the Son of God, born before all creation, and the Son of God, as he appeared of late. Since Hermas expresses more clearly than 1 Pet.[289] the preexistence

---

[286]The Oxford Committee (*The New Testament in the Apostolic Fathers*, 116) is favorable to this viewpoint.

[287]Cf. A Committee of the Oxford Society, *The New Testament in the Apostolic Fathers*, 115.

[288]Cf. above, 148.

[289]Regarding this text of 1 Pet. 1:20, see Charue, *Les Épîtres Catholiques, Épître de saint Jacques*, 448, who says, "Preexistence does not necessarily imply the notion of predestination, and it is not expressed either with the word φανερωθέντος, which can only mean the revelation of divine advice on the stage of the world. However, in the context of 1 Peter, the revelation of Christ is to be understood in terms of a real and already operative preexistence as stated above (1:11)."

of the Son of God, it is, therefore, possible to believe in a simple similarity of idea without being able to assert a literary reference to the Epistle of Peter. Moreover, the similarity with Col. 1:15 must not be overlooked either.

In explaining in Vis. 4.3.4 the symbolism of the four colors on the head of the monster, the woman says, "You who flee this world are the golden section. For, just as gold is tried by fire (ὥσπερ γὰρ τὸ χρυσίον δοκιμάζεται) and becomes useful, so also you who live in the world are tried in it." Numerous are the texts where we find the image of the purification of gold by fire: Ecclus. 2:5; Prov. 17:3; 27:21; Job 23:10; Wis. 3:6; Zech. 13:9; 1 Pet. 1:7 and Rev. 3:18. The metaphor is too common to call for a particular reference to 1 Peter.

I would like to conclude by pointing out the importance of the number of passages of the Epistle of James which have influenced Hermas. But here again, Hermas does not follow the text literally. He is inspired by it; the presence of a similar idea and of identical words and expressions demonstrates that he refers to it.

Hermas may possibly have known 1 Peter, but the texts which could possibly be linked with this epistle do not really speak for a true literary influence.

I have spent much time examining New Testament writings beyond the Gospel of Mt.; the very scope of Hermas's work, and the fact that it assumed knowledge of several writings of the New Testament demanded it. Yet, this analysis was worthwhile because it demonstrated that, if Hermas was above all literarily influenced by Mt., Jn., Paul and James, he relied differently on each one of them.

Of all the synoptics, the Gospel of Mt. had the greatest literary influence on Hermas. With the exception of one passsage in which a Markan influence is rather probable,[290] the Matthean texts influenced Hermas's composition most often and most assuredly. To be sure, many texts of the *Shepherd* can be compared with passages from the other synoptics, but they simply agree with the gospel tradition. Hermas seems to have adopted the Gospel of Mt. as the usual gospel, the common gospel to which to refer. Sim. 5.2[291] is a typical instance in which Hermas assembles and uses several Matthean parables; he generally reverts to the Matthean texts and simply adapts them to his work; he develops them, but not so as to give an explanation or a commentary; he refers to them totally as though Mt. normally comes to mind whenever he has to refer to a gospel.

His literary dependence on John and Paul is quite different and very characteristic. Some texts of their writings have formed the basis and have served as conduits for long developments and full explanations, very often parenetic in nature. In the end, very few texts of John and Paul have played a role in the composition of the *Shepherd*; they generally afford a kind of theme upon which Hermas writes

---

[290]Cf. Mand. 4.1.6; cf. above, 130-31.

[291]Cf. above, 116-19.

variations, a theme which recurs many times in the course of the pericope which develops these texts.[292]

It must also be pointed out that Hermas generally understood these texts of John and Paul in a "moral" sense, or he introduced them in a context dealing with the practice of Christian life and discussed them primarily in the light of the whole Christian life. He abstained from the high theological speculations of John and Paul.

As for the Epistle of James, it influenced the composition of the *Shepherd* principally in the same manner as John and Paul did, such as in Mand. 9.1-7[293] and several verses of Mand. 12.[294] But its influence was also similar to that of Mt., in the sense that Hermas referred to specific texts without commenting upon them at length.

Hermas probably also knew Acts, 1 John, Revelation, and 1 Peter, but the literary influence of these texts was very minimal.

Let me point out again that Hermas did not hesitate to draw his inspiration from the New Testament, from which he borrowed various writings and applied them together to one of his compositions. He never cited literally any of these texts which inspired him, nor did he make explicit reference to the texts of the New Testament.

What remains, therefore, is that of all the gospels, the Gospel of Mt. is, for Hermas, the one to which to turn normally without having to develop and interpret the ideas it expresses. It is well known; it is commonly used; it is within the understanding of everybody.

An overview of chapter 3 reveals that for the Christian apocalyptic literature, the Gospel of Mt. seems to have been the gospel par excellence. Its literary influence is substantial and unrivaled by the other gospels. Thus, the Christian parts of the *Ascension of Isaiah* demonstrate that Mt. was the single influence;[295] the *Odes of Solomon* grant it a privileged place by showing no influence from either Mk. or Lk.[296] Whereas the *Sibylline Oracles* do not show a great affinity with the Gospel of Mt., they do suggest that it is the basis of the tradition on which they depend.[297] The *Apocalypse of Peter*, for as much as the Ethiopic version allows

---

[292]Cf. Jn. 3:5; 14:6 in Sim. 9 (cf. above, 135-42); 1 Cor. 7:8-9, 28, 38, 40 in Mand. 4.4.1-2 (cf. above, 144); Eph. 4:30 and 2 Cor. 7:16 in Mand. 10 (cf. above, 144-45); the Pauline formulas of unity in Sim. 9 (cf. above, 146-47).

[293]Cf. Jas. 1:5-9 (above, 152).

[294]Cf. Jas. 4:7 (above, 154).

[295]Cf. above, 62.

[296]Cf. above, 80.

[297]Cf. above, 98.

definite conclusions, came under its strong literary influence to the point that certain texts follow very closely their Matthean source.[298] Hermas reveals that Mt. is the one to which to turn normally when in need of a gospel. The use of the Matthean parables in the *Shepherd* is remarkable on this point: not only are the sayings of Christ drawn from Mt., but the author also builds on its parables.[299] Yet, none of these writings refer explicitly to Mt. just as they do not cite the gospel literally.

The Gospel of Mk. seems beyond the scope of the apocalyptic literature; other than in one passage in the *Shepherd* where its influence is rather probable, none of its texts have literally inspired the apocrypha. The situation with respect to the Gospel of Lk. is hardly better, except for the *Apocalypse of Peter* in which Hermas combined themes of Lk. with those of Mt., and where he sometimes drew inspiration only from Lk.

With the exception of the *Ascension of Isaiah* and the *Apocalypse of Peter*, all the apocalyptic writings reveal relationships with the fourth gospel. But these relationships take on a peculiar character. Thus, in the *Odes of Solomon*, the literary link with Jn. does not stem from a direct influence of the gospel, but from the identical atmosphere in which they were written. The *Shepherd of Hermas* simply retains some Johannine texts—moreover very few—on which he comments at length according to his personal views; the passages from Jn. serve as themes for long variations of a clearly marked moral character.

Naturally, we had to expect to find in this apocalyptic literature themes which are also present in the Revelation of John.

As for the Pauline writings, traces of their influence are found in the apocalypses; the texts that were used have above all a moral feature, or they are inserted in parenetic contexts. The authors do not proceed along the apostle's profound theological developments.

I have also remarked that some apocalypses referred to the Old Testament and to the apocryphal gospels.

All these observations demonstrate that it was the Gospel of Matthew from which people of the time drew the core of the Christian message. As the second century progresses, Christians notice more and more—and Hermas is eloquent on this point—that the sayings of Christ in Mt. are not the only source of inspiration, but that the use of the Matthean parables to construct an argument entails a very great familiarity with the Gospel of Mt. as a whole. It is the rule of Christian life. The gospel narrative—and the *Sibylline Oracles* demonstrate it particularly—is basically Mt., but with recourse as well to the Old Testament and the apocrypha, and it is Matthew that is in vogue in the Christian literature of the second century.

---

[298]Cf. above, 110-11.

[299]Cf. above, 161.

Editor's Addenda to Chapter 3

Section 1
THE ASCENSION OF ISAIAH

Wolf-Dietrich Köhler (*Die Rezeption des Matthäusevangeliums in der Zeit vor Irenäus*, 303-308) concludes the following with respect to the use of the Gospel of Matthew by the author of the *Ascension of Isaiah*.

1. Passages which show a distinct dependence on Matthew

ASCENSION OF ISAIAH	MATTHEW
3:14	27:62-66
11:3-5	1:15-25
1:4	12:18

2. Passages for which dependence on Matthew is less probable but still possible

ASCENSION OF ISAIAH	MATTHEW
3:13	27:38, 60
3:14a	26:31
3:16	28:2
3:17-18	28:19
4:3	15:13
9:9	22:30
9:14	26:50

3. Passages for which a literary dependence on Mattew is extremely unlikely

ASCENSION OF ISAIAH	MATTHEW
11:11	17:9
11:19	27:2
11:19	27:35
11:22	28:19

Biblia Patristica (*Index des Citations et Allusions bibliques dans la Littérature patristique, Des Origines à Clément d'Alexandrie et Tertullien*, vol. 1 [Paris, 1975] 223-93) lists the following citations or allusions to the Gospel of Matthew in the Ascension of Isaiah.

ASC. ISAIAH	MATTHEW	ASC. ISAIAH	MATTHEW
11:3	1:18	11:5	1:25
11:3	1:19	11:15	2:21
11:2	1:20	11:11	17:9
11:4	1:20	9:9	22:30
11:4	1:24	3:14	26:31

9:14	26:50
11:19	27:2
11:19	27:35
3:13	27:38
3:13	27:60

3:14	27:66
3:16	28:2
3:18	28:19
11:22	28:19
3:17	28:19

Section 2
THE ODES OF SOLOMON

Wolf-Dietrich Köhler (*Die Rezeption des Matthäusevangeliums in der Zeit vor Irenäus*, 371-72) concludes the following with respect to the use of the Gospel of Matthew by the author of the *Odes of Solomon*.

1. Passages for which dependence on Matthew is quite possible

ODES OF SOLOMON	MATTHEW
22:12	16:18

2. Passages for which dependence on Matthew is much less clear

ODES OF SOLOMON	MATTHEW
3:2	19:5
4:13; 5:3	10:8
7:15	3:17; 17:5; 12:18
7:16	11:27
7:17	25:6
14:5	6:13
24:1	3:16
31:6	11:28
31:9	27:35
31:11	7:25
41:15	13:35

3. Passages for which dependence on Matthew is at most theoretically possible

ODES OF SOLOMON	MATTHEW
8:20b-21a	25:34
23:17-18	28:19
42:6	28:19-20
42:7b-8	11:29

Biblia Patristica (*Index des Citations et Allusions bibliques dans la Littérature patristique, Des origines à Clément d'Alexandrie et Tertullien*, vol. 1 [Paris, 1975] 223-93) lists the following citations or allusions to the Gospel of Matthew in the *Odes of Solomon*.

ODES OF SOLOMON	MATTHEW
19:6	1:20
24:1	3:16
7:15	3:17
14:5	6:13
31:11	7:25
4:13	10:8
5:3	10:8
7:16	11:27
31:6	11:28
7:15	12:18
41:15	13:25
22:12	16:18
7:15	17:5
3:2	19:5
7:17	25:6
31:9	27:35

Section 3
THE SIBYLLINE ORACLES

Wolf-Dietrich Köhler (*Die Rezeption des Matthäusevangeliums in der Zeit vor Irenäus*, 309-13) concludes the following with respect to the use of the Gospel of Matthew by the author(s) of the *Sibylline Oracles*.

1. Passages for which dependence on Matthew is probable

SIBYLLINE ORACLES	MATTHEW
1.332	5:17
1.334	2:12
1.345	2:13-21
2.82	9:13; 12:7
6.24-25	27:34
8.476	2:2-9
12.30	2:2-9

2. Passages for which dependence on Matthew is quite possible but not conclusive

SIBYLLINE ORACLES	MATTHEW
1.333	5–7
2.165-66	24:11
2.203, 305	8:12; 13:42, 50; 22:13; 24:51; 25:30
8.105, 231, 350	8:12; 13:42, 50; 22:13; 24:51; 25:30
8.239	24:31
8.272, 286	4:23; 9:35
8.324-25	21:5
8.401	18:8; 25:42

3. Passages for which dependence on Mt. is certainly possible but not obvious

SIB. ORACLES	MATTHEW	SIB. ORACLES	MATTHEW
Prologue 18	1:23	1.353	11:5
1.336-38	3:3	1.356-60	14:21-23
1.342-43	14:6, 10	1.365-66	26:67

1.367-68	27:34, 48	7.69	1:20
1.373	27:29-30	7.134	7:15
1.389-90	24:7	8.86	8:12
1.393-94	24:2	8.190	24:29
2.6	24:7	8.206	11:5
2.179	24:46	8.232	24:29
2.187	11:14	8.270	1:18-23
2.190	24:19	8.273	8:26
2.194	24:29	8.274	14:25
2.200	24:29	8.275	14:19-21
2.241-42	24:30; 25:31	8.287	26:45
2.242	16:27; 25:31	8.288	26:67
2.243	26:64	8.290	27:26
2.244	16:27	8.294	27:29
2.328	22:30	8.305	27:51
2.332	8:12; 13:42, 50; 22:13;	8.306	27:45
	24:51; 25:30	8.326	11:29
3.636	24:7	8.341	24:29
6.4	3:13-17	8.417	25:32
6.13	14:25	8.479	2:1
6.23	27:29	8.481	22:37, 39
7.66	3:13-17		

4. Passages for which dependence on Mt. is improbable and virtually to be excluded

SIBYLLINE ORACLES	MATTHEW
1.339	3:6
1.349	25:46
1.396	13:25
2.154	13:30, 39
2.253	3:12
3.264	13:8
4.15	14:13-21

Biblia Patristica (*Index des Citations et Allusions bibliques dans la Littérature patristique, Des origines à Clément d'Alexandrie et Tertullien*, vol. 1 [Paris, 1975] 223-93) lists the following citations or allusions to the Gospel of Matthew in the Sibylline Oracles.

SIB. ORACLES	MATTHEW	SIB. ORACLES	MATTHEW
Prologue 18	1:18	6.4	3:13-17
8.270	1:18	7.66	3:13-17
7.69	1:20	8.272	4:23
8.479	2:1	2.286	4:23
8.476	2:2-9	1.332	5:17
12.30	2:2-9	7.134	7:15
1.334	2:11	2.203	8:12
1.345	2:15	2.305	8:12
1.339	3:6	2.332	8:12
2.253	3:12	8.86	8:12

8.105	8:12	2.6	24:7
8.231	8:12	3.636	24:7
8.350	8:12	2.165	24:11
8.273	8:26	2.190	24:19
2.82	9:13	2.194	24:29
8.272	9:35	2.200	24:29
8.286	9:35	8.190	24:29
1.353	11:5	8.232	24:29
8.206	11:5	8.341	24:29
2.187	11:14	2.242	24:30
8.326	11:29	8.239	24:31
2.82	12:7	2.179	24:46
3.264	13:8	8.417	25:32
1.396	13:25	8.401	25:41
2.164	13:30	1.349	25:46
2.164	13:39	8.287	26:45
1.342	14:6	2.243	26:64
1.343	14:10	1.365	26:67
6.15	14:13-21	8.288	26:67
1.356	14:17-21	8.290	27:26
8.275	14:19-21	1.373	27:29
1.356	14:25-33	6.23	27:29
6.13	14:25	8.294	27:29
8.274	14:25	1.373	27:30
2.244	16:27	1.367	27:34
8.401	18:8	6.24	27:34
Prologue 47	19:29	1.374	27:45
8.324	21:5	8.306	27:45
2.328	22:30	1.367	27:48
1.393	24:2	1.376	27:51
1.389	24:7	8.305	27:51

Section 4
THE APOCALYPSE OF PETER

Wolf-Dietrich Köhler (*Die Rezeption des Matthäusevangeliums in der Zeit vor Irenäus*, 314-18) concludes the following with respect to the use of the Gospel of Matthew by the author of the Ethiopic version of the *Apocalypse of Peter*.

1. Passages for which dependence on Matthew is very probable

ETHIOPIC APOCALYPSE OF PETER	MATTHEW
chapter 1	24:3
	24:4
	24:5
	24:23-26
	24:27
	24:30
	25:31
	16:27
chapter 2	24:5
chapter 6	25:31, cf. 24:30
chapter 16	17:3
	5:10
	17:4

2. Passages for which dependence on Mt. is very possible, but not really probable

ETHIOPIC APOCALYPSE OF PETER	MATTHEW	AKHMÎM FRAGMENT
chapter 1	24:30a	
	17:2	
	25:32ff.	
chapter 2	24:32	
	13:36	
	24:24	
chapter 3	26:24	
chapter 4	19:26	
chapter 5	8:12	
chapter 6	26:64	
	16:27	
chapter 7	21:32	22 (cf. 28)
chapter 15	17:2-3	7
chapter 16	16:23	
chapter 17	3:17	
	17:5	
	17:5a	
	17:9	
	24:11	1
	5:6	3

3. Passages for which dependence on Matthew is possible but not conclusive

ETHIOPIC APOCALYPSE OF PETER	MATTHEW	AKHMÎM FRAGMENT
chapter 1	16:27	
chapter 2	24:24	
chapter 5	24:29	
	7:15	1
	24:24	
	13:31 et al.	3
	17:2	6

Biblia Patristica (*Index des Citations et Allusions bibliques dans la Littérature patristique, Des origines à Clément d'Alexandrie et Tertullien*, vol. 1 [Paris, 1975] 223-93) lists the following citations or allusions to the Gospel of Matthew in the *Apocalypse of Peter* (references to the Coptic version are noted as well).

APOC. PETER	MATTHEW	APOC. PETER	MATTHEW
chapter 17	3:17	6	17:2-3
3	5:6	1	17:2
16	5:10	16	17:3
Coptic, line 7	7:18	16	17:4
chapter 5	8:12	17 (twice)	17:5
Coptic, line 19	13:11	4	19:2
Coptic, line 27	13:12	1	24:3
chapter 2	13:36	1	24:4
16	16:23	1	24:5
1	16:27	2	24:5
15	17:2-3	1	24:23-26

2	24:24	chapter 1	25:31
1	24:27	3	25:33
5	24:29	3	26:24
1	24:30	6	26:61
6	24:30	Coptic, line 33	26:69-75
2	24:32-33	Coptic, line 22	27:39-44
Coptic, line 27	25:29		

Section 5
THE SHEPHERD OF HERMAS

Helmut Köster (*Synoptische Überlieferung bei den apostolischen Vätern* 242-56) maintains that there are no clear references in Hermas to passages from the synoptic tradition. Although the writings of Hermas contain many passages which agree with material from the synoptic gospels, there are no passages at all that show a clear use of synoptic citations, and the agreements between Hermas and the synoptic gospels can be explained as the result of the important role that Jewish tradition played in both. Although some passages are sufficiently close that a literary dependence on the synoptic gospels is not impossible (Mand. 4.1.6; Sim. 9.20.2-3; 9.29.3; 9.31.2), neither can it be established.

Wolf-Dietrich Köhler (*Die Rezeption des Matthäusevangeliums in der Zeit vor Irenäus*, 125-28) concludes the following with respect to Hermas's use of the Gospel of Matthew.

1. No passages in Hermas for which use of the Gospel of Matthew is probable

2. Passages for which dependence on Matthew is possible

HERMAS	MATTHEW
Vis. 1.1.8	5:28
3.6.5	13:20, 22
3.6.6	19:21-24
Mand. 4.1.1	5:28
4.1.6	19:9
11.16	7:15-16
12.1.2	22:11
12.6.3	10:28
Sim. 5.2.1	21:33
6.3.6b	21:22; 7:2-3
9.13.2	22:11

3. Passages for which dependence on Mt. appears to be at least theoretically possible but is not convincing

HERMAS	MATTHEW
Vis. 3.7.3	13:22
3.8.3	9:22
3.8.9	for the expression συντέλεια τοῦ αἰῶνος
3.9.8	5:35
4.2.6	26:24
Mand. 4.1.6	5:32
Sim. 5.1.5	19:17
5.2.5	25:19
5.2.9	13:27
9.22.3	23:12
9.28.6	5:11

4. Passages for which dependence on Matthew is improbable

HERMAS	MATTHEW		HERMAS	MATTHEW
Vis. 2.2.7	24:21		5.3.2-3	19:17, 21
2.2.8	10:33		5.3.8	5:24
Mand. 5.2.7	12:43		5.5.2	13:38
6.2.4	7:16		5.6.1 and 5.6.4	28:18
7.4	10:28		5.6.2	18:10b
9.4	7:7, 11; 21:22		6.3.6a	16:27
10.1.5	13:22		8.3.2	13:31-32
12.5.4	12:43-45		8.7.6	18:4; 23:6-12
Sim. 3.3	13:24-30		9.12.3	5:20
4.2; 4.4	13:40		9.20.1	13:22
4.6	7:7; 18:19		9.20.2	19:23
5.2.2	25:14		9.21.1	13:20-21
5.2.4	13:7		9.29.1-3 & 9.31.2-3	18:34; 19:14
5.2.6	21:37-38		9.31.6	26:31

Biblia Patristica (*Index des Citations et Allusions bibliques dans la Littérature patristique, Des Origines à Clément d'Alexandrie et Tertullien*, vol. 1 [Paris, 1975] 223-93) lists the following citations or allusions to the Gospel of Matthew in the writings of Hermas.

HERMAS	MATTHEW
Mand. 4.1.6	5:32
Sim. 4.6	7:7
Vis. 2.2.8	10:33
Vis. 3.6.5; Sim. 9.21.1	13:20-21
Vis. 3.6.5; 3.7.3; Mand. 10.1.5	13:22
Sim. 5.5.2	13:38
Sim. 4.6	18:19
Mand. 4.1.6	19:9
Sim. 5.1.5; 5.3.2-3	19:17

Chapter 4

THE NONCANONICAL GOSPELS

This chapter deals with a series of apocryphal gospels, some of which were passed on to us in their entirety, while others survive in a fragmentary state. I propose to study in succession the Unknown Gospel (Papyrus Egerton 2 [editor's addition]), the Gospel of the Hebrews, the Gospel of the Ebionites, the Gospel of the Egyptians, the Gospel of Peter, the Gospel of Matthias, and the Protevangelium of James; I also add the *Kerygma Petri,* which belongs to the genre of the apocrypha.

Section 1
THE UNKNOWN GOSPEL

This section is devoted to a text published in 1935 by H. I. Bell and T. C. Skeat,[1] generally considered as a gospel fragment from the first half of the second century. Since its publication under the title "The Unknown Gospel," it has prompted many articles. Its editors consider it, for the most part, a gospel independent of the canonical gospels: it is a witness to traditions different from theirs. However, critics in general lean more towards assigning to the Unknown Gospel a secondary character.[2]

Since the focus of my attention is the literary influence of the first gospel, I devote the first paragraph to St. Matthew and a second paragraph to the other New

---

[1] *Editio princeps*: H. I. Bell and T. C. Skeat, *Fragments of an Unknown Gospel and Other Early Christian Papyri* (London, 1935). Revised text in *The New Gospel Fragments* (London, 1935). [This fragment is generally known as Papyrus Egerton 2. The text followed in the English translation is that of Edgar Hennecke, *New Testament Apocrypha*, ed. Wilhelm Schneemelcher, ET ed. R. McL. Wilson, 2 vols. (Philadelphia: Westminster Press, 1963) 1:94-96. Editor's note.]

[2] Cf. M. Goguel, "Les fragments nouvellement découverts d'un Évangile du IIme siècle," *RHLR* 15 (1935): 465; M.-J. Lagrange, "Deux nouveaux textes relatifs à l'Évangile," *RB* 44 (1935): 339-43; E. R. Smothers, "Un nouvel Évangile du deuxième siècle," *RSR* 25 (1935): 358-62; J. Huby, "Une importante découverte papyrologique," *EBib* 224 (1935): 763-75; H. Vogels, "Fragments of an Unknown Gospel," *ThRv* 34 (1935): 315; F. C. Burkitt, "Fragments of an Unknown Gospel," *JTS* 36 (1935): 303.

Testament writings.[3]

§1. Saint Matthew

The literary influence of the first gospel on the fragments preserved from the Unknown Gospel seems to have been minimal. Only two texts, one of which comes from a conjectural restoration, are open to comparison with Mt.

1. Pap. Eg. 2, lines 17-20

ἀποκριθεὶς ὁ 'Ιη(σοῦς) εἶ[πεν αὐτο]ῖς· νῦν κατηγορεῖται [ὑμῶν ἡ ἀ]πιστεί[α . . . ἀ]λλο. [. . .

Jesus answered and said unto them, "Now [already] accusation is raised against [your] unbelief. . . ."

The words νῦν κατηγορεῖται ὑμῶν ἡ ἀπιστεία follow the spirit of the canonical gospels: Mt. 21:41; Mk. 12:9; Lk. 20:16; Jn. 8:45-46. Yet, the word ἀ-πιστία is absent from these texts; it refers to the condemnation of the Jews as stated in the Const. Apost. 2.60.3: οἱ μάτην λεγόμενοι 'Ιουδαῖοι . . . οἱ τῆς δυνάμεως τοῦ λογοῦ ἐν τῇ ἀπιστίᾳ αὐτῶν κενωθέντες;[4] 5.16.8: περὶ γὰρ τοῦ ποτε 'Ισραὴλ εἶπεν ὁ κύριος διὰ τὴν ἀπιστίαν αὐτῶν, ὅτι ἀρθήσεται ἀπ' αὐτῶν ἡ βασιλεία τοῦ θεοῦ.[5] Based on this last text, Cerfaux proposed a double conjecture: the first, based on the editio princeps in which the editors read ιλε in line 20, supposes that καὶ ἀρθήσεται ἀφ' ὑμῶν ἡ βασιλεία τοῦ θεοῦ is a sentence inspired by Mt. 21:43; the second comes from the restored text, which reads λλο in line 20 and which recalls Mt. 21:41 in the parable of the murderous vine growers who brand the incredulity of the Jews with infamy. Cerfaux understands καὶ ἡ βασιλεία τοῦ θεοῦ ἄλλοις ἐκδοθήσεται to be under the influence of Mt. 21:41.[6] Let me point out that Lk. 20:16 and Mk. 12:9 end the same parable with the words καὶ δώσει τὸν ἀμπελῶνα ἄλλοις. Cerfaux points out that the conjecture could then also be καὶ δώσει τὴν βασιλείαν ἄλλοις, which is closer to Mk. 12:9 and Lk. 20:16.

---

[3]The relationship between the Unknown Gospel and the canonical writings has been fully examined by L. Cerfaux, "Parallèles canoniques et extra-canoniques de l'Évangile Inconnu," *Le Muséon* 49 (1936): 55-57, to which I refer constantly. See also G. Mayeda, *Das Leben-Jesu-Fragment. Papyrus Egerton 2 und seine Stellung in der urchristlichen Literaturgeschichte* (Bern: Haupt, 1946) 65-77; H. J. Bell, "The Gospel Fragment P. Egerton 2," *HTR* 42 (1949): 53-64.

[4]Cf. Funk, *Patres apostolici*,2:173.

[5]Cf. ibid., 285.

[6]Cf. Cerfaux, "Parallèles canoniques," 59.

2. Pap. Eg. 2, line 32

καὶ [ἰ]δοὺ λεπρὸς προσελθ[ὼν αὐτῷ] λέγει.

And behold a leper drew near [to him] and said. . . .

This sentence is drawn from a narrative of the healing of a leper; the whole narrative finds excellent parallels in Mt. 8:1-4; Mk. 1:40-45; Lk. 5:12-16; 17:12-19. The above sentence is, however, closer to Mt. 8:2 than to the other parallels, and a simple synoptic table demonstrates it clearly.

Pap. Eg. 2, l. 32	Matt. 8:2	Mark 1:40	Luke 5:12
καὶ ἰδοὺ λεπρὸς προσελθὼν αὐτῷ λέγει·	καὶ ἰδοὺ λεπρὸς προσελθὼν προσεκύνει αὐτῷ λέγων·	καὶ ἔρχεται πρὸς αὐτὸν λεπρὸς παρακαλῶν αὐτὸν καὶ γονυπετῶν λέγων αὐτῷ·	καὶ ἰδοὺ ἀνὴρ πλήρης λέπρας· ἰδὼν δὲ τὸν Ἰησοῦν, πεσὼν ἐπὶ πρόσωπον ἐδεήθη αὐτοῦ λέγων·

Except for the verb προσκυνέω, the text of Mt. is there literally; given the similarity of context and the identity of phrases, it is believable that the author begins his narrative just as Mt. does,[7] and that he is, therefore, literarily dependent on the first gospel.

These two passages are the only ones in the Unknown Gospel that imply a literary influence from the Matthean text; however, let us remember that the first is the result of a conjecture. Other texts are commonly found in the gospels and can also be linked with Mt., and I propose to deal with those later.

§2. The Other New Testament Writings

No text of the Unknown Gospel implies the use of either the epistles of St. Paul or the catholic epistles. On the other hand, the use of Mk., Lk., and Jn. is certain. Let me add that some passages have parallels in many gospels, but they do not allow us to determine exactly upon which gospel they depend. This is why I examine in succession the Gospel of Mk., the Gospel of Lk., and the Gospel of Jn., and I conclude with a section on the texts that are in agreement with the synoptic tradition.

A. The Gospel of Mark

In the episode containing the question about the kings, Pap. Eg. 2 (lines 43-47) reads, . . . νόμενοι πρὸς αὐτὸν ἐξ[ετασ]τικῶς ἐπείραζον αὐτὸν λ[έγονετς]: " . . . [ca]me to him to put him to the pro[of] and to tempt him, whilst [they said]. . . . "

The main feature of this episode concerns taxes owed to Caesar: Mt. 22:15-22; Mk. 12:13-17; Lk. 20:20-26.[8] Mk. 10:2 may be given as a parallel because it

---

[7]Cf. ibid., 62.

[8]Cf. ibid., 64.

brings in an insidious question stamped with the formula ἔξεστιν: καὶ προσελθόντες Φαρισαῖοι ἐπηρώτων αὐτὸν εἰ ἔξεστιν ἀνδρὶ γυναῖκα ἀπολῦσαι, πειράζοντες αὐτόν. Variants may bring the text of Mk. 12:14 even closer to the papyrus, for example, ἐλθόντες ἤρξαντο ἐρωτᾶν (or ἐπηρωτᾶν) αὐτὸν ἐν δόλῳ λέγοντες.[9] I may, therefore, point out that this passage follows Mk.'s style, which may have influenced the author of the Unknown Gospel by the way in which he introduces this controversy: the verb πειράζω is present in both Mk. and the apocryphon.

In the same narrative, lines 47-50 continue with [εἶπε οὖν] ἡμεῖν· ἐξὸν τοῖς βα(σι)λεῦσ[ιν ἀποδοῦ]ναι τὰ ἀν[ή]κοντα τῇ ἀρχῇ; ἀπ[οδῶμεν αὐ]τοῖς ἢ μ[ή];: "[Wherefore tell] us: is it admissable [to p]ay to the kings the (charges) appertaining to their rule? [Should we] pay [th]em or not?" This text is literarily dependent on Mk. 12:14: ἔξεστιν δοῦναι κῆνσον Καίσαρι ἢ οὔ; δῶμεν ἢ μὴ δῶμεν; The composite verb ἀποδίδωμι instead of the simple δίδωμι may come from Mk. 12:17: τὰ Καίσαρος ἀπόδοτε Καίσαρι, which easily developed into ἀποδοῦναι τὰ ἀνήκοντα τῇ ἀρχῇ.[10] The resemblance with the apocryphon is even closer if it is read together with D, 346, and the ancient Latin δῶμεν ἢ οὔ,[11] which eliminate the second δῶμεν. In general, Mk.'s expressions are, in fact, found in the Unknown Gospel; and this is particularly true when, after the words "is it permissible to pay to the kings the charges," the repetition of ἀποδῶμεν ἢ μή recalls δῶμεν ἢ μὴ δῶμεν in Mk.; this repetition is missing in Mt. 23:17 and Lk. 20:22.[12]

Let me also add that the word ἐμβιμησάμενος (line 51) is relatively rare, but that it is found in the gospels in Mt. 9:30; Mk. 1:43; 14:15; and Jn. 11:33. It is possible that the author kept this word in mind because of the version of the leper as it is given in Mk. 1:43.[13]

B. The Gospel of Luke

Of all the synoptics, the Gospel of Lk. contains the greatest number of texts that are parallel to the Unknown Gospel.

In the controversy on the scripture, let me first point out two words that are familiar from the vocabulary of Lk. The first is νομικός (line 3), which is found in Lk. 7:30; 10:25; 11:45, 46, 52; 14:3;[14] the second is στραφείς (lines 6-7), which

---

[9]This text is supported by G, W, Θ, fam. 1, cod. 22, fam. 13, etc.; cf. Cerfaux, "Parallèles canoniques," 65.

[10]Cf. Cerfaux, "Parallèles canoniques," 66; the author notes, "Compare 2 Macc. 14:8: πρῶτον μὲν ὑπὲρ τῶν ἀνηκόντων τῷ βασιλεῖ γνησίως φρονῶν, or Const. Apost. 4.13.1 (Funk, 233): πάσῃ βασιλείᾳ καὶ ἀρχῇ ὑποτάγητε . . . πάντα φόβον τὸν ὀφειλόμενον αὐτοῖς ἀποπληρώσατε, and particularly Rom. 13:7: ἀπόδοτε πᾶσιν τὰς ὀφειλάς, τῷ τὸν φόρον τὸν φόρον, κτλ."

[11]The papyrus may have read ἢ οὔ as well as ἢ μή (*The New Gospel Fragments*, 33).

[12]Cf. Cerfaux,"Parallèles canoniques," 66.

[13]Cf. ibid., 67 and n. 23.

[14]This word is also found in Mt.22:35 with the same meaning.

mentions a gesture of Jesus fairly common in Lk. 7:9, 44; 9:55; 10:23; 14:25; 22:61; 23:28.[15]

The attempted arrest is described in lines 22-32: ? ἔ]λκω[σιν] β[αστάσαντες δὲ] λίθους ὁμοῦ λι[θάζω]σι[ν αὐ]τόν· καὶ ἐπέβαλον [τὰς] χεῖ[ρας] αὐτῶν ἐπ᾽ αὐτὸν οἱ [ἄρχον]τες [ἵ]να πιάσωσιν καὶ παρ[αδώ]σω[σι]ν τῷ ὄχλῳ· καὶ οὐκ ἠ[δύναντο] αὐτὸν πιάσαι ὅτι οὔπω ἐ[ληλύθει] αὐτοῦ ἡ ὥρα τῆς παρα-δό[σεως] αὐτὸς δὲ ὁ κ(ύριο)ς ἐξελθὼν [ἐκ τῶν χεί]ρων ἀπένευσεν ἀπ᾽ [αὐτῶν]: " . . . [to gather] stones together to stone him. And the [rul]ers laid their hands on him that they might arrest him and [deliver] him to the multitude. But they w[ere not able] to arrest him because the hour of his betrayal [was] not yet c[ome]. But he himself, the Lord, escaped out of [their han]ds and turned away from them." Lk. 20:17-20 relates as well an attempted arrest, and it contains four elements that are found in the same order in the Unknown Gospel: the first is λίθον; the second is ἐπίβαλεῖν ἐπ᾽ αὐτὸν τὰς χεῖρας; the third is ἐν αὐτῇ τῇ ὥρᾳ; and the fourth is παραδοῦναι. The presence of the word παραδίδωμι in the apocryphon leads to a preference for the text of Lk. over its parallels, Mk. 12:10-13; Mt. 21:42-46; and 22:15-16, which do not have it. Even if Johannine centos which have this apocryphal text may be juxtaposed here, a contact with Lk. is still more probable given the fact that the element παραδίδωμι is missing in these centos, and only the second and third elements mentioned above are found in the same context.[16]

In the narrative of the healing of the leper, lines 33-36 read λέγει· διδάσ-καλε Ἰη(σοῦ) λε[προῖς συν]οδεύων καὶ συνεσθίω[ν αὐτοῖς] ἐν τῷ πανδοχείῳ ἐλ[έπρησα] καὶ αὐτὸς ἐγώ·: "And behold a leper drew near [to him] and said, 'Master Jesus, wandering with lepers and eating with [them was I? pub-licans are thou?] in the inn; I also [became] a le[per].' " The Gospel of the He-brews, 8, provides a remarkable parallel when the man with the shriveled hand says, "caementarius eram, manibus victim quaeritans; precor te, Iesu, ut mihi restituas sanitatem, ne turpiter mendicem cibos."[17] Similar words from the Un-known Gospel constitute an addition to the canonical narrative, and this addition is in the style of Lk. In fact, συνοδεύω is found only in Acts 9:7 in the New Tes-tament; συνεσθίω is read in Lk. 15:2 and Acts 10:41; 11:3;[18] πανδοχεῖον is pe-culiar to Lk. 10:34 in the New Testament.[19]

A statement of Christ to the healed leper is preserved in lines 39-41: ὁ δὲ κ(ύριο)ς εἶπεν αὐτῷ] πορε[υθεὶς ἐπίδειξον σεαυτὸ]ν τοῖ[ς ἱερεῦσι: "Go [thy way and show th]yself to the [priests. . . . " Several gospel parallels come

---

[15]This word is also found in Mt. 16:23; Jn. 1:38; 20:16.

[16]Cf. Cerfaux, "Parallèles canoniques," 60.

[17]Cf. E. Klostermann, *Apocrypha* 2, KlT 8 (1929) 8.

[18]It is also found in 1 Cor. 5:11; Gal. 2:12.

[19]Cf. Cerfaux, "Parallèles canoniques," 63.

to mind:

Pap. Eg. 2, ll. 39-41	Matt. 8:4	Mark 1:44	Luke 5:14	Luke 17:14
πορευθείς	ὕπαγε σεαυτόν	ὕπαγε σεαυτόν	ἀπελθὼν	πορευθέντες
ἐπίδειξον σεαυτὸν	δεῖξον	δεῖξον	δεῖξον σεαυτὸν	ἐπιδείξατε ἑαυτοὺς
τοῖς ἱερεῦσιν.	τῷ ἱερεῖ.	τῷ ἱερεῖ.	τῷ ἱερεῖ.	τοῖς ἱερεῦσιν.

The presence of the words πορευθείς, ἐπίδειξον, and τοῖς ἱερεῦσιν demonstrates a definite literary contact with Lk. 17:14, which is the only one to use the verb πορεύομαι, the composite verb ἐπιδείκνυμι, and the plural οἱ ἱερεῖς.[20]

In the question about the kings, this saying of Christ is read in lines 52-54: τί με καλεῖτ[ε τῷ στό]ματι ὑμ[ῶν δι]δάσκαλον· μ[ὴ ἀκού]οντες ὃ [λ]έγω·: "Why call ye me with yo[ur mou]th Master and yet [do] not what I say?'' The parallel that stands out and upon which the author depends here is Lk. 6:46, which reads, τί δέ με καλεῖτε κύριε κύριε καὶ οὐ ποιεῖτε ἃ λέγω. Except for the word κύριε instead of διδάσκαλον, there is an identity between the Lukan text and the apocryphon; the addition of τῷ στόματι ὑμῶν may have already been influenced by the citation of Is. 29:3, which follows immediately in the text.[21]

C. The Gospel of John[22]

Literary relationships of the Unknown Gospel with the Gospel of Jn. are very numerous.

In the controversy on the scripture, Christ says to his adversaries in lines 7-10, ἐραυ[νᾶτε τ]ὰς γραφάς· ἐν αἷς ὑμεῖς δο[κεῖτε] ζωὴν ἔχειν, ἐκεῖναί εἰ[σ]ιν [αἱ μαρτ]υροῦσαι περὶ ἐμοῦ: "(Ye) search the scriptures in which ye think that ye have life; these are they which bear witness of me.'' The apocryphon takes up almost literally Jn. 5:39: ἐραυνᾶτε[23] τὰς γραφάς, ὅτι ὑμεῖς δοκεῖτε ἐν αὐταῖς ζωὴν αἰώνιον ἔχειν· καὶ ἐκεῖναί εἰσιν αἱ μαρτυροῦσαι περὶ ἐμοῦ. The literary contact is beyond doubt. Some minor differences are still to be mentioned: first of all, the Unknown Gospel reads ἐν αἷς instead of ὅτι . . . ἐν αὐταῖς, but this reading is sustained in Jn. 5:39 according to von Soden's apparatus, Tatian,[24] the manuscripts a, q, ff² of the ancient Latin, Irenaeus, Tertullian, boh. Furthermore, the apocryphon omits αἰώνιον; but this omission is found

---

[20]Cf. ibid., 64, where Cerfaux writes, ''The papyrus is not the only one to do so. The textual tradition of Lk. 5:14 and Mt. 8:4 is also tainted by Lk. 18:14. Tatian, b, ff², syr. cur. (von Soden) read τοῖς ἱερεῦσιν in Lk. 5:14; h and the Syriac tradition in Mt. 8:4.''

[21]Cf. ibid., 67.

[22]Cf. Mayeda, *Das Leben-Jesu-Fragment. Papyrus Egerton 2*, 69-77, who deals with this subject.

[23]With B and S, despite Nestle and von Soden who write ἐρευνᾶτε.

[24]Cf. Vogels, ''Fragments of an Unknown Gospel,'' 314.

in cod. 71 of Jn. and could be explained by the influence of the following verse of Jn., which reads ζωὴν ἔχητε. Finally, the omission of καὶ is common to the apocryphon and to the manuscripts a, q, r of Jn.[25]

Another saying of Jesus is found in this same controversy on the scripture in lines 10-14: μὴ δ[οκεῖτε ὅ]τι ἐγὼ ἦλθον κατηγο[ρ]ῆσαι [ὑμῶν] πρὸς τὸν π(ατέ)ρα μου· ἔστιν [ὁ κατη]γορῶν ὑμῶν Μω(υσῆς) εἰς ὃν [ὑμεῖς] ἠλπίκατε: "Do not think that I came to accuse [you] to my Father! There is one [that ac]cuses [you], even Moses, on whom ye have set your hope." These words are literarily dependent on Jn. 5:45: μὴ δοκεῖτε ὅτι ἐγὼ κατηγορήσω ὑμῶν πρὸς τὸν πατέρα· ἔστιν ὁ κατηγορῶν ὑμῶν Μωυσῆς εἰς ὃν ὑμεῖς ἠλπίκατε. The verb ἦλθον is missing in the entire manuscript tradition of Jn. 5:45. "This addition," notes Cerfaux, "is obviously secondary. Christ did not 'come to accuse his Father,' since this accusation is being held in store for the eschatological future. It can be easily explained by the influence of other passages of Jn., i.e., 5:36-37; 6:39; 8:18."[26] The possessive μου is also missing in the manuscript tradition of Jn. 5:45, but ὁ πατήρ μου is as Johannine as ὁ πατήρ.[27]

Still in the controversy on the scripture, the adversaries of Christ retort in lines 14-17: α[ὐ]τῶν δὲ λε[γόντω]ν ε[ὖ] οἴδαμεν ὅτι Μω(ϋσεῖ) ἐλά[λησεν] ὁ θ(εό)ς[·] σὲ δὲ οὐκ οἴδαμεν [πόθεν εἶ]·: "And when they sa[id]: 'We know that God [hath] spok[en] to Moses,but as for thee, we know not [whence thou art].' . . ." There is no doubt that the author of the apocryphon was inspired by Jn. 9:29: ἡμεῖς οἴδαμεν ὅτι Μωϋσεῖ λελάληκεν ὁ θεός, τοῦτον δὲ οὐκ οἴδαμεν πόθεν ἐστίν. The only pronounced difference, if one may say so, is the fact that these words are addressed to Jesus himself, whereas in Jn. 9:29 the reading that has Jesus in mind is addressed to the man born blind. Let me point out in the Unknown Gospel the adverb εὖ, which is not common in gospel literature, and in Jn. 9:29 the variant ἐλάλησεν for λελάληκεν, supported by various manuscripts.[28]

In a second episode, the Unknown Gospel narrates an attempted arrest of Jesus, in which lines 22-24 state, ἔ]λκω[σιν] β[αστάσαντες δὲ] λίθους ὁμοῦ λι[θάζω]σι[ν αὐ[τόν: " . . . [to gather] stones together to stone him. And the [rul]ers laid their hands on him. . . . " At first glance, one cannot help but think of an influence of Jn. 10:31: ἐβάστασαν πάλιν λίθους οἱ Ἰουδαῖοι ἵνα λιθάσωσιν αὐτόν? Jn. 8:59 could also be mentioned as a parallel, but the verb

---

[25]Cf. Cerfaux, "Parallèles canoniques," 57.

[26]Cf. ibid., 57. Cf. the formula ἦλθον κατηγορῆσαι of the papyrus with the Gos. Eb. 5 (E. Klostermann, *Apocrypha*, 2:14): ἦλθον καταλύσαι τὰς θυσίας and with the Gos. Egypt. 5 (ibid., 2:16): ἦλθον καταλῦσαι τὰ ἔργα τῆς θελείας. This formula may be a Copticism.

[27]Cf. Cerfaux, "Parallèles canoniques," 58.

[28]This reading is supported by Θ, A, 053 (von Soden).

βαστάζω is missing. Cerfaux makes an important remark regarding this text: "It may be possible, however, that the synoptic context has triggered the reminiscence. The context of the parable of the vine growers (Mt. 21:36-46 = Lk. 20:9-19 = Mk. 12:1-2) is inserted between the conclusion of the parable (which speaks of the condemnation of the Jews, parallel in thought to the end of the episode on the controversy on the scripture) and the attempted arrest that this parable involves, the logion on the rejected stone (Mt. 21:42 = Lk. 20:17 = Mk. 12:10). It might be assumed that the papyrus proceeds in the same vein, inserting between the episode of the controversy on the scripture and the episode of the attempted arrest (respectively the verso and recto of the same page whose top and bottom are torn) this logion of the stone, which would lead to the idea of the stoning. A comparison with Lk. might explain the significance of ὁμοῦ, which is enigmatic in the papyrus: Pap.: ὁμοῦ λιθάζωσιν αὐτόν; Lk. 20:6: ὁ λαὸς ἅπας καταλιθάσει ἡμᾶς."[29]

In the same narrative of the attempted arrest, the author of the apocryphon writes in lines 24-29: καὶ ἐπέβαλον [τὰς] χεῖ[ρας] αὐτῶν ἐπ' αὐτὸν οἱ [ἄρχον]τες [ἵνα πιάσωσιν καὶ παρ[αδώ]σω[σι]ν τῷ ὄχλῳ· καὶ οὐκ ἠ[δύναντο] αὐτὸν πιάσαι ὅτι οὔπω ἐ[ληλύθει] αὐτοῦ ἡ ὥρα τῆς παραδό[σεως]: "And the [rul]ers laid their hands on him that they might arrest him and [deliver] him to the multitude. But they w[ere not able] to arrest him because the hour of his betrayal [was] not yet c[ome]." Jn. 7:30 is an excellent parallel: ἐζήτουν οὖν αὐτὸν πιάσαι καὶ οὐδεὶς ἐπέβαλεν ἐπ' αὐτὸν τὴν χεῖρα, ὅτι οὔπω ἐληλύθει ἡ ὥρα αὐτοῦ. Jn. 7:44; 10:39 could also come to mind, but the mention of the hour of Christ's betrayal is missing. Yet, remember that Lk.'s influence seems to be pronounced by the word παραδώσωσιν.[30] I would also like to add that no gospel emphasizes as this one does that Jesus was delivered to the multitude.[31] Instead of τὴν χεῖρα in Jn. 7:30, the apocryphon has τὰς χεῖρας. This reading seems to come from Lk. 20:19. Jn. 7:30, 44 attests to it as well.[32]

Still in the narrative of the attempted arrest, lines 30-31 read, αὐτὸς δὲ ὁ κ(ύριο)ς ἐξελθὼν [ἐκ τῶν χεί]ρων ἀπένευσεν ἀπ' [αὐτῶν]: "But he himself, the Lord, escaped out of [their han]ds and turned away from them." The construc-

---

[29]Cf. Cerfaux, "Parallèles canoniques," 60-61.

[30]Cf. above, 176.

[31]Cf. Cerfaux, "Parallèles canoniques," 61, who writes, "The fact that Jesus is delivered to the multitude (expected to take the initiative in the passion) is contrary to the canonical gospels, but is found in the Gospel of Peter 5 which says of Pilate: καὶ παρέδωκεν αὐτὸν τῷ λαῷ (E. Klostermann, *Apocrypha*, 1:4). The people are the ones who, in this gospel, mistreat and crucify Jesus: οἱ δὲ λαβόντες τὸν κύριον (6).

[32]Cf. Cerfaux, "Parallèles canoniques," 61, in which the author notes, "Judging by its proponents, it is an ancient 'Western' reading: W, fam. 1, cod. 565, Boh., Lat., Syr., etc. (cf. critical apparatus by von Soden)."

tion of the sentence is close to Lk. 4:30.[33] However, the text is literarily closer to Jn. 10:39: καὶ ἐξῆλθεν ἐκ τῆς χείρος αὐτῶν. Moreover, I have already pointed out a reference to Jn. 7:30 in lines 24-29. Now, witnesses of the fourth gospel insert in this verse καὶ ἐξῆλθεν ἐκ τῆς χείρος αὐτῶν after the word πιάσαι.[34] The author is, therefore, still under the Johannine influence. Yet, let me note the presence of the verb ἀπονεύω, which is not found in the New Testament.[35]

I have previously shown that the narrative of the question about the kings is built on the narrative of the tax to Caesar in the synoptics.[36] But there are Johannine reminiscences as well, notably in lines 45-47: διδάσκαλε Ἰη(σοῦ) οἴδαμεν ὅτι [ἀπὸ θ(εο)ῦ] ἐλήλυθας ἃ γὰρ ποιεῖς μα[ρτυρεῖ] ὑπὲρ το[ὺ]ς προφ[ήτ]ας πάντας: ''Master Jesus, we know that thou art come [from God], for what thou doest bears a test[imony] (to thee) (which) (goes) beyond (that) of al(l) the prophets.'' Several Johannine texts are obvious parallels: Jn. 3:2, ῥαββί, οἴδαμεν ὅτι ἀπὸ θεοῦ ἐλήλυθας διδάσκαλος· οὐδεὶς γὰρ δύναται ταῦτα τὰ σημεῖα ποιεῖν ἃ σὺ ποιεῖς ἐὰν μὴ ᾖ ὁ θεὸς μετ' αὐτοῦ; 10:25: τὰ ἔργα ἃ ἐγὼ ποιῶ . . . ταῦτα μαρτυρεῖ περὶ ἐμου; and 5:36: ματρυρίαν μείζω τοῦ Ἰωάννου. The author of the apocryphon was probably inspired by these texts of Jn. which revolve around the formula τὰ σημεῖα (τὰ ἔργα) ποιεῖν.[37] In fact, the sentence includes the words διδάσκαλος, οἴδαμεν ὅτι ἀπὸ θεοῦ ἐλήλυθας, ἃ ποιεῖς, μαρτθρεῖ. Regarding the words μαρτυρεῖ ὑπὲρ τοὺς προφήτας πάντας, Cerfaux notes, ''The testimony of the works presented as superior to the testimony of the prophets is rather unexpected. Tradition presents two opposite tendencies on this subject: sometimes the prophetic argument is emphasized (especially Justin; cf. Kerygma Petri 4, Klostermann, *Apocrypha* 1:16: οὐδὲν ἄτερ γραφῆς λέγομεν); sometimes the prophets are diminished: Jesus is *the* prophet announced by Deut. (18:15) to replace Moses (already in Acts 3:22; 7:37; cf. Clem. Hom. 3.53, de Lagarde, 51): the prophets are not without sin (Gos. Heb. 10, Kostermann, *Apocrypha* 2:6).''[38]

D. The Synoptic Tradition

This section includes different passage that have parallels in the gospels, but for which it is impossible to decide which one of the gospels served as a source of inspiration for the author. The narrative of the healing of the leper is the principal typical example in this regard.

Pap. Eg. 2, lines 36-37: ἐὰν [ο]ὖν [σὺ θέλης] καθαρίζομαι: ''If [thou] therefore [wilt], I am made clean.'' The formula ἐὰν θέλης, δύνασαί με καθα-

---

[33]Cf. ibid., 62.

[34]This text is supported by Θ, the Ferrar group, and the Zion group (von Soden).

[35]Cf. Cerfaux, ''Parallèles canoniques,'' 62, who refers to Justin, Dial. 125, for the verb ἀπονεύω.

[36]Cf. above, 174-75.

[37]Cf. Cerfaux, ''Parallèles canoniques,'' 66.

[38]Cf. ibid.

ρίσαι is found in the synoptics: Mt. 8:2; Mk. 1:40; Lk. 5:12. "The small variation in the papyrus is astonishing," writes Cerfaux; "it seems that he was struck above all by the command of Jesus, καθαρίσθητι, and that he led up to it by replacing δύνασαί με καθαρίσαι with καθαρίζομαι."[39]

Pap. Eg 2, lines 37-39: ὁ δὴ κ(ύριο)ς [ἔφη αὐτῷ] θέλ[ω] καθαρίσθητι· [καὶ εὐθέως ἀ]πέστη ἀπ᾽ αὐτοῦ ἡ λέπ[ρα: "Immediately the Lord [said to him]: 'I will, be thou made clean.' [And thereupon] the leprosy departed from him.'' The formula θέλω καθαρίσθητι is traditional; the author dropped the gesture of the three synoptics: ἐκτείνας τὴν χεῖρα αὐτοῦ ἥψατο.[40] The words καὶ εὐθέως ἀπέστη ἀπ᾽ αὐτοῦ ἡ λέπρα are as different from the synoptics as the words in the synoptics vary from one another, namely, with minute differences which do not affect their meaning. Mt. 8:3 uses the verb ἐκαθερίσθη, Mk. 1:42 and Lk. 5:13 use ἀπῆλθεν (Mk. 1:3 adds καὶ ἐκαθερίσθη), the papyrus uses ἀπέστη. This last verb belongs exclusively in the gospels to the vocabulary of Lk.[41]

As for the episode on the question regarding the kings (lines 42-54), it is built on the outline of the synoptic narrative of the tax owed to Caesar: Mt. 22:15-22; Mk. 12:13-17; Lk. 20:20-26. Cerfaux demonstrates this with the help of a synopsis of the four texts[42] that I reproduce below.

Pap. Eg. 2, ll. 42-54	Synoptics
ἐξεταστικῶς ἐπείραζον	Lk. 20:20: ἵνα ἐπιλάβωνται αὐτοῦ λόγου
	21: ἐπηρώτησαν
διδάσκαλε Ἰησοῦ	διδάσκαλε
οἴδαμεν ὅτι	οἴδαμεν ὅτι
εἶπε οὖν ἡμεῖν	Mt. 22:17: εἰπὸν οὖν ἡμῖν
ἐξὸν τοῖς βασιλεῦσιν	Mk. 12:14: ἔξεστιν . . . καίσαρι
ἀποδοῦναι	δοῦναι
ἀποδῶμεν . . . ἢ μή;	δῶμεν ἢ μὴ δῶμεν;
ὁ δὲ Ἰησοῦς εἰδὼς τὴν δι-άνοιαν αὐτῶν . . . εἶπεν	Lk. 20:23: κατανοήσας (Mk. 12:15: εἰδώς) δὲ αὐτῶν τὴν πανουργίαν εἶπεν
τί με καλεῖτε	Mk. 12:15: τί με πειράζετε.

In lines 50-51, the words ὁ δὲ Ἰη(σοῦς) εἰδὼς [τὴν δι]άνοιαν [αὐτ]ῶν: "But Jesus saw through their [in]tention" are more or less parallel to Mt. 22:18: γνοὺς δὲ ὁ Ἰησοῦς τὴν πονηρίαν αὐτῶν; Mk. 12:15: ὁ δὲ εἰδὼς αὐτῶν τὴν ὑπόκρισιν;[43] and Lk. 20:23: κατανοήσας δὲ αὐτῶν τὴν πανουργίαν.

---

[39]Cf. ibid., 63.

[40]Cf. ibid., 63n.15: "The formula abandoned here reappears in another context of the papyrus (fourth episode). A similar phenomenon is frequently present in the synoptic tradition."

[41]Cf. ibid., 63, where the author points out Lk. 4:13: ὁ διάβολος ἀπέστη ἀπ᾽ αὐτοῦ.

[42]Cf. ibid., 64-65.

[43]Mk. 12:15 has the variant ὁ δὲ Ἰησοῦς: D, G, Θ, fam. 1, fam. 13, etc.

Lines 54-59 state, "Well has Is[aiah] prophesied [concerning y]ou saying: This [people honors] me with the[ir li]ps but their heart is far from me; [their worship is] vain. [They teach] precepts [of men]." Mt. 15:7-9 and Mk. 7:6-7 cite the same passage from Is. 29:13 and introduce it in a way that is identical to the apocryphon which says, καλῶς Ἡ[σ(αῖ)ας περὶ ὑ]μῶν ἐπ[ρο]φ(ήτευ)σεν εἰπών. The variants are common and insignificant. On the other hand, if the citation itself is identical in the two synoptics, it has several differences from the apocryphon; the following table sets them off clearly.

Pap. Eg. 2, ll. 54-59	Mt. 15:8-9	Mk. 7:6-7	Is. 29:13
ὁ λαὸς οὗτος τοῖς	ὁ λαὸς οὗτος τοῖς	According to	Ἐγγίζει μοι ὁ λαὸς οὗτος ἐν
χείλεσιν αὐτῶν	χείλεσιν	B, D, 1071,	τῷ στόματι αὐτοῦ καὶ ἐν
τιμῶσίν με	με τιμᾷ	vet. lat., vg.,	τοῖς χείλεσιν αὐτῶν
ἡ δὲ καρδία αὐτῶν	ἡ δὲ καρδία αὐτῶν	syr. sin. and	τιμῶσίν με ἡ δὲ καρδία
πόρρω ἀπέχει ἀπ᾽	πόρρω ἀπέχει ἀπ᾽	pesh., which	αὐτῶν πόρρω ἀπέχει ἀπ᾽
ἐμοῦ μάτην	ἐμοῦ᾽ μάτην	are like Mt.	ἐμοῦ᾽ μάτην δὲ σέβονταί με
με σέβονται	δὲ σέβονταί με	15:8-9.	διδάσκοντες ἐντάλματα . . .
ἐντάλματα . . .	. . . ἐντάλματα.		

The variant αὐτῶν τιμῶσίν με indicates a return to the LXX against the gospel text. Cerfaux notes in this regard, "This variant in the papyrus agrees with Justin (Dial. 78: Otto, p. 284) and Didasc. Jacobi (Patr. Or. VIII, p. 757). There is a slight hint that leads me to believe that the apocryphon depends on a recension of Isaiah which is not in common circulation: it agrees with Justin (Dial. 78) in placing ἐντάλματα immediately after σέβονταί (με)."[44]

Up to now, I have excluded from all these texts the fifth episode called the "miracle of the Jordan" (lines 60-75), which is very enigmatic. Parallels to it are doubtful. According to Cerfaux's restoration,[45] based on the relationships with the synoptic tradition he demonstrated in the other episodes, and especially with the chapter on the controversies (Lk. 20; Mt. 21-22; Mk. 11-12), he came to think of the parable of the withered fig tree in Mt. 21:18-22; Mk. 11:20-25; and Lk. 17:6, in which the mention of the logion of the mountain is linked to that of the fig tree. This is how the author of the apocryphon was inspired here by these synoptic parallels.

In conclusion, of all the synoptics, the influence of Lk. is beyond doubt and played a leading part in the Unknown Gospel. By and large, we can accept the opinion that the Unknown Gospel depends on Mk. The Matthean influence is less strong than that of Lk., but there is an unmistakable affinity with its vocabulary.[46]

Moreover, there are many literary contacts with the fourth gospel, from which certain texts are drawn almost literally. The author of the apocryphon seems to

---

44Cf. Cerfaux, "Parallèles canoniques,"68.

45Cf. ibid., 69-73.

46Cf. ibid., 74.

have used Jn. to enrich the synoptic basis, adding for his purpose what he found interesting in the Johannine tradition. The author of the apocryphon may have had the fourth gospel in hand:[47] a literary dependence on this canonical gospel is the simplest hypothesis,[48] and it is preferable to the use of a tradition parallel to this gospel.[49]

Section 2
THE GOSPEL OF THE HEBREWS

Saint Jerome attests to the existence of the Gospel of the Hebrews, whose date of composition is generally given as before the year 150. He states that he translated the original text into Greek and Latin.[50] He points out that this gospel was written in Chaldean, namely, Aramaic, but written in Hebrew letters, and that it was used by the Nazareans. Some people, according to Saint Jerome, thought that this gospel was the gospel of Mt.[51] Time has not spared the versions any more than it has the original; only a few fragments survive, preserved in later writings. All the authors emphasize its great affinity with the first gospel.

In keeping with my focus of interest, a first paragraph will concentrate on the Gospel of Mt., and a second paragraph will deal with other New Testament writings.[52]

§1. Saint Matthew

I am concerned here only with the fragments of the Gospel of the Hebrews that can be compared with Mt.

---

[47]Cf. C. H. Roberts, *An Unpublished Fragment of the Fourth Gospel in the John Rylands Library* (Manchester, 1935) cited by Cerfaux, "Parallèles canoniques," 76.

[48]Cf. Cerfaux, "Parallèles canoniques," 76-77, who also emphasizes the anti-Jewish attitude of the apocryphon and its predilections for controversies.

[49]While I acknowledge a dependence on the fourth gospel, I do not accept the conclusions of Mayeda, *Das Leben-Jesu-Fragment. Papyrus Egerton 2,* 69-74, who states that the writer of the Unknown Gospel drew his inspiration only from sources used by Jn.

[50]Cf. Jerome, *De viris ill.* 2: "Evangelium quod appellatur secundum Hebraeos et a me nuper in graecum sermonem latinumque translatum est. . . . "

[51]Cf. Jerome, *Contr. Pelag.* 3.2; in Mt. 12:13.

[52]I follow E. Klostermann's edition of the fragments of the Gospel of the Hebrews in *Apocrypha 2, Evangelien,* KIT 8, 3rd ed. (Berlin, 1929) 5-12; I also refer sometimes to E. Preuschen, *Antilegomena. Die Reste der ausserkanonischen Evangelien und urchristlichen Überlieferungen,* 2nd rev. ed. (Giessen, 1905). [The texts followed in the English translation are those of Montague Rhodes James, *The Apocryphal New Testament* (Oxford: The Clarendon Press, corr. rpr. 1953ff.) 1-8; Hennecke's *New Testament Apocrypha,* 2, and A. F. Findlay's *Byways in Early Christian Literature* (Edinburgh: T.&T. Clark, 1923) 158-65. Editor's note.]

A. Jerome, on Mt. 2:5

> *In Bethlehem Iudaeae.* Librariorum hic error est. Putamus enim ab evange-
> lista primum editum, sicut in ipso Hebraico legimus *Iudae* non *Iudaeae*.
>
> *Bethlehem of Judaea.* This is a mistake of the scribes: for I think it was orig-
> inally expressed by the Evangelist as we read in the Hebrew, "of Judah," not
> Judaea.
>
> [The English translation has been added by the editor from James, p. 4.]

According to Saint Jerome, therefore, the first gospel reads Judah, since the
Gospel of the Hebrews also uses this term. Jerome himself says that Mt. 2:5 is
here telling of the coming of the Wise Men: the chief priests and the scribes, interrogated by Herod on the place where the Christ was to be born, answer, ἐν Βηθ-
λέεμ τῆς Ἰουδαίας.

Did the Gospel of the Hebrews reproduce the Matthean text in its entirety? It
is impossible to say, because Jerome reports only one word from this passage. Yet,
it can be stated that the apocryphon is in agreement here with Mt. 2:5. Jerome
himself has seen this relationship, since he goes back to the reading of the Gospel
of the Hebrews to point out the copyists' error in Mt. 2:5.

B. Jerome, Of illustrious men, 3

> Porro ipsum Hebraicum habetur usque hodie in Caesarensi bibliotheca, quam
> Pamphilus martyr studiosissime confecit. Mihi quoque a Nazaraeis qui in Be-
> roea urbe Syriae hoc volumine utuntur, describendi facultas fuit. In quo a-
> nimadvertendum, quod ubicumque evangelista sive ex persona sua, sive ex
> domini salvatoris veteris scripturae testimoniis abutitur, non sequitur septu-
> aginta translatorum auctoritatem sed Hebraicam. E quibus illa duo sunt: *ex
> Aegypto vocavi filium meum* et: *quoniam Nazaraeus vocabitur.*
>
> Further, the Hebrew itself (*or* original) is preserved to this day in the library
> at Caesarea which was collected with such care by the martyr Pamphilus. I
> also had an opportunity of copying it afforded me by the Nazarenes who use
> the book, at Beroea, a city of Syria. [James, p. 4] To these [namely, the ci-
> tations in which Mt. follows not the Septuagint but the Hebrew original text]
> belong the two: "Out of Egypt have I called my son" and "For he shall be
> called a Nazarean." [Hennecke, p. 146]
>
> [The English translation has been added by the editor from James, p. 4, and
> Hennecke, 1:146.]

According to Jerome, the Gospel of the Hebrews contained these two citations of the Old Testament which are peculiar to Mt. 2:15: ἐξ Αἰγύπτου ἐκάλεσα τὸν υἱόν μου, and 2:23: ὅτι Ναζωραῖος κληθήσεται. It is possible to
believe, therefore, that the apocryphon depends on the first gospel, all the more
since there is no definite Old Testament text that relates the prophecy *Quoniam*

Nazaræus vocabitur.

C. Jerome, on Is. 11:2

Sed iuxta evangelium quod Hebraeo sermone conscriptum legunt Nazaraei: *descendet super eum omnis fons spiritus sancti . . .* porro in evangelio, cuius supra fecimus mentionem, haec scripta reperimus: *Factum est autem, cum ascendisset dominus de aqua, descendit fons omnis spiritus sancti et requievit super eum et dixit illi: Fili mi, in omnibus prophetis expectabam te, ut venires et requiescerem in te. Tu es enim requies mea, tu es filius meus primogenitus, qui regnas in sempiternum.*

According to the Gospel written in the Hebrew speech, which the Nazaraeans read, the whole fount of the Holy Spirit shall descend upon him. . . . Further in the Gospel which we have just mentioned we find the following written: And it came to pass when the Lord was come up out of the water, the whole fount of the Holy Spirit descended upon him and rested on him and said to him: My Son, in all the prophets was I waiting for thee that thou shouldest come and I might rest in thee. For thou art my rest: thou are my first-begotten Son that reignest for ever.

[The English translation has been added by the editor from Hennecke 1:163.]

The parallels that are generally mentioned are Mt. 3:16-17; Mk. 1:10-11; and Lk. 3:21b-22. An influence from Lk. is immediately excluded: the third gospel does speak of the going up from the water, but Mt. 3:16 writes, βαπτισθεὶς δὲ ὁ Ἰησοῦς εὐθὺς ἀνέβη ἀπὸ τοῦ ὕδατος· καὶ ἰδοὺ ἠνεῴχθησαν οἱ οὐρανοί, καὶ εἶδεν πνεῦμα θεοῦ καταβαῖνον ὡσεὶ περιστεράν, ἐρχόμενον ἐπ' αὐτόν· καὶ ἰδοὺ φωνὴ ἐκ τῶν οὐρανῶν λέγουσα· οὗτός ἐστιν ὁ υἱός μου ὁ ἀγαπητός, ἐν ᾧ εὐδόκησα. Mk. 1:10-11 states, καὶ εὐθὺς ἀναβαίνων ἐκ τοῦ ὕδατος εἶδεν σχιζομένους τοὺς οὐρανοὺς καὶ τὸ πνεῦμα ὡς περιστερὰν καταβαῖνον εἰς αὐτόν· καὶ φωνὴ [ἐγένετο] ἐκ τῶν οὐρανῶν· σὺ εἶ ὁ υἱός μου ὁ ἀγαπητός, ἐν σοὶ εὐδόκησα.

The apocryphon does not reproduce literally either of these two texts: an entire part of the pericope finds no correspondence in them. Yet, for the part it has in common with Mt. and Mk., it could have been inspired by one of them: *ascendisset dominus de aqua, descendit . . . spiritus super eum . . . filius meus* may come from Mt. as well as from Mk.: these texts are both sufficiently similar to have suggested the words in the Gospel of the Hebrews. Yet, in the absence of any other apocryphal reference to Mk., as we shall see, it is more logical to think that it depends here on Mt. 3:16-17.

D. (a) Jerome, against Pelag. 3.2

Et in eodem volumine: *Si peccaverit,* inquit, *frater tuus in verbo et satis tibi fecerit, septies in die suscipe eum. Dixit illi Simon, discipulus eius: Septies in die? Respondit dominus et dixit eis: Etiam ego dico tibi, usque septuagies septies. Etenim in prophetis quoque, postquam uncti sunt spiritu sancto, inventus est sermo peccati.*

And in the same book: If thy brother (saith he) have sinned by a word and made thee amends, seven times in a day receive thou him. Simon his disciple said unto him: Seven times in a day? The Lord answered and said unto him: Yea, I say unto thee, unto seventy times seven times. For in the prophets also, after they were anointed by the Holy Spirit, the word of sin was found.

[The English translation has been added by the editor from James, p. 6.]

(b) Cod. ev. 566 Tischendorf, Notitia Cod. Sinait., p. 58

Τὸ ᾿Ιουδαϊκὸν ἑξῆς ἔχει μετὰ τὸ <u>ἑβδομηκοντάκις ἑπτά· καὶ γὰρ ἐν τοῖς προφήταις μετὰ τὸ χρισθῆναι αὐτοὺς ἐν πνεύματι ἁγίῳ εὑρίσκετο ἐν αὐτοῖς λόγος ἁμαρτίας.</u>

The Gospel of the Hebrews reads then after seventy times seven: For even in the prophets after they have been anointed by the Holy Spirit, one still finds in them a word of sin. [Editor's translation.]

Two texts of the synoptics can be compared with the apocryphon. Mt. 18:21-22: Τότε προσελθὼν ὁ Πέτρος εἶπεν αὐτῷ· κύριε, ποσάκις ἁμαρτήσει εἰς ἐμὲ ὁ ἀδελφός μου καὶ ἀφήσω αὐτῷ; ἕως ἑπτάκις; λέγει αὐτῷ ὁ ᾿Ιησοῦς· οὐ λέγω σοι ἕως ἑπτάκις, ἀλλὰ ἕως ἑβδομηκοντάκις ἑπτά, and Lk. 17:4: καὶ ἐὰν ἑπτάκις τῆς ἡμέρας ἁμαρτήσῃ εἰς σὲ καὶ ἑπτάκις ἐπιστρέψῃ πρὸς σὲ λέγων· μετανοῶ, ἀφήσεις αὐτῷ.

The comparison of these texts allows us to infer, insofar as a fragment can be relied on, that the author refers to the episode narrated in the passages cited from the synoptics. It is quite believable that there is a literary contact with both Lk. 17:4 and Mt. 18:21-22. The author may have combined both texts, taking from Lk. 17:4 the words "and if he (your brother) sins against you seven times in the day, and turns to you seven times," and from Mt. 18:21-22 "I do not say to you seven times, but seventy times seven."

As for the particular text added by Cod. ev. 566 and Jerome, it is without parallel in the canonical gospels.

E. Origen, on Mt. 15:14 (only in the Latin text)

Scriptum est in evangelio quodam quod dicitur Secundum Hebraeos, si tamen placet suscipere illud, non ad auctoritatem, sed ad manifestationem propositae quaestionis: *Dixit,* inquit, *ad eum alter divitum: "Magister, quid bonum faciens vivam?" Dixit ei: "Homo, legem et prophetas fac." Respondit ad eum:*

"Feci." Dixit ei: "Vade, vende omnia quae possides et divide pauperibus et veni, sequere me." Coepit autem dives scalpere caput suum et no placuit ei. Et dixit ad eum Dominus: "Quomodo dicis: Legem feci et prophetas? Quoniam scriptum est in lege: Diliges proximum tuum sicut teipsum; et ecce multi fratres tui, filii Abrahae, amicti sunt stercore, morientes prae fame et domus tua plena est multis bonis et non egreditur omnino aliquid ex ea ad eos." Et conversus dixit Simoni, discipulo suo sedenti apud se: "Simon, fili Jonae, facilius est camelum intrare per foramen acus, quam divitem in regnum coelorum."

It is written in a certain Gospel which is called according to the Hebrews (if at least one care to accept it, not as authoritative, but to throw light on the question before us):

The second of the rich men (*it saith*) said unto him: Master, what good thing can I do and live? He said unto him: O man, fulfill (do) the law and the prophets.

He answered him: I have *kept them*. He said unto him: Go, sell all that thou ownest, and distribute it unto the poor, and come, follow me. But the rich man began to scratch his head, and it pleased him not. And the Lord said unto him: How sayest thou: I have kept the law and the prophets? For it is written in the law: Thou shalt love thy neighbour as thyself, and lo, many of thy brethren, sons of Abraham, are clad in filth, dying for hunger, and thine house is full of many good things, and nought at all goeth out of it unto them.

And he turned and said unto Simon his disciple who was sitting by him: Simon, son of Joanna, it is easier for a camel to enter in by a needle's eye than for a rich man *to enter* into the kingdom of heaven.

[The English translation has been added by the editor from James, p. 6.]

Parallels can be read in Mt. 19:16-24; Mk. 10:17-25; and Lk. 18:18-25, whose texts are fairly similar. The author of the Gospel of the Hebrews has probably narrated in his own way the dialogue between the rich young man and Christ. But his composition draws from the Matthean narrative rather than from the others. In fact, the Gospel of the Hebrews mentions "love thy neighbor"; and Mt. 19:19 is the only one among the synoptics to speak of the love of one's neighbor in the story of the young rich man. This indication is sufficient to grant preference to the Matthean text as having served as a basis for the author of the apocryphon, and to exclude the two other synoptics.[53] Moreover, the expression "regnum coelorum" is read in certain witnesses of Mt. as in the Gospel of the Hebrews.[54]

F. A fragment of the *Gospel of the Hebrews* is attested by several witnesses.

---

[53]Joachim Jeremias, *Unknown Sayings of Jesus* (London: SPCK; Greenwich CT: Seabury, 1958; rev. ed. 1964) 34n.1, points out the relationship with Mt.

[54]These witnesses are Z, 1, 1582, 124, 33, 157, 1295, the old Latin, the Vulgate, the Syriac versions cur. and sin.

(a) Origen, on Jn. 2:12

Ἐὰν δὲ προσιῆταί τις τὸ καθ᾽ Ἑβραίους εὐαγγέλιον, ἔνθα αὐτὸς ὁ σωτήρ φησιν· <u>ἄρτι ἔλαβέ με ἡ μήτηρ μου τὸ ἅγιον πνεῦμα ἐν μιᾷ τῶν</u> <u>τριχῶν μου καὶ ἀπήνεγκέ με εἰς τὸ ὄρος τὸ μέγα Θαβώρ,</u> ἐπαπορήσει πῶς μήτηρ Χριστοῦ τὸ διὰ τοῦ λόγου γεγενημένον πνεῦμα ἅγιον εἶναι δύναται.

But if any one admits the *Gospel according to the Hebrews,* where the Saviour Himself says, ''Just now my mother, the Holy Spirit, took me by one of my hairs and carried me away to the great mountain Tabor,'' he will raise the fresh difficulty how the Holy Spirit which had being through the Word can be the mother of Christ.

[The English translation has been added by the editor from Findlay, p. 49.]

(b) Origen, on Jeremiah, homily 15.4

Εἰ δέ τις παραδέχεται τὸ <u>ἄρτι ἔλαβέ με ἡ μήτηρ μου τὸ ἅγιον πνεῦμα</u> <u>καὶ ἀνήνεγκέ με εἰς τὸ ὄρος τὸ μέγα τὸ Θαβώρ καὶ τὰ ἑξῆς,</u> δύναται αὐτοῦ ἰδεῖν τὴν μητέρα.

And if anyone receive that *saying,* ''Even now my mother the Holy Spirit took me and carried me up unto the great mountain Thabor [Findlay, p. 49], and then he is able to see him mother [James, p. 2].

[The English translation has been added by the editor.]

(c) Jerome, on Micah 7:6

Qui legerit Canticum . . . credideritque evangelio, quod Secundum Hebraeos editum nuper transtulimus, in quo ex persona salvatoris dicitur: *Modo tulit me mater mea, sanctus spiritus, in uno capillorum meorum.* . . .

Who will read the Psalm . . . and believe in the gospel, which is called ''According to the Hebrews'' which I have recently translated, in which it is said by the person of the savior: ''Even so did my mother, the Holy Spirit, take me by one of my hairs. . . . '' [Editor's translation.]

(d) Jerome, on Is. 40:9ff.

Sed et in evangelio, quod Iuxta Hebraeos scriptum Nazaraei lectitant, dominus loquitur: *Modo me tulit mea spiritus sanctus.*

In the gospel which is called ''According to the Hebrews,'' which the Nazareans read, the Lord says: ''Even so did my mother, the Holy Spirit, take me. [Editor's translation.]

(e) Jerome, on Ezek. 16:13

> In evangelio quoque Hebraeorum, quod lectitant Nazaraei, salvator inducitur dicens: *Modo me arripuit mater mea spiritus sanctus.*

> Also in the Gospel of the Hebrews, which the Nazareans read, the Savior is brought in saying: "Even so did my mother, the Holy Spirit, snatch me away." [Editor's translation.]

This text of the Gospel of the Hebrews, attested to several times, has been linked to the temptation story, notably Mt. 4:1, 8; Mk. 1:12; and Lk. 4:1; but it is too different from the text of the synoptics to support a literary influence: nowhere in the gospels, in fact, is the Holy Spirit called the mother of Christ.

§2. The Other New Testament Writings

The fragments that have reached us from the Gospel of the Hebrews do not seem to reveal a literary influence from New Testament writings other than Mt. Yet, a few passages need to be mentioned because they are sometimes given as parallels beyond the first gospel.

Haimo of Auxerre, on Is. 53:2 (PL 116:994)

> Sicut enim in evangelio Nazaraeorum habetur *ad hanc vocem domini multa millia Iydaeorum astantium circa crucem crediderunt.*

> As it is said in the Gospel of the Nazaraeans: At this word of the Lord many thousands of the Jews who were standing round the cross became believers.

> [The English translation has been added by the editor from Hennecke, 1:150.]

This text alludes perhaps to a similar event mentioned in Lk. 23:48, but the text of Luke is literarily different.[55]

Two fragments may be compared with the synoptic tradition, but they are not necessarily dependent on any one of the gospels.

Jerome, on Mt. 12:13

> In evangelio, quo utuntur Nazaraei et Ebionitae, quod nuper in Graecum de Hebraeo sermone transtulimus, et quod vocatur a perisque Matthaei authenticum, homo iste, qui aridam habet manum, caementarius scribitur istiusmodi vocibus auxilium precans: *Caementarius eram, manibus victum quaeritans; precor te, Iesu, ut mihi restituas sanitatem, ne turpiter mendicem cibos.*

---

[55]Cf. also Gos. Pet. 25.

In the Gospel which the Nazarenes and Ebionites use (which I have lately translated into Greek from the Hebrew, and which is called by many [or most] people the original of Matthew), this man who has the withered hand is described as a mason, who prays for help in such words as these: "I was a mason seeking a livelihood with my hands: I pray thee, Jesu, to restore me mine health, that I may not beg meanly for my food."

[The English translation has been added by the editor from James, pp. 4-5.]

The episode of the man with a withered hand is common to the synoptics, Mt. 12:13; Mk.3:5; and Lk. 6:10, but none of these relate his words of entreaty.

A second fragment is given twice by Saint Jerome:

Jerome, on Mt. 27:51

In evangelio, cuius saepe facimus mentionem, *superliminare templi infiniti magnitudinis fractum esse atque divisum* legimus.

In the Gospel I so often mention we read that a lintel of the temple of immense size was broken and divided.

[The English translation has been added by the editor from James, p. 5.]

Jerome, letter to Hedibia (ep. 120) 8

In evangelio autem quod Hebraicis litteris scriptum est, legimus non velum templi scissum, sed *superliminare templi mirae magnitudinis corruisse.*

But in the Gospel that is written in Hebrew letters we read, not that the veil of the temple was rent, but that a lintel of the temple of wondrous size fell.

[The English translation has been added by the editor from James, p. 5.]

All three synoptics—Mt. 27:51; Mk. 15:38; and Lk. 23:45b—mention the tearing of the veil of the temple, but not the lintel.

A fragment of the Gospel of the Hebrews can be linked with the fourth gospel (Eusebius, *Eccl. Hist.* 3.39.17): Ἐκτέθειται (Παπίας) δὲ καὶ ἄλλην ἱστορίαν περὶ γυναικὸς ἐπὶ πολλαῖς ἁμαρτίαις διαβληθείσης ἐπὶ τοῦ κυρίου, ἣν τὸ καθ' Ἑβραίους εὐαγγέλιον περιέχει: "He (Papias) has also set forth (or expounded) another story, about a woman accused of many sins before the Lord, which the Gospel according to the Hebrews also contains." [James, p. 2. Editor's note.] The subject matter may be the story of the adulterous woman which Jn. 7:53ff. also relates, but the textual criticism of this passage is a well-known problem.

Another fragment of the Gospel of the Hebrews has sometimes been linked with a text of Paul:

Jerome, Of illustrious men, 2

. . . evangelium quoque quod appellatur Secundum Hebraeos et a me nuper in graecum sermonem latinumque translatum est, quo et Origenes saepe utitur post resurrectionem salvatoris refert: *Dominus autem cum dedisset sindonem servo sacerdotis, ivit ad Iacobum et apparuit ei,* iuraverat enim Iacobus se non comesurum panem ab illa hora, qua biberat calicem domini donec videret eum resurgentem a dormientibus rursusque post paululum: *Adferte, ait dominus, mensam et panem.* Statimque additur: *Tulit panem et benedixit ac fregit et dedit Iacobo iusto et dixit ei: Frater mi, comede panem tuum, quia resurrexit filius hominis a dormientibus.*

Also the Gospel according to the Hebrews, lately translated by me into Greek and Latin speech, which Origen often uses, tells, after the resurrection of the Saviour: ''Now the Lord, when he had given the linen cloth unto the servant of the priest, went into James and appeared to him (for James had sworn that he would not eat bread from that hour wherein he had drunk the Lord's cup until he should see him risen again from among them that sleep),'' and again after a little, ''Bring ye, saith the Lord, a table and bread,'' and immediately it is added, ''He took bread and blessed and brake and gave it unto James the Just and said unto him: 'My brother, eat thy bread, for the Son of Man is risen from among them that sleep.' ''

[The English translation has been added by the editor from James, pp. 3-4.]

There is no canonical writing that relates a similar narrative. The only noteworthy remark is simply that the appearance of Christ to James is mentioned in 1 Cor. 15:7: Ἔπειτα ὤφθη 'Ιακώβῳ, εἶτα τοῖς ἀποστόλοις πᾶσιν.

In brief, most of the fragments of the Gospel of the Hebrews that survive have been influenced by the Gospel of Mt. Given the fragmentary character of the apocryphon, it is difficult to characterize this Matthean influence. We are left with the impression that the apocryphon is nothing more than a derivative of Mt., that the first gospel is its basis. Let me point out, however, that there may have been in one instance a reference to Lk.[56]

Section 3
THE GOSPEL OF THE EBIONITES

Epiphanius attests to the existence of the Gospel of the Ebionites,[57] which is, it seems, to be identified with the Gospel of the Twelve known by Origen.[58] This work, which probably dates from the second half of the second century, is lost. Only a few fragments survive in later writings.[59]

Several of these fragments manifest a definite knowledge and demonstrate the use of the Gospel of Mt. Other fragments witness to an agreement with the syn-

---

[56]Cf. Cod. ev. 566 Tischendorf, 343.
[57]Cf. Epiphanius, Haer. 30.13, PG 41:428.
[58]Cf. Origen,Hom. in Lk. 1. Cf. on this subject Altaner, *Patrology,* 66-67.

optic tradition. Still others assume an influence from the Gospel of Lk. With the same focus of interest, I shall examine first the Gospel of Mt. and then the other New Testament writings.

§1. Saint Matthew

Several fragments admit of literary comparison with the first gospel:

A. Epiphanius, Haer. 30.13.2-3

Ἐν τῷ γοῦν παρ᾿ αὐτοῖς εὐαγγελίῳ κατὰ Ματθαῖον ὀνομαζομένῳ οὐχ ὅλῳ δὲ πληρεστάτῳ ἀλλὰ νενοθευμένῳ καὶ ἠκρωτηριασμένῳ—Ἑβαϊκὸν δὲ τοῦτο καλοῦσιν—ἐμφέρεται ὅτι ἐγένετό τις ἀνὴρ ὀνόματι Ἰησοῦς, καὶ αὐτὸς ὡς ἐτῶν τριάκοντα, ὃς ἐξελέξατο ἡμᾶς. καὶ ἐλθὼν εἰς Καφαρναοὺμ εἰσῆλθεν εἰς τὴν οἰκίαν Σίμωνος τοῦ ἐπικληθέντος Πέτρου καὶ ἀνοίξας τὸ στόμα αὐτοῦ εἶπεν· Παρερχόμενος παρὰ τὴν λίμνην Τιβεριάδος ἐξελεξάμην Ἰωάννην καὶ Ἰάκωβον υἱοὺς Ζεβεδαίου καὶ Σίμωνα καὶ Ἀνδρέαν καὶ Θαδδαῖον καὶ Σίμωνα τὸν ζηλωτὴν καὶ Ἰούδαν τὸν Ἰσκαριώτην, καὶ σε τὸν Ματθαῖον καθεζόμενον ἐπὶ τοῦ τελωνίου ἐκάλεσα, καὶ ἠκολούθησάς μοι. ὑμᾶς οὖν βούλομαι εἶναι δεκαδύο ἀποστόλους εἰς μαρτύριον τοῦ Ἰσραήλ.

In the Gospel that is in general use amongst them, which is called according to Matthew, which however is not whole (and) complete but forged and mutilated—they call it the Hebrew Gospel—it is reported: There appeared a certain man named Jesus of about thirty years of age, who chose us. And when he came to Capernaum, he entered into the house of Simon whose surname was Peter, and opened his mouth and said: As I passed along the Lake of Tiberias, I chose John and James the sons of Zebedee, and Simon and Andrew and Thaddaeus and Simon the Zealot and Judas the Iscariot, and thee, Matthew, I called as thou didst sit at the receipt of custom, and thou didst follow me. You therefore I will to be twelve apostles for a testimony unto Israel.

Even though none of the canonical gospels relates such a statement from Christ, parallels may still be drawn: Mt.4:18-22; 9:9; Mk. 1:16-20; 2:14; Lk. 5:1-11; 27-28. They developed at length what the Gospel of the Ebionites gathered into a single saying of Christ. The words regarding the call of Matthew deserve to be compared with their parallels in Mt. 9:9; Mk. 2:14; and Lk. 5:27-28. Inasmuch as Mt.

---

[58]Cf. Origen,Hom. in Lk. 1. Cf. on this subject Altaner, *Patrology*, 66-67.

[59]I follow E. Klostermann's edition of these fragments, *Apocrypha* 2, *Evangelien*, KlT 8, 3rd ed. (Berlin, 1929) 12-15; I sometimes refer to Preuschen, *Antilegomena*, 8-12. [The text followed in the English translation is that of Edgar Hennecke, *New Testament Apocrypha*, ed. Wilhelm Schneemelcher, ET ed. R. McL. Wilson (Philadelphia: Westminster Press, 1963) 156-58. Editor's note.]

is the only gospel to use the name Ματθαῖον, as opposed to Λευίν in Mk. and Lk., we must conclude that the saying of Christ, which recalls the call of Matthew in the apocryphon, has the Matthean narrative in mind. The fact that the fragment stops specifically at the point of the call of Matthew, and that it does not describe the call of the other apostles, confirms this assessment.

B. Epiphanius, Haer. 30.13.4-5

καὶ ἐγένετο Ἰωάννης βαπτίζων καὶ ἐξῆλθον πρὸς αὐτὸν Φαρισαῖοι καὶ ἐβαπτίσθησαν, καὶ πᾶσα Ἱεροσόλυμα. καὶ εἶχεν ὁ Ἰωάννης ἔνδυμα ἀπὸ τριχῶν καμήλου καὶ ζώνην δερματίνην περὶ τὴν ὀσφὺν αὐτοῦ, καὶ τὸ βρῶμα αὐτοῦ (φησὶ) μέλι ἄγριον, οὗ ἡ γεῦσις ἡ τοῦ μάννα, ὡς ἐγκρὶς ἐν ἐλαίῳ ἵνα δῆθεν μεταστρέψωσι τὸν τῆς ἀληθείας λόγον εἰς ψεῦδος καὶ ἀντὶ ἀκρίδων ποιήσωσιν ἐγκρίδα ἐν μέλιτι.

And it came to pass that John was baptizing; and there went out to him Pharisees and were baptized, and all Jerusalem. And John had a garment of camel's hair and a leathern girdle about his loins, and his food, as it saith, was wild honey, the taste of which was that of manna, as a cake dipped in oil. Thus they [the Ebionites] were resolved to pervert the word of truth into a lie and to put a cake in the place of locusts.

The following parallels are found in Mt. 3:4-5a; Mk. 1:4-6; and Lk. 3:3, 7a.

Gos. Eb. 30.13.4-5	Mt. 3:4-5a	Mk. 1:4-6	Lk. 3:3, 7a
Ἐγένετο Ἰωάννης Βαπτίζων καὶ ἐξῆλθον πρὸς αὐτὸν Φαρισαῖοι καὶ ἐβαπτίσθησαν καὶ πᾶσα Ἱεροσόλυμα. καὶ εἶχεν ὁ Ἰωάννης ἔνδυμα ἀπὸ τριχῶν καμήλου καὶ ζώνην δερματίνην περὶ τὴν ὀσφὺν αὐτοῦ, καὶ τὸ βρῶμα αὐτοῦ (φησὶ) μέλι ἄγριον, οὗ ἡ γεῦσις ἡ τοῦ μάννα, ὡς ἐγκρὶς ἐν ἐλαίῳ.	Αὐτὸς δὲ ὁ Ἰωάννης εἶχεν τὸ ἔνδυμα αὐτοῦ ἀπὸ τριχῶν καμήλου καὶ ζώνην δερματίνην περὶ τὴν ὀσφὺν αὐτοῦ· ἡ δὲ τροφὴ ἦν αὐτοῦ ἀκρίδες καὶ μέλι ἄγριον. Τότε ἐξεπορεύετο πρὸς αὐτὸν Ἱεροσόλυμα καὶ πᾶσα ἡ Ἰουδαία καὶ πᾶσα ἡ περίχωρος τοῦ Ἰορδάνου....	Ἐγένετο Ἰωάννης ὁ βαπτίζων ἐν τῇ ἐρήμῳ κηρύσσων βάπτισμα μετανοίας εἰς ἄφεσιν ἁμαρτιῶν. Καὶ ἐξεπορεύετο πρὸς αὐτὸν πᾶσα ἡ Ἰουδαία χώρα καὶ οἱ Ἱεροσολυμῖται πάντες ... καὶ ἦν ὁ Ἰωάννης ἐνδεδυμένος τρίχας καμήλου καὶ ζώνην δερματίνην περὶ τὴν ὀσφὺν αὐτοῦ, καὶ ἐσθίων ἀκρίδας καὶ μέλι ἄγριον.	Καὶ ἦλθεν εἰς πᾶσαν τὴν περίχωρον τοῦ Ἰορδάνου κηρύσσων βάπτισμα μετανοίας. . . . Ἔλεγεν οὖν τοῖς ἐκπορευομένοις ὄχλοις βαπτισθῆναι ὑπ' αὐτοῦ, . . .

The formulas describing the dress and the food of the Baptist are almost literally identical to those in Mt. The text of Mk. is also fairly close to that of the apocryphon, yet, as a whole, preference goes to Mt.; cf. ἔνδυμα as opposed to ἐνδεδυμένος in Mk.; ἀπὸ τριχῶν as opposed to τρίχας in Mk. Furthermore, like the Gospel of the Ebionites, Mt. 3:7 is the only one to mention the Pharisees among those who come to be baptized.

Nevertheless, I must point out that the apocryphon uses τὸ βρῶμα instead of ἡ τροφή in Mt., and that it adds οὗ ἡ γεῦσις ἡ τοῦ μάννα, ὡς ἐγκρὶς ἐν ἐλαίῳ. Besides, Epiphanius emphasizes this last addition when he points out that the Ebionites belie the text by replacing the locusts with a cake of honey. The apocryphon, therefore, uses the Matthean text on which it is literarily dependent, but, according to Epiphanius, it tampers with it willingly. The beginning of this account seems to be influenced by Mk.

C. Epiphanius, Haer. 30.13.7-8

Καὶ μετὰ τὸ εἰπεῖν πολλὰ ἐπιφέρει ὅτι <u>τοῦ λαοῦ βαπτισθέντος ἦλθε</u> <u>καὶ Ἰησοῦς καὶ ἐβαπτίσθη ὑπὸ τοῦ Ἰωάννου.</u> καὶ ὡς ἀνῆλθεν ἀπὸ τοῦ ὕδατος, ἠνοίγησαν οἱ οὐρανοί, καὶ εἶδεν τὸ πνεῦμα τὸ ἅγιον ἐν εἴδει περιστερᾶς κατελθούσης καὶ εἰσελθούσης εἰς αὐτόν. καὶ φωνὴ ἐκ τοῦ οὐρανοῦ λέγουσα· Σύ μου εἶ ὁ υἱὸς ὁ ἀγαπητός, ἐν σοὶ ηὐδόκησα καὶ πάλιν· Ἐγὼ σήμερον γεγέννηκά σε. καὶ εὐθὺς περιέλαμψε τὸν τόπον φῶς μέγα. ὃ ἰδὼν (φησὶν) ὁ Ἰωάννης λέγει αὐτῷ· Σὺ τίς εἶ, κύριε; καὶ πάλιν φωνὴ ἐξ οὐρανοῦ πρὸς αὐτόν· Οὗτός ἐστιν ὁ υἱός μου ὁ ἀγαπητός, ἐφ' ὃν ηὐδόκησα. καὶ τότε (φησὶν) ὁ Ἰωάννης προσπεσὼν αὐτῷ ἔλεγεν· Δέομαί σου, κύριε, σύ με βάπτισον. ὁ δὲ ἐκώλυσεν αὐτὸν λέγων· Ἄφες, ὅτι οὕτως ἐστὶ πρέπον πληρωθῆναι πάντα.

And after much has been recorded it proceeds: When the people were baptized, Jesus also came and was baptized by John. And as he came up from the water, the heavens were opened and he saw the Holy Spirit in the form of a dove that descended and entered into him. And a voice (sounded) from heaven that said: Thou art my beloved Son, in thee I am well pleased. And again: I have this day begotten thee. And immediately a great light shone round about the place. When John saw this, it saith, he saith unto him: Who are thou, Lord? And again a voice from heaven (rang out) to him: This is my beloved Son in whom I am well pleased. And then, it saith, John fell down before him and said: I beseech thee, Lord, baptize thou me. But he prevented him and said: Suffer it; for thus it is fitting that everything should be fulfilled.

There are two parts to this fragment: the first is parallel to the synoptics, and it ends as we hear for the first time the words that come from heaven; the second includes the remainder of the text, which seems to echo Mt. 3:14. I propose to examine them separately.

(a) The first part finds parallels in Mt. 3:13, 16-17; Mk. 1:9-11; and Lk. 3:21-22.

Gos. Eb. 30.13.7-8	Mt. 3:13, 16-17	Mk. 1:9-11	Lk. 3:21-22
Τοῦ λαοῦ βαπτισθέν-τος ἦλθε καὶ Ἰησοῦς	Τότε παραγίνεται ὁ Ἰησοῦς . . . πρὸς τὸν	. . . ἦλθεν Ἰησοῦς . . . ἐβαπτίσθη . . . ὑπὸ	Ἐγένετο δὲ ἐν τῷ βαπτισθῆναι ἅπαντα

καὶ ἐβαπτίσθη ὑπὸ τοῦ Ἰωάννου. καὶ ὡς ἀνῆλθεν ἀπὸ τοῦ ὕδατος, ἠνοίγησαν οἱ οὐρανοί, καὶ εἶδεν τὸ πνεῦμα τὸ ἅγιον ἐν εἴδει περιστερᾶς κατελθούσης καὶ εἰσελθούσης εἰς αὐτόν. καὶ φωνὴ ἐκ τοῦ οὐρανοῦ λέγουσα· Σύ μου εἶ ὁ υἱὸς ὁ ἀγαπητός, ἐν σοὶ ηὐδόκησα, καὶ πάλιν· Ἐγὼ σήμερον γεγέννηκά σε.	Ἰωάννην τοῦ βαπτισθῆναι ὑπ᾽ αὐτοῦ. . . . εὐθὺς ἀνέβη ἀπὸ τοῦ ὕδατος καὶ ἰδοὺ ἠνεῴχθησαν οἱ οὐρανοί, καὶ εἶδεν πνεῦμα θεοῦ καταβαῖνον ὡσεὶ περιστερὰν, ἐρχόμενον ἐπ᾽ αὐτόν· καὶ ἰδοὺ φωνὴ ἐκ τῶν οὐρανῶν λέγουσα, οὗτός ἐστιν ὁ υἱός μου ὁ ἀγαπητός, ἐν ᾧ εὐδόκησα.	Ἰωάννου. καὶ εὐθὺς ἀναβαίνων ἐκ τοῦ ὕδατος εἶδεν σχιζομένους τοὺς οὐρανοὺς καὶ τὸ πνεῦμα ὡς περιστερὰν καταβαῖνον εἰς αὐτόν· καὶ φωνὴ |ἐγένετο| ἐκ τῶν οὐρανῶν· σὺ εἶ ὁ υἱός μου ὁ ἀγαπητός, ἐν σοί εὐδόκησα.	τὸν λαὸν καὶ Ἰησοῦ βαπτισθέντος καὶ προσευχομένου ἀνεῳχθῆναι τὸν οὐρανὸν καὶ καταβῆναι τὸ πνεῦμα τὸ ἅγιον σωματικῷ εἴδει ὡς περιστερὰν ἐπ᾽ αὐτόν, καὶ φωνὴν ἐξ οὐρανοῦ γενέσθαι· σὺ εἶ ὁ υἱός μου ὁ ἀγαπητός, ἐν σοὶ εὐδόκησα.

Since this synoptic table shows that the narratives of the three synoptics are very similar, it is extremely difficult to determine which one demonstrates the greatest affinity with the apocryphon: sometimes it seems closer to one, and at other times closer to another. So it is that τοῦ λαοῦ βαπτισθέντος recalls ἐν τῷ βαπτισθῆναι ἅπαντα τὸν λαὸν in Lk. 3:21; ἦλθε καὶ Ἰησοῦς καὶ ἐβαπτίσθη ὑπὸ τοῦ Ἰωάννου follows much more Mk. 1:9, which has ἦλθεν Ἰησοῦς . . . καὶ ἐβαπτίσθη . . . ὑπὸ Ἰωάννου. The mention of Jesus coming out of the water is missing in Lk. but is found in Mt. 3:16 and Mk. 1:10; the opening of the heavens is expressed with the verb ἀνοίγω, just as it is in Mt. 3:16 and Lk. 3:21, against σχίζω in Mk. 1:10.[60] The epithet ἅγιον after πνεῦμα is found only in Lk. 3:22; εἴδει has a corresponding element only in Lk. 3:22; εἰσελθούσης is closer to ἐρχόμενον in Mt. 3:16 than to καταβαῖνον in Mk. 1:10; the first saying from heaven is a closer parallel to Mk. 1:11 and Lk. 3:22 than to the usual reading in Mt. 3:17. Let me note, however, that regarding this last text, the manuscript D; the old Latin versions a, d; and the Curetonian, Sinaitic, and Hierosolymite Syriac versions read σὺ εἶ instead of οὗτός ἐστιν.[61]

All these observations are proof enough that it is impossible to decide in favor of one or another of the synoptics. They lead me rather to the solution that the narrative simply follows the synoptic tradition.

(b) Certain words of the second part find a parallel only in Mt. 3:15 and 17, and it seems quite obvious that the Gospel of the Ebionites is literarily dependent on it.

---

[60]Ms. D, the Latin version and the Georgian version read ἠνοιγμένους in Mk. 1:10.

[61]I would like to point out that D and the old Latin have υἱός μου εἶ σύ, ἐγὼ σήμερον· γεγέννηκά σε in Lk. 3:22.

The words from heaven in the apocryphon are the same ones that we read in Mt. 3:17: οὗτός ἐστιν ὁ υἱός μου ὁ ἀγαπητός, instead of σὺ εἶ ὁ υἱός . . . in Mk. 1:11 and Lk. 3:22. In addition, the saying of Jesus is almost identical in Mt. 3:15: ἄφες ἄρτι· οὕτως γὰρ πρέπον ἐστὶν ὑμῖν πληρῶσαι πᾶσαν δικαιοσύνην. Only the word δικαιοσύνη is missing in the fragment. I would also like to point out that the mention of a bright light which surrounds this locality is in agreement with the Latin witnesses in Mt. 3:15, which read *et cum baptizaretur, lumen ingens circumfulsit de aqua, ita ut timerent omnes qui advenerant.*[62]

It is believable that the author of the Gospel of the Ebionites developed the dialogue between Christ and John the Baptist at the baptism of Jesus, in his own way and according to his needs, but that he depended on the text of Mt., from which he takes up certain parts.

D. Epiphanius, Haer. 30.14.5

Πάλιν δὲ ἀρνοῦνται εἶναι αὐτὸν ἄνθρωπον, δῆθεν ἀπὸ τοῦ λόγου οὗ εἴρηκεν ὁ σωτὴρ ἐν τῷ ἀναγγελῆναι αὐτῷ ὅτι Ἰδού ἡ μήτηρ σου καὶ οἱ ἀδελφοί σου ἔξω ἑστήκασιν, (ὅτι) Τίς μού ἐστί μήτηρ καὶ ἀδελφοί; καὶ ἐκτείνας τὴν χεῖρα ἐπὶ τοὺς μαθητὰς ἔφη· Οὗτοί εἰσιν οἱ ἀδελφοί μου καὶ ἡ μήτηρ καὶ ἀδελφαί, οἱ ποιοῦντες τὰ θελήματα τοῦ πατρός μου.

Moreover they (the Ebionites) deny that he was a man, evidently on the ground of the word which the Saviour spoke when it was reported to him: "Behold, thy mother and thy brethren stand without," namely, "Who is my mother and who are my brethren?" And he stretched forth his hand towards his disciples and said: "These are my brethren and mother and sisters, who do the will of my Father."

The parallels are Mt. 12:47-50; Mk. 3:32-35; and Lk. 8:20-21.

Gos. Eb. 30.14.5	Mt. 12:47-50	Mk. 3:32-35	Lk. 8:20-21
Ἰδού ἡ μήτηρ σου καὶ οἱ ἀδελφοί σου ἔξω ἑστήκασιν,	[. . . ἰδού ἡ μήτηρ σου καὶ οἱ ἀδελφοί σου ἔξω ἑστήκασιν ζητοῦντές σοι λαλῆσαι]·[63]	. . . ἰδού ἡ μήτηρ σου καὶ οἱ ἀδελφοί σου καὶ αἱ ἀδελφαί σου ἔξω ζητοῦσίν σε.	. . . ἡ μήτηρ σου καὶ οἱ ἀδελφοί σου ἑστήκασιν ἔξω ἰδεῖν θέλοντές σε. . . .
τίς μού ἐστί μήτηρ καὶ ἀδελφοί;	. . . τίς ἐστιν ἡ μήτηρ μου, καὶ τίνες εἰσὶν οἱ ἀδελφοί μου;	. . . τίς ἐστιν ἡ μήτηρ μου καὶ οἱ ἀδελφοί; . . .	
καὶ ἐκτείνας τὴν χεῖρα ἐπὶ τοὺς μαθητὰς ἔφη· οὗτοί εἰσιν οἱ ἀδελφοί μου καὶ ἡ μήτηρ καὶ ἀδελφαί, οἱ ποιοῦντες τὰ θελήματα τοῦ πατρός μου.	καὶ ἐκτείνας τὴν χεῖρα [αὐτοῦ] ἐπὶ τοὺς μαθητὰς αὐτοῦ . . . ὅστις γὰρ ἂν ποιήση τὸ θέλημα τοῦ πατρός μου τοῦ ἐν οὐρανοῖς, αὐτός μου ἀδελφὸς καὶ ἀδελφὴ καὶ μήτηρ ἐστίν.	ὃς ἂν ποιήση τὸ θέλημα τοῦ θεοῦ, οὗτος ἀδελφός μου καὶ ἀδελφὴ καὶ μήτηρ ἐστίν.	μήτηρ μου καὶ ἀδελφοί μου οὗτοί εἰσιν οἱ τὸν λόγον τοῦ θεοῦ ἀκούοντες καὶ ποιοῦντες.

---

[62]These witnesses are a and g¹.

[63]This verse is present in the manuscripts C, E, F, G, H, D, Θ, and the Vulgate.

Although the narratives of Mt. and Mk. are fairly similar, the Gospel of the Ebionites is literarily dependent on Mt. This is undeniable because it contains the words καὶ ἐκτείνας τὴν χεῖρα ἐπὶ τοὺς μαθητάς, which are present only in Mt. 12:49, and it uses the expression τοῦ πατρός μου from Mt. 12:50, instead of τοῦ θεοῦ in Mk. 3:35.

It follows, therefore, that the first words ἰδοὺ ἡ μήτηρ σου καὶ οἱ ἀδελφοί σου ἔξω ἑστήκασιν have been taken from Mt. 12:47 rather than from Lk. 8:20. In this way the Gospel of the Ebionites sustains the reading of Mt. 12:47, attested by C, E, F, G, H, D, Θ , and the Vulgate.

The only difference with Mt.—this is also true for Mk.—rests in the fact that the apocryphon puts the text of Mt. 12:50 in the plural, reverses the order of the clauses, and drops τοῦ ἐν οὐρανοῖς.

E. Epiphanius, Haer. 30.22.4

Αὐτοὶ δὲ ἀφανίσαντες ἀφ' ἑαυτῶν τὴν τῆς ἀληθείας ἀκολουθίαν ἤλλαξαν τὸ ῥητὸν (P. 8: ὅπερ ἐστι πᾶσι φανερὸν ἐκ τῶν συνεζευγμένων λέξεων) καὶ ἐποίησαν τοὺς μαθητὰς μὲν λέγοντας· Ποῦ θέλεις ἑτοιμάσωμέν σοι τὸ πάσχα φαγεῖν; καὶ αὐτὸν δῆθεν λέγοντα· Μὴ ἐπιθυμίᾳ ἐπεθύμησα κρέας τοῦτο τὸ πάσχα φαγεῖν μεθ' ὑμῶν; πόθεν δὲ οὐ φωραθήσεται ἡ αὐτῶν ῥᾳδιουργία, τῆς ἀκολουθίας κραζούσης ὅτι τὸ μῦ καὶ τὸ ἦτά ἐστι πρόσθετα; ἀντὶ τοῦ γὰρ εἰπεῖν ἐπιθυμίᾳ ἐπεθύμησα αὐτοὶ προσέθεντο τὸ μὴ ἐπίρρημα. αὐτὸς δὲ ἀληθῶς ἔλεγεν· ἐπιθυμίᾳ ἐπεθύμησα τοῦτο τὸ πάσχα φαγεῖν μεθ' ὑμῶν, αὐτοὶ δὲ ἐπιγράψαντες τὸ κρέας ἑαυτοὺς ἐπλάνησαν ῥᾳδιουργήσαντες καὶ εἰπόντες μὴ ἐπιθυμίᾳ ἐπεθύμησα τοῦτο τὸ πάσχα κρέας φαγεῖν μεθ' ὑμῶν;

But they (the Ebionites) abandon the proper sequence of the words and pervert the saying, as is plain to all from the readings attached, and have let the disciples say, "Where wilt thou that we prepare for thee the passover?" and him to answer to that, "Do I desire with desire at this Passover to eat flesh with you?" [Hennecke, p. 158]

From this is their deceit not seen to be a flagrant offence, because what follows cries that the μ and the η have been added. For instead of saying "I desire with a great desire to eat this Passover with you," they have added the adverb μή. For he (Christ) truly said, "I desire with a great desire to eat this Passover with you," but they have written in τὸ κρέας (flesh) and have deceived themselves by acting fraudulently and saying, "Do I desire with desire at this Passover to eat flesh with you?" [Editor's addition to Hennecke.]

This narrative suggests the following parallels: Mt. 26:17b; Mk. 14:12b; and Lk. 22:8b-9, 15.

Gos. Eb. 30.22.4	Mt. 26:17b	Mk. 14:12b	Lk. 22:8b-9, 15
Ποῦ θέλεις ἑτοιμάσω-μέν σοι τὸ πάσχα φαγεῖν; Μὴ ἐπιθυμίᾳ ἐπεθύμησα κρέας τοῦτο τὸ πάσχα φαγεῖν μεθ' ὑμῶν;	Ποῦ θέλεις ἑτοι-μάσωμέν σοι φαγεῖν τὸ πάσχα;	Ποῦ θέλεις ἀπελθόν-τες ἑτοιμάσωμέν ἵνα φάγῃς τὸ πάσχα.	πορευθέντες ἑτοιμά-σατε ἡμῖν τὸ πάσχα, ἵνα φάγωμεν. οἱ δὲ εἶ-παν αὐτῷ· ποῦ θέλεις ἑτοιμάσωμεν; . . . ἐπιθυμίᾳ ἐπεθύμησα τοῦτο τὸ πάσχα φα-γεῖν μεθ' ὑμῶν. . . .

Epiphanius tells us that the Ebionites distorted the text by adding μή and κρέας to the saying of Christ who actually said, ἐπιθυμίᾳ ἐπεθύμησα τοῦτο τὸ πάσχα φαγεῖν μεθ' ὑμῶν. Now, Lk. 22:15 is the only one to report this saying of Christ: if we were to add μή and κρέας, we would have the text of the apocryphon.

As for the first sentence which relates the question of the disciples, it coincides literally with Mt. 26:17b. In this fragment of the apocryphon, therefore, I can observe the literary influence of Lk., and very probably of Mt.

F. Epiphanius, Haer. 30.16.4-5

Οὐ φάσκουσι δὲ ἐκ θεοῦ πατρὸς αὐτὸν γεγεννῆσθαι, ἀλλὰ κεκτίσθαι ὡς ἕνα τῶν ἀρχαγγέλων [καὶ ἔτι περισσοτέρως]. αὐτὸν δὲ κυριεύειν καὶ ἀγγέλων καὶ πάντων (τῶν) ὑπὸ τοῦ παντοκράτορος πεποιημένων, καὶ ἐλ-θόντα καὶ ὑφηγησάμενον ὡς τὸ παρ' αὐτοῖς εὐαγγέλιον καλούμενον περιέχει ὅτι Ἦλθον καταλῦσαι τὰς θυσίας· καὶ ἐὰν μὴ παύσησθε τοῦ θύειν, οὐ παύσεται ἀφ' ὑμῶν ἡ ὀργή.

They say that he (Christ) was not begotten of God the Father, but created as one of the archangels [and to an even greater degree (editor's note)] that he rules over the angels and all the creatures of the Almighty, and that he came and declared, as their Gospel, which is called (according to Matthew? according to the Hebrews?), reports: I am come to do away with sacrifices, and if ye cease not from sacrificing, the wrath of God will not cease from you.

This saying of Christ may allude to the one reported in Mt. 5:17; 9:13; and 12:7. If this be the case, it must be stressed that it has been distorted by the Ebionites.

§2. The Other New Testament Writings

I had the opportunity earlier to mention a fragment in which a literary influence of the Gospel of Lk. is undeniable.[64] I also pointed out certain passages that bear witness to an agreement with the synoptic tradition.[65] This being said, I simply wish to add here other fragments which are parallel to this synoptic tradition.

---

[64]Cf. above, 198.
[65]Cf. above, 192 and 196-97.

1. Epiphanius, Haer. 30.13.6

Ἡ δὲ ἀρχὴ τοῦ παρ᾽ αὐτοῖς εὐαγγελίου ἔχει ὅτι Ἐγένετο ἐν ταῖς ἡμέραις Ἡρῴδου βασιλέως τῆς Ἰουδαίας (ἐπὶ ἀρχιερέως Καϊάφα) ἦλθέν τις Ἰωάννης (ὀνόματι) βαπτίζων βάπτισμα μετανοίας ἐν τῷ Ἰορδάνῃ ποταμῷ ὃς ἐλέγετο εἶναι ἐκ γένους Ἀαρὼν τοῦ ἱερέως παῖς Ζαχαρίου καὶ Ἐλισάβετ· καὶ ἐξήρχοντο πρὸς αὐτὸν πάντες.

And the beginning of their Gospel runs: It came to pass in the days of Herod the king of Judaea, [when Caiaphas was high priest,] that there came [one,] John [by name,] and baptized with the baptism of repentance in the river Jordan. It was said of him that he was of the lineage of Aaron the priest, a son of Zacharias and Elisabeth; and all went out to him.

2. Epiphanius, Haer. 30.14

παρακόψαντες γὰρ τὰς παρὰ τῷ Ματθαίῳ γενεαλογίας ἄρχονται τὴν ἀρχὴν ποιεῖσθαι, ὡς προείπομεν, λέγοντες ὅτι Ἐγένετο, φησίν, ἐν ταῖς ἡμέραις Ἡρῴδου βασιλέως τῆς Ἰουδαίας ἐπὶ ἀρχιερέως Καϊάφα ἦλθέ τις Ἰωάννης ὀνόματι βαπτίζων βάπτισμα μετανοίας ἐν τῷ Ἰορδάνῃ ποταμῷ καὶ τὰ ἑξῆς.

Having cut out the genealogy in Matthew, they (the Ebionites) begin, as we have already said above [editor's translation]: It came to pass in the days of Herod the king of Judaea when Caiaphas was high priest that there came a certain man John by name, baptizing with the baptism of repentance in the river Jordan, etc.

The gospel parallels are Mt. 3:1-2, 5-6; Mk. 1:4-5; and Lk. 3:3, 7. Let me say at once that the mention of the parents of John the Baptist is found only in Lk. 1. Incidentally, I would also like to emphasize that, in commenting that the Ebionites mutilated the genealogy that is found in Mt., Epiphanius must have supposed that they had this gospel and that they used it, since they ventured to mutilate its initial genealogy. I would also like to observe that Epiphanius's second text certainly mentions the high priest Caiaphas.

These fragments do not seem to depend particularly on any one of these parallels; in fact, certain words are found sometimes in one gospel and sometimes in another. Indeed, the introductory phrase, "It came to pass in the days of Herod the king of Judaea, [when Caiaphas was high priest,]" may be in agreement with Lk. 3:1-2, in which the evangelist mentions the precise moment in history when John the Baptist began his activity; we find ἐγένετο in Mk. 1:4; ἐν ταῖς ἡμεραῖς in Mt. 3:1; ἦλθεν in Lk. 3:3; Ἰωάννης βαπτίζων in Mk. 1:4; βάπτισμα μετανοίας in Mk. 1:4 and Lk. 3:3; and ἐν τῷ Ἰορδάνῃ ποταμῷ in Mt. 3:6 and Mk. 1:5.

The author of this apocryphal gospel seems simply to conform to traditional practice by starting his gospel with the preaching of the Baptist.

In conclusion, these few fragments of the Gospel of the Ebionites have revealed a definite literary influence from the Gospel of Mt. and the Gospel of Lk., whose texts were taken up almost literally whenever the Ebionites themselves did not distort the texts. The texts of Mt. that have influenced the apocryphon are more numerous than those of Lk., but this statement must not be taken too seriously since this Gospel of the Ebionites has come down to us only in a fragmentary state.

Finally, I pointed out a clearly marked faithfulness to the synoptic tradition. There is no trace of influence from the New Testament writings other than Mt. and Lk.

Section 4
THE GOSPEL OF THE EGYPTIANS

Clement of Alexandria[66] was the first to attest to the Gospel of the Egyptians, which doubtless dates from the middle of the second century. It was used as a source by several heretical sects: the Encratites used it against marriage;[67] the Naassenes, according to Hippolytus,[68] used it for their theory on the soul and the body; the Sabellians, according to Epiphanius,[69] founded their modalism[70] on it. This composition is lost, but several fragments from it have been preserved in later writings.[71]

These fragments, and they are few in number, do not reveal any literary dependence on the New Testament writings. Preuschen, in his edition, provides a fragment that Klostermann does not mention: Preuschen himself puts this fragment in parentheses, probably to demonstrate his doubts as to its relationship to the Gospel of the Egyptians. Yet I find that this fragment offers some interest with regard to my subject matter, and I propose to examine it.

Clement of Alexandria, Strom. 3.13.91

Εἰ γὰρ ἦν παρὰ θεοῦ εἰς ὃν σπεύδομεν, ἡ τοιαύτη διασκευή, οὐκ ἂν ἐμακάρισεν τοὺς εὐνούχους κτλ.

If such an arrangement [namely, the institution of different sexes] were of God, to whom we aspire, then he would not have praised eunuchs and the prophet would not have said that they are no unfruitful tree (Is. 56:3). . . .[72]

---

[66]Cf. Clement of Alexandria, Strom. 3.9.63; 13.92.

[67]Cf. ibid.

[68]Cf. Hippolytus, Philos. 5.7.

[69]Cf. Epiphanius, Haer. 62.2.

[70]Cf. Altaner, *Patrology*, 66-67.

[71]Cf. Klostermann, *Apocrypha*, 2:15-16; see also Preuschen's edition, *Antilegomena*, 2-3.

[72][The text followed in the English translation is that of Edgar Hennecke, *New Testament Apocrypha*, ed. Wilhelm Schneemelcher, ET ed. R. McL. Wilson (Philadelphia: Westminster Press, 1963) 166-78. Editor's note.]

It is possible that Clement of Alexandria implies that the Encratites read in their gospel the passage in Mt. concerning the eunuchs. If this is so, this passage of the Gospel of the Egyptians would agree with Mt. 19:12: εἰσὶν γὰρ εὐνοῦχοι οἵτινες ἐκ κοιλίας μητρὸς ἐγεννήθησαν οὕτως, καὶ εἰσὶν εὐνοῦχοι οἵτινες εὐνουχίσθησαν ὑπὸ τῶν ἀνθρώπων, καὶ εἰσὶν εὐνοῦχοι οἵτινες εὐνούχισαν ἑαυτοὺς διὰ τὴν βασιλείαν τῶν οὐρανῶν.

Section 5
THE GOSPEL OF PETER

Eusebius already knew of the existence of the Gospel of Peter.[73] A Greek fragment on parchment was discovered during the winter of 1886–1887 by H. Bouriant in a Christian tomb in Akhmîm.[74] It tells the story of the passion and the resurrection which it embellishes with miracles. According to this fragment, the Jews are responsible for the death of Jesus; it is Herod who ordered the crucifixion. The Gospel of Peter contains some traces of docetism. It is commonly acknowledged today that it dates from the first half of the second century.[75]

Still in line with my focus of interest, I examine first the literary relationships of this apocryphon and the first gospel; I then deal with the other New Testament writings.[76]

§1. Saint Matthew

The Gospel of Peter reveals in several places a definite literary influence from the first gospel. Other passages show only a probable influence. Elsewhere the apocryphon narrates in different words a detail or an even peculiar to Mt.'s Passion Narrative or his account of the resurrection of Christ.

---

[73]Cf. Eusebius, Hist. Eccl. 6.12.1-6.

[74]Cf. H. Bouriant, *Mémoires de la Mission Archéologique au Caire* 9 (Paris, 1892) 137-42.

[75]Cf. Altaner, *Patrology*, 66-67.

[76]I follow L. Vaganay's text, *L'Évangile de Pierre*, EBib (Paris, 1930); see also E. Klostermann's edition, *Apocrypha* 1, *Reste des Petrusevangeliums, der petrusapokalypse und der Kerygma Petri*, KIT 3 (Berlin, 1933); see also Preuschen, *Antilegomena*, 15-20. [The text followed in the English translation is that of Edgar Hennecke, *New Testament Apocrypha*, ed. Wilhelm Schneemelcher, ET ed. R. McL. Wilson (Philadelphia: Westminster Press, 1963) 179-87. Editor's note.]

A. Texts in Which a Literary Contact with Matthew Is Definite

1. Gos. Pet. 21

Καὶ τότε ἀπέσπασαν τοὺς ἥλους ἀπὸ τῶν χειρῶν τοῦ κυρίου καὶ ἔθηκαν αὐτὸν ἐπὶ τῆς γῆς. καὶ ἡ γῆ πᾶσα ἐσείσθη καὶ φόβος μέγας ἐγένετο.

And then the Jews drew the nails from the hands of the Lord and laid him on the earth. And the whole earth shook and there came a great fear.

The taking down from the cross is narrated in Mt. 27:59-60; Mk. 15:46; Lk. 23:53; and Jn 19:38. All the synoptics have either the words ἔθηκεν αὐτό or κατέθηκεν αὐτόν that are found in the apocryphon: ἔθηκαν αὐτόν. Yet, I must point out that in the synoptics the body of Christ is laid in a tomb, whereas in Pseudo-Peter the body of Christ is placed on the ground. The term ἧλος, peculiar to Jn. 20:25 in the New Testament, is also significant.

But the most important parallel upon which the Gospel of Peter 21 depends is Mt. 27:51b and 54: καὶ ἡ γῆ ἐσείσθη, καὶ αἱ πέτραι ἐσχίσθησαν . . . ὁ δὲ ἑκατόνταρχος καὶ οἱ μετ' αὐτοῦ τηροῦντες τὸν Ἰησοῦν ἰδόντες τὸν σεισμὸν καὶ τὰ γινόμενα ἐφοβήθησαν σφόδρα, λέγοντες. In fact, the phrase καὶ ἡ γῆ ἐσείσθη of the apocryphon is there literally and in a similar context. Moreover, Mt. is the only evangelist who mentions this fact and the fear that ensued: ἐφοβήθησαν σφόδρα. Pseudo-Peter also mentions this fear: καὶ φόβος μέγας ἐγένετο, and if it does not mention the Roman soldiers, it is because in his narrative they do not participate in the crucifixion.

2. Gos. Pet. 29-30

Ἐφοβήθησαν οἱ πρεσβύτεροι καὶ ἦλθον πρὸς Πειλᾶτον δεόμενοι αὐτοῦ καὶ λέγοντες· παράδος ἡμῖν στρατιώτας, ἵνα φυλάξω(σιν) τὸ μνῆμα αὐτοῦ ἐπὶ τρεῖς ἡμ[έρας], μήποτε ἐλθόντες οἱ μαθηταὶ αὐτοῦ κλέψωσιν αὐτόν, καὶ ὑπολάβῃ ὁ λαὸς ὅτι ἐκ νεκρῶν ἀνέστη, καὶ ποιήσωσιν ἡμῖν κακά.

(The scribes and Pharisees and elders) were afraid and came to Pilate entreating him and saying, "Give us soldiers that we may watch his sepulchre for three days, lest his disciples come and steal him away and the people suppose that he is risen from the dead and do us harm."

In verses 29-33, which introduce the story of the resurrection of Christ, the author seems as concerned as Mt. 27:62-64—the latter maybe less emphatically— to respond to the objection to remove the body of Christ from the tomb. This is why he does not fail to tone up his text with corroborations, reinforcing the narrative of the gospels with noncanonical elements such as the affixing of the seven seals (v. 33).

A literary contact with Mt. 27:62-64 appears to be undeniable: Τῇ δὲ ἐπαύ-ριον, ἥτις ἐστὶν μετὰ τὴν παρασκευήν, συνήχθησαν οἱ ἀρχιερεῖς καὶ οἱ Φαρισαῖοι πρὸς Πιλᾶτον λέγοντες· κύριε, ἐμνήσθημεν ὅτι ἐκεῖνος ὁ πλάνος εἶπεν ἔτι ζῶν· μετὰ τρεῖς ἡμέρας ἐγείρομαι. κέλευσον οὖν ἀσ-φαλισθῆναι τὸν τάφον ἕως τῆς τρίτης ἡμέρας, μήποτε ἐλθόντες οἱ μαθηταὶ κλέψωσιν αὐτὸν καὶ εἴπωσιν τῷ λαῷ· ἠγέρθη ἀπὸ τῶν νεκρῶν, καὶ ἔσται ἡ ἐσχάτη πλάνη χείρων τῆς πρώτης.

First of all, in fact—and this is a significant observation—of all the evangel-ists, Mt. is the only one to mention the request of the high priests and the Phari-sees. Secondly, the apocryphon picks up several words from Mt.: πρὸς Πιλᾶτον, λέγοντες, τρεῖς ἡμέρας, ὁ λαός, νεκρῶν. Finally, one sentence coincides al-most literally with Mt., which says ἐλθόντες οἱ μαθηταὶ κλέψωσιν αὐτόν; Pseudo-Peter simply adds αὐτοῦ after μαθηταί, and this is how he comes to be the most ancient witness to the reading αὐτοῦ, which is absent from ℵ, B, and the Armenian version, but which is supported by all the other uncial manuscripts, by all the minuscules, by the old Latin and the Vulgate, by all the Syriac versions, the Sahidic and Bohairic Coptic, by the Ethiopic and the Georgian versions, by the Latin interpretations of Origen, and by Augustine.

This passage has skillfully taken up enough elements from the Matthean text. Yet the author narrates in his own personal way the dialogue between the priests and Pilate, while demonstrating clearly his dependence on the first gospel.

3. Gos. Pet. 31-33

Ὁ δὲ Πειλᾶτος παραδέδωκεν αὐτοῖς Πετρώνιον τὸν κεντυρίωνα μετὰ στρατιωτῶν φυλάσσειν τὸν τάφον· καὶ σὺν αὐτοῖς ἦλθον πρεσβύτεροι καὶ γραμματεῖς ἐπὶ τὸ μνῆμα. καὶ κυλίσαντες λίθον μέγαν μετὰ τοῦ κεντυρίωνος καὶ τῶν στρατιωτῶν ὁμοῦ πάντες οἱ ὄντες ἐκεῖ ἔθηκαν ἐπὶ τῇ θύρᾳ τοῦ μνήματος. καὶ ἐπέχρισαν ἑπτὰ σφραγῖδας καὶ σκηνὴν ἐκεῖ πήξαντες ἐφύλαξαν.

And Pilate gave them Petronius the centurion with soldiers to watch the se-pulchre. And with them there came elders and scribes to the sepulchre. And all who were there, together with the centurion and the soldiers, rolled thither a great stone and laid it against the entrance to the sepulchre and put on it seven seals, pitched a tent, and kept watch.

This narrative recalls Mt. 27:60b, 65-66: καὶ προσκυλίσας λίθον μέγαν τῇ θύρᾳ τοῦ μνημείου ἀπῆλθεν. . . . Ἔφη αὐτοῖς ὁ Πιλᾶτος· ἔχετε κου-στωδίαν· ὑπάγετε, ἀσφαλίσασθε ὡς οἴδατε. οἱ δὲ πορευθέντες ἠσφαλί-σαντο τὸν τάφον σφραγίσαντες τὸν λίθον μετὰ τῆς κουστωδίας, and Mk. 15:46b: καὶ προσεκύλισεν λίθον ἐπὶ τὴν θύραν τοῦ μνημείου.

Alone among the evangelists, Mt. narrates the coming of the guard to the se-pulchre and the sealing of the stone; this brings immediately to mind that this is the passage to which Pseudo-Peter refers. In fact, in verse 32, the Gospel of Peter transposes Mt.'s episode of the laying in the tomb. Mt. is again the only one to emphasize, within the context of the entombment (27:60b), the size of the grave stone with the use of the epithet μέγας; Mk. points out this characteristic only in the context of the resurrection, when it describes the holy women who converse on their way to the sepulchre. Notice that where the apocryphon reads κυλίσαν-τες λίθον μέγαν, it follows almost literally Mt., which has προσκυλίσας λίθον μέγαν, as opposed to Mk., which reads προσεκύλισεν λίθον.

As for the affixing of the seals, it agrees with Mt. 27:66, since the word σφρα-γῖδας corresponds to σφραγίσαντες in the first gospel. The apocryphon simply describes this episode in greater detail.

I would also like to add the presence of the substantive τάφος in verse 31: this word is peculiar to Mt. in the gospels[77] and is found particularly in the narrative of the laying in the tomb (Mt. 27:60) upon which the Gospel of Peter depends here. One last remark: the word κεντυρίων which the apocryphon uses is found in Mk. 15:39, 44, 45, instead of ἑκατόνταρχος in Mt. 27:54 and ἑκατοντάρχης in Lk. 23:47.

Since the apocryphon definitely uses the Matthean narrative of the coming of the guard to the sepulchre and the sealing of the stone, it is also obvious that its author follows quite freely the text on which he depends. He clearly leaves the impression that he constructs his narrative in his own personal way, while he allows those passages from which he draws certain formulas and certain expressions to show through.

4. Gos. Pet. 45

Ταῦτα ἰδόντες οἱ περὶ τὸν κεντυρίωνα νυκτὸς ἔσπευσαν πρὸς Πει-λᾶτον ἀφέντες τὸν τάφον ὃν ἐφύλασσον καὶ ἐξηγήσαντο πάντα ἅπερ εἶδον ἀγωνιῶντες μεγάλως καὶ λέγοντες· ἀληθῶς υἱὸς ἦν θεοῦ.

When those who were of the centurion's company saw this, they hastened by night to Pilate, abandoning the sepulchre which they were guarding, and reported everything that they had seen, being full of disquietude and saying, "In truth he was the Son of God."

The return of the guards into the city to report to Pilate all that happened recalls a similar episode in Mt. 28:11: Πορευομένων δὲ αὐτῶν ἰδού τινες τῆς κουστωδίας ἐλθόντες εἰς τὴν πόλιν ἀπήγγειλαν τοῖς ἀρχιερεῦσιν ἅπαντα τὰ γενόμενα. There is, however, a difference: whereas in the apocryphon they all go to Pilate during the night before the women come to the sepulchre, in Mt. several men of the guard go to the chief priests at the time when the women are

---

[77]Cf. Mt. 23:27, 29; 27:61, 64, 66; 28:1; and also Rom. 3:13.

already on their way back from the sepulchre; moreover, the apocryphon has the guards return to Pilate whereas Mt. sends them to the chief priests. Yet, two elements need to be emphasized: Mt. 28:11 is the only one to mention this return of the guards to the city; furthermore, the word πάντα in the Gospel of Peter recalls ἅπαντα in Mt. 28:11.

As for the guards' turn of speech, it imitates Mt. 27:54 rather than Mk. 15:39 and Lk. 23:47:

Gos. Pet. 45b	Mt. 27:54	Mk. 15:39	Lk. 23:47
ἀγωνιῶντες μεγάλως καὶ	ὁ δὲ ἑκατόνταρχος καὶ οἱ μετ' αὐτοῦ . . . ἐφοβήθησαν σφόδρα,	. . . ὁ κεντυρίων . . .	. . . ὁ ἑκατοντάρχης . . .
λέγοντες· ἀληθῶς υἱὸς ἦν θεοῦ.	λέγοντες· ἀληθῶς θεοῦ υἱὸς ἦν οὗτος.	εἶπεν· ἀληθῶς ὁ ἄν-θρωπος οὗτος υἱὸς θεοῦ ἦν.	λέγων· ὄντως ὁ ἄν-θρωπος οὗτος δίκαιος ἦν.

Since Lk. 23:47 does not have the adverb ἀληθῶς, it can be discarded. Mt., just like the apocyphon, has the participle λέγοντες and puts the profession of faith in the mouth of all the guards: Mt. says ὁ δὲ ἑκατόνταρχος καὶ οἱ μετ' αὐτοῦ . . . λέγοντες; the Gospel of Peter reads οἱ περὶ τὸν κεντυρίωνα. . . . λέγοντες. The profession of faith itself, ἀληθῶς υἱὸς ἦν θεοῦ, in the apocryphon is slightly closer to Mt. (ἀληθῶς θεοῦ υἱὸς ἦν οὗτος) than to Mk. (ἀληθῶς οὗτος ὁ ἄνθρωπος υἱὸς θεοῦ ἦν). This slight resemblance takes on more weight when it is noted that it is only in the apocryphon and in Mt. that this declaration of faith is accompanied with a feeling of fright: ἀγωνιῶντες μεγάλως in the apocryphon, ἐφοβήθησαν σφόδρα in Mt.[78] Let me emphasize again, however, the word κεντυρίων, which is peculiar to Mk. and to the apocryphon.[79]

All these remarks lead to the conclusion that the language of the guards is literarily inspired by the Matthean text, which it follows fairly freely.

5. Gos. Pet. 46

'Αποκριθεὶς ὁ Πειλᾶτος ἔφη· ἐγὼ καθαρεύω τοῦ αἵματος τοῦ υἱοῦ τοῦ θεοῦ· ὑμῖν δὲ τοῦτο ἔδοξεν.

Pilate answered and said: "I am clean from the blood of the Son of God, upon such a thing have you decided."

It would be difficult to deny that Pilate's answer is, in the narrative, a transposition of Mt. 27:24: ὁ Πιλᾶτος . . . λέγων· ἀθῷός εἰμι ἀπὸ τοῦ αἵματος τούτου· ὑμεῖς ὄψεσθε. In the apocryphon, Pilate's answer is given after the resurrection, whereas the first gospel places it during the trial of Christ. The apocry-

---

[78]Cf. Vaganay, *L'Évangile de Pierre*, 49.
[79]Cf. Mk. 15:39, 44, 45; and Gos. Pet. 31, 32, 38, 45, 47, 49.

phon has not preserved the Semitic turn of Mt., ἀθῷός εἰμι, but has replaced it with the classical word καθαρεύω.

As for the phrase ὑμῖν τοῦτο ἔδοξεν, it may very well remind the Jews of the words in the trial: ὑμεῖς ὄψεσθε. In fact, by placing Pilate's answer after the resurrection, Pseudo-Peter had to change the ὑμεῖς ὄψεσθε into a formula that reminded the Jews of their guilt. Von Schubert links it to Mt. 26:66,[80] in which the high priest addressed his question to the Sanhedrin: τί ὑμῖν δοκεῖ.

The words υἱοῦ τοῦ θεοῦ echo the confession of the guards in the preceding verse of the apocryphon.

The author is far from taking up literally Pilate's words. Nevertheless, the general meaning of his phrase, the opposition between Pilate and the Jews, and the presence of the words τὸ αἷμα are sufficient to determine that it is a literary reminiscence of Mt. 27:24.

6. Gos. Pet. 56

Τί ἤλθατε; τίνα ζητεῖτε; μὴ τὸν σταυρωθέντα ἐκεῖνον; ἀνέστη καὶ ἀπῆλθεν· εἰ δὲ μὴ πιστεύετε, παρακύψατε καὶ ἴδετε τὸν τόπον ἔνθα ἔκειτο ὅτι οὐκ ἔστιν, ἀνέστη γὰρ καὶ ἀπῆλθεν ἐκεῖ ὅθεν ἀπεστάλη.

Wherefore are ye come? Whom seek ye? Not him that was crucified? He is risen and gone. But if ye believe not, stoop this way and see the place where he lay, for he is not here. For he is risen and is gone thither whence he was sent.

These words of the angel to the women who came to the sepulchre recall Mt. 28:5-7; Mk. 16:6-7; Lk. 24:5b-7; and Jn 20:13, 15.

The texts of Lk. and Jn. have not exercised any literary influence, since they do not report the tangible proof of the resurrection, namely, "see the place where he lay." The texts of Mt., Mk., and the Gospel of Peter are very close:

Gos. Pet. 56	Mt. 28:5-6	Mk. 16:6
Τί ἤλθατε; τίνα ζητεῖτε; μὴ τὸν σταυρωθέντα ἐκεῖνον; ἀνέστη καὶ ἀπῆλθεν· εἰ δὲ μὴ πιστεύετε, παρακύψατε καὶ ἴδετε τὸν τόπον ἔνθα ἔκειτο ὅτι οὐκ ἔστιν, ἀνέστη γὰρ καὶ ἀπῆλθεν ἐκεῖ ὅθεν ἀπεστάλη.	. . . μὴ φοβεῖσθε ὑμεῖς, οἶδα γὰρ ὅτι Ἰησοῦν τὸν ἐσταυρωμέ- νον ζητεῖτε· οὐκ ἔστιν ὧδε, ἠγέρθη γὰρ καθὼς εἶπεν· δεῦτε ἴδετε τὸν τόπον ὅπου ἔκειτο.	. . . μὴ ἐκθαμβεῖσθε· Ἰησοῦν ζητεῖτε τὸν Ναζαρηνὸν τὸν ἐσταυρωμένον· ἠγέρθη, οὐκ ἔσ- τιν ὧδε· ἴδε ὁ τόπος ὅπου ἔθηκαν αὐτόν.

I shall mention later that starting with verse 50, the principal source of inspiration for the Gospel of Peter seems to be Mk.[81] The first part of the angel's ex-

---

[80]Cf. H. von Schubert, *Das Petrusevangelium, Synoptische Tabelle nebst Übersetzung und kritischem Apparat* (Berlin, 1893) 22.

[81]Cf. below, 217.

hortation may depend on Mk. as well as on Mt.; their thought is put here into direct discourse, and it has ζητεῖτε of Mt. and Mk., and τὸν σταυρωθέντα, which corresponds to τὸν ἐσταυρωμένον in the two gospels. But the second part of the exhortation, the proof of the resurrection, is expressed in Mt.'s style with which the resemblance is almost word-for-word; indeed, the apocryphon reads ἴδετε τὸν τόπον as does Mt., as opposed to ἴδε ὁ τόπος in Mk.; it uses the words ἔνθα ἔκειτο, which are closer to Mt.'s ὅπου ἔκειτο than to Mk.'s ὅπου ἔθηκαν αὐτόν. It is possible to conclude, therefore, that if the author had the narrative of Mk. in mind in this passage situated after verse 50, he has certainly introduced here a literary reminiscence of Mt.

Let me add that the words ἀπῆλθεν ἐκεῖ ὅθεν ἀπεστάλη may echo Jn. 16:7 in which the subject matter is the departure (ἀπέλθω) of Jesus to join his Father, and numerous Johannine texts (3:17, 34: 5:36, 38; 6:29, 57; 7:28, 29, 33; 8:42; 11:42; 17:3, 8, 21, 23, 25; 20:21), which relate the sending (ἀποστέλλω) of Jesus by the Father.[82] Therefore, in addition to a definite Matthean literary influence, there is a slight Johannine tint.

B. Texts in Which the Literary Influence of Matthew Is Probable

1. Gos. Pet 1

T[ῶν] δὲ Ἰουδαίων οὐδεὶς ἐνίψατο τὰς χεῖρας, οὐδὲ Ἡρῷδης, οὐδὲ [ε]ἷς τῶν κριτῶν αὐτοῦ. κ[αὶ μὴ] βουληθέντων νίψασθαι, ἀνέστη Πειλᾶτος.

But of the Jews none washed their hands, neither Herod nor any one of his judges. And as they would not wash, Pilate arose.

These words easily allow us to infer what happened just before, which was most likely related in the lost part of the manuscript: Pilate had washed his hands and had probably invited the Jews to do likewise; their refusal (μὴ βουληθέντων) suggests it.[83] Now, Mt. 27:24 is the only one to report that Pilate washed his hands, thereby attesting to his innocence for what was about to happen. Mt. reads: ἰδὼν δὲ ὁ Πιλᾶτος ὅτι οὐδὲν ὠφελεῖ ἀλλὰ μᾶλλον θόρυβος γίνεται, λαβὼν ὕδωρ ἀπενίψατο τὰς χεῖρας κατέναντι τοῦ ὄχλου λέγων· ἀθῷός εἰμι. . . . Let me also emphasize that the expression that Mt. uses with reference to Pilate, ἀπενίψατο τὰς χεῖρας, corresponds to ἐνίψατο τὰς χεῖρας in Pseudo-Peter. The fact that Pseudo-Peter uses the simple verb ἐνίψατο instead of the composite verb ἀπενίψατο in Mt. represents his usual style: he clearly prefers the simple

---

[82]Cf. Vaganay, *L'Évangile de Pierre*, 59.
[83]Cf. ibid., 202.

form of verbs.[84] The similarity of expression with Mt. 27:24 thus becomes striking, and the Matthean text seems to have influenced the apocryphon.

2. Gos. Pet. 6

Οἱ δὲ λαβόντες τὸν κύριον ὤθουν αὐτὸν τρέχοντες καὶ ἔλεγον· σύρωμεν τὸν υἱὸν τοῦ θεοῦ ἐξουσίαν αὐτοῦ ἐσχηκότες.

So they took the Lord and pushed him in great haste and said, "Let us hale the Son of God now that we have gotten power over him."

The designated parallels are Mt. 27:27a; Mk. 15:16a; and Jn. 19:16b. Let me immediately state that the canonical gospels do not relate that Jesus was led to torture by executioners who pushed him while running, but that he was led to the praetorium in the presence of soldiers. Moreover, whereas in the Gospel of Peter the executioners are Jews, the canonical narrative presents them as being Roman soldiers.[85]

Pseudo-Peter, I repeat, was partial to the use of simple verbs. He also regularly omitted the name of Jesus, which he replaced with κύριος.[86] The expression λαβόντες τὸν κύριον may, therefore, be linked with that of Mt. 27:27a: παραλαβόντες τὸν Ἰησοῦν, and of Jn. 19:16b: παρέλαβον οὖν τὸν Ἰησοῦν. However, since the remainder of verse 6 of the apocryphon is not found in any of the gospels, it is impossible to maintain with certainty a literary dependence. A dependence on Mt. 27:27a is still probable, for the words παραλαβόντες τὸν Ἰησοῦν are found in Mt. in the context of the scene of the derision, a scene which Pseudo-Peter describes with λαβόντες τὸν κύριν in the verse that immediately follows. The influence of Jn. 19:16b, which does not mention this scene, is, therefore, less probable. I would still like to add that the divine sonship of Christ to which the words of the Jews allude in the apocryphon was, according to the canonical gospels,[87] the religious motive for the death sentence pronounced by the Sanhedrin.

Gos. Pet.8

Καί τις αὐτῶν ἐνεγκὼν στέφανον ἀκάνθινον ἔθηκεν ἐπὶ τῆς κεφαλῆς τοῦ κυρίου.

And one of them (the Jews) brought a crown of thorns and put it on the Lord's head.

---

[84]Cf. ibid., 144, where the author points out a series of cases which demonstrate Pseudo-Peter's clear preference for the simple verb.

[85]Cf. Mt. 27:27, 54; Mk. 15:16, 39; Lk. 23:36, 47; Jn. 19:2, 23, 24, 32.

[86]Cf. Vaganay, *L'Évangile de Pierre*, 113, 205, 222-23.

[87]Cf. Mt. 26:64; Mk. 14:62; Lk. 22:70.

The crowning with thorns is related by Mt. 27:29a; Mk. 15:17b; and Jn. 19:2a.

In the apocryphon, this crowning with thorns takes place on calvary; according to certain manuscripts of Lk. 23:37,[88] which read περιτιθέντες αὐτῷ καὶ ἀκάνθινον στέφανον, it also takes place on calvary.

This crowing with thorns is described with the help of Mk.'s words (ἀκάνθινον στέφανον) and Mt.'s (ἐπὶ τῆς κεφαλῆς). It is, therefore, difficult to decide on a dependence on one gospel over another. Yet, the Gospel of Peter is slightly more in agreement with the first gospel, because the words ἔθηκεν ἐπὶ τῆς κεφαλῆς are closer to ἐπέθηκαν ἐπὶ τῆς κεφαλῆς in Mt. 27:29a, especially if we keep in mind the apocryphon's distinct preference for the simple verb. The formula of Jn. 19:2a, ἐπέθηκαν αὐτοῦ τῇ κεφαλῇ, is not as close to that of the apocryphon.[89]

4. Gos. Pet. 16

Καὶ τις αὐτῶν εἶπεν· ποτίσατε αὐτὸν χολὴν μετὰ ὄξους· καὶ κεράσαντες ἐπότισαν.

And one of them (the Jews) said, ''Give him to drink gall with vinegar.'' And they mixed it and gave him to drink.

The drink given to Christ on the cross is mentioned in Mt. 27:34, 48; Mk. 15:23, 36; Lk. 23:36; and Jn. 19:29-30a.

The text of the apocryphon is much shorter than that of the gospels, and only the Matthean text mentions χολή and ὄξος. Is this a combination of verses 34 and 48 of Mt. 27? This is not impossible. Yet we may wonder whether Pseudo-Peter expressed himself in that way so as to point to the fulfillment of the prophecy of Ps. 69(68):22: καὶ ἔδωκαν εἰς τὸ βρῶμά μου χολὴν καὶ εἰς τὴν δίψαν μου ἐπότισάν με ὄξος in which the words χολή and ὄξος are found. This hypothesis seems all the more probable inasmuch as the following verse shows the author's preoccupation with relating events to prophecies. Indeed, he writes in verse 17: καὶ ἐπλήρωσαν πάντα καὶ ἐτελείωσαν κατὰ τῆς κεφαλῆς αὐτῶν τὰ ἁμαρτήματα: ''And they (the Jews) fulfilled all things and completed the measure of their sins on their head.'' In this text, the verb πληρόω has the same meaning that it very often has in the New Testament: to fulfill the scriptures;[90] if the author is here un-

---

[88]These are the codices D, c, and the Syriac Curetonian version.

[89]The Word πλέξαντες, common to the gospels, is missing in Gos. Pet. 8; on the other hand, the expression ἐνεγκὼν στέφανον is absent in the gospels: a parallel is found in Acts Pil. B, 9.5: ἔφερον στέφανον.

[90]Cf. W. Bauer, *Griechisch-deutsches Wörterbuch zu den Schriften des Neuen Testaments und der übrigen urchristlichen Literatur*, 3rd ed. (Berlin, 1937) col. 1120 [BAG 677b], who gives the following references: Mt. 1:22; 2:15, 17, 23; 4:14; 8:17; 12:17; 13:35; 21:4; 26:54, 56; 27:9; Mk. 14:49; 15:28; Lk. 1:20; 4:21; 21:22; Jn. 12:38; 13:18; 15:25; 17:12; 19:24, 36; Acts 1:16; Jas. 2:23.

der the literary influence of a reminiscence of Jn. 19:29-30a,[91] it is even easier to admit that the point at stake is the fulfillment of the Scriptures of which John speaks explicitly in verse 28. All the commentators of the Gospel of Peter 17 propose the following meaning: the Jews have fulfilled all that Scripture had predicted.[92] Moreover, the fulfillment of the Scriptures is closely connected with their progressive culpability: the words ἐτελείωσαν . . . τὰ ἁμαρτήματα illustrate it, and this turn of phrase is fairly frequent both in the Bible and in the Christian and Rabbinic literature.[93] This would catch, therefore, the author's concern: to bring the events into harmony with the prophecies, and to show that they fulfilled them. It is necessary, therefore, to keep this in mind when we examine the texts that relate these events. The Gospel of Peter 16 would then be doing nothing more than applying this principle. Besides, tradition reveals a similar concern, and Pseudo-Peter may simply be part of the traditional stream.[94]

5. Gos. Pet 19

Καὶ ὁ κύριος ἀνεβόησε λέγων· ἡ δύναμίς μου, ἡ δύναμίς (μου), κατέλειψάς με, καὶ εἰπὼν ἀνελήφθη.

And the Lord called out and cried, "My power, O power, thou hast forsaken me!" And having said this he was taken up.

Mt. 27:46, 50; Mk. 15:34, 37; Lk. 23:46; and Jn. 19:30 are the parallels.

There is a great similarity between the way that Mt. and Mk. introduce the cry of Christ before his death and the way the Gospel of Peter does: Mt. says ἀνεβόησεν, Mk. writes ἐβόησεν. The Matthean text stands out particularly because it contains the compound verb ἀνεβόησεν as does the apocryphon, a fact that is all the more remarkable because Pseudo-Peter is partial to simple verbs, as I have said many times previously. The inclination might, therefore, be to see a literary

---

[91]Cf. Vaganay, *L'Évangile de Pierre*, 62; von Schubert, *Das Petrusevangelium*, 13, also gives this parallel.

[92]Cf. Vaganay, *L'Évangile de Pierre*, 245-47.

[93]Cf. Gen. 15:16; Dan. 8:23; Mt. 23:32; 1 Thess. 2:16; Barn. 5:11; 14:15; Epist. ad Diogn. 9:2; Did. Syr. 22; cf. Strack-Billerbeck, 3:142.

[94]Cf. Vaganay, *L'Évangile de Pierre*, 246: "Tradition has even grouped both episodes of the drink to better show how the prophecy was fulfilled in Jesus (Barn. 7:3: ἐποτίζετο ὄξει καὶ χολῇ; cf. 7:5; Irenaeus, Adv. Haer. 3.19.2: aceto et felle potatur, cf. 4.33.12; 4.35.3; Pred. apost. 82; Tertullien, De spect. 30: felle et aceto potatus, cf. Adv. Jud. 10; Adv. Mk. 4.42; Origen, C. Cels. 2.37; 4.22; Hom. in Mt. 137; Lactantius, Epist. div. inst. 45; Aphraatus, Hom., 17.10; Cyril of Jerusalem, Cat., 13.29; Acta Iohannis, ch. 97; Const. Apost. 5.14.15; Sib. Or. 1:467; 8.303; Acts Pil. A, 1). In the manuscript tradition of the gospels, more than one witness, starting from similar principles, has corrected the original text in Mt. 27:34, A, N, Γ, Δ, 1241, c, f, h, q, Tat.ᵃʳ, syᵖ replacing οἶνον with ὄξος; in Jn. 19:29, Θ, 348 al syᵖ arm add μετὰ χολῆς to ὄξους."

reference to the Matthean text.

Yet this very saying of Christ has an important variant: instead of θεέ μου θεέ μου, Pseudo-Peter says ἡ δύναμίς μου, ἡ δύναμίς μου. This change has led to a series of hypotheses,[95] and the prevailing hypothesis recognizes in the apocryphal text a literal interpretation of Ps. 22:2 (Hebrew), in which אֵלִי may be understood in the etymological meaning of strength.[96]

The verb ἀνελήφθη, which designates the death of Christ, is missing in the gospels. This probably shows a docetic tendency on the part of the author of the apocryphon, which corresponds to the very clear desire to obscure the suffering on the cross (verse 10) and to suppress any complaint (verses 16 and 19).[97]

In other words, the author is probably literarily dependent on the Matthean text. The use of the verb ἀνεβόησεν points this out. The last saying of the savior seems to come from Mt. 27:46, in which ἠλί, ἠλί (אֵלִי) was taken in the etymological sense of strength. Yet the lingering question is that this interpretation of the first words of Ps. 22 may be independent of Mt., as is Aquila's version, which reads ἰσχυρέ μου, ἰσχυρέ μου. If this were so, the verb ἀνελήφθη would have been willingly inserted by the author, in agreement with his docetic tendency.

C. Texts That State in Different Words an Episode Peculiar to Matthew

1. Gos. Pet. 35

Τῇ δὲ νυκτὶ ᾗ ἐπέφωσκεν ἡ κυριακή, φυλασσόντων τῶν στρατιωτῶν ἀνὰ δύο δύο κατὰ φρουράν, μεγάλη φωνὴ ἐγένετο ἐν τῷ οὐφανῷ.

Now in the night in which the Lord's day dawned, when the soldiers, two by two in every watch, were keeping guard, there rang out a loud voice in heaven, . . .

The usual parallel for this passage is Mt. 28:1-2a: ὀψὲ δὲ σαββάτων, τῇ ἐπιφωσκούσῃ εἰς μίαν σαββάτων, ἦλθεν Μαριὰμ ἡ Μαγδαληνὴ καὶ ἡ ἄλλη

---

[95]Cf. Vaganay, *L'Évangile de Pierre*, 255-56, who mentions these hypotheses.

[96]Cf. ibid., 255-56: "In fact, the LXX has often given this meaning to אֵל, and has even rendered it with δύναμις (Gen. 31:29; Prov. 3:27; Mic. 2:1; Neh. 5:5). Moreover, Aquila, in this particular passage of the psalm, did not translate אֵלִי אֵלִי as the LXX did with ὁ θεός, ὁ θεός μου, but with ἰσχυρέ μου, ἰσχυρέ μου, and Eusebius (Dem. evangel. 10.8.30) approved of this translation. Even better, the bishop of Caesarea reinforced it by proposing ἰσχύς μου, ἰσχύς μου. It is not impossible that he understood "power" to mean the natural strength of Jesus, who simply realized that he was getting increasingly weaker and that he was at the point of dying. (G. Jouassard, *L'abandon du Christ par son Père durant la passion, d'après la tradition patristique et les docteurs du XIII siècle* [Lyons,1923] 13)."

[97]Cf. ibid., 257.

Μαρία θεωρῆσαι τὸν τάφον. καὶ ἰδοὺ σεισμὸς ἐγένετο μέγας. . . .

The only common word found here is ἐπέφωσκεν—ἐπιφωσκούσῃ. It is, above all, this chronological detail of the resurrection that has suggested a parallel to the Matthean text. Vaganay notes on the subject, "Up to the chronology of this event, there is nothing to demonstrate a fairly characteristic coincidence between the two texts: the obscure detail in Mt. 28:1: ὀψὲ δὲ σαββάτων, τῇ ἐπιφωσκούσῃ εἰς μίαν σαββάτων, seems to have been expressed clearly, even if falsely interpreted by Gos. Pet. 35."[98]

I would still like to point out that the scene of the resurrection begins in the apocryphon, as it does in Mt., with a loud noise: Gos. Pet. 35: μεγάλη φωνὴ ἐγένετο ἐν τῷ οὐρανῷ, and Mt. 28:2a: καὶ ἰδοὺ σεισμὸς ἐγένετο μέγας.

2. Gos. Pet. 36-37

Καὶ εἶδον ἀνοιχθέντας τοὺς οὐρα[ν]οὺς καὶ δύο ἄνδρας κατελθόντας ἐκεῖθεν πολὺ φέγγος ἔχοντας καὶ ἐγγίσαντας τῷ τάφῳ. ὁ δὲ λίθος ἐκεῖνος ὁ βεβλημένος ἐπὶ τῇ θύρᾳ ἀφ' ἑαυτοῦ κυλισθεὶς ἐπεχώρησε παρὰ μέρος καὶ ὁ τάφος ἠνοίγη καὶ ἀμφότεροι οἱ νεανίσκοι εἰσῆλθον.

. . . and they (the soldiers) saw the heavens opened and two men come down from there in a great brightness and draw nigh to the sepulchre. That stone which had been laid against the entrance to the sepulchre started of itself to roll and gave way to the side, and the sepulchre was opened, and both the young men entered in.

The nearest parallel to this passage is read in Mt. 28:2b-3: ἄγγελος γὰρ κυρίου καταβὰς ἐξ οὐρανοῦ καὶ προσελθὼν ἀπεκύλισεν τὸν λίθον καὶ ἐκάθητο ἐπάνω αὐτοῦ. ἦν δὲ ἡ εἰδέα αὐτοῦ ὡς ἀστραπή, καὶ τὸ ἔνδυμα αὐτοῦ λευκὸν ὡς χιών.

Except for the closeness of ὁ λίθος κυλισθείς with ἀπεκύλισεν τὸν λίθον in Mt., no other word is common to both texts. Even with regard to the stone, it is the angel who rolls it in Mt., whereas in Pseudo-Peter it rolls by itself.

The idea as a whole is similar: the sepulchre is opened, the stone is rolled back, angels intervene, but the analogy is limited to the event. Let me add that the two angels of the resurrection are designated with the same words (δύο ἄνδρες) in Lk. 24:4, and the epithet νεανίσκοι corresponds to Mk. 16:5, which designates the angel with this word in the singular.[99]

---

[98]Cf. ibid., 51. The author notes on 293: "Our apocryphon is only the very ancient testimony of an exegesis taken up by several modern critics (É. Tobac, '"Ὀψὲ δὲ σαββάτων," *RHE* 20 [1924]: 239-43)."

[99]Cf. ibid., 55.

3. Gos. Pet. 44

Καὶ ἔτι διανοουμένων αὐτῶν φαίνονται πάλιν ἀνοιχθέντες οἱ οὐρανοὶ καὶ ἄνθρωπός τις κατελθὼν καὶ εἰσελθὼν εἰς τὸ μνῆμα.

And whilst they (the soldiers) were still deliberating, the heavens were again seen to open, and a man descended and entered into the sepulchre.

Mt. 28:2b again comes to mind: ἄγγελος γὰρ κυρίου καταβὰς ἐξ οὐρανοῦ καὶ προσελθὼν ἀπεκύλισεν τὸν λίθον καὶ ἐκάθητο ἐπάνω αὐτοῦ.

4. Gos. Pet. 47-49

Εἶτα προσελθόντες πάντες ἐδέοντο αὐτοῦ καὶ παρεκάλουν κελεῦσαι τῷ κεντυρίωνι καὶ τοῖς στρατιώταις μηδενὶ εἰπεῖν ἃ εἶδον· συμφέρει γάρ, φασίν, ἡμῖν ὀφλῆσαι μεγίστην ἁμαρτίαν ἔμπροσθεν τοῦ θεοῦ καὶ μὴ ἐμπεσεῖν εἰς χεῖρας τοῦ λαοῦ τῶς Ἰουδαίων καὶ λιθασθῆναι. ἐκέλευσεν οὖν ὁ Πειλᾶτος τῷ κεντυρίωνι καὶ τοῖς στρατιώταις μηδὲν εἰπεῖν.

Then all came to him, beseeching him and urgently calling upon him to command the centurion and the soldiers to tell no one what they had seen. "For it is better for us," they said, "to make ourselves guilty of the greatest sin before God than to fall into the hands of the people of the Jews and be stoned."

The passage of Mt. 28:12-15, unique in the gospels, is usually given as a parallel: Καὶ συναχθέντες μετὰ τῶν πρεσβυτέρων συμβούλιόν τε λαβόντες ἀργύρια ἱκανὰ ἔδωκαν τοῖς στρατιώταις, λέγοντες· εἴπατε ὅτι οἱ μαθηταὶ αὐτοῦ νυκτὸς ἐλθόντες ἔκλεψαν αὐτὸν ἡμῶν κοιμωμένων. καὶ ἐὰν ἀκουσθῇ τοῦτο ἐπὶ τοῦ ἡγεμόνος, ἡμεῖς πείσομεν καὶ ὑμᾶς ἀμερίμνους ποιήσομεν. οἱ δὲ λαβόντες ἀργύρια ἐποίησαν ὡς ἐδιδάχθησαν.

The mere comparison of the texts is enough to demonstrate that a literary contact is out of the question. These two texts are compared solely because they have in common the fact that the Jewish authorities intervened so that the miracle would not be disclosed, and the fact that the soldiers kept silence. But the differences are important: in fact, over and above the gospel narrative, the apocryphon reads that, after the resurrection, the leaders of the Jews recognized their culpability publicly before Pilate. Moreover, the Jews did not intervene directly with the soldiers and did not bribe them, but they addressed themselves directly to Pilate asking him to impose silence on the guards.

Finally, let me point out several words which are present in the Gospel of Peter and peculiar to the Matthean vocabulary: ταφή,[100] ταφός,[101] and the participle

---

[100]Cf. Gos. Pet. 3 and Mt. 27:7, unique in the N.T.

[101]Cf. Gos. Pet. 24, 31, 36, 37, 39, 45, 55, and, in the passion narrative, only in Mt. 27:61, 64, 66; 28:1.

κοιμωμένοι to designate the dead.[102]

The examination of all these texts is conclusive: Pseudo-Peter knew the Gospel of Mt. and was subject several times to its literary influence. There are numerous parallels with the first gospel, and the literary contacts mentioned can be explained only by a dependence of the apocryphon on Mt.

Yet, in almost every case where I concluded that there is a dependence on Mt., I also pointed out the personal individuality of the author and his fairly great freedom towards his source. I also pointed out in various texts which depend on Mt. either a word, or an expression, or a touch coming from the other gospels, as though, while following Mt., Pseudo-Peter came under a certain influence from the other gospels as well.

I also pointed out some parallels with Mt. which do not suppose a literary contact: these texts described events known only in the first gospel, but which the author of the apocryphon narrates in his own way, not drawing any inspiration from the text of Mt. itself.

§2. The Other New Testament Writings.

The Akhmîm fragment shows literary relationships with the three other gospels. In other respects, some passages are rather in agreement with the gospel tradition in a way that it is impossible to determine on which gospel they depend. The Gospel of Peter reveals no knowledge of the New Testament writings except for the gospels. This is why my attention will turn first to Mk., secondly to Lk., thirdly to Jn., and finally to the gospel tradition.

A. The Gospel of Mark[103]

The Gospel of Peter 52-54 reports the conversation of the holy women on their way to the sepulchre: "And they (Mary Magdalene and her friends) feared lest the Jews should see them, and said (ἔλεγον), 'Although we could not weep (κλαῦσαι) and lament on that day when he was crucified, yet let us now do so at his sepulchre. But who will roll away for us the stone also that is set on the entrance to the sepulchre (τίς δὲ ἀποκυλίσει ἡμῖν καὶ τὸν λίθον τὸν τεθέντα ἐπὶ τῆς θύρας τοῦ μνημείου), that we may go in and sit beside him and do what is due? For the stone was great (μέγας γὰρ ἦν ὁ λίθος)—and we fear lest any one see us. And if we cannot do so, let us at least put down at the entrance what we bring (ἃ φέρομεν) for a memorial of him and let us weep and lament until we have again gone home." The only parallel to be mentioned is Mk. 16:3-4: "And they were

---

[102]Cf. Gos. Pet. 41 and, in the gospels, only in Mt. 27:52.

[103]I do not mention again the passages I studied in the paragraph devoted to Mt. in which I have already pointed out a relationship with Mk.

saying (ἔλεγον) to one another, 'Who will roll away the stone for us from the door of the tomb?' (τίς ἀποκυλίσει ἡμῖν τὸν λίθον ἐκ τῆς θύρας τοῦ μνημείου;) And looking up, they saw that the stone (ὁ λίθος) was rolled back; for it was very large'' (ἦν γὰρ μέγας σφόδρα). The fear of the women who came to the sepulchre is found in none of the canonical gospels. Yet their conversation is introduced in the Gospel of Peter, just as it is in Mk., with ἔλεγον. Verse 53 includes Mk.'s words almost literally: τίς ἀποκυλίσει ἡμῖν τὸν λίθον ἐκ τῆς θύρας τοῦ μνημείου. The borrowing is all the more certain inasmuch as the apocryphon retains the composite verb ἀποκυλίσει. The same literary contact is suggested by the words μέγας γὰρ ἦν ὁ λίθος. Let me add that many witnesses of Mk. 16:3-4[104] mention the size of the stone before the narrative of the women's coming to the tomb: τίς ἡμῖν ἀποκυλίσει τὸν λίθον ἀπὸ τῆς θύρας τοῦ μνημείου; ἦν γὰρ μέγας σφόδρα· καὶ ἔρχονται καὶ εὑρίσκουσιν ἀποκεκυλισμένον τὸν λίθον.

The Gospel of Peter is, therefore, a very ancient witness to the so-called western text. Vaganay points out that Pseudo-Peter here betrays its borrowing: "Among all their complaints, we read this (verse 54): μέγας γὰρ ἦν ὁ λίθος· καὶ φοβούμεθα μή τις ἡμᾶς ἴδη. This imperfect tense (ἦν) seems at first glance to be very strange in the mouth of these women who later speak in the present tense (φοβούμεθα). From where may such a mistake come? Obviously from the text of Mk. 16:4: ὁ λίθος ἦν γὰρ μέγας σφόδρα. The imperfect tense is correct in this case because it reflects the narrator's thinking. It should, therefore, have been corrected before being transposed into direct discourse. But one cannot think of everything, and in transposing this parenthetical clause so clumsily, the apocryphal author points at the original with all the more certainty since the resemblance is even more characteristic in certain manuscripts of Mk. 16:4."[105]

The arrival of the women at the sepulchre and their encounter with the angel are narrated in Gos. Pet. 55: "So they went and found (εὗρον) the sepulchre opened. And they came near, stooped down and saw there a young man sitting (καὶ ὁρῶσιν ἐκεῖ . . . καθεζόμενον) in the midst of the sepulchre, comely and clothed with a brightly shining robe (νεανίσκον . . . ὡραῖον καὶ περιβεβλημένον στολὴν λαμπροτάτην), who said to them, . . ." This text is linked with Mt. 28:3; Mk. 16:4-5; Lk. 24:2-5a; and Jn. 20:1, 11-12. But there is no doubt that it is literarily dependent on Mk. 16:5: "And entering the tomb, they saw a young man, sitting (εἶδον νεανίσκον καθήμενον) on the right side, dressed in a white robe (περιβεβλημένον στολὴν λευκήν); and they were amazed." It is only in

---

[104]D, Θ, 81, 565, c, ff², n, the Syriac versions sin. and pesh., Tatian, Eusebius.

[105]Cf. Vaganay, *L'Évangile de Pierre*, 53. Note that the women recall that they were not able to cry (κλαῦσαι) at the tomb; in Jn. 20:11, Mary Magdalene is all tears (κλαίουσα) when she stands at the tomb. Let me add that the verb φέρομεν, which expresses the women's gifts, is read in 24:1, which speaks of these women (φέρουσα).

Mk. 16:5, in fact, that the women see a young man sitting in the tomb. Mk.'s text coincides almost literally with that of the apocryphon. Mk.'s words ὁράω, νεανίσκος are there, and Mk.'s verb καθῆμαι is very close to καθίζω in the Gospel of Peter. Moreover, the latter describes the young man's garment in the style and with words which belong to the second gospel: Gos. Peter has περιβεβλημένον στολήν which is literally present in Mk., and the parallel between λαμπροτάτην in Gos. Pet. and λευκήν in Mk. is obvious.

Gos. Pet. 57 notes the fear of the holy women: "Then the women fled affrighted (φοβηθεῖσαι ἔφυγον)." This simple sentence recalls Mt. 28:8 and Mk. 16:8. It certainly seems that the apocryphon is in literary contact with Mk.'s text: "And they went out and fled (ἔφυγον) from the tomb; for trembling and astonishment had come upon them; and they said nothing to any one, for they were afraid (ἐφοβοῦντο)." Pseudo-Peter has summarized Mk.'s text and has kept both verbs φοβέομαι and φεύγω. Vaganay states: "Everything, even up to Mk.'s brusque and very particular finale in 16:8: ἔφυγον . . . ἐφοβοῦντο γάρ, is found in the apocryphon (v. 57) in a similar form: φοβηθεῖσαι ἔφυγον."[106]

Two texts depend with less certainty on the second gospel: the first is found in Gos. Pet. 3: "Now there stood there Joseph (Ἰωσήφ), the friend of Pilate and of the Lord, and knowing that they were about to crucify him he came to Pilate and begged the body of the Lord for burial (ἦλθεν πρὸς τὸν Πειλᾶτον καὶ ἤτησε τὸ σῶμα τοῦ κυρίου πρὸς ταφήν)." We can immediately take notice of an addition to and a transformation of the narrative of the canonical gospels: Joseph is Pilate's friend, and he comes to ask for the body of Jesus before the crucifixion, and not after the death of the Lord as related by the synoptics (Mt. 27:57-58; Mk. 15:43; Lk. 23:52), which, together with Jn. 19:38, are parallels of the end of verse 3 of the Gospel of Peter. The last words of Pseudo-Peter, ἦλθεν πρὸς τὸν Πειλᾶτον καὶ ἤτησε τὸ σῶμα τοῦ κυρίου πρὸς ταφήν, are certainly not literarily dependent on Jn. 19:38, which reads, ἵνα ἄρῃ τὸ σῶμα τοῦ Ἰησοῦ. Yet, they are very close to the synoptics which are closely related to one another. But there is a clue which leads me to think that the apocryphon follows rather Mk. 15:43, in that it has preserved the paratactic construction of the two propositions in Mk. which reads, εἰσῆλθεν πρὸς τὸν Πιλᾶτον καὶ ἤτήσατο τὸ σῶμα τοῦ Ἰησοῦ. Mt. and Lk., on the other hand, have οὗτος προσελθὼν τῷ Πιλάτῳ ἤτήσατο τὸ σῶμα τοῦ Ἰησοῦ.

The second text whose dependence on Mk. is doubtful is found in Gos. Pet. 59: "But we, the twelve disciples of the Lord, wept and mourned (ἐκλαίομεν καὶ ἐλυπούμεθα), and each one, very grieved for what had come to pass (διὰ τὸ συμβάν), went to his own home." Scholars generally refer this passage to Mk. 16:10, in which Mary Magdalene announces the resurrection to the apostles

---

[106]Cf. ibid., 54.

"mourning and weeping" (πενθοῦσι καὶ κλαίουσιν), but there is no question anywhere of each apostle's returning home. I would like to point out the word συμβάν, which may recall the expression περὶ πάντων τῶν συνβεβηκότων τούτων in Lk. 24:14, in a context which relates the same events.

The Gospel of Peter does not have as many points of contact with Mk. as it does with Mt. The apocryphal author seems to have been influenced by Mk. mostly for the discovery of the empty tomb beginning in verse 50.

I must also stress that in the passage in which dependence on Mk. seems certain, the author discloses personal initiative by adding elements which are absent from the gospel story.

B. The Gospel of Luke[107]

The Gospel of Peter 10 relates the crucifixion: "And they (the Jews) brought two malefactors (δύο κακούργους) and crucified (ἐσταύρωσαν) the Lord in the midst between them (ἀνὰ μέσον αὐτῶν). But he held his peace, as if he felt no pain." The gospel parallels are Mt. 27:35, 38; Mk. 15:24-27; Lk. 23:32-33; and Jn. 19:18. The presence of the word κακοῦργοι, peculiar to Lk. in the gospels,[108] leads us to that gospel. Let me add that Lk. is the only one of the gospels to mention the arrival of the two criminals before the crucifixion of Christ; the other gospels mention it after. Lk's word ἕτεροι is not found here; the word is in any event superfluous to such a writer who draws a bold outline of the events; certain manuscripts of Lk. 23:32 have imitated him.[109] The text of Pseudo-Peter reveals, therefore, a very probable reminiscence of the Lucan text. As for ἀνὰ μέσον αὐτῶν, the nearest text is, once again, Jn. 18:18; but it could be assumed that this is how the apocryphon summarized Lk.'s formula: one on the right, the other one on the left. The silence of Jesus is reported in Mt. 26:63; 27:14; Mk. 14:61; 15:5; Lk. 23:9; and Jn. 19:9, but they do so in a totally different context, during the interrogations before the high priest, Pilate, and Herod. The words "as if he felt no pain" are missing in the gospel narrative and may demonstrate a docetic ulterior motive. Yet, let us recall that the patience of the martyrs is sometimes pointed out in a similar manner by Christian writers.[110]

---

[107]I omit all passages previously studied, which referred to texts in Mt. and Mk. in which a parallel with the Gospel of Lk. has already been pointed out.

[108]Cf. Lk. 23:32, 33, 39.

[109]Cf. Vaganay, *L'Évangile de Pierre*, 235, who mentions c, e, ff², syrˢ.

[110]Cf. ibid., 236, where the author cites the Martyrdom of Saint Polycarp, ch. 8: καὶ μὴ ἐπιστραφείς, ὡς οὐδὲν πεπονθὼς προθύμως μετὰ σπουδῆς ἐπορεύτο, and ch. 2: βασανιζόμενοι τῆς σαρκὸς ἀπεδήμουν οἱ γενναιότατοι μάρτυρες τοῦ Χριστοῦ, or in the Letter of the Christians of Lyons concerning Saint Blandina: μηδὲ αἴσθησιν ἔτι τῶν συμβαινόντων ἔχουσα διὰ τὴν ἐλπίδα (Eusebius, Hist. Eccl. 5.1.56).

Gos. Pet. 13 relates the words of one of the criminals: "But one of the malefactors (τις τῶν κακούργων) rebuked them (the Jews), saying, 'We have landed in suffering for the deeds of wickedness which we have committed (ἡμεῖς διὰ τὰ κακὰ ἃ ἐποιήσαμεν οὕτω πεπόνθαμεν), but this man (οὗτος δέ), who has become the saviour of men, what wrong has he done you ?' (τί ἠδίκησεν ὑμᾶς;)" This retort brings to mind the words of the penitent thief related only in Lk. 23:39-41: "one of the criminals (εἷς δὲ τῶν κακούγων) who were hanged railed at him, saying, 'Are you not the Christ? Save yourself and us!' But the other rebuked him, saying, 'Do you not fear God, since you are under the same sentence of condemnation? And we indeed justly; for we are receiving the due reward of our deeds; but this man has done nothing wrong' (καὶ ἡμεῖς μὲν δικαίως, ἄξια γὰρ ὧν ἐπράξαμεν ἀπολαμβάνομεν· οὗτος δὲ οὐδὲν ἄτοπον ἔπραξεν)."

It is difficult to deny that Lk.'s narrative served as the author's source and had a literary influence on him. In fact, Lk.'s words εἷς δὲ τῶν κακούγων and its pronouns ἡμεῖς and οὗτος are found in the apocryphon. Vaganay argues against those who reject a dependence on Lk.: "To claim otherwise, you must convince yourself that the author has deliberately removed from his narrative the details which could give substance to objections, for example, the heinous banter inviting Jesus to descend from the cross. And so, it all suddenly becomes clear. The impenitent thief is eliminated in Gos. Pet., together with all the other revilers of Calvary. As a result, the penitent thief, who can no longer reprimand his companion, upbraids the Jews. Furthermore, since he can no longer have a conversation with Jesus, who keeps silent on the cross (v. 10), there is a new epilogue to end this story. Everything else faithfully retains Lk's style and goes so far as to show obvious traces of borrowing. Thus the beginning is altogether different from Mark and Matthew (Gos. Pet. 13 εἷς δέ τις τῶν κακούργων = Lk. 23:39 εἷς δὲ τῶν κρεμασθέντων κακούργων). And this is particularly true for the end of the penitent thief's retort (Gos. Pet. 13 = Lk. 23:14), the only part which anyway was useful to Pseudo-Peter and whose elements, in both cases in direct discourse, correspond stroke for stroke. The thieves and Jesus present the same opposition (in Gos. Pet. and in Lk.: ἡμεῖς . . . οὗτος δέ). The penitent thief accepts his torture likewise and recognizes it as legitimate (Gos. Pet.: διὰ τὰ κακὰ ἃ ἐποιήσαμεν οὕτω πεπόνθαμεν = Lk.: ἄξια γὰρ ὧν ἐπράξαμεν ἀπολαμβάνομεν).

And finally, the same testimony is offered in favor of the innocence of the Savior (Gos. Pet.: τί ἠδίκησεν ὑμᾶς; = Lk.: οὐδὲν ἄτοπον ἔπραξεν). Yes, there are certain changes in wording so as to clarify the argument, and some clumsy additions are made for dogmatic reasons. But the general similarity is accurate enough to reveal its source document. From this point of view, the little word ἡμεῖς does not fail to be very suggestive. The penitent thief, who criticizes the other's unjustifiable attack, is as natural in Lk. as he is artificial in Pseudo-Peter, in which the impenitent thief has disappeared from the scene."[111]

Gos. Pet. 28 mentions that the Jewish people realized their error: "But the scribes and Pharisees (Φαρισαῖοι) and elders, being assembled together (συναχθέντες) and hearing that all the people were murmuring (γογγύζει) and beating their breasts (κόπτεται τὰ στήθη) saying, 'If at his death these exceeding great signs have come to pass, behold how righteous he was' (πόσον δίκαιός ἐστιν)." These words recall those of Mt. 27:54, 62 and Lk. 23:47-48. The text in Jn. 7:31-32a has sometimes been mentioned with regard to the murmuring of the people. The beginning of verse 28 is in agreement with the narrative of Mt. 27:62: it includes the same verb συνάγω, but the authorities who come together are different; in the apocryphon, the assembly is comprised of scribes, Pharisees and priests; in Mt., they are the centurion and the guards. The words which follow are not found in the narrative of the synoptics; yet a parallel must be mentioned with Jn. 7:31-32a in which the Pharisees also hear (the same verb ἀκούω), the people murmur (the same verb γογγύζω), and for a similar reason: the miracles. The difference in the contexts is, however, so great that it is difficult to assert a possible literary influence; in the apocryphon, the subject matter is the miracles of Calvary; in Jn. it is the miracles of Christ. Lk. is the only one to mention that the people were beating their breasts; Pseudo-Peter mentions it as well and uses Lk.'s substantive στήθη, but he substitutes the verb κόπτω for τύπτω. Moreover, it is no accident that Jesus' proclamation of innocence is so similar to that in Lk 23:47 (οὗτος δίκαιος ἦν). The apocryphon, therefore, depends very probably on the Lucan text regarding this particular confession of the Jews.

In other sections of the Gospel of Peter, a parallel with Lk. is possible, but it might be bold to assert that a specific text in Lk was the source of influence. Thus, Gos. Pet. 4-5 reads: "And Pilate sent to Herod and begged his body. And Herod said, 'Brother Pilate, even if no one had begged him, we should bury him, since the Sabbath is drawing on. For it stands written in the law: The sun should not set on one that has been put to death.' And he delivered him to the people on the day before the unleavened bread, their feast." This text supposes a friendly relationship between Herod and Pilate, and the name ἀδελφέ may allude to Lk. 23:12.

Gos. Pet. 15 points out the darkness: "Now it was midday and a darkness covered all Judaea (ἦν δὲ μεσημβρία καὶ σκότος κατέσχε πᾶσαν τὴν Ἰουδαίαν). And they became anxious and uneasy lest the sun had already set, since he (Jesus) was still alive. [For] it stands written for them: the sun should not set on one that has been put to death." The following texts are generally mentioned as being more or less parallel: Mt. 27:45; Mk. 15:33; and Lk. 23:44-45a. I must state at once that the fear of having committed a transgression against the law, at the coming of the darkness at noon, is not found in any of the gospels. The Gospel

---

[111]Cf. ibid., 56-57.

of Peter contains the same chronological fact as the synoptics, but without the slightest textual contact. The construction of the sentence ἦν δὲ . . . καὶ σκότος resembles very strongly that of Lk. 23:44: ἦν ἤδη . . . καὶ σκότος; certain manuscripts in Lk. even have the formula ἦν δέ of the Gospel of Peter.[112] The verb ἦν gives preference to Lk. over the other synoptics as having perhaps influenced the apocryphon. There is also the word πᾶσαν in Mt. 27:45, which is applied to the earth, and which is read in Gos. Pet. 15 as applied to Judea. To be sure, the apocryphon stresses the darkness in these and the following verses.[113] And it is a fact that the Church Fathers looked upon the miraculous darkness of Calvary as the fulfillment of the words of Amos 8:9: καὶ ἔσται ἐν τῇ ἡμέρᾳ ἐκείνῃ, λέγει κύριος, δύσεται ὁ ἥλιος μεσημβρίας.[114] The question may be asked whether Pseudo-Peter used the word μεσημβρία of the LXX of Amos to designate noon, and not ὥρα ἕκτη of the synoptics. In this case, the possibility of Lk.'s literary influence still remains, for the author of the apocryphon may have taken and included μεσημβρία from Amos and have introduced it instead of ὡσεὶ ὥρα ἕκτη from Lk.

In Gos. Pet. 25, the Jews confess their error: "Then the Jews and the elders and the priest, perceiving what great evil they had done to themselves, began to lament and to say, 'Woe on our sins, the judgment and the end of Jerusalem is drawn nigh.'" Scholars generally refer to Lk. 23:48; even though these texts are actually too far apart to allow us to believe in a literary contact, the similarity of the episode is fairly striking.

The literary parallels between the Gospel of Peter and Lk. are less numerous and, as a whole, not as well defined as with Mt. and Mk. Yet, I have pointed out several texts which can hardly be explained other than by a literary dependence on the third gospel, especially Gos. Pet. 10 and 13, which drew their inspiration from the episode of the penitent thief, a story which is peculiar to Lk.

C. The Gospel of John[115]

Gos. Pet. 7 narrates the beginning of the scene of the derision of Christ: "And they (the Jews) put upon him a purple robe (καὶ πορφύραν αὐτὸν περιέβαλον) and set him on the judgment seat and said, 'Judge righteously, O King of Israel!'" This reminds us naturally of Mt. 27:28-29b; Mk. 15:17a, 18; Lk. 23:11; and Jn. 19:2b-3. The first words of the apocryphon, καὶ πορφύραν αὐτὸν περιέβαλον,

---

[112]A. Q. R, c, f, vg., syr. cited by Vaganay, ibid., 249.

[113]Cf. ibid., 243-46.

[114]Cf. ibid., 245, in which the author refers to Irenaeus, Ad. Haer. 4.33.12; Tertullian, Adv. Jud. 10; Adv. Marc. 4.42; Cyprian, Testim. 2.23; Eusebius, Dem. evang. 10.6.1; Aphraatus, Hom. 1.11; Cyril of Jerusalem, Cat. 13.25.

[115]I omit those passages which have already been compared with the other gospels, and in which a parallel with the fourth gospel was pointed out.

are so close to Jn. 19:2b, which reads καὶ ἱμάτιον πορφυροῦν περιέβαλον αὐτόν, that a literary dependence is very likely; yet, let me add that Mk. 15:17a includes the word πορφύραν. As for the rest of the sentence, which relates that Christ was made to sit on a judge's bench, it may be a reminiscence of the text of Jn. 19:13. This hypothesis is based on the fact that since Justin relates the same episode in 1 Apol. 35:6 and uses the word βῆμα which is present in Jn. 19:13, he seems to depend on this text and on the grammatically correct possibility of a wrong interpretation of ἐκάθισεν in Jn. 19:13 in the intransitive meaning of "to set on a seat." Instead of understanding Jn. 19:13: "Pilate sat down on the seat," Pseudo-Peter understood it as "Pilate left and put Jesus on the judgment seat."[116]

The sharing of the garments is narrated in Gos. Pet. 12: "And they (the Jews) laid down his garments before him and divided them among themselves and cast the lot upon them (καὶ λαχμὸν ἔβαλον ἐπ' αὐτοῖς)." This feature is read in Mt. 27:35; Mk. 15:24; Lk. 23:34; and Jn. 19:23-24. Ps. 22(21):19 can be added to these texts. Wishing to show the fulfillment of the prophecies in the events of the Passion (verse 17), Pseudo-Peter probably referred here to the text of Ps. 22 (21):19, which inspired the gospels. He may, however, have used the word λαχμός in reminiscence of Jn. 19:24, which used the verb λάχωμεν.[117]

Gos. Pet. 60 reads: "But I, Simon Peter (Σίμων Πέτρος), and my brother (ὁ ἀδελφός μου) Andrew took our nets and went to the sea (θάλασσαν). And there was with us Levi, the son of Alphaeus (ὁ τοῦ 'Αλφαίου), whom the Lord. . . . " This verse closes the Akhmîm fragment; it may have begun the narrative of an appearance of the risen Christ. Jn. 21:1-3 has been mentioned since it opens the narrative with an appearance of Christ to some apostles who are fishing on the lake of Tiberias. Just as in this Johannine text, the subject matter in the apocryphon is a fishing party led by Peter and which takes place on the sea (ἐπὶ τῆς θαλάσσης). Vaganay sees here the most important feature supporting a reference to the fourth gospel.[118] Let me add that the combination of the two words Σίμων Πέτρος appears mostly in Jn.,[119] that the relationship between Simon and Andrew is read in Mt. 4:18 and Mk. 1:16, and that the expression ὁ τοῦ 'Αλφαίου is found in Mk. 2:14.

The literary relationships of the Gospel of Peter are still less numerous with the fourth gospel than with Lk. There is no text in the apocryphon that implies an absolute dependence on Jn. Yet, the few texts I have examined reveal sufficient

---

[116]Cf. Vaganay, *L'Évangile de Pierre*, 72, 156-58, where this hypothesis is developed at length.

[117]Cf. ibid., 239, which points out that this word λαχμός is unusual in classical Greek which uses λαχός, and is quite rare in Hellenistic Greek.

[118]Cf. ibid., 63.

[119]Jn. 1:40; 6:8, 68; 13:6, 9, 24, 36; 18:10, 15, 25; 20:2, 6; 21:2, 3, 7, 11, 15. Mt. points them out in 16:16 and Lk. in 5:8.

literary relationships to allow us to assume that the author of the Gospel of Peter knew the fourth gospel.

D. The Gospel Tradition

This section deals with passages which show an affinity with several of the gospels, but which do not allow us to determine to which one in particular the apocryphon refers. This affinity is attributed to a familiarity with the canonical gospels.

Gos. Pet. 5, "And he (Herod) delivered (παρέδωκεν) him to the people on the day before the unleavened bread, their feast (τῆς ἑορτῆς αὐτῶν)," has parallels in Mt. 27:26b; Mk. 15:15b; Lk. 23:25b; and Jn. 19:16a. They all use the same verb παραδίδωμι to signify that Christ was handed over. I would like to add that Jn. 19:14 and 31 certainly set the crucifixion on the day of the Passover preparation, and that τῆς ἑορτῆς αὐτῶν has a rather Johannine consonance (Jn. 5:1; 6:4; 7:2).

In the scene of the derision of Christ, Gos. Pet. 9 states: "And others who stood by spat (ἐνέπτυον) on his face (ταῖς ὄψεσι), and others buffeted him (τὰς σιαγόνας αὐτοῦ ἐράπισαν) on the cheeks, others nudged him with a reed (καλάμῳ ἔνυσσον αὐτόν), and some scourged him (ἐμάστιζον), saying, 'With such honour let us honour the Son of God.'" In this description of the cruelties imposed upon Christ, certain words are found in the various parallels: Mt. 26:67; 27:26b, 30; Mk. 14:65; 15:15b, 19; Jn. 18:22; 19:1, 3, 34. Thus ἐμπτύω is read in Mt. 26:67; 27:30; Mk. 14:65; 15:19; ῥαπίζω in Mt. 26:67 (Mk. 14:65 and Jn. 18:22; 19:3 have ῥάπισμα); κάλαμος in Mt. 27:30; Mk. 15:19; notice the use of νύσσω, hapax in the New Testament, in Jn. 19:34 in the piercing episode, and the verb μαστιγόω, which is present in Jn. 19:1. We may also wonder together with Vaganay whether, in fact, the author referred implicitly to the prophecy of Is. 50:6 whose fulfillment he wishes to show here. Is. 50:6 has τὸν νῶτόν μου δέδωκα εἰς μάστιγας, τὰς δὲ σιαγόνας μου εἰς ῥαπίσματα, τὸ δὲ πόσωπόν μου οὐκ ἀπέστρεψα ἀπὸ αἰσχύνης ἐμπτυσμάτων. This hypothesis remains valid, especially if we keep in mind that ὄψεις might be a translation, after the manner of Aquila, of the Hebrew פָּנִים, which is found precisely in this passage of Isaiah. In any case it is possible to admit to an undeniable similarity with the gospel tradition, and point out at the same time that the author of the Gospel of Peter may have had in mind the fulfillment of Is. 50:6, certain words of which correspond to the words of the apocryphon, such as μάστιξ, ῥάπισμα, and ἔμπτυσμα.

Gos. Pet. 11: "And when they (the Jews) had set up the cross, they wrote upon it: This is the King of Israel (οὗτός ἐστιν ὁ βασιλεὺς τοῦ Ἰσραήλ)." The inscription on the cross is mentioned in the four gospels: Mt. 27:37; Mk. 15:26; Lk. 23:38; and Jn. 19:19. It is very close to the Matthean form as well as to certain manuscripts of Mk.[120] and of Lk.[121] which have οὗτός ἐστιν ὁ βασιλεὺς τῶν Ἰουδαίων. However, none of the canonical gospels includes the words τοῦ Ἰσραήλ, and various hypotheses have been given by those who have wondered why.[122] Might this substitution come from verse 7, in which a similar expression is found as well? It is no easy task to determine with which of the gospels the author is here in literary contact, since the synoptic texts are quite similar. There might be a slight preference for the Matthean text which has the formula οὗτός ἐστιν, although a similar expression is present as well in the readings of Mk. and Lk.

Among the extraordinary events which followed the death of Christ, Gos. Pet. 20 mentions the rending of the veil in the temple: "And at the same hour (αὐτῆς ὥρας) the veil of the temple in Jerusalem was rent in two (τὸ καταπέτασμα τοῦ ναοῦ." This feature is related in Mt. 27:51; Mk. 15:38; and Lk. 23:45b in practically identical words. In Lk., it is linked with the coming of darkness; in Mt. and Mk., it is related more directly to the death of Christ. Pseudo-Peter also relates this event to the death of Christ with the words αὐτῆς ὥρας. Given the similarity of the texts of the Gospel of Peter and Mt. and Mk., it is impossible to decide with which of these two gospels there is a literary contact.

The burial of Christ is described in Gos. Pet. 23-24: "And the Jews . . . gave his body to Joseph (δεδώκασι τῷ Ἰωσὴφ τὸ σῶμα αὐτοῦ) that he might bury it, since he had seen all the good that he (Jesus) had done. And he took (λαβὼν) the Lord, washed him, wrapped him in linen (εἴλησε σινδόνι) and brought him in his own sepulchre, called Joseph's Garden (κῆπον)." Mt. 27:58-60; Mk. 15:45-46; Lk. 23:53; and Jn. 19:39-41 relate this burial of Jesus. In the narrative of Pseudo-Peter, some elements are added to the canonical narratives: Joseph of Arimathea washes the body before burying it, and the tomb was known by the name "Joseph's Garden." The apocryphon does not follow the narrative of one specific gospel. Verse 23 seems to recall Joseph's approach in his inquiry with Pilate, although the Jews are the ones who return the body of Christ. Let me point out the verb δίδωμι, which has its counterpart only in Mt. with the composite verb ἀποδίδωμι. The participle λαβὼν recalls that in Mt. 27:59, whereas εἴλησε σινδόνι leads us to Mk. 15:46, and the mention of the "Garden" (κῆπος) is found only in Jn. 19:41. Note that the word τάφος is, in this context, found only in Mt.[123] It follows then that the author does not depend on a specific gospel in particular for this entire passage. He follows rather the gospel tradition, which he embellishes with picturesque details in the manner of the apocryphal gospels.

---

[120]Cf. D, r, syr. sin. and pesh.
[121]According to Vaganay, *L'Évangile de Pierre*, 238: A, Q, R, . . . b, f, q, . . . syrᶜ.
[122]Cf. ibid., 238.
[123]Cf. Mt. 27:61, 64, 66; 28:1.

Gos. Pet. 26-27 states,

But I mourned (ἐλυπούμην) with my fellows (τῶν ἑταίρων), and being wounded in heart we hid ourselves (ἐκρυβόμεθα), for we were sought after by them (the Jews) as evildoers and as persons who wanted to set fire to the temple. Because of all these things we were fasting (ἐνηστεύομεν) and sat mourning and weeping (πενθοῦντες καὶ κλαίοντες), night and day until the Sabbath.

The parallels usually mentioned are Mt. 9:14-15; Mk. 2:18-20; Lk. 5:33-35; and Jn. 16:20; 20:19, 26. This is the first time that there appears the pseudonymous author who, if we turn to verse 60, presented himself in the lost part of the apocryphon as the apostle Peter. The behavior of the apostles, as it is described here, is found in none of the gospels, but simple parallels may be drawn with different gospel passages. Thus ἑταῖρος is found in the New Testament only in Mt. 20:13; 22:12; 26:50; and in some manuscripts in 11:16.[124] The verb ἐλυπούμην, particularly if it is linked with verse 23 where the Jews rejoiced (ἐχάρησαν δὲ οἱ Ἰουδαῖοι), may lead us to the prophecy of Christ in Jn. 16:20: ὁ δὲ κόσμος χαρήσεται· ὑμεῖς λυπηθήσεσθε.[125] The verb ἐκρυβόμεθα recalls Jn. 20:19, 26, which describes the apostles living together behind closed doors. Peter and his companions were fasting: Christ had prescribed fasting (Mt. 6:16-18), and had announced that his disciples would fast when the bridegroom would be taken away from them (Mt. 9:14-15; Mk. 2:18-20; Lk. 5:33-35). The apostles' grief after the Passion is described with the participles πενθοῦντες καὶ κλαίοντες, which recall vividly those of Mk. 16:10: πενθοῦσιν καὶ κλαίουσιν.[126]

Gos. Pet. 50-51:

Early in the morning (ὄρθρου) of the Lord's day Mary of Magdala, a woman disciple of the Lord—for fear of the Jews, since (they) were inflamed with wrath, she had not done at the sepulchre of the Lord what women are wont to do for those beloved of them who die—took with her her women friends (τὰς φίλας) and came to the sepulchre (ἦλθε ἐπὶ τὸ μνημεῖον) where he was laid.

This episode finds its parallel in Mt. 28:1; Mk. 16:1-2; Lk. 24:1, 10; and Jn. 20:1. The apocryphon adds details which are not present in the canonical gospels; yet, let me nevertheless point out the word ὄρθρου, which is present in Lk. 24:1; the

---

[124]G, al., vg., syr.

[125]Cf. Vaganay, *L'Évangile de Pierre*, 272.

[126]Cf. ibid., 52, where the author notes, "Although this is a common formula (2 Kings 19:1; Neh. 1:4; 8:9; Mk. 16:10; Lk. 6:25; Jas. 4:9; Rev. 18:11, 15 ff.; Oxyrh. Papyri, 3.528, 9), to find it here is no less curious, all the more so since the same thought is developed again, in a different form, in v. 59: ἐκλαίομεν καὶ ἐλυπούμεθα."

words τὰς φίλας, which in the entire New Testament are read only in Lk. 15:9 in the parable of the lost drachma; and the expression ἦλθε ἐπὶ τὸ μνημεῖον, which is to be linked with Jn. 20:1, ἔρχεται . . . εἰς τὸ μνημεῖον, and Mk. 16:1, ἔρχονταιν ἐπὶ τὸ μνῆμα.

In summary, the following conclusions emerge: first of all, the literary parallels between the Gospel of Peter and the first gospel are much more numerous than with Mk., Lk. and Jn; some texts of the apocryphon can be explained only by a literary dependence on Mt. The other gospels, in varying degrees, have also had a literary influence on Pseudo-Peter. The resemblances of the Gospel of Peter with the canonical gospels are too characteristic to come from the oral tradition which preceded the gospels; these resemblances presuppose existing texts, or at least a tradition based on the gospel texts.

Yet, the author of the apocryphal gospel shows a very personal tendency. Like all authors of apocryphal writings, he does not refrain from changing certain texts and adding details which are missing in the canonical narratives. I often remarked as well that, in a particular verse which seems to be literarily dependent on a specific gospel, we found vague recollections of other gospels, to such an extent that scholars have wondered whether the author followed a harmony of the gospels, namely the *Diatessaron*. [127] Vaganay has demonstrated that the different ways in which the *Diatessaron* and the Gospel of Peter grouped the facts opposes this hypothesis. [128] The fact that the apocryphon adds some features to the canonical narratives and drops others which are just as essential argues against the hypothesis which makes of Pseudo-Peter a harmonizer of the gospels. Likewise, the considerable freedom he uses with those texts that he borrows holds in check the idea that he might be a compiler.

The analysis of the texts leaves us rather with the impression that, first of all, the author of the Gospel of Peter creates a Passion Narrative which suits his anti-Jewish and slightly docetic concerns. Secondly, we are left with the feeling that he does not necessarily use a specific text, but that he rather builds a narrative which is inspired by the gospels, a bit like someone today who sets out to retell the events of the Passion: assembling details, borrowing each feature from various gospels without being able to determine from which gospel such a feature comes; yet, this reconstructed narrative is still influenced by the written texts. Such a hypothesis explains simultaneously both the definite literary relationships and the differences between the texts and the combinations of various texts which belong to different

---

[127]Cf. H. B. Swete, *The Apocryphal Gospel of Peter. The Greek Text of the Newly Discovered Fragment*, 2nd ed. (London, 1893) xx-xxv; F. H. Chase, "Peter (Simon), The Gospel of Peter," in *A Dictionary of the Bible (Hastings)*, 3:776; J. G. Tasker, "Apocryphal Gospels, Peter (Gospel According to)," in *A Dictionary of the Bible (Hastings)*, extra vol., 427-28.

[128]Cf. Vaganay, *L'Évangile de Pierre*, 75-77.

gospels.

It is probable that in early Christianity the story of the passion had been told many times. The author of the Gospel of Peter may possibly have been inspired by one of these narratives, but if that is so, then we must acknowledge that this narrative, which may be traditional, must have been built on the canonical gospels. In any hypothesis, given its large number of literary references to Mt., the Gospel of Peter demonstrates the leading role of the Gospel of Matthew in Christian thought.

Section 6
THE GOSPEL OF MATTHIAS

Origen already mentioned this apocryphal gospel.[129] Eusebius considered it heretical.[130] This work seems to be integral to the Traditions of Matthias, Παραδόσεις Ματθίου, which Clement of Alexandria quoted many times,[131] and which was used by the Gnostics of the School of Basilides.[132] It seems to have stemmed from Egypt, perhaps Alexandria, where it likely appeared in the first half of the second century.[133] Actually lost, this work is known only from a very few fragments which Clement of Alexandria relates to us.[134] I shall deal with only one of the preserved fragments, because it alone shows literary relationships with a text of the New Testament; nevertheless, scholars are not certain that it belongs to the Gospel of Matthias.

Clement of Alexandria, Strom. 4.6.35

> Ζακχαῖον τοίνυν, οἱ δὲ Ματθίαν φασίν, ἀρχιτελώνην ἀκηκοότα τοῦ κυρίου καταξιώσαντος πρὸς αὐτὸν γενέσθαι· Ἰδοὺ τὰ ἡμίση τῶν ὑπαρχόντων μου δίδωμι ἐλεημοσύνην (φάναι) κύριε· καὶ εἴ τινος τι ἐσυκοφάντησα, τετραπλοῦν ἀποδίδωμι. ἐφ᾽ οὗ καὶ ὁ σωτὴρ εἶπεν· Ὁ υἱὸς τοῦ ἀνθρώπου ἐλθὼν σήμερον τὸ ἀπολωλὸς εὗρεν.

> Zacchaeus then (but some say Matthias), a chief tax gatherer, when he heard that the Lord has seen fit to be with him, (said) "Behold, the half of my goods

---

[129]Cf. Origen, Hom. 1 in Lk.

[130]Cf. Eusebius, Hist. Eccl. 3.25.6-7.

[131]Cf. Clement of Alexandria, Strom. 2.9.45; 7.13.82.

[132]Cf. ibid., 7.17.8.

[133]Cf. Altaner, *Patrology*, 71.

[134]I follow the edition of E. Klostermann, *Apocrypha* 2, *Evangelien*, KIT 8, 3rd ed. (Berlin, 1929) 16-18. See also E. Preuschen, *Antilegomena*, 13-14. [The text followed in the English translation is that of Edgar Hennecke, *New Testament Apocrypha*, ed. Wilhelm Schneemelcher, ET ed. R. McL. Wilson (Philadelphia: Westminster Press, 1963) 1:308-13. Editor's note.]

I give in alms, O Lord; and if I have extorted anything from any man, I restore it fourfold.'' Whereupon the Saviour also said ''The Son of Man is come today, and has found that which was lost.''

The parallel which comes readily to mind is Lk. 19:8-10:

Σταθεὶς δὲ Ζακχαῖος εἶπεν πρὸς τὸν κύριον· ἰδοὺ τὰ ἡμίση μου τῶν ὑπαρχόντων, κύριε, τοῖς πτωχοῖς δίδωμι, καὶ εἴ τινός τι ἐσυκοφάντησα, ἀποδίδωμι τετραπλοῦν. εἶπεν δὲ πρὸς αὐτὸν ὁ Ἰησοῦς ὅτι σήμερον σωτηρία τῷ οἴκῳ τούτῳ ἐγένετο, καθότι καὶ αὐτὸς υἱὸς Ἀβραάμ [ἐστιν]· ἦλθεν γὰρ ὁ υἱὸς τοῦ ἀνθρώπου ζητῆσαι καὶ σῶσαι τὸ ἀπολωλός.

And Zacchaeus stood and said to the Lord, ''Behold, Lord, the half of my goods I give to the poor; and if I have defrauded any one of anything, I restore it fourfold.'' And Jesus said to him, ''Today salvation has come to this house, since he also is a son of Abraham. For the Son of Man came to seek and to save the lost.''
[The English translation has been added by the editor.]

The great similarity between the text in the Gospel of Matthias and that in Lk., combined with the fact that this episode is peculiar to Lk., can be explained only by a literary dependence on Lk. In fact, Zacchaeus' spoken words in the apocryphon are almost literally identical to those in Lk. The author of the apocryphal gospel has simply dropped μου after τὰ ἡμίση and τοῖς πτωχοῖς and replaced it with ἐλεημοσύνην. As for the Lord's answer, he shortened it and slightly changed it, but the words ἔρχομαι, ὁ υἱὸς τοῦ ἀνθρώπου, σήμερον, and τὸ ἀπολωλός, which we find there, are sufficient to establish a literary dependence on Lk. for the answer of Christ.

The fragments of the Gospel of Matthias provide nothing new regarding the literary influence of Matthew, which is the focus of this study. The fragment which I have quoted with reservation reveals a literary affinity with Lk.

Section 7
THE PROTEVANGELIUM OF JAMES[135]

Hilgenfeld had already acknowledged in 1850 that this work was put together from pieces that had been rather awkwardly juxtaposed.[136] The first part goes from 28:2 to 29:1, which Harnack called an *Apocryphum Josephi*, in which Joseph speaks in the first person; the second part from chapters 21 to 24 is called the *Apocryphum Zachariae*; and the last part consists of the first sixteen chapters whose

---

[135]For the text of the Protevangelium of James, I follow the edition of C. Michel, *Protévangile de Jacques, Pseudo-Matthieu, Évangile de Thomas*, Textes et Documents, Évan-

title Γέννησις Μαρίας[137] is appropriate for the entire work. As for the composition of these three parts, I adopt Harnack's judgment: the Γέννησις Μαρίας dates from the end of the second century, the *Apocryphum Josephi* goes back to the second century, and the *Apocryphum Zachariae*, in the form in which it appears in the Protevangelium of James, is later than the second century,[138] and according to P. Peeters, somewhat before the sixth century.[139] Since this *Apocryphum Zachariae* appeared later, it presents no interest for this inquiry.

I propose as usual to devote a first paragraph to Saint Matthew, saving the second for the other New Testament writings.

§1. Saint Matthew

Several passages of the Protevangelium of James presuppose a literary influence from the first gospel.

1. Prot. Jas. 11:3

καὶ καλέσεις τὸ ὄνομα αὐτοῦ ᾿Ιησοῦν· αὐτὸς γὰρ σώσει τὸν λαὸν αὐτοῦ ἀπὸ τῶν ἁμαρτιῶν αὐτῶν.

And you shall call his name Jesus; for he shall save his people from their sins.

In the Annunciation narrative—I shall substantiate it later[140]—the Protevangelium of James follows the narrative in Lk.; suddenly, we are faced here with a text, part of which is read in Lk. 1:31: καὶ καλέσεις τὸ ὄνομα αὐτοῦ ᾿Ιησοῦν, but which Mt. 1:21 gives in its entirety: καὶ καλέσεις τὸ ὄνομα αὐτοῦ ᾿Ιησοῦν· αὐτὸς γὰρ σώσει τὸν λαὸν αὐτοῦ ἀπὸ τῶν ἁμαρτιῶν αὐτῶν.

The correspondence with the Matthean text is literal. I doubt, however, that the entire passage of the apocryphon comes from Mt., because the words "you shall call his name Jesus" are addressed in Mt., not to the Virgin, but to Joseph, whereas in Lk., it is the Virgin who hears them from the angel's mouth. Yet, it is quite possible that the author, following as a whole the Annunciation narrative of

---

giles apocryphes 1, 2nd ed. (Paris, 1924). See also G. Rauschen, *Monumenta minora saeculi secundi*, Florilegium Patristicum 3 (Bonn, 1914) 57-84. [The text followed in the English translation is that of Edgar Hennecke, *New Testament Apocrypha*, ed. Wilhelm Schneemelcher, ET ed. R. McL. Wilson (Philadelphia: Westminster Press, 1963) 1:370-74. Editor's note.]

[136]Cf. A. Hilgenfeld, *Kritische Untersuchungen* (Leipzig, 1850) 154.

[137]Cf. C. Michel, *Protévangile de Jacques*, viii-xi.

[138]Cf. A. Harnack, *Die Chronologie der altchristlichen Literatur bis Eusebius*, 1 (Leipzig, 1897) 600ff.

[139]Cf. Michel, *Protévangile de Jacques*, xvii.

[140]Cf. below, 233-34.

Lk., still borrowed the first words of its text; but when he came to the name Ἰησοῦς, he felt the need to explain this name and resorted to the explanation given by Mt., unique in the New Testament. This hypothesis is all the easier to acknowledge inasmuch as the words καὶ καλέσεις τὸ ὄνομα αὐτοῦ Ἰησοῦν link it to Mt.

A literary contact with the Matthean text is compelling; it is confirmed by the fact that in 14:2, as we shall see, the author resorts again to this explanation of the name of Jesus, and definitely depends in that instance on the Matthean text.

2. Prot. Jas. 14:1

φοβοῦμαι μήπως ἀγγελικόν ἐστιν τὸ ἐν αὐτῇ, καὶ εὑρεθήσομαι παραδιδοὺς αἷμα ἀθῷον εἰς κρίμα θανάτου. Τί οὖν αὐτὴν ποιήσω; λάθρα αὐτὴν ἀπολύσω ἀπ' ἐμοῦ.

I fear lest that which is in her may have sprung from the angels and I should be found delivering up innocent blood to the judgment of death. What then shall I do with her? I will put her away secretly.

The expression παραδιδοὺς αἷμα ἀθῷον recalls Judas's confession as he returns the money to the chief priests and to the elders in Mt. 27:4: ἥμαρτον παραδοὺς αἷμα ἀθῷον. In the Protevangelium of James, these words are read in a totally different context; yet their actual identity with the words in Mt., which are without parallel in the New Testament, suggest a literary reminiscence of the Matthean text.

The last phrase of the passage (λάθρα αὐτὴν ἀπολύσω ἀπ' ἐμοῦ) has a parallel only in Mt. 1:19. The Protevangelium of James depends on it, simply transposing the sentence in Mt. into direct discourse: ἐβουλήθη λάθρα ἀπολῦσαι αὐτήν.

3. Prot. Jas. 14:2

Καὶ ἰδοὺ ἄγγελος κυρίου φαίνεται αὐτῷ κατ' ὄναρ λέγων· Μὴ φοβηθῇς τὴν παῖδα ταύτην· τὸ γὰρ ἐν αὐτῇ ὂν ἐκ πνεύματός ἐστιν ἁγίου· τέξεται δὲ υἱόν, καὶ καλέσεις τὸ ὄνομα αὐτοῦ Ἰησοῦν· αὐτὸς γὰρ σώσει τὸν λαὸν αὐτοῦ ἀπὸ τῶν ἁμαρτιῶν αὐτῶν. Καὶ ἀνέστη Ἰωσὴφ ἀπὸ τοῦ ὕπνου καὶ ἐδόξασεν τὸν θεὸν Ἰσραὴλ τὸν δόντα αὐτῷ τὴν χάριν ταύτην, καὶ ἐφύλασσεν αὐτήν.

And behold, an angel of the Lord appeared to him in a dream, saying, "Do not fear because of this child. For that which is in her is of the Holy Spirit. She shall bear a son, and you shall call his name Jesus; for he shall save his people from their sins." And Joseph arose from sleep and glorified the God of Israel who had bestowed his grace upon him, and he watched over her.

The author used Mt. 1:20-24, dropping verses 22-23, which relate a prophecy from the Old Testament. Mt. is the only one to record this dialogue between the angel and Joseph. As the author of the Protevangelium arranges it in his own way, he picks up many passages literally, leaving no doubt concerning the source from which he draws, such as ἰδοὺ ἄγγελος κυρίου κατ' ὄναρ ἐφάνη αὐτῷ λέγων· . . . μὴ φοβηθῇς . . . τὸ γὰρ ἐν αὐτῇ γεννηθὲν ἐκ πνεύματός ἐστιν ἁγίου. τέξεται δὲ υἱόν, καὶ καλέσεις τὸ ὄνομα αὐτοῦ Ἰησοῦν· αὐτὸς γὰρ σώσει τὸν λαὸν αὐτοῦ ἀπὸ τῶν ἁμαρτιῶν αὐτῶν. . . . Ἰωσὴφ ἀπὸ τοῦ ὕπνου.

4. Prot. Jas. 21:1–22:1

And behold, Joseph prepared to go forth to Judaea. And there took place a great tumult in Bethlehem of Judaea. For there came wise men (μάγοι) saying (λέγοντες), ''Where is the [new-born] king of the Jews? For we have seen his star in the east and have come to worship him (ποῦ ἐστιν ὁ τεχθεὶς βασιλεὺς τῶν Ἰουδαίων; εἴδομεν γὰρ αὐτοῦ τὸν ἀστέρα ἐν τῇ ἀνατολῇ καὶ ἤλθομεν προσκυνῆσαι αὐτόν).'' When Herod heard this he was troubled (ἀκούσας Ἡρώδης ἐταράχθη) and sent officers [to the wise men, and sent for the high priests (τοὺς ἀρχιερεῖς) and questioned them, ''How is it written concerning the Messiah (Χριστοῦ)? Where is he born (ποῦ γεννᾶται)?'' They said to him, ''In Bethlehem of Judaea; for so it is written (λέγουσιν αὐτῷ· ἐν Βηθλεὲμ τῆς Ἰουδαίας· οὕτως γὰρ γέγραπται).'' And he let them go. And he questioned the wise men (τοὺς μάγους) and said to them, ''What sign did you see concerning the newborn king?'' And the wise men said, ''We saw how an indescribably greater star shone among these stars and dimmed them, so that they no longer shone; and so we knew that a king was born for Israel. And we have come to worship him.'' And Herod said (εἶπεν), ''Go and seek (ζητήσατε), and when you have found him, tell me, that I also may come to worship him (καὶ ἐὰν εὕρητε, ἀπαγγείλατέ μοι, ὅπως κἀγὼ ἐλθὼν προσκυνήσω αὐτόν).'' And the wise men went forth. And behold, the star which they had seen in the east, went before them (καὶ ἰδοὺ ὃν εἶδον ἀστέρα ἐν τῇ ἀνατολῇ προῆγεν αὐτούς),] until they came to the cave. And it stood over the head of the child [the cave]. And the wise men saw the young child with Mary his mother (εἶδον τὸ παιδίον μετὰ τῆς μητρὸς αὐτοῦ Μαρίαμ), and they took out of their bag gifts (δῶρα), gold, and frankincense and myrrh (χρυσὸν καὶ λίβανον καὶ σμύρναν). And being warned (χρηματισθέντες) by the angel that they should not go into Judaea, they went to their own country by another way (δι' ἄλλης ὁδοῦ ἐπορεύθησαν εἰς τὴν χώραν αὐτῶν). But when Herod perceived that he had been tricked by the wise men (Ἡρώδης ὅτι ἐνεπαίχθη ὑπὸ μάγων) he was angry and sent his murderers and commanded them to kill all the children who were two years old and under (ἀπὸ διετοῦς καὶ κατωτέρω).

This pericope shows a definite literary contact with Mt. 2:1-5, 7-9, 11-12, and 16; I have placed between parentheses all the Greek passages from the Protevangelium of James that are found in Mt.

The author has taken his narrative from Mt. He does not reproduce the Matthean text as such, but he works it over, developing particularly the wonderful feature of the star. Let me add, however, that since this pericope belongs to the part called the *Apocryphum Zachariae,* it is quite probably later than the second century, if not even later.

I would also like to point out that the Protevangelium of James in 23:3 relates the death of Zacharias in the forecourt of the temple of the Lord (εἰς τὰ πρόθυρα τοῦ ναοῦ κυρίου). Mt. 23:35 is the only one to allude to this event; the author may have drawn from this passage of Mt. to compose his text. This passage also belongs to the *Apocryphum Zachariae.*

Finally, let me mention that in Prot. Jas. 10:1, the veil of the temple is designated by the term καταπέτασμα, which is read in the three synoptics: Mt. 27:51; Mk. 15:38; and Lk. 23:45.

In conclusion, it can be stated with certainty that the author of the Protevangelium of James not only knows the Gospel of Mt. but also uses it, borrowing literally certain passages from it, particularly in the infancy narratives.

§2. The Other New Testament Writings

Among the other New Testament writings which have influenced the Protevangelium of James, only the Gospel of Lk., in actual fact, is worth mentioning. This is why I shall first consider the Gospel of Lk., and I shall then group the few texts that have some affinity with the New Testament writings, other than Mt. and Lk.

A. The Gospel of Luke

The passages in the Protevangelium of James which are literarily influenced by Lk. are fairly numerous; they are influenced mostly by its infancy narrative. In general, the author of the apocryphon uses Lk.'s texts in various ways. Sometimes in pericopes in which his narrative is consistent with the canonical narrative he cites Luke almost literally; sometimes in passages added to the Lucan narrative, he develops an idea borrowed from Lk., using its terms and expressions, applying casually Lk.'s sentences to persons other than those referred to in the gospel. Neither does he refrain from enhancing the marvellous nor from changing certain circumstances known in the gospel narrative. In short, he builds a new infancy gospel with the help of material taken from the canonical gospels.

Prot. Jas. 4:1. And behold an angel (ἄγγελος) of the Lord came to her and said, "Anna, Anna, the Lord has heard your prayer (τῆς δεήσεώς σου). You shall conceive and bear (γεννήσεις), and your offspring shall be spoken of in the whole world."

This text is sometimes linked to Lk. 1:13. In the third gospel, the angel's words are addressed to Zechariah and not to Anna and have in mind Elizabeth who will conceive, but not Anna. Yet the author, fabricating this passage all the way through, goes so far as to apply to Anna the angel's words: the words ἄγγελος, ἡ δεήσις σου, and γαννάω lead us to this belief.[141]

> Prot. Jas. 4:2. . . . for an angel (ἄγγελος) of the Lord came down to him and said to him: "Joachim, Joachim, the Lord God has heard your prayer (τῆς δεήσεώς σου). Go down; behold (ἰδού), your wife Anna has conceived [shall conceive] (ἐν γαστὶ λήψεται)."

Lk. 1:13 may have inspired the author. Although the angel's words are addressed to Joachim and not to Zechariah as in Lk., the mention of the angel and the term ἡ δεήσις are found in both cases. In the same vein, the author may have thought of Lk. 1:13 and used it for the angel's words to Joachim, for in that instance the words ἰδού and συλλήμψη ἐν γαστρί are the same. This represents a new method for the author.

> Prot. Jas. 5:1. "Now I know that the Lord God is gracious to me (ἱλάσθη μοι) and has forgiven all my sins (τὰ ἁμαρτήματά μου)." And he went down from the temple of the Lord justified (κατέβη δεδικαιωμένος), and went to his house (ἐν τῷ οἴκῳ αὐτοῦ).

Scholars have thought here of the parable of the publican in Lk. 18:13-14. Given the freedom with which the author of the apocryphon uses the texts of Lk. for narrating events which are peculiar to him, and given the fact of the similarity of the words ἱλάσθητί μοι τῷ ἁμαρτωλῷ, κατέβη δεδικαιωμένος, and εἰς τὸν οἶκον αὐτοῦ, we are justified in concluding that there is a literary dependence.

> Prot. Jas. 5:2. And Anna said, "My soul is magnified (ἐμεγαλύνθη ἡ ψυχή μου) this day."

Anna's words echo the first words of the Magnificat of the Virgin in Lk. 1:46: Μεγαλύνει ἡ ψυχή μου τὸν κύριον. A literary dependence is very probable, given the ease with which the author of the apocryphon, in the parts which are peculiar to him, uses the Gospel of Lk.

> Prot. Jas. 6:3. And Anna sang this song to the Lord God: "I will sing praises to the Lord my God, / for he has visited me and taken away from me the reproach (ἀφείλατο ἀπ' ἐμοῦ τὸ ὄνειδος) of my enemies."

---

[141]Chaps. 2 and 4 of the Protevangelium of James are sometimes linked to 1 Sam. 1 and 2:1, in which is read the story of Elkanah and his wife Hannah; a very general similarity is to be kept in mind.

These words recall Elizabeth's words in Lk. 1:25: ὅτι οὕτως μοι πεποίηκεν κύριος ἐν ἡμέραις αἷς ἐπεῖδεν ἀφελεῖν ὄνειδός μου ἐν ἀνθρώποις. Most likely, there again, the author of the Protevangelium of James is inspired by the Lucan text. The presence of the expression ἀφαιρέω τὸ ὄνειδος, inserted in a sentence whose meaning is similar to that of Lk., suggests it.

Prot. Jas. 10:2. At that time, Zacharias became dumb (ἐσίγησεν Ζαχαρίας).

These words are a vague recollection of the dumbness of Zechariah mentioned in Lk. 1:20-22.

It is especially in the annunciation narrative itself that the Protevangelium of James depends most clearly and indubitably on the Gospel of Lk.

Prot. Jas. 11:1. And she (Mary) took the pitcher and went forth to draw water, and behold, a voice said, "Hail, thou that art highly favoured, [the Lord is with thee, blessed art thou] among women (χαῖρε κεχαριτωμένη, ὁ κύριος μετὰ σοῦ, εὐλογημένη σὺ ἐν γυναιξίν)."

Reading these words, Lk. 1:28, 42 comes readily to mind; the coincidence is literal. But the apocryphon organizes the annunciation narrative its own way, multiplying the marvellous and adding, in particular, an interview between the Virgin and the angel near a fountain. It may not even be necessary to refer to Lk. 1:42, since certain witnesses of Lk. 1:28 use the same sentence that is read in the Protevangelium of James.[142]

Prot. Jas. 11:2-3. And behold, an angel of the Lord (suddenly) stood before her and said, "Do not fear, Mary; for you have found grace before the Lord of all things and shall conceive of his Word." When she heard this she doubted in herself and said, "Shall I conceive of the Lord, the living God, [and bear] as every woman bears?" And the angel of the Lord said, "Not so, Mary; for a power of the Lord shall overshadow you; Wherefore also that holy thing which is born of you shall be called the Son of the Highest. And you shall call his name Jesus; for he shall save his people from their sins." And Mary said, "Behold, (I am) the handmaid of the Lord before him: be it to me according to your word."

Once again, a series of texts in Lk. call for attention: Lk. 1:30, 31, 35, 38.[143] The author takes up the text of Lk., changes it slightly, and, in line with the tendency towards the marvellous in the apocryphal gospels, he develops the most

---

[142]Note that D, C, E, F, G, H, Θ, several minuscules, the Vulgate, and the old Syriac version have in verse 28 the entire phrase with εὐλογημένη.

[143]See what was mentioned above, on 229, regarding the part devoted to Mt. on Prot. Jas. 11.3.

striking elements of the Lucan narrative, namely how Mary expresses her astonishment in 11:2 when she learns that she will give birth to a child. Except for this
passage, the rest of the narrative is found almost literally in Lk.

> Prot. Jas. 12:1. And the priest . . . blessed Mary and said, "Mary, the Lord
> God has magnified your name, and you shall be blessed among all genera-
> tions on the earth (καὶ ἔσῃ εὐλογημένη ἐν πάσαις ταῖς γενεαῖς τῆς
> γῆς)."

The last words are probably fabricated with the help of vague recollections of
the salutation of Elizabeth in Lk. 1:42, in which we find the word εὐλογημένη,
and of the Magnificat in Lk. 1:48, in which we find the expression πᾶσαι αἱ γενεαί.

> Prot. Jas. 12:2. And Mary rejoiced, and went to Elizabeth her kinswoman
> ('Ελισάβετ τὴν συγγενίδα αὐτῆς), . . .

With this sentence, the author of the Protevangelium of James alludes to the
event narrated in Lk. 1:39-40. Moreover, in Lk. 1:36, we learn in the course of
the annunciation narrative that Elizabeth is Mary's kinswoman: καὶ ἰδού, says
the angel to the Virgin, 'Ελισάβετ ἡ συγγενίς σου. . . . The author has condensed the two verses of Lk. into a single sentence.

> Prot. Jas. 12:2. . . . [and when she (Elizabeth) saw Mary], she blessed her
> and said, "Whence is this to me, that the mother of my Lord should come to
> me (πόθεν μοι τοῦτο ἵνα ἔλθῃ ἡ μήτηρ τοῦ κυρίου μου πρός με)? For
> behold (ἰδοὺ γάρ), that which is in me leaped (ἐσκίρτησεν) and blessed
> thee."

This passage takes up literally the words ἰδοὺ γάρ and ἐσκίρτησεν from Lk.
1:43 and Lk. 1:44.

> Prot. Jas. 12:2. . . . and (Mary) raised a sigh towards heaven and said, "Who
> am I, Lord, that all the women [generations] of the earth count me blessed
> (ὅτι πᾶσαι αἱ γενεαὶ τῆς γῆς εὐλογοῦσίν με)?"

The presence of the verb εὐλογέω and of the words πᾶσαι αἱ γενεαί recall
Lk. 1:42 and 1:48, as noticed above regarding 12:1.

> Prot. Jas. 12:3. And she (Mary) remained three months with Elizabeth.

The author refers most likely to Lk. 1:56, in which it is mentioned that Mary
stayed three months with Elizabeth.

> Prot. Jas. 12:3. Day by day her womb grew, and Mary was afraid and went
> into her house and hid herself (καὶ ἔκρυβεν ἑαυτήν) from the children of

Israel.

Lk. 1:24 mentions that Elizabeth hid (περιέκρυβεν), but not Mary. The verb κρύπτω suggests a reference to Lk.; the author again draws freely from Lk. and does not hesitate to apply to the Virgin what the gospel said of Elizabeth.

Prot. Jas. 13:3. But she (Mary) wept bitterly, saying, "I am pure, and know not a man (καὶ ἄνδρα οὐ γινώσκω)."

Lk. 1:34 is the only possible parallel: εἶπεν δὲ Μαριὰμ πρὸς τὸν ἄγγελον· πῶς ἔσται τοῦτο, ἐπεὶ ἄνδρα οὐ γινώσκω. It includes the phrase ἄνδρα οὐ γινώσκω. Although in the Protevangelium of James, Mary addresses Joseph and not the angel, the expression ἄνδρα οὐ γινώσκω is borrowed from Lk. Here again, we touch on the author's operating process: he draws from Lk.'s texts., and he uses them freely to fabricate the parts of his narrative which are peculiar to him.

Prot. Jas. 17:1. Now there went out (ἐγένετο) a decree from the king Augustus (κέλευσις ἀπὸ Αὐγούστου βασιλέως) that all (inhabitants) of Bethlehem in Judaea (πάντας τοὺς ἐν Βηθλεὲμ τῆς Ἰουδαίας) should be enrolled (ἀπογράφεσθαι).

The presence of the words ἐγένετο, Αὐγούστου, and ἀπογάφεσθαι in Lk. 2:1 is enough to acknowledge that the author drew from the text of the third gospel. But once again, he transformed the canonical narrative according to his own purpose and preoccupations; this is demonstrated with the use of κέλευσις ἀπὸ . . . βασιλέως instead of δόγμα παρὰ Καίσαρος, and the words πάντας τοὺς ἐν βηθλεὲμ τῆς Ἰουδαίας instead of πᾶσαν τὴν οἰκουμένην.

Prot. Jas. 19:2. And the midwife said, "My soul is magnified today, for my eyes have seen wonderful things (ὅτι εἶδον οἱ ὀφθαλμοί μου παράδοξα); for salvation (σωτηρία) is born to Israel."

These words echo old Simeon's canticle in Lk. 2:30: ὅτι εἶδον οἱ ὀφθαλμοί μου τὸ σωτήριόν σου. Let me emphasize again the author's freedom: he transposes onto the midwife the words that Lk. put into old Simeon's mouth.

Prot. Jas. 20:4. And Salome was healed as she had requested, and she went out of the cave [justified] (δεδικαιωμένη).

Given that I mentioned above[144] the definite influence of Lk. 18:14 on a passage from the Protevangelium of James, it is all the more believable that the author probably alluded to it once more, inasmuch as the participle δεδικαιωμένη recalls δεδικαιωμένος in Lk.

---

[144]Cf. above, 232.

Both texts which follow belong to the *Apocryphum Zacchariae* whose late date was mentioned above.

Prot. Jas. 22:2. When Mary heard that the children were to be killed, she was afraid and took the child and wrapped him in swaddling clothes (ἐσπαρ-γάνωσεν) and laid him in an ox manger (ἐν φάτνῃ).

The narrative of this episode does not correspond to Lk.'s narrative. Indeed, it is not because of Herod's decree to massacre children less than two years old, but it is rather after the birth of Jesus that the Virgin wrapped him in swaddling clothes and laid him in a manger. Here is what Lk. 2:7 tells us: καὶ ἔτεκεν τὸν υἱὸν αὐτῆς τὸν πρωτότοκον, καὶ ἐσπαργάνωσεν αὐτὸν καὶ ἀνέκλινεν αὐτὸν ἐν φάτνῃ. The presence of the words ἐσπαργάνωσεν and ἐν φάτνῃ speak in favor of a literary dependence on Lk.; the author of the Protevangelium of James simply transforms the texts according to the marvelous concept he has of the birth of Christ.

Prot. Jas. 24:1. And the priests stood waiting for Zacharias (προσδοκῶντες τὸν Ζαχαρίαν), to greet him with prayer and to glorify the Most High.

Scholars have sometimes thought of Lk. 1:21, which mentions that people were waiting for Zechariah (προσδοκῶν τὸν Ζαχαρίαν). Although the context speaks of different events—the Protevangelium of James narrates the episode of Zechariah's death, Lk. narrates what happened when the birth of John the Baptist was announced—the author, according to his method, probably borrowed this expression from the Gospel of Lk.

B. The New Testament Writings Other Than Matthew and Luke

Not the slightest trace of a literary influence of the Gospel of Mk. is found in the Protevangelium of James.

Two texts have been related to the fourth gospel. The first is 16:3: "And the high priest said, 'If the Lord God has not made manifest your sins (Mary and Joseph), neither do I condemn you (οὐδὲ ἐγὼ κρίνω ὑμᾶς).' " This recalls Jn. 8:10-11, which narrates the episode of the adulterous woman. The author may have been inspired by this text in Jn.; the fact that the Virgin and Joseph were accused of having consummated their marriage provided the author with a context more or less similar to that of the adulterous woman; furthermore, the words οὐδὲ ἐγὼ κρίνω ὑμᾶς in the Protevangelium of James correspond to οὐδὲ ἐγώ σε κατακρί-νω in Jn.

The second text is 19:3: "And Salome said, 'As the Lord my God lives, unless I put (forward) my finger (ἐὰν μὴ βαλῶ τὸν δάκτυλόν μου) and test her condition, I will not believe (οὐ μὴ πιστεύσω) that a virgin has brought forth.' " These words which betray Salome's doubt recall strangely those of doubting Thomas in

Jn. 20:25: ἐὰν μὴ . . . βάλω τὸν δάκτυλόν μου . . . οὐ μὴ πιστεύσω. Although
the contexts are different, it is conceivable that the author is referring to Thomas
as the prototype of the doubter. He picked up what he could from Jn.'s words and
adapted it to his own narrative.

Only one passage in the Protevangelium of James presupposes a reference to
the Pauline texts. Prot. Jas. 13:1 reads, "For as Adam was (absent) in the hour of
his prayer and the serpent came and found Eve alone and deceived her (ἦλθεν ὁ
ὄφις καὶ εὗρε τὴν Εὖαν μόνην καὶ ἐξηπάτησεν) and defiled her, so also has
it happened to me." Scholars have given the following parallels: 2 Cor. 11:3; 1
Tim. 2:14; and Gen. 3:13. The words ὁ ὄφις Εὖαν ἐξηπάτησεν invite us to believe in a literary dependence on 2 Cor. 11:3. Yet Gen. 3:13 reads ὁ ὄφις ἠπάτη-
σέν με, and it may also have inspired the author; furthermore, the absence of any
other reference to Paul tilts the scale in favor of the Old Testament text.

Finally, Prot. Jas. 15:2: " . . . and [you] have not bowed your head under
the mighty hand (ὑπὸ τὴν κραταιὰν χεῖρα) . . . ' has the expression ὑπὸ τὴν
κραταιὰν χεῖρα, which is found in 1 Pet. 5:6, but it does not call for a literary
dependence since this epistle simply gives one piece of advice among others and
since this may have been a common expression.

Except for these various texts I mentioned, there is no trace of any other New
Testament writings in the Protevangelium of James.

By way of conclusion, I have pointed out that the author of the Protevangelium
of James, whose intention is clearly to give a detailed and marvelous account of the
birth of the Virgin and of Christ, is inspired by the infancy gospels in Mt. and in Lk.
He cites literally specific passages and is simply inspired by others. The influence of
Lk. is greater than that of Mt., the reason probably being that the third gospel has a
longer infancy narrative in which the author found more material to work.

Section 8
THE KERYGMA PETRI

The Kerygma Petri is not actually an aprocryphal gospel, but since, as its title
claims, it narrates the preaching of Peter, I have classified it among the apocryphal gospels. This writing probably appeared in the first third of the second century, most likely among Egyptian Christians.[145] Clement of Alexandria has
preserved a few fragments.[146] Origen tells us that the gnostic Heracleon referred

---

[145]Cf. Altaner, *Précis de Patrologie*, 60 [not in ET, editor's note].

[146]I follow E. Klostermann's edition, *Apocrypha 1, Reste des Petrusevangeliums, des
Petrusapokalypse und des Kerygma Petri*, KIT 3 (Berlin, 1933) 13-16. See also E.
Preuschen, *Antilegomena*, 88-91. [The text followed in the English translation is that of
Edgar Hennecke, *New Testament Apocrypha*, ed. Wilhelm Schneemelcher, ET ed. R. McL.
Wilson (Philadelphia: Westminster Press, 1963) 2:94-102. Editor's note.]

to it as well, even though he doubted its authenticity.[147] Eusebius rejects it as apocryphal.[148]

None of the preserved fragments reveal a definite literary dependence on any writing of the New Testament. I propose to mention those few to which scholars have sometimes referred because they contain a more or less similar idea.

A. Clement of Alexandria, Strom. 6.6.48

> Αὐτίκα ἐν τῷ Πέτρου κηρύγματι ὁ κύριός φησι πρὸς τοὺς μαθητὰς μετὰ τὴν ἀνάστασιν· ἐξελεξάμην ὑμᾶς δώδεκα μαθητὰς κρίνας ἀξίους ἐμοῦ [οὓς ὁ κύριος ἠθέλησεν], καὶ ἀποστόλους πιστοὺς ἡγησάμενος εἶναι πέμπω ἐπὶ τὸν κόσμον εὐαγγελίσασθαι τοὺς κατὰ τὴν οἰκουμένην ἀνθρώπους γινώσκειν ὅτι εἷς θεός ἐστιν, διὰ [τῆς τοῦ Χριστοῦ] πίστεως ἐμῆς δηλοῦντας τὰ μέλλοντα, ὅπως οἱ ἀκούσαντες καὶ πιστεύσαντες σωθῶσιν, οἱ δὲ μὴ πιστεύσαντες ἀκούσαντες μαρτυρήσωσιν, οὐχ ἔχοντες ἀπολογίαν εἰπεῖν· οὐκ ἠκούσαμεν.

Therefore (that is, to adduce a similar example) in the "Preaching of Peter" the Lord says to his disciples after the resurrection, "I have chosen you twelve because I judged you worthy to be my disciples (whom the Lord wished). And I sent them, of whom I was persuaded that they would be true apostles, into the world to proclaim to men in all the world the joyous message that they may know that there is (only) one God, and to reveal what future happenings there would be through belief on me (Christ), to the end that those who hear and believe may be saved; and that those who believe not may testify that they have heard it and not be able to excuse themselves saying, We have not heard."

Several parallels are usually mentioned: Mt. 10:1-2; 24:14; 28:19; Mk. 3:13-14; 13:10; 16:15-16; Lk. 6:12-13; and Jn. 15:16. They all relate the mission of the apostles in a totally or partially similar fashion. The apocryphon is not literarily dependent on any of them, since its text is too remote from theirs. Furthermore, the parallels do not all consider the mission of the apostles after the resurrection. I simply propose to mention several words or expressions in the aprocryphon which are found in the synoptics: δώδεκα μαθητάς (Mt. 10:1), οἰκουμένη (Mt. 24:14), οὓς ἠθέλησεν (Mk. 3:13: οὓς ἤθελεν αὐτός), ἐπὶ τὸν κόσμον (Mk. 16:15: εἰς τὸν κόσμον ἅπαντα), πιστεύσαντες σωθῶσιν (Mk. 16:16: ὁ πιστεύσας καὶ βαπτισθεὶς σωθήσεται), ἐξελεξάμην ὑμᾶς δώδεκα (Lk. 6:13: ἐκλεξάμενος ἀπ' αὐτῶν δώδεκα; Jn. 15:16: ἐξελεξάμην ὑμᾶς). This simple survey is sufficient to show that the author does not follow a specific text. Let me add that there may be an allusion to Rom. 10:13-18 with the words "to the end that those who hear and believe may be saved; and that those who believe not may testify that

---

[147]Cf. Origen, Comment. in Ioan. 13.17.
[148]Cf. Eusebius, Hist. Eccl. 3.3.2.

they have heard it and not be able to excuse themselves saying, 'we have not heard'.''

B. Clement of Alexandria, Strom. 6.5.43

Διὰ τοῦτό φησιν ὁ Πέτρος εἰρηκέναι τὸν κύριον τοῖς ἀποστόλοις· ἐὰν μὲν οὖν τις θελήσῃ τοῦ Ἰσραὴλ μετανοῆσαι διὰ τοῦ ὀνόματός μου πιστεύειν ἐπὶ τὸν θεόν, ἀφεθήσονται αὐτῷ αἱ ἁμαρτίαι. μετὰ [δὲ] δώδεκα ἔτη ἐξέλθετε εἰς τὸν κόσμον, μή τις εἴπῃ· οὐκ ἠκούσαμεν.

For that reason Peter records that the Lord had said to the disciples, ''If now any one of Israel wishes to repent and through my name to believe in God, his sins will be forgiven him. And after twelve years go ye out into the world that no one may say, 'we have not heard (it)'.''

Lk. 24:47 has been given as a parallel because of the final instructions of Christ to the apostles: ''(Thus it is written) . . . that repentance and forgiveness of sins (μετάνοιαν εἰς ἄφεσιν ἁμαρτιῶν) should be preached in his name (ἐπὶ τῷ ὀνόματι) to all nations (εἰς πάντα τὰ ἔθνη) beginning from Jerusalem.'' Acts 2:38; 3:19; 5:31; and 10:43, in which Peter preaches repentance, the forgiveness of sins, and faith in God may also be mentioned. Let me point out that the apocryphon has Christ himself speaking, which brings us to a similarity with the text of Lk. 24:47

C. Clement of Alexandria, Strom. 6.15.128

Ὅθεν καὶ ὁ Πέτρος ἐν τῷ κηρύγματι περὶ τῶν ἀποστόλων λέγων φησίν· ἡμεῖς δὲ ἀναπτύξαντες τὰς βίβλους ἃς εἴχομεν τῶν προφητῶν, ἃ μὲν διὰ παραβολῶν, ἃ δὲ δι' αἰνιγμάτων, ἃ δὲ αὐθεντικῶς καὶ αὐτολεξεὶ τὸν Χριστὸν Ἰησοῦν ὀνομαζόντων, εὕρομεν καὶ τὴν παρουσίαν αὐτοῦ καὶ τὸν θάνατον καὶ τὸν σταυρὸν καὶ τὰς λοιπὰς κολάσεις πάσας, ὅσας ἐποίησαν αὐτῷ οἱ Ἰουδαῖοι, καὶ τὴν ἔγερσιν καὶ τὴν εἰς οὐρανοὺς ἀνάληψιν πρὸ τοῦ Ἱεροσόλυμα κτισθῆναι (κριθῆναι), καθὼς ἐγέγραπτο ταῦτα πάντα, ἃ ἔδει αὐτὸν παθεῖν καὶ μετ' αὐτὸν ἃ ἔσται. ταῦτα οὖν ἐπιγνόντες ἐπιστεύσαμεν τῷ θεῷ διὰ τῶν γεγραμμένων εἰς αὐτόν.

Wherefore Peter also in the ''Preaching'' speaks about the apostles as follows: ''But we opened the books of the prophets which we had, which partly in parables, partly in enigmas, partly with certainty and in clear words name Christ Jesus, and found his coming, his death, his crucifixion and all the rest of the tortures which the Jews inflicted on him, his resurrection and his assumption to heaven before the foundation (? *better doubtless*: before the destruction) of Jerusalem, how all was written that he had to suffer and what would be after him. Recognizing this, we believed God in consequence of what is written of (in reference to) him.''

At best, these words lead us to a similar idea in Lk. 24:46 and 1 Pet. 1:10-12. But the texts are too remote to enable us to think of a literary influence.

D. Clement of Alexandria, Strom. 6.6.48

Πάσαις δ' ἄνωθεν ταῖς ψυχαῖς εἴρηται ταῖς λογικαῖς· ὅσα ἐν ἀγνοίᾳ τις ὑμῶν ἐποίησεν μὴ εἰδὼς σαφῶς τὸν θεόν, ἐὰν ἐπιγνοὺς μετανοήσῃ, πάντα αὐτῷ ἀφεθήσεται τὰ ἁμαρτήματα.

But concerning all reasonable souls it has been said from the beginning, "All sins which any one of you has committed in ignorance, because he did not know God accurately, will be forgiven him if he come to know (God) and repents."

Acts 17:30 has sometimes been thought of because it states a more or less similar idea in different terms.

E. Clement of Alexandria, Strom. 6.5.39

Πέτρος ἐν τῷ κηρύγματι λέγει· γινώσκετε οὖν ὅτι εἷς θεός ἐστιν . . . ὃς τὰ πάντα ἐποίησεν λόγῳ δυνάμεως αὐτοῦ, τῆς γνωστικῆς ἀρχῆς, τουτέστι τοῦ υἱοῦ.

[Peter says in the "Preaching": (Editor's addition.)] Recognize now that there is one God . . . who has made all things by the word of his power (who is discernible through Scripture, that is to say through the Son).

The Son is also called the δύναμις θεοῦ in 1 Cor. 1:24. Yet let me point out that it is not certain that the expression τουτέστι τοῦ υἱοῦ belongs to the apocryphon; it may belong to Clement of Alexandria.[149]

F. Clement of Alexandria, Strom. 6.5.41

Εἶτα τὸν κολοφῶνα τοῦ ζητουμένου προσεπιφέρει· ὥστε καὶ ὑμεῖς ὁσίως καὶ δικαίως μανθάνοντες ἃ παραδίδομεν ὑμῖν, φυλάσσεσθε καινῶς τὸν θεόν, διὰ τοῦ Χριστοῦ σεβόμενοι· εὕρομεν γὰρ ἐν ταῖς γραφαῖς καθὼς ὁ κύριος λέγει· ἰδοὺ διατίθεμαι ὑμῖν καινὴν διαθήκην, οὐχ ὡς διεθέμην τοῖς πατράσιν ἐν ὄρει Χωρήβ.

He then inserts the keystone to his own inquiry: Learn then, ye also, holily and righteously what we deliver to you and keep it, worshipping God through

---

[149]Klostermann, *Apocrypha,* 1:13, doubts that this expression belongs to Kerygma Petri; Preuschen seems to believe that it is connected with it. [Schneemelcher, in a footnote to this passage in Hennecke, *New Testament Apocrypha,* 2:99, writes, "The words in parentheses are probably an addition made by Clement. The translation rests upon a conjecture of Früchtel." Massaux translates τῆς γνωστικῆς ἀρχῆς by "le principe gnostique," i.e., the gnostic principle. Editor's note.]

Christ in a new way. For we have found in the Scriptures, how the Lord says, "Behold, I make with you a new covenant, not as I made (one) with your fathers in Mount Horeb."

I can only point out that Heb. 8:8 uses the text of Jer. 31:31-34 as well, and that it does seem that the apocryphon draws its inspiration from it.

From the point of view of the literary influence of Mt., the Kerygma Petri brings no interesting information.

To bring this chapter to a close, I propose to review as a whole the noncanonical gospels that I studied. The Gospel of Mt. has the largest number of literary relationships; it is sometimes cited almost literally, sometimes its narrative is embellished, and other times the Matthean narrative is used as a canvas which is embroidered. There are traces of this gospel in all of the apocryphal gospels, except in the few fragments of the Gospel of Matthias.

Lk. comes immediately after Mt. The Gospel of Lk. seems to have exerted a fairly remarkable literary influence. Its influence is even greater than Mt.'s in the Protevangelium of James, but this is probably due to the longer exposition that the third gospel gave to the infancy narrative. It also played a leading part in the fragments of the Unknown Gospel, in which, by contrast, the literary influence of Mt. is tenuous. It is felt also in the Gospel of the Ebionites.

It is especially in the Unknown Gospel that numerous contacts appear, sometimes to the point of being literarily dependent on the fourth gospel. As for Mk., its influence is also evident in the Unknown Gospel.

The perception we get is that the apocryphal gospels which came from Egypt reveal a stronger relationship with Lk. and Jn., such as the Gospel of Matthias, the Protevangelium of James, and the Unknown Gospel. On the other hand, the Palestinian documents, witness the Gospel of the Hebrews, are more faithful to Mt. I must remind the reader, however, that even in the Alexandrian documents, the influence of Mt. is felt.

The Gospel of Peter depends rather on a narrative or on a tradition which was made up from the four gospels. It is literarily dependent on them, and the Gospel of Mt. holds there a privileged position.

Finally, I would like to point out in particular that in comparison with the writings I studied previously, there is a greater tendency in the apocryphal gospels to follow literally the gospel text which is borrowed.

Editor's Addenda to Chapter 4

Section 1
THE UNKNOWN GOSPEL (PAPYRUS EGERTON 2)

Wolf-Dietrich Köhler (*Die Rezeption des Matthäusevangeliums in der Zeit vor Irenäus*, 451-52) concludes the following with respect to the Unknown Gospel (Papyrus Egerton 2). (Papyrus Egerton 2 is cited as in the edition of H. I. Bell and T. C. Skeat, 1935.)

1. Passages for which dependence on Mt. is possible

PAPYRUS EGERTON 2	MATTHEW
11.32	8:2
13.54-59	15:7-9

2. Passage for which dependence on Mt. is theoretically possible but hardly compelling

PAPYRUS EGERTON 2	MATTHEW
11.43–12.53	22:15-18

Biblia Patristica (Index des Citations et Allusions bibliques dans la Littérature patristique, Des Origines à Clément d'Alexandrie et Tertullien, vol. 1 [Paris, 1975] 223-93) lists the following citations or allusions to the Gospel of Matthew in the Unknown Gospel (Papyrus Egerton 2).

PAPYRUS EGERTON 2	MATTHEW
13.32	8:1-4
13.54	15:7-9
11:47ff.	22:15-18

Section 2
THE GOSPEL OF THE HEBREWS

Wolf-Dietrich Köhler (*Die Rezeption des Matthäusevangeliums in der Zeit vor Irenäus*, 270-71) concludes the following with respect to the Gospel of the Hebrews. (The edition of the [supposed] Gospel of the Hebrews cited in this section is that as reconstructed by Philipp Vielhauer.)

1. There are no passages for which dependence on Mt. is probable.

2. Passages for which dependence on Mt. is very possible but in no way compelling

GOSPEL OF THE HEBREWS	MATTHEW
2	3:16-17
7	26:26
5 and 6	5:22; 18:6-7

3. Passages for which dependence on Mt. is improbable

GOSPEL OF THE HEBREWS	MATTHEW
3	4:1, 8
4a.b.	7:7-8; 11:28-29
7	26:27, 29

Biblia Patristica (*Index des Citations et Allusions bibliques dans la Littérature patristique, Des Origines à Clément d'Alexandrie et Tertullien,* vol. 1 [Paris, 1975] 223-93) lists the following citations or allusions to the Gospel of Matthew in the Gospel of the Hebrews.*

GOSPEL OF THE HEBREWS	MATTHEW
Ev.Heb. B 148.52	3:16-17
Ev.Heb. B 148.38	3:16
Ev.Heb. C 67.20	4:1
Ev.Heb. C 67.20	4:8
Ev.Heb. 389.14	7:7-8
Ev. Heb. F 8.20	26:26
Ev.Heb. F 8.17	26:27
Ev.Heb. 8.18	26:29

Section 3

THE GOSPEL OF THE EBIONITES

Wolf-Dietrich Köhler (*Die Rezeption des Matthäusevangeliums in der Zeit vor Irenäus,* 272-87) concludes the following with respect to the Gospel of the Ebionites.

1. Fragments with distinct influence from Mt.

EPIPHANIUS, *Panar.* (= *Haer.*)	MATTHEW
30.13.2-3	8:5, 14; 5:2; 10:2, 3, 4, 6; 9:9-13
30.13.4	3:4-7

*The following notations are used by the editors of *Biblia Patristica* for their references to the Gospel of the Hebrews. Ev.Heb. = Euangelium Hebraeorum in Clemens Alexandrinus, *Stromata,* 3rd ed., ed. O. Stählin and L. Früchtel, GCS 52 (1960) 137, 389. Ev.Heb. B = Euangelium Hebraeorum in Hieronymus, *Commentarii in Isaiam,* ed. M. Adriaen, CCL 73 (1963) 148. Ev.Heb. C = Euangelium Hebraeorum in Origines, *Commentarii in Ioannem,* ed. E. Preuschen, GCS 10 (1903) 67. Ev.Heb. F = Euangelium Hebraeorum in Hieronymus, *De uiris illustribus,* ed. E. C. Richardson, TU 14/1A (1896) 8.

30.13.7	3:13-17
30.14.5	12:48-50
30.16.5	5:17; 9:13; 12:7
30.22.4	26:17

2. Fragment without provable influence from Mt.

EPIPHANIUS, *Panar.* (= *Haer.*)	MATTHEW
30.13.6	3:1

Biblia Patristica (*Index des Citations et Allusions bibliques dans la Littérature patristique, Des Origines à Clément d'Alexandrie et Tertullien*, vol. 1 [Paris, 1975] 223-93) lists the following citations or allusions to the Gospel of the Ebionites.†

GOSPEL OF THE EBIONITES	MATTHEW
350.4	3:4
350.3	3:5-6
350.12	3:5
350.3	3:7
350.13	3:13
351.4	3:14-15
350.14	3:16
350.16	3:17
351.2	3:17
349.7	4:18
354.7	5:17
349.5	8:5
349.6	8:14
349.10-11	9:9
354.7	9:13
349.7	10:2-4
350.1	10:6
351.24	12:48-50
363.4	26:17

Section 4
THE GOSPEL OF THE EGYPTIANS

Wolf-Dietrich Köhler (*Die Rezeption des Matthäusevangeliums in der Zeit vor Irenäus*) does not discuss the Gospel of the Egyptians.

Biblia Patristica (*Index des Citations et Allusions bibliques dans la Littérature patristique, Des Origines à Clément d'Alexandrie et Tertullien*, vol. 1 [Paris, 1975] 223-93) lists the following citations or allusions to the Gospel of the Egyptians.**

---

†The following references to the Gospel of the Ebionites are from Euangelium Ebionitarum in Epiphanius, *Panarion*, ed. K. Holl, GCS 25 (1915) 349-51, 354, 363.

**The following references to the Gospel of the Egyptians are from Euangelium Aegyptiorum copticum, ed. H.-M. Schenke, "Das Aegypter Evangelium aus Nag-Hammadi Codex 3," *NTS* 16 (1969-1970): 196-208.

GOSPEL OF THE EGYPTIANS	MATTHEW
Ev.Aeg.2 206.40	16:28
Ev.Aeg.2 204.19	24:7
Ev.Aeg.2 204.23	24:11
Ev.Aeg.2 204.23	24:24

Section 5
THE GOSPEL OF PETER

Wolf-Dietrich Köhler (*Die Rezeption des Matthäusevangeliums in der Zeit vor Irenäus*, 437-48) concludes the following with respect to the Gospel of Peter.

1. Passages for which dependence on Mt. is quite possible, because the parallels occur in special Matthean material

GOSPEL OF PETER	MATTHEW
1	27:24
21b	27:51b-54
29	27:62-64
30	27:64
32	27:60
33	27:66

2. Passages for which dependence on Mt. is quite possible, although there are synoptic parallels

GOSPEL OF PETER	MATTHEW
3	27:57-58
5c	27:17-19; 27:26
6a	27:27
7b	27:42
9a	26:67
10b	26:63
17	27:25
19a	27:46
23-24	27:58-60
28	27:54
30	27:63; 28:13
31	27:65-66
36	3:16-17
37 and 44	28:2
45	27:54; 28:11-15
46	27:24
47	28:11-15
50	28:1
54	27:60-61

55	28:2-3
56	28:5-6
57	28:8

3. Passages for which dependence on Mt. is not to be totally excluded, but neither is it compelling

GOSPEL OF PETER	MATTHEW
5a	27:57-62
6a	27:42
6b	26:63-64; 27:40
7a	27:28
8	27:29
9	27:30
10a	27:38
11	21:5; 27:37
12	27:35
15	27:45
16	27:34, 48
19b	26:64
20	27:51
22	27:46
26a	17:23
26b	26:61
28	27:19; 28:12
30	16:21; 17:22-23; 20:19
31	27:54
34	27:1; 28:1
35a	28:1
35b and 41	3:17; 17:5
36	28:2-4
38	28:11
59	28:7, 10, 16-17
60	10:2; 16:16

Biblia Patristica (*Index des Citations et Allusions bibliques dans la Littérature patristique, Des Origines à Clément d'Alexandrie et Tertullien*, vol. 1 [Paris, 1975] 223-93) lists the following citations or allusions to the Gospel of Peter.

GOSPEL OF PETER	MATTHEW
9	26:67
1	27:24
46	27:24
17	27:25
7	27:28-29
9	27:30
16	27:34
12	27:35
11	27:37
10	27:38

15	27:45
22	27:45
19	27:46
16	27:48
20	27:50-51
21	27:51
28	27:54
45	27:54
23	27:57-60
3	27:57-58
29	27:62-65
34	28:1
50-51	28:1
53-54	28:2-8
36	28:2-4
44	28:2
47	28:11-15

Section 6
THE GOSPEL OF MATTHIAS

Wolf-Dietrich Köhler (*Die Rezeption des Matthäusevangeliums in der Zeit vor Irenäus*), and *Biblia Patristica* (*Index des Citations et Allusions bibliques dans la Littérature patristique, Des Origines à Clément d'Alexandrie et Tertullien*, vol. 1 [Paris, 1975] 223-93) list no citations or allusions to the Gospel of Matthias.

Section 7
THE PROTEVANGELIUM OF JAMES

Wolf-Dietrich Köhler (*Die Rezeption des Matthäusevangeliums in der Zeit vor Irenäus*, 429-36) concludes the following with respect to the Protevangelium of James.

1. Passages for which dependence on Mt. is quite possible

PROTEVANGELIUM OF JAMES	MATTHEW
9:1	3:16
13:1	26:75
14:1	1:19; 17:6; 27:4
19:1	1:18-20
19:2	4:16; 17:5
19:3	1:23
20:4	17:9
23:3	23:35
24:3	27:51

2. Passages for which dependence on Mt. is theoretically possible but in no way compelling

PROTEVANGELIUM OF JAMES	MATTHEW
9:3	1:24
10:1	27:51
16:3	1:24
17:3	14:15
24:2	23:35

Biblia Patristica (*Index des Citations et Allusions bibliques dans la Littérature patristique, Des origines à Clément d'Alexandrie et Tertullien*, vol. 1 [Paris, 1975] 223-93) lists the following citations or allusions to the Protevangelium of James.

PROTEVANGELIUM OF JAMES	MATTHEW
14:1	1:19
14:2	1:20-21
11:3	1:21
14:2	1:24
21:1	2:1-2
21:2	2:2
21:2	2:3
21:2	2:4-5
21:2	2:7
21:2	2:8
21:3	2:9
21:3	2:11-12
22:1	2:16
9:1	3:16
19:2	4:16
20:2	8:13
19:2	17:5
14:1	27:4
24:3	27:51

Section 8
THE KERYGMA PETRI

Wolf-Dietrich Köhler (*Die Rezeption des Matthäusevangeliums in der Zeit vor Irenäus*), and *Biblia Patristica* (*Index des Citations et Allusions bibliques dans la Littérature patristique, Des Origines à Clément d'Alexandrie et Tertullien*, vol. 1 [Paris, 1975] 223-93 list no citations or allusions to the Kerygma Petri.

Chapter 5

THE AGRAPHA

Certain sayings of Jesus are not found in the gospels, but have been preserved either in the other New Testament writings, in the ancient manuscripts of the canonical gospels, in the works of ecclesiastical writers, or finally in the papyri, notably those of Oxyrhynchus.[1] Many of these agrapha have already been analyzed in the study of the Epistle of Barnabas, 2 Clement, the Gospel of the Hebrews, the Gospel of the Ebionites, and the Unknown Gospel and will not be discussed again. This inquiry is limited to those unauthentic agrapha—and they are fairly numerous—which have been composed under the influence of Mt.

1. No. 28 (Re L 3; Ro 85): Epiphanius, *Haer.* 80.5

ἄξιος γὰρ ὁ ἐργάτης τοῦ μισθοῦ αὐτοῦ καὶ ἀρκετὸν τῷ ἐργαζομένῳ ἡ τροφὴ αὐτοῦ.

For the worker deserves his salary / and sufficient to the one who works is his food. [Editor's translation.]

The second saying, which is believed to be an agraphon, may be a commentary on the first saying drawn from 1 Tim. 5:18, a commentary inspired by a vague

---

[1]Cf. J. Jeremias, *Unknown Sayings of Jesus* (London, 1958) 4-21. For the Agrapha which are scattered in later writings and which belong neither to a noncanonical gospel nor to fragments of the Oxyrhynchus papyri, I follow E. Klostermann's edition, *Apocrypha,* vol. 3, *Agrapha, slavische Josephusstücke, Oxyrh.-Fragment,* KIT 2, 2nd ed. (Berlin, 1911); the agrapha, which are found in the noncanonical gospels and in the Oxyrhynchus papyri are given according to Klostermann's edition, *Apocrypha,* vol. 2, *Evangelien,* KIT 8, 3rd ed. (Berlin, 1929); H. B. Swete, *Zwei neue Evangelinenfragmente,* KIT 31 (Berlin, 1924). See also the older editions of A. Resch, *Agrapha. Aussercanonische Schriftfragmente gesammelt und untersucht,* TU 15/3-4, 2nd ed. (Leipzig, 1906); J. H. Ropes, *Die Sprüche Jesu, die in den kanonischen Evangelien nicht überliefert sind. Eine kritische Bearbeitung des von D. Alfred Resch gesammelten Materials,* TU 14/2 (Leipzig, 1896). For each agraphon, E. Klostermann, in *Apocrypha* 3, adds in parentheses a reference to Resch (Re L for the logia, A for the agrapha) and Ro for Ropes. [The texts followed in the English translation are those of William D. Stroker, *Extracanonical Sayings of Jesus* (Atlanta: Scholars Press, 1989); Edgar Hennecke, *New Testament Apocrypha,* vol. 1 (Philadelphia: Westminster Press, 1963).]

recollection of Mt. 10:10, ἄξιος γὰρ ὁ ἐργάτης τῆς τροφῆς αὐτοῦ, where indeed ἡ τροφὴ αὐτοῦ is found.

2. No. 42 (Ro 117): Talmud, *Tractate Sabbath* 116ab

> The philosopher said, Starting from the day you left your country, the law of Moses has been suppressed and the gospel has been given in which it says: Sons and daughters will inherit together. On the last day . . . the philosopher said to them, As for me, I the gospel have not come to take away the Torah of Moses, but I have come to add to the Torah of Moses. It is written in the Torah: where there is a son, the daughter will not inherit.[2] [Stroker, 174.]

This text quite probably contains a vague literary recollection of Mt. 5:17: Μὴ νομίσητε ὅτι ἦλθον καταλῦσαι τὸν νόμον ἢ τοὺς προφήτας· οὐκ ἦλθον καταλῦσαι ἀλλὰ πληρῶσαι, a text which is unique in the New Testament. The reminiscence seems all the more certain inasmuch as it deals explicitly, as does the first gospel, with the relationship between the law and the gospel.

3. No. 60 (Re L 13; Ro 7): *Clem. Hom.* 12.29

> καὶ ὁ Πέτρος ἀπεκρίνατο, ὅτι ὁ τῆς ἀληθείας προφήτης ἔξη· τὰ ἀγαθὰ ἐλθεῖν δεῖ, μακάριος δὲ (φησὶ) δι' οὗ ἔρχεται· ὁμοίως καί· τὰ κακὰ ἀνάγκη ἐλθεῖν, οὐαὶ δὲ δι' οὗ ἔρχεται.
>
> And Peter answered, The Prophet of truth said, It is necessary for good things to come, and blessed, he says, is the one through whom they come. Likewise it is necessary that evil things come, but woe to him through whom they come. [Stroker, 79.]

This saying of Christ is not found literally in any gospel, but there is an unmistakable affinity with Mt. 18:7, ἀνάγκη γὰρ ἐλθεῖν τὰ σκάνδαλα, πλὴν οὐαὶ τῷ ἀνθρώπῳ δι' οὗ τὸ σκάνδαλον ἔρχεται and Lk. 17:1, ἀνέκδεκτόν ἐστιν τοῦ τὰ σκάνδαλα μὴ ἐλθεῖν, οὐαὶ δὲ δι' οὗ ἔρχεται. The second part of the text agrees especially with the Matthean text in which the words ἀνάγκη ἐλθεῖν and οὐαὶ δι' οὗ ἔρχεται are found; Lk., which has ἀνέκδεκτόν ἐστιν instead of ἀνάγκη, is less close. A literary dependence on the Matthean text is quite possible: the author has merely embellished the gospel saying.

---

[2]Klostermann, *Apocrypha* 3:9, no. 42, gives the German translation of this text of the Talmud: "Der Philosoph sprach: seit dem Tage, wo ihr aus eurem Lande vertrieben seid, ist das Gesetz Mosis aufgehoben und das Evangelium gegeben, in welchem es heisst: Sohn und Tochter sollen zusammen erben, am nächsten Tage . . . sagte der Philosoph zu ihnen: ich habe den Schluss des Evangeliums nachgesehen; da heisst es: ich, Evangelium, bin nicht gekommen wegzutun vom Gesetz Mosis, sondern hinzuzufügen zum Gesetz Mosis bin ich gekommen. Geschrieben steht im Gesetz Mosis: wo ein Sohn ist, soll die Tochter nicht erben.''

4. No. 65 (Re L 14; Ro 8): *Apost. const.* 5.7

λαβόντες ἐντολὴν παρ᾽ αὐτοῦ κηρύξαι τὸ εὐαγγέλιον εἰς ὅλον τὸν κόσμον καὶ <u>μαθητεῦσαι πάντα τὰ ἔθνη καὶ βαπτίσαι εἰς τὸν αὐτοῦ θάνατον</u> ἐπὶ αὐθεντίᾳ τοῦ θεοῦ τῶν ὅλων (ὅς ἐστιν αὐτοῦ πατήρ) καὶ μαρτυρίᾳ πνεύματος (ὅς ἐστι παράκλητος).

. . . and who received the command from him to preach the gospel to all the world, to make disciples of all nations, and to baptize them into his death, by the authority of the God of the universe, who is his father, and by the testimony of the Spirit, who is the comforter. . . . [Stroker, 229.]

The expressions μαθητεῦσαι πάντα τὰ ἔθνη καὶ βαπτίσαι εἰς τὸν αὐτοῦ θάνατον recall Mt. 28:19: πορευθέντες οὖν μαθητεύσατε πάντα τὰ ἔθνη, βαπτίζοντες αὐτοὺς εἰς τὸ ὄνομα τοῦ πατρὸς καὶ τοῦ υἱοῦ καὶ τοῦ ἁγίου πνεύματος. This text repeats literally the formula μαθητεύω πάντα τὰ ἔθνη καὶ βαπτίζω εἰς. There is too great an agreement with this text, which is peculiar to Mt. in the New Testament, not to believe in a literary dependence. The last words εἰς αὐτοῦ θάνατον may have been changed by the author influenced by the Pauline image of baptism.

5. No. 78 (Re L 45; Ro 23): Ps. Ignatius, *Magnesians* 9:3

ὁ μὴ ἐργαζόμενος γὰρ <u>μὴ ἐσθιέτω</u>· ἐν ἱδρῶτι γὰρ <u>τοῦ προσώπου σου</u> φάγῃ τὸν ἄρτον σου φασὶ τὰ λόγια.

Let the one not eat who does not work; for in the sweat of your face you shall eat your bread. [Stroker, 237.]

The words ἐν ἱδρῶτι γὰρ τοῦ προσώπου σου φάγῃ τὸν ἄρτον σου are literally drawn from Gen. 3:19. As for the sentence ὁ μὴ ἐργαζόμενος, μὴ ἐσθιέτω, it is not found in any New Testament writing. The author may have drawn his inspiration from Mt. 10:10, ἄξιος γὰρ ὁ ἐργάτης τῆς τροφῆς αὐτοῦ, where the same idea is found in a negative form.

6. P. Oxy. 1.1-4[3]

[Λέγει ᾽Ιησοῦς· ῎Εκβαλε πρῶτον τὴν δοκὸν
ἐκ τοῦ ὀφθαλμοῦ σου][4]
καὶ τότε διαβλέψεις
ἐκβαλεῖν τὸ κάρφος
τὸ ἐν τῷ ὀφθαλμῷ

---

[3]According to Klostermann, *Apocrypha* 2:19. Cf. also on this papyrus the edition of W. Lock and W. Sanday, *Two Lectures on the "Sayings of Jesus" Recently Discovered at Oxyrhynchus* (Oxford, 1897).

[4]This reconstruction follows Lock and Sanday, *Two Lectures*, 18.

τοῦ ἀδελφοῦ σου.

Jesus said, . . . When you take the beam out of your eye, then you will see clearly to take out the splinter which is in your brother's eye. [Stroker, 134-35.]

The parallels are Mt. 7:5, ὑποκριτά, ἔκβαλε πρῶτον ἐκ τοῦ ὀφθαλμοῦ σου τὴν δοκόν, καὶ τότε διαβλέψεις ἐκβαλεῖν τὸ κάρφος ἐκ τοῦ ὀφθαλμοῦ τοῦ ἀδελφοῦ σου, and Lk. 6:42, ὑποκριτά, ἔκβαλε πρῶτον τὴν δοκὸν ἐκ τοῦ ὀφθαλμοῦ σου, καὶ τότε διαβλέψεις τὸ κάρφος τὸ ἐν τῷ ὀφθαλμῷ τοῦ ἀδελφοῦ σου ἐκβαλεῖν.

In the fragment, the position of the verb ἐκβαλεῖν is identical to the position it occupies in the Matthean text; but Lk. has ἐν τῷ ὀφθαλμῷ as does the fragment, as opposed to ἐκ τοῦ ὀφθαλμοῦ in Mt. and, except for the position of ἐκβαλεῖν, it coincides literally with the agraphon.

7. P. Oxy. 1.23-30[5]

Λ[έγ]ει ['Ιης· ὅπ]ου ἐὰν ὦσιν
[β', οὐκ] ε[ἰσὶ]ν ἄθεοι, καὶ
[ὅ]που ε[ἷς] ἐστιν μόνος,
[λέ]γω· ἐγώ εἰμι μετ' αὐ-
τ[οῦ]. ἔγει[ρ]ον τὸν λίθον,
κἀκεῖ εὑρήσεις με·
σχίσον τὸ ξύλον, κἀγὼ
ἐκεῖ εἰμι.

[Jesus said,] Where there are [three gods, they are] gods. And [where] there is [one] alone [by himself,] I am with him. Lift up the stone and you will find me there; split the wood and I am there. [Stroker, 188 and 193.]

The first sentence may have stretched rather far the text of Mt. 18:20:[6] οὐ γάρ εἰσιν δύο ἢ τρεῖς συνηγμένοι εἰς τὸ ἐμὸν ὄνομα, ἐκεῖ εἰμι ἐν μέσῳ αὐτῶν. Christ uses a fairly similar language when he asserts his presence wherever two or three others are gathered in his name.

8. P. Oxy. 1.36-41[7]

Λέγει 'Ιης· πόλις οἰκοδο-
μημένη ἐπ' ἄκρον
[ὄ]ρους ὑψηλοῦς καὶ ἐσ-

---

[5]According to Klostermann, *Apocrypha* 2:19.
[6]Cf. Jeremias, *Unknown Sayings of Jesus*, 94-96.
[7]According to Klostermann, *Apocrypha* 2:19.

τηριγμένη οὔτε πε-
[σ]εῖν δύναται οὔτε κρυ-
[β]ῆναι.

Jesus said, A city that is built on the top of a high mountain and firmly established can neither fall nor be hidden. [Stroker, 136-37.]

Only Mt. 5:14 in the entire New Testament can be introduced as a parallel: οὐ δύναται πόλις κρυβῆναι ἐπάνω ὄρους κειμένη. There is no doubt that this fragment is in literary contact with this Matthean text; indeed, the words οὐ δύναται, ὄρος, and κρυβῆναι are repeated in Mt., and one may even add the participle οἰκοδομημένη, a reading sustained in Mt. by the Curetonian and Peshitta Syriac versions, and by Hilary. The author of the fragment may have constructed his sentence starting with the text of the first gospel to which he has added several elements peculiar to him.

9. P. Oxy. 654.27-31[8]

Λέγει ᾽Της· [πᾶν τὸ μὴ ἔμπροσθεν τῆς ὄψεώς σου καὶ [τὸ κεκαλυμμένον
ἀπὸ σοῦ ἀποκαλυφ[θ]ήσετ[αί σοι· οὐ γάρ ἐστιν κρυπτὸν ὃ οὐ φανε[ρὸν γενήσεται
καὶ θεθαμμένον ὃ ο[ὐκ ἐγερθήσεται.

Jesus says, "K[now what is be]fore your sight, and [what is hidden] from you will be revealed [to you. For there is nothing] hidden which will not [be made] visi[ble] and nothing buried which [will not be raised up.] [Stroker, 96.]

This logion recalls Mt. 10:26; Mk. 4:22; and Lk. 12:2; the participle κεκαλυμμένον is found only in Mt. 10:26, whereas Lk. 12:2, which has the composite verb συγκεκαλυμμένον, speaks in favor of a literary dependence on the Matthean text.

10. P. Oxy. 654.32-42[9]

[᾽Εξ]ετάζουσιν αὐτὸν ο[ἱ μαθηταὶ αὐτοῦ καὶ
[λέ]γουσιν· πῶς νηστεύ[σομεν καὶ πῶς προσ-
[ευξώ]μεθα καὶ πῶς [ἐλεημοσύνην ποιή-
[σομεν κ]αὶ τί παρατηρήσ[ομεν τῶν παραδο-
[θέντω]ν; Λέγει ᾽Της· [οὐκ ἔσεσθε ὡς οἱ

---

[8]Cf. ibid., 22.

[9]Cf. ibid., 22, in which Klostermann gives the reconstruction which I follow. Regarding this papyrus, cf. B. P. Grenfell and A. S. Hunt, *New Sayings of Jesus and Fragment of a Lost Gospel from Oxyrhynchus,* Egypt Exploration Fund, Graeco-Roman Branch (Oxford, 1904).

[ὑποκρ]ειταί. μή ποιεῖτ[ε ταῦτα φανερῶς,
[ἀλλὰ τ]ῆς ἀληθείας ἀν [τέχεσθε, καὶ ἡ δικαι-
[οσύνη ὑμῶ]ν ἀ[π]οκεκρ[υμμένη ἔστω· λέ-
[γω γὰρ· μα]κάρι[ός] ἐστιν [ὁ ταῦτα ποιῶν ἐν
[κρυπτῷ, ὅτι ἐν φανερ]ῷ ἐστ[αι ὁ μισθὸς αὐτοῦ
[παρὰ τῷ πρι ὅς ἐστ]ιν [ἐν τοῖς οὐρανοῖς.

[His disciples] asked him and said, "How shall we fast, [and how shall we pray] and how [shall we give alms,] and what [diet] should we observe?" Jesus said, "[Do not lie and] do not do [what you hate, for all things will be] manifest [before heaven. For there is nothing hidden which will not be revealed.] Blessed is [the one who does not do these things, for all things will be manifest to the Father who is in heaven.] [Stroker, 24.]

If the reconstruction given by Klostermann is correct, it is obvious that this fragment is under the literary influence of Mt. 6:1-18, a passage which is unique in the New Testament and in which similar ideas concerning justice, almsgiving, prayer and fasting are expressed. Moreover, some words from this fragment are read in this Matthean pericope: ἡ δικαιοσύνη ὑμῶν (6:1), μισθὸς παρὰ τῷ πατρὶ τῷ ἐν τοῖς οὐρανοῖς (6:1), ἐλεημοσύνην ποιέω (6:2, 3), οἱ ὑποκριταί (6:2, 5, 16), ἐν τῷ κρυπτῷ (6:4, 6), προσεύχομαι (6:5, 6, 7), νηστεύω (6:16, 17), ἐν φανερῷ (6:18).[10]

11. P. Oxy. 655.2-8[11]

[ἀ]πὸ πρωὶ ἕ[ως ὀψὲ
[μήτ]ε ἀφ' ἐσπ[έρας
[ἕως π]ρωὶ μήτε [τῇ
[τροφῇ ὑ]μῶν τί φά-
[γητε μήτε] τῇ στ[ο-
[λῇ ὑμῶν] τί ἐνδύ-
[ση]σθε.

[Do not be anxious] from morning until [evening, nor] from evening [until] morning either [for] your food what [you will] eat, [or] for [your] clo[thing], what you [will] put on. [Stroker, 130.]

This passage is in agreement with Mt. 6:25, μὴ μεριμνᾶτε τῇ ψυχῇ ὑμῶν τί φάγητε [ἢ τί πίητε], μηδὲ τῷ σώματι ὑμῶν τί ἐνδύσησθε. οὐχὶ ἡ ψυχὴ πλεῖόν ἐστιν τῆς τροφῆς καὶ τὸ σῶμα τοῦ ἐνδύματος, and Lk. 12:22-23, μὴ μεριμνᾶτε τῇ ψυχῇ τί φάγητε, μηδὲ τῷ σώματι [ὑμῶν] τί ἐνδύσησθε. ἡ γὰρ

---

[10]The reading ἐν τῷ φανερῷ is sustained by E, Δ, 118, 209, 124, 346, 543, 28, 157, 472, 485, 1241, the Latin versions a, b, c, g¹, h, k, the Ethiopic version, and some witnesses of the Armenian version.

[11]Acccording to Klostermann, *Apocrypha* 2:23.

ψυχὴ πλεῖόν ἐστιν τῆς τροφῆς καὶ τὸ σῶμα τοῦ ἐνδύματος.

The gospel texts express an idea identical to that of the fragment. They both use the words τί φάγητε and τί ἐνδύσησθε, whereas ἀπὸ πρωὶ ἕως ὀψὲ μήτε ἀφ' ἑσπέρας ἕως πρωί and στολῇ are absent in Mt. and Lk. A literary contact with Lk. is just as possible as with Mt.; yet, preference is to be given to the Matthean text as having been the canvas upon which the author has built his thought and upon which he is literarily dependent, because the text which follows in this fragment and which belongs to the same context is literarily dependent on a text in Mt. which is also located in the same context.

12. P. Oxy. 655.8-14[12]

> [πολ]λῷ κρεί[σ-
> [σον]ές [ἐστε] τῶν [κρί-
> νων ἅτι[να α]ὐξά-
> νει οὐδὲ ν[ήθ]ει˙.[.
> ἐν ἔχοντ[ες ἔ]νδ[υ-
> μα τί ἐν [. . .] καὶ
> ὑμεῖς;
>
> [You] are of much more value than [the lili]es which grow but do not s[pi]n nor have clothing. What do [you lack]? [Stroker, 139.]

In the same context as the preceding passage, the parallels are Mt. 6:26, 28, οὐχ ὑμεῖς μᾶλλον διαφέρετε αὐτῶν; . . . καταμάθετε τὰ κρίνα τοῦ ἀγροῦ, πῶς αὐξάνουσιν˙ οὐ κοπιῶσιν οὐδὲ νήθουσιν, and Lk. 12:24, 27, πόσῳ μᾶλλον ὑμεῖς διαφέρετε τῶν πετεινῶν . . . κατανοήσατε τὰ κρίνα, πῶς οὔτε νήθει οὔτε ὑφαίνει. The passage in the papyrus is much shorter, but it expresses an idea similar to that of the parallels, while using the word κρίνα and the verb νήθω. Yet, it is literarily dependent on the Matthean text, which is the only one in this context to use the verb αὐξάνω, which the author of the fragment uses as well, as opposed to Lk., which reads, ὑφαίνει. Let me note, however, that certain of Lk.'s manuscripts (P[45], B, ℵ, C, L, Θ, E, F, G, H) support the reading αὐξάνει instead of ὑφαίνει.

13. P. Oxy. 655.14-16[13]

> τίς ἂν προσθ[εί]η
> ἐπὶ τὴν εἰλικίαν
> ὑμῶν;
>
> Who of you can add to his lifespan? [Stroker, 139.]

---

[12]Cf. ibid., 23.
[13]Cf. ibid., 23.

Still in the same context, the parallels are Mt. 6:27, τίς δὲ ἐξ ὑμῶν μεριμνῶν δύναται προσθεῖναι ἐπὶ τὴν ἡλικίαν αὐτοῦ πῆχυν ἕνα, and Lk. 12:25, τίς δὲ ἐξ ὑμῶν μεριμνῶν δύναται ἐπὶ τὴν ἡλικίαν αὐτοῦ προσθεῖναι πῆχυν;

Except for the position of the verb προσθεῖναι, the texts of Mt. and Lk. are identical, save ἕνα in Mt. which is absent in Lk. Since the verb προστίθημι in the fragment is in the same place as in the Matthean parallel, specifically before ἐπὶ τὴν εἱλικίαν, it signals a clue which favors a literary dependence on Mt., particularly if we recall that the preceding text of the same episode was under the literary influence of this gospel.

14. P. Oxy. 655.16-18[14]

αὐτὸ[ς δ]ώσει
ὑμῖν τὸ ἔνδυμα ὑ-
μῶν.

He will give you your clothing. [Stroker, 139.]

Still in the same context, the following parallels may be noted, Mt. 6:30, εἰ δὲ τὸν χόρτον . . . ὁ θεὸς οὕτως ἀμφιέννυσιν, οὐ πολλῷ μᾶλλον ὑμᾶς, ὀλιγόπιστοι, and Lk. 12:28, εἰ δὲ τὸν χόρτον . . . ὁ θεὸς οὕτως ἀμφιάζει, πόσῳ μᾶλλον ὑμᾶς, ὀλιγόπιστοι. The idea is absolutely identical, but the author of the fragment has Jesus replying more directly and more briefly to those who worry about clothing.[15] Since I have given preference to the text of Mt. in the entire preceding context, it is believable that here again it is the text of the first gospel which the author has condensed into this direct answer of Christ.

15. P. Cair. 10735[16]

ἄγγελος κυρίου ἐλάλησεν· Ἰω[σήφ, ἐγερθεὶς
παράλαβε Μαρίαν τὴν γ[υναῖκά σου καὶ
φεῦγε εἰς Αἴγυπτον κοι[

The Angel of the Lord spake: Jo[seph, arise,] take Mary thy w[ife and] flee to Egypt [. . . [Hennecke, 115.]

This text is built on and is literarily dependent on Mt. 2:13: ἰδοὺ ἄγγελος κυρίου φαίνεται κατ᾽ ὄναρ τῷ Ἰωσὴφ λέγων· ἐγερθεὶς παράλαβε τὸ παιδίον καὶ τὴν μητέρα αὐτοῦ, καὶ φεῦγε εἰς Αἴγυπτον. It has the same construction, the idea is similar, and the following expressions from the first gospel

---

[14]Cf. ibid., 23.
[15]Cf. Jeremias, *Unknown Sayings of Jesus,* 86-87.
[16]According to Klostermann, *Apocrypha* 2:24.

are found: ἄγγελος κυρίου, Ἰωσήφ, ἐγερθείς, παράλαβε, and φεῦγε εἰς Αἴγυπτον. The author of the fragment, for reasons which escape me, has simply replaced τὸ παιδίον καὶ τὴν μητέρα αὐτοῦ with τὴν γυναῖκά σου.

16. P. Oxy. 1224, 2r[17]

> κ]αὶ π[ρ]οσεύχεσθε ὑπὲρ
> τῶν ἐχθ]ρῶν ὑμῶν.
> And pray for your enemies. [Stroker, 129 and 201.]

The parallels that come spontaneously to mind are Mt. 5:44, ἀγαπᾶτε τοὺς ἐχθροὺς ὑμῶν καὶ προσεύχεσθε ὑπὲρ τῶν διωκόντων ὑμᾶς, and Lk. 6:27, 28, ἀγαπᾶτε τοὺς ἐχθροὺς ὑμῶν, καλῶς ποιεῖτε τοῖς μισοῦσιν ὑμᾶς . . . προσεύχεσθε περὶ τῶν ἐπηρεαζόντων ὑμᾶς. None of these parallels has literally the sentence of this fragment; both have the word ἐχθρούς, but not as a complement of προσεύχεσθε. The fact that προσεύχεσθε is construed with ὑπέρ might give us a weak clue in favor of a reference to Mt., which has the same preposition as opposed to περί in Lk.

Let me also point out several agrapha to which comparisons with several gospels can be made, such as Mt., without being able to determine upon which gospel they are literarily dependent.

1. No. 4 (Re L 41; Ro 143)[18]
(a) Clem. *Strom.* 1.24.158.2

> αἰτεῖσθε γάρ φησι, τὰ μεγάλα καὶ τὰ μικρὰ ὑμῖν προστεθήσεται.
> For, he says, seek the great things and the small will be added to you. [Stroker, 123.]

(b) Origen, *On Prayer, 14.1*

> κατανοήσωμεν τὸ αἰτεῖτε τὰ μεγάλα καὶ τὰ μικρὰ ὑμῖν προστεθήσεται, καὶ αἰτεῖτε τὰ ἐπουράνια καὶ τὰ ἐπίγεια ὑμῖν προστεθήσεται.
> Let us consider the words: Ask for great things, and small things will be added to you. And ask for heavenly things, and earthly things will be added to you. [Stroker, 124.]

A similar idea is found in Mt. 6:33 and Lk. 12:31. Yet, the words which express it are fairly different, except for the expression ὑμῖν προστεθήσεται, which

---

[17]Cf. ibid., 26.
[18]According to Klostermann, *Apocrypha* 3:3.

is common to the agraphon and to the two gospel parallels. Jeremias also notes the close relationship with the gospel texts, but he considers this saying as an application of the gospels' saying on prayer, an application made by the community.[19] This agraphon may very well have been fabricated and have gotten its inspiration from a primitive logion of which it seems to be a kind of commentary. In Mt.'s context as well as in Lk.'s, the author may have read τὰ μεγάλα and τὰ ἐπουράνια under the word βασιλεία. As for ταῦτα in Mt. and Lk., it describes food and clothing; the author may have defined all these bodily needs by τὰ μικρά and τὰ ἐπίγεια. This agraphon is, therefore, in agreement with the gospel tradition. I would like to add that τὰ ἐπουράνια and τὰ ἐπίγεια constitute an antithesis with a rather Pauline resonance.

2. Pap. Oxy. 654.5-9[20]

[Λέγει Ἰης·
μὴ παυσάσθω ὁ ζη[τῶν τοῦ ζητεῖν, ἕως ἂν
εὕρῃ, καὶ ὅταν εὕρῃ [θαμβηθήσεται, καὶ θαμβηθεὶς βασιλεύσῃ κα[ὶ βασιλεύσας ἀναπα-
ήσεται.

[Jesus says,] Let the one who seeks not cease [seeking until] he finds, and when he finds [he will be amazed, and] when he has been [am]azed he will reign, and [when he has reigned], he will [re]st. [Stroker, 117.]

The conclusion of this logion is cited by Clement of Alexandria, Strom. 2.9.45, who said that he took it from the Gospel of the Hebrews: Ἢ κἂν τῷ καθ' Ἑβραίους εὐαγγελίῳ· Ὁ θαυμάσας βασιλεύσει, γέγραπται· καὶ ὁ βασιλεύσας ἀναπαυθήσεται. The same logion, this time complete, recurs in another passage in Strom. 5.14: Οὐ παύσεται ὁ ζητῶν ἕως ἂν εὕρῃ· εὑρὼν δὲ θαυβηθήσεται· θαμβηθεὶς δὲ βασιλεύσει· βασιλεύσας δὲ ἐπαναπαύσεται. The beginning of the logion recalls Mt. 7:7 and Lk. 11:9, both of which have ζητεῖτε and καὶ εὑρήσετε. Thus, the fragment indicates that it conforms to the gospel tradition, and its words may display a rather secondary extension of the gospel texts themselves.[21] Let me add that the verb θαμβέομαι is peculiar to Mk. in the New Testament.[22] Clement of Alexandria, as mentioned above, affirmed that, at least for the end of the passage, the source was the Gospel of the Hebrews. It is not impossible that the whole passage was dependent on it and that Clement of Alexandria reproduced only part of it.

---

[19]Cf. Jeremias, *Unknown Sayings of Jesus*, 87-89.
[20]According to Klostermann, *Apocrypha* 2:20.
[21]Cf. Jeremias, *Unknown Sayings of Jesus*, 14-15.
[22]Cf. Mk. 1:27; 10:24, 32.

3. P. Oxy. 654.24[23]

The reconstructions of Grenfell-Hunt as well as White and Deissmann both contain the words

πολλοὶ ἔσονται π[ρῶτοι ἔσχατοι καὶ
οἱ ἔσχατοι πρῶτοι·

For many [who are] f[irst] will be [last and] the last first. [Stroker, 95.]

This sentence reminds us of Mt. 19:30; 20:16; Mk. 10:31; and Lk. 13:30. The text of the fragment agrees literally with the texts which are read in Mt. 19:30 and Mk. 10:31. Since Lk. has a longer text, it could not have had a literary influence on it. It is impossible to determine whether the text of Mt. or of Mk. is the one which has exerted its influence on this fragment. I can only note its total agreement with these two gospels.

4. P. Oxy. 840.35-41[24]

ὅπερ
[κα]ὶ αἱ πόρναι καὶ α[ἱ] αὐλητρίδες μυρί-
[ζ]ου[σαι κ]αὶ λούουσιν καὶ σμήχουσι
[καὶ κ]αλλωπίζουσι πρὸς ἐπιθυμί-
[αν τ]ῶν ἀνθρώπων, ἔνδοθεν δὲ ἐκεῖ-
[ναι πεπλ]ήρω[ν]ται σκορπίων καὶ
[πάσης ἀδι]κίας.*

. . . which harlots and flute girls also anoint, wash, wipe, and beautify for the lust of men, whereas within they are full of scorpions and wickedness of

---

[23]According to Klostermann, *Apocrypha* 2:21-22.

[24]Cf. ibid., 24, which refers to Swete, *Zwei neue Evangelienfragmente*, which gives the Greek text on pp. 4 and 5. Regarding this papyrus Oxyrhynchus 840, see also B. P. Grenfell and A. C. Hunt, *Oxyrhynchus Papyri*, vol. 5 (1907) no. 840; Grenfell and Hunt, *Fragment of an Uncanonical Gospel from Oxyrhynchus*, Egypt Exploration Fund, Graeco-Roman Branch (Oxford, London, New York, Toronto, 1908); A. Büchler, "The New Fragment of an Uncanonical Gospel," in *JQR* 20 (1908): 330-46; E. Preuschen, "Das Neue Evangelienfragment von Oxyrhynchus," in *ZNW* 9 (1908): 1-11; E. Schürer, "Fragment of an Uncanonical Gospel," in *TLZ* 33 (1908): 170ff.; A. Sulzbach, "Zum Oxyrhynchus-Fragment," in *ZNW* 9 (1908): 175ff.; L. Blau, "Das neue Fragment von Oxyrhynchos, buch- und zaubergeschichtlich betrachtet," in *ZNW* 9 (1908): 204-15; A. Marmorstein, "Einige Bemerkungen zum Evangelienfragment in Oxyrhynchus Papyri, V, Nᵣ 840," in *ZNW* 15 (1914): 336-38; E. Riggenbach, "Das Wort Jesu im Gespräch mit dem pharisäischen Hohenpriester nach dem Oxyrh. Fragment, V, Nᵣ 840," in *ZNW* 25 (1926): 140-44; J. Jeremias, "Der Zusammenstoss Jesu mit dem Pharisäischen Oberpriester auf dem Tempelplatz. Zu Pap. Ox. V, 840," in *ConNT* 11 (in honorem A. Fridrichsen) (1945): 97-108; Jeremias, *Unknown Sayings of Jesus*, 36-49.

*Stroker reads κακίας (wickedness) instead of Massaux's ἀδικίας (injustice). [Editor's note.]

every kind. [Stroker, 22.]

The entire Oxyrhynchus papyrus no. 840 recalls one of the numerous arguments between the Christ and the Scribes and Pharisees. Similar ideas are found, particularly in this cited passage in which Christ's offensive epithets to the Pharisees are parallel to Mt. 23:25, 33 and Lk. 11:39, and yet without using their words. This depicts, therefore, nothing more than a similar episode.

5. P. Oxy. 1081[25]

Two very similar texts are found in two parts of this fragment.

(a) lines 13-14

ὁ ἔχων ὦτ[α ἀκού]ειν ἀ-
κουέτω.

He who has ea[rs to hea]r, let him hear. [Editor's translation.]

(b) lines 8-10

ὁ ἔχων ὦ[τ]α τ[ὰ ὄντα
πέραν τῶν [ἀ]κο[ῶ]ν ἀ-
κουέτω.

He who has e[ar]s m[ade] to [h]e[a]r . . . let him hear. [Editor's translation.]

The first of these two formulas is frequent in the synoptics: it is read in Mt. 11:15 (the reading of ℵ, C, E, F, G, H, Θ); 13:9 (the reading of C, E, F, G, H, D); 13:43 (the reading of C, E, F, G, H, D); Mk. 4:9, 23; and Lk. 8:8; 14:35.

6. P. Oxy. 1224.2r[26]

ὁ γὰρ μὴ ὢν
κατὰ ὑμ[ῶν ὑπὲρ ὑμῶν ἐστιν.

For he who is not [against you] is for you. [Stroker, 201.]

These words echo Mt. 12:30; Mk. 9:40; and Lk. 9:50, but the sentence of the fragment is found literally only in Lk. Indeed, the text of Lk. has the same pronoun ὑμῶν as in the fragment, as opposed to ἐμοῦ in Mt. and ἡμῶν in the usual reading of Mk. Yet, a reading of Mk. 9:40, sustained by D, E, F, G, H and the Vulgate, also uses the pronoun ὑμῶν; it, therefore, becomes impossible to decide in favor of Lk. or this reading of the second gospel.

---

[25]According to Klostermann, *Apocrypha* 2:25.
[26]Cf. ibid., 26.

As I conclude this argument, I would like to mention the term ἀντίδιχος in P. Oxy. 1224.2r,[27] which is also read in Mt. 5:25; Lk. 12:58; 18:3; as well as 1 Pet. 5:8.

Before drawing this chapter to a conclusion, let me note that several agrapha have been attributed to a gospel or to Christ, whereas they obviously depend on New Testament writings other than the gospels. These agrapha were generally given by ecclesiastical writers who wrote much later, and who, therefore, are outside of my focus of interest.[28] These writers may themselves have been the ones who ascribed these agrapha to Christ.

There are quite a few agrapha in which a literary influence of Mt. is certain. Several texts of the first gospel were adopted almost literally; elsewhere, Matthean sentences have served as a basis for certain fragments.

---

[27]Cf. ibid., 26.

[28]These principal agrapha are found in Klostermann, *Apocrypha* 3, nos. 47, 48, 50, 51, 75, and 82.

Editor's Addendum to Chapter 5

Wolf-Dietrich Köhler (*Die Rezeption des Matthäusevangeliums in der Zeit vor Irenäus*, 453-55) concludes that the following agrapha show knowledge of the Gospel of Matthew.*

PAPYRUS EGERTON 3	MATTHEW
45.4-8	4:5
45.8-12	27:52-53
46.44-46	5:8

PAPYRUS CAIRENSIS 10735	MATTHEW
86	2:13

Biblia Patristica (*Index des Citations et Allusions bibliques dans la Littérature patristique, Des Origines à Clément d'Alexandrie et Tertullien*, vol. 1 [Paris, 1975] 223-93) lists the following citations or allusions to the Gospel of Matthew among the papyri.*

PAPYRUS EGERTON 3	MATTHEW
45.4	4:5
46.44	5:8
45.9	27:52-53

PAPYRUS CAIRENSIS 10735	MATTHEW
86.1	2:13

PAPYRUS OXYRHYNCHURS 840	MATTHEW
488.31	23:16
489.35	23:26

PAPYRUS OXYRHYNCHUS 1224	MATTHEW
492.2	5:44
491.16	9:10
491.18	9:12

---

*The editions cited are A. de Santos Otero, *Los Evangelios apócrifos*, 2nd ed. (Madrid, 1963): 86 for Papyrus Cairensis 10735; H. J. Bell and T. C. Skeat, *Fragments of an Unknown Gospel and Other Early Christian Papyri* (London, 1935) rev. in *The New Gospel Fragments* (London, 1935) for Papyrus Egerton 3; Carl Wessely, Patrologie Orientalis 18.3 (1924): 488-89 for Papyrus Oxyrhynchus 840; and ibid., 490-93 for Papyrus Oxyrhynchus 1224.

Chapter 6

SOME GNOSTIC WRITINGS

The year 1948 marked the discovery of new Gnostic writings of such a nature as to furnish elements essential for the study of Gnosticism.[1] Henceforth, it will be necessary to refer to these writings in order to gain an overall view of this movement. But the publication of these several thousand pages, which encompass forty-three Gnostic treatises lost until then, will demand much time, and we have not yet reached the day that will allow us to draw from this source.* I do not know whether their documentary evidence will be much help for understanding the ancient period which concerns me. For obvious reasons, this chapter does not take into consideration the contents of this Gnostic library but only wishes to scan several Gnostic writings which are definitely authentic and which have been preserved in a generally fragmentary form in later Christian literature. I deliberately do not enter into the labyrinth of Irenaeus's and Hippolytus's accounts; indeed, it is not always easy to determine exactly which part belongs to the Gnostic authors and which part comes from those writers who attacked them.

Except where otherwise stated, I quote those fragments of works by Gnostic authors according to the edition of W. Völker, *Quellen zur Geschichte des christlichen Gnosis,* Sammlung ausgewählter kirchen- und dogmengeschichtlicher

---

[1]On the recent discovery of the new Gnostic writings, see H. C. Puech and J. Doresse, "Nouveaux écrits gnostiques découverts en Égypte," *Comptes rendus de l'Académie des Inscriptions* (conference of 20 February 1948) 89; Togo Mina, "Le papyrus gnostique du Musée Copte," *VigChr* 2 (1948): 129-36; J. Doresse, "Trois livres gnostiques inédits," *VigChr* 2 (1948): 137-60; id., "Nouveaux livres gnostiques coptes découverts en Haute-Égypte" (lecture delivered at the Academy of Inscriptions and Letters on 17 June 1949); id., "Douze volumes dans une jarre," *Les Nouvelles Littéraires* (Paris, 30 June 1949); id., "Une bibliothèque gnostique copte découverte en Haute-Égypte" (lecture delivered at the Royal Academy of Belgium on 4 July 1949) *Bulletin de l'Académie,* 399-413; id., "Une bibliothèque gnostique copte," *La Nouvelle Clio* 1 (Brussels, 1949): 59-70, in which is found a list of the works contained in this library; J. Doresse and Togo Mina, "Nouveaux Textes gnostiques coptes découverts en Haute-Égypte: la bibliothèque de Chénoboskion," *VigChr* 3 (1949): 129-41.

*Editor's note. Since Massaux wrote these words in 1950, a definitive English translation of these writings has been published. See *The Nag Hammadi Library in English,* 3rd ed., ed. James M. Robinson (San Francisco: Harper & Row, 1988).

Quellenschriften 5 (Tübingen, 1932).[2]

The first section is devoted to Basilides and his disciples; the second longer section deals with Valentinus and his school.[3]

Section 1
BASILIDES AND HIS DISCIPLES

Basilides taught in Alexandria from approximately A.D. 120 to 140. He is the author of three works: a gospel, a commentary on this gospel, and Psalms or Odes. Origen mentions the Gospel of Basilides.[4] The Commentary, according to Agrippa Castor as cited by Eusebius,[5] was composed of twenty-four books: some passages are recorded by the author of the *Acta Archelai et Manetis,* by Origen, and by Clement of Alexandria. The third work, Psalms or Odes, is known only by name.[6]

Isidore, ''the legitimate son and disciple of Basilides,''[7] also wrote three books, and, according to Clement of Alexandria, their titles are: ''On the In-grown Soul,[8] ''Ethics,''[9] and ''Explanation of the Prophet Parchor.''[10]

This section consists of two paragraphs: the first is concerned with the Gospel of Matthew, the second with the other New Testament writings.[11]

---

[2]I cite this edition with the abbreviation Vk. followed by two numbers, the first referring to the page, and the second to the line of the passage in question.

[3]I omit Carpocrates and his son Epiphanes, the latter having written a work entitled Περὶ δικαιοσύνης, whose fragments have been preserved by Clement of Alexandria in *Stromata* 3.2.5-9. These fragments do not actually contain any passage suitable for literary comparison with the first gospel; only one text (*Strom.* 3.7.2 = Vk. 35.2-6) may reveal a literary influence from Paul (Rom. 7:7). Cf. Völker, *Quellen zur Geschichte der christlichen Gnosis,* 33.7-35.29. See also O. Stählin, *Clemens Alexandrinus,* Griechische christliche Schriftsteller 15, vol. 2 (Leipzig, 1906) 197, 18-199, 13; 199, 29bis-200, 4; A. Hilgenfeld, *Die Ketzergeschichte des Urchristentums* (Leipzig, 1894): 403-405.

[4]Cf. Origen, *Hom. 1 in Lk.*

[5]Cf. Eusebius, *Hist. Eccl.* 4.7.7.

[6]Cf. Origen, *In Job* 21.2ff.

[7]Cf. Hippolytus, *Philos.* 7.20.

[8]Cf. Clement of Alexandria, *Strom.* 2.20.113.

[9]Cf. ibid., 3.1.2.

[10]Cf. ibid., 6.6.53. Concerning Basilides, see P. J. G. A. Hendrix's monograph, *De Alexandrijnsche haeresiarch Basilides* (Dordrecht, 1926); cf. B. Altaner, *Patrology,* 141.

[11]The texts of the fragments of Basilides and his son Isidore are found in Völker, *Quellen zur Geschichte des christlichen Gnosis,* 39, 20-43, 25; see also H. Beeson, *Hegemonious. Acta Archelaï,* GCS 16 (Leipzig, 1906) chap. 67, 4-12, pp. 96, 10-97, 24; Stählin, *Clemens Alexandrinus,* vol. 2, 174, 21-20; 195, 4-196, 16; 284, 5-285, 3; 286, 3-6; C. H. E. Lommatzch, *Origenis opera omnia,* vol. 6 (Berlin, 1836) 336ff.; Higenfeld, *Die Ketzergeschichte des Urchristentums,* 207-09; 213-17. [The English translations are the work of the editor.]

§1. Saint Matthew

1. Fragment 2 (Clement of Alexandria, *Strom.* 4.82.3; Vk. 40.20-24)

'Ως γὰρ ὁ μοιχεῦσαι θέλων μοιχός ἐστι, κἂν τοῦ μοιχεῦσαι μὴ ἐπιτύχῃ, καὶ ὁ ποιῆσαι φόνον θέλων ἀνδροφόνος ἐστί, κἂν μὴ δύνηται φονεῦσαι, οὑτωσὶ δὴ καὶ τὸν ἀναμάρτητον, ὃν λέγω, ἐὰν ἴδω πάσχοντα, κἂν μηδὲν ᾖ κακὸν πεπραχώς, κακὸν ἐρῶ τῷ θέλειν ἁμαρτάνειν.

For just as he who wishes to commit adultery is an adulterer, even if he did not have the opportunity to commit adultery, and just as he who wishes to commit murder is a murderer, even if he was not able to kill, so it is that if I see suffering the one whom I thought had not sinned, I shall call him evil because he has wished to sin.

The words "he who wishes to commit adultery is an adulterer" echo Mt. 5:28: ὁ βλέπων γυναῖκα πρὸς τὸ ἐπιθυμῆσαι [αὐτὴν] ἤδη ἐμοίχευσεν αὐτὴν ἐν τῇ καρδίᾳ αὐτοῦ.

2. Fragment 7 (Clement of Alexandria, *Strom.* 3.1.1; Vk. 42.18-21)

οἱ δὲ ἀπὸ Βασιλείδου πυθομένων φασὶ τῶν ἀποστόλων μὴ ποτε ἄμεινόν ἐστι τὸ μὴ γαμεῖν ἀποκρίνασθαι λέγουσι τὸν κύριον· οὐ πάντες χωροῦσι τὸν λόγον τοῦτον· εἰσὶ γὰρ εὐνοῦχοι, οἱ μὲν ἐκ γενετῆς, οἱ δὲ ἐξ ἀνάγκης.

The sectarians of Basilides say, "As the apostles wondered whether it was better not to marry," the Lord, they say, answered, "Not everyone understands this saying: for there are eunuchs, some by birth and others by necessity."

This passage definitely refers to Mt. 19:10-12, which is the only one that has a similar narrative. The literary dependence on Mt. is certain. Indeed, the words of Mt., γαμέω, οὐ πάντες χωροῦσι τὸν λόγον τοῦτον, and εἰσὶν γὰρ εὐνοῦχοι, are found in the fragment. Furthermore, the apostles' question, ἄμεινον ἐστι τὸ μὴ γαμεῖν, corresponds to the question in Mt., οὐ συμφέρει γαμῆσαι. Finally, if in this text the sectarians of Basilides seem to distinguish only two types of eunuchs, those by birth and those by necessity, they actually add a third category, οἱ δὲ ἕνεκα τῆς αἰωνίου βασιλείας εὐνουχίσαντες ἑαυτούς,[12] in the commentary they give on this saying of Christ, thus allowing us to assume that they were interpreting the saying of Christ. The three kinds of eunuchs characterized by Mt. are, therefore, present, and the Basilidians explain them in their own way.

---

[12]Cf. Clement of Alexandria, *Strom.* 3.1.4; Vk. 43.2-4.

§2. The Other New Testament Writings

The fragments of Basilides and of his son Isidore do not include any text that may be compared with the gospels of Mk., Lk., or Jn. Several passages may have literary relationships with the Pauline writings.

Fragment 3 (Origen, *In Epist. ad Rom.* 5.1; Vk. 41.13-15) reads, "Dixit enim, inquit apostolus, quia 'ego vivebam sine lege aliquando' hoc est, antequam in istud corpus venirem, in ea specie corporis vixi, quae sub lege non esset, pecudis scilicet vel avis." Origen reported here Basilides's commentary on Rom. 7:9, which he cited literally.

Fragment 7 (Clement of Alexandria, *Strom.* 3.2.1; Vk. 43.6-9) states, "When the apostle said: It is better to marry than to burn (ἄμεινον γαμῆσαι ἢ πυροῦσ-θαι), they said that he meant: So that you may not set your soul on fire night and day, resist and fear so as to remain chaste." This is a commentary on 1 Cor. 7:9.

In the rare fragments of Basilides and his disciples, I mentioned one passage which bears a definite literary dependence on the first gospel; I detected no trace of the other gospels. On the other hand, two texts seem to refer explicitly to the words of Paul, on which Basilides and his disciples commented as being in sympathy with their system, and in which they found a confirmation of their teaching.

Section 2
VALENTINUS AND HIS SCHOOL

Born in Egypt, Valentinus lived in Rome from approximately A.D. 135 to 160. He wrote letters and homilies of which Clement of Alexandria relates small fragments.[13] We are left with only one single fragment[14] of his psalms which are often mentioned.[15] His disciples were Heracleon and Ptolemy in the West and Theodotus in the East. Heracleon composed a commentary on the Gospel of John from which Origen borrowed many passages; two fragments of the commentary have also been preserved by Clement of Alexandria.[16] Epiphanius conveyed Ptolemy's *Letter to Flora*,[17] and Irenaeus has handed down his commentary on the prologue of Jn.[18] Clement of Alexandria has given us citations from Theodotus in his work entitled "Excerpts from Theodotus."[19]

---

[13]Cf. Clement of Alexandria, *Strom.* 2.8.36; 4.13.89ff.

[14]Cf. Tertullian, *De Carne Christi* 17; 20.

[15]Cf. Hippolytus, *Philos.* 6.37.6-8.

[16]Cf. Clement of Alexandria, *Eclog. proph.* 25.1; *Strom.* 4.9.70ff.

[17]Cf. Epiphanius, *Panarion haer.* 33.3-7.

[18]Cf. Irenaeus, *Adv. Haer.* 1.8.5-6.

[19]On all these Valentinian names and sources, see F. Sagnard, *La Gnose valentinienne et le Témoignage de S. Irénée* (Paris, 1947).

I propose to examine in turn the fragments of Valentinus, those of Heracleon, the *Letter of Ptolemy to Flora* and the commentary on the prologue of the fourth gospel by Ptolemy.[20]

§1. The Fragments of Valentinus[21]

A. Saint Matthew

1. Fragment 2 (Clement of Alexandria, Strom. 2.114.3-6; Vk. 58.4-5)

Οὐαλεντῖνος πρός τινας ἐπιστέλλων αὐταῖς λέξεσι γράφει . . . ·
εἷς δέ ἐστιν ἀγαθός, οὗ παρρησία ἡ διὰ τοῦ υἱοῦ φανέρωσις.

Valentinus addressed certain people and wrote to them textually: Only one is good and his expression is the disclosure by the Son.

The beginning of this fragment recalls Mt. 19:17; Mk. 10:18; and Lk. 18:19. Only Mt. uses the expression εἷς ἐστιν ὁ ἀγαθός. A reminiscence of the Matthean text is, therefore, possible.

2. Fragment 2 (Clement of Alexandria, *Strom.* 2.114.3-6; Vk. 58.15-17)

Ἐπειδὰν δὲ ἐπισκέψηται αὐτὴν ὁ μόνος ἀγαθὸς πατήρ, ἡγίασται καὶ φωτὶ διαλάμπει, καὶ οὕτω μακαρίζεται ὁ ἔχων τὴν τοιαύτην καρδίαν, ὅτι ὄψεται τὸν θεόν.

When he, the only good Father, has visited it (this dwelling place of demons which is the heart of man), it is sanctified and shines with light, and this is how he who has such a heart is proclaimed blessed, because he will see God.

Mt. 19:17; Mk. 10:18; and Lk. 18:19 may be mentioned again as parallels to the words ὁ μόνος ἀγαθὸς πατήρ. With this expression, it is clear that Valentinus alludes to the first words of his letter reported above. Now, if there is here a lit-

---

[20]I do not examine the "Excerpts from Theodotus" in which it is difficult to distinguish between what belongs to Theodotus and what belongs to Clement of Alexandria. I cannot, therefore, rely with certainty on this work; for each text, I would have had to decipher what belongs to Theodotus, and this would have taken me too far from my goal. F. Sagnard has attempted a reconstruction of the "Excerpts of Theodotus" in *Clément d'Alexandrie, Extraits de Théodote*, SC 23 (Paris, 1948).

[21]The fragments of Valentinus are found in Völker, *Quellen zur Geschichte der christlichen Gnosis*, 57.18-60.10; see also Stählin, *Clemens Alexandrinus*, vol. 2, 132, 6-16; 174, 3-175; 223, 12-16; 287, 10-15, 21-27; 456, 11-16; P. Wendland, *Hippolytus Werke*, vol. 3 (Berlin, 1906) 167, 14bis-168, 4; 173, 22-25; G. Mercati, "Note di litteratura biblica e cristiana antica," *Studi e Testi* 5 (Rome, 1901) 96; Hilgenfeld, *Die Ketzergeschichte des Urchristentums*, 293-305.

erary reminiscence of Mt. 19:7, it naturally follows that this Gnostic refers to it once again.

The last words of the cited text recall Mt. 5:8, μακάριοι οἱ καθαροὶ τῇ καρδίᾳ, ὅτι αὐτοὶ τὸν θεὸν ὄψονται, with which a literary contact is certain. First of all, let me note that only the first gospel contains this beatitude. Next, the fragment goes on to say "that the heart of man is impure: it is an inn where many evil spirits dwell. But as fate would have it, when he happens to meet the Father who alone is good and who lets his eye dwell upon him, he then shines with light." [22] His heart is purified and happy because he will see God. The entire context is, therefore, about purity of the heart. [23] Now, Mt. 5:8 speaks of it as well. It is, therefore, credible that Valentinus depends here on the text of the first gospel because, in addition, the formula μακαρίζεται ὁ ἔχων τὴν τοιαύτην καρδίαν is equivalent to μακάριοι οἱ καθαροὶ τῇ καρδίᾳ, and ὄψεται τὸν θεόν picks up τὸν θεὸν ὄψονται from Mt.

Out of the nine fragments of Valentinus we have, one of these is definitely literarily dependent on a Matthean text, and another probably constitutes a reminiscence of another passage from the first gospel.

B. The Other New Testament Writings

In the fragments of Valentinus, there is no trace of a literary influence stemming from the other New Testament writings. At best, I can mention in fragment 4 [24] the expression ζωὴ αἰώνιος, which has a rather Johannine tint, [25] and the words τὸ τοῦ θεοῦ ἀόρατον in fragment 5, [26] which resemble fairly well those of Rom. 1:20: τὰ γὰρ ἀόρατα αὐτοῦ (θεοῦ).

Thus, in the few fragments of Valentinus only the first gospel has exercised a definite literary influence.

§2. The Fragments of Heracleon [27]

A. Saint Matthew

1. Fragment 5 (Origen, Comm. on John 6.20ff.; Vk. 66.7-11)

Καὶ προφήτην μὲν καὶ Ἡλίαν ὁ σωτὴρ ἐπὰν αὐτὸν λέγῃ, οὐκ αὐτὸν ἀλλὰ τὰ περὶ αὐτόν, φησί, διδάσκει· ὅταν δὲ μείζονα προφητῶν καὶ ἐν γεννητοῖς γυναικῶν, τότε αὐτὸν τὸν Ἰωάννην χαρακτηρίζει.

When the Savior called him (John the Baptist) a prophet and Elijah, he said that he does not allude to him, but to the things around him; when he calls

---

[22]Cf. Sagnard, *La Gnose valentinienne*, 122-23.

[23]Cf. Vk., 58.6.

[24]Cf. Clement of Alexandria, *Strom.* 4.89.1 (Vk. 58.24).

[25]Cf. Jn. 3:15, 16, 36; 4:14, 36; 5:24, 39; 6:27, 40, 47, 53, 63; 10:28; 12:25, 50; 17:2, 3; 1Jn. 1:2; 2:25; 3:15; 5:11, 13, 20; this expression is also found in Mt. 19:29; 25:46; Mk. 10:30; Lk. 10:25; Acts 13:46, 48; Rom. 2:7; 5:21; 6:22, 23; 1 Tim. 1:16; 6:12; Tit. 1:2; Jude 21.

[26]Cf. Clement of Alexandria, *Strom.* 4.89.6-90.1 (Vk. 59.5-7).

[27]The fragments of Heracleon are found in Völker's edition, *Quellen zur Geschichte*

him greater than the prophets and (the greatest) among the children of women, he then characterizes John himself.

This text can be linked to Mt. 11:9, 11, 14: Ἀλλὰ τί ἐξήλθατε; προφήτην ἰδεῖν; ναὶ λέγω ὑμῖν, καὶ περισσότερον προφήτου . . . ἀμὴν λέγω ὑμῖν, οὐκ ἐγήγερται ἐν γεννητοῖς γυναικῶν μείζων Ἰωάννου τοῦ βαπτιστοῦ· . . . καὶ εἰ θέλετε δέξασθαι, αὐτός ἐστιν Ἡλίας ὁ μέλλων ἔρχεσθαι, and to Lk. 7:26, 28: Ἀλλὰ τί ἐξήλθατε ἰδεῖν; προφήτην; ναὶ λέγω ὑμῖν, καὶ περισσότερον προφήτου . . . λέγω ὑμῖν, μείζων ἐν γεννητοῖς γυναικῶν Ἰωάννου οὐδείς ἐστιν.

While commenting on Jn. 1:20-21, 23, Heracleon refers here to other gospel texts. Is it to Mt., or is it to Lk.? In this case, preference is to be given to the Matthean text, which is the only one to speak of Elijah in this passage, identifying John the Baptist with this prophet. Mt. also says—because of my preceding statement, I shall ignore the parallel in Lk.—προφήτης, ἐν γεννητοῖς γυναικῶν, and μείζων, words which are present in this fragment. These elements are sufficient enough to maintain a definite literary contact of Heracleon with the text of Mt. Let me still add, however, that, according to Heracleon's text itself, it is necessary to distinguish in John the Baptist ''the things around him'' and what he is within himself; one calls him a prophet, and to another, he is more than a prophet. Now, this distinction seems to come from the comparison between Jn. 1:21 and Mt. 11:7-15 from which the fragment takes up some elements word for word.[28]

2. Fragment 10 (Origen, Comm. on John, 6.60; Vk. 68.20-23)

Τὸ μὲν ἀμνὸς τοῦ θεοῦ ὡς προφήτης φησὶν ὁ Ἰωάννης, τὸ δὲ ὁ αἴρων τὴν ἁμαρτίαν τοῦ κοσμοῦ, ὡς περισσότερον προφήτου.

Lamb of God, John says it as a prophet. He who takes away the sin of the world, inasmuch as he is more than a prophet.

The last words recall Mt. 11:9 and Lk. 7:26 in which Christ called John the Baptist: περισσότερον προφήτου. They also recall fragment 5 in which Heracleon reminds us that Christ has called John the Baptist the greatest of the prophets, but in which the expression περισσότερον προφήτου is missing. Now, I demonstrated precisely in fragment 5 that there is a definite literary influence stemming from the verses of Mt. which form the context of Mt. 11:9. I can, there-

---

der christlichen Gnosis, 63, 24-86, 24. See also E. Preuschen, ''Origines Johannes Kommentar,'' vol. 4 of Origen's works, GCS 10 (Leipzig, 1903); O. Stählin, *Clemens Alexandrinus,* vol. 2 (Leipzig, 1906); vol. 3 (1909); Hilgenfeld, *Die Ketzergeschichte des Urchristentums,* 472-98; A. E. Brooke, *The Fragments of Heracleon,* TextsS 1/4 (Cambridge, 1891) 50-103; W. Förster, *Von Valentin zu Heracleon (Giessen, 1928); J. Mouson,* ''La Théologie d'Héracléon'' (Th.D. diss., Catholic University of Louvain, 1949). [The English translations are the work of the editor.]

[28] Cf. Mouson, *La Théologie d'Héracléon,* 191.

fore, reasonably suppose that Heracleon is referring here to Mt. 11:9. The expression περισσότερον προφήτου is one more element which indicates that, while doing an exegesis of the Gospel of Jn., Heracleon draws his inspiration from the first gospel.

3. Fragment 13 (Origen, Comm. on John, 10.33; Vk. 70.17-21)

Concerning the episode of the money-changers in the temple in Jn. 2:13-15, Heracleon wrote,

Οὐ γὰρ ἐκ δέρματος νεκροῦ ἐποίησεν αὐτό, ἵνα τὴν ἐκκλησίαν κατασκευάσῃ οὐκέτι λῃστῶν καὶ ἐμπόρων σπήλαιον, ἀλλὰ οἶκον τοῦ πατρὸς αὐτοῦ.

For he has not made it (the whip) with dead skin, in order to build the Church, nor a cave of bandits and merchants, but the house of his Father.

The end of this passage echoes the same incident narrated by the synoptics: Mt. 21:13, ὁ οἶκός μου οἶκος προσευχῆς κληθήσεται, ὑμεῖς δὲ αὐτὸν ποιεῖτε σπήλαιον λῃστῶν; Mk. 11:17, οὐ γέγραπται ὅτι ὁ οἶκός μου οἶκος προσευχῆς κληθήσεται πᾶσιν τοῖς ἔθνεσιν; ὑμεῖς δὲ πεποιήκατε αὐτὸν σπήλαιον λῃστῶν; Lk. 19:46, γέγραπται· καὶ ἔσται ὁ οἶκός μου οἶκος προσευχῆς· ὑμεῖς δὲ αὐτὸν ἐποιήσατε σπήλαιον λῃστῶν. These parallels cite explicitly the scripture, and they present a text which is a combination of Is. 56:7 and Jer. 7:11. Heracleon has taken up this citation of the narrative of the money-changers in the temple from one of the synoptics. But which one? In face of the similarity of expressions of these synoptics, it is difficult to determine which one ought to be given preference. But, as we shall see, the Gospel of Mt. seems to have been specially used by Heracleon. It is, therefore, credible that here again he borrowed the words λῃστῶν σπήλαιον from Mt. and joined them to those of Jn. 2:16.[29]

4. Fragment 32 (Origen, Comm. on John 13.41; Vk. 77.22-25)

This fragment comments on Jn. 4:35: "Do you not say, 'There are yet four months, and then comes the harvest'? I tell you . . . the fields are already white for harvest." Heracleon notes that Christ speaks of the harvest of young shoots; one harvest will take another four months, but the harvest of which he speaks is ready to be reaped. The harvest is a metaphor for the soul of the believers. Then comes the text:

Ἤδη ἀκμαῖοι καὶ ἔτοιμοί εἰσιν πρὸς θερισμὸν καὶ ἐπιτήδειοι πρὸς τὸ συναχθῆναι εἰς ἀποθήκην τουτέστι διὰ πίστεως εἰς ἀνάπαυσιν, ὅσαι γε ἔτοιμοι.

---

[29]Cf. ibid., 191.

They [the souls of the believers] are already ripe and ready for the harvest, and suited to be gathered into the barn, that is to say, through faith in rest— for those at least who are ready.

The expression συναχθῆναι εἰς ἀποθήκην is read also in Mt. 13:30: τὸν δὲ σῖτον συναγάγετε εἰς τὴν ἀποθήκην μου. When Heracleon speaks of the harvest and of the time of the harvest, he may have thought of the parable of the tares in Mt., which also speaks of the harvest which has come. A literary contact is, therefore, possible. The same remark holds true for fragment 33 in which the same text is found.[30]

5. Fragment 33 (Origen, Comm. on John 13.44; Vk. 78.1-4)

Before examining this passage, it is useful to recall the context in which it is inserted. Having cited Heracleon in fragment 32, Origen finishes the commentary on Jn. 4:35.[31] He then goes on to verse 36 of this same chapter. Wondering how to apply the metaphor of the harvest, he mentions six parallels in the scripture, the second being Mt. 9:37-38. In presenting objections to these parallels, he remarks with regard to the second,

Καὶ ἐρεῖ γε ὁ Ἡρακλέων, τάχα δὲ τούτῳ κατὰ τὴν ἐκδοχὴν ταύτην συμπεριφερόμενός τις καὶ ἐκκλησιαστικός, ὅτι τῷ κατὰ τὸ ὁ θερισμὸς πολύς, οἱ δὲ ἐργάται ὀλίγοι σημαινομένῳ ὁμοίως ταῦτα εἴρηται.

Heracleon will no doubt say, and perhaps some member of the Church as well who agrees with him in this expectation, that the [Johannine] text is meant in a sense which is similar to the one identified with "the harvest is great and the laborers are few."

The last sentence finds precise parallels in Mt. 9:37 and Lk. 10:2, both of which read, ὁ μὲν θερισμὸς πολύς, οἱ δὲ ἐργάται ὀλίγοι. Since the parallels are textually identical, it is difficult to determine which one Heracleon has used. We shall actually see that not one passage of the fragments of Heracleon reveals a definite literary dependence on a text that is peculiar to Lk., whereas this is not the case for Mt. Therefore, whenever passages in Mt. and Lk. have an identical text and are parallel to a passage of Heracleon, it is logical to give preference to the first gospel as being the one on which this Gnostic depends.

6. Fragment 35 (Origen, Comm. on John, 13.49; Vk. 79.4-8)

Still in the commentary on the pericope of the harvest, more particularly in Jn. 4:37, Origen states,

Heracleon said: For the proverb is true if we understand that the sower is someone other than the harvester; the Son of Man indeed sows over the place.

---

[30]Cf. Origen, *Comm. on John* 13.44 (Vk. 78.5-6).
[31]Cf. ibid., 12.42.

And the Savior, who is also the Son of Man, harvests and sends as harvesters the angels, portrayed by the disciples, each toward his own soul (ὁ μὲν γὰρ ὑπὲρ τὸν τόπον υἱὸς ἀνθρώπου σπείρει· ὁ δὲ σωτήρ, ὢν καὶ αὐτὸς υἱὸς ἀνθρώπου, θερίζει καὶ θεριστὰς πέμπει τοὺς διὰ τῶν μαθητῶν νοουμένους ἀγγέλους, ἕκαστον ἐπὶ τὴν ἑαυτοῦ ψυχήν).

Several expressions in this fragment remind us of the commentary on the parable of the good grain and the weeds in Mt. 13:36-48, and more particularly in verses 37: ὁ σπείρων τὸ καλὸν σπέρμα ἐστὶν ὁ υἱὸς τοῦ ἀνθρώπου; 39: οἱ δὲ θερισταὶ ἄγγελοί εἰσιν; and 41: ἀποστελεῖ ὁ υἱὸς τοῦ ἀνθρώπου τοὺς ἀγγέλους αὐτοῦ.

In the commentary on the pericope of the harvest, Heracleon has already drawn his inspiration from the Matthean parable,[32] and he still depends on it here. First of all, indeed, for him as for Mt., the theme is the harvest, the sower is the Son of Man, the angels harvest, the Son of Man sends his angels; and then we find in Heracleon several words from the Matthean passage: σπείρω, υἱὸς ἀνθρώπου, θερισταί, and οἱ ἄγγελοι.[33]

7. Fragment 40 (Origen, Comm. on John, 13.60; Vk. 80.30-81.1)

Origen reports here that in the words of Jn. 4:47, ἤμελλεν ἀποθνήσκειν, Heracleon sees a rebuttal of the assertions of those who claim that the soul is immortal. Then comes the following passage:

εἰς τὸ αὐτὸ συμβάλλεσθαι καὶ τὸ ψυχὴν καὶ σῶμα ἀπόλλυσθαι ἐν γεέννῃ.

The following text focuses on the same goal: the soul and the body perish in gehenna.

Given that Heracleon saw in the text of Jn. 4:47 the falsity of the defenders' opinion on the immortality of the soul, the word τό, which introduces the phrase ψυχὴν καὶ σῶμα ἀπόλλυσθαι ἐν γεέννῃ, indicates that Heracleon is referring here as well to a text, and he adds another text to the text of Jn. in order to prove his views. Now, the added phrase finds parallels in Mt. 10:28: φοβεῖσθε δὲ μᾶλλον τὸν δυνάμενον καὶ ψυχὴν καὶ σῶμα ἀπολέσαι ἐν γεέννῃ, and Lk. 12:5: φοβήθητε τὸν μετὰ τὸ ἀποκτεῖναι ἔχοντα ἐξουσίαν ἐμβαλεῖν εἰς τὴν γέενναν. The examination of these two parallels makes it obvious that Heracleon is literarily dependent on the Matthean text. In fact, the latter has ψυχὴν καὶ σῶμα, ἀπόλλυμι, ἐν γεέννῃ, whereas the Lucan text has neither ψυχή nor σῶμα—this sole last word is mentioned in the preceding verse—nor ἀπόλλυμι.

---

[32]Cf. fragments 32 and 33.
[33]Cf. Mouson, *La Théologie d'Héracléon*, 191.

This passage of Heracleon, which has a literary reference to a text, which in fact is Mt., is significant. It demontrates that, for the readers of this disciple of Valentinus, the gospel of Mt. was sufficiently well known to be able to refer to it without its being necessary to make an explicit notation, and it shows the normative value attributed at that time to the first gospel.

8. Fragment 40 (Origen, Comm. on John 13.60; Vk. 82.4-7)

In the exegesis of the episode of the healing of the son of the official of Capernaum, the following text constitutes the commentary on Jn. 4:53: "and he himself believed and all his household." For Heracleon, these words apply to the angelic order and to those who are more closely linked with it. The question it raises, he says, is the salvation of certain angels, those that have come down upon the daughters of men. And he adds,

καὶ τῶν ἀνθρώπων δὲ τοῦ δημιουργοῦ τὴν ἀπώλειαν δηλοῦσθαι ἐν τῷ οἱ υἱοὶ τῆς βασιλείας ἐξελεύσονται εἰς τὸ σκότος τὸ ἐξώτερον.

As to the demiurge's men, their loss is obvious in the text; the Sons of the kingdom will leave for the outer darkness.

With the expression ἐν τῷ, Heracleon refers certainly to a text;[34] the text which he reconciles here with Jn. 4:53 is Mt. 8:12a, which he drew from the episode of the centurion of Capernaum: Heracleon has, therefore, linked the official of Capernaum with the centurion in Mt. and not in Lk. 7:1-10, because Mt. 8:12a has no parallel in the Lucan narrative.

Mt. 8:12a reads, Οἱ δὲ υἱοὶ τῆς βασιλείας ἐκβληθήσονται εἰς τὸ σκότος τὸ ἐξώτερον. I would like to point out that the variant ἐξελεύσονται instead of ἐκβληθήσονται is supported by ℵ*, k, by the Syriac Curetonian, Sinaitic and Peshitta versions, and by the Ethiopic version. This passage of Heracleon coincides literally with this text which carries the variant ἐξελεύσονται; in his commentary on the fourth gospel, this Gnostic is, by this fact, one of the most ancient witnesses to the reading ἐξελεύσονται in Mt. 8:12a.

9. Fragment 46 (Origen, Comm. on John 20.24; Vk. 84.10-12)

This fragment comments on Jn. 8:44: " . . . your will is to do your father's desires." In the course of his exegesis, Heracleon notes that the designation of "children" is justified threefold: first by birth, then by determination, and finally by merit. He then goes on to explain each of these, and he writes for the third,

ἄξια δέ, καθ' ὃ λέγονταί τινες γεέννης τέκνα καὶ σκότους καὶ ἀνομίας, καὶ ὄφεων καὶ ἐχιδνῶν γεννήματα.

---

[34]Cf. above regarding no. 7.

. . . . and by merit, in a sense whereby some speak of children of gehenna and of darkness and of iniquity, and some speak of the offspring of serpents and vipers.

He then adds,

For these things do not engender their own nature: on the contrary they are the cause of corruption and annihilation for those who are thrown into them (τοὺς ἐμβληθέντας εἰς αὐτά).

Some of the nomenclature in this fragment has been drawn from chapter 23 of Mt., which contains the curses of the Pharisees, notably in verses 15: ποιεῖτε αὐτὸν υἱὸν γεέννης διπλότερον ὑμῶν; 28: ἔσωθεν δέ ἐστε μεστοὶ ὑποκρίσεως καὶ ἀνομίας; and 33: ὄφεις, γεννήματα ἐχιδνῶν; the expression γεννήματα ἐχιδνῶν is also found in Mt. 3:7b and Lk. 3:7b. As for the word σκότος in connection with ἐμβάλλω, it appears in Mt. 8:12, cited above regarding fragment 40, and in Mt. 22:13.

In the judgment which Heracleon pronounces here on the Jews, he seems to be in literary contact with the curses of the Pharisees in Mt. from which he lifted various expressions.

10. Fragment 50 (Clement of Alexandria, Strom. 4.71ff.; Vk. 85.15-86.21)

Explicating this passage, Heracleon, the most esteemed member of the school of Valentinus, writes literally: There is confession in faith and in conduct (ὁμολογίαν εἶναι τὴν μὲν ἐν πίστει καὶ πολιτείᾳ), and confession aloud (τὴν δὲ ἐν φωνῇ). This latter (ἡ μὲν οὖν ἐν φωνῇ ὁμολογία) is the one which is also fulfilled before the authorities, and most people consider it to be the only true confession (ὁμολογίαν), but they are wrong. For even the hypocrites can confess it (ταύτην τὴν ὁμολογίαν καὶ οἱ ὑποκριταὶ ὁμολογεῖν). And in this case, the spoken word (ὁ λόγος εἰρημένος) would not even have a universal meaning since all who are saved have not made their confession aloud (ὡμολόγησαν τὴν διὰ τῆς φωνῆς ὁμολογίαν) before leaving: thus Matthew, Phillip, Thomas, Levi, and many others. Confession aloud (ἡ διὰ τῆς φωνῆς ὁμολογία) is not (then) universal, but occasional. The universal confession which (the Savior) here has in mind, is the one which is fulfilled in works and actions conformed to faith in him; it is followed by occasional confession (ταύτῃ τῇ ὁμολογίᾳ) before the authorities if it is necessary and if reason demands it. For that person will also confess (ὁμολογήσει γὰρ οὗτος) aloud who had loyally confessed beforehand (προομολογήσας) having made provisions to this effect. (The Savior) has spoken very aptly of those who confess in him (τῶν ὁμολογούντων ἐν ἐμοί) and of those who deny him (τῶν ἀρνουμένων τὸ ἐμὲ προσέθηκεν). And in fact, even if they confess him (ὁμολογήσωσιν) aloud, those are the ones who deny him (ἀρνοῦνται) and who do not confess him (μὴ ὁμολογοῦντες) through their acts. And they only confess him (ἐν αὐτῷ ὁμολογοῦσιν) those who live in the confession (ἐν τῇ ὁμολογίᾳ) and act according to him. Through them, he is also the one who confesses (ὁμολογεῖ), for he assumes them into himself and is in turn possessed by them. This is why they can in no way deny him (ἀρνήσασθαι αὐτὸν οὐδέποτε δύνανται); those who are not in him deny him. For in fact he has not said: He who denies in me (ὃς ἀρνήσεται ἐν ἐμοί), but he who denies me (ἐμέ); for no one who is in him denies him. The words "before men" (τὸ δὲ ἔμπροσθεν τῶν ἀνθρώπων) have in mind all at once the saved and the pagans, facing some through confession in life, facing others through confession aloud (καὶ τῇ φωνῇ).

The logion on which Heracleon comments in this passage is not given; but it certainly relates to the logion either in Mt. 10:32-33 or in Lk. 12:8-9. The verb ὁμολογέω and the substantive ὁμολογία which come up frequently in this fragment lead me to these passages; the words ἐν ἐμοί and τῶν ἀρνουμένων ἐμέ lead to them as well. Moreover, if the sentence "for in fact, he has not said, ὃς ἀρνήσεται ἐν ἐμοί, ἀλλ' ἐμέ" recalls the same gospel texts, it provides, however, an important indication in favor of the Matthean text as being the one to which Heracleon refers: indeed, Mt. is the only one to have ὅστις δ' ἂν ἀρνήσηταί με, whereas Lk. does not use the personal form ἀρνήσηται, but rather the participial form ὁ δὲ ἀρνησάμενός με. Now, in general, Heracleon reproduces rather faithfully the text on which he comments, as we have seen with the texts of Jn. upon which he comments and cites to account for it. It is, therefore, credible that the personal form ἀρνήσηται refers to the text of Mt. If I add to these considerations the fact that it has been established that Heracleon is never in a definite literary contact with any text peculiar to Lk., I may conclude with all the more certainty that it is indeed Mt. 10:32-33 which the disciple of Valentinus explicates.

These ten passages which belong to the fifty-one preserved fragments of Heracleon demonstrate clearly the very great use that this author made of Mt. He came under such a profound influence from the first gospel that he used its words to comment on the fourth gospel. In all the great pericopes of Jn., except naturally the prologue, he borrowed from Mt. his principles of interpretation as if Mt. were the norm to which anyone had usual recourse in his time. With respect to the Matthean texts themselves, Heracleon demonstrates a fairly great fidelity, and sometimes even went so far as to reproduce them literally.

B. The Other New Testament Writings

None of the fragments of Heracleon suppose a literary dependence on Mk. In the same vein, I cannot point to any passage where Heracleon has a definite literary contact with Lk. The few texts admitting of comparison with this gospel have an identical parallel in Mt., and since Heracleon usually cites Mt., preference must logically be given to the latter.

Several passages of the fragments reveal a literary affinity with the epistles of Paul.

In fragment 13,[35] expounding on the following words from Jn. 2:13-15: "In the temple he found . . . , " Heracleon writes: "Not in the parvis. This is said so as not to envision that only those who are called, being under the Spirit, are delivered by the Lord, for the sanctuary is the Holy of Holies into which only the high priest enters (τὰ μὲν ἅγια τῶν ἁγίων εἶναι τὸ ἱερόν, εἰς ἃ μόνος ὁ ἀρχιερεὺς εἰσήει)." The last words recall Heb. 9:7, εἰς δὲ τὴν δευτέραν ἅπαξ τοῦ ἐνιαυτοῦ μόνος ὁ ἀρχιερεύς, upon which the author seems to be literarily dependent. Indeed, when we know that, according to Heb. 9:3, the second tent is called Ἅγια Ἁγίων, and that the verb εἰσήει is implied in verse 7 by virtue of verse 6, there is no difficulty to see in Heb. 9:7 the literary source of Heracleon. Besides finding an identical statement in this fragment, the words ἅγια ἁγίων (Heb. 9:3) and εἰς, μόνος, ὁ ἀρχιερεύς, and εἰσήει (Heb. 9:6) are there as well.

Reflecting on Jn. 4:21: "Woman, believe me, the hour is coming when neither on this mountain nor in Jerusalem will you worship," Heracleon says in fragment 20:[36] "Jerusalem is the creation or the creator which the Jews worshiped (Ἱεροσόλυμα δὲ τὴν κτίσιν ἢ τὸν κτίστην, ᾧ προσεκύνουν οἱ Ἰουδαῖοι); but a second explanation is that the mountain represents the creation which the pagans worshiped (τὴν κτίσιν, ἣ [οἱ] ἐθνικοὶ προσεκύνουν), Jerusalem being the creator which the Jews honored." The author expresses an idea similar to that of Rom. 1:25b; Paul describes in this context what has led the pagans into the ignorance of the true God: they adored the creature rather than the creator. The absence of the verb λατρεύω in Heracleon prevents me from believing in a literary contact; I can only point out a simple analogy of thought, although Paul did not distinguish, as did Heracleon, between what the pagans and the Jews adored.

In fragment 22,[37] we read in the commentary on Jn. 4:22 an idea similar to this same text of Rom. 1:25: "They served the creation and not the creator according to the truth (ἐλάτρευον τῇ κτίσει, καὶ οὐ τῷ κατ᾽ ἀλήθειαν κτίστῃ) who is Christ." Let me note here the presence of λατρεύω.

In this same fragment 22, the text states a few lines above,[38] "Salvation comes from the Jews: because he was born in Judea, but not from within them, because he did not take pleasure in all of them" (οὐ γὰρ εἰς πάντας αὐτοὺς εὐδόκησεν). The last sentence brings to mind 1 Cor. 10:5: ἀλλ᾽ οὐκ ἐν τοῖς πλείοσιν αὐτῶν εὐδόκησεν ὁ θεός. Wishing to record the censure of the Jews, the author

---

[35]Cf. Origen, *Comm. on John* 10.33 (Vk. 69.17-20).
[36]Cf. ibid., 13.16 (Vk. 73.28-74.1).
[37]Cf. ibid., 13.19 (Vk. 75.4-5).
[38]Cf. ibid., 13.19 (Vk. 74.23-26).

mentions that the words in Jn., "salvation is from the Jews," do not mean that salvation was born in them, but rather that it was born in Judea. He justifies then his exegesis by resorting to the words of Paul in 1 Cor. 10:5, in which context Paul wished to caution the Corinthians against the spirit of presumption, by putting before their eyes the example of the Israelites who came out of Egypt under the leadership of Moses, but very few of whom reached the promised land: God did not take pleasure in many of them.[39] Besides the very great analogy of the idea of censure, Heracleon and Paul have in common the verb εὐδοκέω; moreover, εἰς πάντας αὐτούς and ἐν τοῖς πλείοσιν αὐτῶν are two expressions which are very close in meaning. A literary contact with Paul seems, therefore, compelling.

Devoted to Jn. 4:24, "and those who worship him must worship in spirit and truth," fragment 24[40] states: "As it is proper, Heracleon thinks, to him who is adored spiritually, not physically. They themselves are Spirit, being of the same nature as the Father since they adore according to the truth and not according to error, following the teaching of the apostle who called this religion a spiritual worship" (καθὰ καὶ ὁ ἀπόστολος διδάσκει λέγων λογικὴν λατρείαν τὴν τοιαύτην θεοσέβειαν). In the last part of this passage, Heracleon refers explicitly to the statement of the apostle which is found in Rom. 12:1: παραστῆσαι τὰ σώματα ὑμῶν θυσίαν ζῶσαν ἁγίαν τῷ θεῷ εὐάρεστον, τὴν λογικὴν λατρείαν ὑμῶν.

In fragment 40,[41] Heracleon explains the episode of the healing of the son of the official of Capernaum. In the course of his exposition, he asserts that the words of Jn. 4:47, "for he was at the point of death," refute the affirmations of those who claim that the soul is immortal. Then he has the following text converge towards the same goal: "The soul and the body perish in gehenna," a text which he draws from Mt. 10:28 as previously shown.[42] Then he continues with, "The soul is not immortal, but it possesses a capacity for salvation; it is the corruptible which puts on incorruptibility, and the mortal which puts on immortality when death will have been swallowed by victory" (αὐτὴν εἶναι τὸ ἐνδυόμενον ἀφθαρσίαν φθαρτὸν καὶ ἀθανασίαν θνητόν, ὅταν καταποθῇ ὁ θάνατος αὐτῆς εἰς νεῖκος). Heracleon, therefore, adds new thought on the immortality of the soul, relying on the text of 1 Cor. 15:53-54, on which he indubitably depends. The parallelism of terms and expressions is, in fact, very strict: τὸ ἐνδυόμενον ἀφθαρσίαν φθαρτόν corresponds to τὸ φθαρτὸν ἐνδύσασθαι ἀφθαρσίαν (1 Cor. 15:53) and to φθαρτὸν ἐνδύσηται ἀφθαρσίαν (1 Cor. 15:54); ἀθανασίαν θνητόν picks up τὸ θνητὸν ἐνδύσασθαι ἀθανασίαν (1 Cor. 15:53) and τὸ θνητὸν ἐνδύσηται ἀθανασίαν (1 Cor. 15:54). In addition, the coincidence is

---

[39]Cf. J. Huby, *Saint Paul, Première Épître aux Corinthiens*, VS 13 (Paris, 1946) 215-16.

[40]Cf. Origen, *Comm. on John* 13.25 (Vk. 75.17-24).

[41]Cf. ibid., 13.60 (Vk. 80.28–89.6).

[42]Cf. above, 275.

almost literal between ὅταν καταποθῇ ὁ θάνατος αὐτῆς εἰς νεῖκος and κατεπόθη ὁ θάνατος εἰς νῖκος in 1 Cor. 15:54.

Still concerning the official of Capernaum, the same fragment 40[43] reads: " 'Go before my child dies' means that the end of the Law is death—the Law which kills because of transgressions" (διὰ τὸ τέλος εἶναι τοῦ νόμου τὸν θάνατον ἀναιροῦντος διὰ τῶν ἁμαρτιῶν). These words recall Rom. 7:13, in which Paul seems to express a similar idea; Heracleon seems to have taken up here very concisely the Pauline teaching: it is not the Law in itself that leads to death, but it is sin as a transgression of the Law. "The agent of malice," writes Cerfaux, "is Sin, which is so coarsely revealed in sin, by means of the precept, and which, at its highest degree, becomes conscious and voluntary sin."[44] With the words ἀναιροῦντος διὰ τῶν ἁμαρτιῶν, Heracleon shows how the Law must be understood; it must be understood that it is the Law that makes transgressions conscious. The presence in this text of the words νόμος, θάνατος, and ἁμαρτία leads me to believe in a literary remembrance of Rom. 6:21 and 7:13.

Fragment 48[45] provides us with the exegesis of Jn. 8:50: "He who seeks and judges is the one who claims justice for me, he is the servant in charge of this mission and he does not carry the sword in vain (ὁ μὴ εἰκῆ τὴν μάχαιραν φορῶν), he is the procurator of the king." The words "he does not carry the sword in vain" do seem to be a literary reminiscence of Rom. 13:4. The literal coincidence of these texts, combined with the fact that both texts speak of an official in charge of pronouncing judgment argue in favor of this hypothesis.

Heracleon, therefore, certainly knew the epistles of Paul. He even returned once explicitly to a sentence of the apostle;[46] he used the Pauline texts in his commentary on the gospel of Jn., sometimes almost literally, and sometimes as a freer source of inspiration while still literarily dependent on them.

No other New Testament writing seems to have influenced Heracleon.[47]

In conclusion, whenever Heracleon commented on the gospel of Jn., he simply revealed the visible "predilection that the disciples of Valentinus have shown towards this gospel, as food for commentary and as a conclusive authority."[48] But

---

[43]Cf. Origen, *Comm. on John* 13.60 (Vk. 81.12-13).

[44]Cf. L. Cerfaux, *Une Lecture de l'Épître aux Romains*, Bibliothèque de l'Institut Supérieur des Sciences Religieuses de l'Université Catholique de Louvain 2 (Tournai, Paris, 1947) 73.

[45]Cf. Origen, *Comm. on John* 20.38 (Vk. 84.31-85.1).

[46]Cf. 278, fragment 24.

[47]Concerning fragment 17 (Origen, *Comm. on John* 13.10; Vk. 71.23-24), it has sometimes been referred to 2 Pet. 1:11, but only because it has the expression ἐπιχορηγέω πλουσίως, and without a compelling literary dependence; only the verb ἐπιχορηγέω is found in 2 Cor. 9:10; Gal. 3:5; Col. 2:9; 2 Pet. 1:5.

[48]Cf. Th. Zahn, *Geschichte des neutestamentlichen Kanons*, vol. 1/2 (Erlangen, Leipzig, 1889) 736.

what is striking above all, is that Heracleon commented on the gospel of Jn. with the help of the gospel of Mt., from which he borrowed his principles of interpretation. Through Heracleon, we arrive at the usual teaching of the Valentinian gatherings in which the place of Mt. must have been privileged;[49] this is how he revealed the common atmosphere of Christianity. The absence of any influence from the other synoptics throws into even greater relief the value that this author, together with the Valentinian school, attached to the first gospel.

Other than the influence of Mt., but to a lesser degree, Heracleon came under the influence of the writings of Saint Paul, to whom he referred sometimes explicitly, and from which he even cited some passages literally.

§3. The Letter of Ptolemy to Flora[50]

A. Saint Matthew

1. 3.5 (Vk. 87.14-17)

Conversely, it is not allowed to ascribe the Law to the unjust Adversary, because it is opposed to injustice. This is the action of those who do not see what is apparent in the words of the Savior: "Any house or city divided against itself, cannot stand" (οἰκία γὰρ ἢ πόλις μερισθεῖσα ἐφ' ἑαυτὴν ὅτι μὴ δύναται στῆναι), declared our Savior.

This saying of Christ can be read in the synoptics in Mt. 12:25; Mk. 3:25; and Lk. 11:17.

Ptolemy	Mt. 12:25	Mk. 3:25	Lk. 11:17
	πᾶσα βασιλεία μερισθεῖσα καθ' ἑαυτῆς ἐρημοῦται,		πᾶσα βασιλεία ἐφ' ἑαυτὴν διαμερισθεῖσα ἐρημοῦται, καὶ οἶ-

---

[49]Mouson, *La Théologie d'Héracléon*, notes on 194, "In light of this conclusion, other signs become all the more intelligible: the terms 'called' and 'elect' which, in Valentinian documents, describe so universally the categories of both the psychic and the pneumatic, and which are also much used by Heracleon (κλῆσις and ἐκλογή), are borrowed from the parable of the marriage feast (Mt. 22:14), a parable which seems to have enjoyed a great popularity in the Valentinian world. Similarly, the comparison given in fragment 28 between the disciples and the foolish virgins of the parable (Mt. 25:1-13) supposes an exegesis of the latter, which was common in the circles of the school. Finally, the πίστις ἀδιάκριτος of the Samaritan (fragment 17) corresponds to the logion in Mt. 21:21: 'Truly, I say to you, if you have faith and never doubt. . . . ' "

[50]I follow G. Quispel's edition, *Ptolémée, Lettre à Flora*, SC 24 (Paris 1949); I also use its numbering system, and, between parentheses, I refer to Völker, *Quellen zur Ge-*

| οἰκία γὰρ
ἡ πόλις μερισθεῖσα ἐφ᾽
ἑαυτὴν ὅτι μὴ δύνα-
ται στῆναι. | καὶ πᾶσα πόλις ἢ οἰκία
μερισθεῖσα καθ᾽
ἑαυτῆς οὐ σταθήσε-
ται. | καὶ ἐὰν οἰκία ἐφ᾽
ἑαυτὴν μερισθῇ, οὐ
δυνήσεται ἡ οἰκία ἐκ-
είνη στῆναι. | κος ἐπὶ οἶκον πίπτει. |

The text of Mt. is the one which has literarily influenced Ptolemy. It is, indeed, the only one which has the words οἰκία and πόλις; Mk. does not have πόλις; in Lk., both οἰκία and πόλις are missing. Moreover, like Ptolemy, Mt. uses the simple verb μερίζω; Lk. uses the composite verb διαμερίζω. Yet, there may be a secondary influence from Mk. with the words ἐφ᾽ ἑαυτήν and οὐ δυνήσεται στῆναι. Let me note that D sustains in Mt. the reading ἐφ᾽ ἑαυτήν instead of καθ᾽ ἑαυτῆς.[51] In the absence of any other reference to Mk. in Ptolemy's letter, it is tempting to attribute the formula μὴ δύναται στῆναι to Ptolemy himself.

2. 4.4 (Vk. 88.19-24)

Having stated that the sayings of the Savior teach that the Law is divided into three parts: one attributable to God, the other to Moses, and the third to the Elders of the people, Ptolemy continues with the demonstration of this affirmation.

On the question of divorce (which was permitted by the Law), the Savior declared to his adversaries: It is because of the hardness of your heart that Moses has allowed the renouncing of one's wife: it was not so at first. For God, he said, has united this couple and what God has united, he said, man cannot set apart.

These declarations of the Savior are read in Mt. 19:7-8, 6; and Mk. 10:3-5, 9.

Ptolemy	Mt. 19:7-8, 6	Mk. 10:3-5, 9
πρὸς τοὺς περὶ τοῦ ἀποστα- σίου συζητοῦντας αὐτῷ, ὃ δὴ ἀποστάσιον ἐξεῖναι νενομ- οθέτητο ὅτι Μωϋσῆς πρὸς τὴν σκληροκαρδίαν ὑμῶν ἐπέτρεψεν τὸ ἀπολύειν τὴν γυναῖκα αὐ- τοῦ· ἀπ᾽ ἀρχῆς γὰρ οὐ γέγονεν οὕτως. θεὸς γάρ, φησί, συνέζευξε ταύτην τὴν συζυγίαν καὶ ὃ συ- νέζευξεν ὁ κύριος, ἄνθρωπος, ἔφη, μὴ χωριζέτω.	⁷λέγουσιν αὐτῷ· τί οὖν . . . δοῦναι βιβλίον ἀποστασίου καὶ ἀπολῦσαι; ⁸ὅτι Μωϋσῆς πρὸς τὴν σκληρο- καρδίαν ὑμῶν ἐπέτρεψεν ὑμῖν ἀπολῦσαι τὰς γυναῖκας ὑμῶν ἀπ᾽ ἀρχῆς δὲ οὐ γέγονεν οὕτως. ⁶ὃ οὖν ὁ θεὸς συνέζευξεν. ἄν- θρωπος μὴ χωριζέτω	⁴Τί ὑμῖν ἐνετείλατο Μωϋσῆς; . . . βιβλίον ἀποστασίου γρά- ψαι καὶ ἀπολῦσαι. ⁵ὁ δὲ Ἰησοῦς εἶπεν αὐτοῖς· πρὸς τὴν σκληροκαρδίαν ὑμῶν ἔγραψεν ὑμῖν τὴν ἐντολὴν ταύτην. ⁹ὃ οὖν ὁ θεὸς συνέζευξεν, ἄν- θρωπος μὴ χωριζέτω.

schichte der christlichen Gnosis, 87, 1-93. See also K. Holl, *Epiphanius, Ancoratus und Panarion*, GCS 25/1 (Leipzig, 1915) 450, 16-457, 21; A. Harnack, *Der Brief des Ptolemaeus an die Flora*, SPAW 25 (1902): 536-41; id., *Ptolemaeus. Brief an die Flora*, KIT 9, 2nd ed. (Bonn-Berlin, 1912).

[51]Cf. S. C. E. Legg, *Evangelium secundum Matthaeum, Novum Testamentum graece sec. textum Westcotto-Hortianum* (Oxford, 1940) ad loc.

A simple glance at this synoptic table is convincing enough that Ptolemy is in definite literary contact with the text of Mt., and not with that of Mk. Everything that Ptolemy said is found in Mt., with two exceptions: the first, θεὸς γὰρ συνέζευξε ταύτην τὴν συζυγίαν, may be Ptolemy's summary of Mt. 19:4-6; the second, κύριος instead of ὁ θεός, may be a variation to avoid a repetition or to emphasize the antithesis with ἄνθρωπος. These two exceptions aside, the entire text of Mt. can be read almost literally in Ptolemy, except for the plural τὰς γυναῖκας ὑμῶν which is replaced with the singular τὴν γυναῖκα αὐτοῦ.

Compared to Mk., on the other hand, the words ἔγραψεν ὑμῖν τὴν ἐντολὴν ταύτην are not found in the letter to Flora; in addition, Ptolemy's sentences ἐπέστρεψεν τὸ ἀπολύειν τὴν γυναῖκα αὐτοῦ, ἀπ᾽ ἀρχῆς οὐ γέγονεν οὕτως and θεὸς γὰρ συνέζευξε ταύτην τὴν συζυγίαν are not present in Mk.

The literary dependence on Mt. 19:6-8 is, therefore, definite. It follows that, in his argumentation on the immediate context, Ptolemy remains in literary contact with Mt., particularly in 4.5 (Vk. 88.25-26), which reads, "Through it, he demonstrates that there is a law from God which forbids separating (χωρίζεσθαι) a wife from her husband, and another from Moses which, because of the hardness of heart (διὰ τὴν σκληροκαρδίαν), allows the breaking off of a marriage.

3. 4.11-13 (Vk. 89.14-21)

The Savior shows clearly that the Ancients intermingled their traditions with the Law: For God, he states, has said: Honor your father and your mother in order to have happiness. But you, he said to the Ancients, you have said: The help you could have received from me is an offering to God. And you have annulled the Law of God through the tradition of your Ancients. This is exactly what Isaiah announced when he said: These people honor me with their lips and their hearts are far from me: they honor me in vain when they teach precepts that are the commandments of men.

Ptolemy referred explicitly to the sayings of the Savior, which are found in Mt. 15:4-9; and Mk. 7:10-11, 13, 6-7.

Ptolemy	Mt. 15:4-9	Mk. 7:10-11, 13, 6-7
ὁ γὰρ θεὸς εἶπεν· τίμα τὸν πατέρα σου καὶ τὴν μητέρα σου, ἵνα εὖ σοι γένηται. ὑμεῖς εἰρήκατε τοῖς πρεσβυτέροις λέγων· δῶρον τῷ θεῷ, ὃ ἐὰν ὠφεληθῇς ἐξ ἐμοῦ,	ὁ γὰρ θεὸς εἶπεν· τίμα τὸν πατέρα καὶ τὴν μητέρα . . . ⁵ὑμεῖς δὲ λέγετε· . . . δῶρον ὃ ἐὰν ἐξ ἐμοῦ ὠφεληθῇς	¹⁰Μωϋσῆς γὰρ εἶπεν· τίμα τὸν πατέρα σου καὶ τὴν μητέρα σου . . . ¹¹ὑμεῖς δὲ λέγετε· . . . κορβᾶν, ὅ ἐστιν δῶρον, ὃ ἐὰν ἐξ ἐμοῦ ὠφεληθῇς

καὶ ἠκυρώσατε τὸν νόμον τοῦ θεοῦ διὰ τὴν παράδοσιν ὑμῶν . . . τοῦτο δὲ ᾿Ησαΐας ἐξεφώνησεν εἰπών· ὁ λαὸς οὗτος τοῖς χείλεσί με τιμᾷ, ἡ δὲ καρδία αὐτῶν πόρρω ἀπέχει ἀπ᾿ ἐμοῦ. μάτην δὲ σέβονταί με, διδάσκοντες διδασκαλίας ἐντάλματα ἀνθρώπων.	⁶. . . καὶ ἠκυρώσατε τὸν λόγον (τὸν νόμον, ℵ*, C) τοῦ θεοῦ διὰ τὴν παράδοσιν ὑμῶν ⁷ὑποκριταί, καλῶς ἐπροφήτευσεν περὶ ὑμῶν ᾿Ησαΐας λέγων· Next follows the text of Is. 29:13, which is identical to that given by Ptolemy.	¹³ἀκυροῦντες τὸν λόγον τοῦ θεοῦ τῇ παραδόσει ὑμῶν ᾗ παρεδώκατε. ⁶καλῶς ἐπροφήτευσει ᾿Ησαΐας περὶ ὑμῶν τῶν ὑποκριτῶν, ὡς γέγραπται ὅτι Next follows the text of Is. 29:13, which is identical to that given by Ptolemy.

This synoptic table clearly shows that the sayings of the Savior to which Ptolemy refers are close to those of Mt. and not of Mk.

First of all, the order of the narrative follows that of Mt.; in Mk., in fact, to follow the order of Ptolemy, we have to read verses 10-11 and 13 before verses 6 and 7. Secondly, just as in Mt. 15:4, Ptolemy says ὁ γὰρ θεὸς εἶπεν as opposed to Μωϋσῆς γὰρ εἶπεν in Mk. 7:10; as in Mt. 15:5 again, Ptolemy has δῶρον ὃ ἐὰν ἐξ ἐμοῦ ὠφεληθῇς, and he does not speak of κορβᾶν, ὅ ἐστιν δῶρον as does Mk. 7:11; again as in Mt. 15:6, Ptolemy has preserved the verbal form ἠκυρώσατε and not ἀκυροῦντες as in Mk. 7:13. In addition, Ptolemy reads τὸν νόμον τοῦ θεοῦ διὰ τὴν παράδοσιν ὑμῶν, supporting the reading of ℵ*, C in Mt. 15:6, as opposed to Mk. 7:13, which has the phrase τὸν λόγον τοῦ θεοῦ τῇ παραδόσει ὑμῶν ᾗ παρεδώκατε. Finally, in his citation of Isaiah, this Gnostic follows the text of Mt. against Is. 29:13 of the LXX, which has the pronoun αὐτῶν after χείλεσιν and the plural τιμῶσίν με, and which reads διδάσκοντες ἐντάλματα ἀνθρώπων καὶ διδασκαλίας at the end.

There is only one difference to mention: Ptolemy has abridged the text of Mt. 15:4 and has added ἵνα εὖ σοι γένηται as a recollection of Deut. 5:16.

4. 5.1 (Vk. 89.26-29)

This part, the Law of God himself, can again be divided into three parts: the pure legislation, which was not mixed with evil, which is called the law par excellence, ''which the Savior came not to destroy, but to fulfill'' (ὃν οὐκ ἦλθε καταλῦσαι ὁ σωτὴρ ἀλλὰ πληρῶσαι).

The last words are literarily inspired by Mt. 5:17: Μὴ νομίσητε ὅτι ἦλθον καταλῦσαι τὸν νόμον ἢ τοὺς προφήτας· οὐκ ἦλθον καταλῦσαι ἀλλὰ πληρῶσαι. In fact, the words ''which the Savior'' refer to the New Economy; moreover, just as in Mt., it is about the Law; finally and above all, we find the words of Mt.: ἔρχομαι, νόμος, καταλῦσαι, and πληρῶσαι, and the opposition οὐκ . . . ἀλλά.

It follows that the word πληρώσεως in 5.3 (Vk. 90.5), in the phrase in which Ptolemy writes: ''The pure but imperfect commandments, needed to be completed by the Savior," also recalls Mt. 5:17.

5. 5.4 (Vk. 90.7-9)

Ptolemy notes that, besides the Law of God, there is a law which is accompanied by injustice, which he qualifies as the law of retaliation and punishment for committing a crime; and this is what he writes about this law:

ὀφθαλμὸν ἀντὶ ὀφθαλμοῦ καὶ ὀδόντα ἀντὶ ὀδόντος ἐκκόπτεσθαι κελεύων καὶ φόνον ἀντὶ φόνου ἀμύνασθαι.

(The law) which exacts an eye for an eye, a tooth for a tooth, and returns death for death.

The expression "an eye for an eye, a tooth for a tooth" recalls Lev. 24:20 and Mt. 5:38, in which it is found literally. Given that this part of the law mixed with injustice has been annulled in the teaching of Ptolemy (5.7), it normally follows that he had the Old Testament in mind here and that he referred to it, just as he did in 5.6, which repeats the commandment of Lev. 24:13: "Thou shalt not kill." Yet, as we shall see later in 6.1 and 2, Ptolemy certainly depended on Mt. for these identical texts, and it is credible that here, as well as for οὐ φονεύσεις in 5.6, he borrowed his text from Mt.

6. 5.7 (Vk. 90.17-21)

This is why, Ptolemy writes, his Son (of God), in his coming, annulled this part of the Law (the one which dealt with injustice) while admitting that it also came from God. Among other things, his acknowledgment of the ancient αἵ-ρεσις is shown by the following words: God said: "He who will damn his father or mother must die" (ὁ θεὸς εἶπεν· ὁ κακολογῶν πατέρα ἢ μητέρα θανάτῳ τελευτάτω).

The last words are parallel to Ex. 21:16; Lev. 20:9; Mt. 15:4; and Mk. 7:10. The reading from Ex. 21:16, sustained by manuscript A, reads: ὁ κακολογῶν πατέρα αὐτοῦ ἢ μητέρα αὐτοῦ θανάτῳ τελευτάτω. Lev. 20:9 does not have τελευτάτω; Mk. 7:10 reads: Μωϋσῆς γὰρ εἶπεν· τίμα τὸν πατέρα σου καὶ τὴν μητέρα σου, καὶ· ὁ κακολογῶν πατέρα ἢ μητέρα θανάτῳ τελευτάτω. Mt. 15:4 uses the same identical text that Ptolemy does. On which parallel does this author depend? First of all, the texts of Ex. and Lev. may be excluded; indeed, we must turn to the New Testament since Ptolemy states that one of the acts of the Son on his arrival was to annul the part of the Law which dealt with injustice, while acknowledging that it came from God; when Ptolemy speaks of the coming of the Son, he, therefore, has in mind the New Economy. Besides, he obviously insists on the expression ὁ θεὸς εἶπεν which, to him, demonstrates that the Son acknowledges that this law comes from God. Now, the expression ὁ θεὸς εἶπεν appears only in the text of Mt. 15:4; indeed, Mk. reads Μωϋσῆς γὰρ εἶπεν.

There is no doubt, therefore, that Ptolemy depended here on the Matthean text, which he cited literally.

7. 6.1-3 (Vk. 91.14-22)

[1] Οὕτως γ᾽ οὖν καὶ αὐτὸς ὁ τοῦ θεοῦ εἶναι νόμος ὁμολογούμενος εἰς τρία διαιρεῖται, εἴς τε τὸ πληρούμενον ἀπὸ τοῦ σωτῆρος (τὸ γὰρ οὐ φονεύσεις, οὐ μοιχεύσεις, οὐκ ἐπιορκήσεις ἐν τῷ μηδ᾽ ὀργισθῆναι μηδὲ ἐπιθυμῆσαι μηδὲ ὀμόσαι περιείληπται)· [2] Διαιρεῖται δὲ καὶ εἰς τὸ ἀναιρούμενον τελείως. τὸ γὰρ ὀφθαλμὸν ἀντὶ ὀφθαλμοῦ καὶ ὀδόντα ἀντὶ ὀδόντος συμπεπλεγμένον τῇ ἀδικίᾳ καὶ αὐτὸ ἔργον τῆς ἀδικίας ἔχον, ἀνῃρέθη ὑπὸ τοῦ σωτῆρος διὰ τῶν ἐναντίων. [3] Τὰ δὲ ἐναντία ἀλλήλων ἐστὶν ἀναιρετικά. ἐγὼ γὰρ λέγω ὑμῖν μὴ ἀντιστῆ-ναι ὅλως τῷ πονηρῷ, ἀλλὰ ἐάν τίς σε ῥαπίσῃ, στρέψον αὐτῷ καὶ τὴν ἄλλην σιαγόνα.

[1] Thus it is, therefore, that the Law which we follow as being that of God is divided into three parts: one part has been brought to perfection by the Savior, (for the commandments, "you shalt not kill, you shalt not commit adultery, you shalt not make false oaths," are understood as forbidding to have fits of anger, to have evil desires, and to swear). [2] Another part is completely abolished, for the commandment, "an eye for an eye, a tooth for a tooth," is mixed with injustice and has an unjust act as a consequence, and has been replaced by the Savior with contrary commandments. [3] Things which are contrary are self-destructive—"But I say to you not to resist at all an evil person, but if someone strikes you, offer him your other cheek."

This passage is nothing but an incisive commentary on Mt. First of all, in fact, the participle πληρούμενον (6.1) refers to Mt. 5:17, in which the verb πληρόω is applied to the Law. The idea, moreover, is identical: it speaks of the Law brought to its perfection by the Savior. I have noted previously Ptolemy's reference to this text.[52] Next, the commandments set forth in 6.1 are found in Mt. 5:21-22, 27-28, 33-34, and I must add immediately that these passages are peculiar to Mt. Mt. 5:21-22 states, Ἠκούσατε ὅτι ἐρρέθη τοῖς ἀρχαίοις· οὐ φονεύσεις . . . ἐγὼ δὲ λέγω ὑμῖν ὅτι πᾶς ὁ ὀργιζόμενος . . . ; and Ptolemy says, οὐ φονεύσεις, which is contained in μηδ᾽ ὀργισθῆναι. Mt. 5:27-28 has Ἠκούσατε ὅτι ἐρ-ρέθη· οὐ μοιχεύσεις. ἐγὼ δὲ λέγω ὑμῖν ὅτι πᾶς ὁ βλέπων γυναῖκα πρὸς τὸ ἐπιθυμῆσαι [αὐτὴν] ἤδη ἐμοίχευσεν; and Ptolemy notes οὐ μοιχεύσεις, which is contained in μηδὲ ἐπιθυμῆσαι. Mt. 5:33-34 says, Πάλιν ἠκούσατε ὅτι ἐρρέθη τοῖς ἀρχαίοις· οὐκ ἐπιορκήσεις . . . ἐγὼ δὲ λέγω ὑμῖν μὴ ὀμόσαι ὅλως; and Ptolemy has οὐκ ἐπιορκήσεις, which is contained in μηδὲ ὀμόσαι.

In each of these three groups of texts in Mt., Christ sets forth a precept of the old Law, followed immediately with the precept of the new Law, which takes the

---

[52]Cf. above, 284.

old precept to its perfection, in such a way that it can be said, as Ptolemy does, that the old precept is contained in the new one.

Finally, the words in 6.2-3 go back to Mt. 5:38-39, in which Christ indeed abolished the old precept of retaliation: Ἠκούσατε ὅτι ἐρρέθη· ὀφθαλμὸν ἀντὶ ὀφθαλμοῦ καὶ ὀδόντα ἀντὶ ὀδόντος. ἐγὼ δὲ λέγω ὑμῖν μὴ ἀντιστῆναι τῷ πονηρῷ· ἀλλ' ὅστις σε ῥαπίζει εἰς τὴν δεξιὰν σιαγόνα [σου], στρέψον αὐτῷ καὶ τὴν ἄλλην.

Ptolemy reproduces this passage of Mt. almost literally, noting very well that the old commandment (Mt. 5:38) and the new (Mt. 5:39) are opposed as contraries, and he concludes that the second abolishes the first.

Several minute differences in the texts ought to be noted. Ptolemy (6.3) has ὅλως, which is absent in Mt.; he uses ἐάν τις (6.3) instead of ὅστις; and he does not mention the right cheek.

Lk. 6:29 presents a parallel to Mt. 5:39. A priori, it could be excluded on the basis that, until now, Ptolemy was in literary contact with the Matthean text in this entire pericope. Furthermore, examination of the text confirms this point of view: first, the context in Lk. bears no opposition with the precept of the old Law, an opposition which is clearly stressed in Mt. and Ptolemy, and which the latter explained in his own way; second, the text itself, τῷ τύπτοντί σε ἐπὶ τὴν σιαγόνα πάρεχε καὶ τὴν ἄλλην, could not have influenced Ptolemy, since he did not use the verbs τύπτω and παρέχω from Lk., but rather the verbs ῥαπίζω and στρέφω from Mt.

There is, therefore, a definite literary contact with the Matthean text.

8.7.5 (Vk. 92.14-15)

ἕνα γὰρ μόνον εἶναι ἀγαθὸν θεὸν τὸν ἑαυτοῦ πατέρα ὁ σωτὴρ ἡμῶν ἀπεφήνατο, ὃν αὐτὸς ἐφανέρωσεν.

For our Savior has said that there is only one God who is good, his Father, whom he has revealed.

The parallels are Mt. 19:17, εἷς ἐστιν ὁ ἀγαθός; Mk. 10:18, οὐδεὶς ἀγαθὸς εἰ μὴ εἷς ὁ θεός; and Lk. 18:19, οὐδεὶς ἀγαθὸς εἰ μὴ εἷς [ὁ] θεός.

The presence of ὁ θεός in Mk. and Lk., and its absence in the usual reading of Mt. do not speak in favor of the Matthean text as a source for Ptolemy. Yet, several readings in Mt. have a text which is identical to Mk. and Lk.;[53] a few even say "pater," a reading which is definitely absent in Mk. and Lk.[54] It is, therefore, practically impossible to decide from which of the gospels Ptolemy drew his in-

---

[53]Cf. the mss. ff², and the Hierosolymite Syriac version.

[54]Cf. b, c, ff², l, m, aur., the Hierosolymite and Curetonian Syriac versions, and the Bohairic Coptic version.

spiration; since his distinct preference until now has been for Mt., the scale tilts to the latter: Ptolemy may have been witness to an ancient reading of Mt. 19:17.

9.7.10 (Vk. 93.6-10)

> I do not get weary of having told you this in a few words, my sister Flora. Even though I have previously been brief, I have still dealt decisively with the subject. When the time comes, these remarks will help you greatly if, like good and beautiful land which has received fertilizing seeds, you show the fruit which stems from them (ἐάν γε ὡς καλὴ γῆ καὶ ἀγαθὴ γονίμων σπερμάτων τυχοῦσα τὸν δι' αὐτῶν καρπὸν ἀναδείξῃς).

In the last words of the letter, a reminiscence of the parable of the sower seems to stand out, especially as it is found in Mt. 13:8, ἄλλα δὲ ἔπεσεν ἐπὶ τὴν γῆν τὴν καλὴν καὶ ἐδίδου καρπόν; Mk. 4:8, καὶ ἄλλα ἔπεσεν εἰς τὴν γῆν τὴν καλὴν καὶ ἐδίδου καρπόν; and Lk. 8:8, καὶ ἕτερον ἔπεσεν εἰς τὴν γῆν τὴν ἀγαθὴν καὶ φυὲν ἐποίησεν καρπόν.

The words γῆ and καρπός are present in the three synoptics; furthermore, καλή is found in Mt. and Mk., and ἀγαθή appears in Lk. But the different verbs in the text of Ptolemy and in the synoptics prevent me from deciding on which gospel Ptolemy shows a literary dependence.

I must point out separately one last text, because it reveals not so much a literary contact as a simple similarity of thought with the gospels: 3.7 (Vk. 88.1-3):

> . . . οἱ μὲν διὰ το ἀγνοεῖν τὸν τῆς δικαιοσύνης θεόν, οἱ δὲ διὰ τὸ ἀγνοεῖν τὸν τῶν ὅλων πατέρα, ὃν μόνος ἐλθὼν ὁ μόνος εἰδὼς ἐφανέρωσε.

> . . . some, because they did not know the God of justice; others, because they did not know the Father of all, who was revealed only by the one who has come and who is the only one to know him.

This passage recalls Mt. 11:27; Lk. 10:22; and Jn. 1:18. These parallels point out that the Father is known only by the Son. The idea is similar, but Ptolemy expresses it with words and expressions which are too different to lead me to believe in a literary contact with any one of these parallels.

In conclusion to this part devoted to the gospel of Mt., it is obvious that Ptolemy very often drew his inspiration from this gospel. He himself disclosed his knowledge of the Matthean text, sometimes even in its details, since he once drew his argument from a simple detail in the text.[55] In general, he was very close to the text of Mt. which he cited almost literally. I pointed out as well that, whenever Ptolemy wrote a passage parallel to the synoptics, preference was given to the first gospel. Furthermore, in the entire Letter to Flora, or at least in what remains of

---

[55]Cf. above, 284-85, regarding 5.7.

it, Ptolemy took up from Mt. those texts which were meant to prove his statements. He turned to the Gospel of Matthew as though it were the norm, yet he never said explicitly that he was referring to it.

B. The Other New Testament Writings

I have previously implied that neither Mk. nor Lk. seems to have had the slightest literary influence on the Letter of Ptolemy to Flora.

3.6 (Vk. 87.18-19) takes up this passage from the fourth gospel: "Moreover, with these words: 'all things were made through him, and without him was not anything made' (πάντα δι' αὐτοῦ γεγονέναι καὶ χωρὶς αὐτοῦ γεγονέναι οὐδέν), the apostle states that the creation of the world is His doing (ἰδίαν)." The words which Ptolemy attributes to the apostle are read in Jn. 1:3: πάντα δι' αὐτοῦ ἐγένετο, καὶ χωρὶς αὐτοῦ ἐγένετο οὐδὲ ἕν (οὐδέν: ℵ, D). The word ἰδίαν is also probably due to Jn. 1:11. The literary contact is indisputable, and I might add that Ptolemy sustains the reading of ℵ, D in Jn. 1:3. Moreover, it is not surprising to find here an allusion to the prologue of Jn.

Ptolemy used the epistles of Paul several times.

He writes in 5.15 (Vk. 91.10-14), "That Passover and unleavened bread were also images; the apostle Paul shows it clearly when he said: Our Passover has been sacrificed; it is Christ, so that you may be unleavened bread, without leaven (καὶ Παῦλος ὁ ἀπόστολος τὸ δὲ πάσχα ἡμῶν, λέγων, ἐτύθη Χριστός, καὶ ἵνα ἦτε, φησίν, ἄζυμοι, μὴ μετέχοντες ζύμης)—by this leaven, Paul means evil—so that you may be a new dough (ἀλλ' ἦτε νέον φύραμα)." Ptolemy refers explicitly to the text of Paul which is read in 1 Cor. 5:7 and which he takes up almost literally; in fact, he has in common with the Pauline verse τὸ πάσχα ἡμῶν ἐτύθη Χριστός, ἄζυμοι, ζύμη, ἵνα ἦτε νέον φύραμα.

6.6 (Vk. 91.28-92.2) reads: "Both the disciples and the apostle Paul have spoken about these three parts (of the Law): in the symbolic part, as already mentioned when speaking of the paschal lamb which was sacrificed for us and of the unleavened bread (ὡς ἤδη εἴπομεν, διὰ τοῦ πάσχα καὶ τῶν ἀζύμων δι' ἡμᾶς δείξας); in the part mixed with injustice, when they said that the law of the ordinances with its prescriptions has been annulled (τὸν νόμον τῶν ἐντολῶν ἐν δόγμασι κατηργῆσθαι); and in the part which is not mixed with the inferior element, when they said: the law is holy and the commandment is holy, just, and good (ὁ μὲν νόμος ἅγιος καὶ ἡ ἐντολὴ ἁγία καὶ δικαία καὶ ἀγαθή)." Ptolemy recalls first that he has previously mentioned that Paul spoke of the paschal lamb and the unleavened bread; this text which he drew from 1 Cor. 5:7 is read in 5.15 in the *Letter to Flora*. He now goes back to other passages in Paul: the first, which applies to the second part of the Law, was taken up literally in Eph. 2:15; the second, valid for the part of the Law which is not mixed with an inferior element, is drawn literally from Rom. 7:12.

In 7.6 (Vk. 92.19-22), Ptolemy speaks of God as placed between the perfect God and the devil, and he states, "On the one hand, such a God would be inferior to the perfect God and below His justice, for he is begotten and not unbegotten: there is in fact only one unbegotten, the Father, from whom all things proceed" (ὁ πατήρ, ἐξ οὗ τὰ πάντα). The expression ὁ πατήρ, ἐξ οὗ τὰ πάντα recalls 1 Cor. 8:6 and Rom. 11:36. It is found literally in 1 Cor., from which it is believable that the author, who knows Paul, has borrowed it. The formula is longer in Rom.

In two passages, Ptolemy seems indeed to be in literary contact with the Epistle to the Hebrews. The first is read in 5.9-10 (Vk. 90.25-32): "For all these things (offerings, circumcision, sabbath, fasting, Passover, and unleavened bread) are only images and symbols which have been transposed when the truth appeared (εἰκόνες καὶ σύμβολα ὄντα, τῆς ἀληθείας φανερωθείσης μετετέθη). In their guise and their corporeal being, they have been abolished (ἀνῃρέθη), but in their spiritual sense, they have been retained (ἀνελήφθη): the names remain, the things are totally changed. Thus the Savior instructed us to make offerings: but it is no longer an offering of animals without reason: it is the offering of spiritual praises, glorification, thanksgiving, union with neighbor, and the doing of good (διὰ τῆς εἰς τοὺς πλησίον κοινωνίας καὶ εὐποιίας)." The second passage is found in 6.5 (Vk. 91.25-28): "These images and symbols are representations of other realities (αἱ γὰρ εἰκόνες καὶ τὰ σύμβολα παραστατικὰ ὄντα ἑτέρων πραγμάτων). It follows then that they are beneficial as long as truth itself is not present (καλῶς ἐγίνοντο μέχρι μὴ παρῆν ἡ ἀλήθεια). But when truth appears (παρούσης δὲ τῆς ἀληθείας), it becomes necessary to operate from the truth and no longer from the image." Both of these texts presuppose a knowledge of the Epistle to the Hebrews whose passages I propose to quote, and which seem to have influenced the thought and expressions of both of Ptolemy's pericopes. Heb. 9:24: "For Christ has entered, not into a sanctuary made with hands, a copy of the true one (ἀντίτυπα τῶν ἀληθινῶν), but into heaven itself." Heb. 9:23: "Thus it was necessary for the copies of the heavenly things to be purified with these rites (τὰ μὲν ὑποδείγματα τῶν ἐν τοῖς οὐρανοῖς), but the heavenly things themselves with better sacrifices than these." Heb. 7:12: "For when there is a change in the priesthood, there is necessarily a change in the law as well (μετατιθεμένης γὰρ τῆς ἱερωσύνης ἐξ ἀνάγκης καὶ νόμου μετάθεσις γίνεται)." Heb. 8:4-5: " . . . priests who offer gifts according to the law. They serve a copy and shadow (ὑποδείγματι καὶ σκιᾷ) of the heavenly sanctuary." The entire typology developed in Heb. 9:9ff. and above all in 10:1 could also be added: σκιὰν γὰρ ἔχων ὁ νόμος τῶν μελλόντων ἀγαθῶν, οὐκ αὐτὴν τὴν εἰκόνα τῶν πραγμάτων. Heb. 13:15-16 also comes to mind: " . . . let us continually offer up a sacrifice of praise to God, that is, the fruit of lips that acknowledge his name. Do not neglect to do good and to share what you have (τῆς δὲ εὐποιίας καὶ κοινωνίας), for such sacrifices are pleasing to God.''[56]

Ptolemy, therefore, reveals a definite knowledge of the Pauline writings which he uses in general by means of quoting them literally to demonstrate his statements. Paul is an authority he regards as trustworthy.

To bring this paragraph on the Letter of Ptolemy to Flora to a close, various facts come to light. First of all, the gospel of Mt. plays a leading part in this letter; the writings of Mt. are the ones to which Ptolemy turns to find the sayings of Christ; this is from where he draws to demonstrate his statements. Whenever Ptolemy is under the literary influence of Mt., he follows the text very closely, he cites it sometimes literally, and even goes so far as to argue over a point with the help of a detail which is peculiar to the Matthean text.[57]

Next, I cannot help but point out the total absence of a reference to Mk. and to Lk., whose influence seems to have been nil.

As for the texts of Paul, Ptolemy refers explicitly to them; he even quotes them literally, and he uses them as an authority which confirms the teaching which he proposes. But the Pauline texts appeared to be fewer in number and were used in a subsidiary way.

§4. Ptolemy's Commentary on the Prologue of Saint John[58]

This exegesis of the Johannine Prologue does not provide any addition to the focus of this study, namely the literary influence of Mt.: there is, in fact, no trace of this gospel to be found.

Since he commented on the Prologue of the first gospel, Ptolemy naturally cited many passages from this Prologue. Like Heracleon, he divided the text in parts, and he started each part with the text of the Prologue which he followed with his explications.

Let me also emphasize a reference to a text of Paul in 5 (Vk. 94.17-18): ''This is what Paul says: everything that becomes manifest is light (πᾶν γὰρ τὸ φανερούμενον φῶς ἐστιν).'' This text is found literally in Eph. 5:14.

By way of closing this chapter, I propose to gather the conclusions that have emerged. If the Gnostics, in particular the Valentinians, paid particular attention to the gospel of Jn., especially its Prologue, I must nevertheless point out that the

---

[56]Cf. F. Sagnard, *La Gnose Valentinienne*, 462; Th. Zahn, *Geschichte des neutestamentlichen Kanons*, 1/2 (Erlangen, Leipzig, 1889) 758-59.

[57]Cf. above, 284-85, regarding 5.7.

[58]The text is found in Völker's edition, *Quellen zur Geschichte der christlichen Gnosis*, 93.11-95.4. See also Holl, *Epiphanius, Ancoratus und Panarion*, 1:426, 1:427, 25; W. W. Harvey, *S. Irenaei libros V adv. Haeres.*, vol. 1 (1857) 75-80.

Gospel of Mt. held for them a definitely preferential position. Indeed, I pointed out that these Gnostics frequently made definite literary references to the first gospel, whereas there is no trace of the other synoptics. In the rare fragments of Basilides, one text of Mt. has exerted its influence. The fragments of Valentinus reveal no literary influence other than that of Mt. As for Heracleon, he commented on the gospel of Jn. in synopsis with the Gospel of Mt.; he gave an exegesis of Jn. with the help of Mt. Ptolemy as well resorted to Mt. to support his statements.

These conclusions imply that the Gospel of Mt. must have been the gospel par excellence to refer to for the sayings of the Savior; it was recognized as the norm. This observation is all the more significant when it has been established that neither Mk. nor Lk. has exerted a literary influence. The Gospel of Mt. was the solid ground upon which to start the exegesis of Jn. or to set forth a teaching. And I might add as well that, most of the time, these Gnostic writers followed the Matthean text very closely, and even went as far as to quote it literally quite frequently.

Other than a definite influence of Mt., but to a lesser degree, I must mention as well that the Gnostics undoubtedly knew and used the Pauline writings, which they quoted literally fairly often and which they used as an authority to confirm the exegesis of a text in Jn. or the teaching in question. It is also interesting to note that, in some cases when they referred to the epistles of Paul, the Gnostics stated explicitly that they resorted to them, whereas they did not when they quoted even literally the Gospel of Mt. This phenomenon is one more clue of the scope and major significance of the first gospel among these Gnostics: Mt. was the source for a saying of the Savior and for his teachings, and there was no need to specify that they resorted to it, for the Gospel of Mt. entirely superseded the other synoptics, provided they were even in existence in the Gnostic communities, because their influence was nil. Through their copious use of Mt., the Gnostic writings bring out the overall atmosphere of Christianity.

This second book presented a survey of many writings of various literary genres: epistles, apocalypses, apocryphal gospels, and Gnostic writings.

The Gospel of Mt. has proven to be the New Testament writing whose literary influence was the most widespread and the most profound in the various works I examined. To all these writers, it took on the role of the gospel par excellence, which encompassed the doctrine and the teachings of Christ as the foundation of Christianity. There was no need to refer to it explictly so as to distinguish it from the others. It was familiar not only to Christian circles, but to Gnostic circles as well. It was the source of inspiration for those who wished to summon the main points of the Christian religion. Certain authors even seem to have used nothing but the first gospel in their writings, excluding the other synoptics, namely *2 Clement*, the *Letter of Polycarp to the Philippians*, the Christian parts of the *As-*

cension of Isaiah, the *Odes of Solomon*, and the Gnostic writings. And when other works, such as the *Martyrdom of Polycarp* and the *Sibylline Oracles*, seem to depend on a gospel tradition rather than on a written gospel, they reveal that this tradition itself was based on the first gospel.

Unlike a Clement of Rome, a Barnabas, or an Ignatius of Antioch, the authors of this period followed more closely the very text of the Gospel of Mt. It is not unusual to find literal quotations in these writings (2 Clement, Polycarp, the Gnostic writings). And some went as far as to grant the first gospel the value of Scripture (2 Clement).

It is also remarkable that the closer these writings are to the end of the second century, the more they drew their inspiration not only from the legislative sayings of Jesus in Mt., but also from other sayings of Christ and from the narratives in this gospel. In this regard, Hermas provides us with excellent proof when he built a long pericope with the help of the Matthean parables. The apocryphal gospels bring us proof which is no less telling: they quote Mt. literally in the infancy narratives, or else they embellish the Matthean narrative itself, or again they draw their own narrative on the backdrop of the Matthean narrative.

There are two facts that especially bring to light the preferential status of Mt. Polycarp, a disciple of John according to the tradition, seems to have known only the first gospel and did not reveal a special affinity with the gospel of his master. Whereas the Gospel of Jn. was the bedside book of the Gnostics, they commented on it with the help of the Gospel of Mt. The first gospel was the solid ground which was used as the point of departure to comment on Jn.

The importance and the predominant role of the first gospel takes on an even brighter light once it is established that the literary influence of Mk. was virtually nil: its presence was felt in the Unknown Gospel, and there was a probable influence in a passage of the *Shepherd of Hermas*. The status of Lk. does not fare any better than that of Mk., except for the Apocalypse of Peter, which combined some information from Mt. and Lk. and which sometimes even drew its inspiration only from Luke. A literary influence from Lk. is also found in the apocryphal gospels, specifically in the Unknown Gospel and in the Protevangelium of James, the latter already belonging to the last decades of the second century. The influence of Lk. in these apocrypha is attributable in part to the wide scope of its infancy narrative of Christ and may possibly be the result of the Alexandrian origin of these non-canonical gospels.

These writings show a literary kinship with the gospel of Jn., but in a form which is altogether different than with Mt. So it is that, in the *Odes of Solomon*, this literary kinship did not come from a direct influence of the gospel, but it is rather to be ascribed to an identical mystical climate. In the *Shepherd of Hermas*, a few texts provided us with themes of long parenetic moral variations. Of all the apocrypha, it is the Unknown Gospel which came under the greatest influence of the fourth gospel. I barely need to remind the reader that Jn. held a privileged place among the Gnostics.

Almost all these writings are witness to the use of the Pauline epistles, either by picking up themes, or by quoting passages almost literally, or even better, by referring to them explicitly such as in the Gnostic writings. Yet, as a general rule, they take from the apostle only those passages of a clearly marked moral nature (Polycarp), or they introduce Pauline texts into moral contexts so that they may serve as a basis for parenetic developments (Hermas, the apocalypses), or again, they appeal to Paul as an authority to confirm the stated teaching such as in the Gnostic writings. Never do they refer to them as a source which is essential to the Christian message. None of these authors follows the apostle in his profound theological developments.

Let me also point out the relatively important standing of 1 Peter in the *Letter of Polycarp to the Philippians*.

All these observations tend to show that the Gospel of Mt. was the one from which to draw the essence of the Christian message and in which to look for the teachings which are the foundation of the religion of Christ. Paul was an authority who confirmed the statement of the teaching, but, in fact, Mt. alone seems to have taken on a normative stature and to have created the climate of popular Christianity. As we approach the end of the second century, in addition to the sayings of Christ in Mt., there appears more and more narrative of this gospel, and the various authors adhered more and more faithfully to the texts themselves. The influence of Lk. grew at the same time, with Mk. still remaining in the shadows.

Editor's Addenda to Chapter 6

Section 1
BASILIDES AND HIS DISCIPLES

Wolf-Dietrich Köhler (*Die Rezeption des Matthäusevangeliums in der Zeit vor Irenäus*, 373-76) maintains that Basilides and his disciples knew and used the canonical Matthew. The following parallels are listed.

BASILIDES	MATTHEW
Clem. Alex., Strom. 3.1.1	19:11-12
Epiphanius, Adv. Haer. 25.5.2	7:6
Clem. Alex., Strom. 4.82.2	5:28

Biblia Patristica (*Index des Citations et Allusions bibliques dans la Littérature patristique, Des Origines à Clément d'Alexandrie et Tertullien*, vol. 1 [Paris, 1975] 223-93) lists the following citation or allusion to the Gospel of Matthew in the writings of Basilides.

BASILIDES	MATTHEW
Explanationes 40.20*	5:28

Section 2
VALENTINUS AND HIS SCHOOL

Wolf-Dietrich Köhler (*Die Rezeption des Matthäusevangeliums in der Zeit vor Irenäus*, 355-65) maintains that the Gnostics knew and used the church's gospels. He draws the following conclusions.

§1.a. The Fragments of Valentinus

1. It is clear that Matthew lies behind the following Gnostic passages as quoted in Irenaeus.

VALENTINUS (according to Irenaeus)	MATTHEW
Haer. 1.1.3	20:1-16
1.3.2	5:18
1.6.1	5:13-14

---

*W. Völker, *Quellen zur Geschichte der urchristlichen Gnosis*, SQS n.s. 5 (Tübingen, 1932) 38-41.

2. It is probable that Matthew lies behind the following Gnostic passages as quoted in Irenaeus.

VALENTINUS (according to Irenaeus)	MATTHEW
Haer. 1.2.5	11:27
1.3.1	13:10-13
1.3.2	10:1
1.3.3	3:13-17; 9:20-22; 10:4; 26:14-16
1.3.5	10:34, 38; 3:12
1.7.2	3:13-17; 27:2
1.7.4	8:9
1.8.2	9:18-26; 26:38-39; 27:46
1.8.3	19:16-30; 13:33
1.8.4	18:12-14

§1.b. Matthew 11:27 in the Gnostics and in Irenaeus

VALENTINUS AND THE GNOSTICS (according to Irenaeus)	MATTHEW
Haer. 4:6	11:27-28

CITATIONS FROM THE GNOSTICS (according to Irenaeus)	MATTHEW 11:27
Haer. 1.20.3	11:27
2.14.7	11:27
4.6.1	11:27

CITATIONS FROM IRENAEUS	MATTHEW 11:27
Haer. 2.6.1	11:27
4.6.1	11:27
4.6.3	11:27
4.6.7	11:27
4.7.4	11:27

§1.c. Marcus and the Marcosians

1. Marcus and the Marcosians probably used the Gospel of Matthew in the following passages.

MARCUS AND THE MARCOSIANS (according to Irenaeus)	MATTHEW
Haer. 1.14.1	18:20
1.20.2	10:5-6; 11:28-29
1.20.3	11:25-27

2. Marcus and the Marcosians quite possibly used the Gospel of Matthew in the following passages.

MARCUS AND THE MARCOSIANS (according to Irenaeus)	MATTHEW
Haer. 1.13.2	13:31-32
1.14.6	17:1-8; 3:16; 27:62; 27:45
1.15.1	3:16
1.15.3	26:64; 3:16
1.16.1	18:12-14
1.18.4	10:2
1.20.2	31:23-27
1.21.2	3:13-27

§1.d. Carpocrates

CARPOCRATES (according to Irenaeus)	MATTHEW
Haer. 1.25.4	5:25-26

Biblia Patristica (Index des Citations et Allusions bibliques dans la Littérature patristique, Des Origines à Clément d'Alexandrie et Tertullien, vol. 1 [Paris, 1975] 223-93) lists only two references under its heading "Valentinus Gnosticus" (p. 45).

VALENTINUS	Völker*	MATTHEW
Fragmenta	58.16	5:8
Fragmenta	58.5-6	19:17

In addition, however, *Biblia Patristica* does list all of the above citations to Valentinus and his school listed by Köhler, but rather as citations or allusions to Irenaeus, *Adversus Haereses,* with the exception of the following, which are not listed.

IRENAEUS	MATTHEW
Haer. 1.8.2	26:39; 27:46
1.20.3	11:27
1.14.1	18:20
1.20.3	11:25-27
1.20.2	21:24-27
1.25.4	5:26

§2. The Fragments of Heracleon

Wolf-Dietrich Köhler (*Die Rezeption des Matthäusevangeliums in der Zeit vor Irenäus,* 351-54) maintains that Heracleon (as reported in Origen) clearly used the Gospel of Matthew.

---

*Völker, *Quellen zur Geschichte der urchristlichen Gnosis.*

1. The following passages reflect clear use of the Gospel of Matthew.

HERACLEON	Völker*	MATTHEW
Fragm. 35	79.4-8	13:37, 39, 41
40	82.6-7	8:12
32	77:24	13:30
40	80.31-81.1	10:28
46	84.11-12	23:15, 28, 33

2. The following passages suggest that Matthew lies behind the passage in Heracleon.

HERACLEON	Völker*	MATTHEW
Fragmenta	85.13	3:11
In Ioannem	82.6	8:12
In Ioannem	80.31ff.	10:28
Fragmenta	86.6-7	10:32-33
Fragmenta	85.16	10:32
In Ioannem	66.6	11:9
In Ioannem	66.8	11:9
In Ioannem	68.21	11:9
In Ioannem	66.9	11:11
In Ioannem	66.30	11:11
In Ioannem	66.35-36	11:11
In Ioannem	66.6	11:13-14
In Ioannem	66.8	11:13-14
In Ioannem	66.16	11:14
In Ioannem	77:24	13:30
In Ioannem	79.4	13:37
In Ioannem	79.4	13:39
In Ioannem	79.4	13:41
In Ioannem	70.19	21:13
In Ioannem	84.11	23:15
In Ioannem	84.11	23:28
In Ioannem	84.11	23:33

§3. Ptolemy

Wolf-Dietrich (*Die Rezeption des Matthäusevangeliums in der Zeit vor Ir- anäus*, 340-50) identifies the following passages in Ptolemy (as found in Epi- phanius, *Panar.* 33.3-7) as parallels to the Gospel of Matthew.

1. The following passages clearly reflect a Matthean background.

---

*Völker, *Quellen zur Geschichte der urchristlichen Gnosis*.

PTOLEMY, FLORA**	MATTHEW
4.4-10	19:6-8
4.11-13	15:4-7
5.1	5:17
6.3	5:39
5.7	15:4
3.5	12:125

2. The following passages are possible parallels but do not reflect a definite Matthean background.

PTOLEMY, FLORA**	MATTHEW
5.13	6:16-18
3.7	11:27
7.5	19:17
7.10	13:8

Biblia Patristica (*Index des Citations et Allusions bibliques dans la Littérature patristique, Des Origines à Clément d'Alexandrie et Tertullien*, vol. 1 [Paris, 1975] 223-93) lists the following citations or allusions to the Gospel of Matthew in Ptolemy.

PTOLEMY, FLORA**	MATTHEW
3.4	5:17
5.1	5:17
5.3	5:17
6.1	5:21
6.1	5:22
6.1	5:27
6.1	5:28
6.1	5:33
6.1	5:34
5.7	5:38-42
6.2	5:38
6.3	5:39
5.13	6:16-18
3.7	11:27
3.5	12:25
7.10	13:8
4.12	15:2
4.11	15:4
5.7	15:4
4.12	15:5-7
4.13	15:8-9
4.4	19:6
4.4	19:8
7.5	19:17

**G. Quispel, *Ptolémée, Lettre à Flora. Analyse, texte critique, traduction, commentaire et index grec*, 2nd ed., SC 24 (Paris, 1966).

Bibliography

CHRISTIAN LITERATURE
OF THE FIRST TWO CENTURIES

IN GENERAL

1. Sources[1]

Aland, Kurt, ed. *Synopsis quattuor evangeliorum locis parallelis evangeliorum apocryphorum et patrum adhibitis.* 13th ed. Stuttgart, 1985 ([1]1963).

Amiot, F. *La Bible apocryphe. Évangiles apocryphes.* Paris, 1952.

Benoit, P. and M.-É. Boismard. *Synopse des quatre évangiles en français avec parallèles des Apocryphes et des Pères.* 3 vols. Paris, 1965/1972/1977.

Bihlmeyer, K. *Die apostolischen Väter.* SAQ 2nd ser. 1/1. Tübingen, 1924. *Neubearbeitung der Funkschen Ausgabe.* 2nd ed. Tübingen, 1956. 3rd ed. 1970.

Bonwetsch, N. *Texte zur Geschichte des Montanismus.* KIT 129. Bonn, 1914.

Bosio, G. *I padri apostolici.* 1. *Dottrina degli Apostoli; S. Clemente Romano; Lettera di Barnaba.* Turin, 1940. 2. *S. Ignazio d'Antiochia, S. Policarpo, Martirio di S. Policarpo, Papia, Lettera a Diognete.* Turin, 1942.

Cameron, R. *The Other Gospels. Non-Canonical Gospel Texts.* Philadephia, 1982.

Cartlidge, D. R., and David L. Dungan, eds. *Documents for the Study of the Gospels.* Cleveland: Collins; Philadelphia: Fortress Press, 1980.

Charles, R. H. *The Apocrypha and Pseudepigrapha.* 2 vols. Oxford, 1913.

Charlesworth, J. H. ed. *The Old Testament Pseudepigrapha.* 2 vols. London, 1983–1985.

de Labriolle, P. *Les sources de l'Histoire du Montanisme.* Textes grecs, latins, syriaques. Fribourg, Switzerland, 1913.

de Santos Otero, A. *Los evangelios apócrifos.* Edición critica y bilingüe. Madrid, 1956. New ed. 1979.

---

[1]I include in the sources editions of texts as well as translations.

Dungan, David L., and D. R. Cartlidge, eds. *Sourcebook of Texts for the Comparative Study of the Gospels: Literature of the Hellenistic and Roman Period Illuminating the Mileau and Character of the Gospels.* 3rd ed. Missoula MT: Scholars Press, 1973 ('1971).

Errandonea, I. *El primer siglo cristiano.* Documentos. Madrid, 1947.

Erbetta, M. *Gli apocrifi del Nuovo Testamento.* 4 vols. Turin, 1966–1981.

Fischer, J. A. *Die Apostolischen Väter. Griechisch und deutsch.* Munich, 1956. = *Die Apostolischen Väter.* Schriften des Urchristentums 1. Darmstadt, ⁸1981.

Funk, F. X. *Patres Apostolici.* 2 vols. Tübingen, 1901.

Geffken, J. *Zwei griechische Apologeten. Leipzig and Berlin, 1907. Repr. Hildesheim, 1970.*

Gli Apocrifi cristiani e cristianizzati. Augustinianum 23. Rome, 1983.

Glimm, F. X., J. M. Marique, and G. G. Walsh. *The Apostolic Fathers. The Fathers of the Church* 1. New York, 1947.

Goodspeed, E. J. *The Apocrypha. An American Translation.* Chicago, 1938.

————. *Die ältesten Apologeten.* Göttingen, 1914 (new ed. 1984).

————. *The Apostolic Fathers. An American Translation.* London, 1950.

Grant, R. M. *Second Century Christianity. A Collection of Fragments.* London, 1946, 1957.

————, ed. *The Apostolic Fathers. A New Translation and Commentary.* 6 vols. London and New York, 1964-68.

Hamman, A. *Naissance des lettres chrétiennes. Odes de Salomon, Lettre de Barnabé, etc.* Paris, 1957 (³1980).

————. *L'empire et la Croix. Épître de Clément, Lettres d'Ignace d'Antioche, Lettre de Polycarpe de Smyrne.* Paris, 1957.

Harvey, W. W. *Irenaeus Lugdunensis Episcopus, Libri quinque adversus Haereses.* 2 vols. Cambridge, 1857.

Hennecke, E. *Neutestamentliche Apokryphen.* 3rd. ed. Tübingen, 1924.

Hennecke, E., and W. Schneemelcher. *Neutestamentliche Apokryphen in deutscher Übersetzung.* 2 vols. 3rd ed. Tübingen, 1959–1964 (⁴1968). ET: *New Testament Apocrypha.* 2 vols. Trans. A. J. B. Higgins et al. Ed. R. McL. Wilson. Philadelphia, London, 1963, 1966.

————. *New Testament Apocrypha.* 2 vols. London and Philadephia, 1963–1965 (repr. 1973).

Hervieux, J. *Was nicht im Evangelium steht.* Aschaffenburg, 1960. ET: *The New Testament Apocrypha.* New York, 1960.

Huck, Albert. *Synopse der drei ersten Evangelien mit Beigabe der johanneischen Parallelstellen [Synopsis of the First Three Gospels with the Addition of the Johannine Parallels].* 13th ed. fundamentally rev. by Heinrich Greeven. Tübingen, 1981.

James, Montague Rhodes. *Apocrypha anecdota. A Collection of Apocryphal Books and Fragments.* Texts and Studies 2/3, 5/1. Cambridge 1893, 1899.

————. *The Lost Apocrypha of the Old Testament, Their Titles and Fragments.* London, 1920.

————. *The Apocryphal New Testament.* Oxford, 1924. Corrected repr. 1953ff.

————. *Latin Infancy Gospels.* Cambridge, 1927.

Kautzsch, E. *Die Apokryphen und Pseudepigraphen des A. T.* 2 vols. Tübingen, 1900.

Kleist, J. A. *The Epistles of St. Clement of Rome and St. Ignatius of Antioch.* ACW 1. Westminster MD, 1946.

──────. *The Didachè, The Epistle of Barnabas, The Epistle and the Martyrdom of St. Polycarp, The Fragments of Papias, The Epistle to Diognetus.* ACW 6. Westminster MD, 1948.

Klijn, A. F. J. *Apostolische Vaders.* 2 vols. Kampen, 1981–1983 (orig. ed. 3 vols. Baarn, 1966–1967).

──────. *Apokriefen van het Nieuwe Testament.* 2 vols. Kampen, 1984–1985.

Klostermann, E. *Apocrypha.* Vol. 2. KIT 8. Berlin, 1929.

──────. *Apocrypha.* Vol. 1. *Reste des Petrusevangeliums, der Petrusapokalypse und des Kerygma Petri.* KIT 3. Berlin, 1933.

Kümmel, W. G., ed. *Jüdische Schriften aus hellenistisch-römischer Zeit.* Gütersloh, 1973–.

Lake, K. *The Apostolic Fathers.* 2 vols. London, 1917.

Lefort, L. T. *Les pères apostoliques en copte.* CSCO 135-36. Louvain, 1952.

Legg, S. C. E. *Evangelium secundum Matthaeum. Novum Testamentum graece secundum textum Westcotto-Hortianum.* Oxford, 1940.

──────. *Evangelium secundum Marcum. Novum Testamentum graece secundum textum Westcotto-Hortianum.* Oxford, 1935.

Lightfoot, J. B. *The Apostolic Fathers.* 5 vols. 1889–1890 (repr. Hildesheim, 1973).

Lightfoot, J. B., and J. R. Harmer. *The Apostolic Fathers.* London, 1891 (repr. Grand Rapids, 1983).

Lommatzch, C. H. E. *Origenis opera omnia.* Vol. 6. Berlin, 1836.

Louvel, F. e.a. *Les écrits des Pères Apostoliques.* Paris, 1963.

Mai, A. *Scriptorum veterum nova collatio.* Vol. 3, pt. 2. Rome, 1828.

Michaelis, W. *Die apokryphen Schriften des Neues Testaments.* 3rd ed. Bremen, 1962.

Michel, C., and P. Peeters. *Évangiles apocryphes.* Textes et Documents 18. 2 vols. Paris, 1911, 1914.

Moraldi, L. *Apocrifi del Nuovo Testamento.* 2 vols. Turin, 1971.

Nestle, E. *Novum Testamentum graece.* 19th ed. Stuttgart, 1949.

New Testament in Greek, The. The Gospel according to St. Luke. Ed. the American and British Committees of the International Greek New Testament Project. Pt. 1, chaps. 1-12. Oxford, 1984.

Otto, J. C. T. *Corpus Apologetarum Christianorum Saeculi Secundi.* 5 vols. Jena, 1847–1874 (repr. Frankfort, 1974).

Preuschen, E. *Antilegomena, Die Reste der ausserkanonischen Evangelien und urchristlichen Überlieferungen.* 2nd ed. Giessen, 1905.

Rauschen, G. *Monumenta minora saeculi secundi.* Florilegium Patristicum 3. 2nd ed. Bonn, 1914.

Resch, A. *Agrapha. Aussercanonische Schriftfragmente gesammelt und untersucht.* TU 15/3-4. 2nd ed. Leipzig, 1906 (repr. Darmstadt, 1974).

Richardson, C. C. *Early Christian Fathers.* The Library of Christian Classics 1. London, 1953.

Riessler, P. *Altjüdisches Schrifttum ausserhalb der Bibel.* Augsbourg, 1928.

Ristow, H. *Die apostolischen Väter.* Ausgew. Texte aus der Geschichte der Christl. Kirche 1. Berlin, 1964.

_____. *Die Apologeten ausgelegt und übersetzt.* Berlin, 1963.

Roberts, A., and J. Donaldson. *The Ante-Nicene Fathers.* Vol. 1. *The Apostolic Fathers.* Vol. 2. *Fathers of the Second Century.* Repr. Grand Rapids, 1979.

Robinson, F. *Coptic Apocryphal Gospels.* Cambridge, 1896.

Rouët de Journel, M. J. *Enchiridion patristicum.* 19th ed. Fribourg-in-Br., 1956.

Ruhbach, G. *Altkirchliche Apologeten.* Gütersloh, 1966.

Ruiz Bueno, D. *Padres apologistas griegos.* Madrid, 1954.

_____. *Padres apostólicos.* Edición bilingüe completa. Madrid, 1965.

Sparks, H. F. D., ed. *The Apocryphal Old Testament.* Oxford, 1984.

Stählin, O. *Clemens Alexandrinus.* Griechische christliche Schriftsteller 15. Leipzig, 1906. Ed. Stählin, O., L. Früchtel, and U. Treu. 3 vols. 2nd-3rd eds. Berlin, 1960–1972.

Tischendorf, C. *Evangelia apocrypha.* 2nd ed. Leipzig, 1876 (repr. Hildesheim, 1966).

Tukker, C. A. *Enige Nieuwtestamentische Apokriefe Geschriften.* Utrecht, 1984.

Wendland, P. *Hippolytus Werke.* Vol. 3. Griechische Christliche Schriftsteller 26. Leipzig, 1916.

Wengst, K. *Didache (Apostollehre). Barnabasbrief. Zweiter Klemensbrief. Schrift an Diognet.* Schriften des Urchristentums 2. Munich and Darmstadt, 1984.

2. Studies

Agulles Estrada, J. *Bienaventurados los puros de corazón. Mt. 5:8 en la teologia greco-cristiana hasta Origenes.* Valencia, 1965.

Aland, K. "Methodische Bemerkungen zum Corpus Paulinum bei den Kirchenvätern des Zweiten Jahrhunderts." In *Kerygma und Logos. Festschrift C. Andresen,* 29-48. Göttingen, 1979.

_____. *Repertorium der greichischen christlichen Papyri.* PTS 18. Berlin, 1976.

Aleith, E. *Paulusverständnis in der alten Kirche.* BZNW 18. Berlin, 1937.

Alsup, J. E. *The Post-Resurrection Appearance Stories of the Gospel Tradition.* Stuttgart, 1975.

Altaner, B. *Précis de Patrologie.* Trans. M. Grandclaudon. Mulhouse, Paris, Tournai, 1941.

Altaner, B., and A. Stuiber. *Patrologie. Leben, Schriften und Lehre der Kirchenväter.* 9th ed. Fribourg-in-Br., 1980.

Altendorf, H. D. "Wiederkunft und Kreuz. Zur auslegung von Matth. 24:30 in der alten Kirche und zur Deutung einiger Kreuzesdarstellungen der frühchristlichen Kunst." Diss., Tübingen, 1966.

Altermath, F. *Du corps psychique au corps spirituel. Interprétation de 1 Cor. 15:35-49 par les auteurs chrétiens des quatre premiers siècles.* BGBE 18. Tübingen, 1977.

Amstutz, J. ΑΠΛΟΤΗΣ. *Eine begriffsgeschichtliche Studie zum jüdisch-christlichen Griechisch.* Bonn, 1968.

Andrews, H. T. *An Introduction to the Apocryphal Books of the Old and New Testament.* Grand Rapids, 1964.

Anger, R. *Ratio qua loci Veteris Testamenti in Evangelio Matthaei laudantur, quid valeat ad illustrandum huius evangelii originem quaeritur.* Vol. 1. Leipzig, 1861.

Aono, T. *Die Entwicklung des paulinischen Gerichtsgedankens bei den apostolischen Vätern.* Bern, 1979.

Arndt, W. F., F. W. Gingrich, and F. W. Danker, eds. *A Greek-English Lexicon of the New Testament and Other Early Christian Literature (Bauer's.)* 2nd ed. Chicago and London, 1979.

Aubineau, M. "Dossier patristique sur Jean 19:23-24. La tunique sans couture du Christ." In *La Bible et les Pères,* 9-50. Strasbourg, 1970.

————. "La tunique sans couture du Christ. Exégèse patristique de Jean 19:23-24." In *Kyriakon. Festschrift J. Quasten,* 1:100-27. Munster-in-Westphalia, 1970. = In *Recherches patristiques,* 351-78. Amsterdam, 1974.

Audet, J. P. "L'hypothèse des Testimonia. Remarques autour d'un livre récent." *RB* 70 (1963): 381-405.

————. "Affinités littéraires et doctrinales du 'Manuel de Discipline.' " *RB* 59 (1952): 219-38; 60 (1953): 41-82.

Aune, D. E. "Early Christian Biblical Interpretation." *EQ* 91 (1969): 89-96.

Baarda, T. *Early Transmissions of Words of Jesus, Thomas, Tatian, and the Text of the New Testament. A Collection of Studies.* Amsterdam, 1983.

Bardenhewer, O. *Les Pères de l'Église, leur vie et leurs oeuvres.* New French ed. completely recast by P. Godet and C. Verschaffel. Vol. 1. Paris, 1905.

————. *Geschichte der altchristlichen Literatur.* Vol. 1. Fribourg-in-Br., 1913 (repr. Darmstadt, 1962).

Bardenhewer, O., T. Schermann, and K. Weymann. *Bibliothek der Kirchenväter.* Kempten and Munich, 1911.

Bardsley, H. J. *Reconstructions of Early Christian Documents.* Vol. 1. London, 1935.

Bardy, G. *La vie spirituelle d'après les Pères des premiers siècles.* Paris, 1935.

————. *La théologie de l'Église de saint Clément de Rome à saint Irénée.* Unam Sanctam 13. Paris, 1945.

————. "La lecture de la Bible aux premiers siècles chrétiens." *Bible et Vie Chrétienne* 2 (1953): 25-39.

Barnard, L. W. *Studies in Church History and Patristics.* Analecta Vlatadon 26. Salonika, 1978.

————. *Studies in the Apostolic Fathers and their Background.* Oxford, 1966.

Bartelink, G. J. M. *Lexicologisch-semantische studie over de tall van de Apostolische Vaders.* Nijmegen, 1952.

Bartsch, H. W. "Entwicklungslinien der frühen Christenheit." *TLZ* 97 (1972): col. 721-34.

Bauer, J. B. *Clavis apocryphorum supplementum complectens voces versionis Germanicae Libri Henoch Slavici / Libri Jubilaeorum / Odarum Salomonis.* Graz, 1980.

Bauer, W. *Das Leben Jesu im Zeitalter der neutestamentlichen Apokryphen.* Tübingen, 1909 (repr. Darmstadt, 1967).

_____. *Rechtgläubigkeit und Ketzerei im ältesten Christentum*. Leipzig, 1934; 2nd ed. Tübingen, 1964. ET: *Orthodoxy and Heresy in Earliest Christianity*. Philadelphia, 1971.

_____. *Griechisch-deutsches Wörterbuch zu den Schriften des Neuen Testaments und der übrigen urchristlichen Literatur*. 5th ed. Berlin, 1958 (³1937, ⁴1949). English ed.: see above, Arndt, Gingrich, and Danker.

_____. "Das Gebot der Feindesliebe und die alten Christen" (1917). In *Aufsätze und kleine Schriften*, 235-52. Tübingen, 1967.

_____. "Matth. 19:12 und die alten Christen" (1914). In *Aufsätze und kleine Schriften*, 253-62. Tübingen, 1967.

Baur, F. C. *Kirchengeschichte der drei ersten Jahrhunderte*. 3rd ed. Tübingen, 1863.

Becker, U. *Jesus und die Ehebrecherin. Untersuchungen zur Text-und Überlieferungsgeschichte von Joh. 7:53-8:11*. BZNW 28. Berlin, 1963.

Benoit, A. "Die Überlieferung des Evangeliums in den ersten Jahrhunderten." In *Evangelium als Geschichte*, ed. V. Vajta, 161-86. Göttingen, 1974.

Bertrand, D. A. *Le baptême de Jésus. Histoire de l'exégèse aux deux premiers siècles*. BGBE 14. Tübingen, 1973.

Beyschlag, K. "Zur Geschichte der Bergpredigt in der Alten Kiche." *ZThK* 74 (1977): 291-322.

Biblia Patristica. Index des citations et allusions bibliques dans la littérature patristique. Vol. 1. *Des origines à Clément d'Alexandrie et Tertullien*. Ed. Equipe de Recherche Associée, Centre d'Analyse et de Documentation Patristique, Strasbourg. Paris, 1975.

Blum, G. G. *Tradition und sukzession. Studien zum Normbegriff des Apostolischen von Paulus bis Irenäus*. Berlin and Hamburg, 1963.

Boismard, M.-É. "Critique textuelle et citations patristiques." *RB* 57 (1950): 388-408.

Bousset, W. *Die Religion des Judentums im späthellenistischen Zeitalte*. HNT Testament 21. Tübingen, 1926.

_____. *Jüdisch-christlicher Schulbetrieb in Alexandria und Rom*. Göttingen, 1914 (repr. Hildesheim, 1975).

Bovon, F. e.a. *Les Actes apocryphes des Apôtres. Christianisme et monde païen*. Geneva, 1981.

Braun, F. M. *Jean le théologien et son évangile dans l'église ancienne*. Études Bibliques. Paris, 1959.

Bruce, F. F. "Eschatology in the Apostolic Fathers." In *The Heritage of the Early Church. Essays in Honor of G. V. Florovsky*, 77-89. Rome, 1973.

_____. *Jesus and Christian Origins outside the New Testament*. 2nd ed. London and Grand Rapids, 1984 (¹1974).

Bultmann, R. *Theologie des Neuen Testaments*. 2 vols. 7th ed. Tübingen, 1977 (¹1948–1953; UTB, 1980; ⁹1984). ET: *Theology of the New Testament*. 2 vols. Trans. Kendrick Grobel. New York, 1951, 1955; London, 1952, 1955. 2 vols. in 1. New York, London, 1965.

Burchard, C. "Das doppelte Liebesgebot in der frühen christlichen Überlieferung." In *Der Ruf Jesu und die Antwort der Gemeinde. Festschrift J. Jeremias*, 39-62. Göttingen, 1970.

Cambe, M. "Les récits de la Passion en relation avec différents textes du IIe siècle." *Foi et Vie* 81 (1982): 12-24.

von Campenhausen, H. *Kirchliches Amt und geistliche Vollmacht in den ersten drei Jahrhunderten.* BHT 14. 2nd ed. Tübingen, 1963 ('1953).

_____. "Die Jungfrauengeburt in der Theologie der alten Kirche" (1962). In *Urchristliches und altkirchliches. Vorträge und Aufsätze,* 63-161. Tübingen, 1979.

_____. *Aus der Frühzeit der Christentums. Studien zur Kirchengeschichte des ersten und zweiten Jahrhunderts.* Tübingen, 1963.

_____. *Die Entstehung der christlichen Bibel.* BHT 39. Tübingen, 1968. French: *La formation de la bible chrétienne.* Trans. D. Appia and M. Dominice. Neuchâtel, 1971. ET: *The Formation of the Christian Bible.* Trans. J. A. Baker. Philadephia, London, 1972.

Carmignac, J. *Recherches sur le "Notre Père."* Paris, 1969.

Cavallera, F. "Les pseudépigraphes et l'ancienne littérature chrétienne." *BLE* 23 (1922): 212-26.

Cerfaux, L. "La première communauté chrétienne à Jérusalem." *ETL* 16 (1939): 5-31.

_____. " 'L'aveuglement d'esprit' dans l'Évangile de Saint Marc." *Le Muséon* 59/1-4 (Louvain, 1946): 267-79.

_____. *La voix vivante de l'Évangile au début de l'Église.* Louvain, Paris, Tournai, 1946.

_____. *Une lecture de l'Épître aux Romains.* Bibliothèque de l'Institut Supérieur des Sciences Religieuses de l'Université Catholique de Louvain 2. Tournai, Paris, 1947.

_____. *La Théologie de l'Église suivant saint Paul.* 2nd ed. Paris, 1948.

Clavier, H. "Brèves remarques sur les commentaires patristiques de Matth. 16:18a." *Studia Patristica* 1:253-61. TU 63. Berlin, 1957.

Committee of the Oxford Society of Historical Theology, A. *The New Testament in the Apostolic Fathers.* Oxford, 1905.

Conzelmann, H. *Geschichte des Urchristentums.* GNT 5. Göttingen, 1969.

_____. *Heiden-Juden-Christen. Auseinandersetzungen in der Literatur der hellenistisch-römischen Zeit.* BHT 62. Tübingen, 1981.

Couard, L. *Altchristliche Sagen über das Leben Jesu und der Apostel.* Gütersloh, 1909.

Credner, K. A. *Beiträge zur Einleitung in die biblischen Schriften.* Halle, 1832.

Cremer, F. G. *Die Fastenansage Jesu. Mk. 2:20 und Parallelen in der Sicht der patristischen und scholastischen Exegese.* BBB 23. Bonn, 1965.

Cross, F. L. *The Early Christian Fathers.* London, 1960.

Crossan, J. D. *Four Other Gospels. Shadows on the Contours of Canon.* Minneapolis, Chicago, New York, 1985.

Crouzel, H. "Le texte patristique de Matthieu 5:32 et 19:9." *NTS* 19. (1971–1973): 98-119.

_____. *L'Église primitive face au divorce. Du premier au cinquième siècle.* Théologie historique 13. Paris, 1970.

Cullmann, O. "Quand viendra le Royaume de Dieu? Le témoignage des écrivains chrétiens du IIe s. jusqu'en 150." *RHPR* 18 (1938): 174-86. = "Wann kommt das Reich Gottes? Zur Enderwartung der christlichen Schriftsteller des zweiten Jahrhunderts." In *Vorträge und Aufsätze 1925–1962*, 535-47. Tübingen, Zurich, 1966.

——. *Les premières confessions de foi chrétiennes.* Cahiers de la Rev. Hist. Phil. Rel. 30. Paris, 1943.

——. *Le Christ et le Temps.* Neufchâtel, Paris, 1947.

——. "Die Tradition und die Festlegung des Kanons durch die Kirche des 2. Jahrhunderts." In *Das Neue Testament als Kanon*, ed. E. Käsemann, 98-108. Göttingen, 1970.

Daniélou, J. *Théologie du Judéo-christianisme.* Paris, Tournai, 1958.

——. *Message évangélique et culture hellénistique aux IIe et IIIe siècles.* Paris, Tournai, 1961.

——. *Études d'exégèse judéo-chrétienne (Les Testimonia).* Paris, 1966.

Dassmann, E. *Der Stachel im Fleisch. Paulus in der frühchristlichen Literatur bis Irenäus.* Munster, 1979.

Davids, A. "Irrtum und Häresie. 1 Clem.-Ignatius von Antiochien-Justinus." *Kairos* n.s. 15 (1973): 165-87.

de Aldama, J. *Maria en la patristica de los siglos I y II.* Madrid, 1970.

de Jonge, M. "Het motief van het gescheurde voorhangsel van de tempel in een aantal vroegchristelijke geschriften. *NedTTs* 21 (1966–1967): 257-76.

Delobel, J. *Logia. Les paroles de Jésus = The Sayings of Jesus. Mémorial J. Coppens.* BETL 59. Louvain, 1982.

de Margerie, B. *Introduction à l'histoire de l'exégèse. 1. Les pères grecs et orientaux.* Paris, 1980.

de Roover, E. R. *L'exégèse patristique de Luc 1:35 des origines à Augustin.* Averbode, 1969.

de Santos Otero, A. *Die handschriftliche Überlieferung der altslavischen Apokryphen.* Vol. 1. PTS 20. Berlin, 1978.

——. *Die handschriftliche Überlieferung der altslavischen Aprokryphen.* Vol. 2. PTS 23. Berlin, 1981.

Descamps, A. "Le Christianisme comme justice dans le Premier Évangile." *ETL* 22 (1946): 5-33.

Dewailly, L. M. " 'Donne-nous notre pain': quel pain? Notes sur la quatrième demande du Pater." *RSPhTh* 64. (1980): 561-88.

Dibelius, M. *Geschichte der urchristlichen Literatur.* New ed. Munich: F. Hahn, 1975.

Dihle, A. *Die goldene Regel. Eine einführung in die Geschichte der antiken und frühchristlichen Vulgärethik.* Göttingen, 1962.

Dölger, F. J. *Antike und Christentum.* 5 vols. Munster, 1929–1936.

Donaldson, J. *The Apostolical Fathers: a Critical Account of Their Genuine Writings and of Their Doctrines.* London, 1874.

Dorneich, M. *Vaterunser-Bibliographie.* Freiburg-in-Br., 1982.

Duchesne, L. *Histoire ancienne de l'Église.* Vol. 1. 6th ed. Paris, 1911.

Dungan, D. L. "The New Testament Canon in Recent Study." *Interpretation* 29 (1975): 339-51.

Dupont, J. *Gnosis. La connaissance religieuse dans les épîtres de saint Paul.* Louvain, Paris, 1949.

Erhard, A. *Die Kirche der Märtyrer, ihre Aufgaben und ihre Leistungen.* Munich, 1932.

Ewald, H. *Geschichte des Volkes Israels bis Christus.* Vol. 6. *Geschichte des apostolischen Zeitalters bis Zerstörung Jerusalem's.* 3rd ed. Göttingen, 1868. Vol. 7. *Geschichte der Ausgänge des Volkes Israël und des nachapostolischen Zeitalters.* 3rd ed. Göttingen, 1868.

Fabbri, E. " 'Agua y Espíritu.' Investigación sobre el Cristo vivificante y el bautismo del Señor en los primeros Padres prenicenos." Diss., Rome, 1956.

Festugière, A. J. *L'idéal religieux des Grecs et l'Évangile.* Études Bibliques. Paris, 1932.

Findlay, A. F. *Byways in Early Christian Literature, Studies in the Uncanonical Gospels and Acts.* Edinburgh, 1923.

Flesseman-van Leer, E. *Tradition and Scripture in the Early Church.* Assen, 1954.

_____. "Het Oude Testament bij de Apostolische Vaders en de Apologeten." *NedTTs* 9 (1954–1955): 230-44.

_____. "Prinzipien der Sammlung und Ausscheidung bei der Bildung des Kanons." *ZThK* 61 (1964): 404-20.

Frank, I. *Der Sinn der Kanonbildung. Eine historisch-theologische Untersuchung der Zeit vom 1. Clemensbrief bis Irenaeus von Lyon.* Freiburg-in-Br., 1971.

Galot, J. *Être né de Dieu. Jean 1:3.* Analecta biblica 37. Rome, 1969.

Geerard, M. *Clavis patrum graecorum.* 1. *Patres antenicaeni.* Turnhout, 1983.

Geffcken, J. *Christliche Apokryphen.* Tübingen, 1908.

Gingrich, F. W. "Prolegomena to a Study of the Christian Element in the Vocabulary of the New Testament and Apostolic Fathers." In *Festschrift R. T. Stamm,* 173-78. Leiden, 1969.

Glover, R. "Patristic Quotations and Gospel Sources." *NTS* 31 (1985): 234-51.

Goodspeed, E. J. *Index patristicus sive clavis Patrum Apostolicorum operum.* Leipzig, 1907 (repr. Naperville IL, 1960).

_____. *The Story of the Apocrypha.* Chicago, 1939.

_____. *A History of the Early Christian Literature.* Chicago, 1942. Rev. and enl. by R. M. Grant. Chicago, 1966.

Goppelt, L. *Christentum und Judentum im ersten und zweiten Jahrhundert.* Gütersloh, 1954.

_____. *Die apostolische und nachapostolische Zeit (Die Kirche in ihrer Geschichte).* 2nd ed. Göttingen, 1966.

Grant, R. M. "The Decalogue in Early Christianity." *HTR* 40 (1947): 1-17. = In *Christian Beginnings: Apocalypse to History.* London, 1983.

_____. *The Letter and the Spirit.* London, 1957.

_____. *The Earliest Lives of Jesus.* London, 1961.

_____. *L'interprétation de la Bible des origines chrétiennes à nos jours,* 49-63. Paris, 1967.

_____. *After the New Testament.* Philadelphia, 1967.

_____. "The Sermon on the Mount in Early Christianity." *Semeia* 12 (1978): 215-30.

Gregory, G. R. "The Reading of Scripture in the Church in the Second Century." *AJT* 13 (1909): 86-91.

Groh, D. E. "Hans von Campenhausen on Canon. Positions and Problems." *Interpretation* 28 (1974): 331-43.

Gry, L. *Dires prophétiques d'Esdras (IV Esdras).* Vol. 1. Paris, 1938.

Gunkel, H. *Die religion in Geschichte und Gegenwart.* 6 vols. Tübingen, 1927–1932.

Hagner, D. A. "The Sayings of Jesus in the Apostolic Fathers and Justin Martyr." In *The Jesus Tradition Outside the Gospels,* ed. D Wenham, 233-68. Gospel Perspectives 5. Sheffield, 1985.

Hahn, F. "Neuorientierung in der Erforschung des frühen Christentums?" *EvTh* 33 (1973): 537-44.

Hamman, A. *Le Pater expliqué par les Pères.* New ed. Paris, 1962.

Hanson, R. P. C. "Biblical Exegesis in the Early Church." In *The Cambridge History of the Bible.* Vol. 1. *From the Beginnings to Jerome,* 412-53. Cambridge, 1970 (pbk. 1975, repr. 1976).

Harnack, A. *Das Neue Testament und das Jahr 200.* Freiburg-in-Br., 1889.

_____. *Die Chronologie der altchristlichen Literatur bis Eusebius.* Vol. 1. Leipzig, 1897 (1893). Rev. ed. Kurt Aland. 2 vols. in 4. *Geschichte der altchristlichen Literatur bis Eusebius.* Leipzig, 1958 (repr. 1968).

_____. *Militia Christi. Die christliche Religion und der Soldatenstand in den ersten drei Jahrhunderten.* Tübingen, 1905.

_____. *Beiträge zur Einleitung in das Neue Testament.* 7 vols. Leipzig, 1906–1916.

_____. *Dogmengeschichte.* 6th ed. Tübingen, 1922.

_____. *Die Mission und Ausbreitung des Christentums in der ersten drei Jahrhunderten.* 2 vols. 4th ed. Leipzig, 1924.

Hasler, V. E. *Gesetz und Evangelium in der alten Kirche bis Origenes. Eine auslegungsgeschichtliche Untersuchung.* Zurich, 1953.

Heinisch, P. *Der Einfluss Philos auf die älteste christliche Exegese (Barnabas, Justin und Clemens von Alexandria). Ein Beitrag zur Geschichte der allegorisch-myst. Schriftauslegung. im christl. Altertum.* ATAbh 1-2. Münster, 1908.

Heitmüller, W. *"Im Namen Jesu."* FRLANT. Göttingen, 1903.

Hennecke, E. "Zur christlichen Apocryphenliteratur." *ZKG* 45 (1926): 309-16.

Henss, W. *Das Verhältnis zwischen Diatessaron, christlicher Gnosis und "Western Text."* BZNW 33. Berlin, 1967.

Hermaniuk, M. *La Parabole Évanglique.* Bruges, Paris, Louvain, 1947.

Hilgenfeld, A. *Kritische Untersuchungen.* Leipzig, 1850.

_____. *Die Apostolischen Väter, Untersuchungen über Inhalt und Ursprung der unter ihrem Namen erhaltenen Schriften.* Halle, 1853.

_____. "Die jüdische Apokalyptik und die neuesten Forschungen." *ZWT* 3 (1860): 301-62.

_____. *Historisch-Kristische Einleitung in das Neue Testament.* Leipzig, 1875.

_____. *Novum Testamentum extra canonem receptum.* 2nd ed. Leipzig, 1877.

_____. *Die Ketzergeschichte des Urchristentums.* Leipzig, 1884.

Hillmer, M. R. "The Gospel of John in the Second Century." Diss., Cambridge MA, 1966.

Hockel, A. *Christus der Erstgeborene. Zur Geschichte der Exegese von Kol 1:15.* Düsseldorf, 1965.

Hoffmann, M. *Der Dialog bei den christlichen Schriftstellern der ersten vier Jahrhunderte.* TU 96. Berlin, 1966.

Houssiau, A. "L'exégèse de Matthieu 11:27b selon saint Irénée *ETL* 19 (1953): 328-54.

James, R. "Notes on Apocrypha." *JTS* 7 (1906): 562-68.

John, J. "The Importance of St. Paul and the Pauline Epistles in Second Century Christian Gnosticism. (Apart from Marcion)." Diss., Oxford, 1984.

Johnson, S. E. "Asia Minor and Early Christianity." In *Christianity, Judaism and Other Greco-Roman Cults. Studies for M. Smith,* pt. 2, 77-145. Leiden, 1975.

Jordan, H. *Geschichte der altchristlichen Literatur.* Leipzig, 1911.

Jouassard, G. *L'abandon du Christ par son Père durant la passion d'après la tradition patristique et les docteurs du XIIIᵉ siècle.* Lyons, 1923.

Kissinger, W. S. *The Sermon on the Mount: A History of Interpretation and Bibliography.* Metuchen NJ, 1975.

Kittel, G. "Der Jakobusbrief und die Apostolischen Väter." *ZNW* 43 (1950–1951): 54-112.

Klein, G. *Der älteste christliche Katechismus und die jüdische Propaganda-Literatur.* Berlin, 1909.

Klevinghaus, J. *Die theologische Stellung der Apostolischen Väter zur alttestamentlichen Offenbarung.* BFChTh 44/1. Gütersloh, 1948.

Klijn, A. F. J. "The Question of the Rich Young Man in a Jewish Christian Gospel." *NovT* 8 (1966): 149-55.

_____. "Patristic Evidence for Jewish Christian and Aramaic Gospel Tradition." In *Text and Interpretation. Studies in the New Testament Presented to M. Black,* 169-77. Cambridge, 1979.

Knoch, O. *Die "Testamente" des Petrus und Paulus. Die Sicherung der apostolischen Überlieferung in der spätneutestamentlichen Zeit.* Stuttgart, 1973.

_____. "Paulus und Petrus in den Schriften der Apostolischen Väter." In *Kontinuität und Einheit für Franz Mussner,* 240-60. Freiburg-in-Br., 1981.

Köhler, W. D. "Die Rezeption des Matthäusevangeliums in der Zeit vor Irenäus." Diss., Bern, 1985.

Köppen, K. P. *Die Auslegung der Versuchungsgeschichte unter besonderer Berücksichtigung der Alten Kirche.* Beiträge zur Geschichte der biblischen Exegese 4. Tübingen, 1961.

Köster, H. *Synoptische Überlieferung bei den Apostolischen Vätern.* TU 65. Berlin, 1957.

_____. "Die ausserkanonischen Herrenworte als Produkte der christlichen Gemeinde." *ZNW* 47 (1957): 220-37.

_____. *Einführung in das Neue Testament.* Berlin, New York, 1980. ET: *Introduction to the New Testament.* 2 vols. Philadelphia, 1982.

Köster, H., and J. M. Robinson. *Trajectories through Early Christianity.* Philadephia, 1971. = *Entwicklungslinien durch die Welt des frühen Christentums.* Tübingen, 1971.

Ko Ha Fong, M. *Crucem tollendo Christum sequi. Untersuchung zum Verständnis eines Logions Jesu in der Alten Kirche.* Münsterische Beiträge zur Theologie 52. Münster, 1984.

Köstlin, K. R. *Der Ursprung und die Komposition der Synoptischen Evangelien.* Stuttgart, 1853.

Kraft, H. *Clavis patrum apostolicorum. Catalolgum vocum in libris patrum qui dicuntur apostolici non raro occurentium.* Munich, Darmstadt, 1963.

Kraft, R. A. "In Search of 'Jewish Christianity' and Its 'Theology.' Problems of Definition and Methodology." In *Judéo-Christianisme. Recherches historiques et théologiques offertes au Card. J. Daniélou,* 109-28. Paris, 1972.

Kramutzky, A. "Über das altkirchliche Unterrichtsbuch: Die zwei Wege oder die Entscheidung des Petrus." *ThQ* 64 (1882): 359-445.

Kroll, J. *Die christliche Hymnodik.* Königsberg, 1921.

Krüger, G. *Geschichte der altchristlichen Literatur in den ersten drei Jahrhunderten.* 2nd ed. Freiburg-in-Br., 1898.

Krüger, P. *Hellenismus und Judentum in neutestamentlichen Zeitalter.* Schriften des Institutum Delitzschianum zu Leipzig 1. Leipzig, 1908.

Kuhn, H.-W. "Jesus als Gekreutzigter in der frühchristlichen Verkündigung bis zur Mitte des 2. Jahrhunderts." *ZThK* 72 (1975): 1-46.

Lampe, G. W. H. "Some notes on the Significance of βασιλεία τοῦ θεοῦ, βασιλεία Χριστοῦ in the Greek Fathers." *JTS* 49 (1948): 58-73.

_____. *The Seal of the Spirit. A Study in the Doctrine of Baptism and Confirmation in the New Testament and the Fathers.* 2nd ed. London, 1967 (¹1951).

_____. *A Patristic Greek Lexicon.* Oxford, 1961–1968.

Laurentin, A. *Doxa. 1. Problèmes de christologie. Études des commentaires de Jean 17:5 depuis les origines jusqu'à St. Thomas d'Aquin. 2. Documents.* Paris, 1972.

Lawson, J. *A Theological and Historical Introduction to the Apostolic Fathers.* New York, 1961.

Lebeau, P. *Le vin nouveau du royaume. Étude exégétique et patristique sur la parole eschatologique de Jésus à la Cène.* Paris, Bruges, 1966.

Lebreton, J. *Histoire du dogme de la Trinité.* 2 vols. Paris, 1919 and 1928.

_____. *La vie chrétienne au premier siècle de l'Église.* Paris, 1927.

Lebreton, J., and J. Zeiller. *Histoire de l'Église primitive depuis les origines jusqu'à nos jours.* Vol. 1. *L'Église primitive.* Paris, 1938.

Lechler, H. *Das apostolische und das nachapostolische Zeitalter.* Haarlem, 1851.

Leipoldt, J., and W. Grundmann. *Umwelt des Urchristentum.* 3 vols. Berlin, 1967–1971.

Lepin, M. *Évangiles canoniques et évangiles apocryphes.* 2nd ed. Paris, 1907.

Liébaert, J. *Les enseignements moraux des Pères apostoliques.* Gembloux, 1970.

Lietzmann, H. *Geschichte der alten Kirche.* Vol. 1. *Die Anfänge.* 2nd ed. Berlin, Leipzig, 1937.

_____. *Messe und Herrenmahl. Eine Studie zur Geschichte der Liturgie.* AKG 8. 3rd. ed. Berlin, 1955 (¹1926). ET: *see* R. D. Richardson, below.

Lindemann, A. *Paulus im ältesten Christentum. Das Bild des Apostels und die Rezeption der paulinischen Theologie in der Frühchristlichen Literatur bis Marcion.* BHT 58. Tübingen, 1979.

Lipsius, R. A. *Die apokryphen Apostelgeschichten und Apostellegenden.* 3 vols. Brunswick, 1885–1890.

Löwenich (von), W. *Das Johannes-Verständnis im zweiten Jahrhundert.* BZNW 13. Giessen, 1933.

Loisy, A. *Histoire du Canon du Nouveau Testament.* Paris, 1891.

Loofs, F. *Dogmengeschichte.* 3rd ed. Halle, 1893.

Lucchesi, E. "Compléments aux Pères apostoliques en copte." *AnBoll* 99 (1981): 395-408.

McFadden, W. "The Patristic Exegesis of 1 Cor. 1:24: 'Christ the Power of God and the Wisdom of God' until the Arian Controversy." Diss., Rome, 1962.

McRay, J. R. "Charismata in the Second Century." In *Studia Patristica* 12:232-37. TU 115. Berlin, 1975.

Manns, F. *Bibliographie du Judéo-christianisme.* Jerusalem, 1979.

―――. *Essais sur le Judéo-Christianisme.* Jerusalem, 1977.

Marshall, S. C. "Δίψυχος: a Local Term?" In *Studia Evangelica* 6:348-61. TU 112. Berlin, 1973.

Massaux, É. *Influence de l'Évangile de saint Matthieu sur la littérature chrétienne avant saint Irénée.* Louvain, Gembloux, 1950 (repr. 1986).

Mees, M. "Das Sprichwort Mt. 6:21/Lk. 12:24 und seine ausserkanonischen Parallelen." *Aug* 14 (1974): 67-89.

Ménard, J. E. "L'interprétation patristique de Jean 7:38." *RUO* 25 (1955): 5*-25*.

Merkel, H. *Die Widersprüche zwischen den Evangelien. Ihre polemische und apologetische Behandlung in der Alten Kirche bis zu Augustin.* Tübingen, 1971.

Meyer, E. *Ursprung und Anfänge des Christentums.* 3 vols. Repr. Darmstadt, 1962 (¹1923).

Morgan, C. S. "The Comparative Influence of the Gospels of Matthew and Luke on Christian Literature before Irenaeus." Diss., Harvard, 1970–1971.

Müller, K., and F. H. von Campenhausen. *Kirchengeschichte.* Vol. 1, pt. 1. 3rd ed. Tübingen, 1941.

Munck, J. "Jewish Christianity in Post-Apostolic Times." *NTS* 6 (1959–1960): 103-16.

Nikolasch, F. *Das Lamm als Christussymbol in den Schriften der Väter.* Vienna, 1963.

Norden, E. *Agnostos Theos. Untersuchungen zur Formengeschichte religiöser Rede.* Leipzig, 1913.

―――. *Die antike Kunstprosa vom VI Jahrhundert v. Chr. bis in die Zeit des Renaissance.* 2 vols. 3rd ed. Leipzig, 1915–1918.

Normann, F. *Christos Didaskalos. Die Vorstellung von Christus als Lehrer in der christlichen Literatur des ersten und zweiten Jahrhunderts.* Münsterische Beiträge zur Theologie 32. Münster, 1967.

―――. *Teilhabe—ein Schlüsselwort der Vätertheologie.* Münsterische Beiträge zur Theologie 42. Münster, 1978.

Norris, F. W. "Ignatius, Polycarp and 1 Clement: Walter Bauer Reconsidered." *VigChr* 30 (1976): 23-44.

Ochagavia, J. *Visibile Patris Filius. A Study of Irenaeus's Teaching on Revelation and Tradition.* OrChrAn 161. Rome, 1964.

O'Hagan, A. P. *Material Re-Creation in the Apostolic Fathers.* TU 100. Berlin, 1968.

Ohlig, K. H. *Die theologische Begründung des neutestamentlichen Kanons in der alten Kirche.* Düsseldorf, 1972.

Orban, A. P. *Les dénominations du monde chez les premiers auteurs chrétiens.* Graecitas Christianorum Primaeva 4. Nimègue, 1970.

Orbe, A. *Cristología gnóstica.* 2 vols. Madrid, 1976.

_____. *Los primeros herejes ante la persecución.* Estudios Valentinianos 5. Rome, 1956.

Otranto, G. "Mattheo 7:15-16a e gli ψευδοπροφῆται nell'esegesi patristica." *VetChr* 6 (1969): 33-45.

_____. "Il sacerdozio commune dei fedeli nei riflessi della 1 Petr. 2:9 (I e II secolo)." *VetChr* 7 (1970): 225-46.

Paulsen, H. "Die Bedeutung des Montanismus für die Herausbildung des Kanons." *VigChr* 32 (1978): 19-52.

Pedersen, S. "Die Kanonfrage als historisches und theologisches Problem." *StTh* 31 (1977): 83-136.

Peterson, E. *Frühkirche, Judentum und Gnosis.* Freiburg-in-Br., 1959.

Pfleiderer, O. *Paulinismus.* 2nd ed. Leipzig, 1890.

Piesik, H. "Die Bildersprache der Apostolischen Väter." Diss., Bonn, 1961.

Pietrella, E. " 'Caro et sanguis regnum Dei possidere non possunt' (1 Cor. 15:50)." *Aevum* 49 (1975): 36-76.

Plummer, A. "The Apocryphal Gospels." *ExpTim* 34 (1923): 473-74.

Pollard, T. E. *Johannine Christology and the Early Church.* Cambridge, 1970.

Prigent, P. "Ce que l'oeil n'a pas vu, 1 Cor. 2:9. Histoire et préhistoire d'une citation." *ThZ* 14 (1958): 416-29.

Puzicha, M. *Christus Peregrinus. Die Fremdenaufnahme (Mt. 25:35) als Werk der privaten Wohltätigkeit im Urteil der Alten Kirche.* Münsterische Beiträge zur Theologie 47. Münster, 1980.

Quacquarelli, A. "Sulla dossologia trinitaria dei Padri apostolici." *VetChr* 10 (1973): 211-41.

Quasten, J. *Patrology.* Vol. 1. Utrecht, Brussels, 1950 (repr. 1975).

Rader, W. *The Church and Racial Hostility. A History of Interpretation of Ephesians 2:11-22.* Beiträge zur Geschichte der biblischen Exegese 20. Tübingen, 1978.

Renan, E. *Histoire des origines du christianisme.* Vol. 6. *L'Église chrétienne.* 3rd ed. Paris, 1879.

Resch, A. "Miscellen zur neutestamentlichen Schriftforschung." *ZKWL* 9 (1888): 232-45.

_____. *Aussercanonische Paralleltexte zu den Evangelien.* Vol. 2. *Matthäus und Markus.* TU 10/2. Leipzig, 1894.

Reuss, É. *Histoire de la théologie chrétienne au siècle apostolique.* Vol. 1. Strasbourg, Paris, 1852.

Richardson, R. D. "Introduction and Further Inquiry." In *Mass and Lord's Supper. A Study in the History of the Liturgy,* by H. Lietzmann, trans. D. H. G. Reeve, 219-702. Leiden, 1953-1979. (ET of Lietzmann, *Messe und Herrenmahl,* ³1955, above.)

Rigaux, B. *L'Antéchrist et l'Opposition au Royaume Messianique dans l'Ancien et le Nouveau Testament.* Gembloux, Paris, 1932.

Ritschl, A. "Über den gegenwärtigen Stand der Kritik der synoptischen Evangelien." *ThJ* 10 (1851): 480-538.

_____. *Die Enstehung der altkatholischen Kirche.* 2nd ed. Bonn, 1857.

Robinson, J. A. *Excluded Books of the New Testament.* London, 1927.

Rondet, H. "Le péché originel dans la tradition. De Clément de Rome à saint Irénée." *BLE* 66 (1965): 241-71.

Rordorf, W. "Le 'pain quotidien' (Mt. 6:11) dans l'histoire de l'exégèse." *Didaskalia* 6 (1976): 221-35.

_____. " 'Wie auch wir vergeben haben unseren Schuldnern' (Mt. 6:12b)." In *Studia Patristica* 10:236-412. TU 107. Berlin, 1970.

_____. "Beobachtungen zum Gebrauch des Dekalogs in der vorkonstantinischen Kirche." In *The New Testament Age. Essays in Honor of Bo Reicke,* ed. W. Weinrich, 2:431-42. Macon, 1984.

Rordorf, W., and A. Schneider. *Die Entwicklung des Traditionsbegriffs in der Alten Kirche.* Bern, Frankfurt, 1983.

Ruts, C. *De Apocriefen uit het N. T.* Vol. 1. *Evangeliën en Kerkstemmen.* Brussels, 1927.

Sabugal, S. "El titulo χριστός en los Padros apostólicos y apologistas griegos." *Aug* 12 (1972): 407-23.

Sachot, M. "Pour une étude de la notion de salut chez les Pères apostoliques." *RevScRel* 51 (1977): 54-70.

Sagnard, F. M. "Holy Scripture in the Early Fathers of the Church." In *Studia Evangelica:* 706-13. TU 73. Berlin, 1959.

Samain, P. "L'Accusation de magie contre le Christ dans les Évangiles." *ETL* 15 (1938): 449-90.

Sand, A. Kanon. *Von den Anfängen bis zum Fragmentum Muratorianum.* Handbuch der Dogmengeschichte 1/3a. Freiburg-in-Br., 1974.

Sanday, W. *The Gospels in the Second Century.* London, 1876.

Sanders, E. P. *The Tendencies of the Synoptic Tradition.* Cambridge, 1969.

Saxer, V. "Leçons bibliques sur les martyrs." In *Le monde grec ancien et la Bible,* 195-221. Paris, 1984.

_____. *Bible et Hagiographie. Textes et thèmes bibliques dans les Actes des martyrs authentiques des premiers siècles.* Bern, 1985.

Schelkle, K. H. *Paulus Lehrer der Väter. Die altkirche Auslegung von Römer 1-11.* Düsseldorf, 1956.

_____. "Zur biblischen und patristischen Verkündigung der Eschatologie (Nach Röm. 13:11-13)." In *Verkündigung und Glaube. Festschrift F. S. Arnold,* 1-15. Freiburg-in-Br., 1958.

Schille, G. "Was ist ein Logion?" *ZNW* 61 (1970): 171-82.

Schneemelcher, W. "Paulus in der griechischen Kirche des zweiten Jahrhunderts." *ZKG* 75 (1964): 1-20. = In *Gesammelte Aufzätze zum Neuen Testament und Patristik*, 154-81. Salonika, 1974.

Schoeps, H. J. *Urgemeinde, Judenchristentum, Gnosis*. Tübingen, 1956.

Schonfield, H. J. *Readings from the Apocryphal Gospels*. London, 1940.

Schürer, E. *Geschichte des jüdischen Volkes im Zeitalter Jesu Christi*. 4th ed. Leipzig, 1909.

Schwartz, E. *Aporien im vierten Evangelium*. Nachrichten der königl. Gesellschaft d. Wissenschaften zu Göttingen. Göttingen, 1907.

Schwegler, A. "Über den Charakter des nachapostolischen Zeitalters." *ThJ* 2 (1843): 176-94.

_____. *Das Nachapostolische Zeitalter in den Hauptmomenten seiner Entwicklung*. 2 vols. Tübingen, 1846.

Seeberg, A. *Der Katechismus der Urchristenheit*. Leipzig, 1903.

_____. *Die Didache des Judentums und der Urchristenheit*. Leipzig, 1908.

Seeberg, R. *Lehrbuch der Dogmengeschicte*. Vol. 1. 3rd ed. Leipzig, Erlangen, 1920.

Sieben, H. J. *Exegesis Patrum. Saggio bibliografico sull' esegesi biblica dei Padri della chiesa*. Sussidi Patristici 2. Rome, 1983.

Simon, M. *Recherches d'histoire judéo-chrétienne*. Paris, The Hague, 1962.

_____. "Réflexions sur le Judéo-Christianisme." In *Christianity, Judaism, and Other Greco-Roman Cults. Studies for M. Smith*, pt. 2, 53-76. Leiden, 1975. = In *Le christianisme antique et son contexte religieux. Scripta varia*, 2:598-621. Tübingen, 1981.

_____. "La Bible dans les premières controverses entre Juifs et Chrétiens." In *Le monde grec ancien et la Bible*, 107-25. Paris, 1984.

Smith, T. V. *Petrine Controversies in Early Christianity. Attitudes towards Peter in Christian Writings of the First Two Centuries*. Tübingen, 1985.

Smitmans, A. *Das Weinwunder von Kana. Die Auslegung von Jo 2:1-11 bei den Vätern und heute*. BGBE 6. Tübingen, 1966.

Soiron, Th. *Die Bergpredigt Jesu*. Freiburg-in-Br., 1941.

Speyer, W. "Die biblische Abstammung Jesu im Urteil der Schriftsteller der Alten Kirche." *Helmantica* 28 (1977): 523-39.

Staerk, W. "Der eschatologische Mythos in der altchristlichen Theologie." *ZNW* 35 (1936): 83-96.

Stahl, A. *Patristische Untersuchungen*. Vol. 1. *Der erste Brief des röm. Clemens*. Vol. 2. *Ignatius von Antiochien*. Vol. 3. *Der Hirt des Hermas*. Leipzig, 1901.

Stanton, V. H. *The Early Use of the Gospels*. Vol. 1 of *The Gospels as Historical Documents*. Cambridge, 1903.

Starck, J. "L'Église de Pâques sur la Croix. La foi à la résurrection de Jésus-Christ d'après les écrits des Pères Apostoliques." *NRTh* 75 (1953): 337-64.

Starowieyski, M. "Les problèmes de systématisation et d'interprétation des évangiles apocryphes." In *Studia Patristica* 18, ed. E. A. Livingstone, 731-37. Oxford, New York, 1982.

314   Massaux: *The Influence of the Gospel of Saint Matthew* (2)

Stegemann, V. "Christentum und Stoizismus im Kampf um die geistigen Lebenswerte im II Jahrhundert nach Christus." *Die Welt als Geschichte* 7 (1941): 295-330.

Steiner, M. *La tentation de Jésus dans l'interprétation patristique de saint Justin à Origène.* Études Bibliques. Paris, 1962.

Strecker, G. "Christentum und Judentum in den ersten beiden Jahrhunderten." *EvTh* 16 (1956): 458-77.

————. "Zum problem des Judenchristentums." Postscript to *Rechtgläubigkeit und Ketzerei,* by W. Bauer (²1934, see above), 245-87.

————. *Das Judenchristentum in den Pseudoklementinen.* TU 70. Berlin, 1981 ('1958).

Strobel, A. "Schriftverständnis und Obrigkeitsdenken in der ältesten Kirche." Diss., Erlangen, 1956.

Supernatural Religion: an Inquiry into the Reality of Divine Revelation. Vol. 1. (No author given.) London, 1879.

Thackeray, J. *The Relation of St. Paul to Contemporary Jewish Thought.* London, 1900.

Thieme, K. *Kirche und Synagoge. Die ersten nachbiblischen Zeugnisse ihrers Gegensatzes im Offenbarungsverständnis: Der Barnabasbrief und der Dialog Justins des Märtyrers.* Olten, 1945.

Thyen, H. *Der Stil der jüdisch-hellenistischen Homilie.* Göttingen, 1955.

Tischendorf, C. *Wann wurden unsere Evangelien?* Leipzig, 1865.

Tison, J. M. "Salus Israel apud Patres primi et secundi saeculi." *VD* 39 (1961): 97-108.

Torrance, T. F. *The Doctrine of Grace in the Apostolic Fathers.* Edinburgh, 1948.

Torrey, C. C. *The Apocryphal Literature.* New Haven, 1945.

Trummer, P. *Anastasis. Beitrag zur Auslegung und Auslegungsgeschichte von 1 Kor. 15 in der griechischen Kirche bis Theodoret.* Vienna, 1970.

Turner, H. E. W. *The Pattern of Christian Truth. A Study in the Relation between Orthodoxy and Heresy in the Early Church.* London, 1954.

Turowski, I. "Geschichte der Auslegung der synoptischen Verklärunggeschichte in vornizänischer Zeit." Diss., Heidelberg, 1966.

Vallberg, V. *Det nya testamentets sanning bestyrckt genom de apostolika fäderna.* Stockholm, 1966.

van den Eynde, D. *Les normes de l'enseignement chrétien dans la littérature patristique des trois premiers siècles.* Gembloux, Paris, 1933.

van Eijk, A. H. C. *La résurrection des morts chez les Pères apostoliques.* Paris, 1971.

van Haelst, J. *Catalogue des papyrus littéraires juifs et chrétiens.* Paris, 1976.

van Unnik, W. C. "De oud-christlijke letterkunde tot Irenaeus." In *Het oudste Christendom en de antieke Cultuur,* 2:84-105. Harlem, 1951.

van Vliet, H. *Did Greek-Roman-Hellenistic Law Know the Exclusion of the Single Witness? The Answer of the Early Christian Writings . . . A Supplement to "No Single Testimony," a Study on the Adoption of the Law of Deut. 19:15 par. into the New Testament (Utrecht 1958 . . .).* Franeker, 1980.

————. "Zur Bedeutung von ταπεινοῦν τὴν ψυχήν bei den Apostolischen Vätern." *ZNW* 44 (1952–1953): 250-55. = In *Sparsa Collecta,* 3:71-76. Leiden, 1983.

Variot, J. *Les Évangiles apocryphes.* Paris, 1878.

Verveijs, P. G. *Evangelium und neues Gesetz in der ältesten Christenheit bis auf Marcion.* Utrecht, 1960.

Vielhauer, Ph. *Oikodomè. Das Bild vom Bau in der christlichen Literatur, vom Neuen Testament bis Clemens Alexandrinus.* Karlsruhe, 1940. 2nd ed. in *Aufsätze zum Nuen Testament,* 2:1-168. Munich, 1979.

_____. *Geschichte der urchristlichen Literatur. Einleitung in das Neue Testament, die Apokryphen und die Apostolischen Väter.* Berlin, 1975 (repr. 1978).

Vischer, L. *Die Auslegungsgeschichte von 1 Kor. 6:1-11. Rechtsverzicht und Schlichtung.* Tübingen, 1955.

Vögtle, A. *Die Tugend-und Lasterkataloge im Neuen Testament.* NTAbh 16/4-5. Münster-in-Westphalia, 1936.

Vokes, F. E. "The Lord's Prayer in the First Three Centuries." In *Studia Patristica* 10:253-60. TU 107. Berlin, 1970.

Völter, D. *Die apostolischen Väter neu untersucht.* Pt. 1. *Clemens, Hermas, Barnabas.* Leiden, 1904.

Volz, P. *Die Eschatologie der jüdischen Gemeinde im neutestamentlichen Zeitalter nach den Quellen der rabbinischen, apokalyptischen, und apokryphen Literatur.* 4th ed. Tübingen, 1934.

Wehofer, T. M. "Untersuchungen zur altchristlichen Epistolographie." Sitzungberichte d. Wiener Akad. Phil.-hist. Kl. 143/17: 102-37. Vienna, 1901.

Weigandt, P. *Der Doketismus im Urchristentum und in der theologischen Entwicklung des zweiten Jahrhunderts.* 2 vols. Heidelberg, 1961.

Wescott, B. F. *A General Survey of the History of the Canon of the New Testament,.* London, 1896.

Wild, E. "Histoire de l'exégèse de la période de Gethsemani Matthieu 26:36-46. Les trois premiers siècles." Diss., Strasbourg, 1975.

Wiles, M. F. "Early Exegesis of the Parables." *SJT* 11 (1958): 287-301.

Wilhelms, E. *Die Tempelsteurperkope Matthäus 17:24-27 in der Exegese der griechischen Väter der Alten Kirche.* Helsinki, 1980.

Willard, C. R. "The Sermon on the Mount in the Writings of the Ante-Nicene Fathers from New Testament Times to Origen." Th.D. thesis, Central Baptist Theological Seminary, Kansas City KS, 1956.

Wilson, R. McL. "Apokryphen II. Apokryphen des Neuen Testaments." In *Theologische Realenzyklopädie* 3:316-62. 1978.

Windisch, H. *Taufe und Sünde im ältesten Christentum.* Tübingen, 1908.

Winling, R. "Une façon de dire le salut: la formule 'Être avec Dieu—Être avec Jésus-Christ' dans les écrits des Pères apostoliques." *RevScRel* 54 (1980): 109-28.

_____. "Une façon de dire le salut: la formule 'Être avec Dieu—Être avec Jésus-Christ' dans les écrits (apocryphes chrétiens compris) de l'ère dite des Pères apostoliques." In *Studia Patristica* 18, ed. E. A. Livingstone, 760-64. Oxford, New York, 1982.

Winter, P. "Matthew 11:27 and Luke 10:22 from the First to the Fifth Century. Reflections on the Development of the Text." *NovT* 1 (1956): 112-48.

Wrege, H. T. *Die Überlieferungsgeschichte der Bergpredigt.* WUNT 9. Tübingen, 1968.

Wright, L. E. *Alterations of the Words of Jesus as Quoted in the Literature of the Second Century.* Harvard Historical Monographs 25. Cambridge MA, 1952.

Wustmann, G. *Die Heilsbedeutung Christi bei den apostolischen Vätern.* BFChTh 9/2-3. Gütersloh, 1905.

Zahn, Th. *Geschichte des neutestamentlichen Kanons.* Erlangen, Leipzig, 1888–1892.

————. *Forschungen zur Geschichte des neutestamentlichen Kanons.* 7 vols. Leipzig, 1891–1929.

Zaphiris, G. *Le texte de l'Évangile selon saint Matthieu, d'après les citations de Clément d'Alexandrie comparées aux citations des Pères et des théologiens grecs du IIᵉ au XVᵉ siècle.* Gembloux, 1970.

Zeegers-van der Vorst, N. *Les citations des poètes grecs chez les apologistes chrétiens du deuxième siècle.* Louvain, 1972.

Zeiller, J. "La vie chrétienne aux deux premier siècles." *RSR* 24 (1934): 513-42.

————. "Les persécutions contre les chrétiens aux deux premiers siècles." Miscellanea hist. A. de Meyer, 1:131-36. 1946.

Zeller, E. "Die älteste Überlieferung ber die Schriften des Lukas." *ThJ* 7 (1848): 528-72.

Ziegler, I. *Der Kampf zwischen Judentum und Christentum in den ersten drei christlichen Jahrhunderten.* Berlin, 1907.

CHRISTIAN LITERATURE
OF THE FIRST TWO CENTURIES
IN PARTICULAR[1]

Second Clement

1. Sources

Crafer, T. W. *Second Epistle of Clement to the Corinthians*. Texts for Students 22. London, 1921.

Graham, H. H., and R. M. Grant. *First and Second Clement*. The Apostolic Fathers. London, 1965.

Hemmer, H.-P. Lejay. *Clément de Rome, Épître aux Corinthiens, Homélie du IIme siècle*. Textes et documents, Les Pères Apostoliques 2. 2nd ed. Paris, 1926.

Knopf, R. *Der Zweite Clemensbrief*. HNT/E. *Die Apostolischen Väter*, 1:151-84. Tübingen, 1920.

Wengst, K. *Didache (Apostellehre). Barnabasbrief. Zweiter Klemensbrief. Schrift an Diognet*. In *Schriften des Urchristentums* 2. Munich and Darmstadt, 1984.

2. Studies

Baarda, T. "2 Clement 12 and the Sayings of Jesus." In J. Delobel, ed., *Logia*, 529-56. = "Early Transmission of Words of Jesus, Thomas, Tatian, and the Text of the New Testament." In *A Collection of Studies*, 261-88. Amsterdam, 1983.

Bartlet, V. "The Origin and Date of 2 Clement." *ZNW* 7 (1906): 123-35.

Di Pauli, A. "Zum sogenannten zweiten Korintherbrief des Clemens Romanus." *ZNW* 4 (1903): 321-29.

Donfried, K. P. "The Setting of Second Clement in Early Christianity." NovTSup 38. Leiden, 1974.

_____. "The Theology of Second Clement. *HTR* 67:35-53.

Frank. A. "Studien zur Ekklesiologie des Hirten, II Klemens, der Didache und der Ignatiusbriefe unter besonderer Berücksichtigung der Idee einer Präexistenten Kirche." Diss. Munich, 1975.

Funk, F. X. "Der sogenannte zweite Klemensbrief." *ThQ* 84 (1902): 349-64.

Hagemann, H. "Über den zweiten Brief des Klemens von Rom." *ThQ* 43 (1861): 509-31.

Harnack, A. "Über den sogennanten zweiten Brief des Klemens an die Korinther." *ZKG* 1 (1877): 264-83; 329-64.

---

[1]This bibliography follows the order of distinct chapters in this book.

—————. "Zum Ursprung der sog. zweiten Clemensbrief." *ZNW* 6 (1905): 67-71.

Harris, R. "The Authorship of the So-Called Second Epistle of Clement." *ZNW* 23 (1924): 193-200.

Knopf, R. "Die Anagnose zum zweiten Clemensbriefe." *ZNW* 3 (1902): 266-79.

Krüger, G. *Bemerkungen zum zweiten Clemensbrief.* Studies in Early Christianity, 419-39. New York, 1928.

—————. "Zu II Klem. 14:2." *ZNW* 31 (1932): 204-05.

Powell, D. "Clemensbrief, zweiter." *Theologische Realenzyklopädie* 8 (1981): 121-23.

Prätorius, W. "Die Bedeutung der beiden Clemensbriefe für die älteste Geschichte der kirchlichen Praxis." *ZKG* 33 (1912): 347-63.

Stanton, G. R. "2 Clement VII and the Origin of the Document." In *Classica et Mediaevalia* 28 (1970): 314-20.

Stegemann, C. "Herkunft und Entstehung des sogenannten zweiten Klemensbriefes." Diss. Bonn, 1974.

Taylor, C. "The Homily of Pseudo-Clement." *JPh* 28 (1903): 195-208.

van Unnik, W. C. "The Interpretation of 2 Clement 15,5." *VigChr* 27 (1973): 29-34.

Völter, D. *Die älteste Predigt aus Rom. Der sogenannte zweite Clemensbrief.* Leiden, 1908.

Windisch, H., *Das Christentum des zweiten Clemensbriefes.* Leipzig, 1921.

Polycarp and the Martyrdom of Polycarp

1. Sources

Bauer, W. *Der Brief des Polykarp von Smyrna an die Philipper.* HNT/E. *Die Apostolischen Väter* 2:282-98. Tübingen, 1920.

Bauer, W., and H. Paulsen. *Die Briefe des Ignatius von Antiochia und der Polykarpbrief.* HNT 18. Tübingen, 1985.

Camelot, P. T. *Ignace d'Antioche. Polycarpe de Smyrne. Lettre. Martyre de Polycarpe.* SC 10. 4th ed. Paris, 1969.

Dehandschutter, B. "Martyrium Polycarpi. Een literair-kritische studie." *BETL* 52. Louvain, 1979.

Fisher, J. A. *Die Apostolischen Väter. Greichisch und deutsch.* Munich, 1956. = *Die Apostolischen Väter.* Schriften des Urchristentums 1. 8th ed. Darmstadt, 1981.

Kleist, J. A. "The Didache. The Epistle of Barnabas. The Epistle and the Martyrdom of Polycarp, etc." *ACW* 6. London, 1948. (Repr. 1961.)

Krüger, G. *Ausgewählte Märtyrerakten.* 4th ed. Tübingen, 1965.

Lazzati, G. *Gli sviluppi della letteratura sui martiri nei primi quattro secoli.* Turin, 1956.

Lelong, A. *Ignace d'Antioche et Polycarpe de Smyrne, Épîtres, Martyre de Polycarpe.* Textes et Documents, Les Pères Apostoliques 3. 2nd ed. Paris, 1927.

Musurillo, H. *The Acts of the Christian Martyrs.* Oxford, 1972.

Schoedel, W. R. *Polycarp. Martyrdom of Polycarp. Fragments of Papias.* The Apostolic Fathers 5. London, 1965.

Zahn, Th. *Ignatii et Polycarpi Epistulae, Martyria, Fragmenta.* Patrum Apostolicorum opera 2. Leipzig, 1876.

2. Studies

Note: As for contributions regarding the date of the Martyrdom of Polycarp, see B. Dehandschutter, "Martyrium Polycarpi."

A. C. "The Epistle of Polycarp to the Philippians." *CQR* 141 (1945): 1-25.

Barnard, L. W. "The Problem of St. Polycarp's Epistle to the Philippians." *CQR* 158 (1962): 421-30. = *Studies in the Apostolic Fathers and their Background,* 31-39. Oxford, 1966.

_____. "In Defence of Pseudo-Pionius's Account of Polycarp's Martyrdom." In *Kyriakon. Festschrift J. Quasten,* 192-204. = "Studies in Church History and Patristics." *Analecta Vlatadon* 26, 224-41. Thessalonica, 1978.

Barnes, T. D. "A Note on Polycarp." *JTS* 18 (1967): 433-47.

_____. "Pre-Decian Acta Martyrum." *JTS* 19 (1968): 509-31.

Baumeister, T. "Die Anfänge der Theologie des Martyriums." *Münsterische Beiträge zur Theologie* 45 (1980): 289-306.

Bovon-Thurneysen, A. "Ethik und Eschatologie im Philliperbrief des Polykarp von Smyrna." *ThZ* 29 (1973): 241-56.

Brind'Amour, P. "La date du martyre de saint Polycarpe (le 23 février 1967)." AnBoll 98 (1980): 456-62.

Campenhausen, H. von. "Polykarp von Smyrna und die Pastoralbriefe" (1951). = "Aus der Frühzeit des Christentums." In *Studien zur Kirchengeschichte des ersten und zweiten Jahrhunderts,* 197-252. Tübingen, 1963.

_____. "Bearbeitungen und Interpolationen des Polykarpmartyriums" (1957). = "Aus der Frühzeit des Christentums." In *Studien zur Kirchengeschichte des ersten und zweiten Jahrhunderts,* 253-301. Tübingen, 1963.

Conzelmann, H. "Bemerkungen zum Martyrium Polykarp." In *Ak. Wiss.* Göttingen Phil. Hist. Kl. 2. Göttingen, 1978.

Dahl, N. A. "Der Erstgeborene Satans und der Vater des Teufels (Poly 7,1 und Joh 8,44)." In *Apophoreta. Festschrift für E. Haenchen,* 70-84. Berlin, 1964.

Dehandschutter, B. "Le Martyre de Polycarpe et le développement de la conception du martyre au deuxième siècle." In *Studia Patristica* 18:659-68. Ed. E. A. Livingstone. Oxford and New York, 1982.

Den Boeft, J., and J. Bremmer. "Notiunculae martyrologicae III. Some Observations on the Martyria of Polycarp and Pionius." *VigChr* 39 (1985): 110-30.

Frei, W., "Bischof Polykarp von Smyrna und die beginnende Heiligenverehrung." *IKZ* 72 (1982): 207-17.

Glasson, T. F. "Hort's Rendering of Passages from Ignatius and Polycarp." *CQR* 167 (1966): 302-09.

Grant, R. M. "Polycarp of Smyrna. *ATR* 28 (1946): 137-48.

Guillaumin, M. L. "En marge du 'Martyre de Polycarpe.' Le discernement des allusions scripturaires." In *Forma Futuri. Studi in onore del Cardinale M. Pellegrino,* 462-69. Turin, 1975.

Harrison, P. N. *Polycarp's Two Epistles to the Philippians*. Cambridge, 1936.

Hilgenfeld, A. "Polykarp von Smyrna." *ZWT* 17 (1874): 305-45.

_____. "Das Martyrium Polykarp's von Smyrna." *ZWT* 22 (1879): 145-70.

_____. "Der Brief des Polykarpus an die Philipper." *ZWT* 29 (1886): 180-206.

Lallemand, A. "Le parfum des martyrs dans les Actes des martyrs de Lyon et le Martyre de Polycarpe." *Studia Patristica* 16. TU 129:186-92. Berlin, 1985.

Lipsius, R. A. "Der Märtyrertod Polykarp's." *ZWT* 17 (1874): 188-214.

Mathiesen, R., and R. F. Allen. "An Early Church Slavonic Translation of the Martyrdom of St. Polycarp." *HTR* 72 (1979): 161-63.

Meinhold, P. "Polykarpos." In *Paulys Realenzyclopädie der classischen Altertumwissenschaft* 21/2 (1952): cols. 1662-93.

Müller, H. "Eine Bemerkung zum Martyrium Polycarpi." *TGl* 2 (1910): 669-70.

Nielsen, C. M. "Polycarp, Paul and the Scriptures." *ATR* 47 (1965): 199-216.

Prete, S. "'Confessioni Trinitarie' in alcuni Atti dei Martiri del sec. II (Giustino, Apollonio, Policarpo)." *Aug* 13 (1973): 469-82.

_____. "In incorruptibilitate ἀφθαρσία Spiritus s. (Mart. Polyc. 14,2)." *Aug* 20 (1980): 509-21.

Reuning, W. *Zur Erklärung der Polykarpmärtyriums*. Darmstadt, 1917.

Rordorf, W. "Zum Problem des 'grossen Sabbats' im Polykarp- und Pioniusmartyrium." In *Pietas. Festschrift B. Kötting*, 245-49. Münster, 1980.

Saxer, V. "L'authenticité du Martyre de Polycarpe. Bilan de 25 ans de critique." *Mélanges de l'École française de Rome. Antiquité* 94 (1982): 979-1001.

Schwartz, J. "Note sur le Martyre de Polycarpe de Smyrne." *RHPR* 52 (1972): 331-35.

Schweitzer, V. "Polycarp von Smyrna über Erlösung und Rechtfertigung." *ThQ* 86 *(1904): 91-109.*

Simonetti, M. "Alcune osservazioni sul martirio di S. Policarpo." *Giornale Italiano di Filologia* 9 (1956): 328-44.

Steinmetz. P. "Polykarp von Smyrna über die Gerechtigkeit." *Hermes* 100 (1972): 63-75.

Völter, D. *Polykarp und Ignatius und die ihnen zugeschriebenen Briefe neu untersucht. Die apotolischen Väter* 2. Leiden, 1910.

The Apocalypses

General

Dehandschutter, B. "Judentum und Christentum. Das Problem der Frühchristlichen Apokalypsen." *Ebraismo, Ellenismo, Cristianesimo* 1 (1985): 261-66. = Archivio di Filosofia 53.

Grébaut, S., "Littérature éthiopienne pseudo-clémentine." *ROC* 2/5(15) (1910): 197-214; 307-17.

Hennecke E., and W. Schneemelcher. *Neutestamentlische Apokryphen in deutscher Übersetzung*. 2 vols. 3rd ed. Tübingen, 1959–1964 (⁴1968). ET: *New Testament Apocrypha*. 2 vols. Trans. A. J. B. Higgins et al. Ed. R. McL. Wilson. Philadelphia, London, 1963, 1966.

Lücke, F. *Versuch einer vollständigen Einleitung in die Offenbarung des Johannes und die apokalyptische Literatur*. 2nd ed. Bonn, 1852.

Reitzenstein, R. *Poimandrès. Studien zur griechisch-aegyptischen und frühchristlichen Literatur*. Leipzig, 1904.

───────. *Hellenistische Wundererzählungen*. Leipzig, 1906.

Schwarte, K. H. "Apokalyptik. Apokalypsen V. Alte Kirche." *Theologische Realenzyklopädie* 3 (1978): 257-75.

Vielhauer, P. "Apokalyptik des Urchristentums. 1. Einleitung." In E. Hennecke–W. Schneemelcher, *Neutestamentliche Apokryphen in deutscher Übersetzung* 2:428-54. 3rd ed. Tübingen, 1959–1964 (⁴1968).

The Ascension of Isaiah

1. Sources

Barton, J. M. T. "The Ascension of Isaiah." In *The Apocryphal Old Testament*, H. F. D. Sparks, ed. 775-812. Oxford, 1984.

Basset R. *Les Apocryphes éthiopiens traduits en français*. Vol. 3. *L'Ascension d'Isaïe*. Paris, 1894.

Charles, R. H. *The Ascension of Isaiah*. London, 1900.

───────. *The Apocalypse of Abraham, and the Ascension of Isaiah*. London, 1919.

Dillman, A. *Ascensio Isaïae aethiopice et latine*. Leipzig, 1877.

Flemming, J., and H. Duensig. "Die Himmelfahrt des Jesaja." In E. Hennecke–W. Schneelmelcher, *Neutestamentliche Apokryphen in deutscher Übersetzung* 2:454-68. 3rd ed. Tübingen, 1959–1964 (⁴1968).

Grenfell, B. P., and A. S. Hunt. *The Amherst Papyri, Part I, The Ascension of Isaiah*, 87-92, 98-139. London, 1900.

Jolowicz, H. *Die Himmelfahrt und Vision des Propheten Jesaia aus dem Aethiopischen und Lateinischen in's Deutsch übersetz*. Leipzig, 1854.

Knibb, M. "Martyrdom and Ascension of Isaiah." In *The Old Testament Pseudepigrapha*, ed. J. H. Charlesworth, 2:143-76. London, 1983–1985.

Tisserant, E. *Ascension d'Isaïe*. Traduction de la version éthiopienne avec les principales variantes des versions grecques, latines et slaves. Documents pour l'Étude de la Bible. Paris, 1909.

2. Studies

Bauckham, R. J. "Synoptic Parousia Parables Again." *NTS* 29 (1983):129-34.

Bosse, A. "Zur Erklärung der Apokalypse der Asc. Jesaïae." *ZNW* 10 (1909): 320-23.

Burch, V. "Material for the Interpretation of the Ascensio Isaiae." *JTS* 21 (1920): 249-65.

Charlesworth, J. H. *The Pseudepigrapha and Modern Research* (+ bibl.), 125-30. Missoula MT, 1981.

Erbetta, M. "Ascensione di Isaia 4,3 è la testimonianza più antica del martirio di Pietro." *Euntes Docete* 19 (1966): 427-36.

Flusser, D. "The Connection between the Apocryphal 'Ascensio Isaiae' and the Dead Sea Scrolls." *Bulletin of the Israel Exploration Society* 17 (1952-53): 28-46.

——————. "The Apocryphal Book of 'Ascensio Isaiae' and the Dead Sea Sect." *Israel Exploration Journal* 3 (1953): 30-47.

Heussi, K. "Die Ascensio Isaiae und ihr vermeintliches Zeugnis für ein römisches Martyrium des Apostels Petrus." *Wissenschaftliche Zeitschrift Jena* 12 (1963): 269-74.

Leonardi, C. "Il testo dell' Ascensio Isaiae nel Vat. Lat. 5750." *Cristianesimo nella storia* 1 (1980): 59-74.

Martin, F. "Ascension d'Isaïe, c. I, v. 8." *Orientalische Literaturzeitung* 11 (1908): 220-22.

Norelli, E. "La resurrezione di Gesu nell' Ascensione di Isaia." *Cristianesimo nella storia* 1 (1980): 315-66.

Pesce, M., ed. *Isaia, il diletto e la chiesa. Visione ed esegesi prefetica cristiano-primitiva nell' Ascensione di Isaia.* Brescia, 1983.

Philonenko, M. "Le 'Martyre d'Ésaïe' et l'histoire de la secte de Qoumrân." *Pseudépigraphes de l'Ancien Testament et manuscrits de la mer Morte* 1:1-10 (Cahiers d'histoire et de philosophie religieuses 41). Paris, 1967.

Odes of Solomon

Note: Regarding the Odes of Solomon, I did not specify the numerous contributions on the origin and the original language of the Odes. See:

Brock, S. P. "Syriac Studies 1960–1979, a Classified Bibliography." *Parole de l'Orient* 5 (1973): 393-465; cf. 454-56.

——————. "Syriac Studies 1971–1980, a Classified Bibliography." *Parole de l'Orient* 10 (1981-82): 291-412; cf. 394-96.

Charlesworth, J. H. *The Pseudepigrapha and Modern Research*, 189-94. Missoula MT, 1981.

Drijvers, H. J. W. *East of Antioch. Studies in Early Syriac Christianity.* London, 1984. [= Collected essays.]

1. Sources

Bauer, W. "Die Oden Salomos." In E. Henneck–W. Schneemelcher, *Neutestamentliche Apokryphen in deutscher Übersetzung* 2:576-625. 3rd ed. Tübingen, 1959–1964 (⁴1968).

Bernard, J. H. *The Odes of Solomon. JTS* 12 (1910): 1-31. = *Texts and Studies.* Cambridge, 1912.

Charlesworth, J. H. *The Odes of Solomon*. Oxford, 1973. = SBL Texts and Translations. Pseudepigrapha Series. Missoula MT, 1977.

_____. "Odes of Solomon." *The Old Testament Pseudepigrapha*, ed. J. H. Charlesworth, 2:725-71. London, 1983–1985.

Diettrich, G. *Die Oden Salomos, unter Berüchtsichtigung der überlieferten Stichengliederung*. Berlin, 1911.

Emerton, J. A. "The Odes of Solomon." In *The Apocryphal Old Testament*, H. F. D. Sparks, ed., 683-731. Oxford, 1984.

Harris, R. *The Odes and Psalms of Solomon*. Cambridge, 1909.

Harris, R., and A. Mingana. *The Odes and the Psalms of Solomon, re-edited for the Governors of the John Rylands Library*. 2 vols. Manchester, London, New York, Bombay, Calcutta, Madras, 1916.

Labourt, J., and P. Batiffol. *Les Odes de Salomon. Une oeuvre chrétienne des environs de l'an 100-120*. Paris, 1911.

Lattke, M. *Die Oden Salomos in ihrer Bedeutung für Neues Testament und Gnosis*. 3 vols. Fribourg-Göttingen, 1979-81.

Smirnov, A. *Die Psalmen Salomos nebst den Oden Salomos*. Die alttestamentliche Apokryphen. Fasc. 3. Kasau, 1906.

Testuz, M. *Papyrus Bodmer* 10-12. Cologny-Geneva, 1959.

Ungnad, A., and W. Staerk. *Die Oden Salomos*. KlT 64. Berlin, 1933.

2. Studies

Aune, D. E. "The Odes of Solomon and Early Christian Prophecy." *NTS* 28 (1982): 435-60.

Bouquet, A. C. "The Odes of Solomon." *Th* 8 (1924): 197-206.

Braun, F. M. "L'énigme des Odes de Salomon." *Revue thomiste* 57 (1957): 597-625.

Bruston, C. "Les plus anciens cantiques chrétiens: les Odes de Salomon." *RTP* 44 (1911): 465-97.

_____. "Quelques observations sur les Odes de Salomon." *ZNW* 13 (1912): 111-16.

Charlesworth, J. H. "Qumran, John and the Odes of Solomon." In id., *John and Qumran*, 107-36. London, 1972.

_____. "Haplography and Philology: A Study of Ode of Solomon 16:8." *NTS* 25 (1978-79): 221-27.

Charlesworth, J. H., and R. A. Culpepper. "The Odes of Solomon and the Gospel of John." *CBQ* 35 (1973): 298-322.

Clemen, C. "Die neuentdeckten Oden Salomos." *ThR* 14 (1911): 1-19.

Connolly, R. H. "The Odes of Solomon: Jewish or Christian." *JTS* 13 (1912): 298-309.

_____. "Greek the Original Language of the Odes of Solomon." *JTS* 14 (1913): 530-38.

Conybeare, F. C. "The Odes of Solomon Montanist." *ZNW* 12 (1911): 70-75.

_____. "Note on the Odes of Solomon." *ZNW* 14 (1913): 96.

D'Alès, A. "Les Odes de Salomon." *Études* 129 (1911): 753-70.

Daniélou, J. "Odes de Salomon." *Supplément au Dictionnaire de la Bible* 6 (1960): cols. 677-84.

Drijvers, H. J. W. "Kerygma und Logos in den Oden Salomos dargestellt am Beispiel der 23 Ode." In *Kerygma und Logos. Festschrift C. Andresen*, 163-72. Göttingen, 1979.

Frankenberg, W. *Das Verständnis der Oden Salomos.* BZAW 21. Giessen, 1911.

Franzmann, M. "The Odes of Solomon, Man of Rest." *Orientalia Christiana Periodica* 51 (1985): 408-21.

Fries, S. A. "Die Oden Salomos, montanistische Lieder aus dem 2. Jahrhundert." *ZNW* 12 (1911): 108-25.

Gamber, K. "Die Oden Salomos als frühchristliche Gesänge beim heiligen Mahl." *Ostkirchliche Studien* 15 (1966): 182-95.

Gressman, H. "Die Oden Salomos." *Deutsche Literaturzeitung* 32 (1911): cols. 1349-56.

──────────. "Les Odes de Salomon." *RTP* n.s. 1 (1913): 195-227.

──────────. *Ode Salomos 23.* Ak. Berl. Berlin, 1921.

Grimme H. "Die 19. Ode Salomos." *TGl* 3 (1911): 11-18.

Gunkel, G. H. "Die Oden Salomos." *ZNW* 11 (1910): 291-328.

Harnack, A. *Ein jüdisch-christliches Psalmbuch aus dem ersten Jahrhundert.* TU 35/4. Leipzig, 1910.

Haussleiter, J. "Der judenchristliche Charakter der 'Oden Salomos'." *ThLB* 31 (1910): cols. 265-76.

Headlam, A. C. "The Odes of Solomon." *CQR* 71 (1911): 272-97.

Hora, E. "Die Oden Salomos." *TGl* 5 (1913): 128-40.

Kittel G. "Die Oden Salomos überarbeit oder einheitlich, mit 2 Beilagen. 1. Bibliographie der Oden Salomos; 2, Syrische Konkordanz der Oden Salomos." BWANT 16. Leipzig, 1914.

Lattke, M. "The Apocryphal Odes of Solomon and the New Testament Writings." *ZTW* 74 (1982): 294-301.

McNeil, B. "The Odes of Solomon and the Sufferings of Christ." In *Symposium Syriacum 1976*, 31-38. OrChrAn 205. Rome, 1978.

──────────. "The Odes of Solomon and the Acts of Thomas." *OrChr* 67 (1983): 104-22.

Merrill, E. H. "Odes of Solomon and the Acts of Thomas: a Comparative Study." *Journal of the Evangelical Theological Society* 17 (1974): 231-34.

Mingana, A. "Quelques mots sur les Odes de Salomon." *ZNW* 15 (1914): 234-53; 16 (1915): 167-90.

Reinach, S. "Les Odes de Salomon." *RHR* 62 (1910): 279-94.

Slee, H. M. "A Note on the Sixteenth Ode of Solomon." *JTS* 15 (1914): 454.

Spitta, F. "Zum Verständnis der Oden Salomos." *ZNW* 11 (1910): 193-203; 259-91.

Staerk, W. "Kritische Bemerkungen zu den Oden Salomos." *ZWT* 52 (1910): 289-306.

Stölten, W. "Gnostische Parallelen zu den Oden Salomos." *ZNW* 13 (1912): 29-58.

Strachan, R. H. "The Newly Discovered Odes of Solomon and their Bearing on the Problem of the Fourth Gospel." *ExpTim* 22 (1910): 7-14.

Vaccari, A. "Le Ode di Salomone." *CivCatt* 1 (1912): 21-36.

van Unnick, W. C. "A Note on Ode of Solomon 34, 4." *JTS* 37 (1936): 172-75. = *Sparsa Collecta* 3:3-6. Leiden, 1983.

Willey, D. "The Odes and Psalms of Solomon." *JTS* 14 (1913): 293-98.

Zahn, Th. "Die Oden Salomos." *NKZ* 21 (1910): 667-701; 747-77.

The Sibylline Oracles

1. Sources

Alexandre, C. Χρησμὰ Σιβυλλιακά. *Oracula Sibyllina*. 2nd ed. Paris, 1853.

Bouché-Leclercq, A. "Oracles Sibyllins." *RHR* 7 (1883): 236-48; 7 (1884): 220-33.

Collins, J. J. "Sibylline Oracles." In *The Old Testament Pseudepigrapha*, ed. J. H. Charlesworth, 1:317-472. London, 1983–1985.

Friedlieb, J. B. *Die sibyllinischen Weissagungen vollständig gesammelt nach neuer Handschriften-Vergleichung.* Leipzig, 1852.

Geffcken, J. "Die Oracula Sibyllina." *Griechische Christliche Schriftsteller* 8:352. Leipzig, 1902. (Repr. Amsterdam, 1967.)

Kurfess, A. "Christliche Sibyllinen." In E. Hennecke–W. Schneemelcher, *Neutestamentlische Apokryphen in deutsche Übersetzung* 2:498-528. Tübingen, 1959–1963 (⁴1968).

——————. *Sibyllinische Weissagungen.* Urtext und Übersetzung. Munich, 1951.

Lods, A., *Evangelii secundum Petrum et Petri Apocalyseos quae supersunt.* Paris, 1893.

——————. *L'Évangile et l'Apocalypse de Pierre avec le texte grec du livre d'Hénoch.* Paris, 1893.

Nahrung, J. C. *Neue Bücher sibyllinischer Prophezeiungen aus der griechischen in die deutsche Sprache übersetz.* Halle, 1819.

Terry, M. S. *The Sibylline Oracles.* New York, 1890.

2. Studies

Alexandre, C. *Excursus ad Sibyllina.* Paris, 1858.

Badt, B. *Ursprung und Text des 4. Buches der sibyllinischen Orakel.* Breslau, 1878.

Bauer, J. B. "Oracula Sibyllina 1 323 ab." *ZNW* 47 (1956): 284-85. = *Scholia biblica et patristica*, 143-44. Graz, 1972.

——————. "Die Messiasmutter in den Oracula Sibyllina." *Marianum* 18 (1956): 1-7. = *Scholia biblica et patristica*, 151-57.

Bousset, W. "Sibyllen, Sibyllinen und sibyllinische Bücher." *Realencyclopädie für protestantische Theologie und Kirche.* 3rd ed. (1906) 18:265-80.

Charlesworth, J. H. *The Pseudepigrapha and Modern Research* (+ bibl.), 184-88. Missoula MT, 1981.

Collins, J. J. *The Sibylline Oracles of Egyptian Judaism*. Missoula MT, 1972. [= Sib. Or. 3.]

_____. "The Sibylline Oracles." In *Jewish Writings of the Second Temple Period*, ed. M. E. Stone, 357-82. Assen–Philadephia, 1984.

Ewald, H. *Abhandlung über Entstehung, Inhalt und Werth der sibyllinischen Bücher*. Göttingen, 1858.

Fehr, E. *Studia in Oracula Sibyllina*. Upsala, 1893.

Geffcken, J. *Komposition und Entstehungszeit der Oracula Sibyllina*. TU 33/1. Leipzig, 1902.

Hildebrandt, A. "Das römische Antichristentum zur Zeit der Offenbarung Johannis und des 5 sibyllinischen Buches." *ZWT* 17 (1874): 57-95.

Hilgenfeld, A. *Jüdische Apokalyptik*. Jena, 1857.

_____. "Die jüdischen Sibyllen und der Essenismus." *ZWT* 14 (1871): 30-59.

Holzinger, K. "Erklärungen zu einigen der umstrittensten Stellen der Offenbarung Johannis und der Sibyllinischen Orakel mit einem Anhange über Martial 12:33." *SAH* 216/3. Vienna, 1936.

Kurfess, A. "Sibyllinische Weissagungen. Eine literar-historische Plauderei." *ThQ* 117 (1936): 351-66.

_____. "Wie sind die Fragmente der Oracula Sibyllina einzuordnen." *Aevum* 26 (1952): 228-35.

Nikiprowetzky, V. *La troisième Sibylle*. Paris–The Hague, 1970. [217-25: Or. Sib. 3.1-96 est-il d'origine chrétienne?]

Noack, B. "Der zeitgeschichtliche Hintergrund der Oracula Sibyllina." *Studien zum Neuen Testament und seiner Umwelt*. Series A2:167-90. Linz, 1976.

van der Horst, P. W. *The Sentences of Pseudo-Phocylides*. Leiden, 1978.

Volkmann, R. *De Oraculis Sibyllinis*. Leipzig, 1853.

Zahn, Th. "Über Ursprung und religiösen Character der sibyllinischen Bücher 4; 5; 8.1-216; 12; 13." *ZKWL* 7 (1886): 77-87.

The Apocalypse of Peter

1. Sources

De Gebhardt, O. *Das Evangelium und die Apokalypse des Petrus*. Leipzig, 1893.

De Groot, Y. C. "De Openbaring van Petrus." *Apokriefen van het Nieuwe Testament* 2:205-209. Kampen, 1984–1985.

Klostermann, E. *Apocrypha, I, Reste des Petrusevangeliums, der Petrusapokalypse und des Kerygma Petri*. KlT 3. Berlin, 1933.

Kunze, J. *Das neuaufgefundene Bruckstück des sog. Petrusevangeliums übersetzt und beurteilt*. Leipzig, 1893. Corrected and reedited study in *Neue Jarb. für deutsche Theol.* 2 (1893): 583-604; 3 (1894): 58ff.

Maurer, C., and H. Duensing. "Offenbarung des Petrus." In E. Hennecke–W. Schnee-melcher, *Neutestamentliche Apokryphe in deutscher Übersetzung*, 2:468-83. 3rd ed. Tübingen, 1959–1964 (⁴1968).

Mingana, A. "The Apocalypse of Peter." *BJRL* 14 (1930): 182-297.

2. Studies

Bauckham, R. J. "The Two Fig Parables in the Apocalypse of Peter." *JBL* 104 (1985): 269-87.

Bonwetsch, N. "Zur Apokalypse des Petrus." *ThLB* 33 (1912): 339-56.

Buchholtz, D. D. "Your Eyes will be Opened: a Study of the Greek (Ethiopic) Apocalypse of Peter." Diss. Claremont, 1984.

Chapuis, P. "L'Évangile et l'Apocalypse de Pierre." *RTP* 28 (1893): 338-55.

Cowley, R. W. "The Ethiopic Work which is Believed to Contain the Material of the Ancient Greek Apocalypses of Peter." *JTS* 36 (1985): 153-57.

Dieterich A. *Nekya. Beiträge zur Erklärung der neuentdeckten Petrusapokalypse*. Leipzig, 1893.

Fiensy, D. "Lex Talionis in the Apocalypse of Peter." *HTR* 76 (1983): 255-58.

Funk, F. X. "Fragmente des Evangeliums und der Apokalypse des Petrus." *ThQ* 75 (1893): 255-63; 266-77, 349; 76 (1894): 324.

Harnack, A. *Die Petrusapokalypse in der alten abendländischen Kirche*. TU 13/1:71-73. Leipzig, 1895.

_____. *Bruchstücke des Evangeliums und der Apokalypse des Petrus*. TU 9/2. Leipzig, 1893.

Harris, J. R. *A Popular Account of the Newly-Recovered Gospel of Peter*. London, 1893.

James, M. R. "A New Text of the Apocalypse of Peter." *JTS* 12 (1910): 36-54.

_____. "The Rainer Fragment of the Apocalypse of Peter," *JTS* 32 (1931): 270-78.

Marmorstein, A. "Jüdische Parallelen zur Petrusapokalypse." *ZNW* 10 (1909): 292-300.

Nau, F., "Notes sur 'un nouveau texte de l'Apocalypse de saint Pierre'." *ROC* 15 (1910): 441-42.

Petersen, E. "Das Martyrium des H. Petrus nach der Petrus-Apokalypse (1953)." *Frühkirche, Judentum und Gnosis*, 88-91. Fribourg-in-Br., 1959.

_____. "Die 'Taufe' im Acherusischen See (1955)." *Frühkirche, Judentum und Gnosis*, 310-32. Fribourg-in-Br., 1959.

Simms, A. E. "Second Peter and the Apocalypse of Peter." *The Expositor*, 5th series 8 (1898): 460-71.

Spitta, F. "Die Petrusapokalypse und der zweite Petrusbrief." *ZNT* 12 (1911): 237-42.

The Shepherd of Hermas

1. Sources

Bonner, C. *A Papyrus Codex of the Shepherd of Hermas (Sim. 2-9) with a Fragment of the Mandates.* Ann Arbor MI, 1934.

Bueno, R. *El Pastor de Hermas.* Madrid, 1947.

De Gebhardt, O., and A. Harnack. *Hermae Pastor graece addita versione latina recentiore e codice Palatino.* Patrum Apostolicorum opera 3. Leipzig, 1887.

Dibelius, M. *Der Hirt des Hermas.* HNT/E. *Die Apostolischen Väter* 4. Tübingen, 1923.

Gaâb, E. *Der Hirte des Hermas.* Basel, 1866.

Hilgenfeld, A. *Hermae Pastor graece integrum ambitu primum.* 3rd ed. Leipzig, 1887.

Joly, R. *Hermas. Le Pasteur.* SC 53bis. 2nd ed. Paris, 1968.

Lebreton, J. "Le texte grec du Pasteur d'Hermas d'après les papyrus de l'Université de Michigan." *RSR* 26 (1936): 464-67.

Lefort, L. Th. "Le Pasteur d'Hermas, en copte sahidique." *Le Muséon* 51 (1938): 239-76.

Lelong, A. *Le Pasteur d'Hermas.* Textes et Documents. *Les Pères Apostoliques.* Paris, 1912.

Snyder, G. F. *The Shepherd of Hermas. The Apostolic Fathers. A new Translation and Commentary.* London, New York, 1964–1968.

Whittaker, M. *Die apostolischen Väter.* 1. *Der Hirt des Hermas.* Griechische christliche Schriftsteller 47. 2nd ed. Berlin. 1967.

Zahn, Th. *Der Hirte des Hermas.* Gotha, 1868.

2. Studies

Barberet, F. "La formule ζῆν τῷ θεῷ dans le Pasteur d'Hermas." *RSR* 46 (1958): 379-407.

Barnard, L. W. "The 'Shepherd' of Hermas in Recent Study." *Heythrop Journal* 9 (1968): 29-36.

_____. "Hermas, The Church and Judaism." In *Studies in the Apostolic Fathers and Their Background,* 151-63. Oxford, 1966.

_____. "The Early Roman Church, Judaism, and Jewish-Christianity." *ATR* 49 (1967): 371-84.

Bardy, G. "Le Pasteur d'Hermas et les livres hermétiques." *RB* 8 (1911): 391-407.

Barnes, W. E. "Hermas, a Simple Christian of the Second Century" (A Lecture). London, 1923.

Bauckham, R. J. "The Great Tribulation in the Shepherd of Hermas." *JTS* 25 (1974): 27-40.

Baumgärtner, P. *Die Einheit des Hermas-Buchs.* Fribourg, 1889.

Bausone, C. "Aspetti dell' ecclesiologia del Pastore di Hermas." *Studia Patristica* 11:101-106. TU 108. Berlin, 1972.

Brüll, A. *Der Hirt des Hermas nach Ursprung und Inhalt untersucht.* Fribourg-in-Br., 1882.

Carlini, A. "La tradizione manuscritta del Pastor di Hermas e il problema dell' unità di composizione dell' opera." In *Festschrift zum 100-jährigen Bestehen der Papyrussammlung der österreichischen Nationalbibliothek. Papyrus Erzherzog Rainer (P. Rainer Cent.)* 1:97-100. Vienna, 1983.

Chadwick, H. "The New Edition of Hermas." *JTS* 8 (1957): 274-80.

Cirillo, L. "La christologie pneumatique de la cinquième parabole du 'Pasteur' d'Hermas (Par. 5.6,5)." *RHR* 184 (1973): 25-48.

_____. "Erma e il problema dell' apocalittica a Roma." *Cristianesimo nella storia* 4 (1982): 1-31.

Clark, K. W. "The Sins of Hermas." In *The Gentle Bias and Other Essays,* 30-47. Leiden, 1980.

Coleborne, W. "The Shepherd of Hermas. A Case for Multiple Authorship and Some Implications." *Studia Patristica* 10:65-70. TU 107. Berlin, 1970.

D'Alès, A. "La discipline pénitentielle d'après le Pasteur d'Hermas." *RSR* 2 (1911): 105-39; 240-65.

_____. "A propos du Pasteur d'Hermas." *Études* 132 (1912): 79-94.

Edmunson, G. "The Date of the Shepherd of Hermas." *The Expositor* 24 (1922): 162-76.

Folgado Florez, S. "El binomio Cristo-Iglesia en el 'Pastor' de Hermas." *La Ciudad de Dios* 185 (1972): 639-70.

Ford, J. M. "A Possible Liturgical Background to the Shepherd of Hermas." *Revue de Qumran* 6 (1969): 531-51.

Frei, H. A. "Metanoia in 'Hirten' des Hermas." *IKZ* 64 (1974): 118-39; 65 (1975): 120-38; 176-204.

Funk, F. X. "Die Einheit des Hirten des Hermas." *ThQ* 81 (1899): 321-60.

_____. "Zum Pastor Hermä." *ThQ* 85 (1903): 639-40.

Ghedini, G. "Nuovi codici del Pastore di Erma." *SCatt* 62 (1934): 576-580.

Giet, S. "L'apocalypse d'Hermas et la pénitence." *Studia Patristica* 3:214-18. TU 78. Berlin, 1961.

_____. *Hermas et les Pasteurs.* Paris, 1963.

_____. "Un courant judéo-chrétien au milieu du IIᵉ siècle?" *Aspects du Judéo-Christianisme,* 95-111. Paris, 1965.

_____. "Les trois auteurs du Pasteur d'Hermas." *Studia Patristica* 8:10-23. TU 93. Berlin, 1966.

_____. "De trois expressions: Auprès de la tour, la place inférieure, et les premiers murs, dans le Pasteur d'Hermas." *Studia Patristica* 8:24-29. TU 93. Berlin, 1966.

_____. "Pénitence ou repentance dans le Pasteur d'Hermas." *Revue de droit canonique* 17 (1967): 15-30.

_____. "À propos de l'ecclésiologie du Pasteur d'Hermas." *RHE* 63 (1968): 429-37. Lund, 1966.

Grobel, K. "Shepherd of Hermas, Parable 2." In *Vanderbilt Studies in Humanities* 1:50-55. Nashville 1951.

Gronewald, M. "Ein verkannter Hermas-Papyrus (P. Jand. 1.4 = Hermae Pastor, Mand. 11.19-21; 12.1, 2-3)." *Zeitschrift f. Papyrologie u. Epigraphik* 40 (1980): 53-56.

Haas, C. *De Geest bewaren. Actergrond en functie van de pneumatologie in de paraenese van de Pastor van Hermas.* The Hague, 1985.

Hamman, A. "La signification de σφϱάγις dans le Pasteur d'Hermas." *Studia Patristica* 4:286-90. TU 79. Berlin, 1961.

Hanson, A. T. "Hodayoth 6 and 8 and Hermas Sim. 8." *Studia Patristica* 10:105-08. TU 107. Berlin, 1970.

Hilhorst, A. *Sémitismes et latinismes dans le Pasteur d'Hermas.* Nimegue, 1976.

Hoh, J. "Die Busse im Pastor Hermae." *ThQ* 111 (1930): 253-88.

Holtzmann, H. "Hermas und Johannes." *ZWT* 18 (1875): 40-51.

Joly, R. "Judaïsme, christianisme et hellénisme dans le Pasteur d'Hermas." *La Nouvelle Clio* 5 (1953): 394-406.

——————. "La doctrine pénitentielle du Pasteur d'Hermas et l'exégèse récente." *RHR* 147 (1955): 32-49.

——————. "Hermas et le Pasteur." *VigChr* 21 (1967): 201-18.

Lake, K. "The Shepherd of Hermas." *HTR* 18 (1925): 279-80.

Lappa-Zizicas, E. "Cinq fragments du Pasteur d'Hermas dans un manuscript de la Bibliothèque Nationale." *RSR* 53 (1965): 251-56.

Lenaerts, J. "Un papyrus du Pasteur d'Hermas: P. Jand. 1.4." *Chronique d'Égypte* 54 (1979): 356-58.

Lipsius, R. A. "Der Hirt des Hermas und der Montanismus." *ZWT* 8 (1865): 266-308.

MacMillan, K. D. "The Shepherd of Hermas, Apocalypse or Allegory?" *PTR* 9 (1911): 61-64.

Marin, M. "Sulla fortuna delle Similitudini 3 et 4 di Erma." *VetChr* 19 (1982): 331-40.

Mazzini, I. "Il codice Urbinate 486 et la versione palatina del Pastore di Erma." *Prometheus* 6 (1980): 181-88.

Michaels, J. R. "The 'Level Ground' in the Shepherd of Hermas." *ZNW* 59 (1968): 245-50.

Moxnes, H. "God and His Angel in the Shepherd of Hermas." *StTh* 28 (1974): 49-56.

O'Hagan, A. P. "The Great Tribulation to Come in the Pastor of Hermas." *Studia Patristica* 4:305-11. TU 79. Berlin, 1961.

Osiek, C. "Wealth and poverty in the Shepherd of Hermas." *Studia Patristica* 18:725-30. Ed. E. A. Livingstone. Oxford–New York 1982.

——————. "Rich and Poor in the Shepherd of Hermas. An Exegetical-Social Investigation." In CBQMS 15. Washington, 1983.

Pernveden, L. *The Concept of the Church in the Shepherd of Hermas.* Lund, 1966.

Peterson, E. "Beiträge zur Interpretation des Visionen im Pastor Hermae." *OrChrAn* 13 (1947): 624-35. = In *Frühkirche, Judentum, und Gnosis*, 254-70. Fribourg-in-Br., 1959.

——————. "Die Begegnung mit dem Ungeheuer (1954)." In *Frühkirche, Judentum, und Gnosis*, 283-309. Fribourg-in-Br., 1959.

—————. "Kritische Analyse der fünften Vision des Hermas (1958)." In *Frühkirche, Judentum, und Gnosis,* 271-84. Fribourg-in-Br., 1959.

Puech, A. "Observations sur le Pasteur d'Hermas." *Studi dedicati alla memoria di Paolo Ubaldi,* 83-85. Milan, 1937.

Reiling, J. "Hermas and Christian Prophecy. A Study of the Eleventh Mandate." Nov-TSup 37. Leiden, 1973.

Schläger, G. "Der Hirt des Hermas, eine ursprünglich jüdische Schrift." *NTTijd* 16 (1927): 327-42.

Schweitzer, V. "Der Pastor Hermae und die opera supererogatoria." *ThQ* 57 (1904): 539-56.

Seitz, O. J. F. "Afterthoughts on the Term 'Dipsychos'." *NTS* 4 (1957-58): 327-34.

Sgherri, G. "Textkritische Bermerkungen zu Hermas 51.5." *VigChr* 31 (1977): 88-93.

Ström, A. V. "Allegorie und Wirklichkeit im Hirten des Hermas." *Arbeiten u. Mitteil. aus dem neutest.* Seminar zu Uppsala 3. Upsala, 1936.

Tanner, R. G. "Latinisms in the Test of Hermas." *Colloquium* 4 (1972): 12-23.

Taylor, C. *The Witness of Hermas to the Four Gospels.* London, 1892.

—————. "The Two Ways in Hermas and Xenophon." *Journal of Philology* 21 (1893): 243-58.

—————. "Hermas and Matth. 18:19f." *JTS* 7 (1906): 268-69.

Treu, K. "Ein neuer Hermas-Papyrus." *VigChr* 24 (1970): 34-39.

Turmel, J. "Le pasteur d'Hermas." *Annales de la philosophie chrétienne* 148 (1904): 26-52.

Turner, C. H. "The Shepherd of Hermas and the Problem of its Text." *JTS* 21 (1920): 193-209.

van Bakel, H. A. *De Compositie van den Pastor Hermae.* Amsterdam, 1900.

van Deemter, R. *Der Hirt des Hermas, Apokalypse oder Allegorie?* Delft, 1929.

van Landschoot, A. "Un second témoin éthiopien du Pasteur d'Hermas." *Byzantion* 32 (1962): 93-95.

Völter, D. "Die Visionen des Hermas, die Sibylle und Clemens von Rom." *Ein Beitrag zur Geschichte der Altchristl. Literatur.* Berlin, 1900.

Wilson, J. C. *Toward a Reassessment of the Milieu of the Shepherd of Hermas. Its Date and its Pneumatology.* Durham NC, 1977.

Wilson, W. J. "The Career of the Prophet Hermas." *HTR* 20 (1927): 21-62.

Winter, F. J. "Sittliche Grundanchauungen im 'Hirten' des Hermas." In *ZKWL* 5 (1884): 33-46.

Zahn, Th. *Hermae Pastor e Novo Testamento illustratus* 1. Göttingen, 1867.

THE NONCANONICAL GOSPELS

1. Sources

Bonaccorsi, G. *Vangeli apocriphi* 1. Florence, 1948.

De Santos Otero, A. *Los evangelios apócriphos. Edición crítica y bilingüe.* Madrid, 1956. (New ed. 1979.)

Erbetta, M. *Gli apocrifi del Nuovo Testamento.* 4 vols. Turin, 1966–1981.

Hennecke E., and W. Schneemelcher. *Neutestamentlische Apokryphen in deutscher Über-setzung.* 2 vols. 3rd ed. Tübingen, 1959–1964 (⁴1968). ET: *New Testament Apocry-pha.* 2 vols. Trans. A. J. B. Higgins et al. Ed. R. McL. Wilson. Philadelphia, London, 1963, 1966; rpr. 1973.

Klijn, A. F. J. *Apokriefen van het Nieuwe Testament.* 2 vols. Kampen, 1984–1985.

Tischendorf, C. *Evangelia Apocrypha.* 2nd ed. (Leipzig, 1876). Repr.: Hildesheim, 1966.

Tukker, C. A. *Enige Nieuwtestamentische Apokriefe Geschriften.* Utrecht, 1984.

2. Studies

Barnard, L. W. "The Church and Judaism." In *Studies in the Apostolic Fathers and their Background,* 151-63. Oxford, 1966.

_____. "The Early Roman Church, Judaism, and Jewish-Christianity." *ATR* 49 (1967): 371-84.

Barns, J. "A Coptic Apocryphal Fragment in the Bodleian Library." *JTS* 11 (1960): 70-76.

Bauckham, R. J. "A Bibliography of Recent Work on Gospel Traditions Outside the Ca-nonical Gospels." In *Jesus Tradition,* ed. D. Wendham, 405-19. Gospel Perspectives 5. Sheffield, 1985.

_____. "The Study of Gospel Traditions Outside the Canonical Gospels: Problems and Prospects." In *Jesus Tradition,* ed. D. Wendham, 369-403. Gospel Perspectives 5. Sheffield, 1985.

Bauer, J. B. "Die Entstehung apokrypher und das Nazaräerevangelium." *Bibel und Li-turgie* 38 (1965): 268-71.

_____. "Sermo Peccati. Hieronymous und das Nazaräerevangelium." *BZ* 4 (1960); 122-28. = *Scholia biblica et patristica,* 226-32. Graz, 1972.

_____. "Die neutestamentlichen Apokryphen." *Die Welt der Bibel* 21. Düsseldorf, 1968.

Baur, F. C. *Kritische Untersuchungen über die Evangelien,* 571-82. Tübingen, 1847.

Beyschlag, K. *Die verborgene Überlieferung von Christus.* Hamburg-Munich, 1969.

Bigaré, C. "Les Apocryphes du Nouveau Testament." *Introduction à la Bible* 3/5:179-211. Paris, 1977.

Charlesworth, J. H. *The Pseudepigrapha and Modern Research,* 125-30; 184-88 (+ bibl.). Missoula MT, 1981.

Cheek, J. L. "The Apocrypha in Christian Scripture." *JBR* 26 (1958): 207-12.

Daniel-Rops, H. *Die apokryphen Evangelien des Neuen Testaments.* Zurich, 1956.

Finegan, J. *Hidden Records of the Life of Jesus. An Introduction to the New Testament Apocrypha.* Philadelphia, 1969.

Goguel, M. "Les fragments nouvellement découverts d'un Évangile du IIe siècle." *RHLR* 15 (1935): 465.

Huby, J. "Une importante découverte papyrologique." *Études* 204 (1935): 763-75.

Kesich, V. "Christ's Temptation in the Apocryphal Gospels and Acts." In *St. Vladimir's Seminary Quarterly* 5 (1961): 3-9.

Kline, L. L. *The Sayings of Jesus in the Pseudo-Clementine Homilies.* Missoula MT, 1975. = *ZNW* 66 (1975): 223-41.

Köster, H. "Apocryphal and Canonical Gospels." *HTR* 73 (1980); 105-30.

_____. Überlieferung und Geschichte der frühchristlichen Evangelienliteratur." In *Aufstieg und Niedergang der römischen Welt II. Principat* 25/2 (1984): 1463-542.

Lagrange, M. J. "Deux nouveaux textes relatifs à l'Évangile." *RB* 44 (1935): 339-43.

Lowe, M. "'Ιουδαῖοι of the Apocrypha. A Fresh Approach to the Gospels of James, Pseudo-Thomas; Peter and Nicodemus." *NovT* 23 (1981): 56-90.

Mara, M. G. "I vangeli apocrifi negli scrittori ecclesiastici." *Aug* 23 (1983): 41-55.

Mees, M. "Petrustraditionen im Zeugnis kanonischen und ausserkanonischen Schriftums." *Aug* 13 (1973): 185-203.

_____. "Das Paradigma vom reichen Mann und seiner Berufung nach den synoptikern und dem Nazaräerevangelium." *VetChr* 9 (1972): 245-65.

_____. "Herrenworte und Erzählstoff in den judenchristlichen Evangelien und ihre Bedeutung." *Aug* 23 (1983): 187-212.

Muñoz Iglesias, S. "Los Evangelios de la Infancia, y las infancias de los héroes." *Estudios Biblicos* 16 (1957): 5-36.

Nock, A. D. "The Apocryphal Gospels." *JTS* 11 (1960); 63-70.

Roberts, C. H. *An Unpublished Fragment of the Fourth Gospel in the John Rylands Library.* Manchester, 1935.

Schmidt, K. L. *Kanonische und Apokryphe Evangelien und Apostelgeschichten.* Basel, 1944.

Schneckenburger, H. *Über den Ursprung des ersten kanonischen Evangeliums,* 105-71. Stuttgart, 1834.

Schneemelcher, W. "Bemerkungen zum Kirchenbegriff der Apokryphen Evangelien." In *Ecclesia. Opstellen aangeboden aan J. N. Bakhuizen van den Brink,* 18-32. The Hague, 1959. = *Gesammelte Aufsätze zum Neuen Testament und Patristik,* 139-53. Thessalonica, 1974.

Seitz, O. J. F. "Afterthoughts on the Term 'Sipsychos'." *NTS* 4 (1957-58): 327-34.

Sint, J. A. "Am Rande der vier Evangelien. Zu den Apokryphen des Neuen Testaments." *Bibel und Leben* 1 (1960): 186-92.

Smothers, E. R. "Un nouvel évangile du deuxième siècle." *RSR* 25 (1935): 358-62.

Stroker, W. D. "Examples of Pronouncement Stories in Early Christian Apocryphal Literature." *Semeia* 20 (1981): 133-41.

Tobac, É. Ὀψὲ δὲ σαββάτων. *RHE* 20 (1924): 239-43.

Turrado, L. "Maria en los Evangelios Apócrifos." *Cultura Biblica* 11 (1954): 380-90.

Vanovermeire, P. " 'Livre que Jésus-Christ a révélé à ses disciples.' Étude sur l'apocryphe, connu sous le nom 'd'Epistula Apostolorum,' premier témoin de l'influence littéraire du quatrième Évangile sur la littérature chrétienne de la première moitié du second siècle." Diss. Paris, 1962.

Walterscheid, J. *Das Leben Jesu nach den neutestamentlichen Apokryphen.* Düsseldorf, 1953.

Wenham, D., ed. *The Jesus Tradition Outside the Gospel.* Gospel Perspectives 5. Sheffield, 1985.

Wright, D. F. "Apocryphal Gospels: the 'Unknown Gospel' (Pap. Egerton 2) and the Gospel of Peter." In *Jesus Tradition Outside the Gospels,* ed. D. Wenham, 207-32. Gospel Perpective 5. Sheffield, 1985.

Wright, L. E. *Alterations of the Words of Jesus as Quoted in the Literature of the Second Century,* 91-102 (Jewish-Christian Gospels); 108-14 (Pap. Eg. 2). Harvard Historical Monographs 25. Cambridge MA, 1952.

Zahn, Th. "Kleine Beiträge zur evangelischen Geschichte. 1. Der Zerrisene Tempelvorhang." *NKZ* 13 (1902): 729-56.

The Unknown Gospel (Papyrus Egerton 2)

Bell, H. J. "The Gospel Fragment P. Egerton 2." *HTR* 42 (1949): 53-64.

Bell, H. J., and T. C. Skeat. *Fragments of an Unknown Gospel and Other Early Christian Papyri.* London, 1935. Rev. text in *The New Gospel Fragments.* London, 1935.

Burkitt, F. C. "Fragments of an Unknown Gospel." *JTS* 36 (1935): 303.

Cerfaux, L. "Parallèles canoniques et extracanoniques de 'L'Évangile inconnu' (Pap. Egerton 2)." *Le Muséon* 49 (1936): 55-77. = In *Recueil Lucien Cerfaux,* 1:279-99. Gembloux, 1954.

Crossan, J. D. *Four Other Gospels. Shadows on the Contours of Canon,* 63-87; 123-81. Minneapolis-Chicago-New York, 1985.

Gallizia, U. "Il P. Egerton 2." *Aegyptus* 36 (1956): 29-72; 178-234.

Jeremias, J. "Unbekanntes Evangelium mit Johanneischen Einshlägen (Pap. Egerton 2)." In *Neutestamentliche Apokryphen in deutscher Übersetzung,* 1:58-61. 3rd ed. Tübingen, 1959–1964 (⁴1968).

Mayeda, G. *Das Leben-Jesu-Fragment. Papyrus Egerton 2 und seine Stellung in Der Urchristlichen Literaturgeschichte.* Bern, 1946.

Neirynck, F. "Papyrus Egerton 2 and the Healing of the Leper." *ETL* 61 (1985): 153-60.

Vogels, H. "Fragments of an Unknown Gospel." *ThRv* 34 (1935): col. 315.

Wright, D. F. "Apocryphal Gospels: the 'Unknown Gospel' (Pap. Egerton 2) and the Gospel of Peter." In *Jesus Tradition Outside the Gospels,* ed. D. Wenham, 207-32. Gospel Perpectives 5. Sheffield, 1985.

Wright, L. E. *Alterations of the Words of Jesus as Quoted in the Literature of the Second Century,* 91-102 (Jewish-Christian Gospels); 108-14 (Pap. Eg. 2). Harvard Historical Monographs 25. Cambridge MA, 1952.

Gospel of the Hebrews

Adeney, W. F. "The Gospel According to the Hebrews." *The Hibbert Journal* 3 (1904-1905): 139-59.

Barnes, A. S. "The Gospel According to the Hebrews." *JTS* 6 (1905): 356-71.

Brock, S. "A New Testimonium to the 'Gospel according to the Hebrews'." *NTS* 18 (1971-1972): 220-22.

Burch, V. "The Gospel According to the Hebrews: Some New Matter Chiefly from Coptic Sources." *JTS* 21 (1920): 310-15.

Dodd, J. F. *The Gospel According to the Hebrews.* London, 1933.

Dunkerley, R. "The Gospel According to the Hebrews." *ExpTim* 39 (1928): 437-42; 490-95.

Ehrhardt, A. A. T. "Judaeo-Christians in Egypt, the Epistula Apostolorum and the Gospel of the Hebrews." *StEv* 3:360-82. TU 88. Berlin, 1964.

Fabbri, E. "El bautismo de Jesús en el Evangelico de los Hebreos y en el de los Ebionitas." *Revista de Teologia* 6 (1956): 35-56.

Franck, F. "Über das Evangelium der Hebräer" *TSK* 21 (1848): 369-422.

Handman, R. *Das Hebräer-Evangelium. Ein Beitrag zur Geschichte und Kritik des Hebräischen Matthäus.* TU 5/3. Leipzig, 1888.

Hennecke E., and W. Schneemelcher. *Neutestamentliche Apokryphen in deutscher Übersetzung.* 2 vols. 3rd ed. Tübingen, 1959-1964 (⁴1968). ET: *New Testament Apocrypha.* 2 vols. Trans. A. J. B. Higgins et al. Ed. R. McL. Wilson. Philadelphia, London, 1963, 1966.

Hilgenfeld, A. "Das Evangelium der Hebräer." *ZWT* 6 (1863): 345-85.

_____. "Das Hebräer-Evangelium in England." *ZWT* 27 (1883): 188-94.

_____. "Das Hebräer-Evangelium und sein neuester Bearbeiter." *ZWT* 32 (1889): 280-302.

Lagrange, M. J. "L'Évangile selon les Hébreux." *RB* 31 (1922): 161-81; 321-49.

_____. "Deux nouveaux textes relatifs à l'Évangile." *RB* 44 (1935): 339-43.

Nestle, E. "Ein altdeutsches Bruchstück aus dem Hebräer-Evangelium." *ZNW* 10 (1909): 183-84.

Nicholson, E. B. *The Gospel According to the Hebrews.* London, 1879.

Nösgen, K. F. "Das Hebräer-Evangelium und sein neuester Bearbeiter." *ZKWL* 10 (1889): 499-519; 561-78.

Quispel, G. "Das Hebräerevangelium im gnostischen Evangelium nach Maria." *VigChr* 11 (1957): 139-44.

_____. "The Discussion of Judaic Christianity." *VigChr* 22 (1968): 81-93. = *Gnostic Studies* 2:146-58. Istanbul, 1975.

_____. " 'The Gospel of Thomas' and the 'Gospel of the Hebrews'." *NTS* 11 (1965-1966): 371-82.

_____. "Jewish-Christian Gospel Tradition." In *Gospel Studies in Honor of E. L. Johnson.* ATRSup 3 (1974): 112-16.

Riggenbach, E. "Zum Hebräerevangelium." *ThLB* 29 (1908): cols. 447-48.

Robinson, J. A. "Three Notes on the Gospel to the Hebrews." *The Expositor* 5th ser. 5 (1897): 194-200.

Schmidtke, A. "Zum Hebräerevangelium." *TLZ* 33 (1908) col. 436.

_____. "Zum Hebräerevangelium." *ZNW* 35 (1936): 24-44.

Winkler, G. "Das Diatessaron und das Hebräer-Evangelium, ihr Verhältnis zueinander." In *3rd Symposium Syriacum. OrChrAn* 22:25-34. Rome, 1983.

Gospel of the Ebionites

Bertrand, D. A. "L'Évangile des Ébionites: une harmonie évangélique antérieure au Diatessaron." *NTS* 28 (1980): 548-63.

Boismard, M.-É. "Évangile des Ébionites et problème synoptique (Mc 1:2-6 et par)." *RB* 23 (1966): 321-52.

Hennecke E., and W. Schneemelcher. *Neutestamentlische Apokryphen in deutscher Übersetzung.* 2 vols. 3rd ed. Tübingen, 1959–1964 (⁴1968). ET: *New Testament Apocrypha.* 2 vols. Trans. A. J. B. Higgins et al. Ed. R. McL. Wilson. Philadelphia, London, 1963, 1966.

Lentzen-Deis, F. "Ps 2.7 ein Motiv früher 'hellenistischer' Christologie? Der Psalvers in der Lectio varians von Lk. 3:22 im Ebionäerevangelium und bei Justinus Martyr." *ThPh* 44 (1969): 342-62.

Neirynck, F. "Une nouvelle théorie synoptique (À propos de Mc 1:2-6 et par.)." *ETL* 44 (1968): 141-53. = "Jean et les Synoptiques. Examen critique de l'exégèse de M.-É. Boismard." *BETL* 49:299-311. Louvain, 1979.

Waitz, H. "Das Evangelium der zwölf Apostel (Ebionitenevangelium)." *ZNW* 13 (1912): 338-48; 14 (1913): 38-64; 117-32.

Gospel of the Egyptians

Hennecke E., and W. Schneemelcher. *Neutestamentlische Apokryphen in deutscher Übersetzung.* 2 vols. 3rd ed. Tübingen, 1959–1964 (⁴1968). ET: *New Testament Apocrypha.* 2 vols. Trans. A. J. B. Higgins et al. Ed. R. McL. Wilson. Philadelphia, London, 1963, 1966.

Hornschuh, M. "Erwägungen zum 'Evangelium der Ägypter', ins besondere zur Bedeutung seines Titels." *VigChr* 18 (1964): 6-13.

Roberts, C. H. *Manuscript, Society, and Belief in Early Christian Egypt.* Schweich Lectures 1977. London, 1979.

Schneckenburger, H. *Über das Evangelium der Aegypter. Ein historisch-kritischer Versuch.* Bern, 1834.

Gospel of Peter

1. Sources

Mara, M. G. *Évangile de Pierre*. SC 201 (Paris, 1973).

Maurer, C. *Petrusevangelium*. In E. Hennecke–W. Schneemelcher, *Neutestamentlische Apokryphen in deutscher Übersetzung*, 1:188-24. Tübingen, 1959–1964 (⁴1968).

2. Studies

Amann, E. "Apocryphes du Nouveau Testament, Évangile de Pierre ou selon Pierre." *Supplément du Dictionnaire de la Bible*, 1:476-77.

Baljon, J. M. S. *Het evangelie en de openbaring van Petrus*. Utrecht, 1896.

Battomley, G. *The Acts of S. Peter*. London, 1933.

Bouriant, H. "Fragments du text grec du livre d'Énoch et de quelques écrits attribués à saint Pierre." In *Mémoires publiés par les membres de la Mission archéologique française au Caire*, 9/1:137-42. Paris, 1892.

Cabrol, F. "La découverte du manuscrit d'Akhmîm: l'évangile et l'apocalypse de saint Pierre et le livre du prophète Énoch." *Revue des Facultés catholiques de l'Ouest* (1893): 570-90.

Cassels, W. R. *The Gospel According to Peter: a Study by the Author of "Supernatural Religion."* London, 1894.

Craig, W. L. "The Guard at the Tomb." *NTS* 30 (1984): 273-81.

Crossan, J. D. *Four Other Gospels. Shadows on the Contours of Canon*, 123-81. Minneapolis-Chicago-New York, 1985.

De Bruyne, D. "Deux citations apocryphes de l'Apôtre Pierre." *JTS* 24 (1933): 395-96.

Denker, J. *Die theologiegeschichtliche Stellung des Petrusevangeliums. Ein Beitrag zur Frühgeschichte des Doketismus*. Frankfurt, 1975.

Dibelius, M. "Die alttestamentlichen Motive in der Leidensgeschichte des Petrus- und des Johannes-Evangeliums." *Botschaft und Geschichte* 1:221-47. Tübingen, 1953.

Duchesne, L. "L'Évangile de Pierre." *Bulletin Critique* 13 (1893):101-06.

Fuchs, A. *Das Petrusevangelium*. Linz, 1978.

Funk, F. X. "Fragmente des Evangeliums und der Apokalypse des Petrus." *ThQ* 75 (1893): 255-63; 266-77, 349; 76 (1894): 324.

Gardner-Smith, P. "The Gospel of Peter." *JTS* 27 (1926): 255-71.

—————. "The Date of the Gospel of Peter." *JTS* 27 (1926): 401-407.

Grant, R. M., and G. Quispel. "A Note on the Petrine Apocrypha." *VigChr* 6 (1952): 31-32. = In R. M. Grant. *Christian Beginnings: Apocalypse to History*. London, 1983.

Harnack, A. *Die Petrusapokalypse in der alten abendländischen Kirche*. TU 13/1:71-73. Leipzig, 1895.

—————. *Bruchstücke des Evangeliums und der Apokalypse des Petrus*. TU 9/2. Leipzig, 1893.

Harris, J. R. *A Popular Account of the Newly-Recovered Gospel of Peter*. London, 1893.

Headlam, A. C. "The Akhmîm Fragments." *The Classical Review* 7 (1893): 458-63.

Hilgenfeld, A. "Das Petrusevangelium über Leiden und Auferstehung Jesu." *ZWT* 36 (1893): 1:439-55; 2:220-67.

Jacquier, E. "L'Évangile selon saint Pierre." *L'Université catholique* (15 Sept. 1893): 5-29.

Johnson, B. A. "Empty Tomb Tradition in the Gospel of Peter." Diss. Harvard, 1965.

——————. "The Gospel of Peter: Between Apocalypse and Romance." *Studia Patristica* 16:170-74. TU 129. Berlin, 1985.

Klijn, A. F. J. "Het Evangelevan Petrus en de Westerse tekst." *NedTTs* 15 (1961): 264-69.

——————. "Fragmenten uit de prediking van Petrus." *Apostolisch Vaders* 2:113-21. Kampen, 1981-83. (Orig. ed. 3 vols. Baarn, 1966–1967.)

Koch, E. "Das Petrusevangelium und unser kanonischen Evangelien." *Kirchliche Monatsschrift* 15 (1896): 311-38.

Lambiasi, F. "I criteri di autenticita storica dei Vangeli applicati ad un apocrifo: il Vangelo di Pietro." *Biblia e Oriente* 18 (1976): 151-60.

Lejay, P. "L'Évangile de Pierre." *Revue des Études Grecques* 6 (1893): 59-84; 267-70.

Lods, A. *Evangelii secundum Petrum et Petri Apocalypseos quae supersunt.* Paris, 1892.

——————. *L'Évangile et l'Apocalypse de Pierre avec le texte grec du livre d'Hénoch.* Paris, 1893.

Lowe, M. "'Ιουδαῖοι of the Apocrypha. A Fresh Approach to the Gospels of James, Pseudo-Thomas; Peter and Nicodemus." *NovT* 23 (1981): 56-90.

Lührmann, D. "POx 2949: EvPt 3-5 in einer Handschrift des 2./3. Jahrhunderts." *ZNW* 72 (1981): 216-26.

McCant, J. W. "The Gospel of Peter. The Docetic Question Reexamined." Diss. Emory, 1978.

——————. "The Gospel of Peter: Docetism Reconsidered." *NTS* 30 (1984): 258-73.

McGiffert, A. C. "The Gospel of Peter." *Papers of the American Society of Church History* 6 (1894): 99-130.

McPherson, J. "The Gospel of Peter." *ExpTim* 5 (1894): 556-61.

Mara, M. G. *Évangile de Pierre.* SC 201. Paris, 1973.

Martineau, J. "The Gospel of Peter." *The Nineteenth Century* 33 (1893): 905-26; 34 (1894): 633-56.

Maurer, C., and H. Duensing. "Petrusevangelium." In E. Hennecke-W. Schneemelcher, *Neutestamentlische Apokryphen in deutscher Übersertzung,* 1:118-24. 3rd ed. Tübingen, 1959–1964 (⁴1968).

Moulton, J. H. "The Gospel of Peter and the Four." *ExpTim* 6 (1892-93): 299-300.

Perler, O. "L'Évangile de Pierre et Méliton de Sardes." *RB* 71 (1964): 584-90.

Robinson, J. A., and M. R. James. *The Gospel According to Peter and the Revelation of Peter.* 2nd ed. London, 1892.

Sabatier, A. *L'Évangile de Pierre et les évangiles canoniques.* Paris, 1893.

Schenk, W. "Das 'Matthäusevangelium' als Petrusevangelium." *BZ* 27 (1983): 58-80.

Schubert (von), H. *Die Composition des pseudopetrinischen Evangelien-fragments.* Berlin, 1893.

_____. *Das Petrusevangelium, Synoptische Tabelle nebst Übersetzung und kritischem Apparat.* Berlin, 1893. ET: *The Gospel of St. Peter, Synoptical Tables with Translation and Critical Apparatus.* Trans. Jay MacPherson. Edinburgh, 1893.

Séméria, J. B. "L'Évangile de Pierre." *RB* 3 (1894): 522-60.

Soden (von), H. "Das Petrusevangelium und die kanonischen Evangelien." *ZThK* 3 (1893): 52-92.

Stanton, V. H. "The Gospel of Peter, Its Early History and Character Considered in Relation to the History of the Recognition in the Church of the Canonical Gospels." *JTS* 3 (1900): 1-25.

Stocks, H. "Zum Petrusevangelium." *NKZ* 13 (1902): 276-314; 511-42.

Swete, H. B. Εὐαγγέλιον κατὰ Πέτρον. *The Akhmîm Fragment of the Apocryphal Gospel of St. Peter.* London, 1893.

_____. *The Apocryphal Gospel of Peter. The Greek Text of the Newly Discovered Fragment.* 2nd ed. London, 1897.

Turner, C. H. "The Gospel of Peter." *JTS* 14 (1913): 161-95.

Usener, H. "Eine Spur des Petrusevangeliums." In *Kleine Schriften*, 4:417-21. Repr. of the 1912–1913 ed. Osnabrück, 1965.

Vaganay, L. "L'Évangile de Pierre." *EBib.* Paris, 1930.

van Manen, W. C. "Het Evangelie van Petrus." *ThT* 26 (1893): 317-33; 379-432; 517-72.

_____. "Het Evangelie van Petrus." *Tekst en vertaling.* Leiden, 1893.

Völter, D. *Petrusevangelium oder Aegypterevangelium?* Tübingen, 1893.

_____. "Petrusevangelium oder Aegypterevangelium?" *ZNW* 6 (1905): 368-72.

Vouaux, L. *Les Actes de Pierre.* Paris, 1922.

Waitz, H. "Apocryphen des Neuen Testamentes, Das Petrusevangelium." *Realencyclopädie für protest. Theologie und Kirche* (3rd ed.) 23:86-87.

Walter, N. "Eine vormatthäische Schilderung der Auferstehung Jesu. Anhang: Zur Literarkritik und zur traditionsgeschichtlichen Bedeutung des Petrus-Evangeliums." *NTS* 19 (1972–1973): 415-19.

Wright, D. F. "Apocryphal Gospels: the 'Unknown Gospel' (Pap. Egerton 2) and the Gospel of Peter." In *Jesus Tradition Outside the Gospels*, ed. D. Wenham, 207-32. Gospel Perspectives 5. Sheffield, 1985.

Zahn, Th. *Das Evangelium des Petrus.* Erlangen and Leipzig, 1893.

The Gospel of Matthias

Puech, H. C. *Das Evangelium nach Matthias. Die Traditionen des Matthias.* In E. Hennecke–W. Schneemelcher, *Neutestamentliche Apokryphen in deutscher Übersetzung* 1:224-28. Tübingen, 1959–1964 (⁴1968).

The Protevangelium of James

1. Sources

De Strycker, E. *La forme la plus ancienne du Protévangile de Jacques.* Subsidia hagiographica 33. Brussels, 1961.

──────────. "Le Protévangile de Jacques. Problèmes critiques et exégétiques." *StEv* 3:339-59. TU 88. Berlin, 1964.

Testuz, M. *Papyrus Bodmer V. Nativité de Marie.* Cologne and Geneva, 1958.

2. Studies

Amann, E. *Le Protévangile de Jacques.* Paris, 1910.

Birdsall, J. N. "A Second Georgian Recension of the Protevangelium Jacobi." *Le Muséon* 83 (1970): 49-72.

Canal-Sánchez, J. M. "Antiguas versiones latinas del Protoevangelio de Santiago." *Ephemerides Mariologicae* 18 (1968): 431-73.

Castro, M. G. "Los apócrifos marianos." *La Ciencia Tomista* 77 (1950); 145-75.

Cothénet, É. "Protévangile de Jacques." *Supplément au Dictionnaire de la Bible* (1972) 8:1374-84.

Daniels, B. L. "The Greek Manuscript Tradition of the Protevangelium Jacobi." Diss. Duke, 1956.

De Aldama, J. A. "Fragmentos de una versión latina del Protoevangelio de Santiago y una nueva adaptación de sus primeros capitulos." *Biblica* 43 (1962): 57-63.

──────────. "Poluplousios dans le Protévangile de Jacques et l'Adversus Haereses d'Irénée." *RSC* 50 (1962): 86-89.

──────────. "El Protevangelio de Santiago y sus problemas." *Ephemerides Mariologicae* 12 (1962): 107-30.

──────────. "Un nuevo testigo indirecto del Protoevangelio de Santiago." *Studia Patristica* 12:79-82. TU 115. Berlin, 1975.

De Strycker, E. "Le Protévangile de Jacques. Problèmes critiques et exégétiques." *StEv* 3:339-59. TU 88. Berlin, 1964.

──────────. "Une ancienne version latine du Protévangile de Jacques (Montpellier, École de médecine, ms. 55ff. 179-182v), avec des extraits de la Vulgate de Matthieu 1-2 et Luc 1-2." *AnBoll* 83 (1965): 365-402. = *La forme la plus ancienne du Protévangile de Jacques.* Subsidia hagiographica 33. Brussels, 1961.

──────────. "De Griekse handschriften van het Protevangelie van Jacobus." In *Mededelingen van de Koninklijke Vlaamse Academie voor Wetenschappen, Letteren en Schone Kunsten van België, Klasse der Letteren* 30 (1968): 3-46.

Di Segni, R. "Rapporti con tradizioni rabbiniche di una narrazione apocrifa sull' infanzia di Maria (Protevangelio di Giacomo, Capitulo 6)." *Henoch* 5 (1983): 235-41.

Emmi, B. "Tentativo d'interpretazione del dialogo tra Anna e la serva nel Protoevangelo di Giacomo (3,11-5, 5)." *Studia Patristica* 7:184-93. TU 92. Berlin, 1966.

Fuchs, A. *Konkordanz zum Protoevangelium des Jakobus*. Linz, 1978.

Garitte, G. "Le 'Protévangile de Jacques' en géorgien." *Le Muséon* 70 (1957): 233-65.

_____. "Protevangelii Jacobi versio Arabica antiquior." *Le Muséon* 86 (1973): 377-96.

Klawek, A. "Motivum immobilitatis naturae in Protoevangelio Jacobi." *Collectanea Theologica* 27 (1936): 327-37. Lemberg.

Mehlmann, J. "Protoevangelium Jacobi c. 21,2 in liturgia citatium." *VD* 39 (1961): 50-51.

Michel, C. "Protévangile de Jacques, Pseudo-Matthieu, Évangile de Thomas." *Textes et Documents, Évangiles apocryphes* 1. 2nd ed. Paris, 1924.

Peretto, L. "Testi sacri nel Protovangelo di Giacomo." *Rivista biblica Italiana* 3 (1955): 174-78; 235-56.

_____. "Recenti ricerche sul protovangelo di Giacomo." *Marianum* 24 (1962): 129-57.

_____. "La 'Natività di Maria'." *Marianum* 22 (1960): 176-96.

Perler, O. "Das Protoevangelium des Jakobus nach dem Papyrus Bodmer 5." *FZPhTh* 6 (1959): 23-35.

Quecke, J. "Lk 1,34 in den alten Übersetzungen und im Protoevangelium des Jakobus." *Biblica* 54 (1963): 499-520.

Smid, H. R. *Protevangelium Jacobi. A Commentary*. Assen, 1965.

van Stempvoort, P. A. "De bronnen van het thema en de stijl van het Protevangelium Jacobi en de datering daarvan." *NedTTs* 16 (1961): 18-34.

_____. "The Protevangelium Jacobi, the Sources of its Theme and Style and their Bearing on its Date." *StEv* 3:410-26. TU 88. Berlin, 1964.

Kerygma Petri

Dobschütz (von), E. *Das Kerygma Petri.* TU 11/1. Leipzig, 1893.

Grant, R. M., and G. Quispel. "A Note on the Petrine Apocrypha." *VigChr* 6 (1952): 31-32. = R. M. Grant. "The Decalogue in Early Christianity." *Christian Beginnings: Apocalypse to History.* London, 1983.

Klijn, A. F. J. "Fragmenten uit de prediking van Petrus." *Apostolische Vaders* 2:113-21. Kampen, 1981-83. (Orig. ed. 3 vols. Baarn, 1966–1967.)

Mara, M. G. "Il Kerygma Petrou." *Studi e materiali di storia delle religioni* 38 (1967): 314-42.

Nautin, P. "Les citations de la Prédication de Pierre dans Clément d'Alexandrie, Strom. 6.5,39-41." *JTS* 25 (1974): 98-105.

Paulsen, H. "Das Kerygma Petri und die urchristliche Apologetik." *ZKG* 88 (1977): 1-37.

Reagan, J. N. *The Preaching of Peter. The Beginning of Christian Apologetic.* Chicago, 1923.

Rordorf, W. "Christus als Logos und Nomos. Das Kerygma Petrou in seinem Verhältnis zu Justin." In *Kerygma und Logos. Festschrift C. Andresen,* 424-34. Göttingen, 1979.

Schneemelcher, W. "Das Kerygma Petrou." In E. Hennecke–W. Schneemelcher, *Neutestamentliche Apokryphen in deutscher Übersetzung* 2:58-59. 3rd ed. Tübingen, 1959–1964 (⁴1968).

Agrapha

1. Sources

Grenfell, B. P., and A. S. Hunt. *The Amherst Papyri. Being an Account of the Greek Papyri. 1.* London, 1900.

──────. *The Oxyrhyncus Papyri* 5. London, 1907.

──────. *New Sayings of Jesus and Fragment of a Lost Gospel from Oxyrhynchus.* Egypt Exploration Fund, Graeco-Roman Branch. Oxford, 1904.

──────. *Fragment of an Uncanonical Gospel from Oxyrhynchus.* Egypt Exploration Fund, Graeco-Roman Branch. Oxford, London, New York, Toronto, 1908.

Hennecke E., and W. Schneemelcher. *Neutestamentliche Apokryphen in deutscher Übersetzung.* 2 vols. 3rd ed. Tübingen, 1959–1964 (⁴1968). ET: *New Testament Apocrypha.* 2 vols. Trans. A. J. B. Higgins et al. Ed. R. McL. Wilson. Philadelphia, London, 1963, 1966.

Klostermann, E. *Apocrypha. 3. Agrapha.* KIT 11. 2nd ed. Berlin, 1911.

Lock, W., and W. Sanday. *Two Lectures on the "Sayings of Jesus" Recently Discovered at Oxyrhynchus.* Oxford, 1897.

Resch, A. *Agrapha. Aussercanonische Schriftfragmente gesammelt und untersucht.* TU 15/3-4. 2nd ed. Leipzig, 1906 (repr. Darmstadt, 1974).

Roberts, C. H. *An Unpublished Fragment of the Fourth Gospel in the John Rylands Library.* Manchester, 1935.

Swete, H. B. *Zwei Neue Evangelienfragmente.* KlT 31. Bonn, 1908.

2. Studies

Bauer, J. B. "Agraphon 90 Resch." *ZNW* 62 (1971): 301-03.

Büchler, A. "The New Fragment of an Uncanonical Gospel." *JQR* 20 (1908): 340-46.

Delobel, J. "Luke 6:5 in Codex Bezae: the Man who Worked on Sabbath." In *À cause de l'Évangile. Études sur les Synoptiques et les Actes offertes au P. J. Dupont*, 453-77. Lectio Divina 128. Paris, 1985.

_____. "The Sayings of Jesus in the Textual Tradition. Variant Readings in the Greek Manuscripts of the Gospels." In *The Sayings of Jesus: Memorial J. Coppens*, 431-57. BETL 59. Louvain, 1982.

Donovan, J. *The Logia in Ancient and Recent Literature.* Cambridge, 1924.

Harnack, A. "Über einiger Worte Jesu, die nicht in den kanonischen Evangelien stehen." *Sitzungberichte der Akademie Berlin* 1 (1904): 170-208.

Hofius, O. "Unbekannte Jesusworte." In *Das Evangelium und die Evangelien*, ed. P. Stuhlmacher, 355-82. WUNT 28. Tübingen, 1983.

_____. "Agrapha." *Theologishe Realenzyklopädie* 2 (1978): 103-10.

Jeremias, J., *Unbekannte Jesusworte.* ATANT 16 (1948). Zurich.

_____. "Der Zusammenstoss Jesu mit dem pharisäischen Oberpriester auf dem Tempelplatz. Zu Pap. Ox. v, 840." In *Coniectanea Neotestamentica XI in honorem A. Fridrichsen*, 14-144. 1947.

_____. "Zur Überlieferungsgeschichte des Agraphon 'Die Welt ist eine Brücke'." *Nachr. Ak. Wiss. Gött.* 4 (1953): 95-103.

_____. "The Saying of Jesus about the Bridge." *ExpTim* 69 (1957): 7-9.

_____. *Unknown Sayings of Jesus.* Trans. R. H. Fuller. New York, 1957 (²1964).

_____. *Les Paroles inconnues de Jésus.* Lectio Divina 62. Paris, 1970.

Jeremias, J., and O. Hofius. *Unbekannte Jesusworte.* ATANT 16. Zurich, 1948 (3rd ed. Gutersloh, 1963).

Karawidopulos, J. "Ein Agraphon in einem liturgischen Text der griechischen Kirche." *ZNW* 62 (1971): 299-300.

Käser, W. "Exegetische Erwägungen zur Seligpreisung des Sabbatarbeiters Lk. 6:5d." *ZThK* 65 (1968): 414-30.

Mees, M. *Ausserkanonische Parallelstellen zu den Herrenworten und ihre Bedeutung.* Quaderni di "Vetera Christianorum" 10. Bari. 1975.

_____. "Formen, Strukturen und Gattungen ausserkanonischen Herrenworte." *Aug* 14 (1974): 459-88.

Nepper-Christensen, P. "Das verborgene Herrnwort (Eine Untersuchung über 1 Thess. 4:13-18)." *StTh* 19 (1965): 136-54.

Paulsen, H. "Papyrus Oxyrhynchus 1.5 und die ΔΙΑΔΟΧΗ ΤΩΝ ΠΡΟΦΗΤΩΝ." *NTS* 25 (1978–1979): 443-53.

Rengstorf, K. H. "'Geben is seliger denn Nehmen'. Bemerkungen zu dem ausserevangelischen Herrenwort Apg. 20,35." In *Die Leibhaftigkeit des Wortes. Festschrift A Köberle*, 23-33. Hamburg, 1958.

Riggenbach, E. "Das Wort Jesu im Gespräch mit dem pharisäischen Hohenpriester nach dem Oxyrh. Fragment. 5, no 840." *ZNW* 25 (1926): 140-44.

Ropes, J. H. *Die Sprüche Jesu die in den kanonischen Evangelien nicht überliefert sind.* TU 14/2. Leipzig, 1896.

Sahlin, H. "Die Welt is eine Brücke." *ZNW* 76 (1956): 286-87.

Schürer, E. "Fragment of an Uncanonical Gospel." *TLZ* 33 (1908): cols. 170 ff.

Schwarz, G. "ἔγειραι, καὶ σωθήσῃ." *ZNW* 76 (1985): 129-30. See J. Karawidopulos.

Wright, L. E. *Alterations of the Words of Jesus as Quoted in the Literature of the Second Century*, 75-90. Harvard Historical Monographs 25. Cambridge MA, 1952.

——————. "Die ausserkanonischen Herrenworte als Produkte der christlichen Gemeinde." *ZNW* 47 (1957): 220-37.

Oxyrhynchus

Note: Regarding the bibliography of the Papyrus Oxyrhynchus, see J. A. Fitzmyer, "The Oxyrhynchus Logoi of Jesus and the Coptic Gospel according to Thomas," *TS* 20 (1959): 505-60, repr. in *Essays on the Semitic Background of the New Testament*, 355-433 (London, 1971), with "Additional Bibliography 1969"; K. Aland, *Repertorium der griechischen christlichen Papyri*, 37-72 (Berlin, 1975); and also D. M. Scholer, *Nag Hammadi Bibliography 1948–1969*, Nag Hammadi Studies 1 (Leiden, 1971), and Scholer's annual supplements in NovTSup. (1971ff.). Add:

Englezakis, B. "Thomas Logion 30." *Studia Patristica* 16:152-62. TU 129. Berlin, 1985.

Wright, L. E. *Alterations of the Words of Jesus as Quoted in the Literature of the Second Century*, 103-107; 119-27. Harvard Historical Monographs 25. Cambridge MA, 1952.

Studies

Blau, L. "Das neue Fragment von Oxyrhynchos, buch- und zaubergeschichtlich betrachtet." *ZNW* 9 (1908): 204-15.

Marmorstein, A. "Einige Bemerkungen zum Evangelienfragment in Oxyrhynchus Papyri, Vol. 5, no 840." *ZNW* 9 (1914): 336-38.

Paulsen, H. "Papyrus Oxyruncus 1.5 und die ΔΙΑΔΟΧΗ ΤΩΝ ΠΡΟΦΗΤΩΝ." *NTS* 25 (1978-79): 443-53.

Preuschen, E. "Das neue Evangelienfragment von Oxyrhynchus." *ZNW* 9 (1908); 1-11.

Sulzbach, A. "Zum Oxyrhynchus-Fragment." *ZNW* 9 (1908): 175-76.

Gnosticism

Note: Regarding the basic bibliography on Basilides, Isidorus, Valentinus, Heracleon, and Ptolemy, see M. Geerard, *Clavis patrum graecorum*, vol. 1 (Turnhout, 1983) 61-65; see also D. M. Scholer, *Nag Hammadi Bibliography 1948-1969*, Nag Hammadi Studies 1 (Leiden, 1971), and Scholer's annual supplements in NovTSup (1971ff.). Add:

Poffet, J. M. *La méthode exégétique d'Heracléon et d'Origène commentateurs de Jean 4: Jésus, la Samaritaine et les Samaritains*. Paradosis 27. Fribourg, 1985.

Whittaker, J. *Studies in Platonism and Patristic Thought*. London, 1984.

1. Sources

Brooke, A. E. *The Fragments of Heracleon*, 50-103. Texts and Studies 1/4. Cambridge, 1891.

Harnack, A. *Ptolaemaeus, Brief an die Flora*. KIT 9. 2nd ed. Bonn, Berlin, 1912.

Holl, K. *Epiphanius, Ancoratus und Panarion*. GCS 25/1. Leipzig, 1915.

Preuschen, E. *Origene's Johannes Kommentar*. Vol. 4 of Origen's works. GCS 10. Leipzig, 1903.

Quispel, G. *La Lettre de Ptolémée à Flora*. SC 24. Paris, 1939.

Sagnard, F. *Extraits de Théodote*. SC 23. Paris, 1948.

Völker, W. *Quellen zur Geschichte der Christlichen Gnosis*. Tübingen, 1932.

2. Studies

Barth, C. *Die Interpretation des Neuen Testaments in der Valentinianischen Gnosis*. TU 37/3. Leipzig, 1911.

Bousset, W. *Hauptprobleme der Gnosis*. FRLANT 10. Göttingen, 1907.

Burkitt, F. C. *Church and Gnosis. A Study of Christian Thought and Speculation in the Second Century*. New York, Cambridge, 1932.

Casey, R. P. "Two Notes on Valentinian Theology. 1. Valentinian Myths. 2. The Eastern and Italian Schools of Valentinianism." *HTR* 23 (1930): 275-98.

——————. "The Study of Gnosticism." *JTS* 36 (1935): 45-59.

Cerfaux L. "La gnose simonienne, nos principales sources." *RSR* 15 (1926): 498-511; 16 (1926): 5-20; 265-85; 481-503.

——————. "Gnose préchrétienne et biblique." *Dictionnaire de la Bible, Supplément*, 3:659-701. Paris, 1938.

De Faye, E. *Introduction à l'étude du gnosticisme au IIe et IIIe siècle*. Paris, 1903.

——————. *Gnostiques et Gnosticisme*. 2nd ed. Paris, 1925.

Dibelius, O. "Studien zur Geschichte der Valentinianer." *ZNW* 9 (1908): 230-47; 329-40.

Doresse, J. "Trois livres gnostiques inédits." *VigChr* 2 (1948): 137-60.

——————. "Nouveaux livres gnostiques coptes découverts en Haute Égypte." Presentation given at the Académie des Inscriptions et Belles Lettres on 17 June 1949.

——————. "Douze volumes dans une jarre." *Les Nouvelles Littéraires* (Paris, 30 June 1949).

——————. "Une bibliothèque gnostique copte." *La Nouvelle Clio* 1 (1949): 59-70. Brussels.

——————. "Une bibliothèque gnostique copte découverte en Haute Égypte." Presentation given at the Académie Royale de Belgique on 4 July 1949. In *Le Bulletin de l'Académie*, 399-413.

Doresse, J., and T. Mina. "Nouveaux textes gnostiques coptes découverts en Haute Égypte: la bibliothèque de Chénoboskion." *VigChr* 3 (1949): 129-41.

Förster, W. *Von Valentin zu Herakleon*. Giessen, 1928.

Harnack, A. *Der Brief des Ptolemaeus an die Flora. Eine religiöse Kritik am Pentateuch im 2 Jahrhundert*, 507-45. SPAW 25. Berlin, 1902.

Heinrici, G. *Die Valentinianische Gnosis und die Heilige Schrift*. Berlin, 1871.

Hendrix, P. J. G. A. *De Alexandrijnsche haeresiarch Basilides*. Dordrecht, 1926.

Jonas, H. *Gnosis und spätantiker Geist. 1. Die mythologische Gnosis*. FRLANT 51. Göttingen, 1934 (³1964).

Leisegang, H. *Die Gnosis*. 2nd ed. Leipzig, 1936.

Mina, T. "Le papyrus gnostique du Musée Copte." *VigChr* 2 (1948): 129-36.

Mouson, J. "La Théologie d'Héracléon." Diss. Louvain, 1949.

Müller, K. *Beiträge zum Verständnis der valentinianischen Gnosis*, 179-204. Nachrichten d. königl. Gesellsch. d. Wissensch. zu Göttingen. Göttingen, 1920.

Puech, H. Ch. "Où en est le problème du Gnosticisme?" *Revue de l'Université de Bruxelles* 29 (1934): 137-58.

Puech, H. C., and J. Doress. "Nouveaux écrits gnostiques découverts en Égypte." Comptes rendus de l'Académie des Inscriptions, session of 20 Feb. 1948, 89.

Quispel, G. "The Original Doctrine of Valentine." *VigChr* 1 (1947): 43-73.

——————. "La lettre de Ptolémée à Flora." *VigChr* 2 (1948): 17-56.

Reinach, S. "Observations sur Valentin et le valentinisme." *Revue Archéologique* 14 (1921): 131-45.

Sagnard, F. *La gnose Valentinienne et le témoignage de Saint Irénée*. Paris, 1947.

Steffes, J. P. *Das Wesen des Gnotizismus und seine Verhältnis zum katholischen Dogma*. Paderborn, 1922.

Torm, F. "Das Wort γνωστικός." *ZNW* 35 (1936): 70-75.

Völker, W. *Herakleons Stellung in seiner Zeit im Lichte seiner Schriftauslegung*. Halle, 1922.

Indexes

AUTHORS

REFERENCES TO THE OLD TESTAMENT

REFERENCES TO THE NEW TESTAMENT

The first column refers to passages from the New Testament; the second pertains to works studied whose passages reveal a literary influence; an asterisk indicates where a literary influence is certain; the third refers to pages in this volume.

27:4	*Prot. Jas. 14.1	229		28:11	Asc. Is. 3:14	61
27:7	Gos. Pet. 3	213			Gos. Pet. 45	204-205
27:11	Sib. Or. 8.292-295	87-88		28:12-15	Gos. Pet. 47-49	213-14
27:14	Ode 31.10	79		28:18	Herm., Sim. 5.6.1 & 4	125
	Gos. Pet. 10	217			Sim. 5.7.3	125
27:24	Gos. Pet. 1	207-208		28:19	Asc. Is. 3:17-18a	55-56
	*Gos. Pet. 46	205-206			Ode 23.17-18	65
27:26	Gos. Pet. 5	222			Kerygma Pet.	238-39
	Gos. Pet. 9	222			*Agraphon 65	251
27:27	Gos. Pet. 6	208		28:19-20	Ode 42.6	65-66
27:28-29	Gos. Pet. 7	220				
27:29	Sib. Or. 8.292-295	87-88		**Mark**		
	Gos. Pet. 8	208-209		1:4-5	Gos. Eb.	199
27:30	Gos. Pet. 9	222		1:4-6	Gos. Eb.	193-94
27:34	Sib. Or. 8.303	89		1:9-11	Gos. Eb.	194-96
	Gos. Pet. 16	209-10		1:10	Ode 24.1-3	78-79
27:35	Ode 31.9	79		1:10-11	Gos. Heb.	185
	Sib. Or. 8.302	88-89		1:11	Ode 7.15	77
	Gos. Pet. 10	217		1:12	Gos. Heb.	188-89
	12	221		1:16	Gos. Pet. 60	221
27:37	Gos. Pet. 11	222		1:39	Sib. Or. 8.272	84-85
27:38	Asc. Is. 3:13	61		1:40	Unkn. Gos. 32; 36-37	174,180-81
	Gos. Pet. 10	217		1:42	Unkn. Gos. 37-39	181
27:45	Sib. Or. 8.305-306	89-90		1:43	Unkn. Gos. 51	175
	Gos. Pet. 15	219-20		2:14	Gos. Eb.	192-93
27:46	Gos. Pet. 19	210-11			Gos. Pet. 60	221
27:48	Sib. Or. 8.303	89		2:17	2 Clem. 2:4	3-6
	Gos. Pet. 16	209-10		2:18-20	Gos. Pet. 26-27	224
27:50	Gos. Pet. 19	210-11		3:5	Herm., Man. 4.2.1	131-32
27:51	Sib. Or. 8.305-306	89-90			Gos. Heb.	189-90
	Gos. Heb.	190		3:13-14	Kerygma Pet.	238-39
	*Gos. Pet. 20	223		3:25	Ptolemy 3.5	279-80
	21	202		3:32-35	Gos. Eb.	196-97
	Prot. Jas. 10.1	231		3:34-35	2 Clem. 9:11	9-10
27:52	Gos. Pet. 41	214		4:3-20	Ode 17.13	78
27:54	*Gos. Pet. 21	202		4:7	Herm., Sim. 5.2	116-19
	28	219		4:8	Ptolemy 7.10	286
	*45	204-205		4:9	P. Oxy. 1081	260
27:57-58	Gos. Pet. 3	216		4:16-20	Herm., Vis. 3.6.5	121-22
27:58-60	Gos. Pet. 23b-24	223		4:18	Herm., Vis. 3.7.3	122-23
27:59-60	Gos. Pet. 21	202		4:18-19	Herm., Man. 10.1.5	124
27:60	Asc. Is. 3:13	61			Sim. 9.20.1	126
	*Gos. Pet. 31-33	203-204		4:22	P. Oxy. 654.27-31	253
27:62	Gos. Pet. 28	219		4:23	P. Oxy. 1081	260
27:62-64	*Gos. Pet. 29-30	202-203		5:34	Herm., Vis. 3.8.3	123
27:65-66	Asc. Is. 3:14	61		6:7	Sib. Or. 8.272	84-85
	*Gos. Pet. 31-33	203-204		6:35-49	Sib. Or. 8.273-278	85-86
28:1	Gos. Pet. 50-51	224		6:45-52	Ode 39.9	79
28:1-2	Gos. Pet. 35	211-12		6:52	Herm., Man. 4.2.1	131-32
28:2	Asc. Is. 3:16	61		7:6	2 Clem. 3:5	7
	Gos. Pet. 44	213			Herm., Man. 12.4.4	127
28:2-3	Gos. Pet. 36-37	212		7:6-7	Unkn. Gos. 5459	181-82
28:3	Gos. Pet. 55	215			Ptolemy 4.11-13	281-82
28:6	*Gos. Pet. 56	206-207				
28:8	Gos. Pet. 57	216				

18:13	Mart. Pol. 7:3	49		23:9	Ode 31:10	79
18:13-14	*Prot. Jas. 5.1	232			Sib. Or. 8.292-295	87-88
18:14	Herm., Sim. 8.7.6	129			Gos. Pet. 10	217
	*Prot. Jas. 20.4	235		23:11	Gos. Pet. 7	220-21
18:16	Herm., Sim. 9.29.3	126-27		23:12	Gos. Pet. 4-5	219
	Sim. 9.31.3	127		23:18	Mart. Pol. 3:2	49
18:18-25	Gos. Heb.	186-87		23:25	Gos. Pet. 5	222
18:19	Val., Fragm. 2	267-68		23:28	Unkn. Gos. 6-7	175-76
18:20	Herm., Sim. 5.3.2-3	129		23:32-33	Gos. Pet. 10	217
18:22	Herm., Sim. 5.3.3	124-25		23:33	Asc. Is. 3:13	61
18:22-25	Herm., Vis. 3.6.6	122			Sib. Or. 8.302	88-89
18:24	Herm., Sim. 9.20.2	119-20		23:34	Asc. Is. 9.14	58
	Sim. 9.20.3	120			Ode 31:9	79
18:38-39	Ode 42:15	79			Gos. Pet. 12	221
18:42	Herm., Vis. 3.8.3	123		23:35	Asc. Is. 8:7	62
19:8-10	*Gos. Matthias	226-27		23:36	Sib. Or. 8.303	89
19:10	2 Clem. 2:7	10			Gos. Pet. 16	209-10
19:12-27	Herm., Sim. 5.2	116-19		23:37	Gos. Pet. 8	208-209
19:29-38	Mart. Pol. 8:1	47-48		23:38	Gos. Pet. 11	222-23
19:37-38	Ode 7.16b-17	77-78		23:39-41	Gos. Pet. 13	218
19:46	2 Clem. 14:1	16		23:42	Pol., Phil. 6:3	35
	Heracleon, Fragm. 13	270		23:44	Sib. Or. 8.305-306	89-90
20:9-10	Herm., Sim. 5.2	116-19		23:44-45	Gos. Pet. 15	219-20
20:16	Unkn. Gos. 17-20	173		23:45	Sib. Or. 8.305-306	89-90
20:17-20	*Unkn. Gos. 17-20	176			Gos. Heb.	190
20:20-26	Unkn. Gos. 42-54	181			Gos. Pet. 20	223
20:23	Unkn. Gos. 50-51	181			Prot. Jas. 10:1	231
20:36	Asc. Is. 9:9	62		23:46	Gos. Pet. 19	210-11
21:7	Pol., Phil. 6:3	35		23:47	Gos. Pet. 45	204-205
	Apoc. Pet. 1	99-100		23:47-48	*Gos. Pet. 28	219
21:8	Asc. Is. 4.6, 9	60		23:48	Gos. Heb.	189
	Apoc. Pet. 1	100-101			Gos. Pet. 25	220
	2	103		23:52	Gos. Pet. 3	216
21:9	Asc. Is. 3:22	60		23:53	Asc. Is. 3:13	61
21:16	Asc. Is. 3:29	60			Gos. Pet. 21	202
21:27	Asc. Is. 10:12	61			23b-24	223
	Apoc. Pet. 1	101-102		24:1	Gos. Pet. 50-51	224-25
	6	105		24:2-5	Gos. Pet. 55	215-16
21:29-30	Apoc. Pet. 2	102-103		24:4	Asc. Is. 3:16	61
21:30	Herm., Sim. 4.2-4	115-16			Gos. Pet. 36-37	212
22:3	Asc. Is. 4:3	62		24:5-7	Gos. Pet. 56	206-207
22:8b-9	Gos. Eb.	197-98		24:10	Gos. Pet. 50-51	224-25
22:15	*Gos. Eb.	197-98		24:14	Gos. Pet. 59	216-17
22:27	Pol., Phil. 5:2	32-33		24:46	Kerygma Pet.	239-40
22:29-30	Ode 20:7b-8	78		24:47	Kerygma Pet.	239
22:42	Mart. Pol. 7:1	46-47				
22:46	Pol., Phil. 7:2	31-32				
22:47	Asc. Is. 4:3	62		**John**		
22:52	Mart. Pol. 7:1	46-47		1:1	Ode 41:14	67
22:61	Unkn. Gos. 6-7	175-76			Herm., Sim. 9.12.2-3	160
22:63-65	Sib. Or. 8.287-289	86-87		1:3	*Ptolemy 3.6	287
22:67	Sib. Or. 8.292-295	87-88		1:4	Ode 3:9	70
22:69	Asc. Is. 11:32	61		1:5	Ode 18:6	67
	Apoc. Pet. 6	105		1:9	Ode 12:7	68
23:3	Sib. Or. 8.292-295	87-88			Apoc. Pet. 2	103

15:53-55	Ode 15:8-9	74
15:55	*Sib. Or. 8.414-415	96
15:58	Pol., Phil. 10:1	39-40

2 Corinthians

3:2	Pol., Phil. 11:3	42
4:1	Herm., Man. 9.8	132
4:14	*Pol., Phil. 2:2	35-36
	Asc. Is. 3:18	61
4:16	Herm., Man. 9.8	132
4:17	2 Clem. 19:4	18
5:4	Asc. Is. 4:16	61
5:6	Mart. Pol. 2:2	50
5:10	Pol., Phil. 6:2	37
6:7	Pol., Phil. 4:1	36
6:10	Herm., Sim. 2.5	157
6:13	2 Clem. 11:6	20
6:16	2 Clem. 9:3	17
	Herm., Sim. 9.13.5-7	146
6:18	2 Clem. 1:4	18
7:10	*Herm., Man. 10.2.4	145-46
8:21	Pol., Phil. 6:1	39
11:2	Sib. Or. 8.291	97
11:3	Prot. Jas. 13.1	237
11:15	Herm., Sim. 6.3.6	125
12:19	Herm., Sim. 9.13.5-7	146
13:11	2 Clem. 17:3	20

Epistle to the Galatians

1:1	Asc. Is. 3:18	61
2:2	Pol., Phil. 9:2	39
3:27	Ode 7:3b-6	68
4:4-5	2 Clem. 1:4	18
	Ode 3:7	73
4:6	Asc. Is. 10:6	59
4:9	Mart. Pol. 1:1	50
4:26	Pol., Phil. 3:3	38
	Asc. Is. 3:15	62
4:27	2 Clem. 2:1	19
5:14	Pol., Phil. 3:3	36
5:17	Pol., Phil. 5:3	43
6:7	*Pol., Phil. 5:1	36
6:9	Herm., Man. 9.8	132
6:10	2 Clem. 9:7	20

Epistle to the Ephesians

1:20	Asc. Is. 11:32	61
	3:18	61
1:20-21	Herm., Sim. 5.6.1	125
	and 4	
1:23	2 Clem. 14:2	17-18
2:5	*Pol., Phil. 1:3	35
2:8	Ode 9:5	74
	Herm., Vis. 3.8.3	123

2:8-9	*Pol., Phil. 1:3	35
2:10-22	Herm., Sim. 9.4.3	146-47
2:15	*Ptolemy 6.6	287
2:16	2 Clem. 14:2	17-18
2:19	Ode 3:6	73
	6:3	73
2:21-22	Herm., Sim. 9.13.5-7	146
3:9	Herm., Sim. 5.5.2	149
	Sim. 7.4	149
3:10	Asc. Is. 9:15; 10:11;	59
	11:16	
3:13	Herm., Man. 9.8	132
3:14-19	Ode 32:1	74
3:20	Mart. Pol. 20:2	50
4:3-6	Herm., Sim. 9.17.4	147
	Sim. 9.18.4	147
4:4	2 Clem. 14:2	17-18
4:9	Sib. Or. 8.310-11	98
4:9-10	Ode 22:1	78
4:12	Herm., Sim. 9.13.5-7	146
4:15-16	Ode 17:15-17	71
4:18	2 Clem. 19:2	20
4:22	2 Clem. 1:6	20
4:24	Ode 33:12	74
4:25	2 Clem. 1:6	20
	Herm., Man. 3.1	147-48
4:26	*Pol., Phil. 12:1	38
4:30	Herm., Man. 3.4	146
	*Man. 10.1.2	144-45
	*Man. 10.2.1-6	145
	*Man. 10.3.2	145
4:32	Pol., Phil. 5:2; 6:1	44
5:5	Pol., Phil. 11:2	42
5:14	*Ptolemy, Comm. 5	289
5:15	2 Clem. 19:2	21
5:23	2 Clem. 14:2	17-18
	Ode 17:15-17	71
5:28-32	2 Clem. 14:2	17-18
6:6	2 Clem. 13:1	21
6:18	Pol., Phil. 12:3	40-41

Epistle to the Philippians

1:11	Herm., Sim. 9.19.2	158
1:27	Pol., Phil. 5:2	38-39
2:2	2 Clem. 17:3	20
2:4	Mart. Pol. 1:2	50
2:8-9	Ode 41:11-13	73
2:9-10	Herm., Sim. 5.6.1	125
	and 4	
2:10	Asc. Is. 10:15	59
2:16	Pol., Phil. 9:2	39
2:18	Ode 8:1	73
3:1	Ode 8:1	73
3:15	Herm., Vis. 3.13.4	150

2:13	2 Clem. 12:1	21
2:14	Pol., Phil. 6:3	44

Epistle to the Hebrews

1:2	Herm., Sim. 9.12.2-3	160
1:3	Asc. Is. 11:32	61
2:10	2 Clem. 20:5	16
2:13	Ode 31:4	74
3:12	Herm., Vis. 2.3.2	149
	Vis. 3.7.2	149
4:3	Ode 28:3	71
4:4	Ode 16:12	74
4:12	Ode 12:5	74
4:16	Mart. Pol. 10:1	50
5:7	Pol., Phil. 6:3	41
5:13	Pol., Phil. 9:1	41
6:4-6	Herm., Man. 4.3.1	148
6:18	Ode 3:10	73
6:20	Pol., Phil. 12:2	40
7:3	Pol., Phil. 12:2	40
8:1	Asc. Is. 11:32	61
8:5	*Ptolemy 5.9-10	288
8:8	Kerygma Pet.	240-41
9:3-7	*Heracleon, Fragm. 13	276
9:23-24	*Ptolemy 5.9-10	288
9:28	Asc. Is. 4:13	60
10:12	Asc. Is. 11:32	61
10:23	2 Clem. 11:6	20
11:33	Herm., Vis. 2.2.7	134
	Man. 12.3.1	134
	Man. 12.6.2	134
	Sim. 9.13.7	134
12:1	2 Clem. 1:6	20
12:2	Asc. Is. 11:32	61
	2 Clem. 20:5	16
12:11	Herm., Sim. 9.19.2	158
12:22	Asc. Is. 3:15	62
12:28	Pol., Phil. 6:3	41
13:15-16	Ptolemy 5.9-10	288-89
13:17	Herm., Sim. 9.31.6	149
13:18	2 Clem. 16:4	20

Epistle of James

1:5-6	Herm., Sim. 2.5	157
1:5-9	Herm., Man. 9.1-7	151-52
1:8	Herm., Man. 2.3	159
	Man. 5.2.7	159
1:12	Asc. Is. 8:26	62
	*Herm., Vis. 2.2. 7	156-57
	Sim. 8.2.1	158
	Sim. 8.3.6	158
	Sim. 8.4.6	158
1:17	Herm., Man. 9. 11	152-53
	*Man. 11.5	153

1:21	Herm., Sim. 6.1.1	155
1:26	Herm., Man. 12.1.1	159
1:27	Herm., Man. 2.7	159
	Man. 8.10	157
	Sim. 1.1.8	157
	Sim. 5.7.1	159
2:1-13	Asc. Is. 3:25	60
2:5	Herm., Sim. 2.5	157
2:7	*Herm., Sim. 8.6.4	155-56
2:14	Herm., Sim. 8.9.1	158
2:19	*Herm., Man. 1.1	150-51
3:1-12	Herm., Vis. 2.2.3	158-59
3:2	Herm., Man.12.1.1	159
3:8	Herm., Man. 2.3	159
	Man. 5.2.7	159
3:15	Herm., Man. 9.11	152-53
	*Man. 11.5	153
3:18	Herm., Sim. 9.19.2	158
4:4	2 Clem. 6:3	22
4:5	Herm., Man. 3.1	157
	Sim. 5.6.5	157
4:7	*Herm., Man. 12.2.4	153-54
	*Man. 12.4.6-7	153-54
	*Man. 12.5.2	153-54
4.11	2 Clem. 4:3	22
4:12	*Herm., Man. 12.6.3	154-55
	*Sim. 9.23.4	156
5:1	Herm., Vis. 3.9.6	157
5:4	Herm., Vis. 3.9.6	157
5:5	Herm., Sim. 6.1.6	159
5:7-11	2 Clem. 20:3	22
5:11	Herm., Vis. 1.3.2	159
5:19-20	2 Clem. 15:1	21-22
5:20	2 Clem. 16:4	22

1 Peter

1:7	Herm., Vis. 4.3.4	161
1:8	*Pol., Phil. 1:3	42
1:10-12	Kerygma Pet. 4	239-40
1:12	*Pol., Phil. 1:3	42
1:13	*Pol., Phil. 2:1	43
1:17	Apoc. Pet. 1	102
	Herm., Sim. 6.3.6	125
1:20	Herm., Sim. 9.12.2-3	160
1:21	*Pol., Phil. 2:1	43
	Phil. 12:2	44
2:1	2 Clem. 1:6	20
2:5	Herm., Sim. 5.3.8	129
2:6	Sib. Or. 8.254b-255	94-95
2:8	Sib. Or. 8.246	97
2:11	*Pol., Phil. 5:3	43
2:12	Pol., Phil. 10:2	44
2:13-14	Mart. Pol. 10:2	50
2:22	*Pol., Phil. 8:1	43-44

6:8	Herm., Vis. 4.1.10	143-44	12:16-17	Ode 22:5	69
6:11	Asc. Is. 4:16	61	12:17	Herm., Sim. 5.1.5	142
6:13	Sib. Or. 8.190	81-82	13:2	Ode 22:5	69
6:14	Sib. Or. 3.81b-82	96	13:4	Ode 22:5	69
7:3	Ode 42:14	70	13:8	Apoc. Pet. 17	110
7:9	Asc. Is. 4:16	61	13:11	Ode 22:5	69
7:13-14	Asc. Is. 4:16	61	13:13-14a	Sib. Or. 3.63-70	93
8:6	Sib. Or. 8.239-240	84	14:1	Ode 42:14	70
8:8	Sib. Or. 8.239-240	84	14:12	Herm., Sim. 5.1.5	142
8:10	Sib. Or. 8.239-240	84	14:14	Herm., Sim. 8.2.1	143, 158
8:12	Sib. Or. 8.239-240	84		Sim. 8.3.6	158
9:1	Sib. Or. 8.239-240	84		Sim. 8.4.6	158
9:4	Ode 42:14	70	15:3	Mart. Pol. 14:1	50
9:6	Sib. Or. 8.353	95-96	16:7	Mart. Pol. 14:1	50
9:13	Sib. Or. 8.239-240	84	16:13	Ode 22:5	69
9:17	Herm., Sim. 8.2.1	143, 158	17:8	Apoc. Pet. 17	110
	Sim. 8.3.6	158	19:9	Ode 20:7b-8	78
	Sim. 8.4.6	158	19:10	Asc. Is. 7:21	58-59
9:20	2 Clem. 1:6	23	19:15	Sib. Or. 8.248	95
10:7	Sib. Or. 8.239-240	84	19:19-20	Apoc. Pet. 2	104
11:7	Herm., Vis. 4.1.6	143	19:20	Asc. Is. 4:14	61
11:17	Mart. Pol. 14:1	50	20:2	Ode 22:5	69
12:1	Herm., Sim. 8.2.1	143, 158	20:4	Ode 42:14	70
	Sim. 8.3.6	158	20:10	Asc. Is. 4:14	61
	Sim. 8.4.6	158	20:12	Apoc. Pet. 17	110
12:3	Sib. Or. 8.88	96	20:13	Apoc. Pet. 4	110
12:3-4	Ode 22:5	69	20:15	Apoc. Pet. 17	110
	Herm., Vis. 4.1.6	143	21:2	Asc. Is. 3:15	62
12:5	Sib. Or. 8.248	95		Herm., Vis. 4.2.1	143
12:7	Ode 22:5	69	21:27	Apoc. Pet. 17	110
	Herm., Sim. 8.3.3	143	22:1-2	Ode 20:7	69
12:9	Ode 22:5	69	22:8	Asc. Is. 7:21	58-59
12:10	Herm., Sim. 5.6.1	125	22:12	2 Clem. 11:6	17
	and 4		22:17	Ode 30:1, 2, 5	67-68
12:13	Ode 22:5	69		6:10-11, 18	67-68
			22:20	Ode 7:16b-17	77-78

Lightning Source UK Ltd.
Milton Keynes UK
UKHW010447250820
368770UK00001B/4